MANAGEMENT BY JAPANESE SYSTEMS

MANAGEMENT BY JAPANESE SYSTEMS

Edited by
Sang M. Lee
Gary Schwendiman

PRAEGER

PRAEGER SPECIAL STUDIES • PRAEGER SCIENTIFIC

Library of Congress Cataloging in Publication Data

Main entry under title:

Management by Japanese systems.

Bibliography: p.
Includes index.
1. Management — Japan — Addresses, essays, lectures. 2. Comparative management — Addresses,
essays, lectures. 3. Management — United States —
Addresses, essays, lectures. I. Lee, Sang M., ⌇⌇
1939–   II. Schwendiman, Gary. ⌇⌇
HD70.J3M26   658'.00952   82-7612
ISBN 0-03-062051-1   AACR2

To Tosca and Amy Lee

To Todd, Heidi, Lisa, Wendy, and Julie Schwendiman

Published in 1982 by Praeger Publishers
CBS Educational and Professional Publishing
a Division of CBS Inc.
521 Fifth Avenue, New York, New York 10175 U.S.A.

© 1982 by Praeger Publishers

23456789   052   987654321

Printed in the United States of America

Preface

There has been widespread publicity about the "economic and social miracle" of Japan. The gross national product of Japan exceeds $1 trillion, second only to that of the United States. Japan's crime rate is the lowest in the world. Life expectancy is the highest in the world, and infant mortality the lowest. The unemployment rate is less than 2 percent; population growth, about 1 percent. The Japanese society is said to be built on trust, having an extremely low ratio of lawyers to total population.

Recently, Japan has outperformed other countries in most of the sophisticated technological areas, excelling in electronics, ship building, and production of cameras, watches, video recorders, and the like. Japan has achieved these miracles while importing many critical raw materials from abroad. The Japanese worker earns almost twice as much as his counterpart in France, and Parisian dress designers concede that Japan has now overtaken France as a market for high fashion. In many sectors of industry, Japanese wages have also surpassed those of Britain and are approaching wage levels in the United States and West Germany.

Behind the economic and social miracle of Japan, there are newly developed management philosophies and operation systems, and diligent workers. The Japanese management systems have turned around many failing business organizations in the United States. American executives flock to Japan to study Japanese manufacturing systems, quality control methods, and employee relations policies. Could Japan's formula for success be implanted in the United States? We believe so. Many people think that the Japanese success can be attributed to Japan's culture and favorable business environment. However, there exist in Japan many new management and operating systems that are unique and innovative. We must study how these systems could be adapted by American corporations.

In Japan, almost every aspect of life in the West, especially in the

v

493463

United States, has been studied, turned over, imitated, improved, adapted, and finally absorbed. Thus, the Japanese can draw upon an all-pervading knowledge of Western culture, preferences, politics, economics, and management systems. How many American managers have acquired a deep understanding of Japanese preferences?

To facilitate our understanding of Japanese management systems and also provide a forum to study the transferability of these systems to the United States, the first international Japan-United States Business Conference was organized. It was held October 4–7, 1981, on the University of Nebraska-Lincoln campus, and attracted about 300 leading management scholars, business executives, and administrators of schools of business administration from the United States and Japan. Some of the best-known experts in the field of study who participated in the seminar are:

Professor Ezra Vogel, Harvard (author of *Japan as Number One*)

Professor William Ouchi, UCLA (author of *Theory Z*)

Leighton Smith, Arthur Andersen, Tokyo

Professor Motoo Kaji, University of Tokyo

Dean Eugene Kelley, Penn State University

Professor Jinichiro Nakane, Waseda University, Tokyo

Dr. Dick Nanto, Library of Congress

Edward Hay, Fram Corporation

Professor Toshiyuki Tamura, Tokyo Metropolitan University

This book is based on the best original papers presented at the conference and those specially written for this volume. Currently, there is no book that deals exclusively with Japanese management systems. This particular volume emphasizes the following key issues:

1. Overall Japanese management style
2. Various aspects of quality circles
3. Japanese operations management systems
4. Japanese marketing systems
5. Comparative analysis of Japanese and American management
6. Transferability of Japanese management systems to the United States

This book includes a number of empirical as well as conceptual studies by well-known Japanese or American scholars. Their insights are based on broad and profound understanding of Japanese management systems. We believe the most important contribution of this book lies in the discussion of transferability of Japanese management approaches to U.S. corporations.

This book is directed toward two basic markets. It is intended as a text for management theory, comparative management, and organization theory and practice at the upper undergraduate and graduate levels; in addition, it can serve as a reference book for practicing managers and staff personnel in various organizations.

We would like to express our thanks to all of the contributors to this book. We are especially grateful to those who made the first Japan-United States Business Conference a big success: President Ronald Roskens, Chancellor Martin Massengale, and Vice President Alan Seagren of the University of Nebraska; Governor Charles Thone; Ambassador Yoshio Okaware; Chairman of the Board T. Takeshita, President Kichiro Ando, and Robert Summers of Kawasaki Motors Corporation, USA; Dr. Carl Halvarson of College and University Partnership Program; our Japanese colleagues Professors Motoo Kaji, Motofusa Murayama, Toshiyuki Tamura, Jinichiro Nakane, Norio Aoyama, and others; and other distinguished colleagues in the profession.

We express our sincere thanks to our efficient office staff, who made all arrangements for the conference and typed many different versions of the papers: Joyce Anderson, Jane Chrastil, Cindy LeGrande, Angela Sullivan, Billie Lefholtz, Linda Rock, and Mary Best. We give our love to our family members who shared with us the burden of long hours throughout the process of this project.

Sang M. Lee
Gary Schwendiman

Contents

Contents

Part I

JAPANESE MANAGEMENT SYSTEMS

This part is devoted to the discussion of broad Japanese concepts that are essential in understanding the working of Japanese management systems. Dick K. Nanto, in "Management, Japanese Style," presents an overview of Japanese management principles and practices. The chapter focuses on the Japanese concept of the firm as a community, the emphasis on the group instead of the individual, the priority placed on human instead of functional relationships, and the treatment of top management personnel as generalists. These principles of Japanese management are then used to explain various characteristics of Japanese enterprises, such as labor relations, quality control, market share, export drive, harmony, paternalism, consensus decision making, and dispersion of responsibility.

Thomas Patrick Cullen suggests in his chapter, "Development and Use of the Functional Informal Group in the Japanese Organization," that Japanese management systems are a response to a business philosophy that emphasizes the ability of the organization to respond to changes in the environment. One important factor in the success of Japanese management is the unique way in which the organization defines and utilizes the group. Differentiation and specialization within the organization are moderated by a communication and decision participation system emphasizing organizational rather than task orientation. The result is a lessening of negative outcomes associated with intraorganizational coalitions.

Ronald Greenwood and Robert H. Ross, in "Early American Influence on Japanese Management Philosophy: Scientific Management Movement in Japan," point out that the history of Japanese management

1

philosophy has been ignored by American management writers. Most American writers concentrate on Japanese culture and history to give a basis for the modern Japanese management philosophy. Japanese theorists, however, have had a long and strong contact with the philosophies of the Western world and were greatly influenced by scientific management, as this chapter will show.

Ian Maitland, in his chapter "Organizational Structure and Innovation: The Japanese Case," attempts to identify the structural features of large Japanese firms that have facilitated rapid technological innovation. For this purpose, the process of innovation is decomposed into two stages: "origination" and "adoption." The argument is advanced that the structure of the Japanese firm is optimally adapted to the adoption of innovations, but is ill-suited for their origination. As long as Japan was in a catch-up phase this situation did not slow the rate of technological change, since Japanese firms systematically imported technologies pioneered overseas; but, now that Japan has closed the gap, the organizational structure of the large Japanese firm may impede attempts to develop an indigenous capacity to originate major technological advances.

1

Management, Japanese Style

DICK KAZUYUKI NANTO

Suppose the leaders of an aboriginal tribe that was interested in entering the age of industry asked you how to organize and run a factory. Most likely you would bring out staffing charts and speak of job descriptions, the division between management and labor, and the need for clarity, responsibility, and specific objectives. The leaders would probably nod their heads in agreement.

Suppose someone else came along and asked the leaders why they did not organize their factory along the lines of their tribe. After all, a tribe is able to accomplish considerable work. It has a natural sort of hierarchy and is able to inspire and motivate people even to the point of going to war for it, while concurrently providing a sense of community that meets many social and psychological needs of its members.

"But," the leaders ask, "who will be in charge of seeing that the work gets done?" "Oh, there will be leaders," the person answers, "but the workers generally will monitor themselves." "Who will have the responsibility if something goes wrong?" respond the leaders. "No one in particular will; everyone will. All will share the same fate." The tribal leaders shake their heads in disapproval. "I thought that was a serious proposal," they say, as they return to the security of organizational charts.

As the world approaches the twenty-first century, however, some of the benefits of a quasi-tribal organization are being rediscovered. Such a

Views expressed are solely those of the author and should not be attributed to the Congressional Research Service.

system not only is able to produce goods and services efficiently, but also adapts to change and addresses sociological and psychological needs of its members. A prime example of this type of organization can be found in a typical Japanese big business.

THE CHALLENGE

Americans are engaged in a process of discovery about Japan's economy that is turning up some startling surprises. The impetus behind this process has been the phenomenal success of Japanese business in export markets. Japanese firms producing steel, ships, watches, cameras, semiconductors, automobiles, and consumer electrical appliances have jolted the trading world into taking notice. When one's survival in the marketplace is being threatened, one is inclined to sit up and listen.

In many quarters, the initial reaction to Japan's export success was a refusal to believe that Japanese business competitiveness could be real. Many took refuge in the convenient illusion that Japanese market penetration had to be based on some "unfair" advantage from government subsidies, cheap labor, or dumping. Until recently, for example, many top Detroit executives had never even been in a Japanese car (Wiegner 1981, p. 129). As long as such views prevailed, many U.S. firms could look to the government for relief from Japanese competition and not feel compelled to alter the way their businesses were operated.

Once these illusions were disproven, however, people began to ask more penetrating questions. What makes large Japanese corporations efficient? Japanese companies marshal human resources in complex organizations to produce goods that are technologically advanced, of high quality, and reasonably priced; how at the same time do they maintain labor-management relations that produce relatively high worker satisfaction and a low number of days lost because of industrial disputes?* How can growth in Japanese manufacturing productivity continue to outstrip that in other industrialized countries? How can Japanese companies continue to compete in markets when they suffer the disadvantages of remoteness, lack of raw materials, and high costs of land, and are subject to considerable linguistic and cultural handicaps?

No single answer can suffice for all these questions. Recently, however, scholars are discovering that part of the answer lies in the way the Japanese manage their enterprises (Pascale and Athos 1981, p. 22). Japan

---

*In 1979, 930,304 working days were lost in Japan, compared with 35,467,300 in the United States.

seems to have developed a managerial system particularly appropriate to tackling the problems of the 1980s.

The elements of Japanese management are not unique, at least no more so than individual parts of a Porsche sports car. Yet in each case the synergistic action of the parts and the way they perform in competition invite closer scrutiny.

Consider the story of the farmer whose son had just graduated from college in agronomy and was offering a steady stream of unsolicited advice. Like that farmer, most American managers already know how to manage a lot better than they actually do. The last thing they need is more advice. Yet studying managerial styles against the background of Japanese culture can highlight points that might otherwise not be apparent. The suspicion is growing among some U.S. scholars, government officials, and managers, moreover, that in the postindustrial, high-technology world of the future, the Japanese management system may even be superior to the American one Rehder 1979).

Of course, Japanese companies are not the only well-managed companies in the world. Indeed, two recently published books on the subject conclude that the most characteristic aspects of Japanese management can be found in many successful U.S. companies. Firms such as IBM, Intel, Eli Lilly, Hewlett-Packard, and United Airlines employ a style of management similar to that of the Japanese (Ouchi 1981; Pascale and Athos 1981). Firms that perform well year after year appear to have a lot in common.

The Japanese themselves trace many of their professional management techniques to the United States. Japanese have been students of American management for a long time. Most Japanese textbooks on management contain considerable material from U.S. authors. Peter Drucker's *Practice of Management* was a best seller among Japanese businessmen (Noda 1970, p. 54). Virtually any entering class at the best U.S. schools of business will include some Japanese students ("Japan Gives" 1981; Tsuchiya 1974). Japanese used to joke that a B.A. degree meant "Been in America" (Lohr 1981, p. 15). Perhaps an MBA degree meant "Many-times Been in America."

Until recently, however, Americans generally did not reciprocate Japanese interest in U.S. management practices. Americans had little access to information about management in Japan, and seemed to care little about the subject. Students of Japanese management, however, claim that Americans can learn much from Japanese organizational practices. These techniques, like other Japanese products, are exportable.

Even if U.S. firms do not adopt Japanese-style management practices, American business should be aware of them. By understanding Japanese strengths and weaknesses, U.S. business can design better corporate strategies to compete with Japanese firms (Puri and Bhide 1981, p.

20). U.S. governmental organizations that must cope with problems of worker productivity and morale can also find the Japanese experience illuminating.

Even well-managed companies can improve their practices through Japanese-style methods. General Motors was reported to have been so pleased with an experiment in worker participation patterned along Japanese lines that it undertook 160 organizational changes of this nature at plants throughout the country (Lohr 1981, p. 58). Recently, Westinghouse Electric Corporation dispatched some 500 employees (including 50 to 60 union leaders) to study Japanese industry. As a result of what they learned, Westinghouse has spent millions of dollars on altering its factories to incorporate Japanese methods (Lehner 1981, p. 44).

This chapter presents a brief overview of the principles and practices of management most characteristic of the Japanese model, derives some important results of the model, and provides some comparisons with typical U.S. practices. Although specific techniques are discussed, the focus is on broad principles and their results. In the interest of conserving space, most of this study is devoted to discussing Japanese, not American, management style.

As a word of caution, in the real world no pure American or pure Japanese management model exists. One defect of international comparisons is the temptation to sweep with a single broom or paint with a single stroke. In each country there are firms with characteristics that cover the spectrum of possible types. Japanese in large corporations, however, tend to believe that the ideal exists and often behave accordingly.

JAPANESE MANAGEMENT

Japanese management style has been called Theory Z (Ouchi 1981), in contrast to Theory X or Y;* and "organic type" of management, in contrast to the American "system type" of management (Yamagata 1978, p. 34); and the art of Japanese management (Pascale and Athos 1981). Japanese themselves call it *Nihonteki keiei* or Japanese management, which will be used here (Hazama 1971; Iwata 1977).

The cofounder of the Honda Motor Company once remarked that American and Japanese management are 95 percent alike, yet differ in all important respects (Ouchi 1981). The 95 percent tends to be common

---

*A theory X manager assumes that people are fundamentally lazy and irresponsible, and need constant watching. A theory Y manager assumes that people are fundamentally hard-working and responsible, and need only to be encouraged and supported.

knowledge. This chapter focuses on the 5 percent, the important differences.

In a nutshell, Japanese management can be characterized by three basic principles. These are: (1) an emphasis on the group rather than the individual; (2) an emphasis on human rather than functional relationships; and (3) a view of top managers as generalists and facilitators rather than as decision makers. These broad principles manifest themselves repeatedly in Japanese management practices and produce interesting results.

Emphasis on the Group

Instead of the rugged individualism so idealized in the United States, Japanese hold to the aphorism that "the nail that sticks up gets hammered." Japanese relish life in groups. In the corporate world, the Japanese enterprise becomes a social as well as economic group that is quasi-tribal and permeates the lives of its employees (Nakane 1970, pp. 19–22).

Akio Morita, the president of Sony Corporation, once described his firm as a ship. Every person on the ship shares the same fate. If one falters and causes the ship to sink, all will suffer (Morita 1981). The president of Nippon Steel, describing the difference between American and Japanese management, said that, while a U.S. corporation is regarded as a cold, impersonal economic unit, the Japanese unit is regarded as a community with a common destiny ("Japanese Managers" 1977, p. 130).

By focusing on the group instead of the individual, Japanese corporations are able to unleash considerable energy of the type usually reserved for college athletics, nationalism, or religion. Japanese companies seem to be able to elicit worker attitudes similar to school spirit, patriotism, and religious fervor.

The Japanese focus on the group does make intuitive sense. Anyone who belongs to a professional group knows that evaluations by those outside the group or even monetary rewards (especially fixed salaries) usually are not the primary motive for achievement. The evaluation of peers — those who cannot be fooled — tends to be paramount. Such peer pressure can be a major motivation toward excellence.

Of course, the host society of Japanese enterprises is much more group-oriented than is American Society. Japanese tend to exert themselves with the most effort when the merit of the group as a whole is in question (Arai 1971, p. 119). When a Japanese man is asked his occupation, he will usually answer that he is a Sony or Hitachi man, not that he is an accountant, sales person, or business manager. Japanese often refer to their nation as "our country" (*waga kuni*) and non-Japanese as "outside people" (*gaijin*). In the Japanese psyche is a concept of inside (*uchi*) and outside (*soto*) that not only defines one's membership in a group but determines how one speaks to and interacts with others. (Iwata 1977, pp. 60–65).

Japanese corporations reinforce this group consciousness through a variety of methods. The first is to emphasize the permanence of the group. Those who are recruited into the core group of an enterprise enter with the understanding that they are joining for life.

In pay and incentives for workers, semiannual bonuses, which account for nearly a third of yearly salary, depend partly on company profits or on the financial health of the group. While remuneration for top management in U.S. firms often is tied to profits, salaries for workers generally do not have such an explicit link. Japanese workers, moreover, usually have more access to financial data on the operation of the company and are more aware of how their actions affect profitability.

An extreme case of reliance on group work can be found at the Toyota Motor Company. Toyota assigns production quotas to work teams. On any given shift, production lines do not stop until the day's quota has been filled, which occasionally entails overtime work without pay. Exceeding the quota, conversely, brings extra compensation. Salaries, not only for actual production workers but also for clerical personnel, are tied to each day's production. Supervisors at Toyota have been known to assist on the assembly line to meet the production quota; then they take their paperwork home to complete (Kamata 1980).

Japanese auto makers often point out that any worker who finds anything defective in the product has the right and obligation to shut down the whole assembly line. Shutting down the assembly line, however, does not necessarily reduce the number of cars the work team is required to finish that day. The peer pressure is tremendous, therefore, for each individual in the group to achieve 100 percent quality control and efficiency. Each person depends on each other person to do the job well. If one person slacks off or does not show up for work, it places a burden on others (Kamata 1980).

Under such peer pressure, it is little wonder that few Japanese workers take all their vacation time each year. Absenteeism tends to be low in Japanese firms. A plant of the Kyoto Ceramic Company in Japan goes so far as to read the names of the previous day's absentees each morning before the assembled work force (Bylinsky 1981, p. 70).

Group cohesion is buttressed by morning calisthenics, company songs, recitations of the company creed, and other activities. Company parties, after-hour revelry in bars, company recreation, and a constant direction of energies toward competitors outside the enterprise also solidify the group. The "us against them" mentality in a Japanese company is likely to refer to the company against its competitors — not the workers against management.

An emphasis on broad social goals and service to society further enhances group consciousness. A recurrent theme in orientation lectures for new recruits in Japanese companies is that they have become full adults in society (*shakaijin*). They now have a chance in working for the company to serve society and to earn its esteem (Clark 1979, p. 138).

This theme of contribution to society is emphasized in the goals and songs of Japanese companies. Such a sense of mission can bind people together. The Hitachi company song states, "We are Hitachi men, roused and ready/ To promote the happiness of others" (Dore 1973, p. 52). The Matsushita workers' song begins with "For the building of a new Japan/ Let's put our strength and mind together" (Kahn 1970, p. 110). The Ueda Bank principles contain the sentence "Intent on the spirit of service, we will contribute to public welfare and social prosperity" (Rohlen 1974, p. 36). This concept of mission in Japanese companies facilitates a type of management by ideology.

Japanese companies also emphasize a united company spirit through company traditions, history, atmosphere, and discipline. This identification with the company culture creates a bond that serves the organization well both in good times and in bad. If such a company must face difficulties, it usually can rely on the wholehearted support of its employees (Arai 1971, p. 67).

Maintaining group relations takes time, patience, and resources. Japanese put in long hours at the office or in after-hours discussions at bars or restaurants. Japanese corporations budget sizable funds for entertainment, expense accounts, and group activities. While such expenditures are not uncommon in U.S. companies, the difference is that Japanese firms allocate a sizable proportion of such funds for use by the employees for themselves. In 1980, Japanese businesses spent $14.2 billion on entertainment (only 60 percent of which was tax deductible)—more than the nation budgeted for national defense ("Japanese Companies" 1981). U.S. firms can hardly be expected to duplicate the lavishness of Japanese entertainment accounts, but allocating more funds for internal social expenses could return high dividends.

The strength of group identity gives rise to some interesting operational characteristics of Japanese businesses. These include the existence of enterprise unions, quality control, promotion criteria, corporate strategy, and a strong export drive.

A. *Enterprise unions* Ozaki

A primary motivator of company consciousness in Japan is the enterprise union—organized along company lines instead of by trades. The union itself justifies its existence through the firm. Members of the union are expected to rise through the management ranks of the company. In some cases, management salary increases are determined by settlements with the union (Yamagata 1978).

Enterprise unions in Japan developed out of the special circumstances following World War II, but fit well into Japan's business structure. In the rush to democratize Japan, the Allied Occupation forces found that fostering labor unions at the enterprise level was the fastest and most convenient way to organize labor (Japan Institute of Labor 1979, p. 8).

In the 1950s, enterprise unions learned some harsh lessons about how prolonged strikes can backfire. Since enterprise unions can close down a firm but not an industry, lengthy strikes resulted in the firm's loss of market share and threatened the solvency of the company itself. In the case of the National Automobile Workers' Union in its strike against Nissan Motors in 1953, the union actually lost its membership and was dissolved. As a result, Japanese enterprise unions now seriously consider the financial position of the company, its market share, and its ability to compete in international markets before they resort to long strikes (Sumiya 1973, pp. 76–77). In the business sector, strikes generally are short and work lost is often made up. (Public-sector unions, however, tend to be more militant and often resort to strikes or slow-down tactics.)

In a one-day strike against an American subsidiary in Japan, for example, the union gave management six weeks notice of the walkout, afterward cleaned up the coffee cups and cigarette butts, and the following day made up the lost production with no overtime. When queried as to why the union members acted in such an inexplicable manner, a worker answered that the strike was necessary to let management know they had serious grievances. The worker stated, however, that the company belonged to the union members too, and they did not want to give the idea that they were disloyal (Ouchi 1981, p. 11).

Experiences such as this are not unusual. Strikes in the private sector often begin on Saturday afternoon and end on Monday morning. They are usually intended to be a show of force. Hence, they are generally conducted before negotiations begin, not after talks have broken down. It is little wonder that Japanese companies preferred that their subsidiaries in the United States not be organized by U.S. trade unions.

B. Quality control

The group ethic — along with sharing of fate and a close identification with the products of the firm rather than the output of the individual within the firm — naturally gives rise to a group-oriented system of quality control. The Japanese also feel that the person "on the spot," or in the case of an enterprise, the individual worker, probably knows more than anyone else about how to solve the problems at hand. Japanese enterprises, therefore, tend to place the responsibility for quality control primarily on the worker. Workers are trusted to monitor their own quality. Each worker in an assembly process also inspects the quality of the product arriving from stations up the assembly line and is expected to stop the line when tolerances are not met.

The best-known vehicle for implementing worker-based quality control has been the quality circle (or what Americans prefer to call participative management). This is a group of eight to ten workers who concentrate on identifying problems in their work area, statistically analyzing the problem, and proposing a permanent solution (Cole 1979). Quality circles recognize that quality control is a joint responsibility and that solutions often require joint effort. In the automobile industry, for example, Japan's quality control circles are estimated to have saved 12.4 hours, yielding a productivity advantage of $213, per car when compared with traditional American practices (Harbour and Associates, Inc. 1980).

The Japanese fetish for high quality also stems from some historical and cultural factors. First, as members of a homogeneous society, Japanese people tend to be extremely status-conscious. The mass media regularly identify which products are of the highest quality, so that customers can buy them for their snob appeal. Second, the Japanese themselves had to live through the poor-quality, "Made in Japan" era. They learned how to search for quality and understand consumer frustrations when quality is missing. Third, Japanese hold to the idea that there is only one right way to do anything. For centuries, left-handed children were forced to learn to hold their chopsticks in their right hands, since this was regarded as the only proper way. Children spend endless hours studying calligraphy and learning the "correct" way to write Chinese characters.

In most cases, what is considered the correct way is also the most efficient way. Time and motion studies are popular, not only for manufacturers but for people in every endeavor. Even ditch diggers have a methodical way of shoveling dirt that conserves energy and produces a pattern of shoveled soil that is aesthetically pleasing. In department stores, clerks must wrap packages in such a way that only one piece of tape is needed. These attitudes carry over to assembly lines and enhance quality control.

Promotion criteria

Because groups tend to be permanent in Japan, promotion within the group can give rise to hostilities and rivalries that could destroy the fabric of the organization. Considerations of equity, therefore, receive heavy weight during the early career of individuals. Japanese promotion criteria explicitly take into account age and length of service. This policy favors internal promotions, which are important in maintaining the morale of employees. It also recognizes the respect for seniority prevalent throughout Japanese society.

During the first several years with a firm, all individuals are moved up the salary ladder together, even though their performance is being critically monitored, and high achievers are receiving the best job assignments. Inevitably, moving up a hierarchy requires that some receive promotions while others do not. In the typical Japanese case, before persons are moved ahead of those who entered the firm at the same time, they have been evaluated thoroughly in many different situations and a strong consensus exists as to their qualifications.

Young recruits know that each of them has a clear shot at becoming a high executive in the company, because promotions are from within. They are therefore willing to put up with slow promotions in the beginning on the promise of considerable rewards later. Each recruit, moreover, is assigned a senior (*sempai*) who gives advice, lets the employee know he or she is wanted, and plays a major role in determining whether the recruit eventually is promoted (Ouchi 1981, pp. 58–60; Rohlen 1974, pp. 123–29; Nakane 1970, p. 26 ff.).

Obviously, such a system is more difficult to implement in the United States, where job mobility is greater and fast promotions are considered necessary to retain good people. Rapid turnover and bidding for people among firms, however, can result in lower employee morale, less commitment to the company, an emphasis on immediate results, and managers who may be specialists in some aspects of a corporation (usually finance) but lack expertise in the basics of the products they produce.

Corporate strategy

The permanence of the individual worker's relationship with the employing company manifests itself in Japanese corporate strategy through: (1) a long-term outlook for marketing and product development; (2) a preference for growth; and (3) an emphasis on market share.

There has been nearly unanimous indictment of U.S. industry's focus on short-term performance indicators, such as quarterly profits and stock value. Even U.S. corporations speak of the "tyranny of Wall Street."

Japanese firms also must perform well in the short run; but with less interfirm mobility, and with the need to provide for one's livelihood during the autumn of one's working life, Japanese managers have a strong incentive to look farther down the road. More than maximizing short-term profits, the incentive for Japanese managers is propelling the firm forward by growth and development. Their future hangs solely with the company. To sacrifice future opportunities by currently underinvesting in research and development, process technology, or market development would be considered short-sighted indeed.

Two practices in addition to company loyalty reinforce Japanese companies' impetus to grow. The first is the policy of promoting from within. As managers work their way up the system's hierarchy, fewer and fewer positions exist. If a company is growing, more promotions become available.

The second is the practice of retiring all but the most senior people at the early age of 55 or 60 with lump-sum payments but no (or paltry) pensions. With seniority wage increases and permanent employment, early retirement is necessary to keep wage costs under control. Retirees, however, usually move to smaller firms as temporary employees. The larger the company, the more it will be able to impose on its suppliers or subsidiaries to hire its retirees — many of whom then work as contacts with their former firm. By pushing economic growth, Japanese managers tend to be preparing a landing place for their inevitable "fall from heaven" (*amakudari*).

Another aspect of Japanese corporate strategy is the focus on market share, instead of profitability, as a measure of business success. The rationale for this strategy relates to a parallel focus on the growth and longevity of the enterprise but also to some peculiarities of the Japanese system.

In the 1930s, Matsushita Electric gave explicit recognition to the importance of market share. The conventional wisdom of the time was to emphasize recouping investments as quickly as possible. Matsushita, however, reduced prices as soon as higher production volumes generated cost savings. This practice tends to increase market share and establish barriers to entry for competitors who find small margins unattractive (Pascale and Athos 1981, p. 30). Other Japanese firms have followed the Matsushita lead.

Market share is a highly competitive measure of performance. Market share is a manifestation of all the desirable attributes of a company. Any firm that is maintaining or increasing its market share, even if profits are dismally low, has a good chance of existing for a long time. Any firm losing market share, even if it is profitable in the short run, eventually could be forced out of the market. An increasing market share also usually is accompanied by growing production volume. This allows a firm to move down its experience curve and lower its costs of production.

Japan's business history is replete with case histories of fierce battles for market share. Producers who lost the battle have usually been forced to withdraw from the market. In the hand calculator industry, for example, the number of producers dropped from more than 40 to fewer than five.

A structural peculiarity common in Japanese industrial organization favors an emphasis on market share. Japanese firms tend to be highly specialized when compared with their Western counterparts. Toyota and Nissan make motor vehicles and little else. Compare them with General Motors or Ford, with their diversity of interests. Ford, for example, produces motor vehicles, communications equipment, tractors, steel, and glass. It also develops land, provides credit, and writes insurance.

Japanese firms tend to focus on a specific line of products and subcontract out inputs and often even marketing. (Some notable exceptions exist.) This lack of diversification is caused, first, by the permanence of managers in the company group who often lack the skills necessary to branch out into other industries. Second, it arises from the common assumption in Japan that a firm should belong to an industry and make its contribution to society through its efforts in that industry — even if that industry is in decline (Clark 1979, pp. 56–57). If, in the exceptional case, a firm branches out into another industry, it generally will do so by establishing a wholly owned subsidiary that will be given considerable autonomy. Toyota Motors, for example, is now larger than and fairly independent of its parent, Toyoda Looms.

This industry specialization means that if a firm is losing market share, it is losing its only means of livelihood. The market risks of such a firm are not spread as broadly as is typical for firms in other industrialized countries. Japanese firms, therefore, tend to protect their market share with ferocious tenacity.

E. Exports

The permanence of the group, a lack of specialization, the need to grow, and the stress on market share all interact to propel Japanese firms into foreign markets.

During the quarter century following the end of World War II, when the Japanese economy was growing at real rates exceeding 10 percent per year, companies experienced real growth each year without relying extensively on exports. During the 1970s, however, as the Japanese economy matured and growth rates slowed down, firms were forced to look more to foreign markets, to expand and to reduce risks.

Maintaining a permanent staff introduces considerable rigidity into an organization in the face of changing economic conditions. Without the option of laying off workers during periods of slack demand, Japanese firms are confronted by tremendous pressures to maintain production. Firms have adjusted somewhat to this system by hiring temporary and part-time workers or relying on overtime during boom periods, by retaining the right to shift workers to various jobs as economic conditions change, by extensive subcontracting, by adjusting payments of bonuses or salaries, and by keeping the staff of permanent employees lean. Following the oil crisis of 1973, for example, Toyo Kogyo, in the face of plummeting demand for its Mazda cars equipped with rotary engines, shifted 1,100 clerical workers to sales (Pearlstine 1975).

None of this flexibility, however, compares with export markets as a way to reduce risk. Not only can export markets reduce fluctuations in demand, but they offer opportunities for growth that simply do not exist within the Japanese economy. Japan, for example, exports more than 70 percent of its output of cameras and watches, more than 50 percent of its output of automobiles and video tape recorders, more than 40 percent of its machine tools, and 25 percent of its steel (Japan Economic Journal 1981). The focus on export markets, moreover, forces Japanese firms to be competitive internationally and to be at the forefront with new products and technology. Success in international markets also assures the survival of the company and of the group.

Emphasis on Human Relationships

The second major Japanese management principle is the emphasis on human rather than functional relationships. American organizations tend to view people as tools to fill slots that have specific job descriptions. People can be used like machines to accomplish overall objectives of the firm. Indeed, one of the wonders of the Western-style company is its ability to organize a diversity of individuals with different skills, backgrounds, and loyalties into an efficient production system.

In Japan, however, the permanence of the group forces managers to place more emphasis on people than on the system. In the final analysis, it is people, not buildings or organizational charts, that actually make up a company. At the University of Chicago, a story is told that a newly appointed president at his first faculty meeting referred to the teachers as employees of the university. A senior professor stood up, begged to differ with the president, and said, "We are not employees of the university. We are the university!" Japanese would agree wholeheartedly.

Japanese companies place great weight on the quality of the people in the organization and on maintaining harmonious relations among them. This emphasis on human relations can be seen in careful recruitment practices, a concern for the whole employee, harmonious resolution of conflicts, and ambiguity in expressing differences, which minimizes hurt feelings and allows for face saving.

Careful recruitment

While companies in any industrialized nation place considerable emphasis on recruitment, Japanese companies commit exceptionally large amounts of time and resources to attracting talented workers. Because of permanent employment and the lack of a professional managerial class in Japan, the future of the company rests on the quality of the personnel the company is able to attract at the entry level.

Recruitment in Japan tends to be centralized, with the president of the company often personally interviewing the candidates to be hired. Virtually all new recruits in Japan are hired directly after graduation from schools and universities. Japanese rely heavily on schools to select the students with the best minds, who will then be offered the best jobs in government or business. The largest and most prestigious companies can hire from the best and most prestigious universitites (Dore 1973, pp. 46–50). This tyranny of schools reaches all the way down to kindergarten, where entrance examinations are given to children as young as four years old.

Recruitment difficulties provide another reason that Japanese firms feel they must continually grow. If a company can be among the top few firms in its industry, it is better able to recruit the best talent from among the best universities. If not, it will have to resign itself to hiring from lower-rated schools.

The problem with lower-rated schools is not that their students are less bright, because many are essentially as smart as their colleagues in the more prestigious universities. The difficulties come later when the entering recruits rise in the company hierarchy and have to deal with counterparts in other companies and in the government. In a country like Japan, which prefers face-to-face dealings, having classmates in high places helps immensely. Some Japanese companies even send their employees to U.S. business schools, not just to learn American methods but to make contacts with future senior managers of U.S. business ("Japan Gives" 1981).

Concern for the whole employee

Japanese paternalism and focus on social as well as economic relationships stem partly from Japan's early industrial period, when textile mills had to build dormitories, furnish a healthy diet, and provide for the moral, intellectual, and physical well-being of young workers. Japanese feel that social and ethical as well as economic closeness creates an atmosphere of mutual trust, intimacy (nonsexual), and understanding (Ouchi 1981, pp. 51–55).

The Hitachi Company, for example, provides company housing, recreation and sports facilities, a concert auditorium, a monthly magazine designed to teach morality and ethics, a mutual aid fund (80 percent company-funded) that provides gifts of money for weddings, births, and deaths, classes on various subjects, and generous expense accounts for entertaining (Dore 1973, pp. 201–21, 268). Managers often serve as go-betweens in arranging marriages and take interest in the personal lives of their workers. Occasionally a senior manager actually will delegate some of his official corporate work to allow himself to devote more time to his corporate social obligations, such as attending weddings (Arai 1971).

Americans are likely to consider Japanese paternalism as reaching too far into the privacy and independence of the individual. Indeed, many Americans would find it difficult even to talk about spiritual values with their colleagues. The Japanese company, however, sees itself as responsible for the development of the whole person. Since an employee most likely will be with a particular company for most of his or her working life, that development appears to justify the expense and time it requires.

c. Harmonious resolution of conflicts

Every organization has conflicts that must be resolved in order for work to proceed. Many Americans favor adversarial resolution of conflicts, where individuals will "lay their cards on the table" and "battle it out" regardless of the emotional toll on the participants. A frequent approach to motivation also is to "go down to the mill and kick derrières." American bureaucratic organization, moreover, tends to give rise to fierce internal struggles, with people maximizing their owns goals instead of the group's.*

The Japanese approach is clear: harmony within, competition without. People resent being humiliated, publicly scolded, or fired. They will go to great lengths to defend themselves against any such action and will in the process dissipate considerable energy that could better be directed toward external competition. Japanese companies attempt to minimize this internal conflict by emphasizing harmony (wa) (Wallace 1972, pp. 46–51; Pascale and Athos 1981, pp. 101–2).

This harmony is more than a state of being. It is a quality of relationships. It refers to the cooperation, trust, sharing, warmth, morale, and hard work of efficient, pleasant, and purposeful fellowship (Rohlen 1974, p. 47).

Harmony often requires ambiguity. The Japanese have a multitude of ways of saying no. Japanese use ambiguity and indirection instead of outright refusal. Differences tend to be worked out through long discussions and an attempt to understand the viewpoints of others. In such a process, no one has to "lose face" or be humiliated. What many Americans attribute to inscrutability in the Japanese is actually their way of refusing politely.

Organizations seek clarity and certainty, but human relationships in-

---

*Japanese group consciousness also can lead to sectional rivalries in organizations.

volve ambiguity, reading between the lines, and uncertainty. Corporate executives, such as Harold Green of ITT, often have sought clarity and certainty by brute force, but what is achieved by such means generally comes at a considerable cost in terms of human relations (Pascale and Athos 1981).

Internal harmony is difficult to maintain forever without some release. Conflicts, even in Japanese organizations, inevitably arise. One method Japanese use to release pent-up frustrations is getting drunk together. When a man is drunk, he is allowed to say virtually anything with impunity. The next morning no one remembers what was said, but the person has had a legitimate chance to "get it off his chest."

Harmony is furthered by eliminating distinctions between managers and workers. Japanese firms generally have no executive restrooms, lunch rooms, or even parking spaces. (In Japan, however, artificial distinctions are often unnecessary, because Japanese language and behavior require use of honorifics or bowing that recognizes status.) Even at the Honda motorcycle plant in the United States, for example, labor and management eat in the same cafeteria, and executives have no reserved parking spaces. Employees are called associates, and executives wear the same uniforms as the workers (Kanabayashi 1981).

Managers as Generalists

In the United States, managers are considered to be highly knowledgeable professionals and decision makers who are able to lay out problems, make difficult choices, and accomplish objectives. Decisions generally flow from the top down and are often decentralized. Responsibility is narrowly assigned. Problems can be addressed and choices made quickly.

In Japan, top management is rich in experience and has been with the company for a long time. Managers tend to be generalists and facilitators — much like the elders of a tribe. (Entrepreneurs, such as Morita of Sony, are exceptions.) Problems are usually solved by groups in which a consensus is arrived at through long hours of discussion and consideration of alternatives. Actual decisions tend to be made by middle managers after consultation with superiors and then circulated for final approval. The decision-making process tends to be slow, but the implementation generally is fast. Responsibility is widely dispersed, and the system is highly flexible.

The manager as a symbolic leader and facilitator

Japanese management skills tend to be oriented more toward people than to a profession. The Japanese managers who rise, with the exception of entrepreneurs, tend to be those who are bright, can work well with groups, and manage people well. Since future managers are recruited directly from undergraduate colleges, professional associations tend to be weak. Much of the advanced training of managers is done in-house.

Since age is an explicit consideration in promotion, managers tend to be older than their subordinates and richer in experience. Their major duty is to maintain harmony in the group and facilitate decision making and implementation. They also often are responsible for the long-term and nonrecurrent strategic planning.

The founder of Matsushita once observed: "When you have 100 employees, you are on the front line. Even if you yell and hit them, they follow you. But if the group grows to 1,000, you must not be on the front line but stay in the middle. When the organization grows to 10,000, you stay behind in awe and give thanks" (Yamada 1980, quoted in Pascale and Athos 1981, p. 46).

The career path of rising young executives is likely to include posts in most of the major areas of the enterprise, both to gain first-hand experience in various phases of the operation and to become acquainted with persons working in those areas. Career paths tend to be nonspecialized, but since Japanese firms tend to be highly specialized, a person who rises to become a director has had time to become thoroughly familar with virtually all operations of the company.

B. Management by consensus – see Dickerman

Perhaps the most widely discussed aspect of Japanese management is consensual or participative decision making. Such decision-making modes have received considerable attention by scholars. They conclude that a consensus approach, as compared with individual decision making, often yields decisions that are more creative and that can be implemented more effectively (Ouchi 1981, p. 43).

Americans often view consensus decision making as something akin to the group that created a camel when it was charged with designing a horse. Japanese, however, with their emphasis on the permanence and harmony of the group, feel that decision making that explicitly allows those concerned to express openly their views and to attempt to understand the positions of others will work better in the long run. Those whose ideas were not accepted, moreover, will tend to support the final decision, because it was arrived at in a fair and open manner.

The vehicle for formalizing the decision is the *ringisho*. This is a document outlining the decision that circulates among sections so that each section head can note his approval with his name stamp. The responsibility for devising the proposal often falls on a younger member of the department directly involved. He is expected to have fresh ideas that he then can discuss with more-senior managers. Often the young person will make mistakes, which are tactfully pointed out by senior people. Some of the ideas, however, are accepted (Arai 1971, pp. 131–35).

By the time the *ringisho* has been sent both laterally and upward through the organization for approval, it literally is covered with name stamps. By then the president has little choice but to add his stamp of approval. One president complained that the only way he could express his disapproval of a *ringisho* was to stamp his name upside down (Yoshino 1968, p. 262).

This form of decision making requires centralization and considerable face-to-face contact among managers. In Japan, since most major corporate headquarters are located around Tokyo, this is no major problem. With multinational corporations, however, the time required to get approval for a decision can be a major handicap.

In 1981, the employees of the Sanyo Corporation's subsidiary in California voted to unionize. One of their grievances was that it took too long to get decisions from Tokyo on such elementary matters as whether employees would receive discounts on merchandise.

C. Responsibility

Responsibility under a system of consensus decision making tends to be widely dispersed. In a bureaucracy, when something goes wrong the question asked is "Who is responsible?" In Japan, the question is "Where did we go wrong?" Scapegoating is pointless (Wallace 1972, p. 47).

In a sense, however, Japanese decision making places more responsibility on employees than does a system that works from the top down. Japanese demand responsibility all the way down to the blue-collar workers on the factory floor. In Japanese factories, the attitude of "let the bosses take the losses" is virtually unheard of. Everyone is in the boat together.

A Japanese-type system, therefore, tends to bring everyone into the decision-making mechanism and into the process of improving the competitive position of the firm. In making decisions, harmony and the maintenance of group relations are kept in the forefront. The responsibility for the decision rests with all employees.

SUMMARY

This chapter has presented an overview of the major contours of Japanese management principles and practices, along with selected comparisons with those considered typical of American thinking. These are summarized in Table 1.1.

TABLE 1.1   Characteristics of Japanese and American Management Styles

JAPANESE	AMERICAN

1. Emphasis on group
    Permanence of group
    Same fate shared by all
      employees
    Group incentives
    Group against outsiders
 	
    Some results:
      Enterprise unions
      Monitoring of quality by
        workers
      Age and length of service as
        important promotion
        criteria
      Corporate strategy that favors
        longevity, market share,
        exports
	1. Emphasis on individual
	    Transitory nature of group
	    Own fate determined by each
	      employee
	    Individual incentives
	    Individual against others
	
	    Some results:
	      Trade unions
	      Monitoring of quality by in-
	        spectors
	      Age and length of service
	        only partly related to
	        promotion
	      Corporate strategy that favors
	        short term rate of profit,
	        known markets

2. Emphasis on human relationships
    "Lifetime" employment and
      recruiting
    Harmonious resolution of con-
      flicts
    Wholistic concern for
      employees
    Desire for indirection, ambiguity
    No formal distinctions between
      managers and workers
	2. Emphasis on functional relation-
	     ships
	    Short-term employment and
	      recruiting
	    Adversarial resolution of con-
	      flicts
	    Segmented concern for
	      employees
	    Desire for clarity, brute integrity
	    Frequently sharp distinctions
	      between managers and
	      workers

3. Managers as generalists
    Manager as social and symbolic
      leader
    Manager as facilitator
    Management by consensus
    Decisions that come from
      middle up
    Centralization
    Wide dispersion of responsibil-
      ity
    Nonspecialized career paths
	3. Managers as specialists
	    Manager as professional
	    Manager as decision maker
	    Management by objectives
	    Decisions that come from top
	      down
	    Decentralization
	    Narrow assignment of respon-
	      sibility
	    Specialized career paths

The overriding characteristic of Japanese management appears to be its emphasis on the firm as a community whose members share a permanent bond and common fate. The firm also emphasizes its role of service to society.

The three primary principles of Japanese managerial style are an emphasis on the group instead of the individual, an emphasis on human instead of functional relationships, and the treatment of top management as generalists.

The emphasis on the group gives rise to group incentives, a direction of energies toward external competitors and not internal rivalries, enterprise unions, worker-based quality control, seniority-based promotions, corporate longevity, the maintenance of market share, and a strong export drive.

The emphasis on human rather than functional relationships gives rise to lifetime employment, careful recruiting, harmonious resolution of conflicts, a concern for the whole employee, indirection and ambiguity when required to save face, and fewer differences between managers and workers.

The emphasis on the manager as a facilitator and generalist rather than a specialist results in a system of decision making that relies heavily on middle management, tends to be highly centralized, and disperses responsibility widely.

The Japanese system seems to be able to motivate workers to increase productivity and to accept rapid technological change. It also reduces tendencies toward featherbedding or counterproductive work rules, and forces firms to compete in international markets. The system is not without problems, but workers seem to be reasonably content, and the results of the system in terms of success in international markets can hardly be disputed.

REFERENCES

Arai, S. 1971. *An Intersection of East and West, Japanese Business Management.* Tokyo, Rikugei.

Bylinsky, G. 1981. "The Japanese Score on a U.S. Fumble." *Fortune*, June 1, pp. 68–72.

Clark, R. 1979. *The Japanese Company.* New Haven: Yale University Press.

Cole, R. E. 1979. "Made in Japan — Quality Control Circles." *Across the Board*, Vol. 16 (November), pp. 72–78.

Dore, R. 1973. *British Factory — Japanese Factory.* Berkeley: University of California Press.

Drucker, P. F. 1980. "Learning from Foreign Management." *Wall Street Journal*, June 4, p. 28.

Gohara, H. 1966. *Ringiteki Keiei to Ringi Seido (The Ringi System and Management).* Tokyo: Toyo Keizai Shimposha.

Pegels, C. 1984. Japan vs. the West. "Implications for mgmt". Kluwer-Nijhoff Publishing.

Harbour and Associates, Inc. 1980. *Comparison and Analysis of Automotive Manufacturing Productivity in the Japanese and North American Automotive Industry for the Manufacture of Subcompact and Compact Cars.* Berkeley, Mich.: Harbour and Assoc.

Hazama, H. 1971. *Nihonteki Keiei (Japanese Management).* Tokyo: Nihon Keizai Shimbunsha.

International Labour Office. 1980. *Year Book of Labour Statistics.* Geneva: International Labour Office.

Iwata, R. 1977. *Nihonteki Keiei no Hensei Genri* (The Underlying Principles of Japanese Management). Tokyo: Bunshindo.

Japan Economic Journal. 1981. *Industrial Review of Japan/1981.* Tokyo: Nihon Keizai Shimbun.

"Japan Gives the B-schools an A — for Contacts." 1981. *Business Week,* Oct. 19, pp. 132–33.

Japan Institute of Labor. 1979. *Japanese Industrial Relations,* ser. 2. Tokyo: Japan Institute of Labor.

"Japanese Companies Throw a Good Party." 1981. *Wall Street Journal,* Dec. 9, p. 34.

"Japanese Managers Tell How Their System Works." 1977. *Fortune,* November, pp. 126–32, 136–38.

Kahn, Herman. 1970. *The Emerging Japanese Superstate, Challenge and Response.* Englewood Cliffs, N.J.: Prentice-Hall.

Kamata, S. 1980. "The Dark Side of Toyota, the Wonderland." *Sekai,* March, pp. 23–26. Translated in *Summaries of Selected Japanese Magazines.* American Embassy, Tokyo, January, 1981.

Kanabayashi, M. 1981. "Honda's Accord, How a Japanese Firm is Faring on Its Dealings with Workers in the U.S." *Wall Street Journal,* Oct. 2, pp. 1, 25.

Lehner, U. C. 1981. "Japanese Factories Are Points of Interest to Foreign Tourists Studying Technology." *Wall Street Journal,* Sept. 3, p. 44.

Lohr, S. 1981. "Overhauling America's Business Management." *New York Times Magazine,* January 4, pp. 14–17, 42–62.

Morita, A. 1981. "West Meets East at Sony." Speech at the Conference on Management, Productivity, and Reindustrialization: East Meets West, April 2, Washington, D.C.

Nakane, C. 1970. *Japanese Society.* Berkeley: University of California Press.

Noda, N. 1970. "How Japan Absorbed American Management Methods." In *Modern Japanese Management,* ed. British Institute of Management, pp. 29–66. Tonbridge, Kent: British Institue of Management.

Ouchi, W. 1981. *Theory Z.* Reading, Mass.: Addison-Wesley.

Pascale, R. T., and Athos, A. G. 1981. *The Art of Japanese Management.* New York: Simon and Schuster.

Pearlstine, N. 1975. "Hanging Together, Japan's Establishment Rushes, More or Less, to Aid Mazda's Maker." *Wall Street Journal,* March 24, pp. 1, 25.

Puri, T., and A. Bhide. 1981. "The Crucial Weaknesses of Japan Inc." *Wall Street Journal,* June 8, p. 20.

Rehder, R. R. 1979. "Japanese Management: An American Challenge." *Human Resource Management* 18 (Winter):63–70.

Rohlen, T. 1974. *For Harmony and Strength*. Berkeley: University of California Press.

Sumiya, M. 1973. "Contemporary Arrangements: An Overview." In *Workers and Employers in Japan*, ed. K. Okoshi et al., pp. 49–88. Tokyo: University of Tokyo Press.

Tsuchiya, M. 1974. *Ha-ba-do Bijinesu Suku-ru Nite (At the Harvard Business School)*. Tokyo: Chuo Koronsha.

Wallace, W. M. 1972. "The Secret Weapon of Japanese Business." *Columbia Journal of World Business* 7 (Nov.-Dec.):43–52.

Wiegner, K. K. 1981. "It's the Response That Counts." *Forbes*, Nov. 23, pp. 123–29.

Yamada, M. 1980. "Soshiki to Keiei." In *Sangyo Shakai to Nihonjin (Industrial Society and Japanese)*, ed. B. Masao and K. Masamura. Tokyo: Chikuma Shabo.

Yamagata, G. 1978. Interview by author, October, Tokyo.

Yang, C. Y. 1977. "Management Styles: American vis-à-vis Japanese." *Columbia Journal of World Business* 12 (Fall):23–31.

Yoshino, M. Y. 1968. *Japan's Managerial System*. Cambridge, Mass.: M.I.T. Press.

2

Development and Use of the Functional Informal Group in the Japanese Organization

THOMAS PATRICK CULLEN

INTRODUCTION

Within the past decade, a significant change has taken place in the American workforce. Equal opportunity legislation, the women's movement, and government-mandated affirmative action programs have focused increasing attention on the differences in cultural values within our society. Little attention, however, has been given to the effect of these heterogeneous values within the workplace.

Industrial competition from other nations, particularly Japan, raises questions about the relationship between cultural values and organizational effectiveness. Industrial efficiency in Japan can no longer be explained as the result of postwar rebuilding of plants or as an outcome of the availability of a cheap labor force. To a large degree, modern plant technology is a product of the last decade. Per capita wages in Japan now approach or exceed those in the United States.

Current popular business literature suggests that the Japanese productivity marvel is the result of a unique management style and philosophy. U.S. industry has responded to the Japanese challenge by importing some of these management techniques, notably the concept of quality control circles.

Management scholar William Ouchi cautions against the "management fad" of implementing "quality control circles" unless there is a management commitment to adapt to the principles underlying the concept. While Ouchi sees this commitment largely as the organization's philosophical orientation, his message is clear. The techniques employed by Japanese management are shaped by other organizational processes and properties (Ouchi 1980).

Other scholars suggest that organizational theory has paid too little attention to the relationships among organizational activities, processes, and properties and the cultural values of the individuals within the organization (Connor and Becker 1975). The emphasis on values in the Japanese organization and the relationship of values to organizational processes are components of the success of quality control circles and Japanese management systems.

The Western world tends to view Japan as a culturally homogeneous society. While the ethnic and racial minority groups of U.S. society are perhaps more evident, there is a diversity of cultural subgroups within Japanese society. That diversity represents a wide range of value systems associated with political and economic orientations as well as ethnic origins and historical social class structure. The Japanese management system tends to homogenize these diverse value systems, and the resultant unity of values within the organization is one of the great strengths of Japanese management.

Former United States Ambassador to Japan James D. Hodgson finds the Japanese industrial model a paradox, for "though it does not know the Western rules, [it] seems to win all the games." Harmony is valued over justice, and relationships are considered more important than individual rights (Hodgson 1978). The Japanese know the Western rules. They have added to those rules, and the addition is implicit in Hodgson's comment. A consensus of values is perhaps the key rule in Japanese organizations, and their management systems are designed around that rule.

Cultural change, whether nation-wide or within the social microcosm of an organization, is a necessary factor of economic progress (Kellert et al. 1967). Whereas the American tendency is to preserve and protect a diversity of cultural orientations, the Japanese seem to view cultural diversity as an impediment to achievement of organizational objectives.* While the popular notion is that it is the individual, and the in-

---

*Kellert et al. (1967) assert that "those more willing and able to accept the direction of [cultural] change will experience less psychological strain than those either unwilling or unable to accept this direction" (p. 410). The American "protection" of cultural diversity may, in fact, result in additional strain as necessary changes occur.

dividual's values, that are protected in the American system, individuality is perhaps as much a factor of group processes in Japan as it is in the Western world.

Individual expression, beliefs, attitudes, and behaviors are largely regulated by the individual's referent groups. This is a pancultural phenomenon. While referent groups may be selected because they share the individual's attitudes and values, it is the group that helps develop and sustain those values and attitudes in society (Bem 1977).

Thus, the importance of a general concurrence of norms and values, even at the cost of "suppression" of individual rights, is not limited to the culture of Japan. Through its emphasis on the relationship between group norms and values and organizational processes, however, the Japanese organization consciously develops referent groups as a means of encouraging a direction of cultural change within the organization that supports the objectives of the organization.

Management scholar Chester Barnard feels that informal groups within a formal organization function as referent groups for individuals. According to Barnard, the informal group serves to maintain cohesiveness and provide a vehicle for communications. Far from suggesting that informal groups are a necessary evil in organizations, Barnard asserts that the informal group serves as an important referent group for values, and thus promotes individual feelings of personal integrity, self-respect, and independent choice. Thus the informal group forms the basis for cooperation within the organization (Barnard 1978).

Despite the importance of informal groups in organizational functioning, there is little research suggesting that organizational processes affect the development of informal groups within the organization, or that the organization might encourage development of informal groups in such a way that the referent power of the informal group would parallel the legitimate power of the formal group. Such parallel development would permit exploitation of the strengths of the informal group in the interest of achieving organizational objectives.

The development of what might be called a "functional informal group" is an essential objective of Japanese management. Unlike the American approach, which seeks a cohesiveness of task orientation, the Japanese approach emphasizes a heterogeneity of task orientations within the functional, decision-making groups of the organization. Thus there is a homogeneity of values and norms that serves as the basis of group functioning. The organization benefits from better utilization of the communications, maintenance, and referent-group properties of functional informal groups.

The development of the functional informal group, in the Japanese model, is an outcome of the training philosophy and system of Japanese organizations, organizational socialization, and maintenance of peer groups in a cadre system within the organization. While cultural norms and values, in Japanese society, may support the system, research in the United States indicates that the positive outcomes are not culture-bound. The relationship among these Japanese management processes may have implications for U.S. management.

HORIZONTAL TRAINING: SPECIALIZATION VERSUS GENERALIZATION

The Japanese concept of industrial training can be called "horizontal training," for the training system encourages acquisition of a variety of task skills at the expense of skill specialization. The individual is trained in most, if not all, tasks at the entry level — not within a single department, but throughout the organization. Only when the employee has been exposed to a wide variety of entry-level positions and tasks does that individual move to the next level of specialization. The horizontal training of the individual continues through each defined level within the organization. While the form of the organization is pyramidal, and thus the range of task exposure may be increasingly limited as the employee moves up the hierarchy, the training system develops generalists, not specialists.

This horizontal training process is an integral part of the organizational socialization of the employee. Employees are normally hired at specified intervals, usually once a year. Virtually all employees, regardless of education or previous experience, start at the lowest levels of the organization. While the process of training in a variety of tasks is similar to an apprenticeship program, the Japanese form of horizontal training, unlike traditional apprenticeship programs, is not tied to any specific skill.

An apprenticeship program is intended to achieve a vertical accumulation of skills. Skills must be mastered at each level before one can be trained at the next higher level. The Japanese concept equates the training process with ability to handle increasing levels of responsibility, not increasing complexity of skills. Thus it is not unusual for a top-level management employee to be moved to a field in which he has no experience. It is assumed that if the individual is able to handle the responsibility at that level, an intimate knowledge of the tasks involved is not of great importance and can be easily learned.

There are, of course, certain cases in which a high degree of specialization is critical to an organization. Computer specialists are a good example. To a large degree, such highly technical fields are often excluded from the organization. Services generally are contracted from another company, which, in turn, tends to produce generalists within the specialty. The other approach is to treat specialists as exceptional cases within the organization. They may enter the organization at higher levels, but their careers are limited by their specialty, and their participation in organizational decision making is far more restricted than is the case with the generalist.* The subcontracting of highly specialized tasks seems, however, to be the predominant practice.

The basic trade-off of skill specialization for skill generalization reflects the Japanese philosophical definition of an effective organization as one that successfully exploits a changing environment. The predominant Western model, based on specific and perhaps conflicting goals, is more in the Weberian tradition, that of maximizing productivity within each defined, rational unit of the organization. It assumes that maximization of the efficiency of each of the parts of the organization results in maximization of organizational efficiency. The tendency of Japanese firms to use subcontractors reflects their environmental orientation, for use of subcontractors can be reduced in times of recession without affecting the fabric of an organization. Generalists can be used to take advantage of shifts in the economy, as their usefulness to the organization is not limited by their specialty.

The Japanese organization's objective is to maximize the fit between the organization and an environment of scarce resources, so as to maximize the acquisition and use of those resources. It is not surprising, as Japan has always been a country of scarce natural resources, that its industrial orientation should be towards maximization of acquisition and use of material resources, as well as maximization of use of human resources. Thus the Japanese model is well suited to an era of perceived or actual global scarcity of natural resources, and, not surprisingly, is more productive than the Western model of task goals and task efficiency. †

While Japanese management is often seen as suppressing individuality, industrial psychologist Chris Argyris (1957) argues that task specialization has the same effect. He asserts that task specialization inhibits the self-actualization of the individual. According to Argyris, as the highly specialized employee is called on to exhibit only a few superficial abilities. Thus who one is becomes less important than what one can do. The Japanese argument against task specialization is concerned with the ability of the organization to adapt to a changing environment, rather than with

---

*This is the observation of Japanese sociologist Chie Nakane. In a reply to a question following a lecture at Cornell University in 1980, Nakane indicated that highly specialized employees may start at higher salaries, but that their percentage of annual salary increase is generally below that of others in the organization.

†Hall (1980) contends that any basic approach to management effectiveness may be classified as either a resource acquisition model or a goal model.

questions of individual expression. The notion Argyris proposes, that specialization inhibits integration of the individual into the organization, is one that would appeal to Japanese management.

Sociologist Robert Merton (1967) contends that empathy is a factor in the underlying social structure of an organization. According to Merton, development of empathy is limited by the degree to which the social structure encourages and provides opportunities for the individual to understand the conflicting nature of various roles and tasks within the organization. Development of organizational empathy is an important objective of the horizontal training process. Specialization may be dysfunctional in this regard, in that it inhibits development of interdepartmental empathy.

There certainly are contrary arguments supporting the concept of specialization over generalization in the training process. Specialized skills lend themselves to development of specialized goals, and the employee can be asked to perform more-difficult tasks. Performance has been found to be related to both goal specificity and goal difficulty. However, this research, by psychologist Edwin Locke (1968), focuses only on the relationship between intention and goals. It does not attempt to specify a causal relationship. Locke's research assumes a management orientation toward a goal model of organizational efficiency. The Japanese model, based on resource acquisition and utilization, deemphasizes the goal orientation in favor of an efficiency and effectiveness model stressing the decision-making process.

The horizontal training philosophy of the Japanese, stressing generalization, results in a more flexible work force, as the employee is better able to analyze the conflicting nature of various task coalitions within the organization. Thus the individual is more apt to consider those orientations as a part of the decision-making process, because of the empathy developed as a function of the training process. The training philosophy also is reflected in the Japanese view of the functional group, as well as in the way that the group is involved in the decision-making process.

GROUP DEVELOPMENT: THE JAPANESE MODEL

In the Japanese model, group cooperation is the essence of organizational effectiveness. This spirit of cooperation or group harmony (*wa* in Japanese) is one of the principal objectives of the horizontal training system. Popular management literature outside Japan usually translates *wa* as "group harmony," but often fails to appreciate fully the Japanese concept of the "group."

The group, not the individual, is the basic design unit of the Japanese organization. This is not an exclusively Japanese notion. Psychologist Harold Leavitt (1977) has proposed that group membership provides numerous benefits to both the individual and the organization. These include satisfaction of membership needs, enlarging the range of activities available to the individual, creation of an atmosphere of independence, promotion of innovation, improved decision-making processes, improved control, and improved communication. Leavitt therefore suggests that organizations should be developed with groups as the basic design units. Perhaps more importantly, he argues that a group design orientation will result in planned groups while inhibiting the formation of unplanned groups.

The development of planned groups, within the organization, is one of the great strengths of the Japanese management system. The horizontal training system and the concurrent organizational socialization in the Japanese model result in formal groups with the characteristics of informal groups. That development, however, is contingent upon the definition of a group within the organization.

As is the case with the training and socialization processes in the Japanese organization, group definition tends to be horizontal rather than vertical in nature. Task-bounded groups are subordinate to responsibility-level groups. This is an important difference between Western and Japanese orientations. Whereas the Western organization tends to organize within functional task groups, the Japanese organization is made up of hierarchical levels of groups composed of individuals at similar levels of responsibility. These horizontal groups function at all levels of responsibility and participate in the decision-making process at all levels of responsibility; the result is that the decision-making process is less influenced by the task orientation than it is in the Western model.

All employees in a Japanese organization, regardless of individual differences in education, age, or experience, normally start at entry level, with the same degree of responsibility, and tend to move through the hierarchy of the organization at the same pace. As a result, groups of peers are defined at the earliest stages of employment. This peer organization of new recruits is a more effective form of organizational socialization than is task organization (Schein 1977).

The potential danger of a peer-group organization is that such groups may develop norms contrary to those of the organization (Schein 1977). It is possible, however, to deemphasize the individual's psychological identification with the task group, through the horizontal training process as well as by providing the individual with a variety of task experiences. In this way the organizational norms, not the norms of the task group, are reinforced. Those norms and values are common throughout the training experience. Thus the diversity of task experiences is designed to produce a homogeneity of values and norms within any given peer group, for the peer group, rather than the task group, becomes the critical referent group.

On the other hand, a vertical orientation results in reinforcement of a psychological identification with a task group. The Hawthorne experiments have shown that, for whatever reason, a limitation of work environment attitudes is one of the social influences that can result in productivity norms that are below maximum (Roethlisberger and Dickson 1939). Psychologist Leon Festinger's theory of social comparison (1954) would suggest that if there is a deemphasis of task-group identification, with an increase in peer-group interaction, the resulting longitudinal inadequacy of performance criteria will cause the individual to seek comparison with the peer group rather than the task group.

A vertical orientation, with its emphasis on specialized skill acquisition as well as upward mobility within the organization dependent on those skills, results in a group categorization of individuals by task group. Turf protection and intergroup conflict are the inevitable results, as the individual comes to favor the task ingroup over other-task outgroups (Wilder and Thompson 1980). Skill training, in a vertical system, favors this identification with a skill-bounded ingroup. As a referent group, the skill-bounded ingroup owes less allegiance to the organization than it does to the skill. The norms and values that the group develops are bounded only by the minimal acceptable standards of the industry. Protection of production and other norms are important as a means of preserving avenues of interorganizational mobility.

A vertical system also implies a change of referent groups as the individual progresses through higher skill levels. This change in referent groups is an integral part of the Western system of socialization (Lieberman 1977).

The Japanese system, however, seeks to maintain the peer group as a constant referent group. The multiplicity of roles included in the training process serves to reinforce and solidify norms and values unique to the organization, making interorganizational movement a less viable option. While interorganizational movement in Japan is rare, its relationship to the development of organizationally specific norms and values and deemphasis of task-specific norms and values may be more circular than causal.

The horizontal training philosophy assumes that specific tasks are rather simple and easily learned. For this reason, highly skilled tasks are treated not as the norm but as the exception. Within this limitation, productivity is seen as related to the decision-making process more than to tenure. The Western orientation, at least with low-skill jobs, seems to focus not on increasing productivity with tenure, but on amortizing the cost of initial training over a longer period of time.

There are status differences within any given work group in the

Japanese organization. As new recruits are brought into the organization, the more senior peer groups have relatively more status within the task group. This results in a gradual and subtle increase in responsibility over time, related to the seniority of the peer group rather than to task proficiency. Thus even at the lowest levels of the organization there are status differentiations. The unique aspect of the Japanese orientation is that these differences in status are related not to the task group, but to the peer group.

Sociologist Ruth Benedict (1938) sees this gradual changing of roles and status sequences as mitigating the difficulties that arise from a sudden change in role or status. Merton (1967) calls this system of role gradation "anticipatory socialization," noting:

> In effect, by orientation to the norms of prospective statuses, the individual engages in trial behavior and tends to move at a pace which is controlled by the responses of those in his current role set (p. 439).

In the Japanese organization the role set is defined first as the peer group. The norms and values of the peer group and of the individuals within the peer group are reinforced by these trial behaviors and the response of the peer group to those behaviors. The change of roles is gradual, paced by the movement of the individual through the organizational hierarchy. This change in values and socialization to organizational norms is further reinforced by hiring processes. These tend to perpetuate *gakubatsu* (school cliques) and the promotion of individuals by seniority of their peer group (*nenko joretsu*). Individuals also are reinforced by the lifetime employment philosophy (*shushin koyo*) of most Japanese organizations. Again, however, these relationships may be circular rather than causal. These relationships are also an integral part of the decision-making process of Japanese organizations.

THE DECISION-MAKING PROCESS: PARTICIPATIVE BUREAUCRACY

The organizational uniformity of norms and values, an objective of horizontal training and socialization processes as well as an outcome of the development of peer groups as principle referent groups, appears to be a situation that encourages overconformity. Merton (1967, pp. 251–52) suggests that such overconformity tends to lead to a strict devotion to rules, interferes with adaptation to special conditions, and replaces a relativistic approach to the decision-making process with an absolutistic approach.

The Japanese model sees overconformity a danger. However, it is overconformity to norms and values of task groups that is of concern to the Japanese. As the Western vertical system results in a task group that is industry-wide, and thus transcends organizational boundaries, the Japanese view is that overconformity to the task group may inhibit organizational effectiveness. Merton would agree, as he asserts that organic solidarity of any highly differentiated social system is dependent on a similarity of the persistent values and attitudes within that society (Merton 1967, pp. 252–53).

The American value of participative democracy has given rise to a philosophy of participative management. The "human relations" school of management theory, typified by "theory Y" (McGregor 1960), argues that integration of the individual into the organization is best achieved by a participative management style. McGregor's theory, however, does not distinguish between the reality of participation and the perception of participation. Democracy, as it is practiced, may be based more on perception than on reality; democracy may respond more to special interest groups than to the will of the majority. The perception of participation, however, is maintained through the electoral system.

Merton asserts that perception is far more important than reality. In his view, many (if not all) social processes are governed by what he calls "the Thomas Theorem," which is based on the writings of sociologist W. I. Thomas. Thomas wrote that "if men define situations as real, they are real in their consequences" (Merton 1967, p. 475). Merton (1967, p. 20) proposes that, for the individual, effects are caused not by change but by the means employed to produce the change.

Horizontal training and socialization both contribute to increasing the perception of involvement in the decision-making process without yielding the ultimate power of top-level management.

The importance of perception of involvement is not a culture-bound principle. Research in Western countries has shown that less specific individual roles and more-complex tasks lead to a perception of more autonomy on the job (Grimes, Klein, and Schull 1972). While there is no specific research supporting the notion that generalized training leads to a perception of increased task complexity, it seems reasonable to assert that the Japanese tendency to avoid specificity of objectives could lead to perception of a more complex task than would task objectives with readily quantifiable effectiveness measures.

Autonomy has often been cited as a goal of participative management and job-enrichment principles, and the concept has a certain logical appeal. A decrease of bureaucratic imperatives should lead to feelings of autonomy and an increase in ability to respond to an uncertain environment. Bureaucracy in the Japanese model, however, does not encourage autonomy, but does encourage participation in the decision-making process.

Japanese management uses a system known as *ringisho* as the principal decision-making, communications, and participation vehicle (Dickerman 1974, pp. 14–15). Normally a plan or proposal originating at a middle or lower responsibility level is reviewed first at the originating level. This review, like all others, is carried out by the peer group. Thus a variety of task orientations is part of the input. Comments representing these various views accompany the proposal through each of the responsibility levels. At all levels, individuals have an opportunity to contribute their thinking to the final decision, which is made at the top level. A suggestion or proposal originating at the top management level and circulated through lower responsibility levels through the *ringisho* system is unlikely to be contradicted at lower levels, although that does happen.

This lack of actual autonomy, as an aspect of the decision-making process, also does not appear to be limited to the culture of Japan. S. B. Bacharach and M. Aiken (1976), working in the United States, have shown that autonomy is negatively related to perceptions of participation in the decision-making process. They speculate that a lack of autonomy may make integration of the individual into the decision-making process easier. The Japanese *ringisho* system provides the individual with a clearly defined role in the decision-making process. When individuals know the "rules" by which they must participate, individual participation may be less ambiguous (Bacharach and Aiken 1976).

Research by Bacharach and Aiken (1976) also indicates that less skill specialization and less routine tasks result in a perception among lower-level employees of having more influence in the decision-making process. The horizontal training process tends to lessen the routine nature of lower-level positions in the organization, at least over a period of time. Thus the collective experience of working in a number of differentiated task classifications results, for each individual, in a perception of nonroutine work; that, in turn, results in a perception of participation and influence in the decision-making process.

The perception of influence and participation in the decision-making process also has a basis in the communications structure that evolves as a result of the horizontal training and socialization processes and as a result of the development of the peer referent group. In the Japanese organization, the peer group is most influential in the decision-making process. As promotion to higher levels of responsibility is a function of tenure, individuals with similar responsibilities tend to be from the same peer group. This "old boy network" serves to promote open communication channels. While much of the communications research in Western countries is limited to the vertical group orientation of Western management, open communications channels have been shown to facilitate exchange of task-relevant information, thus facilitating job performance (Bacharach and Aiken 1976).

Operational decision making in the Japanese organization is largely influenced by the discussion meetings that take place among peer groups. The operational decision makers, grouped by responsibility title (starting with *kakaricho* or section chief, and ascending through *kacho*, *jicho*, and *bucho* or department head) meet and interact at each of those responsibility levels to discuss operational questions, regardless of the task affected by the problem. Decision making at a policy level is similarly influenced by interdepartmental consultation and peer-group meetings at higher responsibility levels.

These peer-group meetings are often held in the absence of a superior, and are therefore conceptually similar to an "all-channel communications network." While this communication network, lacking a central authority, tends to be less efficient in solving simple problems, overall group satisfaction is greater in an all-channel network than in a network built around an individual in a centralized position (Leavitt 1951). The absence of a superior from the discussion process has been found to result in more-open discussion and in an increase in the number of correct solutions to problems produced by the group (Maier and Solem 1952).

The nature of the promotion and advancement processes in the Japanese organization also contributes to the quality of the communications process. Not only is a diversity of task responsibilities represented, at each of various responsibility levels; there also is the knowledge by those participating in the group discussion that they may soon be in the positions other individuals now occupy. Thus, insistence on a solution that favors one task group by denying another task group an equitable share of the available resources is not viewed as a good solution by any of those participating. Coalition interests of task groups become subordinated to the objectives of the organization as a whole.

The benefits that are gained through use of the peer-level participative discussion process are not necessarily culture-bound. Research in the United States has shown that an open communications system, with relatively few restraints on interactions, results in more-flexible and more-confident groups (Ziller 1958). The use of the peer group, as the discussion and decision participation group, results in an empathy within the group as well as a similarity in the ways that group members categorize events, objects, and concepts. Psychologist Harry Triandis (1959) contends that these characteristics lead to more effective communication.

A unique theory of motivation hypothesizes that motivation is a socially constructed phenomenon, and therefore is best viewed as an interpersonal information processing system, rather than as a need satisfaction system (Bacharach and Aiken 1976). Within this framework, the Japanese use of peer groups and the role of peer groups in the decision-making process may be seen to increase individual motivation.

In terms of perceived influence on the decision-making process, research indicates that, among middle-level managers, lateral communication and downward communication are better predictors of perceived influence than is upward communication (Bacharach and Aiken 1976). It is among these middle levels of responsibility (*kakaricho* to *bucho*) that the Japanese organization most encourages peer-group participation in the decision-making process. The more traditional Western model normally uses interdepartmental communication only at higher levels of the organization.

The distinguishing feature of the Japanese organization, however, is the use of the horizontal group, with the frequent interdepartmental transfer of employees, as the principal means of defining the groups that will participate in the decision-making process. Thus, the functional informal group replaces the formal task-defined group in the decision-making process. At the same time, these functional informal groups serve in the capacities suggested by Barnard (1978), and provide the basis for cooperation without necessarily destroying the task group spirit (*shudan ishiki*), which can be applied to specific tasks within the organization.

The cooperative basis, which results from the use of the functional informal group in the decision-making process, provides the basis for *wa* (group harmony) within the Japanese organization. Group harmony, in the Japanese organization, is an important factor in the effectiveness of the organization. Unlike the Western organization, however, the Japanese model seeks to maximize harmony in intergroup relations and minimize the formation of coalitions within the organization.

INTERGROUP RELATIONSHIPS

In an environment of scarce resources, the Japanese organizational model seeks to maximize utilization of all resources as well as to maximize adaptation to a changing environment. To achieve this objective, the potential of any single element of the organization may be subordinated to the potential of the organization. It is for this reason that the Japanese place such importance on intergroup relationships. *Wa* (group harmony), as an objective of the Japanese management process, is better defined as "organizational harmony."

The peer-group system is designed to maximize intergroup contact, resulting in a decrease in intergroup bias (Wilder and Thompson 1980). The Japanese emphasis on meetings of peer groups assures intergroup contact of task groups at several levels of responsibility. The continual movement of personnel among various task groups, especially at lower levels, as a part of the training process, decreases the cohesiveness of the task group and favors the cohesiveness of the peer group through a sharing of the training and work experience (Dion 1979).

A similarity of goal commitment is encouraged both by the emphasis on peer groups and by the organizational reward system. The semiannual bonus, paid by most Japanese organizations, is based on overall organizational performance. The bonus is shared using a formula that ignores relative performance of task units, but that does recognize relative responsibility and tenure in the organization. All members of a similar peer group are rewarded equally. This sharing of an organizational goal has proven an effective, non-culture-bound means of reducing tension among groups in an organization (Sherif 1958).

The informal nature of the peer group is encouraged by the promotion system and by the continual interaction of peers in the training, socialization, and decision participation process. The frequency of contact and interaction contributes to the formation of informal groups (Shaw 1977). The Japanese organization takes the further step of formalizing the development of those groups and of exploiting the benefits of informal groups toward a more effective organization.

As the attitudes and experiences of the peer-group members are similar, there is agreement within the group about the nature of the relationship of intergroup interaction and the legitimacy of the hierarchical authority and control imposed on intergroup relationships. This uniformity of attitudes about the pattern of control, rather than the specific level of control, is related to both performance and job satisfaction (McMahon and Ivancevich 1976).

Increased control has been seen as a factor leading to increased efficiency. Increased control in the Japanese model depends, not on the imposition of control systems per se, but on increased participation and mutual, peer-level influence, as well as a greater degree of integration of the individual into the organization (Tannenbaum 1962).

The peer-group influence and participation in the decision-making process are not evident in the Japanese organization until the individual reaches the first responsibility level (*kakaricho*). This may take as long as seven years in a typical organization.* Before that point, conformity is expected, encouraged, and rewarded. The employee, therefore, does not reach the first level of responsibility without a history of conforming to organizational norms and values.

Nonconformance, however, is permitted once the employee reaches a designated responsibility level, and it is encouraged if it contributes to the peer-group discussion of possible solutions to problems. This combination of a history of conforming to organizational norms, together with mutual

---

*Allen Dickerman (1974) notes that a typical promotion pattern in a Japanese organization requires seven years of general work, six years at the *kakaricho* level, seven years as a *kacho*, and 13 or more years as a *bucho*.

respect for competence among peers, makes the nonconforming behavior more effective and more influential when it occurs (Hollander 1960).

Whereas the Japanese emphasis on intergroup harmony (wa) discourages individualism with respect to organizational norms, the individual's behavior is not bounded and restricted by the norms of the task group. In this respect, the Japanese system is less repressive of individual behavior than is the American system. It generates novel ways of doing tasks. It injects a measure of creativity into the organization that may exceed what is possible when input is limited by "the way it has always been done."

The peer-group concept also allows for nonconforming behavior in a nonthreatening forum. As the peer group is charged with arriving at a group decision, the individual is not forced to make a commitment from which there is no retreat. The ultimate group decision is the face-saving device that permits individual expression without threat of reprisal. The ringisho system is the device that permits the individual to express a view not shared by other members of the peer group.

Conflict between groups is further decreased by the emotional identification that accompanies the informal nature of the peer group. The similarity of experiences within the organization, the high level of interaction among individuals who comprise the peer group, and an all-channel communication system within the peer group result in increased individual attraction to the group (Ferguson and Kelley 1964).

The intergroup emphasis, through the vehicle of the peer group, lessens the individual's identification with the product of the task group and increases the individual's identification with the product of the organization. The individual is likely to perceive the competitor as another organization, rather than as another group within the organization. The implications for organizational effectiveness in maintaining intergroup harmony are evident.

SUMMARY

The horizontal training system, socialization process, and group-development philosophy of Japanese management result in the formation of functional informal groups within the organization. In addition to playing an integral part in the decision-making process of the organization, these functional informal groups benefit the organization in a communications capacity and in the maintenance of organizational cohesiveness. Because these groups serve as referent groups, and together with other aspects of the organization promote feelings of personal integrity, self-respect, and participation, they form the basis for intergroup harmony within the organization.

The Japanese management system is one that depends on organizational growth, for it demands the continual promotion of large numbers of peers through the various responsibility levels of the organization. Individual growth, however, is not limited to the parent organization. The relationship between a parent organization and subsidiary subcontractors (ko-gaisha — literally, "children companies") provides additional routes for upward mobility of the individual.

The dysfunctional nature of overconformity of values within the organization is balanced by an emphasis on diversity of task orientations and experiences, drawn together in the participative decision-making process.

The Japanese management system, emphasizing harmony within the organization, focuses individual attention on competition outside the organization, developing a conception of the organization as a whole, rather than as a coalition of special interests.

One might speculate that the Japanese system tends to develop a motivational drive based on affiliation as a factor that directs need achievement within the organization. In our Western quest to "self-actualize," we may have paid insufficient attention to the needs of individuals to belong, needs that are emphasized in the Japanese organization. Fulfillment of these needs may be at least partially responsible for what is commonly known as the Japanese productivity marvel. Lack of emphasis in Western organizations on support of these needs to belong may be at least partially responsible for what is known as the American productivity dilemma.

REFERENCES

Argyris, Chris. 1957. "The Individual and the Organization: Some Problems of Mutual Adjustment." *Administrative Science Quarterly* 2, no. 1:1–24.

Bacharach, S. B., and M. Aiken. 1976. "Structural Process Constraints on Influence in Organizations: A Specific Level of Analysis." *Administrative Science Quarterly* 21:623–42.

Barnard, Chester. 1978. "Informal Organizations and Their Relation to Formal Organizations." In *Classics of Organizational Behavior*, ed. Walter E. Natemeyer, pp. 239–43. Oak Park, Ill.: Moore.

Bem, Daryl J. 1977. "Referent Groups." In *Psychological Foundations of Organizational Behavior*, ed. Barry M. Staw, pp. 205–9. Santa Monica, Calif.: Goodyear.

Benedict, Ruth. 1938. "Continuities and Discontinuities in Cultural Conditioning." *Psychiatry* 1 (1938):161–67.

Connor, P. E. and B. W. Becker. 1975. "Values and the Organization: Suggestions For Research." *Academy of Management Journal* 18:559–61.

Dickerman, Allen. 1974. *Training Japanese Managers*. New York: Praeger.

Dion, K. L. 1979. "Status, Equity, Sex Composition of Group, and Inter-Group Bias." *Personality and Social Psychology Bulletin* 5:240–44.

Ferguson, C., and H. Kelley. 1964. "Significant Factors in Overevaluation of Own-Group's Product." *Journal of Abnormal and Social Psychology* 69:223–28.

Festinger, Leon. 1954. "A Theory of Social Comparison Processes." *Human Relations* 7:114–40.

Grimes, A. J., S. M. Klein, and F. A. Schull. 1972. "Matrix Model: A Selective Empirical Test." *Academy of Management Journal* 15:9–31.

Hall, Richard T. 1980. "Effectiveness Theory and Organizational Effectiveness." *Journal of Applied Behavioral Science* 16, no. 4:536–45.

Hodgson, James D. 1978. Untitled chapter. In *Unfinished Business: An Agenda for Labor, Management and the Public*, ed. A. J. Siegel and D. B. Lipsky, pp. 23–28. Cambridge, Mass.: M.I.T. Press.

Hollander, E. P. 1960. "Competence and Conformity in the Acceptance of Influence." *Journal of Abnormal and Social Psychology* 61:365–70.

Kellert, Stephen, Lawrence K. Williams, William F. Whyte and Giorgio Alberti. 1967. *Cultural Change and Stress in Rural Peru*. Ithaca, N.Y.: New York State School of Industrial and Labor Relations, Cornell University, Reprint Series no. 232.

Leavitt, H. J. 1951. "Some Effects of Certain Communications Patterns on Group Performance." *Journal of Abnormal and Social Psychology* 46:38–50.

Leavitt, H. J. 1977. "Suppose We Took Groups Seriously. . ." In *Psychological Foundations of Organizational Behavior*, ed. Barry M. Staw, pp. 397–406. Santa Monica, Calif.: Goodyear.

Lieberman, Seymour. 1977. "The Effects of Changes in Roles on the Attitudes of Role Occupants." In *Psychological Foundations of Organizational Behavior*, ed. Barry M. Staw, pp. 224–32. Santa Monica, Calif.: Goodyear.

Locke, E. A. 1968. "Toward a Theory of Task Motivation and Incentives." *Organizational Behavior and Human Performance* 3:157–89.

Maier, N. R. F., and A. R. Solem. 1952. "The Contribution of a Discussion Leader to the Quality of Group Thinking: Effective Use of Minority Opinions." *Human Relations* 5, no. 3:277–88.

Merton, Robert K. 1967. *Social Theory and Social Structure*. New York: The Free Press.

McGregor, Douglas. 1960. *The Human Side of Enterprise*. New York: McGraw-Hill.

McMahon, J. T., and J. M. Ivancevich. 1976. "A Study of Control in a Manufacturing Organization: Managers and Non-managers." *Administrative Science Quarterly* 21:68–83.

Ouchi, William. 1980. *Theory Z: How American Business Can Meet the Japanese Challenge*. Reading, Mass.: Addison-Wesley.

Roethlisberger, F. J., and W. J. Dickson. 1939. *Management and the Worker*. Cambridge, Mass.: Harvard University Press.

Schein, Edgar H. 1977. "Organizational Socialization and the Profession of Management." In *Psychological Foundations of Organizational Behavior*, ed. Barry M. Staw, pp. 210–24. Santa Monica, Calif.: Goodyear.

Shaw, Marvin E. 1977. "An Overview of Small Group Behavior." In *Psychological*

    Foundations of Organizational Behavior, ed. Barry· M. Staw, pp. 358–96. Santa Monica, Calif.: Goodyear.

Sherif, Muzafer. 1958. "Superordinate Goals in the Reduction of Intergroup Conflict." *American Journal of Sociology* 63, no. 4:349–56.

Tannenbaum, A. S. 1962. "Control in Organizations: Individual Adjustment and Organizational Performance." *Administrative Science Quarterly* 7:236–57.

Triandis, Harry C. 1959. "Cognitive Similarity and Interpersonal Communication." *Journal of Applied Psychology* 43(1959):321–26.

Wilder, David A., and John E. Thompson. 1980. "Intergroup Contact with Independent Manipulations of Ingroup and Outgroup Interaction." *Journal of Personality and Social Psychology* 38, no. 4:589–603.

Ziller, R. C. 1958. "Communication Restraints, Group Flexibility and Group Confidence." *Journal of Applied Psychology* 42:346–52.

3

Early American Influence on Japanese Management Philosophy: The Scientific Management Movement in Japan

RONALD G. GREENWOOD *and* ROBERT H. ROSS

INTRODUCTION

Japan is looked upon as not only a leading industrial nation, but also one possessing highly developed management skills. Only in the last 20 years have Americans accepted Japan as a sophisticated competitor. Yet Japan has had a sophisticated management structure dating at least back to the 1930s. How else can the great industrial productivity of Japan's World War II effort be explained?

The study of Japanese management usually emphasizes the strong morality found in the culture and the apparent absence of conflict in deci-

We gratefully acknowledge the assistance of Ichiro Ueno, President of SANNO Institute of Business Administration, Tokyo, for sharing and assisting with information for this article. We also express appreciation to Professor Ernest Dale for sharing private documents on Yoichi Ueno. Yoichi Ueno has also been transcribed Yoichi Uyeno or Yoiti Ueno.

sion making. Less emphasized, but frequently alluded to, is the Japanese social acceptance of wealth and profit, each having an honorable position. These virtues are all inherent in the philosophies of Taylor, Gilbreth, and most of the scientific management theorists. Taylor and Gilbreth both thought that the incorporation of scientific management would bring about less conflict between management and labor, because scientific management would bring about fairness of treatment and increase the amount of wealth for all people.

Although books and articles are being generated to "explain" present industrial and administrative Japan to Western eyes, very little has been written about the historical influence Western management theory has had on Japan.

The philosophies of Taylor, the Gilbreths, and especially Emerson had a major impact on Japanese industrial production. This chapter will trace the early influence of Western management scholars on Japan and the work of Yoichi Ueno, who was not only a leading Japanese interpreter of Western philosophy but also a major management philosopher in his own right.

JAPANESE AWARENESS
OF SCIENTIFIC MANAGEMENT

The year 1981 marked the seventieth anniversary of the discovery by Yukinori Hoshino, director of Japan's Kajima Bank of Osaka, of Western management theory. Hoshino, while visiting the United States, first encountered Frederick W. Taylor's work and was so impressed by Taylor's writing that he obtained permission to translate *The Principles of Scientific Management*, which Taylor had published only that year. In 1912 or 1913 Hoshino's translation was distributed in Japan (*Chronological History*, p. 2; Hayward 1951, p. 6). Also, in 1911 Toshiro Ikeda, through an American correspondence-course pamphlet, was moved to publish "The Secrets of Eliminating Useless Exertions." We are told that this was "published in the narrative style of a workman and it was said to have sold some million copies" (*Chronological History*, p. 1).

It was 1912 when Yoichi Ueno launched a monthly psychology journal, *Shinri Kenkyo*, for which he authored the paper "On the Efficiency." Here the accomplishments of Taylor, Gilbreth, and C. B. Thompson were described. It was also in this journal that Hugo Munsterberg's writings were first translated into Japanese. In the same year Jujiro Iseki published a special edition of his magazine on "Scientific Management" (*Chronological History*, p. 1).

These were the first two descriptions of the "Taylor" philosophy of efficiency to be published in Japan.* It was also in 1912 that Professor Shoji Ishimaru (affiliation as yet unknown) gave lectures about efficiency at various stops along the South Manchuria Railway.

In 1914 Yoichi Ueno published his introduction to psychology, *Shinri-gaku Tsugi*. Although not a management book, it gave Ueno national standing and would be a springboard from which he was to launch a major consulting business. Later, after studying the work of the Gilbreths, Ueno was able to appreciate the psychological foundation upon which their management philosophy was based. Ueno's book also introduced Sigmund Freud's work to Japan.

In the next year, 1915, the Japan Ceramic Company, Nihon-Toki Kabushiki Kaisha, published a booklet whose title translates roughly as "On the Study of Jobs." Although much of this booklet was based on experiences of the firm, it was also greatly influenced by the Taylor philosophy.

Between 1915 and 1920 the influence of Western management philosophy slowly spread in Japan. In 1917 the commercial College of Otaru became the first college in Japan with a scientific management chair (*Chronological History*, p. 4). The technical College of Port Arthur offered lectures by Masaharu Ishiwara on industrial management, starting in 1918. He is given credit for the term *Seisan Kogaku*, production engineering (*Chronological History*, p. 4).

Two important works were published in 1918: *Efficiency of Factory Economy* by Hazime Katsuda and *The Truth of Efficiency* by Yasaburo Simonaka. It appears, as will be shown shortly, that these two publications were translations of American books.

Yoichi Ueno wrote to Frank Gilbreth and started a long friendship with the Gilbreth family. It is unclear when this happened; Yoichi's son Ichiro places the date of the first letter as "around 1910" (Ichiro Ueno 1982), and Yoichi believed it happened "if I am not mistaken, sometime in 1917" (Uyeno 1953, p. 2). In Yoichi Ueno's own words:

One day, I came upon an article of photographing, a physical motion in an American magazine and wanted to know the detailed methods. So, I wrote a letter to the writer asking how it was done. It happened to be that the writer was Mr. Frank B. Gilbreth, the pioneer of motion study.

A letter from an unknown Japanese youth seemed to have aroused an interest in Mr. Gilbreth. He told me later that he had pleasant chats over the letter with his wife, Dr. Lillian M. Gilbreth. Various materials about the problem were kindly sent to me, in 1919. I wrote a book "*On Psychology of Ef-*

*It is unclear whether the Ueno article was published in 1912, as his son lists a 1913 article entitled "How to Improve Efficiency" (Ichiro Ueno 1980b). This may be the same article listed above or a different one.

ficiency of Individuals and Business" (Hito Oyobi Jigyo Nohritso No Shinri), using these materials in which I devoted a chapter introducing his methods. This book was so popular that editions after the edition were sold out (Yoiti Ueno 1931, p. 2).

A publication of the All Japan Efficiency Federation, the Japan International Congress of Scientific Management (CIOS) member of which Yoichi Ueno was president, made an important point about this book.

> Although many other publications were made hitherto, concerning management, they were chiefly literal translations of American authors. With this book, efficiency may be said to have been expounded in pure Japanese for the first time. It was written in easy Japanese. The large part of the book was so new to the public that it went through many editions (*Chronological History*, p. 5).

Between 1913 and 1918, Ueno lectured on the psychology of advertisements at the Wesenda University.

By 1919, Dr. Tetsuzo Watanabe was lecturing on factory management at the Tokyo Imperial University and Riichi Tokikuni published *The Theory and Practice of Scientific Management* and *Industrial Psychology*, which we assume are translations of C. B. Thompson's *The Theory and Practice of Scientific Management*, published 1917, and either H. Munsterberg's *Business Psychology* or Lillian Gilbreth's *The Psychology of Management*.

YOUCHI UENO, JAPAN'S FIRST MANAGEMENT CONSULTANT

Ueno's lectures on the psychology of advertisements for Waseda University brought him to the attention of Seijiro Nakao, advertising manager of the Lion Tooth-Powder Company. His successful seminars to the advertising section of Lion, in 1920, led to his being invited to study the various operations in the manufacturing department. The invitation fortuitously coincided with Ueno's growing interest in scientific management. In a 1953 speech to the National Efficiency Convention in Japan, Ueno remembered (and we believe this is his own English translation of the speech):

> I first picked up the packing operation of tooth powder. After mixing of materials, a certain amount of powder was put in a paper bag with a small shovel by hand, the mouth of it was turned down. Then the bag was put in a outer paper bag and sealed. Half a dozen of them placed in a carton and tied crosswise with a string. These were again placed in a wooden box. These packing operations were done all by hand at that time.

The time and motion study was tried by me at the first time in my life, as exactly as it was explained in textbooks of Scientific Management. Side by side with female workers, I myself tried the operation among a pretty cloud of the powder for some time. A plan of improvement hit upon me I asked the plant manager to lend me 15 of the female workers to see how this plan would work. This was consented. I remember that I could hardly sleep the night before the improved operation would be put into practice, lest I should find what I had studied might prove an academic theory impracticable in factory.

The day came, I organized 15 workwomen in a unit and the operation started. To my great joy the work went on smoothly [and the] packing operation carried on with increased productivity. The new operation was adopted formally. The length of the conveyor was shortened to half as long. One whole working room became vacant. The production greatly increased in spite of 15 minutes rest were given once in the forenoon and in the afternoon. The production was still much higher than before. Calculating the results in terms of profit, I proposed to dispose the increased profit ¼ to the company, ¼ to the consumer, ¼ to the labourers concerned and ¼ to the fund to be used for management improvement hereafter" (Uyeno 1953, pp. 4–5).

The profit-sharing proposal was flatly refused by Lion's top management. Nonetheless, Ueno was able to increase production by 20 percent, with 30 percent less space and a reduction of the workers' day by one hour (*Chronological History*; Ichiro Ueno 1982). This was the first recorded use of management consulting in Japan and the first Japanese use of motion and time study.

With the completion of the Lion Tooth-Powder work, Ueno was invited by the Osaka Chamber of Commerce to lecture on factory management, a lecture that centered on his work for Lion. In the audience was Taichi Nakayama, owner of Nakayama Taiyodo Company, a toilet articles manufacturer, and Ueno was hence invited to continue his scientific management work. Success at Nakayama led him to the Fukusuke Tabi Company, maker of Japanese socks. Here it took two weeks for a lot of tabi, socks, to go from cutting of the cloth to the finished product. The socks spent most of the time in the inspecting department. Studying the flow of work, Ueno was able to design a method that cut the time, from start to finish, to three days. Ueno notes, "What I had done, if expressed in present day terms, was to change the production by lots to production by flow work. There was no such term as 'flow work'. It was 1920 that the term 'Fliess-Arbeit' was first used in Germany" (Uyeno 1953, p. 8).

Ueno's next step was a direct result of his consulting. The president of Kyoto Imperial University, Masataro Sawayanagi, held small seminars where each participant had to talk about what each was studying. Sawayanagi was so impressed by the Ueno research that he introduced Ueno to the Kyochokai (Society for the Promotion of Coordination of Capital and Labor) in 1919. The Kyochokai officials were also impressed by Ueno's work and, sensing the possibilities of scientific management, sent Ueno to the United States and Europe to learn all he could.

In the United States, Ueno called on his old correspondence friend Frank Gilbreth (Ichiro Ueno 1981a) and became the first Oriental student to attend the Gilbreth school. Ueno also met Carl Barth, William Leffingwell, Wallace Clark, Dwight Merrick, Morris Cooke, King Hathaway, and others (Ichiro Ueno 1982; Uyeno 1953). It is known that Ueno became friends with Harrington Emerson, although we do not know how they first met. Ueno mentions Emerson's espousal of physiognomy while both were attending the *Society of Efficiency International* meeting in Detroit in April 1922 (Ichiro Ueno 1980b; 1981b; Yoichi Ueno 1925). His return trip was by way of Europe, where he investigated the management movement there.

Upon his return to Japan, the Kyochokai organized the Research Institute of Industrial Efficiency in 1922. In 1924 a lack of funds caused the Kyochokai to close the institute; through private enterprise Ueno reopened it. He was its head until 1942.

While at the research institute in 1922, Ueno was invited to share the principle lecturing responsibilities with Toshiro Ideka in a two-month training course for management engineers in Tokyo. This was also a first in Japan: the extended management development course beyond a formal university. A year later a similar course was offered in Osaka.

In 1923, Ueno helped organize the National Japan Federation of Efficiency Engineers, which immediately began publishing a monthly magazine. The magazine, whose title changed in 1927 to *Sangyo Noritsu* ("industrial efficiency" or "industrial management"), published many of Ueno's writings.

Carl Barth visited Japan in 1924 and was invited to lecture at a short course on efficiency or management. The term "efficiency," as used by Emerson, was more widely used in Japan than the term "management" at this time (Ichiro Ueno 1982). This was the first American management specialist to speak on the subject to a Japanese audience. A year later (in 1925), the Japanese branch of the Taylor Society was formed, with Yoichi Ueno acting as its first president. He served in that capacity until 1936.

THE MAP OF MANAGEMENT HISTORY

The 4th International Congress of Scientific Management (CIOS) was held in Paris, June 19–20, 1929, with Yoichi Ueno leading the first Japanese contingent to attend a CIOS meeting. He was representing both the Japan Efficiency Federation and the Japanese branch of the Taylor Society. It was at a special reception held in honor of Mrs. Frederick Taylor that Ueno presented her with a map of management history. This map, designed by Masashige Yagyu under the direction of Ueno, gives good insight into how

Japanese management experts viewed the evolution of the philosophy of management. From this Japanese viewpoint, only Americans had had major impacts on management theory, at least at the time the map was drawn in 1929.

The map is approximately 21 inches by 31 inches, and was constructed "to help beginners and students in the field of Scientific Management to effectively understand at a glance the development of Scientific Management in its earlier state" (Yoichi Ueno 1929).

Yagyu, reflecting upon the map, wrote in 1978, "By way of map design, it was drawn as though it somehow looked like the East Coast of the U.S. (New York, Washington, etc.). Time is represented by the vertical axis and the physical space horizontally, in which 'rivers' stand for people (management pioneers) and 'cities' their writings" (Yagyu).

In 1929, *Sangyo Nortiso (Industrial Efficiency)* printed "How to Read the Map of Management," giving the following explanation (see Figure 3.1):

1. Longitude represents years starting with 1856 at the top down to 1929 on the bottom.
2. Latitude represents nations that have been influenced by Scientific Management, those nations being listed at the bottom of the map.
3. Geographical features represent the following: River — Personalities involved in Scientific Management (the Journal article suggests rivers are representing Gantt, Thompson, Vance, Hathaway, Cooke, etc., yet only Hathaway and Cooke of this group are on this map).
   Main River — the life of Mr. F. W. Taylor.
   Lake, Cities — Key events, affairs, developments, etc. in the development of Scientific Management.
   Roads — Relationships between the above.
4. The main river starts in 1856 with the birth of Mr. Taylor in Pennsylvania and quickly flows through the plains of Midvale and Bethlehem.
5. The river continues through major cities which represent the books *A Piece Rate System*, *Shop Management*, and *Principles of Scientific Management*, each written by Mr. Taylor.
6. In 1915 the river reaches the sea signifying the death of Mr. Taylor.
7. The river on the left side of the map represents Emerson's school of thought and the river on the right represents Gilbreth's school of thought with the space between them and Taylor's 'river' showing the relative closeness of their ideas.
8. The first International "L'Organisation Scientifique du Travail"

FIGURE 3.1

L'HISTOIRE GRAPHIQUE DE L'ORGANISATION SCIENTIFIQUE DU TRAVAIL (1856 — 1929)
Par Masashige Yagyu, revised par Yoiti Ueno.

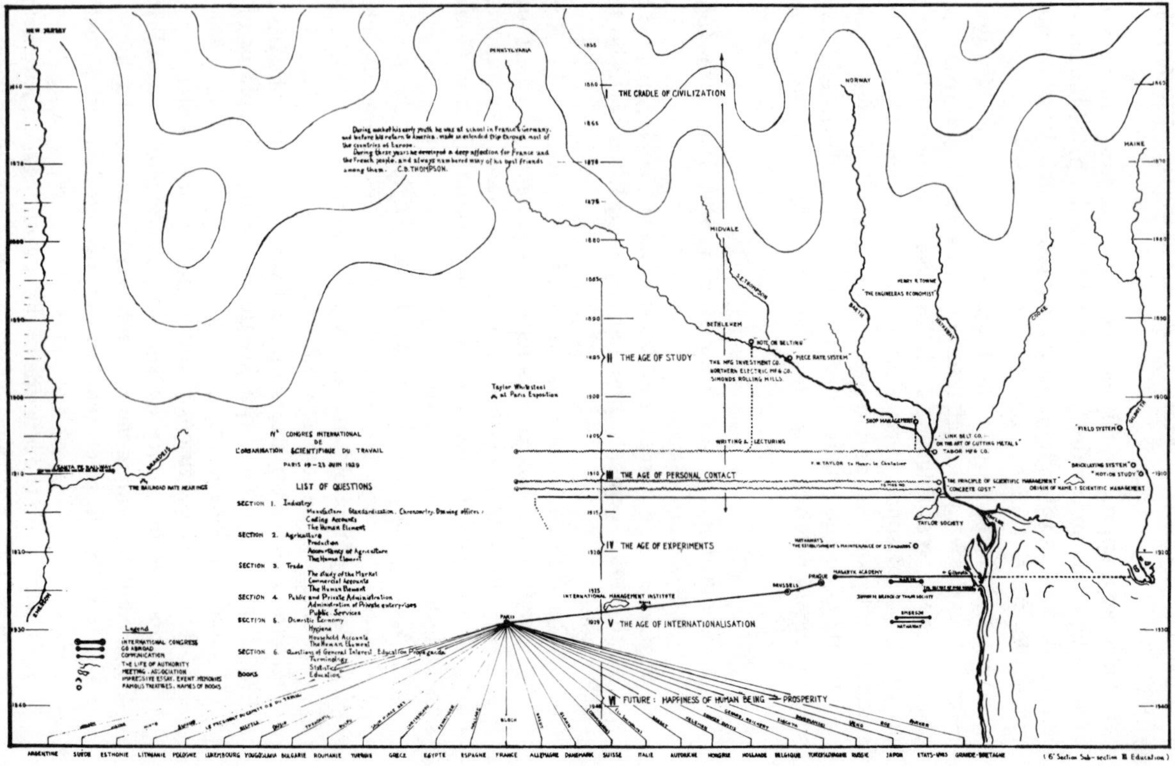

Conference was held in Prague. The fourth one represented on the map was scheduled in June 1929 in Paris. As representatives from 35 countries were scheduled to be present, the 35 were listed at the bottom of the map. The agenda for the fourth conference was listed on the left section of the map.

9. "To read the history of a particular country's development in the field of Scientific Management, let us use France as an example, find France on the bottom of the map and then follow the line up the years to where we find a quotation from Thompson. This quotation, 'During much of youth . . .' explains the roots of Scientific Management Studies in France."

10. In 1911, Mr. Taylor presented his book, *Principles of Scientific Management,* to Mr. Henry Le Chaterlier. At the same time, Mr. Taylor sent his book to Mr. Yukinori Hoshino in Japan. Mr. Hoshino's translation of that book made it the first of Mr. Taylor's books to be published in Japan. Thus, his translation started the Scientific Management movement in Japan.

11. In 1925, the Japan Charter of the Taylor Society was established, as represented by a lake on the map (Yoichi Ueno 1929).

The three main rivers show the main thrusts of scientific management: the Taylor, Gilbreth, and Emerson approaches. The Taylor and Gilbreth streams are close and empty into the same "ocean," but the Emerson stream is far afield and empties into who knows where. Emerson's concern was much more with the total organization, whereas Taylor and Gilbreth concentrated on the efficiency of the "workers" at the bottom of the organization. The stream for Emerson starts in 1853 with his birth in Trenton, New Jersey. His connection with Louis Brandeis is noted; it came about through Emerson's Santa Fe Railway work and his involvement with the Railroad Rate Hearing of 1911. (The Brandeis stream is much too short, as he was born in 1856.)

The Gilbreth stream begins, properly, with Frank's birth in Maine in 1868. We can assume that the tributary joining the Gilbreth stream is Frank's "partner for life," Lillian, although her name is not listed. If that is correct, then the map is off by 15 years, as Frank and Lillian did not meet until June 1903. Nonetheless, three of the Gilbreth books are listed: *Field System* (1908), *Bricklaying System* (1909), and *Motion Study* (1911).

The Taylor stream is the main stream, and starts in 1856 with Taylor's birth in Pennsylvania. The map notes his Bethlehem work and his 1893 "Note on Belting" paper, delivered to the American Society of Mechanical Engineers (ASME). Sanford E. Thompson is shown as entering the Taylor stream in the 1890s. It might be noted that the map is in error , as Thompson did not work for Midvale as suggested. (Gantt did work at Midvale, although he is not on the map.)

"Piece Rate System," Taylor's 1895 ASME paper, is graphically presented, then an unnamed stream flowing just before "Shop Management" (perhaps Gantt?); the 1903 Taylor ASME paper "Shop Management" is properly placed.

A long stream starting in 1860 in Norway denotes the birth of Carl Barth, a long and trusted Taylor friend who met Taylor long before 1908, as implied on the map, and is shown flowing into the Taylor stream. Barth was associated with Taylor and the Taylor system, and he was assigned to put the system in place in both the Link Belt and the Tabor manufacturing companies, as shown on the map.

Taylor's books *The Principles of Scientific Management* and *Concrete Cost* (with S. E. Thompson) are shown, as are his connections with the Manufacturing Investment Company (which employed S. E. Thompson), Northern Electric Manufacturing Company, and Simonds Rolling Mills (which employed Gantt). Both Morris L. Cooke and "King" Hathaway (associated with Midvale, Link Belt, and Tabor) are shown as well.

One wonders why the "process" approach of the Frenchman Henri Fayol was not considered on the map. Perhaps Ueno and Yagyu had not as yet become acquainted with his work — as Fayol was not well known to the English-speaking world and everything on the map was from an American viewpoint. Yet some other well known process-approach theorists of this period are also ignored, such as the Englishman Oliver Sheldon and the Americans Russell Robb and Henry S. Dennison. The behavioralists are also conspicuously missing, as no mention of Hugo Munsterberg, Walter Dill Scott, Bernard Muscio, or Mary Parker Follett was made. Yoichi Ueno was well aware of Munsterberg's employment tests and other industrial psychological works, as he had translated much of his work for the Japanese reader. Max Weber's work on bureaucracy is also not considered for the map.

This map gives good insight into what Japanese management leaders considered important: what they thought important was placed on this map, what they did not see as important is missing from the map. The map, therefore, indicates who influenced Japanese management theorists — Taylor, Gilbreth, and Emerson, while the European and nonscientific managers did not seem to have much influence.

JAPAN MANAGEMENT THEORISTS AFTER THE CIOS MEETING

Shortly after the CIOS meeting in 1929, Japan hosted the World Industrial Conference, in October in Tokyo. Among the distinguished guests were Dr. Lillian Gilbreth (Yost 1949), Francesco Mauro (president of CIOS), Professor Joseph Roe (NYU), Wilfred Lewis (president of Tabor Manufacturing), Harrington Emerson, and King Hathaway (*Chronological History*). Emerson and Hathaway traveled throughout Japan and lectured often. Also in 1929, Ueno published his translation of Wallace Clark's *Gantt Chart* and his original *Essays on the Industrial Efficiency (Sangyo Nohyitsu-Ron)*.

In 1930 the Japanese branch of the Taylor Society, under Ueno, organized a trip to the United States for a party of 14 leading Japanese businessmen. Harlow S. Person, as president of the Taylor Society, coordinated the trip. It was an overwhelming success.

Ueno next turned to translating all of Taylor's works. In 1932 his translations of *The Principles of Scientific Management, Shop Management,* and *A Piece Rate System* were published, along with other Taylor articles and letters (Ichiro Ueno 1982). Prefaces were written by Barth, Hathaway, and Merrick. Ueno was the editor of the 1930 *Office Worker's Manual (Jimu Hikkei)* and the 1939 *Management Handbook (Nohritsu Handbook)*. In 1948 he published *Principles of Management*, an original work on his philosophy.

Yoichi Ueno continued to be active. In 1939 he organized an industrial mission to the United States, covering about 100 shops in two months. In 1941 he founded the Japan Efficiency School (Nihon Nohritsu Gakko), which closed during World War II. After the war, he was asked to act as a commissioner in designing the civil government of Japan. In 1951 the Japan Efficiency School reopened with Ueno as president, a position he held until his death on October 15, 1957, at the age of 74. Today that school is the SANNO Institute of Business Administration, with Yoichi Ueno's son, Ichiro Ueno, as president.

CONCLUSION

Although Japan's unique social-economic culture was a major influence in the formation of Japan's similarly unique management philosophy, early American scientific management also had an impact on that philosophy. The works of Taylor, Gilbreth, and Emerson were early accepted as proper theories in Japan. Yoichi Ueno was an early advocate and interpreter of American scientific management, and he spent most of his life fitting it to the Japanese culture.

REFERENCES

Chronological History of Japan's 40 Odd Years of Management. [Ca. 1954] Tokyo: All Japan Efficiency Federation. Probably prepared by Yoichi Ueno.
Hayward, Elizabeth Gardner. 1951. *A Classified Guide to the Frederick Winslow*

Taylor Collection. Hoboken, N. J.: The Stevens Institute of Technology.

Ueno, Ichiro. 1982. "Yoichi Ueno, 1883–1957, Japan." In *The Golden Book of Management*, 2d ed. New York: American Management Association. Forthcoming.

_____. 1981a. Letter to Ronald G. Greenwood, January 19. This letter contains a translation of Yoichi Ueno's "Diary of A Day with Mr. Gilbreth (1921)."

_____. 1981b. Letter to William F. Muhs, January 26.

_____. 1980a. Letter to Ronald G. Greenwood, September 1.

_____. 1980b. Letter to William F. Muhs, June 20.

Ueno, Yoichi. 1929. "How to Read The Map of Management History." Translated by Ichiro Ueno. *Sangyo Noritsu* 12, no. 11. *Sangyu Noritsu (Industrial Efficiency)* is a journal of Nihon Noritsu Rengokai, the Japan Federation of Efficiency Engineers.

_____. 1925. "The Great Physiognomy Dispute as Centered Around Emerson." In *Noritsu Gakusha No Tabi Nikki (The Traveling Diary of an Efficiency Engineer)*, trans. Ichiro Ueno, pp. 340–43.

Ueno, Yoiti. 1931. "Compte rendu de l'activité en faveur de L'O.S.T. au Japon." In *L'Organisation Scientifique Du Travail IV Congres International Paris, 1929*, pp. 227–28. Paris: Comité National de L'Organisation Francaise.

_____. 1930. "The Scientific Management Discussions." *Bulletin of the Taylor Society* 15, no. 1 (February):43–45.

Uyeno, Yoichi. 1953. "Japan's 40 Years of Scientific Management and I." Reprint of speech delivered at the 5th National Efficiency Convention, held at Matsuyama city in May 1953. Yoichi Ueno is believed to have translated this English copy himself.

Yagyu, Masashige. [Ca. 1978.] Letter to Ichiro Ueno. Translated by Ichiro Ueno for authors. No date given other than "Mr. Yagyu's letter, two years ago."

Yagyu, Masashige, and Yoiti Ueno. "L'Histoire graphique de l'organisation scientifique du travail 1856–1929." In the Frederick Winslow Taylor Collection, Stevens Institute of Technology, Hoboken, N.J.

Yost, Edna. 1949. *Frank and Lillian Gilbreth: Partners for Life*. New Brunswick, N.J.: Rutgers University Press.

4

Organizational Structure and Innovation: The Japanese Case

IAN MAITLAND

The large Japanese enterprise presents a promising site for considering the relationship between organizational structure and innovation. This is so because the remarkable growth of the Japanese economy over the last two decades has been driven largely by rapid "adoption of advances in knowledge" (Denison and Chung 1976, pp. 125–30). The agents of this process have been Japan's larger firms (Patrick and Rosovsky 1976, p. 23). This capability of the larger firms has only partially yielded to economic explanation, usually being attributed to residual, noneconomic factors (Ohkawa and Rosovsky 1973, Ch. 9).

WILSON'S THEORY OF INNOVATION IN ORGANIZATION

A partial theory of the relationship between organizational structure and innovation has been proposed by James Q. Wilson (1966). He has sketched the implications for innovativeness of one structural property, namely "organizational diversity." Wilson hypothesized that the effects of greater

The author is grateful to J. P. Miller for his helpful criticism.

organizational diversity are contradictory: while it stimulates an organization's capacity to generate proposals for innovation, it inhibits its capacity to adopt and implement them. In view of these compensating effects, Wilson pessimistically concluded that his analysis could yield little in the way of empirical propositions: "This . . . may explain why the evidence on whether large or small organizations are more innovative is inconclusive" (p. 205).

Can Wilson's theory then help shed any light on the high rate of innovation in the large Japanese enterprise? On the face of it, the Japanese case presents some serious difficulties. While the theory would lead us to expect that the advantage of the large Japanese enterprise has consisted of its superior capacity to generate proposals for innovation, in fact this is not the case. These firms have relied almost entirely on the importation of foreign techniques (Caves 1976, p. 518; OECD 1972, para. 212; Ohkawa and Rosovsky 1973, p. 89). What has distinguished these firms has been their extraordinary capacity to assimilate innovations (Abegglen 1973, p. 39; Galenson 1976. According to Wilson's theory the greater organizational diversity of these firms would have been expected to constrain the adoption of innovations.

In spite of these apparent anomalies, I believe the Japanese case conforms to Wilson's model of innovation in organizations. To substantiate this belief, I propose to review certain distinctive structural characteristics of the large Japanese enterprise.

ORGANIZATIONAL DIVERSITY AND THE ADOPTION OF INNOVATIONS

Wilson defines organizational diversity as "a function of both the complexity of the *task structure* and the *incentive system*" (1966, p. 198). The task structure is "the sum of all tasks, or one-man duties, in the organization" and the incentive system is "the sum of all rewards given to members" (pp. 198–99). These two components of organizational diversity affect the rate at which innovations are adopted in the following manner. A more complex task structure means a greater diffusion of power within the organization as "detailed control of members' activities by the organization [becomes] difficult."* The more complex the incentive system, the greater

---

*It should be remarked that this hypothesis is grounded in a long tradition of organizational analysis. Selznick (1948) has proposed that formal organizations be conceptualized as "cooperative systems" because power is so dispersed that compliance is essentially voluntary. See also Selznick (1948) on "authority leakage" and Allison (1971) on "fractionated power."

the probability of some interest(s) being adversely affected by a proposed innovation.* As a consequence, a greater number of wills have to be concerted before an innovation can be adopted; but at the same time the likelihood of opposition to the innovation from some quarter is much increased. The interaction of these two effects of organizational diversity has the result of drastically curtailing the adoption of innovations by the organization (pp. 202–4).

What causes organizational diversity? The task structure increases in complexity "as the number of different tasks increases and as the proportion of nonroutine tasks increases" (p. 198). Since a larger organization affords greater opportunity for specialization of functions, size is generally associated with a more complex task structure. A more complex task structure in its turn is a principal source of increased complexity of the incentive system:

> One important source of an increase in the complexity of the incentive system is an increase in the complexity of the task structure. . . . If the task structure becomes more complicated, it will in the typical case require the creation within the organization of subunits . . . normally result[ing] in the generation of subunit loyalties among members of the organization (p. 199).

This point should be noted, because I intend to argue that one of the distinctive structural features of the large Japanese enterprise is the way it has uncoupled the incentive system from the task structure, so that in spite of its size it has been able to retain a fairly simple incentive system hospitable to the adoption of innovations.

Wilson identified a further source of increase in the complexity of the incentive system, independent of the task structure. That is, the number of groups, inside or outside the organization, with which each organizational member is affiliated. Such groups may complicate the incentive system by providing rewards that are not under direct organizational control (pp. 199–200). I intend to show that in the Japanese firm such ties are rarer than in the West, and that, where they do exist, they tend to be weaker and/or congruent with the incentive system of the firm.

---

*For some relevant literature on this point, see Selznick (1943) on "bifurcation of interest" and March and Simon (1958) on "differentiation of goals" and "differentiation of individual perceptions."

SIMPLIFYING THE INCENTIVE SYSTEM

How the Incentive System Is Uncoupled from the Task Structure

What aspects of the organization of the Japanese enterprise insulate its incentive system from the growing complexity of its task structure? In a few words, the answer is the relative unimportance of tasks as a basis for rewards. This is in sharp contrast with Western practice.

The Japanese enterprise is organized so as to minimize an employee's identification with a task, function, or set of skills. Consider the following features:

1. Unlike their Western counterparts, Japanese "employees are not hired for specific jobs, nor do they apply for specific jobs" (Abegglen 1973, p. 24). Moreover, in the course of his employment "a regular employee tends not to reject jobs or occupations in order to pursue a preferred job or occupation. Rather, he is always ready to move from one job to another, at the will and request of the company" (Wilson 1966, p. 406).
2. The practice of "lifetime employment" divorces security of employment from the marketability of an employee's skills (Abegglen 1973, p. 24).
3. Compensation too is divorced from skill or function, depending as it does primarily on length of service (Abegglen 1973, p. 24; Dore 1973, p. 225).
4. There is a much weaker correlation between rank and function (Glazer 1976, p. 885).
5. "Continuous training" further minimizes dependence on a particular set of skills (Drucker 1971, pp. 217–25).
6. Possession of a skill does not guarantee that an employee can find comparable employment elsewhere, because the "permanent employment" system has displaced any real labor market (Dore 1973, p. 72).
7. Union membership also deemphasizes skill or task, since unions tend to be enterprise ones, not organized along craft or occupational lines. Solomon Levine has pointed out that the combination of diverse elements in these unions has "made it difficult to undertake serious attempts to alter the basic wage relationships even within the enterprise. Rather, in order to retain unity, collective bargaining has had to be concerned mainly with broad common issues" (1965; see also Okochi, Karsh, and Levine, 1974, p. 502).

8. Skill as a source of identity is weaker because "a smaller proportion of Japanese technical manpower . . . is trained at the graduate level" (Peck 1976, p. 580).

9. Informal groups within the Japanese concern, such as *habatsu* (cliques), tend not to be based on the division of labor but rather on other ties such as common birth place or school (Yoshino 1968, p. 208). This contrasts with the Western pattern (for example, Dalton 1959, pp. 53–54).

The preceding examples show how the incentive system in the Japanese firm is largely independent of the task structure. Security of employment, compensation, rank, informal ties, and even social identity have been severed from position in the task structure. Dore has commented that terms like technician and craftsman have no precise equivalents in Japanese (1973, p. 60). This means changes may be made to the task structure (namely, to accommodate innovations) that leave the established incentive system relatively undisturbed, thus provoking little resistance. (For remarks in a similar vein about the relationship between innovation and security, see Blau 1955, pp. 183–200; Moore 1951, pp. 241–49). It also means that differentiation of the task structure need not give rise to a more complex incentive system.

Minimization of Competing Statuses

The complexity of the incentive system of the Japanese firm is further restrained through the suppression or neutralization of social ties that could be a source of rewards not under the firm's control. Various features of the Japanese firm have the effect of abridging the employee's status-set and making his employment his dominant status to a degree unknown in the West. As long as one is careful to avoid imputations of purpose, it is fair to remark that the Japanese firm more than the Western approaches Lewis Coser's concept of the "greedy institution." "They seek exclusive and undivided loyalty and they attempt to reduce the role of competing roles and status positions. . . . They exercise pressures on component individuals to weaken their ties, or not to form any ties, with other institutions or persons that might make claims that conflict with their own demands" (Coser 1974, pp. 4, 8). What are the distinctive features of the Japanese firm that accomplish results of this sort?

1. Clearly the "permanent employment" system, once again, is crucial: "A worker must have a strong concern for the viability of

an institution in which he plans to spend his working life" (Galenson 1976, p. 625).

2. In Japan "national professional organizations of engineers and the like are rather weak; the professional is typically tied to his firm where he has received his training, and is less of an independent agent" (Glazer 1976, p. 880).

3. The practice of "continuous training" within the firm generally precludes the development of external ties. Some of these training programs qualify as schools officially certified by the Ministry of Education (Tsuda 1974, p. 406). Not surprisingly then, a smaller proportion of Japanese technical manpower has been trained at graduate level at a university (Peck 1976, p. 580). Dore reports that neither professional associations nor trade unions have a role in setting standards of technical competence (1973, p. 73).

4. Japan has a much higher ratio of engineers to scientists than the United States, the United Kingdom, or France (Peck 1976, p. 580). A study has found that U.S. engineers more are likely to be oriented to their employers than to professional values and goals (Goldner and Ritti 1967, pp. 491–94). The Japanese case is no exception: Peck has noted the "preferences of Japanese engineers for the esteem which is to be gained within the company from immediate technical success. . . . [In contrast] American researchers on the long term projects were motivated by the prospect of publication and scientific reputation" (1976, p. 564).

5. Peck's report of the "lack of large staffs of basic researchers in Japanese firms" (1976, p. 574) also assumes importance in light of the finding that dependence on research is correlated with weak organizational control (Miller 1967).

6. The same inward orientation is displayed at the board level: the board of directors is "predominantly, if not exclusively, staffed by full-time operating executives" (Yoshino 1968, p. 210).

7. The prevalence of enterprise unions means that union membership is to a striking degree congruent with membership in the firm. "The status of permanent or regular worker coincides exactly with union membership and, ideally, the consciousness of union members is not distinguished from that of the worker's status as employee. Accordingly, the Japanese worker appears to be more sensitive to the prosperity of the enterprise than will typically be the case with his Western counterpart" (Okochi, Karsh, and Levine 1974, p. 502).

8. Permanent or regular workers in the large Japanese enterprise form a privileged caste or "quasi-elite force" (Dore 1973, p. 70) in a dual-structure economy.

9. The relationship between the enterprise and the employee is more diffuse than is the custom in the West. "The wide range of company activities suggests that enterprises are not only economic institutions pursuing profit but are also social security institutions caring for the life of each employee" (Okochi, Karsh, and Levine 1974, p. 502).

10. Informal linkages within the firm tend to be vertical in character and thus more likely to supplement the formal structure than to obstruct it (Drucker 1971, pp. 228–34; Yoshino 1968, p. 218).

11. Finally, the nature of the formal organization of the Japanese enterprise is caught well by Dore in his comparison of a British and a Japanese firm: "English Electric is much more like a federation of semi-autonomous product divisions; Hitachi more like a centralized empire" (1973, p. 228).

THE ORIGINATION OF INNOVATIONS IN THE JAPANESE FIRM

So far we have considered the implications of organizational structure only for the likelihood that innovations will be adopted. Wilson distinguished two other stages in the process of innovation, namely "conception" and "proposal" (1966, p. 200), which I intend to treat jointly as the "origination" of innovations. According to Wilson's theory we would expect a relatively simple incentive system, such as exists in the large Japanese enterprise, to exert a drag on the origination of innovations.

The effect of the structural features noted above is to inhibit the development of internal or external reference or membership groups that might compete with the firm for the loyalty of employees. As a consequence, the Japanese employee approximates closely Gouldner's definition of a "local," that is one "high on loyalty to the employing organization, low on commitment to specialized role skills and likely to use an inner reference group orientation" (1957). The Japanese company, as Glazer has noted, is characterized by a high degree of commitment to a "common value system" (1976, p. 877). While that commitment may be functional for the adoption by the workforce of changes ordered by top management,* there is reason to believe that it is dysfunctional for the origination of innovations within the firm. Such a firm will largely have eliminated internal diversity of

---

*It is not being argued here that this structure is *inherently* more suited to the adoption of innovations. This near monopoly of rewards could equally well be used to obstruct change. It all depends on top management's attitude toward innovation.

viewpoints and will be insulated from outside developments that might stimulate suggestions for change. Wilbert Moore has remarked that "the withering away of all outside relationships, e.g., with 'professional peers,' may promote integration, but will stem the flow of new ideas" (1951, p. 92).

Evidence suggests that this is just what has happened. Yoshino has commented that the efficiency of top management suffers from a lack of broader perspectives. He also believes that the emphasis placed on harmony within the enterprise has limited its ability to innovate (1968, Ch. 7). In a review of studies of Japanese factory organization, Glazer noted a virtual absence of learning between firms in the same industry (1976, p. 879). Peck has reported that Japanese engineers are familiar with their own companies' capabilities and problems but less so with practices in other companies and university research in their specialties (1976, p. 579). Ohkawa and Rosovsky have remarked that the history of Japanese economic modernization has been "virtually devoid of core inventions" (1973, p. 226).

CONCLUSION

In spite of the limitations outlined in the preceding section, the large Japanese enterprise has a remarkable record of innovation. How has it avoided the trap described by Wilson? The answer has already been suggested: the Japanese firm has not attempted to originate its own innovations, preferring to rely on advances developed outside, especially by research leaders overseas. This practice has amounted to a corporate and national policy. We have already noted the lack of large research staffs and the preponderance of engineers in Japanese firms. In addition, Peck has reported that the development of new products consumes a smaller proportion of companies' research and development efforts than in the United States; research managers regard their resources as fully committed to the modification and improvement of existing products. Nationally, a smaller proportion of research and development resources goes to academic basic-science establishments; Japan's educational system is appropriate to a catch-up phase rather than to research leadership (Peck 1976, pp. 544, 563, 581, 580).

This "strategy of number two," as Patrick and Rosovsky have called it, has consisted of "continually searching the world for the best new ideas and inventions and using their own skills to embody them rapidly in commercially and economically attractive goods and services" (1976, p. 902). This policy has meant that the Japanese enterprise's task has been limited to the application of ideas already tried and proven. As noted, Wilson hypothesized that the structural conditions that encourage the process of origination of innovations are also the ones that impede the adoption of innovations. His theory would suggest then that the peculiar advantage of the Japanese enterprise lies in the fact that it is freed from the necessity of balancing these contradictory demands on its structure. It has been able to sustain an exceptionally high rate of innovation because its structure is optimally adapted to the requirements of absorbing innovations.*

REFERENCES

Abegglen, James. 1973. *Management and the Worker, The Japanese Solution.* Tokyo: Sophia University. New York: Kodansha.

Allison, Graham T. 1971. *Essence of Decision.* Boston: Little Brown.

Blau, Peter M. 1955. *The Dynamics of Bureaucracy.* Chicago: University of Chicago Press.

Burns, Tom, and G. M. Stalker. 1961. *The Management of Innovation.* London: Tavistock.

Caves, Richard E. 1976. With the collaboration of Masu Uekusa. "Industrial Organization." In *Asia's New Giant, How the Japanese Economy Works*, ed. Hugh Patrick and Henry Rosovsky, pp. 459–524. Washington, D.C.: Brookings Institution.

Coser, Lewis. 1974. *Greedy Institutions.* New York: Free Press.

Dalton, Melville. 1959. *Men Who Manage.* New York: John Wiley.

Denison, Edward F., and William K. Chung. 1976. "Economic Growth and Its Sources." In *Asia's New Giant, How the Japanese Economy Works*, ed. Hugh Patrick and Henry Rosovsky, pp. 63–152. Washington, D.C.: Brookings Institution.

Dore, Ronald. 1973. *British Factory — Japanese Factory.* Berkeley: University of California Press.

Downs, Anthony. 1966. *Inside Bureaucracy.* Boston: Little Brown.

Drucker, Peter F. 1971. *Men, Ideas and Politics.* New York: Harper & Row.

Galenson, Walter. 1976. With collaboration of Konosuke Odaka. "The Japanese Labor Market." In *Asia's New Giant, How the Japanese Economy Works*, ed. Hugh Patrick and Henry Rosovsky, pp. 587–672. Washington, D.C.: Brookings Institution.

Glazer, Nathan. 1976. "Social and Cultural Factors in Japanese Economic Growth." In *Asia's New Giant, How the Japanese Economy Works*, ed. Hugh Patrick and Henry Rosovsky, pp. 813–96. Washington, D.C.: Brookings Institution.

Goldner, Fred H., and R. R. Ritti. 1967. "Professionalization as Career Immobility." *American Journal of Sociology* 72:489–502.

Gouldner, Alvin W. 1957. "Cosmopolitans and Locals: Toward an Analysis of La-

---

*Wilson's model of innovation differs in some important respects from Burns and Stalker's (1961, esp. pp. 119–25). In my view, their paradigm suffers from its failure to distinguish between the stages involved in the process of innovation and the structural conditions appropriate to each.

tent Social Roles — I."*Administrative Science Quarterly* 2:281–306.

Levine, Solomon B. 1965. "Labor Markets and Collective Bargaining in Japan." In *The State and Economic Enterprise in Japan*, ed. William W. Lockwood, pp. 633–37. Princeton: Princeton University Press.

March, James, and Herbert Simon. 1958. *Organizations*. New York: Wiley.

Merton, Robert K. 1957. *Social Theory and Social Structure*, rev. ed. Glencoe, Ill.: The Free Press.

Miller, George A. 1967. "Professionals in Bureaucracy: Alienation Among Industrial Scientists and Engineers." *American Sociological Review* 32:755–67.

Moore, Wilbert E. 1951. *Industrial Relations and the Social Order*. New York: Macmillan.

OECD. 1972. *The Industrial Policy of Japan*. Paris: OECD.

Ohkawa, Kazushi, and Henry Rosovsky. 1973. *Japanese Economic Growth*. Stanford, Calif.: Stanford University Press.

Okochi, Kazuo, Bernard Karsh, and Solomon B. Levine. 1974. "The Japanese Industrial Relations System: A Summary." In *Workers and Employers in Japan*, ed. Kazuo Okochi, Bernard Karsh, and Solomon B. Levine, pp. 485–512. Princeton, N.J.: Princeton University Press.

Patrick, Hugh, and Henry Rosovsky. 1976. "Japan's Economic Performance: An Overview" and "Prospects for the Future and Some Other Implications." In *Asia's New Giant, How the Japanese Economy Works*, ed. Hugh Patrick and Henry Rosovsky, pp. 1–62 and 897–924. Washington, D.C.: Brookings Institution.

Peck, Merton J. 1976. "Technology." In *Asia's New Giant, How the Japanese Economy Works*, ed. Hugh Patrick and Henry Rosovsky, pp. 525–86. Washington, D.C.: Brookings Institution.

Selznick, Philip. 1948. "Foundations of the Theory of Organization." *American Sociological Review* 13:25–35.

_____. 1943. "An Approach to a Theory of Bureaucracy." *American Sociological Review* 8:47–54.

Tsuda, Masumi. 1974. "Personnel Administration at the Industrial Plant Level." *Workers and Employers in Japan*, pp. 399–440.

Wilson, James Q. 1966. "Innovation in Organization: Notes Toward a Theory." In *Approaches to Organizational Design*, ed. James D. Thompson. Pittsburgh: University of Pittsburgh Press.

Yoshino, M. Y. 1968. *Japan's Managerial System, Tradition and Innovation*. Cambridge, Mass.: M.I.T.

Part II

QUALITY CIRCLES

Quality circles represent comprehensive programs intended to improve human resources through the worker's involvement and participation in functional decision making. There are millions of Japanese workers involved in quality circles, and many view these systems as the key behind the phenomenal Japanese success. This section includes three chapters that discuss the philosophy, working, and consequences of quality circles.

Jo Ann Hranac and Kathleen C. Brannen, in "The What, Where, and Whys of Quality Control Circles," first define quality control (QC) circles and describe the QC circle process. The development of the QC circle philosophy is traced from its roots in post-World War II Japan to its current status in the industrial world. Certain differences between U.S. industrial management style and Japanese industrial management style are then discussed. U.S. industrial management is shown to be based on "scientific management" and Theory X. Japanese industrial management is pictured as a Theory Y style based on cultural, sociological, and economic aspects of the Japanese society.

Robert E. Callahan's chapter, "Quality Circles: A Program for Productivity Improvement through Human Resource Development," presents the philosophy and the basic principles utilized to develop and implement a comprehensive quality circle program. The author believes that quality circles are comprehensive programs for improving productivity through improved methods of human resource management that stress employee development and employee involvement in work-area decision making.

George W. Jacobs contributes "Quality Circles and Japanese Management: Participation or Paternalism?" Here Japanese management systems are discussed through an analysis of quality circles. Jacobs concludes that Japanese systems are more typically paternalistic than participative, in the customary sense, but that unexplored differences in the cultural frame of reference may justify the apparent Japanese emphasis on participative aspects and deemphasis of paternalistic aspects, particularly in media accounts. A constructive approach to the issue is proposed, centering on objective consideration of the facts, avoidance of premature evaluation or judgments, and awareness of crucial differences in the relevant cultural contexts.

5

The What, Where, and Whys of Quality Control Circles

JO ANN HRANAC *and* KATHLEEN C. BRANNEN

An article recently appeared in *Time* describing how Japanese cars are taking over the European auto market. The article closed with this "warning": "The Japanese now have 21% of the U.S. auto market. European automakers, like their American counterparts, will have to face the Japanese challenge by obtaining more cooperation from often fractious labor unions, boosting productivity, and turning out cars that can compete with the Japanese in price and appeal" ("Slippery Roads" 1981). Ironically, one of the means by which Americans (and perhaps Europeans) might be able to accomplish some of these goals would be by using a Japanese "invention"—the quality control circle.

What is a quality control circle? The purpose of this chapter is to answer this question and related questions: How did the concept develop? Why is it successful in Japan? Can it be implemented in the United States?

WHAT IS A QUALITY CONTROL CIRCLE?

A quality control circle (QC circle) is a small group of employees doing similar work under one supervisor and meeting regularly to identify, analyze, and solve product quality problems (Rieker 1977). QC circles are voluntary, and this is one of the most important characteristics of a circle. Theoretically, the ideal size of a circle is eight to ten people, and the circle generally meets weekly.

Training is another very important aspect of QC circles. Leaders are first trained in the concepts and techniques of the QC circle program. The first several meetings of a new circle are spent training the circle members, familiarizing them with the basic QC circle techniques in which the leader has been trained. Training for both leaders and members involves learning the techniques of giving a management presentation and learning how to use brainstorming, cause-and-effect diagrams, Pareto diagrams, histograms, check sheets, graphs, sampling, and control charts to analyze effectively the sources and causes of quality problems.

Once the training is completed, the real function of the circle begins. First, the circle members identify the problems in their work area and decide which is the most significant problem. After they have decided upon a problem to investigate first, they gather data about the problem, find the cause or causes, and arrive at a solution. Generally, they then present their findings and recommendations to management, implement their solutions, or both.

The following steps are an outline and summary of this QC circle process:

1. Determine what problem to solve and why that problem needs to be solved.
2. If it is a general problem, choose a specific part of that problem and find out as much as possible about it.
3. Analyze the data gathered about the problem, to sort out the true cause from the noncontributory factors.
4. Determine what solution or actions to take to solve the problem.
5. Develop a plan for initiating those actions.
6. Carry out the plan; that is, take the corrective action (if authorized to do so).
7. Check to see if the problem is really solved.
8. Set up a system to be sure the problem remains solved.
9. Investigate and resolve other aspects of the problem if they are significant (Rieker 1977).

Quality control circles are basically a type of participative problem solving and, as such, are based on the concept that people will take more interest and pride in their work if they are allowed to have an input to decisions made about their work. Increased interest and pride will result in improved quality. QC circles affirm that management believes the individual doing the job knows more about it than anyone else and can suggest the changes necessary for improving it. QC circles are broadly based on the Theory Y style of management.

The following characteristics summarize a successful QC circle program:

1. A people-building philosophy is emphasized — that is, training and development of QC circle members.
2. Participation in the QC circle is voluntary.
3. Leaders get participation from everyone.
4. Members help others to develop.
5. Projects are circle, not individual, efforts.
6. Training is provided to both workers and management.
7. Creativity is encouraged.
8. Projects are related to members' work.
9. Management is supportive.
10. A consciouness devoted to quality improvement develops (Rieker 1977).

HOW DID THE QC CIRCLE DEVELOP?

The quality control circle movement officially started in Japan in 1962. However, the roots of the movement go back farther than that, to the post-World War II era, when Japan was faced with massive reconstruction and the desire to upgrade the reputations of Japanese products in the international markets. The concepts and techniques of modern quality control were introduced to Japan in 1946 by the U.S. forces of occupation. It was believed that these methods would help Japan during its reconstruction process. The Union of Japanese Scientists and Engineers (JUSE) took over the primary responsibility for domestic education in statistical quality control and opened a six-month quality control basic course in 1949. However, most Japanese literature gives credit for the first formal training in modern quality control to Dr. Deming's lectures in statistical methodology (1950) and Juran's courses on management of quality control (1954).

The Japanese, with their desire for learning and self-sufficiency, took these principles and adapted them to their own work situations. In the latter part of the 1950s, industrial managers gradually recognized the need for company-wide involvement in quality control and extended quality control training from managers and engineers to foremen and line workers. Training was conducted throughout the country over the radio, through newspapers, and through books. The most important feature of the whole movement was this extension to line workers. In April 1962, the magazine *Gemba to QC (QC for the Foreman)* was published. In May 1962, the first quality control circle was registered at the QC circle headquarters of JUSE, in Tokyo. Table 5.1 outlines the history of the QC circle movement in Japan from that time up to the mid 1970s (Asao 1976).

Table 5.1 lists one of the significant events of 1970 as the publication by JUSE of "Fundamentals of the QC Circle." This publication was important to the development of a favorable attitude towards QC circles. "Fun-

TABLE 5.1   Highlights of QC Circle Movement

1962	Apr.	*Gemba to QC (QC for the Foreman)* begins its quarterly publication. Formation and registration of QC circles are solicited by JUSE.
1962	May	The first QC circle is registered.
1962	Nov.	The first foreman QC conference is held (JUSE).
1963	May	The first QC circle conference is held.
1964	Jan.	*Gemba to QC* is changed into a monthly publication.
1964	Sep.	Regional chapters are organized.
1965	Nov.	FQC award is established (JUSE).
1967	Feb.	QC basic course for foremen starts (JUSE).
1968	Apr.	The first QC circle team (1 FQCT) visits United States (JUSE).
1970	Nov.	"Fundamentals of the QC Circle" is published.
1970	Nov.	QC correspondence course for foremen starts (JUSE).
1971	June	The first QC circle cruising seminar starts (JUSE).
1971	Aug.	The 200th QC Circle Conference is held.
1971	Nov.	QC Circle Grand Prize is established and the first All Japan Competition Conference is held.
1972	Aug.	The number of circles registered reaches 50,000.
1973	Jan.	*Gemba to QC* is renamed "FQC."
1973	May	The 300th QC Circle Conference is held.
1973	Nov.	The number of circles registered reaches 60,000.
1974	Oct.	The 400th QC Circle Conference is held.
1975	July	The number of circles registered reaches 70,000.
1975	Dec.	The 500th QC Circle Conference is held.

Source: Hranac, Jo Ann, and Kathleen C. Brannen. 1976. In *QC Circles: Applications, Tools and Theory*, ed. Davida M. Amsden and Robert T. Amsden. Milwaukee, Wisc.: American Society for Quality Control.

damentals of the QC Circle" presented the following as the major purposes of the QC circle movement in Japan:

1. Elevation of leadership and capability of the first-line supervisors: it should be achieved through their own efforts toward self-development.
2. Elevation of the morale of every worker and the permeation of quality consciousness throughout workers on the shop floor: they are established by the participation of all workers in the QC circle activities.
3. Formation of a core in every workshop: core members are linked with each other in the activities of company-wide control of the aspects and attainment of company goals, assurance of quality, day-to-day control of manufacturing processes, and so on (Kondo 1976).

With these favorable attitudes, it is fairly easy to see why the number of QC circles in Japan (both registered and unregistered) has been increasing since 1962. It is now estimated that one out of every eight Japanese employees is involved in QC circles; that means approximately 4–5 million people participate (Cole 1980). In fact, it is also estimated that over 50 percent of Japanese firms in the private sector with more than 30 employees are involved in some form of worker participation in decision-making or small-group activities ("Quality Concept" 1979).

Although this increasing number of QC circles represents a tremendous commitment by the Japanese people to the QC circle program, the results seem to be worthwhile:

1. At Nippon Kokan K.K., there are 8,000 workers in 1,480 circles. This program accounted for more than $86 million in cost savings in 1978.
2. Sharp Corporation's Tenri plant reports productivity up an average of 30 percent every six months for the last few years, and attributes much of the improvement to QC circle activity.
3. Nissan Motor Company has 4161 circles, which tackled more than 30,000 projects in 1978, resulting in savings of about $2.4 million ("Quality Control Circles" 1979).

WHY DO QC CIRCLES WORK IN JAPAN? CAN THEY BE SUCCESSFULLY IMPLEMENTED IN THE UNITED STATES?

Quality control activities in Japan may have an advantage over those in the United States because of inherent differences in Japanese and U.S. management philosophies. To understand these differences, one must first review the history of the assembly line in the United States and then to examine the U.S. management philosophies underlying the use of the assembly line.

In 1903, Frederick Taylor presented his paper "Shop Management" to the American Society of Mechanical Engineers and "scientific management" was born. Time and motion studies became almost an exact science, especially for the industrial engineer. Certainly when these concepts were introduced at the turn of the century they were innovative. Engineers drew up work standards and operators simply manufactured products according to the standards. This was probably a good system at the time, since few people besides the engineers had any education in this field (Ishikawa 1976). However, since then, industrial technology has been making steady progress while humanity or humaneness has also been gaining importance in society. Unfortunately, the Taylor system still prevails in U.S.

industry. We have become highly structured and controlled in the workplace; creativity has been discouraged in production jobs because "scientifically speaking," it must have a negative effect on efficiency and output. Operators are little better than mechanical equipment.

While the instrument responsible for mechanizing work in the United States is the assembly line, that instrument is really a concrete example of the prevalent U.S. industrial management philosophy. It is a "Theory X" management style. American managers tend to believe that improved efficiency and productivity come from top management through better education and broader perspective. An adversary relationship between workers and management is considered inevitable. There is a lack of trust, and the interests seem to be incompatible. Management discounts worker cooperation. In fact, in the early 1970s, a major study supported by the U.S. Department of Health, Education, and Welfare reported that the most consistent complaint of American workers was the failure of superiors to listen to them when they wanted to propose better ways of doing their jobs. "Workers feel that their bosses demonstrate little respect for their intelligence; superiors are said to feel that the workers are incapable of thinking creatively about their jobs (Cole 1979).

Consider now the Japanese manager. He views his employees as resources that, if cultivated (trained), will yield economic returns to the firm. The Japanese industrial management style is "Theory Y." The roots of this attitude or style fall into three categories: cultural, sociological, and economic.

The cultural aspect involves the Confucianist doctrine of human perfectability, with its belief in the potential of every person. Belief in everyone's potential permits every individual to participate in QC circles. This is in contrast to the Judeo-Christian heritage of the United States, which emphasizes human weakness and limitations and may discourage individual creativity.

To look at the sociological aspect one must examine the matters of racial, ethnic, and religious differences between the Japanese managerial and working classes. Japan is relatively homogeneous in all of these areas; this allows Japanese managers to realize that average workers are not so different from themselves. Again, this is in sharp contrast to the makeup of labor and management in the United States, where management is largely white, Anglo-Saxon, and Protestant, and labor is composed of diverse racial, religious, and ethnic groups. American managers see labor as "different" and thus inferior; if labor is inferior, an investment in training is not worthwhile.

Finally, the economic aspect is fairly obvious. Since World War II, Japanese managers have operated in an economy characterized by a high growth rate. Additionally, in Japan the company has traditionally supplied lifelong employment for the worker, thereby increasing the worker's sense of loyalty to the company. These two facts allow investments in training to be easily recouped. In the United States, with its poor growth rate and high rate of turnover, employers are likely to view employees as interchangeable or temporary parts, not worth the investment of training (Cole 1980).

It seems that quality control circles are a natural outgrowth of Japanese management style. However, in light of the differences between Japanese and U.S. management, can the QC circles be successfully implemented in the United States? Many reasons have been proposed for why QC circles will not work in the United States, and why they are so successful in Japan. These arguments have already been mentioned; they are summarized as follows:

1. QC circle activities are a cultural phenomenon. Japan's culture and traditions create a unique environment favorable to the development of QC circles. (The United States has neither such a culture nor such traditions.)
2. Participation and humanistic industrial practices are prerequisites. In Japan, management attitudes, labor-management relations, lifetime employment methods of training, and other factors all contribute to the growth of QC circles. (The United States operates under Theory X management style, not Theory Y as in Japan.)
3. The way the quality control system is organized is decisive. In Japan, quality control involves everyone — from top management to line workers. Everyone receives training and everyone has an input. (U.S. quality control decisions come from the top down.)
4. There must be strong motivation for change. Japan wanted to change the image that "Made in Japan" conveyed. This was a national objective that everyone — managers and workers — wanted to help achieve. (As yet, the United States has no such national objective.) (Rubenstein 1976).

Traditional management practices in U.S. industry would seem to support the argument that QC circles are unique to Japan. However, with an increasing emphasis in the United States on the quality of worklife, and with shifting attitudes of management towards labor, the concept could become workable in the United States. A strong motivation for change, as mentioned above, may be the key to successful implementation. With U.S. productivity declining and the economy in poor condition, something will have to change. The motivation may already be present.

However, just as Japan adapted QC statistical methods to its own purposes and came up with QC circles, some adaption will have to be made to fit this concept to the needs of American management and workers — and there will be problems to overcome. Basic problems are the relationship of managers to workers, resistance of unions, workers' lack of education in quality practices, and management philosophy or resistance toward such programs.

Of those problems, the major ones seem to be middle management and union resistance. Unions were never much of a problem in Japan, but in the United States, unions can be very suspicious of a program with "control" in the title. Middle-management resistance can take several forms. In all cases, all workers must be made to feel a part of the action so that they can feel they contributed to the success or failure of an effort (Cole 1979).

Other problems concern keeping the program voluntary and giving adequate rewards. A U.S. company will have to pay overtime wages for circle work done outside normal working hours. This is not always the case in Japan, where lifelong employment means long-term commitment and an investment in the future of the company. In the United States, rewards must be more immediate (Cole 1980).

Even with these roadblocks and problems, there is still reason for optimism. Currently, the QC circle concept is in use in over 100 U.S. firms of different sizes, in a variety of industries and technologies. Examples of these include American Airlines, Honeywell Corporation, Ford Motor Company, General Motors Company, Lockheed Missile and Space Company, and Rockwell International (Cole 1980). Unfortunately, it is too soon to make definitive evaluations of the success of QC circles in U.S. industry.

CONCLUSION

With all of the problems mentioned and not mentioned, the worth of QC circles might be questioned. However, the results Japan has achieved with its QC circles are significant. The primary objective of QC circles is to solve quality and other work-related problems. This objective has been and is being attained in Japan. Other results, however, are increases in motivation, improved attitudes, and the formation of a sense of personal worth and integrity for the individual employee. With problems of absenteeism, labor turnover, and decreasing productivity in the United States, it might be wise to consider that part of the cause of these problems could be poor worker attitude. QC circles deal not only with the quality of production, but also with the quality of working life. They give a feeling of worth to employees by allowing them to have some input to their work. Input and respect may be just the incentives U.S. labor needs to "get back down to business".

Quality control circles are not a panacea for quality and productivity problems. Nevertheless, they may be a forward step toward meeting the Japanese challenge.

REFERENCES

Asao, Masashi. 1976. "Role of JUSE for QC Circle Movement." In *QC Circles: Applications, Tools and Theory*, ed. Davida M. Amsden and Robert T. Amsden, p. 31. Milwaukee, Wisc.: American Society for Quality Control.

Cole, Robert E. 1980. "Learning from the Japanese: Prospects and Pitfalls." *Management Review* (September):25–39.

———. 1979. "Made in Japan—Quality Control Circles." *Across the Board*, November, p. 74.

Ishikawa, Kaoru. 1976. "Conclusion." In *QC Circles: Applications, Tools and Theory*, ed. Davida M. Amsden and Robert T. Amsden, p. 164. Milwaukee, Wisc.: American Society for Quality Control.

Kondo, Yoshio. 1976. "The Roles of Manager in QC Circle Movement." In *QC Circles: Applications, Tools and Theory*, ed. Davida M. Amsden and Robert T. Amsden, pp. 43–45. Milwaukee, Wisc.: American Society for Quality Control.

"A Quality Concept Catches on Worldwide." 1979. *Industry Week*, April 16, p. 125.

"Quality Control Circles Pay Off Big." 1979. *Industry Week*, October 29, pp. 17–19.

Rieker, W. S. 1977. *Quality Control Circles Study Guide—Internorth*. Saratoga, Calif.: Quality Control Guides.

Rubenstein, S. P. 1976. "QC Circles and U.S. Participative Movements." In *QC Circles: Applications, Tools and Theory*, ed. Davida M. Amsden and Robert T. Amsden, pp. 157–62. Milwaukee, Wisc.: American Society for Quality Control.

"Slippery Roads." 1981. *Time*, January 12, p. 65.

6

Quality Circles: A Program for Productivity Improvement through Human Resources Development

ROBERT E. CALLAHAN

INTRODUCTION

Why Improve Productivity

As high inflation continues to plague the U.S. economy despite years of conventional government efforts to control it, there is one word that is getting increasing attention among business executives, government officials, and labor-management experts. That single word is productivity — the measure of output in relation to the input of labor, materials, and money. Increasing productivity has been called the "sleeper" in the bag of tricks economists offer to improve the economy (Miller 1978).

The problem with U.S. productivity is that it has been stagnated since 1973, contributing not only to inflation but to a corresponding stagnation

The author is grateful to Rodney E. Motonaga, coordinator/facilitator at Boeing Commercial Airplane Company, Fabrication Division, for his efforts and comments during the writing of this paper.

in the standard of living. According to the President's Council of Economic Advisors, it is not just a cyclical slowdown but a significant decline that must be reversed if the nation is to deal with spiraling wages and prices, keep up with the increasing price of imported oil, reduce unemployment, improve profits, and pave the way for solid business growth. Even labor leaders are now generally supportive of the idea of trying to improve productivity, viewing it as a way to preserve both the union and workers' jobs ("Productivity" 1978).

History shows that productivity gains have been a key factor in U.S. economic growth. Between 1947 and 1966, productivity, as measured by output per hour in the private sector, grew at a rate of 3.2 percent per year. However, since 1967, the growth has slowed to only 1.6 percent per year (Kutscher, Mark, and Norsworthy 1977). U.S. productivity growth is now the lowest among all the major industrial nations of the world including Japan — the leader with a growth rate of 8.5 percent per year (American Productivity Center 1979), West Germany, Sweden, France, Canada, and Italy. This confirms suspicions that the United States is becoming increasingly noncompetitive in international markets. While the United States still has the highest level of total output per employee, the other industrialized nations are threatening to surpass the United States in less than a decade (American Productivity Center 1979).

During the years of strong productivity growth, workers and their families became accustomed to generous increases in real income. The U.S. standard of living rose dramatically, average work schedules were shortened, and leisure time increased. Over a period of time, everyone came to expect an annual improvement in their real incomes. As productivity growth slowed in 1967, however, real income gains began to fall below individual and collective expectations. In an effort to sustain past patterns of real income growth, wages were pushed up, setting inflationary pressures in motion. The accelerated inflation cycle that still dominates the economy began in 1968.

Challenge for Today's Manager

Actions by both government and the private sector can be taken to revitalize productivity. The government should adopt policies that encourage the increasing of capital investments and research and development expenditures. Additionally, the government should objectively equate the costs with the benefits of many regulations of such agencies as Occupational Safety and Health Administration (OSHA), Environmental Protection Agency (EPA), and Equal Employment Opportunity Commission (EEOC) that have had considerable negative impacts on productivity. However, regardless of these and other actions that the government could take, its lack of action in recent years indicates that it is time for the private sector to take the initiative. In fact, it has been suggested that, in a capitalistic society, the best long-term solution to the problem lies with the private sector. The responsibility therefore falls on the shoulders of management. Solving national economic problems begins with improving productivity in one's own firm — certainly an important challenge for today's managers.

It is a considerable challenge because managers can no longer rely on traditional methods for improving productivity. After all, substitution of capital for labor in the United States is getting progressively more difficult, especially with the recent dramatic growth of service industries. It must be recognized that the greatest potential for productivity improvement lies in the human dimension of productivity. The problem is that while times have changed and workers' needs have changed, management style and practicing philosophy have remained largely unchanged. Management can no longer afford to maintain the status quo.

Need for Change in Management Style

There remains in the United States a considerable residue of the Frederick Taylor system of shop management, which is based upon the concept of separating planning from execution. The Taylor system was spectacularly successful in increasing shop productivity, and was a major contributor to making the United States the world leader in productivity. Circumstances for workers have since changed. Employees now have education, valuable experience, and creativity that could be utilized on the job. However, under the division of work inherent in the Taylor system, they are severely limited in using these assets.

Additionally, today's workers are more inclined to self-expression. Work is viewed as less of a necessary evil. More and more hourly workers have become aware of the inherent contradiction between participating as a full citizen in society and being treated as an extreme subordinate in the traditional authoritarian structures of today's organization. The democratic concepts of self-fulfillment and participation envisioned for society as a whole are not being responsively met at the work place (Kassalow 1977).

As a result, many employees have uncooperative attitudes — they lack motivation and commitment to the organization. This not only deprives the company of full human resource utilization, but also deprives employees of their right to satisfaction on the job. The strategy for winning employee commitment calls for management to rely not on power, which is rapidly becoming an impotent tool of direction, but on the philosophies of participative management and human resources development.

The Human Resources Model of Management Theory and Human Resources Development

The managerial style required is one that puts into practice the human resources model of management theory, which has been proposed under various titles, including McGregor's (1960) "Theory Y," Miles' (1975) "Human Resources Model," Likert's (1967) "System 4," and Schein's (1970) "Complex Man." This model assumes that work is not inherently distasteful, that people want to contribute to meaningful goals that they have helped to establish, and that most people can exercise far more responsible self-direction and self-control than their present jobs demand. Employees are looked upon as reservoirs of potential talent and management's responsibility is to learn how best to tap such resources. A manager must create an environment in which all members may develop and contribute to the limits of their ability. The manager needs to encourage participation on important matters, continually broadening subordinate self-direction and control. This, plus the completion of more meaningful tasks, can in large measure determine the level of satisfaction on the job. It is assumed that good and meaningful performance leads to satisfaction — not the reverse (Steers and Porter 1975, pp. 17–19).

Human resources development refers to educational training and development activities, which often are necessary to achieve the goal of the human resources model of management theory — the goal of enabling workers to achieve meaningful performance that reflects their utmost ability. Human resources development, in effect, enhances the value of human resources assests by developing individuals so they may contribute to the limits of their ability, participate responsibly in decision making, and communicate effectively.

Practical Implementation

With the human resource model, management theory has come of age, but practical implementation is still in its infancy — or at least has been until now. Its concepts have been taught in business colleges and management seminars for many years and are not unfamiliar to most managers. Certainly, in some cases, the lack of strong attempts to implement the concepts was due to personal preferences for maintaining the status quo. Yet, in many cases, managers were, and still are, at a loss to determine a practical method or program for implementing the concepts. Techniques such as management by objectives, work-team concepts, sensitivity training, organizational development, and job enrichment have been prescribed by experts in our country. Yet, for various reasons, none of these have had widespread success.

Now a number of major U.S. companies are adopting a proven Japanese productivity improvement program called quality circles. Inherent in this program is the instilling of a management process that reflects the concepts of the human resources model of management theory. Quality circles, in effect, seems to be a practical solution to the problem of implementing that management theory within a company.

Quality circles are credited with much of Japan's success in improving product quality and overall productivity while simultaneously developing a dedicated work force. Although the Japanese developed the quality circles program back in the early 1960s, management experts in our country long ignored the program since they believed that cultural differences limited its applicability to the Japanese. However, in 1974, bold management people at Lockheed Missiles and Space Company successfully implemented the program in their firm and succeeded in proving that quality circles are just as applicable in this country. Currently, quality circles are in operation in more than 150 companies in the United States, up from only 60 companies a year ago (Beardsley 1980).

Despite the fact that the quality circles program has been shown to be suitable for U.S. businesses, it has gained limited exposure outside of technical journals and magazines of such organizations as the American Society for Quality Control (ASQC) and the American Institute of Industrial Engineers (AIIE).

Purpose of This Study

The purpose of this study was to investigate thoroughly the quality circles program — both the concept and its implementation. This investigation was conducted through an extensive literature search and contact with individuals who have had actual experience with implementing and conducting such a program. The merits of the program as well as its suitability for U.S. companies were evaluated.

QUALITY CIRCLES PROGRAM

Description

The quality circles program is a comprehensive program for improving productivity through improved methods of human resource management that stress employee development and employee involvement in work-area decision making. It is a program that instills a desirable management process reflecting the philosophy that motivation comes from within the indi-

vidual and that management's task is to create the proper work environment for allowing the employee's inner motivation to respond best. This
management process conveniently utilizes work-area problem solving as its
vehicle and provides the employee with the training and development necessary for effective participation.

The quality circles concept centers on the total involvement of all employees in improving the way work is done. Employees voluntarily meeting
in "circle" groups actually identify problems, analyze them, recommend
solutions to management, and implement solutions when possible. It is an
effective method for involving an organization's employees in assuming responsibility for "quality"—the quality of their work, their work environment, their professional growth, and their personal development. The
name quality circles was so derived.

The program emphasizes long-term results—productivity improvement resulting from permanent increases in employee motivation and commitment to the organization. This emphasis results in a focus on the subtle
and usually neglected human dimension of productivity, a virtually untapped area. Although considerable short-term cost savings may result
from problem solutions, these are merely supplemental benefits attributable to the chosen management process vehicle of quality circles.

Quality Circles Philosophy   *Part II*

The entire quality circles concept is based on trust, respect, and caring for
people. The individual worker is recognized as a human being with the in-
tellect and desire to participate in solving work-related problems. Moreover, the worker is believed to have the capacity and desire to grow and develop to become better than she or he already is.

The philosophy recognizes that employees are the job experts who
know best how to make their jobs easier and utilize their time more efficiently. In addition, it is believed that employees are anxious to contribute
their expertise. This philosophy restores a critical but long since removed dimension—the opportunity to think, to commit one's mind as well as one's
hands to the job. By allowing the individual to contribute expertise and
creative ideas, quality circles create in the individual a sense of participation, contribution, and belongingness. Also, investment of employees' time
and interest in problem solving results in their personal commitment to
making the solutions work.

To the benefit of both the employee and the organization, quality
circles provide participants with opportunities for taking on greater responsibilities, utilizing their capabilities more fully, doing interesting and
challenging work, and gaining recognition for achievement. Moreover, the

training program and involvement in circle activities lead to professional and personal growth. These are the intrinsic job factors that Herzberg (1966) identified in his famous "two-factor theory" as being the significant sources of employee motivation and satisfaction.

Origin in Japan

The Japanese industrial community of the early 1960s is credited with the concept of quality circles. For most major innovations, a suitable environment must be present; it must create a need and be receptive to the resolution of that need. Such was the case in postwar Japan.

The nature of Japan's government following World War II was such that its national leaders had to be recruited from its business enterprise. The economy needed to be strengthened, and managerial methods were adopted at the highest levels of government. Japan quickly emerged as a leader in international trade. Japanese products were inexpensive and readily available, but they also developed a reputation for poor quality and workmanship. The unique position of Japan's new leaders, with their ties to both government and industry, led to a national movement aimed at improving the quality of Japanese products. Various strategies were carried out, one of which led to the advancement and widespread adoption of the quality circles concept. At that time the name "quality control circles" was used because improving product quality was the primary goal.

In the United States, the usual approach to improving product quality was to train and educate the technical staff—either during university training or during seminars. The technical staff was then expected to use various techniques and secure the cooperation of management and the workers in getting improvements implemented. With quality circles, the Japanese used a different approach. They trained the workers, as well as management and the technical staff, in the techniques. The intent was that the workers themselves would use the techniques. This would reduce communication problems, reduce resistance to change, and permit the people most familiar with the problems to do the work. Then, after a team of workers had selected, analyzed, and solved a problem, they would present their proposed solution to management and the technical staff. This approach emphasized thousands of people working on problems rather than an elite group of engineers and managers telling the thousands (Konz 1979).

Quality circles were a natural outgrowth of Japanese management philosophy and human relations policies. The country's lack of natural resources had forced the Japanese to optimize returns from their only resource—their people. Japanese management philosophy, characterized as management by consensus, placed emphasis on the flow of information, initiative, and decision making from the bottom up, with the managers serving as facilitators in the decision-making process.

As mentioned previously, the Japanese first called the program quality control circles or QC circles since they began working on it from the point of view of product quality. Then they included cost with product quality. More recently, the program name was changed to quality circles when the whole emphasis was switched to the "quality of working life" (Patchin 1979).

The Japan Union of Scientists and Engineers (JUSE) coordinated the implementation of quality circles throughout Japan. JUSE was instrumental because it dispensed training material and was the source for a variety of training programs in quality circles for all levels of an organization, from executives to workers. JUSE still provides these services today, and in addition, provides a center for registration of circles and tracking of growth in the movement. It provides continuing stimulation by means of publication of periodicals and books featuring an exchange of problem solutions and solution methodology. It also sponsors regional, national, and international conferences (Rieker 1979).

JUSE estimates that registration in quality circles has grown in Japan from 20 circles with 400 members in December 1962, to 16,000 circles with 200,000 members in 1968, and to a phenomenal 88,000 circles with over 700,000 members in 1978 (American Productivity Center 1979). Various estimates put the total involvement of registered and unregistered circle membership up to 10 million workers.

At the Kobe Steel Company alone, there are a total of 2,046 circles with 19,654 members representing 92 percent of the total work force (Pabst 1972). This figure illustrates the magnitude of support of quality circles that is seen among both employers and employees in Japan.

Introduction to the Western World

Relatively little quality circles progress occurred outside of Japan until the early 1970s. In 1973 a team of managers from Lockheed Missiles and Space Company studied the concept in Japan. They were excited by what they saw and were convinced that quality circles were right for the Western world. Lockheed's team returned with training materials obtained from JUSE and immediately proceeded to translate and "Americanize" the program into a basic program for circle members. In addition, they developed a management introduction program and more extensive programs for the trainers. They were very careful not to depart drastically from the Japanese model.

According to Donald Dewar, one of the team members, the developmental phase was a very trying one:

> Not a day passed without one or more people admonishing me that my career was on the line for getting involved in the "Japanese" program. "It may work in Japan, but it will never work here because the Japanese are different," was the often given advice. It was difficult for all of us closely associated with the program to not let this advice adversely affect our enthusiasm. Another favorite remark was, "If this program was capable of working in the U.S., it would have been picked up years ago." Fortunately, middle management support was there and the program forged ahead (1979a).

In November 1974, a pilot program was launched at Lockheed. This much publicized pilot program attracted the attention of many companies in the United States and elsewhere in the Western world. The American Society for Quality Control (ASQC) was primarily responsible for the publicity that resulted from the Lockheed quality circles program. Hundreds of inquiries were received by Lockheed for information on the program and dozens of visitors came to see the program first-hand, including Dr. Ishikawa of JUSE (Dewar 1979a).

The program proved to be a success. The cost savings alone attributed to problems that were solved exceeded $750,000 after the first year of operation. These saving were realized with the 15 circles that were in existence at the end of the first year. However, because the circles grew to that number over the year, the equivalent number of circles was closer to eight or nine. The 15 circles in operation at the end of the first year were in several diverse areas of manufacturing—six in electronic shops, five in mechanical shops, three in composites fabrication, and two in manufacturing paperwork areas (Dewar 1976). Some of the results were:

- 95% felt that the program should be continued.
- 90% of the members felt that communications within the work team has improved as a result of the QC experience.
- Over 80% said the program had made a positive impact on the quality of workmanship with their work team.
- Over three-quarters of the members felt that the program had made their jobs more enjoyable.
- Similarly, a majority of the circle members (70%) felt the quality of their workmanship had improved as a result of the program.
- Four out of every five circle members felt that the cost of the program was justified by improvements in the quality of the products turned out by their organizations.
- About a quarter of the members have given of their own time—lunches, breaks, or after hours—in behalf of the program (Dewar 1976).

By 1976, after two years in operation, Lockheed documented cumulative savings of $2,844,000 with an average equivalent number of 15 circles. In one area of operation, rejects were reduced from 25 to 30 per 1,000 hours to less than six per 1,000 hours (Yager 1979).

In 1977, the quality circle program expanded to 33 circles with three full-time facilitators (trainers). Lockheed's management team felt that the program had been sufficiently tested.

Although less than a half dozen companies began getting involved with quality circles in 1977, the program has been growing since. Some of the more than 150 U.S. companies now using quality circles include Honeywell, Tektronix, Westinghouse, Solar Turbines International, Control Data, Hughes Aircraft, Rockwell International, Lockheed, Martin Marietta, Hewlett Packard, TRW, General Motors, Shell Oil, Champion Paper, Sperry Vickers, Harley Davidson, Champion Spark Plug, Ford Aerospace, J. C. Penney, and Firestone.

Growth outside Japan has not been limited to the United States. The quality circles movement has spread throughout Asia, South America, and Europe. Volvo of Sweden and Volkswagen of Brazil both use the program.

Quality Circles Program Structure

Program structure can vary, but a typical quality circles program is organized as shown in Figure 6.1. The organization is comprised of circles, leaders, facilitators, and a steering committee.

Circles

Forming the perimeter of the organizational wheel, as Figure 6.1 illustrates, can be any number of individual circles. Each circle can consist of three to 15 members, but seven to ten is considered the ideal size. Membership in circles is strictly voluntary. All members of a circle share a common work-related experience and most often report to the same supervisor. Circles usually meet for an hour each week on company time. Members are trained in problem identification and analysis techniques. Upon completion of training, the circle members then proceed to identify, analyze and resolve their work-related problems. They recommend solutions to management and actually implement solutions when possible.

Leaders

Leaders, an integral part of the program, are almost always the immediate supervisors of the circle members. Under the facilitator's supervision,

FIGURE 6.1   Quality Circles Program Structure

Source: Compiled by the author.

leaders conduct the training of circle members. The leaders also prepare agendas for circle meetings. Most importantly, the leaders insure that circle activities follow the prescribed quality circles process (which will be described in detail shortly).

The leader roles are delegated to supervisors so that the current authority structure is utilized, thereby avoiding the risk of creating an authority conflict.

Facilitators

Facilitators are a key element and can greatly influence the success or failure of a quality circles program. They work in close liaison with the steering committee and circle leaders to coordinate circle operations. Each facilitator oversees a number of circles and attends all meetings of those circles. Facilitators work especially closely with the leaders and members of new circles until they build their own momentum. An important role for facilitators is to insure that the circle leaders operate within the prescribed quality circles process. Facilitators are responsible for maintaining accurate records. These may show problem-solving methods that would be valuable to other circles or may be useful for future reference. Circles rely on the facilitator to coordinate and obtain input from necessary functional support groups, arrange for management presentations, and take care of other, similar matters.

Facilitators train new leaders and conduct management orientation seminars on a periodic basis. Another function of the facilitator is to keep management abreast of program status and to respond to requests from outside the organization to lecture on the subject. Facilitators are the most active promoters of the program.

Facilitators usually are on the staff of a high-level manager who is a strong supporter of the program. The authority level to which the facilitators report to is an important consideration, since they are expected to counsel supervisors and managers concerning quality circle matters.

When the program expands enough to require a number of full-time facilitators, the position of a coordinator may be added to the program structure. The coordinator, as supervisor of the facilitators, would then be the one reporting directly to the high-level manager. The coordinator would provide administrative backing to support the facilitators and serve as chairperson of the program steering committee.

Steering committee

As Figure 6.1 illustrates, the steering committee forms the central hub of the organizational wheel. The committee is generally composed of representatives of all major functional areas of the operation plus the facilitators. A designated committee chairperson guides committee meetings to predetermined objectives, and decisions are reached by democratic process. Under the committee's direction, the policies and procedures of the entire program are established and implemented. The committee determines what areas will be off-limits to circle activities. These off-limits areas usually include wages and salaries, company benefits, interpersonal conflicts, and anything directly concerning union contracts. The committee also coordinates the important training program needed for all members within the program structure. Additionally, the committee guides program expansion.

Communication plays a vital role in the success of a circles program. Being the guiding force of the program, the committee must continually publicize to employees, both inside and outside the organization, the activities and progress of individual circles. The objective is to maximize acceptance of the program and participation in it.

The committee is not intended to be an autocratic governing body. It should be a steering committee, not a driving committee. Naturally, this group will have to set up some of the boundaries. However, much of the program's success will depend on the interaction of all the components pictured in the organization chart.

A large company could eventually have more than one steering committee. There could be a corporate-level steering committee along with lower-level steering committees that operate closer to actual quality circle activities.

Quality Circles Process

The quality circles process is a term referring not only to the way circles operate, but, more importantly, to the management process that is involved in circles operation. The fundamental quality circles operation, as outlined in Figure 6.2, consists of four basic steps: problem identification, problem selection, problem analysis and resolution, and solution recommendation.

Problem identification

Identification of problems and themes for the circle to work on can come from the members themselves, from management, or from any other source in the company. The greater the number of problems that the circle has to choose from, the greater its opportunity to select a meaningful and challenging problem to work on.

Problem selection

Problem selection is a definite prerogative of the circle. The circle group itself, with each member including the circle leader having but one equal vote, arrives at such decisions on a democratic basis. By being permitted to select the problems they are to work on, the circle members receive assurance that this is their program.

Problem analysis and resolution

Having selected a problem to work on, the circle then proceeds to analyze it. The circle is expected to use as many of the problem-analysis techniques

FIGURE 6.2   Quality Circles Process

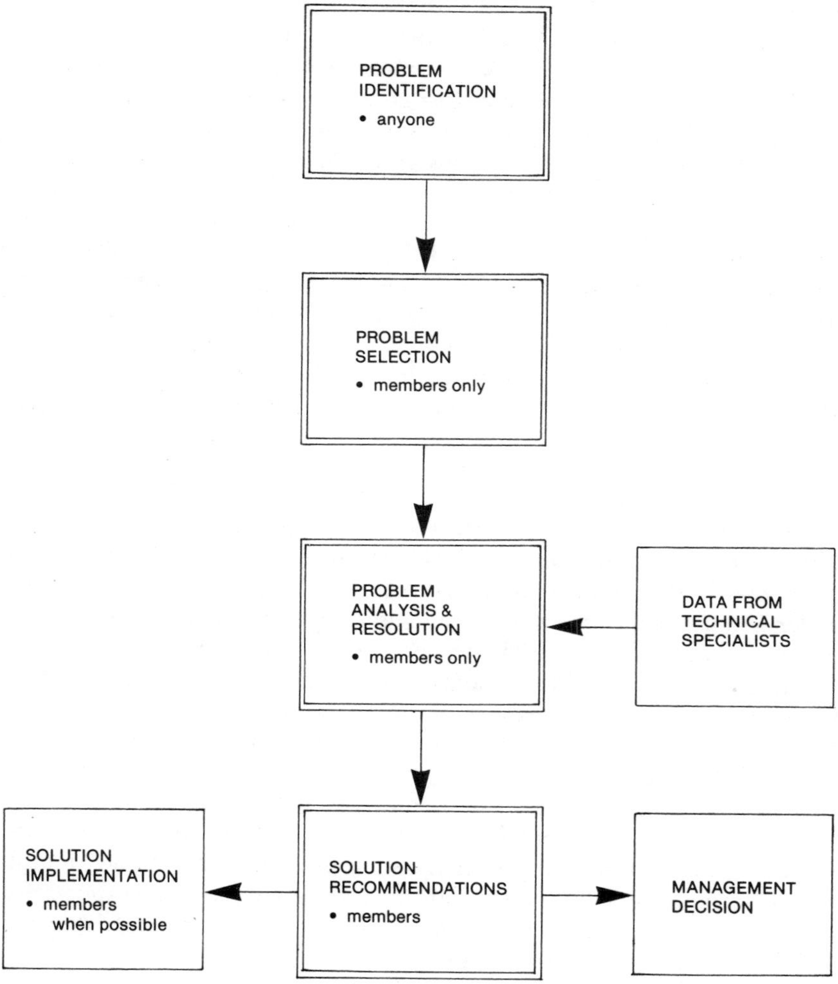

```
                    ┌─────────────────────┐
                    │  PROBLEM            │
                    │  IDENTIFICATION     │
                    │  • anyone           │
                    └─────────────────────┘
                              │
                              ▼
                    ┌─────────────────────┐
                    │  PROBLEM            │
                    │  SELECTION          │
                    │  • members only     │
                    └─────────────────────┘
                              │
                              ▼
          ┌─────────────────────┐        ┌──────────────────┐
          │  PROBLEM            │◄───────│  DATA FROM       │
          │  ANALYSIS &         │        │  TECHNICAL       │
          │  RESOLUTION         │        │  SPECIALISTS     │
          │  • members only     │        └──────────────────┘
          └─────────────────────┘
                     │
                     ▼
┌──────────────┐  ┌─────────────────────┐   ┌──────────────────┐
│ SOLUTION     │  │  SOLUTION           │   │  MANAGEMENT      │
│ IMPLEMENTATION│◄─│  RECOMMENDATIONS    │──►│  DECISION        │
│ • members    │  │  • members          │   └──────────────────┘
│   when possible │ └─────────────────────┘
└──────────────┘
```

Source: Compiled by the author.

that were covered in training as practical. Thorough analysis is expected; the circle members are required to gather the necessary data.

There may be instances when data from technical specialists is required. When this occurs, it becomes the facilitator's responsibility to obtain the necessary data from a technical specialist or to arrange that the specialist attend a circle meeting. When the latter occurs, it is important that the specialist be familiarized with the quality circles concept before attending the circle meeting. The facilitator must caution the specialist not to utilize superior technical knowledge to take over and monopolize the circle meeting. Neither should the specialist go away after the meeting and solve the problem. The technical specialist is, in essence, called upon as a consultant, while the circle retains responsibility for solving the problem.

Once a problem is selected, resolution of that problem rests entirely with the circle members. Even the circle leader may have to be reminded periodically by the facilitator that the leader is not to solve the problem for members. Unless the privilege of problem resolution is reserved for the circle members, the program will have little meaning for them. The experience of actual problem resolution is vital for creating the sense of accomplishment that leads to satisfaction. As with problem selection, all decisions concerning problem resolution are made on a democratic basis.

Solution recommendation

Having arrived at the solution, the circle members make their recommendation directly to management, using a powerful communication technique called the management presentation. The facilitator and circle leader will invite the appropriate managers to attend. During the management presentation, the leader and members of the circle will describe to management the project they have been working on and what recommendations they wish to make concerning it. Circle members explain why particular actions were taken and use charts to lead the audience through the main steps of analysis. The members will even tell management how much the solution will save the company in terms of costs. Then management will review the solution and respond with a decision within a reasonable length of time. If management approves the solution, efforts are made to implement it as soon as possible. If the solution is rejected, it becomes the responsible manager's obligation to attend the next circle meeting and explain, in person, the reasons for the decision.

An exception to the above events occurs when the solution is of such a nature that the decision to implement it would normally be within the purview of the circle leader/supervisor. In such a case, the circle does have the authority to implement the solution even before making a management presentation. Still, management must be kept informed of what is going on, and management presentations will be held periodically to inform management of the circle's accomplishments.

Management presentations serve as one of the strongest means of providing recognition to circle members for their accomplishments. For many members, the management presentation is really the pay-off. They consider it an hour during which they can communicate directly, face to face, with management. It promotes communication between the management and worker levels and improves morale.

Following implementation of a solution, the circle closely monitors effects of that solution for a reasonable period of time, usually about a month. If for some reason, the problem persists, it is again analyzed, until it is properly rectified.

Basic Problem-Solving Techniques

Through the formal training provided in circle meetings, members develop expertise in utilizing a broad spectrum of techniques aimed at solving problems. The initial basic techniques taught to circle members can be grouped into six major categories: brainstorming, cause-and-effect diagramming, Pareto analysis, data gathering, graphics, and presentations.

Brainstorming

Brainstorming is a semiformal, structured process used to list all possible causes for a problem under consideration. Quality circle activities use this technique not only for problem solving, but also for problem identification. Basically, it is a procedure that provides the means for all circle members to make inputs in a disciplined, receptive environment. There are five basic rules that govern a brainstorming session:

1. No criticism is allowed — evaluation comes later.
2. Every attempt is made to maximize the number of ideas.
3. No judgment or evaluation of ideas is made during the brainstorming session.
4. To encourage participation, only one idea at a time is presented by each member until all ideas are exhausted.
5. Building ideas on other ideas is encouraged (American Productivity Center 1979).

Cause-and-effect diagramming

Briefly stated, this technique consists of defining an occurrence (effect) and then reducing it to its contributing factors (causes). Dr. Kaoru Ishikawa of the University of Tokyo is credited with developing this technique in 1950 (Amsden, Beardsley, and Rehg 1976). The relationship of all the contributing factors is illustrated on a structure Ishikawa calls a "fishbone," as shown in Figure 6.3. The principal factors, or causes, are listed first; then they are

FIGURE 6.3   Cause-and-Effect Diagram

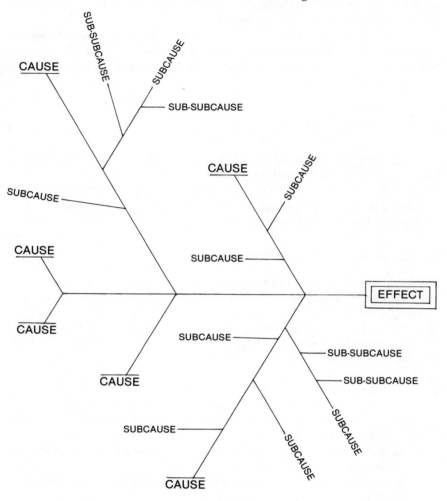

Source: Compiled by the author.

reduced to their subcauses, sub-subcauses, and so on. The causes are identified during brainstorming sessions.

There are essentially five steps in constructing a cause-and-effect diagram:

1. Identify in clear, concise terms the "effect" for which causes are to be sought.

2. Establish goals for the brainstorming activities.
3. Construct the framework upon which the causes are to be listed, in a place where it is visible to all participants.
4. Write all the causes on the diagram as they are suggested during the brainstorming session.
5. "Incubate" the completed diagram by keeping it displayed for a time to encourage the addition of suggestions not made originally (Amsden, Beardsley, and Rehg 1976, p. 247).

Pareto analysis

This process is derived from Pareto's Law, named after Vilfredo Pareto, an Italian economist who wrote early in the twentieth century. Pareto's Law presents the concept that any occurrence resulting from a multitude of causes is primarily a result of the impact from a minor percentage of all the causes. Emphasis on Pareto's Law forces the circle to concentrate on the vital few instead of the trivial many. This law is similar to the 80/20 rule, which means that 80 percent of a particular problem is usually the result of only 20 percent of the possible causes. Graphic techniques, as illustrated in Figure 6.4, are used to facilitate the Pareto analysis process (Blakely, Amsden, and Amsden 1976).

Data gathering

The process of data gathering requires a knowledge and use of sampling procedures, frequency diagrams, checksheets, and control charts. These techniques are rather easy to learn and apply.

Graphics

While this may not be a technique for solving problems, it is an integral part of the analytical and presentation process. Circle members learn how to transfer the numbers and data generated during their investigation into a pictorial or graphic form for clarification, trend determination, and presentation to upper management.

Presentations

The importance of presentation techniques cannot be overemphasized. The reason is that thoughts, ideas, analyses, recommendations, and solutions must be effectively communicated, especially when presentations are made to management. Circle members are taught the techniques of preparing a presentation and are encouraged to give oral presentations of

FIGURE 6.4   Pareto Chart

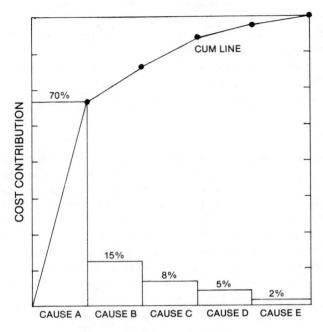

Source: Compiled by the author.

their ideas to the circle group to develop proficiency. Obviously, this can have significant benefits to leadership development and training of circle members.

Training Program

The single most important and unique feature of quality circles is the training program. There are four specific approaches, based upon needs of each group being educated — the managers, facilitators, leaders, and circles. To impress upon the reader the magnitude of the training program, the one developed and in use at Lockheed will be described.

Management training

This level of training is done mainly in what is called the "management introduction." The introduction is a two-hour session conducted twice a year to introduce managers and supervisors to the philosophy behind quality circles, their responsibilities concerning the program, and the benefits to be derived from the program. It is not enough for management to sit back and let the quality circle program develop. Managers must learn at the outset of the program and be periodically reminded that their continued open support is absolutely essential. Included in each management introduction is a sizeable segment dedicated to showing qualitative and quantitative results to date (Beardsley 1976).

Facilitator training

The facilitator training consists of two 40-hour courses presented in a formal classroom atmosphere and in actual practice. The facilitator, being the key to the program, deserves and receives the most complete training in the curriculum. Each of the 40-hour courses is designed to be conducted in five working days. The first course contains large doses of group dynamics, motivation theory, problem-solving techniques, and communications. Upon completion of the first facilitator course, the student has been introduced to knowledge and skills required to start a quality circles program and carry it through its first five months of operation. The second 40-hour facilitator course provides training in advanced quality circles techniques. Emphasis is placed upon enhancing the facilitator's teaching skills. The majority of time in this course is spent in role playing, case studies, and practical application of the techniques (Beardsley 1976).

Leader training

Leader training is no less important than the facilitator training, but by necessity is more concentrated. Each supervisor who volunteers and is selected as a leader candidate receives a 24-hour leader-training course. This course is normally conducted in three installments — one eight-hour day per week for three consecutive weeks. Leader training consists of essentially the same material studied by the facilitator. Training is not as extensive because the leader has a far narrower field of responsibility than does the facilitator.

Another facet of leader training is the monthly leader meetings. These meetings are used to compare notes on circle activities, to learn new techniques and methods, and to become proficient in the techniques already acquired (Beardsley 1976).

Circle training

Basic circle member training is conducted during the initial eight weekly circle meetings. During these training sessions, the typical 60-minute meeting is structured to allow ten minutes to review the previous meeting, 20 minutes for presentation of new material, and 30 minutes for practical application of techniques.

Circle member training does not actually end with completion of basic training sessions. The concept of continuous learning most aptly applies to the circle members. Throughout the life of the circle, the members are exposed to one form of training or another (Beardsley 1976).

Training aids

Lockheed developed its own audiovisual training packages that cover the basic training courses. Each of the eight packages is made up of 30 to 40 35 mm slides and a 20- to 30-minute tape cassette.

Also developed was an instructor guide, which provides a detailed outline of each subject, in lesson plan format, to serve as a guide for the facilitator. It contains specific behavioral objectives to be met, research assignments, discussion points, related instructor activities, and related trainee activities.

In addition, there are three other documents that are an integral part of the program. These are the facilitator guide, the leader handbook, and the member guide. The facilitator guide is a 200-page book containing virtually all the information required to establish and maintain a quality circles program. It serves as the course textbook for the first facilitator course. The leader handbook is a smaller document that serves as an invaluable aid to the supervisor who is acting as a circle leader. It contains considerable information on the day-to-day operation of a circle. The member guide is a three-ring binder that contains an illustrated introduction to quality circles. It also contains segments for notes, training records, and so on. Each circle member is provided this workbook guide upon joining (Beardsley 1976).

Additional Features of Quality Circles

Widespread applicability

Although quality circles have been applied most often to manufacturing organizations, they have been used successfully in the fields of banking, insurance, merchandising, and government. They can be effective wherever people work, regardless of industry.

Management acceptance

Management is more receptive to quality circles than to other "people" programs because the program expense can be justified on the cost savings resulting from problem solutions alone. Most companies report an average program cost-to-paycheck ratio of one to five as a result of the cost savings.

Supervisor development

Supervisors serving as circle leaders make noticeable improvements. Robert Patchin, Northrop's administrator of productivity improvement, reported that Northrop's supervisors had learned to structure their thinking and learned to communicate better — not only downward, but upward. He added, "It's been a big surprise to the people above them to find that these supervisors make more sense now. They don't come in with frustrations and concerns, but they come in with answers and ideas" (Patchin 1979).

Member self-development and maturity

Quality circles, featuring a comprehensive training program for circle members, serve to enhance their professional growth and personal development. Members attain a level of "maturity" that creates an atmosphere more conducive to participative management styles.

Group process

Quality circles depend on a group process. There is a social structure present, and consequently many social needs can be met. Not only will the individual members learn to work with others on a routine basis, but they may become part of the social unit of the circle. The group provides an immediate opportunity for recognition of individual abilities and achievements.

PROGRAM IMPLEMENTATION

Implementation Outline

The implementation of a quality circles program is a major undertaking of the organization and should be planned very thoroughly. The following implementation outline will provide general guidance and direction towards developing an effective plan. The sequence of steps need not be followed precisely.

There are fourteen steps in the implementation outline:

1. Research and evaluate.
2. Make the decision to start.
3. Select a facilitator.

   4. Establish a steering committee.
   5. Create an operating procedure.
   6. Develop training material.
   7. Notify the unions.
   8. Train middle management.
   9. Select pilot circle areas.
  10. Select leaders.
  11. Train leaders.
  12. Collect baseline data.
  13. Solicit members.
  14. Start circle meetings.

Step 1 — Research and evaluate

During this step, it is important that a thorough understanding of the basics of program theory and operation be gained. A literature search and attendance at one or more seminars conducted by proponents of quality circles are in order. The References section of this chapter can serve as an invaluable guide for locating most of the pertinent literature.

In addition, it would be helpful to visit companies that are conducting successful, sustained quality circle programs. During such a visit, ask to witness an actual circle meeting. Arrangements can usually be made in an organization that you know has a quality circles program by contacting the facilitator heading the program.

Step 2 — Make the decision to start

The decision to start is usually made by a management committee. It is extremely important that the committee gain understanding of and commitment and support for the circles concept at the highest management level of the organization, or at least the highest level in the department or division where the pilot program will be implemented. Lack of top management support for a program of this nature can lead to failure.

Step 3 — Select a facilitator

Since the facilitator is the individual responsible for coordinating and directing quality circle activities within the organization, the selection of the right person for the first facilitator position is critical to the success of the program. The chosen person must be a good communicator — effective at listening, easily conversant and relaxed with all levels of the company organization. She or he must also be an effective writer, as well as being people-oriented and wanting an extremely challenging job. The facilitator's initiative and ingenuity can go a long way toward creating a successful program.

It would be desirable for the initial facilitator to have an educational background in the areas of behavioral science, psychology, and/or industrial engineering. Background experiences in education and training, industrial engineering, and/or general supervision would be of benefit.

The facilitator usually is on the staff of a high-level manager who is a strong supporter of the program. In some companies, the facilitator reports to the company president. In large manufacturing organizations, the facilitator commonly reports to the director of manufacturing, the director of quality control, or the director of industrial relations (Dewar 1979c). It is important that all of management consider the facilitator a staff person for quality circle activities. The authority level to which the facilitator reports to is an important consideration, since she or he is expected to counsel supervisors and managers on quality circle matters. The higher the facilitator's authority level, the easier that job will be.

According to Jefferson Beardsley, a quality circles consultant, a full-time facilitator should not be expected to start more than five of six new circles initially. Beardsley also recommends that 15 be the maximum number of mature circles that each facilitator oversees (Beardsley 1977).

Step 4—Establish a steering committee

Representatives from major functional areas within the company should be members of the steering committee. In a manufacturing organization, it is common to have representatives from manufacturing, quality control, industrial relations, industrial engineering, manufacturing engineering, production control, and purchasing. The facilitator should be included in the steering committee. The person selected to be chairperson of the committee should be one who will encourage and support a free flow of ideas, rather than one who is so dominant that other members feel intimidated into accepting only the chairperson's thinking. The chairperson must sincerely believe in the value of quality circles.

The involvement of all members of the steering committee is important. Their egos must be involved in guiding the program to a successful operation. The inclusion of representatives from the various functional areas will help eliminate the possibility that some elements of the organization will feel that the program is something that is being done to them rather than with them. It tends to foster a widespread feeling of ownership of the program and will lessen the chance that any element of the organization will be unresponsive or antagonistic to the circles program.

The ideal size of a steering committee is seven or eight representatives. Fifteen should be the maximum number since no more can be heard from in each meeting. Involvement and participation are just as important at the level of the steering committee as on the circle level (Dewar 1979c).

Step 5 — Create an operating procedure

The steering committee should write and publish an operating procedure containing an overall policy statement concerning program objectives along with procedures to guide the day-to-day operation.

In arriving at the policy statement, the committee must reflect the organization's primary goals or reasons for initiating the quality circles program. It is not uncommon for middle management personnel and circle members alike to question top management's motives, and in the absence of a policy statement, all are left to their own suspicions. Such a statement serves to provide continuity of purpose as well as a point of departure in the event of a change in management's emphasis. Since each circle member will be given a copy of the operating procedure, the policy statement must be written in easily readable language and in a manner that does not sound manipulative.

The burden of composing the operating procedure will usually fall on the facilitator. With advice from the steering committee as required, the facilitator should draw up the basic operating procedure and submit it to other members of the steering committee. All committee members should be encouraged to make suggestions and modifications. The final version of the operating procedure will become the official document for conducting the program.

Step 6 — Develop training materials

Because training is truly the heart of any successful quality circle program, the development of effective training materials is critical. There is little room for compromise in terms of their quality. A number of companies have succeeded in developing their own effective training materials. Given the necessary time, a resourceful facilitator can gather enough information through a literature search and visit to companies with successful programs to develop suitable training materials that cover the basic quality circle techniques described earlier. Development of such materials, however, can certainly be time-consuming and expensive.

There is an alternative. Training materials, and even the initial training of the facilitator and the circle leaders, are available through consultants in the field. The use of consultants will be discussed further.

Step 7 — Notify the unions

In unionized companies, involvement of the workers in problem solving even on a voluntary basis requires some management-union interaction, since participative problem solving is contrary to the traditional role of the workers. There must be careful coordination with union leadership to avoid the classical image of management wanting to get more out of the workers without proper compensation. The union should therefore be apprised at this time of the intent to implement quality circles in the organization. Usually it is a matter of education — making certain that union leaders fully understand the people-building aspects of the program. An open dialogue should be continued throughout the development, implementation, and maturity stages.

The voluntary nature of the program is an important reason that unions generally do not oppose quality circles. However, in no way should the importance of acceptance by the unions be minimized, for problems certainly can develop if unions are ignored.

Step 8 — Train middle management

Middle management must not be bypassed in the introduction of the circles program. A concerted training program is necessary so that middle management personnel will fully understand the philosophy behind quality circles, their responsibilities concerning the program, and the benefits to be derived from it. Their strong support for the program and support for supervisors functioning as circle leaders is important for program success.

Step 9 — Select pilot circle areas

The steering committee should select the areas where the initial circles are to be started. There might be strong inclination to start each circle in a different environment, to demonstrate the applicability of quality circles. An important consideration here is that the more thinly the initial circles are spread through different departments, the greater the task of the facilitator, who must orientate the management personnel involved. Spreading the circles thinly could also result in too great a demand for additional circles when the time for program expansion is reached.

In departments having more than one working shift, consider starting some of the circles on the off shift, so as not to make the off-shift employees feel left out. If supervisors in these departments rotate shifts on a regular basis, having circles established on different shifts in the same department would enable the circle leaders (supervisors) of those circles to rotate duty between circles.

Step 10 — Select leaders

Having selected the areas where the initial circles are to be started, the steering committee, with help from middle management in the areas chosen, should then select the circle leaders. The supervisors chosen to be leaders of the initial circles should be ones who are the most participative in their style of management and have established good rapport with their work groups. Although the leaders selected for the initial circles almost always accept, they should be allowed to decline the selection for any reason.

Step 11 – Train leaders

Leader training, conducted by the facilitator, is usually accomplished in a 16- to 24-hour training course. The leaders will have to be thoroughly familiarized with the quality circles concept, philosophy, and background history. In addition, the leaders should be trained in the member-training curriculum, motivation theory, communications, leadership, and group dynamics.

Step 12 – Collect baseline data

Sooner or later, management will want measurement data to prove just how effective the program is. Consequently, baseline measurement data should be recorded before starting the program. These measurement data should be in such areas as productivity, cost, quality, absenteeism, and employee attitudes. Later on in the program, the same indicators will be remeasured. Improvements will be clearly indicated when these new data are compared with the baseline data.

Step 13 – Solicit circle members

Circle members are solicited by the leader during a member solicitation meeting that usually lasts an hour. The employees that the supervisor/leader invites to the meeting should be performing similar work, under that supervisor.

The supervisor/leader will call the meeting to order and explain that a quality circle will be starting in that area. A description of a quality circle should follow, along with an explanation of the program objectives. The leader can state a belief in the program philosophy and then introduces the facilitator, who could give an overview of the quality circle program and some background history. The leader should then describe in detail how the circle will operate in the particular work area. The functional manager should then be called upon to say a few words regarding his or her support for the program. Next, a few minutes could be spent answering questions from the audience. To capitalize on the enthusiasm that is usually gener-ated at this time, there could be a call for a show of hands by those interested in volunteering to join the circle. Attendees who do not volunteer during the meeting should be allowed a few days to give it further consideration (Beardsley and Dewar 1977).

Step 14 — Start circle meetings

With all of the groundwork completed, circle meetings can now commence and member training can finally begin.

Important Implementation Considerations

Use of a consultant

A competent quality circles consultant can certainly make program implementation expedient by sharing expertise. Assistance and guidance can be given to the steering committee. In addition, the consultant can conduct the initial management orientation session, train the facilitator and circle leaders, and provide the necessary training materials and training aids. This could result in tremendous savings in both time and costs for the company. Perhaps the best approach might be to contact one or more consultants immediately following the decision to start a quality circles program. Most consultants offer one-day, on-site executive seminars that will familiarize management with the quality circles concept as well as with the services the consultants have to offer.

One of the best ways to select a competent consultant is to rely on recommendations from satisfied customers. Most consultants are willing and pleased to provide names of past clients so they can be contacted.

Financial rewards

A question of major concern to most organizations when planning a quality circles program is whether financial rewards for circle members should be incorporated.

Currently in the United States, there are companies with successful programs that provide no financial rewards whatsoever. Control Data and International Harvester Solar Turbines are examples of two such companies. Then there are companies that provide financial rewards through the company suggestion system. Westinghouse and Northrup Aircraft Company are two such companies. Lastly, there are companies that provide financial rewards through a profit-sharing plan — Tektronix and Honeywell, for example. All of the above-mentioned companies have successful circles programs and, interestingly enough, all of them believe that they are handling financial rewards in the proper way. There is a definite lack of consensus as to the best method.

In the literature, the only person who has come forward with a strong opinion is Robert E. Cole, director of the Center for Japanese Studies at the University of Michigan. Cole states that the lack of a lifetime employment system in the United States and the resultant absence of long-term commitment to the organization mean that workers expect their rewards to be somewhat immediate. Hence, he claims that recognition is not a substitute for monetary awards and that attempts to use it as such in the U.S. environment seem likely to fail (Cole 1980b).

For a company with a profit-sharing plan, a reward mechanism is already in effect and no action need be taken. It is really quite an ideal reward method since everyone shares in the benefits derived from increased productivity and profits.

For a company with a paying suggestion system, an easy and popular solution to the financial reward question seems to be the practice of putting circle suggestions into the existing suggestion system, with all circle members sharing equally in the rewards. The disadvantage here, in comparison with profit sharing, is that only circle members are rewarded. Fellow nonmember workers may have helped the circle in data gathering, for example, but will not be rewarded for their efforts. This might tend to cause hard feelings and to cause the nonmember workers to resist implementation of solutions.

For a company without a paying suggestion system or a profit-sharing plan, the decision can be difficult. Keep in mind that it is difficult to do away with financial rewards once a precedent is set. There are external influences to be considered also. For example, it might be difficult to operate a circles program having no financial rewards when programs of other companies providing lucrative rewards are being publicized.

CONCLUSIONS AND RECOMMENDATIONS

In conclusion, quality circles represent a practical system or management process into which the Japanese successfully incorporated the basic principles of modern management theory. The system was developed through a clever combination of management skills, statistical techniques, behavioral concepts, group processes, and organizational concepts.

The genius of the quality circles system is its problem-solving vehicle. Many of the other motivational techniques fail to ask the participants to identify and solve problems, and thereby miss the opportunity to tap participants' creativity and enlist their support for what they have created. By asking individuals to be creative and to improve their jobs through the solving of work-related problems, quality circles cut to the heart of motivation.

The circle does not per se motivate the worker, but it creates the environment for the worker to become self-motivated.

The quality circles program is not a response to specific problems.
Rather, it is a process whereby circle members continually scrutinize technical aspects of the job and thus are constantly developing improvements. This monitoring behavior scans the environment for opportunities,
does not wait to be activated by a problem, and does not stop its activities
when a problem has been found and solved. This represents a rare quality
and constitutes an enormous asset where operative.

Quality circles represent a unique form of job enrichment. They differ from Swedish job-reform activities such as the production group, in that
there are no requirements for large investments to rearrange the factory.
With quality circles, work and its organization continue as usual. The
thrust of quality circles' action is solving work-related problems through
scientific, data-based principles that are used by the employees themselves.
Workers who are part of a circle are actively engaged, not just in doing
their jobs, but also in influencing their own work situation for the good.
For many it is the first time they have been able to affect their work life in a
positive way.

The management presentation element of quality circles is certainly a
unique and outstanding feature. This feature was, understandably, conceived by the Japanese because of the particular importance they place on
recognition. Numerous published articles describing experience with
quality circles in this country reveal that managers are often surprised at
the enthusiasm displayed by circle members during management presentations. The point here is that recognition as a motivational tool is often
underestimated by U.S. managers. Through the management presentation, quality circles provide a specific and much needed mechanism for
management to provide recognition to circle members for their accomplishments. It is imperative that management recognize and respect the
members for what they are — thinking and feeling employees who have the
potential to contribute immensely to the success of the company.

The true emphasis of quality circles is not on short-term dollars-and-
cents results, as with most management programs. Instead, the program
centers on creating a management style that works towards the goals of the
employees as well as goals of the organization, creating a win-win situation.

For the employees, the goals are in the areas of improved job satisfaction and quality of work life. Quality circles allow attainment of these goals
by making the job a stage on which the enlargement of competence, self-
control, and sense of accomplishment can occur. The job itself, with its
challenge and excitement, coupled with the possibility of personal growth,
becomes central to the motivation stimuli.

Success in this country in creating the proper management style rests on management's willingness to release some of its decision-making authority to those lower levels where the information is, thus encouraging a decision-making process that works from the bottom up. This delegation of decision-making authority relates to matters that have been widely regarded as management prerogatives in the past.

A consequence of the quality circles process is that industrial engineers and technical specialists will have to accept the surrendering of some of their long-standing functions. This results from the creation of a competitive force on matters that have been the professionals' monopoly since the origin of the Taylor system. The advantage of having thousands of circle members, rather than an elite group, working on problems is obvious. There are not enough managers, engineers, and technical specialists to tackle the enormous number of problems or improvement opportunities that are out on the work floor. The engineers and technical specialists can keep from feeling threatened by realizing that the majority of problems that circles solve occur at a relatively low level. These professionals are thus freed to do what is, for them, more challenging work.

Even if the solutions arrived at by technical specialists could sometimes be better than those arrived at by workers, there is one overbearing advantage of having the workers solve the problem — workers will more enthusiastically implement solutions they can claim as their own. Resistance to change can cause the best solution in the world to become useless.

Quality circles provide a much needed vehicle for unlocking the potential for worker contribution to the organization. Most managers are aware that workers possess untapped abilities and information. To unlock their full potential, management must be firmly committed to a people-building philosophy and have a sincere desire to help employees to grow and develop. This necessitates management's endorsement of human resources development. Giving workers training in problem analysis will not only enable them to solve problems more quickly but also enable them to solve problems that they would not otherwise be capable of solving. Training also is a sure way to communicate in a clear fashion that management is truly committed to a people-building philosophy. It instills the thought that management believes that the workers are worth training and worth investing in. Providing opportunities through quality circles for continuous learning, along with encouragement of participation in idea generation and problem solving, will help the workers to grow and develop. This will build employee loyalty to the organization and return tremendous benefits in the long term.

The writer believes that the present business and economic climate in the United States is conducive to the adoption of programs such as quality circles. The strategy of striving for full human resource utilization seems to be the logical one for U.S. companies to follow, since human resources represent the last remaining major untapped source for productivity improvements. Also, employees and union leaderships seem to be increasingly concerned about helping to turn the economy around. For the first time in history, it seems that the general public, in just recent months, has come to recognize the existence of a national productivity problem. Americans are beginning to feel world leadership in the standard of living slipping away. They are beginning to feel the existence of U.S. industries, and their jobs as well, threatened by foreign competition. While the Japanese worked as a nation to improve product quality, the growing national effort in the United States is to improve productivity. There is a definite growing need for a mechanism such as quality circles.

The writer has but one caution to offer concerning quality circles. It should be pointed out that although the quality circles system has proven itself beyond a doubt in Japan, most of the experiences with circles in this country have been quite shallow. Few companies have had the circles in operation for more than two years. It may thus be premature to say that their applicability in the United States has been "proven." No reports of scientific research studies on their application have appeared. The reports in the literature, however, have been extremely positive. One thing is certain: quality circles will be undergoing continual minor adaptation to suit U.S. conditions.

The greatest attraction of the quality circles program is the simplicity of its basic principles. Although many of the same elements are embodied in other popular management techniques, no other technique has succeeded in combining all of the particular elements of quality circles. Quality circles could conceivably be the best available long-term solution to an organization's problems.

REFERENCES

American Productivity Center. 1979. *The Key to Productivity Improvement: Employee Involvement.* Houston: Author. N.p.

Amsden, Davida M., and Robert T. Amsden. 1980. "A Look at QC Circles." *Tooling and Production* (June):102–6.

———. "QC Circles, KT, Etc." 1978. *American Society for Quality Control 32nd Annual Technical Conference Transactions*, pp. 211–15. Chelsea, Mich.: Litho Crafters.

———. 1976. "QC Circles: A Challenge to ASQC." *American Society for Quality Control 30th Annual Technical Conference Transactions*, pp. 224–28. Chelsea, Mich.: Litho Crafters.

Amsden, Robert, Jefferson Beardsley, and Virgil Rehg. 1976. "QC Circle Workshop: Cause and Effect Diagrams, A Most Useful Tool." *American Society for Quality Control 30th Annual Technical Conference Transactions*, pp.

224-48. Chelsea, Mich.: Litho Crafters.

Beardsley, Jefferson F. 1980. Personal communication to Rodney E. Motonaga, July. Beardsley is a quality circles consultant.

———. 1977. *Quality Circles Facilitator Manual.* Redmond, Calif.: J. F. Beardsley and Associates, International Inc. N.p.

———. 1976. "Training in the Lockheed QC Circle Program." *American Society for Quality Control 30th Annual Technical Conference Transactions,* pp. 257–60. Chelsea, Mich.: Litho Crafters.

Beardsley, Jefferson F., and Donald L. Dewar. 1977. *Quality Circles.* Redmond, Calif.: J. F. Beardsley and Associates, International, Inc. N. p.

Bhote, Keki R. 1979. "Blueprint to Recapture Quality Leadership for America." *American Society for Quality Control 33rd Annual Technical Conference Transactions,* pp. 795–99. Chelsea, Mich.: Litho Crafters.

Blakely, Edward D., Davida M. Amsden, and Robert T. Amsden. 1976. "QC Circle Workshop: Pareto Analysis." *American Society for Quality Control 30th Annual Technical Conference Transactions,* pp. 236–43. Chelsea, Mich.: Litho Crafters.

Bluestone, Irvin. 1976. "A Changing View of the Union-Management Relationship." *Vital Speeches of the Day,* December 1, pp. 122–24.

Cole, Robert E. 1980a. "Learning from the Japanese: Prospects and Pitfalls." *Management Review* (September):22–28.

———. 1980b. "Will QC Circles Work in the U.S.?" *Quality Progress* (July):30–33.

Dewar, Donald L. 1979a. "Can Quality Circles Make it in the Western World?" *American Society for Quality Control 33rd Annual Technical Conference Transactions,* pp. 681–84. Chelsea, Mich.: Litho Crafters.

———. 1979b. "A Human Approach to Motivation and Productivity." *American Institute of Industrial Engineering 1979 Spring Annual Conference Proceedings,* pp. 161–64. N. p.

———. 1979c. *Quality Circles: Answers to 100 Frequently Asked Questions.* N. p. Philadelphia: Walker Lithograph.

———. 1976. "Measurement of Results—Lockheed QC Circles." *American Society for Quality Control 30th Annual Technical Conference Transactions,* pp. 249–52. Chelsea, Mich.: Litho Crafters.

Gottschalk, Earl C., Jr. 1980. "U.S. Firms, Worried by Productivity Lag, Copy Japan in Seeking Employees' Advice." *Wall Street Journal,* February 21, p. 44.

Hanley, Joseph. 1980. "Our Experience with Quality Circles." *Quality Progress* (February):22–24.

Herzberg, Frederick. 1966. *Work and the Nature of Man.* Cleveland: World Publishing Company.

"Japanese Managers Tell How Their System Works." 1977. *Fortune,* November, pp. 126–38.

Juran, J. M. 1978. "Japanese and Western Quality—A Contrast." *Quality Progress* (December):10–18.

Kassalow, Everett M. 1977. "White-Collar Unions and the Work Humanization Movement." *Monthly Labor Review* (May):9–13.

Konz, Stephan. 1979. "Quality Circles: Japanese Success Story." *Industrial Engineering* (October):24–27.

Kraar, Louis. 1975. "The Japanese are Coming—With Their Own Style of Management." *Fortune*, March, pp. 116–20.

Kutscher, Ronald E., Jerome A. Mark, and John R. Norsworthy. 1977. "The Productivity Slowdown and the Outlook to 1985." *Monthly Labor Review* (May): 3–8.

Likert, Rensis. 1967. *The Human Organization*. New York: McGraw-Hill.

McDermott, T. C. 1977. "The Human Dimension in Productivity." *Vital Speeches of the Day*, March 1, pp. 306–9.

McGregor, Douglas. 1960. *The Human Side of Enterprise*. New York: McGraw-Hill.

Miles, Raymond E. 1975. *Theories of Management*. New York: McGraw-Hill.

Miller, G. William. 1978. "Higher Output: Key to a Bolder Economy." *Enterprise: Journal of the National Association of Manufacturers* (November):18–19.

Mitchell, Edward V. 1980. "Planning and Implementing a Quality Circles Program." Paper presented at the 1980 Golden Gate Conference of the American Society for Quality Control, San Mateo, Calif., January 19.

Nelson, Joani. 1980. "Quality Circles Becomes Contagious." *Industry Week*, April 14, pp. 99–103.

Pabst, William R., Jr. 1972. "Motivating People in Japan." *Quality Progress* (October):14–18.

"A Partnership to Build the New Workplace." 1980. *Business Week*, June 30, pp. 99–101.

Patchin, Robert I. 1979. "Northrup's Formula for Productivity Leadership." Paper presented at the 1979 National Aerospace Conference, sponsored by the American Institute of Industrial Engineers, Anaheim, Calif., January 17–19.

"Productivity: Whipping Inflation Through Increased Output, An Interview with Dr. C. Jackson Grayson." 1978. *Association Management*, October, pp. 20–23.

Quong, Harry. 1977. "QC Circle—Evolution or Revolution." *American Society for Quality Control 31st Annual Technical Conference Transactions*, pp. 258–61. Chelsea, Mich.: Litho Crafters.

Rehg, Virgil. 1976. "QC Circle Workshop: Application." *American Society for Quality Control 30th Annual Conference Transactions*, pp. 229–33. Chelsea, Mich.: Litho Crafters.

Rieker, Wayne S. 1980. "Quality Control Circles: Key to Employee Performance Improvement." *American Institute of Industrial Engineering 1980 Spring Annual Conference Proceedings*, pp. 364–78. N. p.

_____. 1979. "The QC Circle Phenomenon—An Update." *American Society for Quality Control 33rd Annual Technical Conference Transactions*, pp. 689–94. Chelsea, Mich.: Litho Crafters.

_____. 1976. "What is the Lockheed Quality Control Circle Program?" *American Society for Quality Control 30th Annual Technical Conference Transactions*, pp. 253–56. Chelsea, Mich.: Litho Crafters.

Rosow, Jerome M. 1977. "Quality of Working Life and Productivity." *Vital Speech-*

es of the Day, June 1, pp. 496–98.

Sayles, Leonard R., and George Strauss. 1977. *Managing Human Resources.* Englewood Cliffs, N. J.: Prentice-Hall.

Schein, Edgar. 1970. *Organizational Psychology.* Englewood Cliffs, N.J.: Prentice-Hall.

Sherwin, Douglas S. 1972. "Strategy for Winning Employee Commitment." *Harvard Business Review* (May–June):37–47.

Sibson, Robert E. 1976. *Increasing Employee Productivity.* New York: AMACOM.

Steers, Richard M., and Lyman W. Porter. 1975. *Motivation and Work Behavior.* New York: McGraw-Hill.

Swartz, Gerald E., and Vivian C. Constock. 1979. "One Firm's Experience with Quality Circles." *Quality Progress* (September):14–16.

"Talking in Circles Improves Quality." 1977. *Industry Week*, February 14, pp. 57–59.

Veen, B. 1977. "Integration of TCQ and Motivation Programs." *American Society for Quality Control 31st Annual Technical Conference Transactions*, pp. 107–115. Chelsea, Mich.: Litho Crafters.

Wieland, George F., and Robert A. Ullrich. 1976. *Organizations: Behavior Design and Change.* Homewood, Ill.: Richard D. Irwin.

Yager, Ed. 1979. "Examining the Quality Control Circle." *Personnel Journal* (October):682–84.

7

Quality Circles and Japanese Management: Participation or Paternalism?

GEORGE W. JACOBS

INTRODUCTION

It is fashionable in current comparisons of Japanese and U.S. industry to describe the characteristic style or mode of Japanese leadership in industry as participative, democratic, or paternalistic. Typically, these characterizations are being directed toward the same reality, as perceived. If there is but one leadership style in evidence in Japan (and there is some evidence to the contrary), a relevant question today is which conception of style is more accurate, more realistic, and more meaningful. Are all three perhaps equally representative labels or models for the reality described?

It is the central purpose of this chapter to deal objectively with this issue and to suggest a realistic, useful answer to the question. The perspective proposed, then, should serve to aid those concerned and involved with these Japanese-American comparisons, for one reason or other. Specifically, it should help to clarify the thinking of persons responsible for the introduction of Japanese industry and Japanese methods and techniques, such as quality circles, into the industrial picture in the United States. Certainly it is pertinent to the image and success of a quality circle program in this country for those participating to be aware of and to understand the implications of quality circles for the management of their organizations and their relationships to individual jobs and the work environment. The background for the development of this suggested perspective is the leadership literature of the past 40-odd years, encompassing theory, research, and practice, principally in a domestic context.

Because of their current popularity and recent interest in their underlying philosophy, techniques, and operation, quality circles, sometimes called quality control or QC circles, will be used as a central focus of this analysis. The assumption here, which is an admitted oversimplification, is that Japanese QC circles as practiced generally represent the key attributes of Japanese management and leadership.

The broad questions to be resolved are primarily ones of description. First, what is the dominant or characteristic leadership style evident in Japanese industry? Second, what is participative management, what is democratic management, and what is paternalistic management; and are they identical, substantially equivalent, overlapping in some way, or mutually distinct possibilities? Third, which conception, then, best describes the Japanese mode, or would another label be more accurate? A secondary or implied issue arising from this analysis, which is not specifically addressed herein, is the question of the transferability of an effective, preferred Japanese style of management from Japan to U.S. locations, either in Japanese-owned industries or in U.S. companies.

One caveat is in order for undertakings of this sort, which involve conceptualization and word pictures of reality or truth. It must be recognized and accepted that one is not dealing directly with truth as such in the present situation, but merely with abstract theoretical concepts or models, one of which will perhaps best describe the particular reality that is of concern here. After all, does "participative management" really exist, in truth, in reality? The term may well describe reality, but in truth it may be used in multiple ways to describe many different realities in a variety of settings. Not doubt it will fit or accurately reflect some situations better than others, and it will prove more useful in some circumstances and for some purposes than others. This suggests also that one is facing here a question of relatives rather than absolutes.

All models are imperfect representations of reality, and all are abstract, which means merely that they are thinking tools. These are characteristics of models — not faults of models. If the models are realistic enough and useful for the purpose intended, and if their value is commensurate with their cost, they can be highly beneficial in analysis and understanding of some significant real-world phenomenon, such as the topic at hand.

THREE STYLES OF LEADERSHIP

Before attempting to match a label to the Japanese mode of management, as reflected in the widely heralded, enthusiastically endorsed quality circle technique, it should be helpful to clarify the three labels under consideration — participative, democratic, and paternalistic. Again, it must be noted that the terms do not have true definitions as such, but must be defined in such a way that they are realistic, useful, and meaningful in the context in which they are employed. In other words, each is itself a model at best, and differing models of each have been described in the leadership literature.

The Participative Style

Likert's ideal System IV is an example of the participative style. He describes a "participative group" climate or style or management system, clearly distinguishing it from a "consultative" style and others yet more distant from the participative end of the continuum (Likert 1967). Tannenbaum and Schmidt's classic range of leader behaviors, on the other hand, clearly recognizes as legitimate and realistic a broad span of possibilities for subordinate participation in decisions, depending on the degree or amount of involvement in the process (Tannenbaum and Schmidt 1958). They do not, however, emphasize the "participation" concept, as their focus is on characterizing behaviors rather than styles — a fine distinction at best in their presentation.

Clearly, in the example above, Tannenbaum and Schmidt's implied definition of participation encompasses Likert's consultative style or System III in addition to System IV. It also clearly relates the concept to the managerial decision-making process, not to just any decisions made in the organization. This is significant in that one can readily observe a quite different meaning being attached to the term in much popular use, particularly in the Japanese management context. This alternative model reflects degree of involvement in group processes rather than actual sharing of or involvement in carrying out managerial responsibilities for the success of the organization. From the perspective of traditional "participative management" in the United States, which remains highly valid in every respect, the redefinition of the concept in the alternative model is a distracting corruption — one that muddies the conceptual waters and renders otherwise healthy debate on the issues unproductive.

Participation must mean what it has always meant: a question of organizational structure. A key dimension of structure is the distribution or allocation of authority to make decisions and take actions for the organization. In a real sense, delegation of authority by and from a manager is necessary for participation to occur. Depending upon the amount of authority delegated, the degree of participation can be great, as in Likert's System IV, or small. In this context and for the present purposes, the question of degree of involvement in group processes without the delegation of additional authority to the group, whether explicit or implied, is irrelevant and confusing. It is another issue altogether.

The Democratic Style

Democracy, too, has a traditional or standard meaning, and again, there appears to be no reason to corrupt it in practice or in media treatments of the subject. One can treat a democratic style as relative, with a meaning essentially equivalent to a participative style, and this is often done. This is loose language, however, and does not allow for the precision in communication that is possible and desirable. After all, there are many who want to know — and many who need to know — precisely what *is* Japanese management?

Democratic leadership means having decisions made for the group by the group, each member having an equal vote. The leader's own contribution to the decision is equated with that of each other group member. While this is a narrow definition, democracy is a narrow concept, and it is neither realistic nor useful to broaden it to convey a range of meanings. Lewin et al., in their historic boys'-club experiments in the 1930s, attached this meaning to the term, and it remains valid in the present circumstance (Lewin, Lippitt, and White 1939).

What is the relationship of participative and democratic styles? A democratic style, as narrowly defined, is at one end of the range of possibilities within the participative category of styles, as broadly defined. Although sometimes used synonymously, when precision is not at issue, the concepts overlap but do not coincide. A very small amount of participation, such as when a manager "sells" a decision to the group or bases a decision partly on some minor inputs from group members, obviously does not qualify in any way as democratic decision making.

The Paternalistic Style

A paternalistic leadership style, while rarely to be found incorporated into a continuum of styles under that designation, is clearly represented by Likert's System II (Likert 1967). His nomenclature is "benevolent authoritative," sometimes referred to elsewhere in the literature as a benevolent autocrat leader style. This mode reflects fully the characteristics of the more extreme authoritarian, autocratic, or dictatorial style, which Likert describes more colorfully as System I, "exploitive authoritative," except that the more "hard-nosed, boss-type" leader is replaced by the "nice, but stern, father-figure type."

The assumptions underlying both styles are essentially the same, and these are embodied in McGregor's "Theory X": that the subordinates require direction and control for productive effort and generally dislike and seek to avoid work (McGregor 1960). The flavor of paternalistic management, then, is pure nonparticipation in managerial decision processes, a family-type group in which the head is sole authority, the viability and maintenance of the group as dominant themes or goals, and the subordination of individual freedom and potential to the norms and values of the group, as articulated in those directives and prescriptions of the patriarch.

These distinctions among the three conceptions of leadership style are representative of the viewpoints and approaches of the published authorities in the field of leadership, at least in a general sense. The models of three distinct styles, then, are realistic, and their usefulness here remains to be demonstrated.

ANALYSIS

At this point the obvious question is whether any of the three styles aptly describes what is known about Japanese management, specifically as reflected in the design and operation of the quality circle technique in Japanese industry. Perhaps a useful first question is whether any can be ruled out as an apt description. Based on what is known and what has been written about the character of the Japanese situation, it would appear that the democratic style could be eliminated from consideration, for practical purposes. Neither the specific methodology in practice nor the fundamental philosophy or theme of democratic management, according to the model described herein, characterizes the form of management system that appears most typical of the Japanese.

Once only participative and paternalistic styles remain, the distinctions come into sharper focus. It is useful here to reemphasize that such sharp distinctions do exist, by any reasonable definitions, and that the two styles are clearly in opposition rather than virtually synonymous, as the terms are sometimes used.

It is not at all apparent that Japanese management systems or Japanese quality circle programs involve any significant amount of decentralization, delegation of additional authority, power equalization, or change in organizational structure when such programs are initiated. The alternative definition of participation, meaning involvement in group processes, appears to fit the more typical situation in which the circle concept is employed. No participation in the sense of the basic definition or model, therefore, is in evidence. The type of participation emphasized is equivalent to that suggested in learning theory, in the so-called learning principle that one learns, or learns more, by participating in an activity, or by being actively involved in doing it, than by looking on from the sidelines.

At the same time, it is eminently evident that the "family" characteristics of the paternalistic style are most dominant throughout the typical Japanese industrial establishment. Although the philosophical flavor of the central role of patriarch, and an essentially subservient role of subordinates, is not emphasized or highlighted in descriptions of Japanese organizations, some basic requirement for a strong, omnipotent, protective leader in a highly centralized authority role, to preside over the industrial "family," is inescapable. In such a family, a patriarch's authority is unquestioned. How he uses it, and how authority as such is employed in day-to-day operations, is another question altogether — an empirical question, and as yet unanswered in a verifiable sense. Obviously, the rights, needs, values, and freedom of individuals in Japanese "families" are secondary concerns, and this is the accepted, specified mode of life in Japanese industrial society. It is the cultural norm, which establishes the ground rules and constraints under which businesses operate and individuals pursue life's necessary work activities. It is, in short, a paternalistic system rather than a participative one.

The analysis outlined above would be incomplete without the introduction of an additional, albeit crucial, variable — one that suggests the possibility, at least, of a valid alternative view or perspective. The variable is, of course, the cultural setting. Obviously, in drawing from the U.S. literature, primarily, relying on American experience as the frame of reference, basing conclusions on a typically American value system, and utilizing American language, terms, and models to express the central conceptualizations at issue, an unavoidable bias is introduced into the analysis. Surely, the Japanese system is better described as paternalistic rather than participative based on American models and American criteria. In this country, and from an American perspective, the paternalistic model is a rather accurate fit for some variety of purposes.

The question that must be posed here, however, is whether the same continuum of leadership styles referred to on this side of the Pacific can weather the trip abroad, to the shores of Japan. Do "participative" and "paternalistic" mean the same thing there as they do here? Do they stand in the same relation to each other there, as they are practiced there, that they do in the United States? Does "style of leadership" carry the same weight, incorporate the same dimensions, and communicate the same value perspective in Japan as in the United States?

While the answers are not readily known, it is readily known that Japan and the United States represent two very different cultures, and in these two cultures many aspects of life are different. Therefore, it is reasonable to conclude that what might be true, or accurate, or reasonable, in one cultural context, may not fit similarly into the other distinctive context. The foregoing analysis, then, must be qualified as culture-specific.

CONCLUSION

In the United States, open, critical evaluation is as much a part of every-day life as breakfast. Americans tend to view things in terms of good-bad, better-worse, like-dislike, and so on. The Japanese person is thought to be conscious of personal image; face saving, image protection, and confrontation avoidance are dominant themes. This suggests that the American tendency to evaluate participation as good and paternalism as bad, and the tendency of some persons today to regard the Japanese system as good and the American system as inferior, represent dangerously oversimplified and largely inaccurate models of reality. These good-bad models not only are distracting for constructive dialogue, but are potentially destructive and generally not helpful for purposes of either description and understanding or system design.

It is proposed here, therefore, that evaluative conclusions relative to these issues be withheld in the anticipation that ultimately the facts will speak for themselves. Meanwhile, constructive approaches to the development and clarification of the key issues, based on realistic, useful, and meaningful models of the phenomena involved, can accelerate progress for all concerned.

REFERENCES

Lewin, Kurt, R. Lippitt, and R. K. White. 1939. "Patterns of Aggressive Behavior in Experimentally Created Social Climates." *Journal of Social Psychology*, 10:271–99.

Likert, Rensis. 1967. *The Human Organization: Its Management and Value*. New York: McGraw-Hill.

McGregor, Douglas. 1960. *The Human Side of Enterprise*. New York: McGraw-Hill.

Tannenbaum, Robert, and Warren H. Schmidt. 1958. "How To Choose a Leadership Pattern." *Harvard Business Review* (March-April):95–101.

Part III

JAPANESE OPERATIONS MANAGEMENT SYSTEMS

Behind miraculous Japanese economic growth and success in international trade, there are many innovative operations management systems in factories and plants. This part presents five chapters that deal with Japanese operating systems.

Jinichiro Nakane, in "Japanese Production Systems," discusses two important production control systems—Kanban and material requirements planning (MRP). Then he develops the environmental characteristics that are important for efficient application of Kanban and MRP.

Richard J. Schonberger contributes "Inventory Control in Japanese Industry." Western industry has amassed numerous prescriptions for catching up with the Japanese. Until recently, most lists of these prescriptions omitted Japanese just-in-time (JIT) inventory control, sometimes called Kanban. JIT inventory controls are simple, require little use of computers, and in some industries can provide far tighter controls on inventory than are attainable via U.S. computer-based approaches. Furthermore, Japanese JIT leads to significantly higher quality and productivity, and provides visibility for results so that worker responsibility and commitment are improved.

Robert W. Hall's chapter, "The Toyota Kanban System," points out that the objective of the Toyota Kanban system is to trim manufacturing into a streamlined flow of material with very little inventory and very little lead time. It embodies a "pull system" of production control, which is used to stimulate productivity improvements. The processes and layout are revised to overcome the problems that make inventory necessary. The most important conditions for use of the system are that production be convertible to fixed routings for material flows; and that it be possible to level the final assembly schedule, which means making a small amount of every product every day to level material flow coming into final assembly.

C. Carl Pegels, in "The Kanban Production Management Information System," describes the Kanban production management information system, how it is used, what types of Kanbans are used, how the desirable number of Kanbans can be determined, and how the Kanban system can be implemented by a U.S. firm. The two types of Kanbans discussed in this chapter are production and conveyance Kanbans. To illustrate a possible implementation scenario, three sets of in-process inventory situations are shown to illustrate how in-process inventory can be reduced through use of Kanbans.

Steven A. Melnyk and Phillip L. Carter contribute "Viewing Kanban as an (s,Q) System: Developing New Insights into a Japanese Method of Production and Inventory Control." The authors focus upon Kanban, a Japanese-developed system of control. In examining the operation of this system, they found that Kanban does not embody any new procedures. Instead, Kanban incorporates procedures and techniques previously found in traditional Order Point/Order Quantity (x,Q) system; with this finding, a better appreciation and understanding of Kanban can be developed. Kanban has succeeded because Japanese management has been able to restructure the manufacturing environment so as to satisfy the critical system assumptions imposed by (s,Q) systems, such as Kanban.

8

Japanese Production Systems

JINICHIRO NAKANE

INTRODUCTION

Before the 1973 oil crisis, most Japanese companies could improve productivity by increasing volumes and by replacing old equipment with new equipment. The high economic growth allowed these practices. At that time, management's responsibility was only to produce a high volume of high quality and to focus on growth and market share. Therefore, management did not worry about high inventories, high indirect labor expense, and long lead time.

After the oil crisis, economic growth stagnated, and almost all companies realized that they could not keep their profit high in the near future. Thus they began to look at new ways of production management. Over the past few years, two types of profitable manufacturing control systems have come into use. One is the Kanban system, which was developed by the Toyota Corporation; the other is the material requirements planning (MRP) system, which was developed in the United States. This chapter will cover the background of Kanban and MRP, giving examples of the characteristics, functions, and benefits of conversion to the Kanban and MRP systems.

Also discussed will be the types of industries and environments where each has been observed to work best, and conclusions that can be drawn.

YESTERDAY'S PRODUCTION MANAGEMENT

In Japan, most companies started with project-type or job shop-type production. Many companies used project-type production control systems, not only "make-to-order" companies but also "make-to-stock" companies. We call this type of system a Seiban system. Seiban systems predominated in Japanese companies in the past, and today many companies still use Seiban systems although they no longer work well.

Companies under the Seiban system are simply order launching and expediting. Production plan generates planned orders; after that, the expediting system tries to determine what material is really needed and when.

TODAY'S PRODUCTION MANAGEMENT

To avoid the disadvantages of the Seiban system, Seiban users have tried to improve their system by using computers or have taken other steps. They generally have had little success. To answer the need for a useful system that broke away from the Seiban system, Toyota Motor Company developed the Kanban system. Many companies (especially repetitive manufacturing companies) have now installed the Kanban system. These companies can be found in the electronic, machinery, chemical and, of course, automobile industries. Other companies are studying the matter.

In the Kanban system, the leveling of production is essential to success. The Toyota people and other users of the Kanban system have made drastic reforms to level production. Leveling of production is attained in two ways. One is by production planning and scheduling. The other is by redesigning the manufacturing processes, that is, by minimizing lot size and set-up time. That change allows flow-type manufacturing processes using general-purpose equipment. The outline of production planning and scheduling by the Kanban system is shown in Figure 8.1.

Another way leveling of production can be realized is through redesigning the manufacturing processes and improving manufacturing operations. If lot size and set-up time are minimized, leveling of production can be minimized, resulting in lead time and inventory minimization.

Production can be done as smoothly as possible within a small range by Kanban production planning and reform of manufacturing processes. Fluctuation of the production rate does occur to some degree (say ± 10% of one day's average requirements). To cope with the fluctuations, order release in the Kanban system is as shown in Figure 8.2.

The production control department issues the final assembly schedule and Kanban (cards), which are traveling production authorizations. The

FIGURE 8.1

Production Planning & Scheduling

Long-range Production Planning
↓
Long-range Capacity Planning
↓
Annual Production Planning
↓
Middle-range Capacity Planning
↓
Monthly Production Planning
↓
Monthly Capacity Planning
↓
Production Scheduling
(for FIA)
↓
Order Release
(by Final Assembly Line by day)

Source: Compiled by the author.

Kanban card stays with the container. When the succeeding (user) department uses the items in the container, and it is emptied, the container and the Kanban card are returned to the preceding (supplier) department. That department in turn must produce one container's worth and send it to the using department, under certain lead time and delivery schedule rules. This is why the Kanban system is a "pull" system. The user department triggers production by the supplying department.

FIGURE 8.2   Order Release by Kanban System

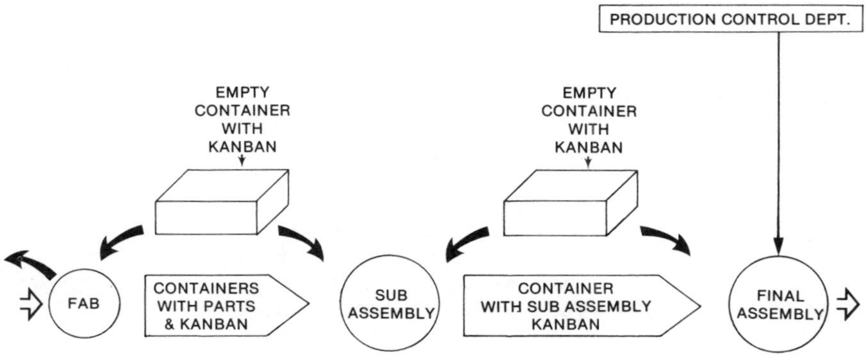

Source: Compiled by the author.

The Kanban card is a form of order card. It indicates the timing and quantity for order releasing to each work center. Except for the final assembly line, the Kanban card is used as a turn-around system. The key point is how many Kanban cards are permitted to circulate on the factory floor, or at the subcontractor or vendor. Generally speaking, the number of Kanban cards is calculated as in Figure 8.3. In this formula, values of PV (policy variable) are decided by the factory manager and are used as indicator of the shop's (W/C's) capability of improvement.

In the Kanban system, the production rate is leveled by day within the month. The production rate, however, may vary with the monthly production plan. To cope with this, companies try to get flexible production capacities through redesigning of manufacturing processes, relayout, promoting mixed-flow lines, flexible automation, and tuning-up of multifunctional workers.

Kanban users believe that the system always is transient, always improving. It enforces good plant operational practices. Small-group improvement activities (SGIA — nearly the same as quality control circles) are very important. In areas such as quality control, zero defects, and industrial engineering, shop people take the initiative. In this case, staff people help and support them. In SGIA, the goal is to "minimize the number of Kanban," that is, to reduce the number of Kanban cards in circulation. By doing this, shop people find the problems that they themselves should improve. Thus lead times and inventories are reduced through SGIA.

Kaban users have benefited greatly from inventory and lead-time reductions and, of course, cost reductions. Figures 8.4 and 8.5 show the beneficial results of the Kanban system for Company X.

FIGURE 8.3   Calculation of Number of Outstanding Kanban Cards

$$\left. \begin{array}{c} \text{NUMBER} \\ \text{OF} \\ \text{KANBAN} \\ \text{CARDS} \end{array} \right\} = \frac{AD(WT + PT)(1 + PV)}{CQ}$$

WHERE:

AD = Average daily demand for the month
WT = Waiting time
PT = Processing time for one container
CQ = Container quantity—limited to maximum of
        10% of day's demand
PV = Policy variable—determined by management
        and checked by each W/C manager

Source: Compiled by the author.

FIGURE 8.4

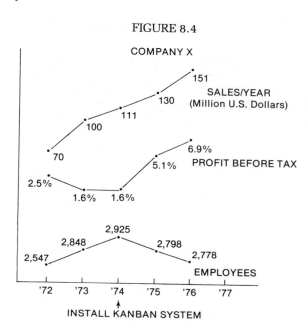

Source: Compiled by the author.

FIGURE 8.5   Company X Inventory Reductions

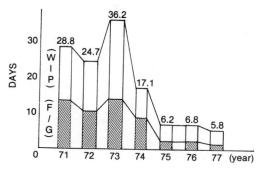

Source: Compiled by the author.

MRP VERSUS THE KANBAN SYSTEM

This section presents a comparative analysis of the relations between MRP and Kanban systems from the viewpoint of production control (see Tables 8.1–8.3). The difference between the two is related to their application areas. The Kanban system is suitable to repetitive manufacturing, while MRP systems are applicable to semirepetitive and nonrepetitive production. If there are large numbers of engineering change orders and if there are large fluctuations in the day-to-day production rate, there is a need for discrete timing of order releasing and time-phasing of requirements. Under these conditions, it is necessary to introduce MRP approaches. The similarities of and differences between the systems from the standpoint of their environment and background are summarized in Tables 8.4 and 8.5.

TOMORROW'S PRODUCTION MANAGEMENT

Were are we going? In the 1980s, the future of production control systems is clear. Figure 8.6 shows the general applicability of the two systems. In repetitive production, the number of Kanban system users will be increasing, and they will be tuning up their systems. Others, in nonrepetitive production, such as project production or job production, will install MRP.

Many companies are involved in semirepetitive production. They will find that a combination of MRP and Kanban systems will be best for them. Figure 8.7 shows general applicability.

Basically, in the marriage of MRP and Kanban systems, the MRP concept is applied to the planning phase and Kanban is applied to the shop floor control phase.

TABLE 8.1

BASIC FUNCTION OF PRODUCTION CONTROL	MRP SYSTEM	KANBAN SYSTEM

Planning priorities	Key point
	  Plan each item through
	  time-phasing based
	  on MPS
		Key point
		  Plan production rate
		  per day of each item
		  through leveling of
		  monthly production

	Planning
	  Centralized planning
	Planning cycle
	  Week (in general)
		Planning
		  Centralized planning
		Planning cycle
		  Month

TABLE 8.2

BASIC FUNCTION OF PRODUCTION CONTROL	MRP SYSTEM	KANBAN SYSTEM
Planning capacities	Calculate capacity requirements and take action to satisfy them (infinite loading)	Set each W C capacity by cycletime (Adjust manufacturing process to meet requirements)

Note: Cycletime = $\dfrac{\text{Number of working hours per day}}{\text{Number of requirements per day}}$

TABLE 8.3

BASIC FUNCTION OF PRODUCTION CONTROL	MRP SYSTEM	KANBAN SYSTEM
Shop floor control Controlling capacities Controlling priorities	Input/output control concept Dispatching list	Adjust capacities through overtime, extra labor First come, first served rule by Kanban

TABLE 8.4

	MRP	KANBAN
Basic concept	Plan-oriented (MPS-oriented production)	Plan-oriented Cycletime production
Transparency	Formal system	Formal system
WIP inventory	Permit planned lead-time inventory	Accept minimum WIP inventory (instead of planned lead time)

TABLE 8.5

	MRP	KANBAN
Development of the system	As a production control system	As a total production system (includes design of production process, OC, IE, etc.)
Fine tuning of the system	Education	Improvement mechanism by Kanban
Appropriate type of production	Without any restriction	Repetitive (item production rate)

FIGURE 8.6 Applicability in Japan

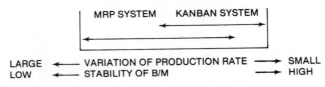

Source: Compiled by the author.

FIGURE 8.7 Where Are We Going?

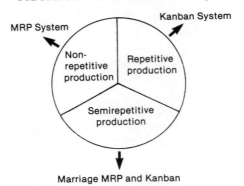

Source: Compiled by the author.

In Japan, in all cases, when companies install production control systems, they also carry out improvement activities, such as quality control circles, production engineering, industrial engineering, and so forth.

REFERENCES

Nakane, J., and T. Yoshiya. 1979. "MRP vs. KANBAN System." *Bulletin of the System Science Institute* 10, Waseda University, pp. 91–98.

One, T. 1978. *Toyota Seisan Hoshiki*. Diamond Bar, Calif.: Diamond Publishing.

Wight, Oliver. 1974. *Production and Inventory Management in the Computer Age.* Hampshire, England: Gower Press.

Yamada, M., and K. Fujita. 1979. *"Koteikaizen no Jissai."Kojokanri*, 25, no. 8:121, 128.

Yoshiya, T., and J. Nakane. 1977. "MRP system." Tokyo: Nikkankogyo.

9

Inventory Control
in Japanese Industry

RICHARD J. SCHONBERGER

Western journalists, economists, and others who have reported to the Western public on the subject of Japanese industrial success have told us about dedicated workers, decision making by consensus, the formation of work groups into quality control (QC) circles, Japanese trading companies, high literacy rates, and Japan, Inc. Until recently, little has been said about Japanese expertise in controlling inventories, and we hear little about Japanese production methods other than use of robots.

This chapter examines the central importance of Japanese inventory control techniques and unique production methods. An attempt is made to show that the "hand-to-mouth" parts control practices perfected by the Japanese lead to higher quality with less scrap, which smooths production and improves productivity. Worker motivational improvements are derivative benefits in the cause-effect sequence. Environmental forces that have encouraged Japanese resourcefulness now exist in other industrialized countries, which suggests that Western industry should adopt Japan's outlook if not its methods.

JUST-IN-TIME INVENTORY CONTROL

Until recently Western knowledge and awareness of Japanese material control and manufacturing methods was meager and spotty. However, in 1981 many production and inventory management people (including professors and students) found opportunities to attend workshops and seminars on the subject. Published materials are starting to be available (for example, Hayes 1981; Moden 1981; Sugimori et al. 1977), and professional organizations are becoming aggressive in spreading the message. For example, in 1979 the American Production and Inventory Control Society (APICS) established the Repetitive Manufacturing Group (with members from over 80 companies), which has sponsored educational and informational activities concerning Japan's repetitive manufacturing management procedures. In June 1979, the Repetitive Manufacturing Group conducted a two-day "Just-in-Time Workshop." The workshop was held in Lincoln, Nebraska, to allow close investigation of the just-in-time (JIT) inventory management program in operation at the Kawasaki motorcycle plant in that city.

JIT appears to be at the core of Japanese material control methods (APICS 1981; Hay 1981). The JIT idea is to deliver subassemblies just in time to go into final assemblies, fabricated parts just in time to go into subassemblies, and raw materials just in time to go into fabricated parts. Among other advantages, JIT avoids having parts delivered before they are needed, only to sit idle gathering carrying charges.

For the high-volume repetitive producer, JIT is accomplished by frequent delivery of parts in small numbers, ideally piece for piece. For parts to be delivered in small numbers, they also must be made and bought in small numbers. Thus, JIT parts delivery requires small production and purchase lot sizes. Japanese ways of dealing with the set-up costs that lead to large lot sizes are considered later.

The APICS Repetitive Manufacturing Group has focused its interest on certain JIT approaches that are known to be in use by Japanese repetitive producers. Toyota's Kanban approach and Yamaha's PYMAC or synchro-MRP received most of the attention and have been written up (APICS 1981). Though Kanban and synchro-MRP seem generally suitable only for certain high-volume original equipment manufacturing (OEM) companies, the JIT *concept* is not similarly limited. Any manufacturer that is able to cut its lot sizes and deliver frequently is moving in the general direction of just-in-time and can expect to realize some of the benefits: direct inventory carrying cost reduction, scrap/quality improvements, and productivity increases. It is incorrect to speak of having or not having a JIT system; JIT is a target to move toward rather than an either/or option.

In addition to the intraplant benefits of JIT, the concept also may yield improvements in the flow of finished goods from plants to distribution centers. The idea is to extend JIT forward so that there is pressure on the factory to match daily output to daily sales, model by model. The ideal factory would be configured and scheduled to run mixed models in final assembly and in subassembly and fabrication as well. Ingenuity is required to cut set-up time bottlenecks and to try to balance the processes for high utilization where the schedule calls for a mixture of different models with different run times.

JIT may also be applied backward to suppliers and suppliers of suppliers. For example, a JIT plant may negotiate purchase agreements that call for frequent deliveries, sometimes several times daily. In early 1980, Kawasaki Motors, USA, launched a multifaceted JIT purchase program, primarily aimed at lowering purchase order quantities and getting more frequent deliveries from suppliers. Numerous ingrained U.S. buying and freight-handling practices resist Kawasaki's JIT purchasing efforts, however. Kawasaki buyers are trying to overcome the resistance via missionary work to sell suppliers and shippers on the JIT purchasing concepts (Schonberger 1981). There have been modest successes, which suggest that the JIT purchasing idea may spread to other companies as more firms hear about it and become acquainted with its potential.

Today the Japanese no longer are alone among nations concerned about conserving materials and other resources. The OPEC oil shock of 1971 and the raw materials shortages in about 1973 delivered a stern conservation message to the world as a whole. North America still has wide open spaces for warehouses, but the jacked-up prices of the materials themselves have altered the economics of inventory retention. However, direct inventory cost savings are by no means the only benefits of JIT. Equally important or maybe more important are benefits in the areas of scrap, quality, rework, worker attitude, and responsibility. These benefits tend to snowball following a strong JIT commitment.

THE JIT CAUSE-EFFECT CHAIN

There is no need for the Japanese to teach us about the benefits of work in progress (WIP) inventory control. We know, thanks especially to Plossl and Wight (1967, p. 308), that WIP inventory reductions lead to more-responsive customer service, more-accurate forecasts, fewer dispatching and communications problems, and decreased need for production control staff. The question is *how to attain* tight WIP inventory control. Material requirements planning helps, but is it the ultimate, or do the Japanese have JIT methods that offer even tighter control?

Material Requirements Planning

The MRP crusade of APICS in the 1970s profoundly altered production and inventory management practices in many Western companies. In MRP the proper time to release orders for component parts is computer-calculated based on schedules for making higher-level parts and assemblies. The MRP goal of correct timing of parts orders is consistent with Japanese JIT goals. Indeed the Japanese use MRP, in addition to Kanban (cards) and other devices, for signaling the need for more parts. While MRP usually is able to reduce buffer stocks via correct order timing, it fails to cut lot-size inventories. By contrast, Japanese JIT focuses upon lot-size inventories, with buffer inventory reductions a secondary effect.

Leading MRP users have attained impressive WIP inventory reductions. In an APICS-sponsored study, 422 surveyed MRP companies claimed an average 4.3 inventory turns after implementing MRP, as compared with 3.2 turns before MRP (Schroeder et al. 1980). This degree of improvement does not compare, however, with turnover improvements reported by Japanese JIT companies. Toyota people, for example, have stated that Toyota's working assets, including inventories, were turned 63 times in 1970 (Sugimori et al. 1977), as compared with 6 turns for each of two U.S. competitors in the automobile industry.

Besides MRP's inability to effect lot-size reductions, the typical planning frequency of MRP is an impediment to the attainment in MRP companies of the inventory reductions achieved with Japanese JIT. MRP plans are typically regenerated once a week, which means that timing of component orders is correct only to the week. By contrast, Japanese JIT procedures, such as Kanban, can trigger orders in time increments of less than an hour. Net-change (as opposed to regenerative) MRP is capable of replanning orders by the day or hour, but in many operating environments the data-processing cost and cost of system "nervousness" for such exactitude are high — as compared, for example, with the triggering of orders by releasing Kanban (cards).

Until recently the conventional Western wisdom was that WIP inventory control benefits are in reduced carrying cost, administrative cost, and delivery time or lead time. Now, thanks to people like Deming and Juran, Western industry is becoming sensitized to the view that WIP inventory reductions lead also to higher quality and less rework. Perhaps we have tended to be unaware of these quality effects because they tend not to be obvious when the inventory reductions are comparatively modest, as in MRP. With the dramatic inventory reductions attained in Japanese JIT plants, the quality/rework benefits become highly visible.

Indirect Benefits of JIT

The reason that minimum lot sizes — the JIT approach — lead to lower scrap and better quality may be simply explained: If a worker makes only one of a given part number and passes it to the next worker immediately, the first worker will hear about it right away if the part does not fit. Thus, defects are discovered right away and their causes are nipped in the bud; production of large lots high in defects is avoided.

Derivative effects of better quality and less scrap are: (a) less wasted material; (b) fewer labor hours spent on rework, which directly improves the productivity of labor; (c) smoother output rates, which cut buffer inventories (providing still greater parts control); and (d) fast feedback on defects, which raises worker awareness of defect causation. These linked benefits form the JIT cause-effect chain shown in Figure 9.1. Factor (a), less material wasted, is self-explanatory, but the other factors warrant elaboration.

Factor (b), less rework and more productivity, is explained as follows

FIGURE 9.1   Effects of JIT Inventory Management

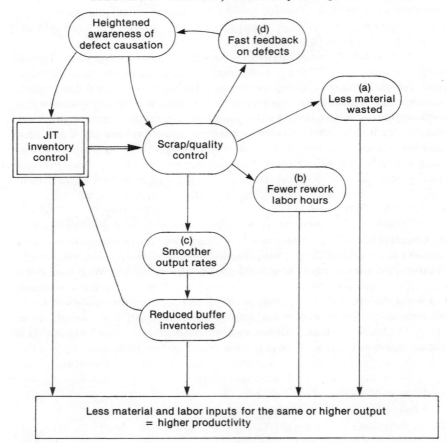

Source: Compiled by the author.

by William Conway, chief executive officer at Nashua Corporation (Ringle 1981).

> As quality goes up, so does productivity. Consider the impact on overall levels of productivity if everyone and every machine in your company performed properly the first time, every time. The same number of employees would be handling much larger volumes of work.
>
> The high cost of inspection would be directed into productive activities. Rework, downgrading, scrapping would be eliminated. Administrative efficiency would be much higher.

Some of the same reasoning applies to factor (c), smoother output rates. As was stated elsewhere, "Studies indicate that the average worker in the U.S. today makes a real contribution only about half the time. The other half is wasted on such things as rework, waiting for parts, or problems caused by worn tools" ("What Can America Do" 1981). Eliminating defect causation and delivering *good* parts smoothly reduces the need for buffer stocks between processes; less buffer inventory further tightens JIT inventory control, and the effects recycle through the cause-effect chain of Figure 9.1.

Regarding factor (d), fast feedback on defects, we may turn to B. F. Skinner's principles of reinforcement. We may expect that workers who quickly learn the effects of their workmanship will become naturally motivated to improve. Such naturally motivated workers sometimes even organize into voluntary production or quality improvement groups, such as QC circles.

As is indicated in the rectangle at the bottom of Figure 9.1, reduction in material and labor inputs for a given output level means higher productivity. With JIT, the output level is likely to rise rather than stay the same, since labor freed from rework may stay busy making more good parts. Furthermore, cumulative JIT effects, including better visibility of problems, may lead to improved worker understanding and acceptance of the need for work assignment flexibility, so that workers may be reassigned as necessary to stay productive. If the factory customarily makes days' or weeks' supply at a time, workers become accustomed to staying at a given job for the days or weeks necessary to complete the given lot, and inventory banks before each work station hide the sorts of problems that in a JIT plant tend to require worker flexibility for fast resolution. In Japanese JIT plants the problems are not covered up by inventories, and the benefits of lower inventories, lower scrap and rework, and so forth are so visible that restrictive work rules are difficult to rationalize. Perhaps the cooperative tendencies of Japanese unions may be partially explained by these visibility effects of JIT.

JIT PLANT CONFIGURATIONS

When the pursuit of just-in-time inventory management is vigorous, the character of the plant changes, and the most apparent changes are likely to be in the physical configurations of plant work spaces. Five rather distinct plant configurations may be identified along the continuum from large-lot to JIT operations. Most JIT plants will have some processes in each of the five configurations, but will be evolving toward configurations that are closer to pure JIT.

The five configurations are shown in Figure 9.2. The figure refers to the example of motorcycle frame welding, but it applies as well to other motorcycle parts and processes and also to other industries. Each successive configuration is more streamlined physically — in equipment, in layout, and in handling aids. "Shop paper" involved in order control is also progressively more streamlined as you proceed from configuration a to configuration e.

Configuration a, the job shop, is the least streamlined. The general-purpose welding equipment in the example requires considerable set-up time to get ready to weld each job-lot of a given motorcycle frame size. Production runs tend to be long — days or weeks — in order to amortize the high set-up costs, and considerable space is needed to store the cycle stocks of work in process (WIP) inventories. Welding booths are loaded, not scheduled, and a good deal of shop paper is needed to sort out priorities for jobs in queue at each booth, to account for WIP inventories, and to control job-lot movements between booths.

Relayout of the job-shop welding booths into dedicated lines, configuration b, follows the group technology (GT) approach to layout (Burbridge 1975), which is widely employed in Japan. Significant reductions in WIP inventory and shop paper obtain when GT/dedicated welding lines are implemented. As Figure 9.2b shows, the inventory of welding jigs and fixtures has disappeared; the reason is that welding jigs and fixtures are specially configured for particular sizes of motorcycle frames and are permanently positioned in a location for one of the dedicated lines. More significantly, there are no WIP inventories between one booth and the next. (There are racks of tubing stock from the punch presses, but that is punch press inventory, not welding WIP.) Frame parts are passed one piece at a time down a given line, stopping at each booth along the way to have one or more additional pieces welded in place. Frame movement from booth to booth within welding is pure just-in-time. Welding makes only one type of contribution to WIP inventory, namely, a buffer stock of finished frames, shown by the box with the x.

The simplicity of piece-for-piece processing requires little shop paper. Documentation is reduced to a daily schedule for each line. The daily

FIGURE 9.2   Plant Configurations: *a*, welding booths, job-shop configuration;
b, dedicated welding lines (group technology); *c*, dedicated lines,
Kaban-driven; *d*, dedicated lines, physically linked forward; *e*,
single line running mixed models.

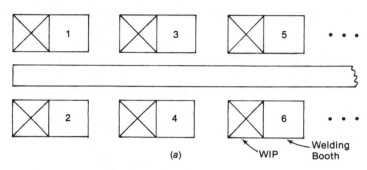

(*a*)

Notes:
1. WIP = several days' supply at each booth.
2. Lead time = several days.
3. Shop paper for every booth: job orders; dispatch list;
   move tags.

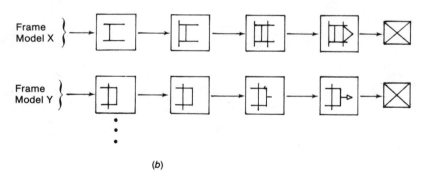

(*b*)

Notes:
1. Completed frames = 1–2 days' (max.) buffer stock.
2. Lead time = 1–4 hours.
3. Shop paper for each line: daily schedule.

(*continued*)

137

FIGURE 9.2   *(continued)*

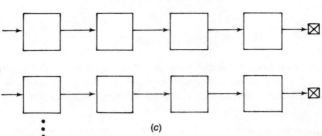

(c)

Notes:
1. Completed frames = a few standard containers' full.
2. Shop paper for each line: one Kanban per empty container (from next work center—paint).

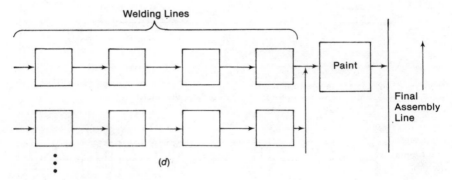

(d)

Notes:
1. Shop paper for welding and paint: none.

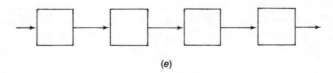

(e)

Notes:
1. Single line simplifies JIT linkages with upstream and downstream processes.
2. Shop paper options: daily schedule; Kanban; none—physical link with next process.

Source: Adapted from Schonberger, Sutton, and Claunch (1981).

schedule calls for running the same number of each frame model as is needed in final assembly a day or two later. All welding lines will not necessarily need to run all day every day, and workers need to be flexible to move from line to line as the schedule changes.

Configuration c employs GT/dedicated lines, like b, but the Toyota Kanban system or a variation thereof is introduced to cut the buffer inventories of completed frames. Kanban (cards) replace the daily schedule. In the Kanban system, component parts may not be made unless triggered by a notice from a downstream work center — paint, in this case — that parts are running short. In any plant, parts usage in the downstream work center will vary from hour to hour and day to day because of equipment, material, labor, and other problems. A daily schedule, as in configuration b, cannot anticipate the timing of such irregularities and therefore provides safety stock or safety time, which in Figure 9.2b is shown as a one- or two-day buffer stock of completed frames. The Kanban approach of Figure 9.2c cuts the buffer to a few standard containers' full (perhaps one or more hours' worth) of completed frames. The mechanism is the Kanban, which acts to coordinate the production rate of the producer in one part of the plant with the user in another. Derivative benefits include fewer schedulers and their accouterments (including computing cycles), since shop-floor dispatching of Kanban replaces daily scheduling. (Kanban system procedures and variations are more fully explained in APICS [1981]; Moden [1981]; Sugimori et al. [1977].)

Figure 9.2d shows the fourth configuration, dedicated lines physically linked forward (to paint, in the example). Shop paper, even Kanban, is eliminated, since movements of parts (welded frames) are physically controlled rather than controlled by paper. End-of-process inventories of welded frames may be cut to zero if the weld lines end where painting begins. Otherwise, the welded-frame inventories would consist of frames hanging on conveyors (moving storage) on the way to paint.

The final configuration, a single line running mixed models, is shown in Figure 9.2e. Welding processes are still arranged, via GT, into the production line configuration, except that the dedicated lines are consolidated into a single line capable of running mixed models. Mixed model processing may require extensive tooling changes. For one thing, jigs, dies, cutting tools, and fixtures may need to be redesigned to cut set-up times to where there is hardly any delay in changing to a different model. Final assembly lines tend to be easiest to configure this way, since assembly is generally labor-intensive and labor is inherently flexible. Set-up may involve little more than grabbing a different hand tool and part. Semi-labor-intensive processes — for example, the welding of tube parts into motorcycle frames — are more difficult to configure for mixed models; ingenuity is needed to design versatility into the jigs and fixtures so that they can hold different sizes of tubing in different ways for different models. Capital-intensive production, such as in machine shops, is more resistant to mixed-model scheduling; nevertheless, Toyota, Kawasaki, and other Japanese manufacturers have made great strides in developing effective and often inexpensive accessories for quick set-up of machine tools. (See especially the comments on carousel die storage platforms made out of common roller conveyor, which reduced punch press set-up time from hours to minutes, as reported in Schonberger, Sutton, and Claunch [1981]. See, also, discussion of similar innovations at Toyota in Sugimori et al. [1977].)

Line balancing is a special challenge in mixed-model operations because different models have different work contents. Line balancing solution methods are well known in Western industry. However, there are rather few Western companies that have tried to establish mixed model lines, and so mixed-model line balancing is not so familiar. Some discussion of mixed-model line balancing may be found in Moden (1981) and Schonberger, Sutton, and Claunch (1981).

The mixed-model, single-line configuration will sharply reduce the number of stations, amount of equipment, and required floor space. Inventory will also be reduced, because there is buffer inventory at the end of only one mixed-model line rather than several buffers at the end of several dedicated lines. Furthermore, it is easier for the downstream process (for example, paint) to communicate or physically interact with a single line, an advantage that makes it easier to introduce Kanban or to link the processes physically. A single line also simplifies interaction with preceding work centers and may cut buffer stocks of parts coming from those work centers. There is also less need for supervision and shop-floor control, since workers stay put at a single line. By contrast, with multiple dedicated lines it is common for workers to be moved from line to line during the day to make the different models. (The workforce may be kept busy, but the facilities in the dedicated lines are underutilized.)

JIT'S FUTURE IN WESTERN INDUSTRY

To restate a point made earlier, the oil and material shocks of the 1970s served to instill a resource-conserving consciousness in all countries. The Japanese have a head start in developing and implementing controls on material resources, and though we in the United States recognize the need, it is not easy for us to break our extravagant habits and follow the Japanese lead.

Fortunately, the Japanese mechanisms for pursuing JIT material controls are not at odds with Western management thought. Western developments in scientific management, quality control, materials management, and manufacturing planning focus on effective use of labor, materials, and plant capacity along with high product quality, just as modern Japanese JIT management does. Lifetime employment, group decision making, and other Japanese cultural traits are very different but do not seem to be necessary antecedents to the pursuit of JIT.

For example, Kawasaki Motors in Nebraska has devised a JIT approach that emphasizes progression toward JIT plant configurations, with changes developed and implemented following the "quick-and-dirty" mode of decision making that is traditional in the United States. The plant manager, an American, ushered in the JIT program in early 1980 and proceeded to implant the JIT objective in everyone's thinking; he gave the JIT program impetus and direction by issuing the following statement about plant configuration: "I envision the whole plant as a series of stations on the assembly lines, whether physically there or not."

Foremen, engineers, material managers, and most other white-collar employees were to use their own individual ingenuity to arrive at ways to move toward the plant vision and JIT objective. The individualistic decision-making process is prone to implementation difficulties, which the Japanese tend to avoid via consensus reached through extensive group discussion. However, an overall plant vision serves as a guide and heuristic device, which may act as a rough surrogate for group consensus mechanisms.

Kawasaki's JIT program is still very new, but there have been a few promising steps in pursuit of the plant vision. One is relayout and retooling of frame welding into dedicated lines, as in Figure 9.2b. Another is physical merger of differential subassembly with one of the motorcycle assembly lines to achieve physically linked processes, as in Figure 9.2d. (See Schonberger [1981] and Schonberger, Sutton, and Claunch [1981] for further discussion of these and other JIT-oriented measures.)

JIT thinking at Kawasaki, Nebraska, had been incorporated into plant management in small ways over the years as a natural outgrowth of close association with Kawasaki, Japan. A full JIT commitment, however, dates back only to January 1980, when Lincoln management decided to abandon plans to implement MRP. The JIT program made rather little progress until 1981, when several changes began to bear fruit. Employee attrition had been about equal to productivity improvements, so that output could grow at a rate of 10–20 percent per year without hiring, but in the spring of 1981, output had increased beyond the attrition rate, which created excess labor. The extra workers were employed in rebuilding subassembly areas, painting walls, caulking joints, and so forth.

Kawasaki, Nebraska, does not have a program to involve blue-collar labor in JIT brainstorming, QC circles, suggestions, or other such involvement mechanisms, presumably in the belief that plant configuration changes promise large and immediate productivity improvement and therefore warrant management's full attention. Labor involvement may come later. (Juni Noguchi, general manager of the Union of Japanese Scientists and Engineers, states that "workers and foremen can solve only 15 percent of all quality control problems. The rest must be handled by management or the engineering staff" (Deming and Gray 1981). In the meantime the youthful workforce has "cut its teeth" in a JIT-oriented plant, and has performed the labor to change the plant configurations. The lower inventories, lower scrap, lower rework, higher quality, and increasing productivity are visible. The workforce is developing the proper mind set for smooth implementation of more extensive JIT measures, and it may not make much difference whether the ideas come from blue- or white-collar workers — or from Japan.

CONCLUSION

Somehow the JIT story was missed by Western newspeople and even by most industrial delegations that visited Japanese industry in recent years. The JIT story is out now, and the news is spreading quickly. U.S. manufacturers are generally eager to find out what can be borrowed from the Japanese. Productivity managers have been appointed and many QC circles have been formed. Perhaps these organizational efforts need to receive more direction, especially via greater understanding of the JIT philosophy. Ways to achieve quality and productivity improvement will vary from plant to plant — but inventory control is a good place to begin.

REFERENCES

APICS (American Production and Inventory Control Society), Repetitive Manufacturing Group. 1981. "Driving the Productivity Machine: Production Planning and Control in Japan," ed. Robert W. Hall.

Burbridge, John L. 1975. *The Introduction of Group Technology*. New York: Wiley/Halstead.

Deming, W. E., and Christopher S. Gray. 1981. "Japan: Quality Control and Innovation." *Business Week*, July 13, pp. 17–44.

Hay, Ed. 1981. "Planning to Implement Kanban." Presentation to APICS Repetitive Manufacturing Group, Just-in-Time Workshop, Lincoln, Nebraska, June.

Hayes, Robert H. 1981. "Why Japanese Factories Work." *Harvard Business Review* (July–August):57–66.

Moden, Yasuhiro. 1981. "What Makes the Toyota Production System Really Tick?" *Industrial Engineering* (January):36–46.

Plossl, G. W., and O. W. Wight. 1967. *Production and Inventory Control*. Englewood Cliffs, N. J.: Prentice-Hall.

Ringle, William M. 1981. "The American Who Remade 'Made in Japan'." *Nation's Business*, February, pp. 67–70.

Schonberger, Richard J. 1981. "Just-in-Time Purchasing." Working paper, Department of Management, University of Nebraska-Lincoln, September.

Schonberger, Richard, Doug Sutton, and Jerry Claunch. 1981. "Kanban ('Just-in-Time') Applications at Kawasaki, USA." *1981 Conference Proceedings*, American Production and Inventory Control Society, Boston, October 6–9.

Schroeder, Roger G., John C. Anderson, Sharon E. Tupy, and Edna M. White. 1980. "A Study of MRP Benefits and Costs." Working paper, Department of Management Sciences, Graduate School of Business Administration, University of Minnesota, May.

Sugimori, Y., K. Kusunoki, F. Cho, and S. Uchikawa. 1977. "Toyota Production System and Kanban System: Materialization of Just-in-Time and Respect-for-Human System." *International Journal of Production Research* 15, no. 6: 553–64.

"What Can America Do To Solve Its Productivity Crisis?" 1981. *World*, Winter, pp. 21–31.

10

The Toyota Kanban System

ROBERT W. HALL

About 20 years ago Toyota Motor Company began developing methods to achieve some of the effects of automation without investing much money. These slowly evolved into the Kanban system. Today most of the leading Japanese manufacturers in appropriate product lines use a very similar system. The system is intended to achieve many objectives based on moving production in a smooth flow. It should improve quality, increase worker morale, increase labor productivity, decrease waste — in short, trim manufacturing into the most competitive stance possible.

The ideas behind Kanban are to investigate the true reasons for problems and to overcome those problems at the shop-floor level. The way to do this is by reducing inventory until the causes of problems are exposed. Japanese companies never wish to live in the comfort of excess inventories because these inventories allow managers to deceive themselves about the true effectiveness of their operation.

The philosophy behind Kanban is to review continuously what can be done to improve operations. To provide visibility, Toyota began to use cards. *Kanban* in Japanese means card. Hence the name of the system, a name that has become the generic term to describe all similar systems in Japan. However, one should not be deceived into thinking that there is magic in the card system. The cards are one of the less important aspects of the system, but, by intent, they are one of the most visible components of it.

The Kanban system promotes repetitive manufacturing. It is a natural system for controlling production of a volume of items that are the same, or very similar. It is not so applicable to such industries as shipbuilding or locomotive production. A great many complex variations in the end items are possible with Kanban, but the system does not work very well where unique products must be built using irregular lot sizes. Kanban promotes repetitive manufacturing in an uninterrupted flow.

Kanban is thought of in two ways, a narrow sense and a broad sense. Narrowly defined, Kanban is a procedure using cards to operate a "pull system" of material control that links all supplying operations to a final assembly line. More broadly defined, Kanban is a method for greatly reducing lead times, decreasing inventory, and improving productivity by linking all production operations together in a smooth uninterrupted flow. The ultimate goal is conversion of raw material to finished products with lead times equal to processing times, thus eliminating all queue time for material and all idle inventory. Automation is thereby simulated.

THE KANBAN CARD SYSTEM

Each work center is defined and has an inbound stock point and an outbound stockpoint. Two types of cards are used: A *move card*, which authorizes the taking of one standard container of a specific part from one work center to another; and a *production card*, which authorizes a producing work center to produce another standard container of parts to replace one that was just taken.

Parts are kept only in standard containers, and only one card goes on each container. Containers full of parts come into the inbound stockpoints with move cards attached. When one of these containers is selected for use, the move card is detached and sent back to the supplying work center to authorize replenishment. Each move card is used for just one part and circulates between a single pair of work centers. (See Figure 10.1.)

In each outbound stockpoint, standard containers full of parts should have production tickets attached. When a container is picked to go forward, the production ticket is removed and the move ticket is attached. The detached production ticket stays at the same work center, where it authorizes production of another standard container of parts to replace the one just taken. The production card is attached to a refilled container, which is placed in the outbound stockpoint ready for pick-up. The lot size equals the container size.

This system begins with the inbound stockpoints of the final assembly line. It allows the final assembly line to pull material from supplying work centers as needed, and some of those work centers may be outside suppliers. The work centers from which material is drawn then pass on the requirements for material to the work centers supplying them, in a linkage all the way back to the outside suppliers.

FIGURE 10.1   The Kanban Card System: · · · · · · · move card flowpath; - - - - - production card flowpath.

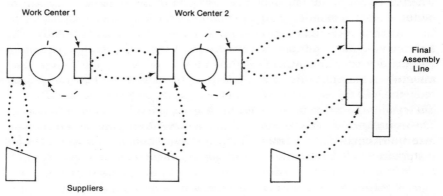

Source: Compiled by the author.

CARD SYSTEM RULES

The following rules apply to the use of the card system:

1. A container full of parts should always have a card attached.
2. Using work centers always come pick up the parts from the supplying work centers.
3. Parts are never to be taken without using a move card.
4. Parts should never be produced without the authorization of an
   unattached production card.
5. Standard containers are always to be used. They should always be
   filled with the correct number of parts.

   If the rules are observed, the work-in-process inventory level of a
specific part cannot exceed the level authorized by the total number of
cards issued for that part. The cards control the work-in-process inventory
level. The fewer the cards, the less inventory.
   The purpose of the cards is to provide visibility of inventory level on
the plant floor. When this system is used, virtually no inventory should be
in storerooms. All of it should be on the plant floor and visible. Other means
of visible control practiced with Kanban are:

1. A status board on all final assembly lines shows by the hour how
   many units have been completed compared with the day's
   schedule.
2. An electronic status board (called *andon* in Japan) is prominently
   located in the plant. It shows which work centers are operating

and which are down. It may also show the running rate of various models in final assembly.

3. Lights on machines signal that a machine has malfunctioned, that it needs a tool change, or that it is time for a regular inspection of a part.

KANBAN PRODUCTIVITY IMPROVEMENT PROCEDURE

The most important function of Kanban is the promotion of productivity through streamlining the flow of production. The card procedure is incidental to this process, and is not used on all parts, but it gets everyone's attention. Much streamlining of the production flow is necessary before the card procedure can work in its most basic sense. Therefore, *after* great change has already taken place, the cards are used in the following way to stimulate productivity and automation further:

1. Issue the cards and start the process.
2. Withdraw cards if material will flow smoothly without them. This reduces the level of work-in-process inventory to that needed to buffer operations from each other.
3. Withdraw one or two additional cards from circulation for a part number in an area where improvement seems possible. Problems usually occur with that part, such as the need to work overtime or a shortage of the part. Everyone watches for the root cause of these problems to devise methods of operating at the new, lower level of inventory.
4. Department management, workers, or staff specialists make changes to solve the observed problems. They may change the work procedure, cut set-up times, modify equipment, or alter the schedule sequence.
5. After consolidating the improvements from one round of the card procedure, one or two more cards for the same part number are removed from circulation and another round begins.

GOALS AND ASSUMPTIONS OF THE KANBAN SYSTEM

To be successful, a Kanban plant must meet the assumptions below. However, when the program is initiated, no plant meets them. At the outset they are goals. When starting the program, each plant must decide whether attainment of the goals is realistic.

The schedule must be level, which means not only that every day's workload must be equal, but that every day's schedule must be very nearly identical. That is, the sequence of models or items to be assembled every day must be almost the same for an extended period. This makes Kanban applicable to the regular schedules of repetitive manufacturing, not to irregular work demands in a job shop, a matter to be examined in detail when beginning Kanban.

The level schedule must be frozen for a period of time. Usually this period is about a month. To do this, the company should be able to use the final assembly schedule as the master schedule. This requires getting the cumulative lead time of material flowing into final assembly short enough that parts need not be stocked at an intermediate level.

Routings must be fixed. This is necessary in order to define the system of outbound and inbound stock points. This in turn allows all fabrication schedules to follow closely the final assembly schedule.

A large number of set-ups must be performed daily. This is necessary if all operations are to make a small amount of everything needed every day. Consequently, set-up times must be very short.

Lot sizes must be small and fixed in order to use the standard containers. A rule-of-thumb goal is to have lot sizes for every part that are no more than one-tenth of a day's use.

The plant must run according to the level schedule. The system will tolerate ± 10 percent deviation on a given day, but over a week the actual production should be ± 0 percent to schedule. The cards allow a little ebb and flow in the schedule. Several other actions are necessary to attain uninterrupted flow:

1. The quality level of production must be high, with very little rework. (The reason Japanese stop the process to correct quality problems is that a temporary stop avoids a big interruption further along in the process.)
2. The equipment must function. This requires diligent preventive maintenance.
3. The assembly line sequence should not be broken for special products. Where these are necessary, they are run at the end of a day, or at the end of one frozen schedule period before starting a new one.

The schedule should not be made with a view to labor utilization. This system requires workers who can perform many different jobs. That prevents a labor shortage or an unexpected absence from interrupting the flow.

The workforce must participate in making improvements. There are too many small problems for staff people to see them and correct them all.

The proper goal of the workforce is precision work, not hurried work. Kanban requires that the right work be done, not that workers go as quickly as they can.

The system should be extended to suppliers. Inventory cannot be reduced much if the suppliers continue to deliver in large quantities. Parts and materials delivered by suppliers should, if possible, be in standard containers ready for production use, and delivery schedules must be reliable.

IMPLEMENTATION OF KANBAN

The major benefits of Kanban come from two sources: leveling the schedule to allow a smooth, uninterrupted flow of material; and modifying equipment and the methods of work to provide a smooth uninterrupted flow of material.

Project teams implementing Kanban in Japan stress the second source of benefit. An enormous amount of process change is necessary to make the project a success. Kanban is regarded as primarily a method of achieving process change, and only secondarily as a method for controlling the flow of material.

The steps in implementation are:

1. Get the total commitment of top management. The few Kanban consultants in Japan will not bother to come to a plant otherwise.
2. Get a good working relationship with the workforce. The program has no chance without strong leadership at the shop-floor level. This means that at a minimum the employees must have guaranteed employment, understanding of the program, and participation in the improvement. (Japanese companies all make full use of their small employee groups when implementing Kanban. They develop their quality control circles into well-trained improvement groups to spot and correct the problems that require buffer inventory. To provide a fast response to worker suggestions, most companies have a highly visible form of management by objectives [MBO] at the shop-floor level. Staff members, supervisors, and foremen all have lists of suggestions, projects, and actions taken. Many of these are placed on plant bulletin boards so workers can see progress being made. Some employee groups even use MBO procedures within the group. Process improvement is a high-profile activity in Kanban.)
3. Start with the final assembly line. Unless the final assembly schedule can be leveled and made almost identical each day, guidance is limited for the rest of the program. This means reducing the change-over times in final assembly until models can be

mixed in assembly. It means using standard containers and setting up exact locations for each different part to be placed.

4. Working back from the final assembly lines, reduce set-up times and lot sizes in the fabrication areas to match the lot sizes needed in assembly. Remove inventory from storerooms. (Often the first move made is to cut lot sizes so as to apply pressure to reduce set-up times.)

5. Balance fabrication rates with assembly rates, which can be done after set-up times are reduced. First, add or convert capacity; Kanban uncovers capacity shortfalls. Second, provide spare capacity in all areas. Inventory is stored capacity. If any operation starts to fall behind schedule for any reason, it can catch up only if spare capacity is never used of any other purpose.

6. Extend Kanban to the suppliers. First, stabilize the schedule given to suppliers. Remove the inventory needed for variance in transport times by telling suppliers the times of day or the days you want materials to arrive. Second, require frequent deliveries of small lots in standard containers. Third, establish a good quality-assurance relationship with them. They must know exactly what is expected in order to deliver high-quality parts every time, so tell them immediately when there are problems. Fourth, visit their plant and advise them on how to set up their operations to phase in with yours.

CAN KANBAN WORK IN THE UNITED STATES?

No one really knows whether Americans can institute Kanban to the same extent as the Japanese. Certainly the physical principles of the system are the same for Americans as for Japanese. Americans can therefore achieve many improvements by the following: level schedules, fixed routings, reductions of set-up time, reduced lot sizes, reduced lead times, and the reduction of inventories to a point where the problems in production are obvious enough that operations can be better balanced with each other.

Several factors are not physically the same between Japan and the United States. Distances between plants and suppliers are longer and truck sizes are larger, which makes the economics of shipping a more trouble-some factor. Also, U.S. equipment tends to be less flexible in general, so Americans may start with more problems in achieving set-up time reductions.

Great improvements are possible if Americans follow Kanban principles, but manage things their own way. To compete with the Japanese on their terms would mean adopting several of the major features of Japanese management, and that means spanning a considerable cultural gap. That is the source of most skepticism.

Of the many cultural differences, two appear to be critical obstacles to Kanban. Americans serious about using the method to its fullest will have to become sensitive to two points. The first is individualism. Japanese work in groups, and the company and the workforce make long-term commitments to each other. American companies lay off workers in downturns, and the managers often job-hop so much that no one can be sure that a policy in place this year will still be in place next year. To get ahead, the manager often finds it inexpedient to give due credit to subordinates. However, Kanban requires long-term commitment, and it must be substantially executed by the shop-floor workforce. Therefore, members of a Kanban project team must expect to consume several years of their lives in the project, and the floor workers must know that they will receive some of the benefit of their contribution.

This boils down to long-term management contracts and policies of no lay-offs for the floor workforce. Major shop-floor improvements cannot occur without true leadership at the shop-floor level — long hours and shirt-sleeve work. The workers and their leaders must have confidence in each other. That is necessary whether there is a union or not.

The second point to consider is impatience. It takes a while to become acquainted with these methods and their implications. Americans often think that what is seen at the first observation is all there is to know. Much damage can be done by jumping into such a comprehensive program without clearly understanding where it is to lead. The detailed steps required for implementation must be worked out piece by piece in each plant. Advice: Do a great deal of studying before beginning. Visit Japan if possible. Work with those already involved in Kanban if possible. Demonstrations are better than written materials.

Emotional preparation is also vital. In Japan every company implementing Kanban starts with an extensive campaign to prepare the workforce before beginning, down to the extent of having smile campaigns and housekeeping campaigns. Kanban is difficult in Japan, and the workers and project team members need as many small victories as possible to sustain them through the difficult states. The improvements come from workforce development, and the project can go no faster than the workforce can adapt to it.

11

The Kanban Production Management Information System

C. CARL PEGELS

INTRODUCTION

The Kanban production management information system is a subsystem of the Japanese manufacturing planning and control system that is referred to by Monden (1981) as the Toyota production system. Kanban is deceptively simple, yet implementation of Kanban is considered to be one of the more difficult projects confronting managers of U.S. firms who are considering the Kanban system.

Kanban is the Japanese word for tags or cards. The word is used because of the cards that are attached to in-process-inventory containers or groups of parts. Kanban also means billboard and is used as such as a means of communication for production control information in the plant.

The Kanban cards contain considerable information and are used over and over again. To protect them in the factory environment they are usually kept in transparent rectangular vinyl envelopes.

There are essentially two types of Kanbans in use. One is the production or production-order Kanban. The other is the conveyance or withdrawal Kanban. In this chapter the terms production Kanban and conveyance Kanban will be used. There are other types of Kanbans in use in Japanese plants. For instance, a special type of conveyance Kanban is used to order parts or subassemblies from parts suppliers. It is called a supplier Kanban. In addition to the routine information, it also contains delivery instructions, including times of day to deliver, and exact locations for deliveries.

In this chapter we shall discuss the functions of both production and conveyance Kanbans and how they can be used, not only as a tool to maintain minimum in-process-inventory levels, but also as a means of reducing inventory in existing high in-process-inventory situations common in U.S. plants.

The Kanban formula for determining the desirable in-process formula, as used by Toyota, will also be described and discussed. Finally, we shall describe the efforts being made in a U.S. plant to introduce Kanban.

FUNCTIONS OF PRODUCTION AND CONVEYANCE KANBANS

A Kanban production and inventory control management information system has multiple purposes. The primary purpose is to maintain inventory, and especially in-process and supplier inventory, at as low a level as possible. A secondary purpose is to communicate production planning information downward into the production chain. That is, the system of Kanban tags communicates production requirements downward from the final end-product assembly to prior operations producing the parts, components, and subassemblies that make up the end product. This downward communication does not take place in a discontinuous and periodical (weekly or daily) pattern, but in a nearly continuous pattern (approximately every hour or few hours) through the medium of the Kanban tags.

To illustrate how a Kanban system works, we shall use the case of two consecutive operations in a production process for the manufacture of a part or component. The two operations will be identified as operations A and B. They are physically separated and the output of operation A must be material handled by fork truck or other means to operation B. Standard size containers are used to move the in-process inventory from operation A to operation B. To make this illustration more vivid, let us assume that one container of in-process inventory satisfies the required end-product output rate for one hour. Hence, in an eight-hour shift, eight containers of in-process inventory would have to be processed by and moved between operations A and B.

Figure 11.1 illustrates the above scenario. To ensure that no delays will occur, a considerable amount of in-process inventory is stored both at the output side of operation A and at the input side of operation B. Note that each stored conveyor has either a production Kanban (PKB) or a con-

FIGURE 11.1 Kanban Installation

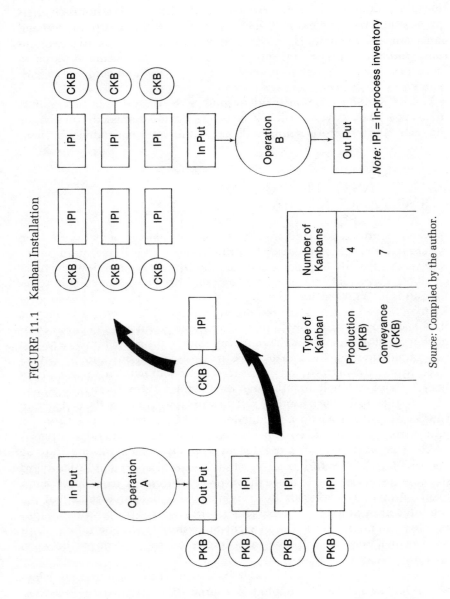

Type of Kanban	Number of Kanbans
Production (PKB)	4
Conveyance (CKB)	7

Note: IPI = in-process inventory

Source: Compiled by the author.

veyance Kanban (CKB) attached to it. The only exception is the input container at operation B that is being emptied while operation B is going on. Also note that production Kanbans are attached only to those containers stored at the output side of operation A. As soon as a container is moved away from operation A, the production Kanban is removed from the container and replaced with a conveyance Kanban. All in-process-inventory containers stored at the input side of operation B have conveyance Kanbans attached to them.

The amount of in-process inventory allowed between operations A and B is determined and controlled by the sum of the number of production Kanbans and conveyance Kanbans. Note that there are a total of four production Kanbans and seven conveyance Kanbans visible on the illustration. We shall assume that the sum of 11 Kanbans is the maximum allowed. Since every container with in-process inventory must have a Kanban attached to it, the 11 Kanbans, therefore, set the limit on the amount of in-process inventory between operations A and B.

When a container is moved from the output side of operation A the production Kanban is replaced with a conveyance Kanban. When this occurs the operator of operation A has authorization to produce another container of operation A's output. Note that the container at the output end of operation A must have a production Kanban attached to it. The free or unattached production Kanban is, therefore, an authorization to produce an additional container of in-process inventory.

Based on the above description of the Kanban production and inventory management information system, it now should become clear to the reader how this system can be used to achieve its primary purpose of in-process-inventory control. In-process-inventory control or reduction can be achieved by gradually reducing the number of production Kanbans and conveyance Kanbans in circulation between a given pair of two operations. In Figure 11.2 a scenario is presented where the number of production Kanbans has been reduced to two and the number of conveyance Kanbans has been reduced to two, for a total of four Kanbans in circulation. Using the Kanban system for inventory control has enabled management to reduce the in-process inventory between operations A and B from a maximum of 11 containers to a maximum of four containers.

It must be pointed out that a drastic reduction of in-process inventory, as portrayed in the scenario described above, is feasible only if other operational and management changes are made. The lower in-process inventory will require close coordination of both operations A and B and possibly the intermittent assignment of the operators of operations A and B to other tasks whenever the output rate of one or both operations does not coincide with the required in-process-inventory flows.

Although two production Kanbans plus two conveyance Kanbans

FIGURE 11.2 Kanban Installation

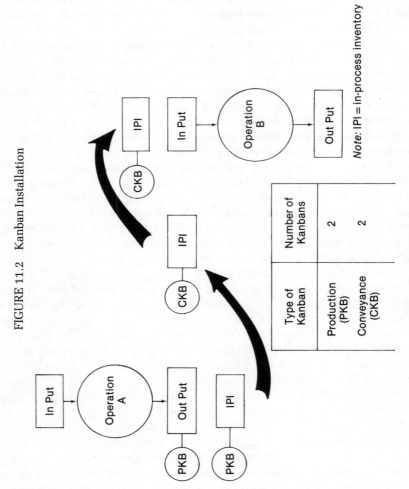

Note: IPI = in-process inventory

Type of Kanban	Number of Kanbans
Production (PKB)	2
Conveyance (CKB)	2

Source: Compiled by the author.

may seem like a substantial reduction in in-process inventory between operations A and B, it is not the absolute minimum in-process-inventory level attainable under the Kanban production and inventory management information system. In Figure 11.3, the absolutely minimum level of in-process inventory attainable under the Kanban system is illustrated. Note that there are only one production Kanban and one conveyance Kanban. Hence, maximum in-process inventory has been reduced from 11 containers to two containers. At this low level it is imperative that the operators of both operations A and B are trained for and assigned to alternative tasks in addition to operations A and B to utilize their production time.

In the above scenario we have shown how the Kanban production and inventory management information system can reduce and control in-process-inventory levels and simultaneously communicate the production requirements to the preceding operations. The scenario used illustrated only one link in the chain of operations in a production process. A production process normally consists of numerous operations. In addition, parts fit into components, parts and components fit into subassemblies, and finally parts, components, and subassemblies fit into end-product final assemblies. All of the processes required to move from raw material or supplier-supplied parts, components, and subassemblies to the end-product final assembly constitute series of links that are connected in tree-like chains from the bottom up. For each link the Kanban system as illustrated in the above scenarios functions as a production and inventory management information and control system. Although the concept of the Kanban system is simple, its implementation along all the links of the tree-like chains is quite an accomplishment, one not easily attainable. To implement the Kanban system, therefore, will be the challenge of the 1980s for U.S. manufacturing firms.

THE ECONOMIC PRODUCTION-LOT SIZE APPROACH TO THE KANBAN SYSTEM

As was pointed out in the previous section, application of the Kanban system will require production operators who are trained in multiple tasks. These multiple tasks may consist not only of an ability to operate several different types of machines, but could also require an ability to perform change-over set-up operations that may be necessary to make possible the performance of several alternate operations on the same piece of equipment and machinery.

In the typical U.S. production operation, the change-over set-ups described above would also be necessary under similar circumstances, but

FIGURE 11.3   Kanban Installation

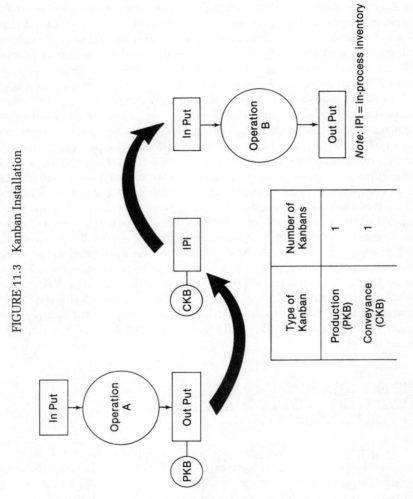

Type of Kanban	Number of Kanbans
Production (PKB)	1
Conveyance (CKB)	1

Note: IPI = in-process inventory

Source: Compiled by the author.

in U.S. plant in-process inventories would be allowed to build up; as a result, change-over set-ups would be rather infrequent and would usually be performed by a specialized set-up mechanic. Under the Kanban system the change-over set-ups would be much more frequent and would most likely have to be performed by the operator of the machine or equipment.

With the frequent change-over set-ups the machine or equipment could be shut down almost constantly unless the time required to perform the change-over set-up were drastically reduced. Under the Japanese Kanban implementation system the change-over set-up times have been drastically reduced. This has been accomplished by the application of various work simplification methods, such as the use of tool and die carousels to store the machine tools and dies near the machine. In addition, special installation guides and fixtures have been incorporated into the machines to facilitate the tool and die removal and installation process.

With all the changes the Japanese have instituted there still remains the unanswered question of how much change-over set-up costs can be traded off against inventory holding costs. We shall try to illustrate this question with an example and show graphically how the economic production quality formula can be applied to the question to determine the degree to which in-process inventory should be reduced.

The economic production quantity formula determines the economic production-lot size that should be run between change-over set-ups if the production rate, the demand rate, the change-over set-up cost, and the in-process inventory holding cost are known. The production-lot size, Q^*, is determined by the formula

$$Q^* = \sqrt{\frac{2\,SDP}{H(P-D)}}$$

where S   is the change-over set-up cost per set-up
H   is the inventory holding cost per unit per month
D   is the demand rate in units per month
P   is the production rate in units per month (assuming continuous production during regularly scheduled operating hours)

The economic production quantity formula is derived from the total cost (per month) formula,

$$TC(Q) = \frac{SD}{Q} + \frac{HQ(P-D)}{2P}$$

where $TC(Q)$ is total cost per month for change-over set-up cost and inventory holding costs.

The economic production quantity formula is illustrated in Figure

11.4 for values of the model parameters of S = \$450; H = \$0.10; D = 3,000 units; and P = 12,000 units. The parameters generate an economic production quantity of

$$Q^* = \sqrt{\frac{(2)\ 450(3000)(12000)}{(0.10)(9000)}} = 600 \text{ units}$$

By applying extraordinary efforts, management was able to reduce the set-up time and reduce the cost for changing over the operation from \$450 to \$50, only one-ninth of the original cost. The new order quantity, with the revised change-over cost, then becomes

$$Q^* = \sqrt{\frac{(2)(50)(3000)(12000)}{(0.10)(9000)}} = 200 \text{ units}$$

Hence, to reduce the economic production-lot size from 600 units to 200 units, or to reduce the lot size to one-third of the original, it was necessary to reduce the change-over set-up cost to one-ninth the original cost. Implementing a Kanban production and inventory management information system, therefore, requires that the change-over set-up costs be drastically reduced.

The results derived from the above illustration show that to reduce

FIGURE 11.4   Economic Lot Size Determination

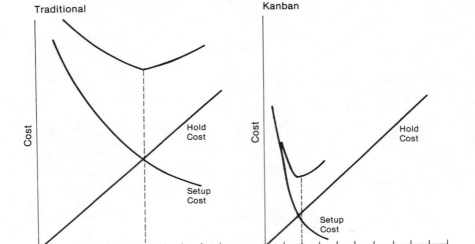

Source: Compiled by the author.

the economic production-lot size by a factor of n (3 in the example) requires that the change-over set-up cost be reduced by a factor of n^2 (9 in the example). To reduce the economic production-lot size by a factor of 6, (that is, to reduce the economic production-lot size to 100 units from 600 units) requires that the change-over set-up cost be reduced by a factor of 36, which requires an actual set-up cost of $450 \div 36 = \$12.50$.

TOYOTA'S KANBAN FORMULA

Toyota developed a formula for determining the number of production Kanbans and conveyance Kanbans in circulation. The formula is empirically based and provides a means of comparing the number of Kanbans in circulation in various locations and departments of the organization (Sugimori et al. 1979).

The Kanban determination formula is of the form

$$n = \frac{D(T_p + T_w)\alpha}{m}$$

where n   is number of production and conveyance Kanban in circulation
      D   is production requirement in units per shift
      T_p is processing time for production requirement D measured in terms of shifts
      T_w is delay time for change-over set-ups and transportation measured in terms of shifts
      α is a policy variable >0, which usually has a value about 1
      m is number of units per container, usually less than 10 percent of D

The maximum inventory in circulation between two operations, M, can now be expressed in terms of m and n as follows:

$$M = mn$$

The two time variables, T_p and T_w, jointly determine the lead time. Hence, maximum inventory, M, can be reduced by reducing demand, D, lead time, $T_p + T_w$, or the policy variable, α. Since demand is an exogenous variable, management has control only over lead time, which includes processing time, transportation time, and change-over set-up times. The policy variable is normally set at a value of one, and adjusted when necessary and feasible.

Suppose we have two production operations for which we want to determine the desirable number of production Kanbans and conveyance Kanbans in circulation. Production requirements per eight-hour shift amount to 1,000 units. Processing time, T_p, for the 1,000 units is three hours, or three-eighths of an eight-hour shift. Delay time for producing the 1,000 units amounts to about one hour, or one-eighth of an eight-hour shift. The policy variable, α, is set equal to 1, and the capacity of the containers equals 50 units per container. Applying the Kanban determination formula then provides

$$m = \frac{1000(3/8 + 1/8)(1)}{50} = 10 \text{ Kanbans}$$

Based on the formula, ten Kanbans should be in circulation. These can now be divided into production Kanbans and conveyance Kanbans. For instance, management may decide to use six production Kanbans and 4 conveyance Kanbans.

Total maximum inventory in circulation between the two processes amounts to M = mn = 50 (10) = 500 units. If management decides to reduce the inventory in circulation, it can modify the policy variable, α. If α is set at 0.80, then the number of Kanbans in circulation will amount to n = 8 and total maximum inventory will be reduced to M = 400 units.

KANBAN IN USE AT KAWASAKI, LINCOLN, NEBRASKA

Kanban production and inventory management information systems are commonplace in Japan but are still largely conversation pieces or topics for study in the United States. There are, however, exceptions, and one of these exceptions will be discussed below. The information presented below was obtained from a presentation by Dennis Butt at a productivity conference sponsored by Productivity, Inc., of Stamford, Connecticut (Butt 1981). He was at that time the plant manager of Kawasaki's Lincoln, Nebraska, manufacturing facilities. The discussion of an installed Kanban system will deal with the Kawasaki Kanban system in use at Kawasaki's Lincoln plant.

The interesting aspect of Kawasaki's adoption of the Kanban system is that the system was adopted following the use of a traditional American production and inventory scheduling system for a period of about five years. Since the opening of the Lincoln plant, Kawasaki's production and inventory control system had utilized a material requirements planning (MRP) system. In the early part of 1980, Kawasaki, Lincoln dropped the MRP system and switched to a modified Kanban system. The use of the Kanban system was facilitated to some extent because its Japanese feeder plants utilized the Kanban system. However, since Kawasaki, Lincoln had to depend on many distant suppliers from Japan, the use of the Kanban system was also considerably more difficult.

The first step Kawasaki, Lincoln took was to reduce all orders to lots of 200 units. Also, instead of painting parts in batches, fixtures were designed to allow the painting of parts in sets, thus ensuring that parts for a given vehicle would have uniform colors but also ensuring the availability of complete sets of parts at the right time. In the stamping areas, press workplaces were redesigned so that all dies for a given press could be stored on a carousel right next to the press.

All parts withdrawn from storage were withdrawn under the Kanban method in small lot sizes. Most important subassemblies were also ordered in small batches with limited lead times. For vehicle engines only a three-day inventory was maintained. Similar small inventories were maintained for other imported subassemblies. Since defective items were virtually non-existent on imported parts, the three-day buffer stock was needed only to protect Kawasaki from the potential delays in trans-Pacific and U.S. surface transportation.

The supplier of seats for Kawasaki vehicles was in Lincoln and delivered its supplies on a daily basis. Only enough inventory was kept on hand to carry production to the next daily delivery.

With the above changes plus numerous others, Kawasaki, Lincoln was able to operate the manufacturing plant with less than three weeks of inventory. Their inventory turnover after less than one year of Kanban implementation had been reduced to 20 inventory turns per year. Further improvements in reducing inventory were planned and expected.

The above illustration shows how one small-to-middle-sized U.S. plant was able to convert from the traditional production and inventory system to a Kanban system. This feat was accomplished in a plant that employed 550 people. The plant produced six different products divided into 40 models and was able to produce 100,000 units per year.

CONCLUSIONS

This chapter provides an overview of the Kanban production and inventory management information system. The Kanban system has two primary purposes. The first is minimization of in-process and supplier inventories and the second is communication of production requirements within a plant and from a plant to supplier firms.

The two common Kanbans were discussed and their use illustrated. They are the production Kanban (PKB) and the conveyance Kanban (CKB). Both have to perform their special functions and together they limit the amount of inventory that is in circulation.

An illustration was presented of how the gradual withdrawal of Kanbans in circulation can serve to reduce in-process inventories. The illustration showed how under one scenario the number of Kanbans in circulation was reduced from 11 to two.

Next we presented the economic production order formula to illustrate how, through reduction of change-over set-up costs, the use of Kanbans can be justified based on the traditional trade-off of change-over set-up cost versus inventory holding cost.

The formula used by Toyota to determine the number of Kanbans in circulation was presented, explained, and illustrated. The illustration showed how a modification of the formula also shows the maximum inventory level under the Kanban system.

Finally, application of the Kanban system in a U.S. setting was presented. Although the application of Kanban took place in a plant owned by a Japanese firm, the setting of the plant, the work force, and plant management were all traditional American.

REFERENCES

Butt, Dennis. 1981. "Just-in-Time in Lincoln, Nebraska — Why and How." Productivity Seminar presentation, Productivity Seminar, February 23, Chicago.

Monden, Yasuhiro. 1981. "Adaptable Kanban System Helps Toyota Maintain Just-in-Time Production." *Industrial Engineering*, May, pp. 29–46.

Sugimori, Y., K. Kusunoki, F. Cho, and S. Uchikawa. 1979. "Toyota Production System and Kanban System — Materialization of Just-in-Time and Respect-for-Human System." Paper presented at Fourth International Conference on Productivity Research, Tokyo.

12

Viewing Kanban as an (s,Q) System: Developing New Insights into a Japanese Method of Production and Inventory Control

STEVEN A. MELNYK *and* PHILLIP L. CARTER

INTRODUCTION

The success of Japanese firms in recent years has become a perplexing problem for many American business people and production managers. To the American production manager, the success reported by Japanese manufacturing operations, combined with the poor performance reported by some U.S. manufacturing firms, has led to a close examination of Japanese manufacturing practices and procedures. These examinations have attempted to identify new procedures developed by the Japanese that are applicable to the U.S. environment. They have also attempted to identify the reasons behind the strong performance of the Japanese manufacturing industry.

One system that has received much recent attention is the Kanban method of production and inventory control, as developed and practiced at

Toyota Motor Company. Since its formal introduction to the American audience (Sugimori et al. 1977), Kanban has been the subject of both published articles (such as Monden 1981b) and conferences (for example, the
Detroit American Production and Inventory Control Society (APICS) Conference, 1980; Midwest American Institute for Decision Sciences (AIDS),
1981). Interest in Kanban has been heightened, in part, by Toyota's
acknowledgment that Kanban is a crucial element in the company's efforts
to remain competitive by eliminating waste (in the form of excess inventory, surplus equipment, and unnecessary work), by controlling costs, and
by improving productivity.

Much of this recent attention dealing with Kanban has focused upon
the mechanics of Kanban. This is a natural orientation, reflecting both a
lack of familiarity with Kanban and a resulting desire to understand its
method of operations. A close examination of Kanban uncovers an important observation: despite its Oriental origins, Kanban uses a method of control familiar to most students of production and inventory control. In
its basic form, Kanban is a modified version of the traditional Order
Point/Order Quantity, or (s,Q), system.

Once Kanban is viewed as an (s,Q) system, its method of operation
can be more easily understood. For example, Kanban equivalents of the
traditional (s,Q) reorder point and order quantity can be identified. Furthermore, this view of Kanban enables the manager to anticipate Kanban's
potential limitations. Finally, if one views Kanban as an (s,Q) system, the
real contribution of Japanese production management to the practice of inventory control can be identified.

In the past, the record of U.S. companies using (s,Q)-based systems
has not been encouraging. These systems have been held accountable for
such problems as high inventory levels (especially at the component level)
and low service levels. The poor performance of (s,Q) systems has been a
significant factor behind the development and growth of alternative
systems of production and inventory control, such as material requirements planning (MRP). In contrast, Kanban's performance has been very
encouraging. One reason for its success is the approach taken by Japanese
management toward the manufacturing environment and production and
inventory control. In U.S. industry, there is a tendency to view the manufacturing environment as a constraint. As a result, the control systems
used are adjusted to fit the specific environment. The use of Kanban indicates that Japanese management views the manufacturing environment
as variable. The environment is adjusted to fit the requirements of the
specific control system being used.

It is the primary intent of this chapter to develop and to expand upon
the concept of Kanban as an (s,Q) system. In developing this view of Kan-

ban, the chapter will begin by describing the manufacturing setting in which Kanban is found. Next, the mechanics of Kanban will be described. This description will then be used to provide a basis for distinguishing those practices and procedures that identify Kanban as an (s,Q) type of system. Finally, the (s,Q) view of Kanban will be used to identify the reasons for the success of Kanban.

REPETITIVE MANUFACTURING— THE SETTING FOR KANBAN DESCRIBED

Toyota is concerned with the control of production and inventory within a specific manufacturing environment—that of repetitive manufacturing. Repetitive manufacturing involves the high-volume fabrication, machining, testing, and assembly of discrete products. Repetitive manufacturing is concerned with standard items. That is, the products are either made of a standard design (as with box wrenches and spark plugs) or assembled to order from standard options (as with automobiles). Production within this setting is characterized by three important factors:

1. Capacity is dedicated and tooling is likely to be specialized for building a specific type of product.
2. Routings are fixed. Units flow through work centers arranged in the same sequence in which operations must be performed. Balancing production rates among work centers becomes important and is often a consideration in equipment design.
3. Processing times at each work center are short and queues are small. Work-in-process inventory is relatively low (Hall 1981).

A well-designed repetitive manufacturing system should generate an uninterrupted flow of materials from receiving, through all operations, to the final stage, shipping.

Repetitive manufacturing systems are unlike either process industries or job shops. In contrast to the process industry (which is concerned with fluids, powders, and processes involving chemical actions), repetitive manufacturing deals with discrete units of products. Furthermore, job shops are differentiated by their lower volumes, flexible machines, and varied routings.

As a result of these differences, the production and inventory control techniques used in repetitive manufacturing typically differ from those found in job shops and process industries. Two key practices common to many repetitive manufacturing firms are:

1. Daily run schedules (for example, 200 units per day) are used to plan and control production. In contrast, job shops typically use work or shop orders.

2. A minimum of paperwork is used. Production counts are made at key points in the flow and inventory is relieved by exploding the bills of material against these counts (that is, backflushing). The volume of production effectively precludes the use of work orders and the recording of all inventory transactions (Hall 1981).

The preceding descriptions suggest that, without major modifications, an MRP system, with its emphasis on shop orders and inventory accuracy, would not be suitable for a repetitive manufacturing firm. This seems to be the case. Repetitive manufacturing companies that have attempted to implement MRP systems have succeeded only in burying themselves in paperwork. Nonetheless, repetitive manufacturing systems are very complex and interrelated and require a complex information system to maintain control. It is, therefore, somewhat surprising that Toyota has been able to plan and control inventories with a system such as Kanban, a system that, being essentially an (s,Q) system, is much less "powerful" and sophisticated than MRP. Before the reasons for this situation can be identified, it is necessary first to understand how Kanban works.

KANBAN – UNDERSTANDING THE MECHANICS

The term "Kanban" has confused some American managers. It has been taken to mean, at various times: a system of control cards; the "day-to-day" system of production and inventory control; and the entire production and inventory control system present at Toyota. Within this chapter, the term "Kanban" will be used to denote a system designed for the day-to-day, on-floor control of production and inventory. In controlling these activities, Kanban relies upon a series of control cards.

Kanban is only one element within the total production and inventory control system used at Toyota. One of the major goals of this total system is to satisfy daily and monthly production objectives while also eliminating "needless" waste in the form of unused capacity (both human and machine) and excess inventory (Sugimori et al. 1977). This goal embodies Toyota's view of the three primary objectives of production and inventory control, as defined by Wight (1974, p. 14): (1) customer service; (2) minimum inventory investment; and (3) maximum plant operating efficiency.

The Toyota system attempts to achieve these objectives by means of "just-in-time" production, which has been defined as "producing the necessary units in the quantity at the necessary time" (Monden 1981b, p. 38). The concept of just-in-time production is similar to the major operating objective of MRP (Orlicky 1970, p. 20). Like MRP, the total production and inventory control system at Toyota attempts to manage all manufacturing inventory so that it is always in process, with every component being immediately used upon its completion or receipt. However, the Toyota system and MRP achieve this objective by means of very different operating procedures. MRP attempts explicitly to coordinate production by extensive use of bills of materials, lead-time estimates, inventory records, and the master production schedule (MPS). The result is the creation and maintenance of a credible time-phased set of component net requirements. In contrast, the system at Toyota relies upon the Kanban system.

In controlling these functions on the floor, Kanban uses a series of control cards. In general, these cards are used to "act as an information system to harmoniously control the productive quantities in every process" (Monden 1981b, p. 42). Specifically, these cards are used to regulate such activities as the withdrawal of component inventory, the initiation of replenishment orders, and the withdrawal of needed raw material in advance of the issuance of a component replenishment order. Furthermore, these cards link the parent and component production processes together. Within Kanban, there are two specific control cards that play a very important role.

The first type of control card is the conveyance (Sugimori et al. 1977) or withdrawal (Monden 1981b) Kanban. The major task of the conveyance card is to generate component demand by authorizing moves from component inventory to the parent assembly or fabrication area. In authorizing these moves, the conveyance card also indicates the type and quantity of inventory to be withdrawn.

The second major type of control card is the production (Sugimori et al. 1977) or production-ordering (Monden 1981b) Kanban. In contrast to the conveyance card, the production card controls the supply of component parts. Specifically, it authorizes a replenishment order to be released to the component work centers. It also identifies the type of component and the amount to be produced.

The replenishment quantity found on the production card has several important characteristics. First, it is set, by management, at a predetermined quantity. Second, this fixed replenishment quantity is small by U.S. production standards. It is frequently no more than a single component (in the case of an expensive component) or a container of components.

The Kanban production and inventory control system is extremely simple to use. The conveyance card links the higher-level (that is, parent) process to the component inventory. At the parent stage, a conveyance card is released whenever components are withdrawn from inventory. The conveyance card is than attached to a container of components at the component work center and serves as an authorization to move the container to the parent work center.

The operation of Kanban is diagramed in Figure 12.1. Production cards are released when the components authorized by the conveyance cards are withdrawn. The production cards are taken off these removed

FIGURE 12.1   Operation of Kanban

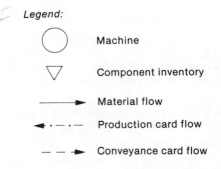

Legend:

◯   Machine

▽   Component inventory

——▶   Material flow

◀·—·—   Production card flow

— —▶   Conveyance card flow

Source: Compiled by the author.

containers and deposited at the component work center area. When picked up by operators from the component work center, these cards become the dispatching information for this department. The component work center is responsible for replenishing the withdrawn inventory as soon as possible. The priority of orders to be completed at the work center is determined by the order in which the production cards are received — that is, first come, first served (FCFS) (Sugimori et al. 1977, pp. 560–62).

Toyota's experience with Kanban has been extremely successful. The operation of the Kanban system has been characterized by low work-in-process inventory, high inventory turns, and extremely high service levels. Furthermore, under Kanban, there is an almost continuous flow of cards and component inventory between the higher and component work centers. This continuity of flow is due, in part, to the small order quantities used.

From this description, it is evident that Kanban is a reactive system. This reactive characteristic, when combined with predetermined reorder points and fixed order quantities, leads to the primary thrust of this chapter: Kanban and the traditional (s,Q) system function almost identically. A brief review of the (s,Q) system before the discussion of these similarities will prove useful.

THE (s,Q) SYSTEM: A REVIEW

The (s,Q) or Order Point/Order Quantity system is a well-known system of inventory control. Under various alternative titles — such as the Q-system (Starr and Miller 1962) and the (Q,r) system (Hadley and Whitin 1963) — this system and its operating procedures have been repeatedly described in numerous textbooks and articles. It has also been one of the more widely used inventory control systems found in actual industrial use (Davis 1975).

Initially designed for use within single-stage/single-product settings, the (s,Q) system embodies a reactive, operationally simple method of inventory control. That is, the (s,Q) system does not attempt to anticipate future changes in demand. This system is based upon the use of a predetermined reorder point (s), a fixed replenishment order quantity (Q), and continuous review of the net inventory position (inventory on order plus inventory in stock).

Whenever item demand and the subsequent withdrawal of inventory occur, the net inventory position is checked to determine if s has been reached. Once s is reached, a replenishment order for a predetermined, fixed order quantity (Q) is released. Frequently, this replenishment quantity is based upon an economic order quantity (EOQ). The production process producing the item is then responsible for replacing the inventory within the standard lead time.

The (s,Q) system generally has not performed well within most U.S. manufacturing settings. This system has been held responsible for a wide range of problems, including late deliveries, excessive inventory (especially at the component levels), and unsatisfactory productivity. The poor performance of the (s,Q) system can be traced to the operating assumptions made by it and the costs imposed when deviations from these assumptions occur.

The following are some of the key assumptions underlying the (s,Q) system:

1. The average demand rate changes very little with time.
2. Actual demand is probabilistically distributed around the average demand.
3. A replenishment order of size Q is placed when the inventory position exactly reaches the reorder point, s.
4. Replenishment time is constant, or, if not, orders are received in the same order as they are placed.
5. The average level of back orders is negligibly small when compared with the average level of on-hand stock.
6. Demand forecast errors are normally distributed about the average demand (Peterson and Silver 1979, pp. 256–57).

The performance of an (s,Q) system is graphically summarized in Figure 12.2.

As numerous authors have pointed out (Eilon 1964; Orlicky 1970; 1975; Plossl and Wight 1970; Wight 1974), very few manufacturing environments satisfy these assumptions. To use an (s,Q) system in an environment that does not meet the above assumptions, organizations have typically added extra safety stock (that is, stock more than that needed to buffer against lead time and demand uncertainty). This excess stock adds greatly to the inventory carrying cost, but only marginally improves service levels.

As a result, the (s,Q) system has been found to be an extremely expensive and unsatisfactory system to use under conditions of: high desired service levels; highly variable, lumpy, and difficult-to-predict demand; long replenishment lead times; large replenishment quantities (indicating relatively high set-up costs); and high lead-time uncertainties. Such conditions are frequently encountered within U.S. manufacturing settings.

FIGURE 12.2   Performance of an (s,Q) System

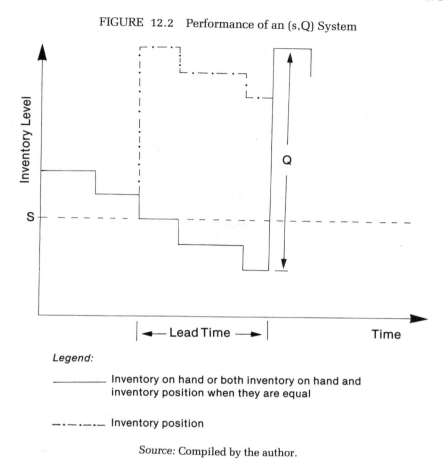

Legend:

———————— Inventory on hand or both inventory on hand and
inventory position when they are equal

—.—.—.— Inventory position

Source: Compiled by the author.

KANBAN AS AN (s,Q) SYSTEM

Kanban, like the (s,Q) system, is essentially a reactive system. Both systems
attempt to replenish inventory, not in anticipation of future orders, but as
soon as the inventory is depleted. Furthermore, both assume continuous
review, predetermined reorder points, and fixed replenishment quantities.
Kanban, as an (s,Q) system, can be best demonstrated by referring to
Figure 12.1.

Consider first the inventory of parts in front of a work center as the inventory to be managed. Assume that there are N standard containers in inventory at *a*, each with n parts, and that all of the conveyance cards are at-

tached. That is, no containers are in the process of moving from the previous work center (that is, from *b* to *a*). Initially, the inventory position at *a* is equal to Nn — that is, Nn (on hand) plus O (on order).

When a container is picked to start the processing of parts (that is, when inventory moves from *a* to *A*), the inventory position at *a* falls, momentarily, to $(N - 1)n$. As the conveyance card is removed and a reorder of Q, where Q is equal to n, is issued, the inventory position at *a* moves to $(N - 1)n$ (on hand) plus n (on order). This is equivalent to the previous inventory position of Nn. This inventory behavior is shown graphically in Figure 12.3. Thus Kanban always tries to maintain an inventory position of Nn. The replenishment lead time is determined by the move time from the feeding work center (that is, from *b* to *a*).

Because each container has the same number of parts, removing a container always drops the inventory position to the reorder point. Thus, each time a container is removed, a reorder should be, and is, placed. The

FIGURE 12.3   Inventory Behavior of Kanban

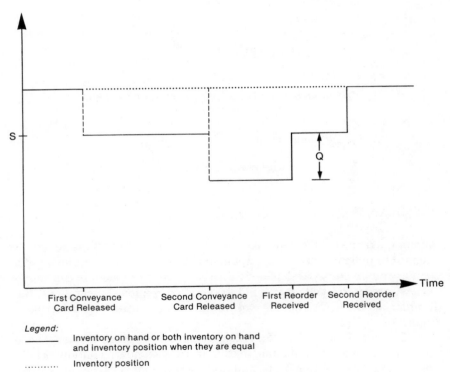

Legend:

_____ Inventory on hand or both inventory on hand and inventory position when they are equal

.... Inventory position

Source: Compiled by the author.

use of standard containers makes it unnecessary to track the inventory position continuously in Kanban.

The inventory of finished components at the preceding, or feeding, work center (that is, from B to b) can be similarly analyzed. For this inventory, the conveyance card generates a demand and the production card generates the reorder. The replenishment lead time includes processing time.

The preceding discussion demonstrating the equivalence of Kanban and an (s,Q) system raises an interesting question: why has Kanban performed so well, while the (s,Q) system has generally failed? The answer lies in the ability of Japanese management to structure a manufacturing environment conducive to Kanban's operation. This ability to manage the environment has been most pronounced in the areas of demand management and lead-time management. The major contribution of Japanese management lies in these areas.

ASSESSING THE CONTRIBUTIONS OF JAPANESE MANAGEMENT

Demand Management

Management at Toyota has been extremely successful in controlling the demand at both the end-item level (as represented by the final assembly schedule) and the component level. The result of this control has been that the component stages are presented with an environment in which (1) demand is constant, known, and relatively uniform; and (2) depletion of inventory is gradual.

End-item demand

The management of demand has focused upon the smoothing of end-item production. This smoothing of production has affected, in turn, three important elements of end-item demand: (1) within the current production month, the variability of production plans from day to day; (2) the regularity with which a demand for components occurs; and (3) the regularity with which a particular end item is scheduled for assembly.

At Toyota, a three-month production-planning horizon is used (Monden 1981a). Within this planning horizon, the first month's total production is frozen. Within this frozen time horizon, significant effort is made, when setting each day's production plan, to ensure that there is relatively little day-to-day variation in the production plans. By so arranging production, Toyota is able to gain several important advantages.

The task of planning daily production within each month is greatly simplified since it has to be done only once. Furthermore, the ability to plan for the most effective utilization of capacity is enhanced. Finally, production personnel, as a result of their familiarity with the daily production plans, can identify production problems much more quickly and remedy them.

When the daily production plan has been established, the next step in leveling production is calculating the cycle time for each model. The cycle time identifies the time interval that must be maintained between assemblies of the same-model end item if the total model production for the model is to be met. The cycle time is calculated using the following two equations (Monden 1981b, pp. 39–41):

$$\text{Necessary output per day} = \frac{\text{Necessary output per month}}{\text{Operating days per month}}$$

$$\text{Cycle time} = \frac{\text{Operating hours per day}}{\text{Necessary output per day}}$$

Finally, the order in which the various models are to be assembled is determined. When arranging the order, the intent is to ensure, for each model, that the time between assemblies of a particular model is equal to the cycle time for that model. This arrangement of model assembly can be seen better from the following discussion:

> Suppose there is a production line which is required to produce 10,000 Coronas, with 20 eight-hour operating days in a month. The 10,000 Coronas consist of 5,000 sedans, 2,500 hardtops and 2,500 wagons. Dividing these numbers by 20 operating days results in 250 sedans, 125 hardtops and 125 wagons per day. Moreover, eight-hour operation means all of these units are produced in 480 min.
>
> The cycle time will be 1 min, 55 sec for a sedan, 3 min, 50 sec each for the hardtop and wagon. In other words, the Corona line can and must convey one sedan in 1 min, 55 sec, and each unit of hardtop or wagon in 3 min, 50 sec. The sedans will be conveyed every one-unit interval, while the hardtops and wagons will be conveyed every three-unit intervals. The final output is then: sedan, hardtop, sedan, wagon, sedan, hardtop, sedan, wagon, etc. (Monden 1981b, pp. 41–42).

In practice, the preceding arrangement creates a unique demand environment. Since production is frozen over the month and daily production plans are almost identical, demand becomes known, constant, and relatively uniform in nature. Furthermore, because the order of assembly is arranged so as to meet the cycle-time requirements, the demand for components becomes continuous, with a gradual depletion of inventory. In addition, the component demand of each model occurs with a known and regular frequency. These demand conditions are conducive to the successful use of any (s,Q) system.

Component demand

Control of demand at the component level is achieved through Kanban's use of small replenishment quantities. The use of small replenishment quantities greatly reduces the degree of lumpiness present in the demand faced by components. As Orlicky (1975, pp. 25–29) and others have pointed out, most (s,Q) systems, when applied to multistage processes, generate discrete (that is, lumpy) component demand. This lumpiness can be attributed to the replenishment quantities issued. These quantities, when issued at the parent level, become part of the component's demand. If these higher-level quantities are large, demand is no longer continuous and constant. To cope with this deviation in assumptions, the (s,Q) typically increases the s. However, such lumpiness can be reduced by using, as Kanban does, small replenishment quantities.

Lead-Time Management

Management at Toyota has succeeded in implementing several measures directed at controlling replenishment lead times. These measures have reduced both mean lead time and the occurrence of lead times exceeding the production standards. The reduction of the mean replenishment lead time, for example, can be attributed to the reduction of component set-up times.

Significant effort has been expended in reducing set-up times (Sugimori et al. 1977). This effort has involved both production engineering and worker involvement (through such vehicles as small-group improvement activities [SGIA]). As a result, set-up times for such departments as pressing have fallen to three minutes from a previous level of 15 minutes (Monden 1981b, p. 42). Such reductions enhance the operation of Kanban in at least two significant ways.

First, small set-up times and costs are consistent with the very small replenishment quantities demanded by Kanban. An advantage offered by small replenishment quantities is a reduction in the total inventory carrying costs incurred by the system. In return, the number of set-ups required is greatly increased. Therefore, through a reduction of the set-up times and costs, the penalty acquired because of Kanban's use of a continuous replenishment policy is greatly reduced. (This relationship between the total costs and set-up cost can be seen better if an EOQ-based analysis is used.)

Second, the reduction in set-up times and replenishment quantities also reduces the mean replenishment lead time. Replenishment lead time is the sum of several different components — queue time, transit time, and so on (Wight 1974, p. 108). One such component is processing time, which is itself a function of the order quantity. When the order quantity is reduced (assuming that there are no offsetting changes in the other components), lead time is reduced. This decrease, in turn, allows s to be reduced.

The reduction in lead time variances can be attributed to the presence of such activities as the *Yo-i-dan* system (Monden 1981b, pp. 44–45). This system is designed to ensure that all processes required for the completion of a component are finished within the allocated cycle time. This process of monitoring is done by means of an *andon* board. For example, when each worker involved in the production of a component completes a task, the worker signals this fact by pressing a button, thus lighting a lamp on the *andon* board. If all processes are not completed (that is, lit) by the end of the established cycle time, the entire line is stopped until the remaining processes are completed. This system, by indicating to the entire system a worker's failure to meet the cycle, discourages positive lead-time variances. Without such variances, both the need for safety stock and the level of s can be reduced. When lead time is controlled, the ability of the user to forecast replenishment lead times is greatly enhanced.

It should be noted that the procedures discussed within the preceding sections are not the only practices designed to control lead times and end-item demand. The practices mentioned here have been selected because they illustrate the measures implemented by management to restructure the manufacturing environment for most-effective operation of a given system of control. This restructuring constitutes the unique contribution of Kanban.

ADVANTAGES OF VIEWING KANBAN AS AN (s,Q) SYSTEM

By viewing Kanban as an (s,Q) system, the reader can begin to anticipate the potential weaknesses present in Kanban. For example, a critical element in Kanban's operation is the ability of management to control demand and lead times. If these elements can not be controlled and Kanban becomes exposed to large fluctuations in either end-item demand or replenishment lead times, it, like most (s,Q) systems, can be expected to perform poorly. To combat these fluctuations, Kanban must rely upon either safety stocks (and higher s levels) or constant direct human intervention.

CONCLUSION

The major intent of this paper has been to show that Kanban is essentially an (s,Q) system. This view of Kanban has been developed for several reasons. It facilitates a quicker understanding of the mechanics of Kanban. It also shows that Kanban, despite its foreign origins, is not based upon principles new to most American practitioners of production and inventory control. Finally, this view of Kanban has enabled this chapter to identify the unique contribution of Kanban (and Japanese management) to operations management.

By treating the manufacturing environment as a variable and the production and inventory control system as a constant, the Japanese have significantly departed from the approach taken by most American managers. The Japanese approach does underline an important fact involving the manufacturing setting, a fact frequently forgotten by most American managers. In the short run, the manufacturing environment is frequently a constraint. In the long run, however, this setting is a variable and can be changed if management wishes to change it.

The findings of this paper coincide with the conclusions reported by several recent studies dealing with Japanese approaches to operations management (for example, Hayes 1981; Wheelwright 1981). These studies have concluded that the key to the Japanese success lies not in the development of new techniques but in the better application of existing techniques and systems. This paper has shown that Kanban embodies a better application of the traditional (s,Q) system.

REFERENCES

Davis, Edward W. 1975. "A Look at the Use of Production Inventory Techniques: Past and Present." *Production and Inventory Management* 16, no. 4:1–19.

Eilon, S. 1964. "Dragons in Pursuit of the EBQ." *Operational Research Quarterly* 15, no. 4:347–54.

Hadley, G., and T. M. Whitin. 1963. *Analysis of Inventory Systems.* Englewood Cliffs, N. J.: Prentice-Hall.

Hall, R. W. 1981. *Driving the Productivity Machine: Production Planning and Control in Japan.* Washington, D.C.: American Production and Inventory Control Society.

Hayes, R. H. 1981. "Why Japanese Factories Work." *Harvard Business Review* 59, no. 4:56–66.

Monden, Y. 1981a. "Kanban System for Just-in-Time Production." Oral presentation at Midwest American Institute for Decision Sciences Annual Meeting, April 16.

_____. 1981b. "What Makes the Toyota Production System Really Tick?" *Industrial Engineering* 13, no. 1:36–46.

Orlicky, J. A. 1975. *Material Requirements Planning*. New York, N.Y.: McGraw-Hill.

_____. 1970. "Requirements Planning Systems." *International Technical Conference: Proceedings, October 7–9, 1970*, pp. 228–39. Cincinnati: American Production and Inventory Control Society.

Peterson, R., and E. A. Silver. 1979. *Decision Systems for Inventory Management and Production Planning*. New York, N.Y.: John Wiley & Sons.

Plossl, G. W., and O. W. Wight. 1970. "Designing and Implementing a Material Requirements Planning System." *International Technical Conference: Proceedings, October 7–9, 1970*. Cincinnati: American Production and Inventory Control Society.

Starr, N. K., and D. W. Miller. 1962. *Inventory Control: Theory and Practice*. Englewood Cliffs, N.J.: Prentice-Hall.

Sugimori, Y., K. Kusunoki, F. Cho, and S. Uchikawa. 1977. "Toyota Production System and Kanban System: Materialization of Just-in-Time and Respect-for-Human System." *International Journal of Production Research* 15, no. 6:553–64.

Wheelwright, S. C. 1981. "Japan — Where Operations Really are Strategic." *Harvard Business Review* 59, no. 4:67–74.

Wight, O. W. 1974. *Production and Inventory Management in the Computer Age*. Toronto: Macmillan of Canada.

Part IV

JAPANESE MARKETING SYSTEMS

One important but often neglected aspect of Japanese success is the marketing process. Business success cannot exist without effective marketing systems. These are the subject of the next three chapters.

Allan C. Reddy and C. P. Rao contribute "The Japanese Marketing Challenge." The authors point out that Japanese firms have borrowed important marketing concepts from the Western world. By imitating and improving on Western concepts of marketing, the Japanese firms have rapidly become more competitive with U.S. businesses—from autos to high-technology equipment. This chapter explores the unique strengths of Japanese firms and whether U.S. firms can benefit from Japan's distinctive marketing approaches.

Eugene J. Kelley and Kate E. Huntington, in "Effective Marketing Systems: A Japan-United States Challenge," present a framework for effective strategic marketing planning and management applicable to both Japanese and U.S. business organizations. This framework suggests how social values and environmental concerns may be integrated with market-oriented organizational strategy and objectives. The process described is directed toward the goal of satisfying consumer-citizens and market segments, through viewing marketing as part of a total system of business and social action.

The third chapter in this section is "The Role of Japanese Sogoshosha (General Trading Companies)," by Norio Aoyama. The author discusses the unique marketing and management features of Sogoshosha that have played a vital role in Japanese economic growth and international trade.

13

The Japanese Marketing Challenge

ALLAN C. REDDY *and* C. P. RAO

The successful challenge of Japanese firms in U.S. and other foreign markets is a growing embarrassment for U.S. business firms and the U.S. government. The balance of trade between the two countries has been increasingly in favor of Japan in the past two decades. Furthermore, the major thrust of Japanese exports to the United States is in machinery (producer goods) and automobiles, whereas the U.S. exports to Japan consist mainly of agricultural products and raw materials.

During the period from January to July 1980, Japan's exports to the United States were $17.674 billion, while U.S. exports to Japan were $14.195 billion. Machine tools and machinery constituted 52 percent of the total Japanese exports to the United States and automobiles represented 23 percent, for a total in these two categories of 75 percent of all exports from Japan to the United States ("Japan-U.S. Trade" 1980, p. 4).

What factors led Japan to achieve an astounding success in world markets? How did Japan accomplish this within a short period after its devastating loss in World War II? The answers to these questions have equal significance for both rich and poor nations. The purpose of this chapter is to examine in broader terms the underlying reasons for Japanese marketing success world-wide, with particular reference to U.S. markets.

TRADITIONAL EXPLANATIONS

The traditional explanations, falling, as they do, somewhere between biases and half-truths, are unsatisfactory. The following reasons are frequently mentioned. Japan, due to its limited resources, must essentially depend on imports of foodstuffs and raw materials; to make up for the cost the Japanese had to be successful in exporting their goods. A second reason given is that Japan spends very little on its defense; therefore, the Japanese government has more time and money to concentrate on its industrial development. Third, the Japanese firms, in collaboration with their government, practice "dumping" (selling below their cost in foreign markets), thereby destroying present and potential competition. Fourth, the government in Japan is not so strict about implementing antitrust laws. This tendency helped Japanese firms and trading companies to grow as large as necessary to achieve large-scale economies. Naturally, a part of this benefit is passed on to the buyers through lower prices. Finally, the cost of labor in Japan is much lower than in the United States and other Western nations; therefore, the Japanese goods are cheaper.

As indicated earlier, most of the above explanations are far from satisfactory. For instance, Japan is not the only country in the world with limited resources. There are many nations that have limited resources but do not have the economic prosperity of Japan today. Although certain Japanese firms have been found to be "dumping" in U.S. markets, in the long run selling below the cost of production is unprofitable to anyone. Also, the allegation of lax enforcement by the Japanese government of its antimonopoly legislation is not entirely true; the Japanese government sees that competition among Japanese firms at home and abroad is well maintained. Finally, with Japan's ever increasing standard of living, the cost of labor in Japan is no longer lower. This is why Japan is relocating labor-intensive industries from the mainland to neighboring Hong Kong, Malaysia, Singapore, and Taiwan.

Japan clearly is not having a free ride in foreign markets. Something more than immediately meets the eye accounts for Japanese marketing successes. Japan accomplished its success methodically using the managerial skills of planning, direction, and control, while optimally utilizing the inherent skills and virtues of its homogeneous population. Also, the Japanese have demonstrated their mastery in the use of the "marketing concept," a widely recognized modern management concept. According to this concept, business firms should first find out the customers' wants and needs, and then satisfy them through the creation of appropriate products and services — certainly not the other way around (Kotler 1980, p. 31). How else can one explain the number-one position of Japanese firms in many lines of business, such as machine tools, automobiles, shipbuilding, steel, electronics, cameras, and motorcycles? Japanese firms have outperformed the Swiss in watchmaking, the Germans in cameras, and now the Americans in automobiles and many other products.

The American response to the Japanese challenge has been haphazard at best. Some U.S. firms discarded unproductive lines and concentrated on fewer product lines; some diversified into other businesses. None of the U.S. firms seriously challenged the aggression. The U.S. government's spasmodic response did not hamper the Japanese invasion of U.S. markets either. This is best illustrated by a few abortive efforts to develop a foreign trade policy based on frequent dollar devaluations and the establishment of import quotas for certain categories of products (autos, for example) where U.S. business is seriously threatened by foreign competition. When the dollar is devalued, however, Japan can buy raw materials more cheaply. In addition, the Japanese firms always find new methods of cutting production costs and thereby still offer their products at lower prices. Their American counterparts, feeling that they are temporarily protected by lower export prices, do not have the same pressure to produce more economically. Conversely, when quotas are set, the Japanese producers quickly move into higher-quality and higher-priced product lines (such as luxury models in autos), thus maintaining the established quotas but increasing the dollar value of their exports to the United States.

TEN REASONS FOR JAPANESE SUCCESS

In the following pages, the ten reasons that Japan has succeeded in its marketing strategy are described. The list is by no means exhaustive. It is intended to cover only the factors considered to be the most important underlying reasons for Japan's economic upsurge.

Emphasis on Long-Term Planning and Market-Share Strategy

Japanese firms emphasize long-term planning and market share even if losses are involved initially. For example, in the 1960s, when Japanese Toyotas and Datsuns were first introduced in the U.S. West Coast market, only a few of them were sold. There appeared to be no demand for them against the large and luxurious American automobiles and somewhat established European makes. The Japanese firms, without giving up hope, went on building up their market share in a slow but steady manner. When the gas crunch came in the 1970s, the wheel of fortune turned in the favor of the Japanese auto makers. Today, not only are millions of Toyotas and

Datsuns sold each year in the United States, but other Japanese makes, such as Honda, Mazda, and Subaru, have become household names. The Japanese have built a reputation for quality, service, availability, and low prices. It is the same story in regard to the dominance of other industries by Japanese firms.

In contrast, the U.S. firms have been concentrating on short-term goals and immediate profits even if dissatisfied customers are the result. A familiar question in U.S. business circles is "What is the bottom line?" A major reason for this short-term attitude of U.S. firms is that professional managers in U.S. business, to feel secure in their jobs, want to "play it safe" by showing profits to investors each and every quarter. Unfortunately, this sort of philosophy costs U.S. business a great deal. The whimsical modern consumer is not convinced to buy a particular product by "Buy American" slogans, but by quality, price, service, and other considerations, regardless of who makes the product.

"Export-Push" Factors

The "export-push" factors are defined by Monroe as "Japanese actions and tactics that have been major catalytic agents in the country's export growth" (1978, p. 192). These factors do not include events or conditions outside Japan that may have stimulated demand for Japanese products. The major export factors are:

1. building of exports through market-share objectives
2. implementing of a marketing strategy based on the "marketing concept"
3. efficient and careful planning from beginning to end in export promotion
4. competitive pricing
5. generous financing terms and conditions
6. competitive product design or redesign

The keen interest of Japanese firms and trading companies in building up exports has become an extension of ongoing competition within the domestic markets for market shares. Japanese companies compete vigorously with one another to gain advantage in foreign markets, just as they do in Japan. Once a customer has been won over, however, there is little or no effort by other Japanese firms to woo the customer away. Each company tends to respect another's turf.

How do Japanese companies build up market shares? First, thorough analyses are made of product design, performance, and other characteristics deemed essential for success in a given region or country. When the companies have done their homework and made necessary modifications or additions to existing plants and equipment, sales and promotion campaigns begin. A small segment of a market is target-tested first. Once operations have been established there, the distribution network and dealerships are expanded systematically in other locales. All the while, close contact is maintained between company representatives in the United States and their colleagues at company headquarters in Japan. In this way, necessary adjustments are made in the products produced and reports are prepared about proper regulation of the flow of exports in relation to market demand.

Among other factors, the use of pricing and liberal financing terms for dealers and customers has become a very important tool. Finally, if Japanese firms perceive a threat to their present or emerging market position, they are likely to respond by updating or redesigning their product line, thereby pulling ahead of the challenger (a Japanese or foreign firm).

"Import-Pull" Factors

An equally significant role is played by import-pull factors — considerations internal to the United States. They are:

1. changes within the U.S. competitive environment
2. changes in customer attitudes
3. policy decisions or actions by U.S. firms and government
4. positions taken by U.S. labor that have afforded foreign producers a better opportunity for gaining and holding increased market shares (Monroe 1978, p. 192)

Actually, the export-push and import-pull factors work in unison. Their combined effect can be compared to the action of the blades of a pair of scissors. Which is more important at a particular point in time can hardly be determined (Monroe 1978, p. 206).

Changes within the U.S. competitive environment have come about since World War II, when the U.S. government began Keynesian economic measures to boost aggregate demand. Maintaining full employment through increased government spending to build aggregate demand became a national objective. With more governmental intervention in the economy, free enterprise and competitive systems have found more and more regulations curbing the freedom of American firms.

Modern consumers are more knowledgeable about the various products that are available in the marketplace. Besides, they are confident that somehow they will be able to repay their debts as the government is trying to maintain a full-employment policy. In short, American consumers are most optimistic about the future and rarely fail to curtail their consumption habits, thus providing vast markets for a variety of goods.

An important import-pull factor is the ever declining quality of U.S.-made products relative to those from Japan. The poor quality and workmanship can be attributed to changing values in American life. Emphasis has shifted from hard work to easy life, and from saving to spending. Moreover, through frequent and costly strikes, American workers have won many of their demands for higher wages, fringe benefits, and job security from their employers without corresponding increases in productivity.

The short-term mentality of U.S. management policies has cut quickly into the ability of American firms to survive in the long run and to compete in national and international markets. Finally, government policies intended to stimulate new investment or encourage modernization of existing production patterns have tended to be slow in coming and in certain major industries have not come at all. On the contrary, the government has provided a growing number of welfare programs to meet certain socioeconomic objectives and also to buttress aggregate demand. This pattern of action and inaction by government has been a significant import-pull factor.

The Role of Japanese Government

The Japanese government is single-minded in its efforts to make Japanese firms competitively strong. It provides the necessary infrastructure and a favorable climate for growth, both internal and international. The government discourages imports (the formidable multilayered Japanese distribution system is another barrier to imports ["Marketing in a Maze" 1978]). Government help is provided for quick resolution of conflicts between firms and between management and unions; and government financing through direct and indirect methods is made available wherever appropriate. In a nutshell, in the years since World War II, the Japanese government has been pursuing economic growth with a passion that U.S. government has reserved for fighting communism. Japan has turned a higher proportion of its GNP and intellectual effort to basic internal development than has the United States. The Japanese government's cooperation with Japanese business firms can hardly be compared with the U.S. government's attitude toward U.S. business firms.

Efficient Bureaucracy

The efficiency of the bureaucracy in Japan contributes to the role of Japanese government. This may sound a little odd to the Western observer, to whom bureaucracy generally connotes red tape, delays in execution of policies and projects, and so forth. In Japan, the bureaucrats are carefully selected and well trained for their positions, so that they remain in them for a longer period than is usual in the West. These bureaucrats become dedicated to the purpose of building the nation.

Fortunately Japan, unlike many other countries, shows considerable continuity in its succession of political leaders. Since they rarely interfere with the main trends of governmental policies, they work in harmony with the efficient bureaucracy. On the other hand, with each presidential change in the United States, there will be considerable changes in policy and personnel in the federal government.

The supportive attitude of Japanese bureaucracy toward Japanese business firms is exemplified by the function of the Ministry of International Trade and Industry (MITI). In fact, the MITI officials are so solicitous and persistent in their efforts to develop Japanese industry that they are called *koiku mama* — overanxious mothers who hover around their children, pushing them to work hard and study well. MITI takes bold steps in restructuring Japanese industry so as to place it in areas where Japan will have an upper hand.

Cooperative Labor Unions

Labor unions have existed in Japan only since the U.S. occupation of Japan after World War II. Although Japan has its share of costly labor strikes, the important point to note is the harmonious relationship between management and unions. Generally, workers develop a strong sense of identification with their firms. That feeling is due partly to modest differences between managers and workers — workers have no rich capitalist class above them whose lifestyle is essentially different from theirs.

The cooperativeness of unions is best seen in the case of their unquestioned acceptance of modern innovations that may in fact threaten labor employment. However, a typical Japanese worker believes in innovations that help the firm to make profits. Since many Japanese firms have profit-sharing plans, the worker gets part of the benefit.

Research and Development Thrust

Japanese are known as the world's best copiers of others' inventions. Most of the present technology in Japan is borrowed from the United States or Europe. In that way, Japan gets more for its research funds, because others have already borne the major burden of developing new inventions.

Japan is turning more to basic and innovative research, contrary to its past practice of concentrating only on adaptive research. Furthermore, it is devoting more effort to areas with high potential economic pay-off. Japan now has as many people engaged in nonmilitary research as does the United States (Vogel 1979, p. 136). The U.S. government, on the other hand, spends a high proportion of research and development dollars on military, space, or basic research.

Unique Management Style

Besides an emphasis on formal management development programs (Yoshino 1968, p. 243), two noteworthy features of the Japanese management styles are their risk-taking attitudes and their reward structures. In Japanese organizations, unlike those in the United States, risk taking is a collective process. Thus, if a business venture or a management program fails, the responsibility is shared by the firm and does not fall on an individual manager. For this reason, the propensity to take risks is strong in Japanese firms. In U.S. firms, failure in job performance can mean loss of a job, but under Japanese management style, even an incompetent employee tags along because of the job permanency feature of the system.

The reward system is also different in Japan. Rewards are paid to groups and not to individuals, thereby assuring wider worker participation and support for management. More than 50 percent of wages are paid through periodic bonuses.

Another unique feature of the Japanese management is the *ringi* system of decision making (Yoshino 1968, pp. 165–66). Everyone from the bottom on up participates in decision making, with programs initiated at the bottom level. Once top management approves the plan, it goes back to the lower-level employees for implementation.

Exports as a Survival Strategy

The extremely unfavorable geographical and topographical features of Japan make it hard for the country to survive without exports. Japan is about the size of Montana but has 116 million people (half as many as the United States) packed into it, making the country the world's most densely populated. Three-fourths of Japan's population lives around its major cities, causing extreme crowding and associated problems. Only one-sixth of the land is arable. Even with its highly productive methods of farming, Japan can produce only one-third of the food it requires.

Japan is also devoid of any valuable minerals. Furthermore, the country is prone to frequent and severe earthquakes. These formidable conditions left the Japanese people no alternative but to raise themselves above hardships by becoming practical, innovative, frugal, and hardworking. Because Japan has to pay for much-needed food and raw materials, the nation has from early times developed expertise in manufacturing finished goods and exporting them. The export consciousness of the country is visible even in consumption behavior — the Japanese export premium-quality goods and consume relatively inferior-quality goods in their home market. In contrast, most high-quality U.S. products are sold in U.S. markets, while the inferior-quality or "no frills" goods are exported to other nations (Mauser 1980, p. 97).

The Japanese Character

A nation's strength depends greatly on its people. Fortunately, the Japanese are a homogeneous group. They speak one language, share many customs and traditions as part of a single culture, and have only two major religions — Shintoism and Buddhism. The high respect of Japanese for their elders and superiors and the samurai-like Japanese dedication to work are quite exemplary.

Most important of all is the undivided loyalty of the Japanese to their country. As stated in a government communication to the people:

> Loyalty to the State requires citizens to show love for it in the right way. Indifference to the existence of one's own nation, and disregard for its values, amounts to hatred of one's own nation (cited in Stone 1969, p. 189).

Other admirable characteristics of the Japanese are patience, persistence, an ability to work hard, and a saving nature — all of which have been particularly useful in building modern Japan.

Stone's words may be appropriate to sum up the extraordinary accomplishment of Japan: "The Japanese as a nation are simply determined to be outstanding in the world and have chosen to achieve this position by economic development. After the Pacific War, the military lost face and the businessman carries the flag" (1969, p. 188).

CONCLUSION

In conclusion, the complexities of the present international environment, compounded by conflicting interests at home, make it difficult for the United States to alter its course quickly and establish protective measures against foreign competition. Nevertheless, it is imperative that the United States begin making necessary policy changes immediately to allow time for fruition of these changes. The basic purpose of this chapter, therefore, is to highlight the underlying factors in the Japanese success in U.S. markets. It is hoped that analyzing the strengths of competitors will help show the obvious weaknesses within the U.S. economic system.

An important moral can be drawn from the story of Japan: the determination of the people as citizens of the country to lift their nation from poverty to prosperity is of extreme importance. This is a lesson both rich and poor nations ought to learn. If there were better understanding among government, unions, consumers, and other powerful groups in this country, a new american dream far exceeding the Japanese miracle might just be possible.

REFERENCES

"Japan-U.S. Trade Expanding During 1980." 1980. *Japan and the Southeast*, September.

Kotler, Philip. 1980. *Marketing Management: Analysis, Planning, and Control*. Englewood Cliffs, N.J.: Prentice-Hall.

"Marketing in a Maze: Japan's Complicated Distribution System Hinders Foreign Companies' Efforts to Sell Goods There." 1978. *Wall Street Journal*, May 3, p. 44.

Mauser, Ferdinand F. 1980. "The Marketing Fraternity's Short Fall." *Journal of Marketing* 44, no. 4 (Fall):97–98.

Monroe, Wilbur F. 1978. *Japanese Exports to the U.S.: Analysis of "Import-Pull" and "Export-Push" Factors*. Washington, D.C.: U.S.-Japan Trade Council.

Stone, Peter B. 1969. *Japan Surges Ahead*. New York, N.Y.: Praeger.

Vogel, Ezra F. 1979. *Japan as No. 1: Lessons for America*. Cambridge, Mass.: Harvard University Press.

Yoshino, Michael Y. 1968. *Japan's Managerial System: Tradition and Innovation*. Cambridge, Mass.: The MIT Press.

14

Effective Marketing Systems: A Japan-United States Challenge

EUGENE J. KELLEY *and* KATE E. HUNTINGTON

THE CHALLENGE: EFFECTIVE MARKETING SYSTEMS

Can the marketing systems of Japan and the United States adapt to meet the changing problems and opportunities of a turbulent, rigorously competitive international marketing environment? Can Japanese and American marketing executives and scholars meet a basic challenge of the 1980s and improve the effectiveness of marketing systems?

In recent years, business and management literature has been filled with comparative analyses of the Japanese and U.S. managerial processes. This research, emphasizing the internal operations of the organization, focuses on how decisions are made and what impact they have on productivity and profitability. With few exceptions, investigations have centered on the organizational philosophies that guide typical Japanese and U.S. firms.

One such comparison is that of William Ouchi (1981; see also Ouchi and Jaeger 1978). He describes three ideal types of work organizations. The first, Type A, is said to represent the American organization, and the second, Type J, the Japanese. The primary dimensions of each are outlined below.

Type A (American)	*Type J (Japanese)*
short-term employment	lifetime employment
individual decision making	consensual decision making
individual responsibility	collective responsibility
rapid evaluation and promotion	slow evaluation and promotion
explicit, formalized control	implicit, informal control
specialized career path	nonspecialized career path
segmented concern	holistic concern

Ouchi then goes on to describe a third ideal work organization, Type Z, as an emergent form particularly suited to the United States today.

Such a comparative approach to organizational systems is crucial to the understanding and improvement of the managerial process as it relates to productivity, participative management, work relations, employee welfare, and the quality of work life. However, marketing systems analyses go beyond the welfare of the individual firm. In this study we would like to ← I'd set aside the organizational-level disparities inherent in the operations of Japanese and U.S. business, to examine marketing's role in corporate strategy, business decisions, and society. Japan and the United States are similar in a number of ways, such as the societal environment, the function and mission of organizations, and evolving consumer-citizen patterns (see Table 14.1).

Marketing's role and function in society is to transcend organizational differences. Thus a marketing system developed to take into account society and the individual as well as the organization will be appropriate for both Japanese and American firms. The purpose of this chapter is to present ← PAPER a conceptual framework for effective decision making. The structure discussed can integrate marketing insights, information, and ideas into any organization's marketing analysis and management process.

TABLE 14.1   Similarities of Japanese and U.S. Systems

SOCIETY	ORGANIZATIONS	CONSUMER-CITIZENS
Mass consumption	Corporate goals	Rising expectations
High degree of indus- trialization	International orientation Professional manage-	Environmental concerns Quality-of-life issues
High degree of techno- logical advancement	ment concerns Marketing-systems	Evolving perceptions of need
Changing values and expectations	orientation	

Marketing's Responsibility

Marketing shares the responsibility for making decisions that affect the nature of a firm's corporate and divisional strategy and planning, products or services, targeted customers, competitive positions, and market growth. An important factor in every marketing decision is the impact on corporate and strategic business-unit profitability. Another fundamental and often overlooked aspect of marketing decisions is the impact on societal well-being as perceived by those internal and external to the organization — employees, investors, government officials, customers, and noncustomers — who may be affected by the decisions. While many businesses have largely chosen to minimize societal issues, others are progressing on this front. If a firm does not willingly face questions of societal impact, it will be forced to do so by regulators, consumers, or competitors.

Many groups are affected by marketing decisions. Each group having a stake in the outcome may evaluate the decision, problem, or consequence from a different perspective. Marketing managers develop and evaluate marketing actions according to the traditional criteria of profitability and satisfying the internal organization. Now the public's judgments must be included as well. Techniques designed to improve the quality of marketing management's strategic decision-making process through greater emphasis on social consequences are needed.

Traditional Constraints

Before discussing how the marketing decision-making process might be improved, let us consider why it is so difficult to develop and maintain effective marketing systems. Inside organizations, there is a lack of incentive for farseeing, socially responsible decision making on the part of the individual manager. Rewards for socially responsible behavior have not been built into organizations' evaluation systems. In fact, many managers believe such behavior may prove detrimental to their own success and to the profitability of their firm in the face of less-accountable competition.

Externally, marketing is surrounded by a rapidly changing environment. The marketplace, as a system of exchange, has always been central to the survival of societies. Since societal changes necessarily affect the marketplace structure, an understanding of such effects is essential for efficient and progressive marketplace systems. In both Japan and the United States, new consumer groups are emerging, in part because of changing population structures, rising education levels, and increases in female employment. As the primary needs of consumer groups are better fulfilled, perceptions of higher-level needs begin to surface. Industrialized societies such as ours, with marketing systems based on the principles of mass consumption, have succeeded in satisfying perceived needs, creating new wants, satisfying them, and so on. In the United States, this continuous process of producing more and more has been referred to as the "psychology of entitlement." Consumers expect and believe they are entitled to whatever they want, and demand satisfaction. Organizations have eagerly supplied the desired products and services, in order to compete successfully.

Unfortunately, the environment has not adjusted well to such levels of growth. World-wide we are now experiencing energy and material shortages, increasing pollution, inflation, increased government regulation, and consumerism. Evidently, society can no longer handle the present pressures of demand and the costs of supply without detrimental consequences to the well-being of individuals and the environment. Marketing systems must be redesigned to account for the externalities previously ignored and to reward behavior consistent with environmental constraints.

The discipline of marketing, as a science designed in part to improve marketplace relations, is extremely young in thought and practice. It has, however, passed through many stages. The development of the marketing concept, in the late 1950s, has had the most pronounced effect on marketing's orientation. It claimed to shift the focus from the product and the needs of the seller to the needs and wants of the buyer (Bagozzi 1976). Yet the marketing concept was developed to serve the consumer during a certain period and under certain economic, political, environmental, and social conditions. Although it appeared to be so successful in past decades, it is, in its present form, unable to cope with and provide for societies in today's environment.

The current marketing emphases in the United States are still closely tied to the marketing concept and are focused on short-term results. With few notable exceptions, marketers are concerned with micro issues — the theories, processes, and tactics of the individual firm. Marketing is perceived as a management discipline (Elgin and Mitchell 1977). Although more thought is being given to the consumer, marketing remains a seller science, a tool used by firms to help them accomplish their objectives.

Since most business enterprises evaluate success on the basis of short-term performance, marketing has also taken on a short-term orientation, particularly in the United States. It focuses on how the seller can sell better today. It has a specific problem-solving orientation concerned with routine occurrences in the marketing process and day-to-day, quarter-to-quarter operations.

Much marketing action is of a "how-to" nature. Marketers are concerned with how to improve an existing product, how to make a more eye-appealing package, and how to create a more persuasive advertisement.

Marketing has become individualistic by adhering to the doctrine that its role in society is to satisfy the wants and needs of the consumer. Each firm attempts to satisfy each consumer in the short term. More and more products are developed with little differentiation other than packaging and promotion.

Marketers must now look at the long-term implications of their theory and practice. They need to study the aggregate nature of entire marketing systems, and how each subsystem fits within this aggregate. Marketing can no longer ignore the societal impacts of its actions. Rather than concentrating only on how to do something better, marketing must also consider what to do and why to do it. Marketers must consider questions such as these: Who is affected by our decisions and in what ways? What products serve the well-being of all consumers, users and nonusers alike? Are there both economic and social needs for a proposed product or service? What information will allow consumers to make better decisions? What technological processes and products will be least damaging to the environment?

In essence, marketing has followed a reductionist path in its theory, methodology, and practice. It has minimized its contacts with management, other areas of business enterprise, and society. It has refused to share responsibility for the social externalities that are the consequences of these necessary interactions. Marketing has "adopted a value-free technological orientation that focuses on direct output-input relations ignoring side-effects, diseconomies, etc." (Fisk, Arndt, and Grønhaug 1978).

THE TASK: INCORPORATING SOCIAL VALUES AND ENVIRONMENTAL CONCERNS

A holistic approach to marketing is now required. Marketing must be examined not as a lone entity, but as one of the interacting subsystems of an organization whose actions influence and are influenced by society. It has been said that "good science alters reality in a predetermined direction, and then we are back at our starting point" (Fisk, Arndt, and Grønhaug 1978). If we assume marketing is a developing science, we must realize that marketing does and will alter reality, and we must be willing to take responsibility for such change.

Macromarketing Issues

In order for marketing to advance in a more responsible direction, greater emphasis must be placed on macromarketing issues. This is not to say that micromarketing activities should be ignored. These activities exist but should receive attention from the proper perspective, as interacting elements within larger macromarketing systems. In a macromarketing state-of-the-art review, macromarketing is referred to as "studies of large patterns of exchange relationships . . . [which] yield both 'private' and 'public' benefit and cost consequences, triggering a corresponding set of reward or penalty sanctions imposed by people experiencing the consequences of marketing activities" (Fisk and White 1981, p. 173). Macromarketing considers the consequences for all groups having a stake in an outcome, rather than for the immediately identifiable marketing constituencies only.

The scope of macromarketing has not been clearly defined. Specific conceptualizations vary, from "networks of relationships and societal patterns of marketing systems" (Heede 1978), to "intranational and international exchange systems and social benefits and costs that result from exchange" (Kelley and Huntington 1981b); but one fundamental concern of macromarketing is the quality of life. Quality-of-life concerns are now a basic force for change in world society.

Consumer quality-of-life concerns, aspirations, and expectations, in conjunction with changing individual and social values, will necessarily alter the practice and teaching of marketing in the decades to come. If marketing's role is to serve society and individuals through the creation and delivery of a standard of living, which now extends to the quality of life, the consideration of quality-of-life issues is essential for the progress of marketing as a discipline (Kelley and Huntington 1981a).

Marketing must address the issues that consumers perceive to be the most important to their well-being. It can no longer see the consumer as a means to an end, namely profit. Consumers' concern for themselves is much greater than their concern for any company's product or profitability. While marketing behavior affects consumers, consumers are in turn making decisions that have unquestionable impacts on marketing. Consequently, marketing must research how beliefs and values are formed, the process by which they change, the speed of this evolution, and how these social values affect consumer decision making.

Difficulties arise during investigation of social values, particularly with respect to macromarketing decision making. Values must be elicited from more than one individual and then aggregated into a preference structure (Kotler 1980). Rethans (1981) notes, however, that the aggregation of individual values is one form of the central problem of social choice and has been treated in the social choice literature. Marketers may gain useful insights from this research. While adopting a macromarketing perspective is a serious challenge, it is the route to strategic marketing planning for more-productive and more-progressive marketing in the future. It is in essence the beginning of a value-based marketing system, which, if supported by larger organizations whose corporate values coincide with the values of society, will lead to more-effective decisions and less undesirable results.

A FRAMEWORK FOR EFFECTIVE STRATEGIC MARKETING DECISIONS

How can marketing systematically analyze changes in social values and other environmental areas and incorporate them into its strategic process? Looking at the wider environment in which corporate and marketing decisions are made is the starting point for more-efficient and more-effective analysis, planning, and control. A conceptual framework for examining environmental changes and quality-of-life concerns is thus proposed.

Change will be explored at three levels: universal environmental forces, organizational change systems, and consumer-citizen quality-of-life ideals. Each level is analyzed in terms of technological, social, economic, and political change. Although each level is appraised separately here, it must be emphasized that this examination is a holistic process (Kelley and Huntington 1981a). Societal forces at large, their impact on the function of

FIGURE 14.1   Environmental Changes and Quality of Life

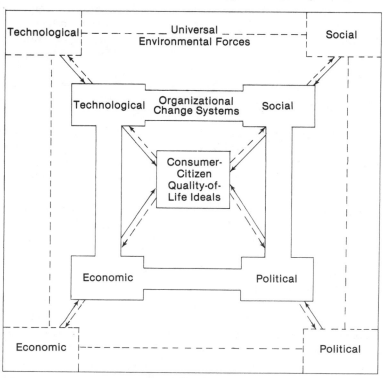

Source: Compiled by the author.

organizations, and their impact on individual consumers are observed. This process also moves in the opposite direction, from consumer to organization to environment. The organization must be responsive to both environmental and consumer-citizen changes.

A brief overview of each level of analysis is presented, highlighting important elements of technological, economic, political, and social change.

Universal Environmental Forces

Universal environmental forces affect and are affected by society in general. These forces may interact differently with each industry and organization. Each manager must examine the consequences of such interplays within the realm of his or her own industry or competitive environment to determine the implications for a particular organization and its competitors.

Technological changes include material and energy shortages, which may require a slower, more selective growth. The advancement of global information systems increases the amount of international technological transfer possible. How do the world-wide shortages affect industry growth rates? Which industries are taking advantage of technological transfer systems for greater productivity with more cost efficiency and less waste?

Perceptions of social entitlement increase support for cultural, sexual, and racial equality. Quality-of-life concerns, improved universal education, and consumerism are on the rise. How do industries adapt to such pressures?

Economic concerns such as world-wide inflation and stagnation necessitate international interdependence for progressive development. Growth with equity and a global money fund may be fundamental to this advancement. Which industries will rely most heavily on one another in such a turbulent economy?

Global security may require more regulation for environmental protection, arms control, and international governance. How will such increased controls affect industry operations?

Organizational Change Systems

Once universal environmental force interactions at the industry level are explored, the focus narrows to how these forces may affect particular strategic areas of an organization. One objective is to evaluate the systems within the organization that foster systematic observation of change, allow for adaptability to change, and anticipate and influence change. These sys-

FIGURE 14.2   Universal Environmental Forces

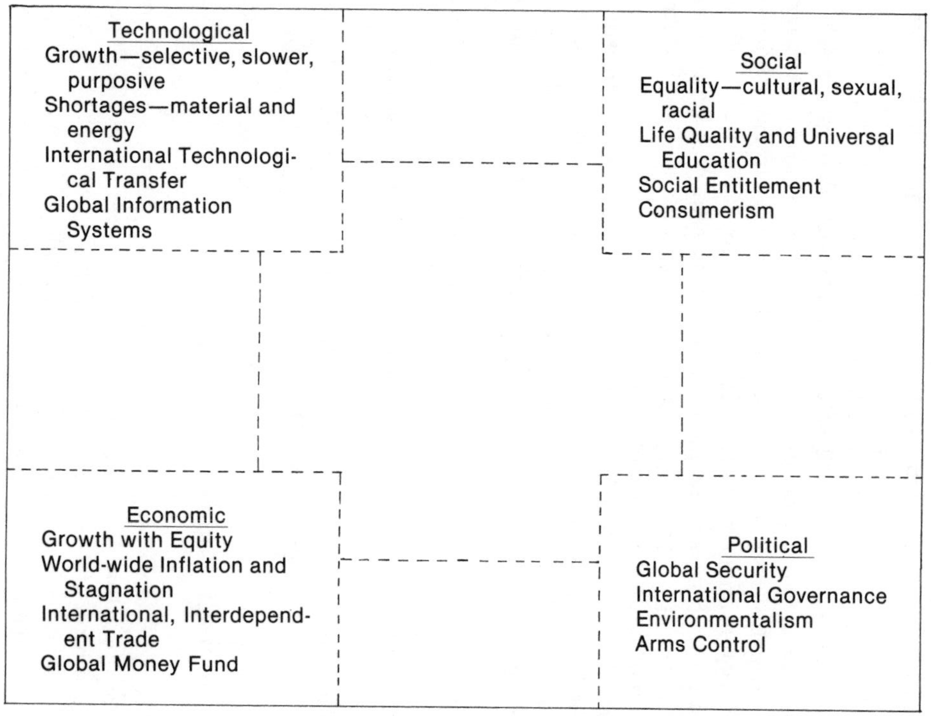

Technological
Growth—selective, slower,
    purposive
Shortages—material and
    energy
International Technologi-
    cal Transfer
Global Information
    Systems

Social
Equality—cultural, sexual,
    racial
Life Quality and Universal
    Education
Social Entitlement
Consumerism

Economic
Growth with Equity
World-wide Inflation and
    Stagnation
International, Interdepend-
    ent Trade
Global Money Fund

Political
Global Security
International Governance
Environmentalism
Arms Control

Source: Compiled by the author.

tems of change operate at corporate, strategic business-unit or divisional, functional, and individual levels. One must identify the strengths and weaknesses of an organization in each of these areas.

A system designed for continuous technological assessment may be employed to insure appropriate technology for more-selective growth. Systematic resource monitoring, the use of renewable resources and recyclable products and materials, and pollution reduction can become elements of an organization's strategic plan. Highly specialized management information systems and telecommunications can promote international technology and resource sharing for increased productivity.

Social responsibility willingly accepted rather than grudgingly adopted is necessary. Quality-of-life indicators may be constructed for organizational evaluation and development. Quality of work life may be enhanced through better understanding of employee needs. Productivity may be increased through greater employee participation in decision making, and through continuous training programs, career advancement information, and management development sessions.

Multinational growth for economic recovery appears more necessary each day. Success is contingent, however, on the behavior of both developed and less developed countries. Decentralization and shared control may be to the advantage of all. Entrepreneurial spirit and creativity will be required to adapt to a turbulent economy.

Conflicts abound in the political sector. The international barriers to trade must be removed to insure purposive growth and global security. Government and consumer groups are pushing for increased regulation for environmental protection. Business espouses self-regulation and less interference from government. Justifiable solutions based on competence, confidence, and respect warrant closer government-business associations.

Consumer-Citizen Quality-of-Life Ideals

Organizations have been analyzed to discover systems in which there are inherent opportunities to adapt to and influence change. The focus now rests, as it ultimately should, on the individual consumer and market segment. It must be emphasized, however, that all individuals and all groups having a stake in an outcome must receive attention from the marketing organization.

For example, the marketing organization must determine what factors most influence the consumer's health and safety values. Technologies that support the health and safety of consumer-citizens should be developed, promoted, and employed.

FIGURE 14.3 Organizational Change Systems

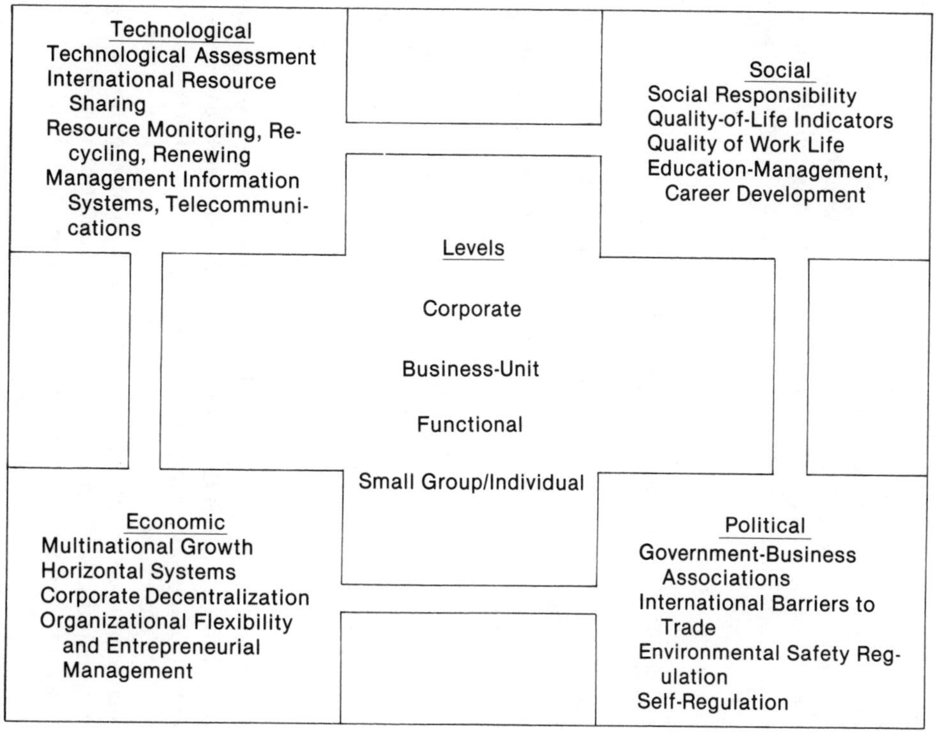

Technological
Technological Assessment
International Resource
  Sharing
Resource Monitoring, Re-
  cycling, Renewing
Management Information
Systems, Telecommuni-
cations

Social
Social Responsibility
Quality-of-Life Indicators
Quality of Work Life
Education-Management,
  Career Development

Levels
Corporate
Business-Unit
Functional
Small Group/Individual

Economic
Multinational Growth
Horizontal Systems
Corporate Decentralization
Organizational Flexibility
  and Entrepreneurial
  Management

Political
Government-Business
  Associations
International Barriers to
  Trade
Environmental Safety Reg-
  ulation
Self-Regulation

Source: Compiled by the author.

203

The organization should place emphasis on learning, leisure, and the family. Development of business organizations has long been thought of as a precursor of the breakdown experienced by these social organizations. Through increased effort and interest in these areas, the organization can become a natural domain for, rather than a detriment to, social development.

Consumers increasingly feel a need for personal contribution and self-respect. Instead of nullifying these desires, organizations can encourage and reward them, for a more productive, resourceful society.

Perceptions of personal comfort and security depend in part on the sense of stability among and within nations. Political harmony and equal and justified opportunity to pursue comfort through the acquisition of high-quality products and services are social goals based on individual rights and freedom.

The Integration Process

How might this integrative structure complement an organization's management process?

Kotler (1980) suggests the following representation of the strategic management process:

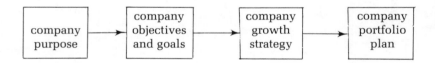

Systematic analysis of the wider environment can provide useful information at each stage of this process. Corporate renewal can be one function of such analysis, keeping the company's purpose, objectives, and goals continuously clear and consistent with the conditions of the environment. A company must systematically identify growth opportunities and plan its business portfolio. New growth strategies and investment possibilities may appear with the additional information on the environment and values of society.

How can this analysis be beneficial to the marketing manager? In order for a company to develop and maintain a well-balanced portfolio, marketing must continue to generate and develop new ideas. This requires an effective strategic marketing process. Kotler (1980) suggests visualizing the process as follows:

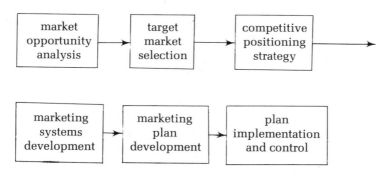

Marketing has the responsibility of assessing the sales potential of the attractive opportunities relevant to a company's purpose. Marketing must then determine the most profitable approach to market entry, since each market has many more consumer groups than any one firm can serve. Systematically taking into account the forces affecting industry, organization, and individuals will lead to innovation based on selective excellence. Appropriate segmentation is the key to such excellence. In the past, segmentation has been based on variables such as demographics — age, sex, income, occupation, education, religion, and social class; psychographics — life style and personality; and behavior — purchase occasion, benefits sought, user status, and usage rates (Kotler 1980). These are all necessary and useful bases for segmenting markets. However, they may be complemented by another segmentation variable, which is based on an understanding of consumer-citizen values and societal well-being.

The quality of life of an individual is a holistic combination and interaction of personal, social, economic, environmental, and international relationships that affect individual well-being and perceptions of well-being (Kelley and Huntington 1981a). Opportunities abound for serving forerunner consumer groups who are especially sensitive to environmental

FIGURE 14.4   Consumer-Citizen Quality-of-Life Ideals

Technological Health and Safety	Social Learning, Leisure, Family
Economic Personal Contribution, Self-Respect	Political Personal Comfort and Security

Source: Compiled by the author.

change and concerned with how such change will affect the quality of their lives. In the years ahead, millions of consumers may move beyond materialistic values and choose an outwardly more simple and inwardly richer life style, an alternative that has been described as "voluntary simplicity" (Nickels and Hill 1977). Avraham Shama (1981) has said that the consumer movement for voluntary simplicity is growing rapidly, and there are increasing opportunities to satisfy individuals who prefer fewer, smaller, more functional, high-quality products and smaller, personalized stores, innovative outlets, and cooperative buying. To allow particular organizations to identify these opportunities, market segments may be defined in terms of consumer-citizen demographics, psychographics, behavior, and quality-of-life ideals. Quality-of-life ideals may be evaluated with respect to the interactions and consequences of technological, social, economic, and political change.

On the basis of this segmentation, evolving threats and opportunities may be revealed, and marketing strategies guiding expenditure levels, marketing-mix elements, and resource allocation can then be developed for proper positioning for a competitive advantage.

To illustrate this opportunity assessment process, let us consider the food and agriculture industries. The factors affecting these industries do not give great cause for optimism. It is estimated that food production will be 90 percent higher in 2000 than in 1970. There is serious deterioration of agricultural soils world-wide due to erosion, loss of organic matter, and desertification. Within the next three decades, 20 percent of all plant and animal species will become extinct (*Global 2000 Report* 1980).

Rising population, food shortages, and soaring costs have resulted in a demand for improved technology to increase food yield world-wide while minimizing the detrimental effects on the environment from fertilizers, pesticides, and herbicides. Organizations should assess their present technologies, explore international resource sharing, and improve recycling capabilities.

These environmental forces are also influencing consumer food-consumption habits. Consumers are eating less meat, spending less on nonessential food items, and experimenting with alternatives to traditional food-consumption habits. There is a rising consumer segment especially concerned with health and nutrition. There are ample opportunities to serve this health-conscious market by producing less expensive, more nutritious foods with more natural ingredients and fewer preservatives and chemical additives. There is also greater demand for more "do-it-yourself" devices such as food processors, bean-sprouting jars, and juicers. Many Americans interested in healthier living are adopting Japanese traditions, enjoying soybean-based products such as tofu and miso and seawood products such as kelp.

In this example, it is apparent that organizations involved with food products may be able to segment further their present markets for new opportunities by basing segmentation partly on social values and concerns. Understanding the social values of this emerging segment will have implications for marketing strategy. It is likely that these consumers prefer informative advertising and functional packaging, and that they can be reached through smaller retail outlets. In summary, service in this market has great potential for both corporate profitability and world-wide well-being.

THE REWARDS: INCREASED PROFITABILITY AND SOCIETAL WELL-BEING

This chapter has explored how the changing environment affects industries, organizations, and individuals, and how organizations that systematically monitor such change can benefit from the emerging opportunities. Within this design we examined how effective marketing systems are essential to an organizational management process for change.

The science of marketing is in a continuous process of evolution. It has passed through phases emphasizing production, distribution, sales, management, and social concerns. It has borrowed theories, methodologies, and applications from the behavioral sciences, economics, and mathematics. It has been criticized by many as lacking foundation and direction. Yet the evolution of marketing dynamics has been progressive rather than unstable; each stage built on the strengths and weaknesses of past stages.

One result of this continuous growth has been the development of many marketing definitions. Each in turn has outgrown its primary usefulness. One of the most contemporary conceptualizations of marketing is Kotler's (1980) societal marketing concept:

> A management orientation which holds that the key task of the organization is to determine the needs and wants of target markets and to adapt the organization to delivering the desired satisfactions more effectively and efficiently than its competitors in a way that preserves or enhances the consumers' and society's well-being. (p. 35)

Another conceptualization is Mulvihill's (1980) new definition of marketing:

> Marketing is a total system of business activities that plan, price, promote, and distribute want-satisfying products and services to consumers so that they may have a quality of life which is culturally and aesthetically rewarding with the least possible environmental cost. (p.7)

While both definitions cover extremely important and timely issues, we do not believe there can be only one descriptive definition of marketing. One may be so narrow as to inhibit progress, another so broad as to prohibit guidance. We also do not believe that any one definition of marketing can remain viable for a long time. Thus, rather than defining what marketing is, we will state what we believe marketing can become as it develops for a progressive and relevant future. The tasks of marketing in a complex interdependent global society are to:

1. monitor and adapt on a continuous basis to the changing values of individual consumers, market segments, groups with special concerns, and social groups
2. present consumer-citizen concerns to the total organizational unit so that organizational purposes, objectives, strategies, and plans are formulated and revised with market opportunity in focus
3. satisfy consumption wants through creativity and innovation, as effectively and efficiently as feasible within environmental constraints and actual and potential organizational capability
4. anticipate possible and probable environmental and value changes, acting responsibly to influence such change for the well-being of society

If marketing can continuously anticipate and align itself with environmental forces and societal values, performing to satisfy consumer-citizens effectively and efficiently within dynamic environmental and organizational systems, then it may not only function as a system of exchange but also become a system of responsible change. Marketing can foster progressive thinking for purposive growth within the organization. By capitalizing on new opportunities, marketing can enhance the quality of life world-wide.

Japanese and American marketers must not only search for what they can learn from one another, but explore how they can move into the future together and how they can collectively work for better service to Japanese, American, and world societies.

REFERENCES

Arndt, J. 1978. "The Marketing Thinking of Tomorrow." In *Future Directions For Marketing*, ed. G. Fisk, J. Arndt, and K. Grønhaug. Cambridge, Mass.: Marketing Science Institute.

Arndt, J., and T. Helgesen. 1981. "Marketing and Productivity: Conceptual and Measurement Issues." In *The Changing Marketing Environment: New Theories and Applications*, ed. K. Bernharde, I. Dolich, M. Etzel, W. Kehoe, T. Kinnear, W. Perreault, Jr., and K. Roering. Chicago: American Marketing Association.

Bagozzi, R. P. 1976. "Science, Politics, and the Social Construction of Marketing." In *Proceedings*, ed. K. L. Bernhardt. Chicago: American Marketing Association.

Elgin, D., and A. Mitchell. 1977. "Voluntary Simplicity: Lifestyle of the Future?" *The Futurist* (August):200.

Fisk, G., J. Arndt, and K. Grønhaug. 1978. *Future Directions for Marketing*. Cambridge, Mass.: Marketing Science Institute.

Fisk, G., and P. D. White. 1981. "Macromarketing: A State of the Art Review." In *Review of Marketing 1981*, ed. B. M. Enis and K. J. Roering. Chicago: American Marketing Association.

The Global 2000 Report to the President: Entering the Twenty-First Century. 1980. Vol. 2. Washington, D.C.: Government Printing Office.

Heede, S. 1978. "Reductionist versus Holistic Definition of Social Responsibility for Marketing." In *Future Directions for Marketing*, ed. G. Fisk, J. Arndt, and K. Grønhaug. Cambridge, Mass.: Marketing Science Institute.

Kelley, E. J., and K. E. Huntington. 1981a. "Futurize Marketing Courses To Prepare Today's Students for Tomorrow's Careers." *Marketing News*, July 24, p. 1.

————. 1981b. "Marketing and Expansion of Quality of Life." In *Marketing and the Future*, ed. D. F. Mulvihill. Chicago: American Marketing Association.

Kotler, P. 1980. *Marketing Management: Analysis, Planning and Control*. Englewood Cliffs, N.J.: Prentice-Hall.

Mulvihill, D. F. 1980. "Environmental Aspects of Marketing in the Future." In *Marketing and the Future*, ed. D. F. Mulvihill. Chicago: American Marketing Association.

Nickels, W. G., and R. Hill. 1977. "Is Marketing What the Textbooks Say? — A New Definition of Macro and Micro Marketing." In *Proceedings of the 1977 Macromarketing Conference*, ed. P. D. White and C. S. Slater. Boulder, Co.: University of Colorado.

Ouchi, W. G. 1981. *Theory Z: How American Business Can Meet the Japanese Challenge*. Reading, Mass.: Addison-Wesley.

Ouchi, W. G., and A. M. Jaeger. 1978. "Type Z Organization: Stability in the Midst of Mobility." *Academy of Management Review* 3:305.

Rethans, A. J. 1981. "Generic Problems Confronting Macromarketing Decision-making." Unpublished working paper, The Pennsylvania State University.

Shama, A. 1981. "Coping with Stagflation: Voluntary Simplicity." *Journal of Marketing* 45:120.

Webster, F. E. 1981. "Top Management's Concerns about Marketing; Issues for the 1980's." *Journal of Marketing* 45:9.

15

The Role of Japanese Sogoshosha (General Trading Companies)

NORIO AOYAMA

The Sogoshosha are unique to Japan; no comparable enterprises exist in other countries. Their development can be traced to the following factors: (1) Japan's heavy reliance on raw material and fuel imports (the nation's material-importing, manufactured-goods-exporting structure); (2) the growth of industrial groups and competition among them; (3) the natural aptitude of Japanese people for the division of labor between manufacturing and trading; and (4) lifetime employment and corporate loyalty.

Now that the Japanese economy seems to be entering a mature stage, with its main strength shifting from heavy industries to knowledge-intensive, less-material-consuming, advanced-technology industries, Sogoshosha must find new opportunities by serving the interests of other nations. Will they succeed in changing the mentality of their management and employees? Will they overcome the problems arising from changing sociocultural factors?

CHARACTERISTICS OF SOGOSHOSHA

Japanese Sogoshosha, formerly referred to as general trading companies, are now often called integrated trading companies. Characterizing marks that separate Sogoshosha from the rest of trading companies in Japan are:

(1) huge amounts of sales; (2) a great variation within a Sogoshosha in commodities handled; and (3) high foreign trade ratios. Nine trading firms — Mitsubishi, Mitsui, C. Itoh, Marubeni, Sumitomo, Nissho-Iwai, Toyo Menka, Kanematsu-Gosho and Nichimen — are classified as Sogoshosha.

Mitsubishi Corporation, the largest of them, handled more than ¥13.9 trillion ($63 billion) worth of goods and services in the year ending March 1981. Even the ninth, Nichimen Company, had sales of more than ¥2.6 trillion ($12 billion). (See Table 15.1.) The total sales of the nine integrated trading companies exceeded ¥72.6 trillion ($330 billion) — equivalent to 30.2 percent of the nation's GNP.

Sogoshosha handle almost all kinds of commodities — oil, coal, ores and other natural resources, iron and steel, nonferrous metals, machinery, foods, textiles, chemicals, lumber, pulp and paper, and so on. "From instant noodles to nuclear reactors or missiles" used to be the catchword of their diversification.

TABLE 15.1   Japanese Integrated Trading Companies (as of March 1981)

COMPANY NAME	SALES (YEN)	SALES (DOLLARS)	CURRENT EARNINGS (YEN)	FOREIGN TRADE RATIO (PERCENT)	TOTAL ASSETS (YEN)	NET WORTH (YEN)	NET WORTH RATIO (PERCENT)
Mitsubishi Corporation	13,937	63.4	41.4	58	4,348	265	6.1
Mitsui and Company	12,667	57.6	35.6	56	4,231	192	4.5
C. Itoh and Company	10,705	48.7	13.2	54	2,699	87	3.2
Marubeni Corporation	10,185	46.3	17.4	62	2,657	113	4.2
Sumitomo Shoji	9,655	43.9	29.5	47	1,822	104	5.7
Nissho-Iwai Company	6,585	29.9	13.3	60	1,804	57	3.2
Toyo Menka	3,283	14.9	3.5	61	1,045	33	3.1
Kanematsu-Gosho	2,955	13.4	0.6	48	1,008	23	2.3
Nichimen Company	2,612	11.9	5.4	68	822	26	3.1

Notes: (1) Amounts are in billions of yen or dollars. (2) Dollar amounts converted at 220 yen = 1 dollar. (3) Foreign trade ratio = imports + exports + third-country transactions/sales

Source: Nikkei Kaisha Joho (Japan Economic Journal's Business Corporation Data)3 (June 1981).

They have a high ratio of foreign trade to total sales, ranging from 47 percent to 68 percent (see Table 15.1). Based on an arbitrary figure of 50 percent for exports from and imports into Japan, Sogoshosha account for over 60 percent of Japan's foreign trade, or 10 percent of the world's trade.

SOURCES OF SOGOSHOSHA'S TRADING STRENGTH

As seen above, Sogoshosha have enormous power and influence in trade. Their strength, while based on a number of factors, lies mainly in their ability to (1) gather information; (2) organize business networks and teams; and (3) arrange financing.

The ability of Sogoshosha to gather information is now almost legendary. Through subsidiaries, branches, and representative offices throughout the world, they gather all kinds of information — not only business news but also political, social, and other information. They all have world-wide telecommunication networks so that information obtained can be transmitted and used to best advantage. One Japanese integrated trading company spent ¥3.5 billion ($16 million) on telecommunications in fiscal 1978.

In recent years, Sogoshosha have shown an increasing tendency to act as organizers for enterprises of various industries, especially in overseas ventures — plant exports, direct manufacturing investments, and resources development. Now, more often than previously, they become equity participants in these ventures, thereby protecting their trading interests.

Sogoshosha borrow heavily, as can be seen from Table 15.1. The main bank of a Sogoshosha — the financial nucleus of the industrial group of which that Sogoshosha is the trading arm — extends a large line of credit to the rest of the Sogoshosha on favorable terms because the credit is essential for the growth of the group as a whole.

Massive credits enable Sogoshosha to use financing as a means to increase and strengthen their trading interests — through making loans or acquiring equities in overseas projects, or extending credits to smaller manufacturers.

THE DEVELOPMENT OF SOGOSHOSHA

A number of factors contributed to the birth and development of Sogoshosha in postwar Japan. *Economic factors* included (1) the scarcity of natural resources in Japan; (2) governmental economic policies aimed at promoting heavy and chemical industries; and (3) formation of industrial groups and competition among them. *Sociocultural factors* involved were

(1) the participation of able workers in trading companies; (2) the natural aptitude of Japanese people for the division of labor between manufacturing and trading; and (3) lifetime employment and corporate loyalty.

There is no doubt that the scarcity of natural resources in Japan was the principal cause of its economic structure, which depends on importing raw materials and exporting manufactured goods. In spite of the handicap of few natural resources, the Japanese government vigorously pursued the policy of heavy and chemical industrialization, and this gave trading companies enormous opportunities to broaden their scope of operation.

During the 1950s and 1960s, the foundation of Sogoshosha was established through a rapid increase in imports of raw materials and fuel for iron, steel, and other material-producing industries. The handling of raw materials particularly suits Sogoshosha, because it offers economies of scale, stability, and related business opportunities. The formation of industrial groups around large city banks and the keen competition among these groups also accelerated the growth of Sogoshosha.

Capable employees have been attracted to trading companies, partly because of the memory of great merchants of the past, and partly because the successful commercial education that has existed since the Meiji era has motivated students to embark on great adventures abroad. Once taken into a trading organization, Japanese people seem especially capable of adapting themselves to the role given to them — serving customers, especially those of manufacturing industries. The traditional class distinctions — warriors (now government officials) at the top, followed by farmers, manufacturers, and merchants — may have some bearing on the smooth functioning of the division of labor between manufacturing and trading.

Finally, lifetime employment and corporate loyalty were essential to the development of Sogoshosha. Long-term planning and lasting personal relationships with customers — characterizing marks of Sogoshosha — would not have been possible without these conditions.

Some of the factors mentioned above are unique to Japan, and without them business enterprises comparable with Sogoshosha are not likely to come into existence. Under different conditions, trading companies will of necessity develop differently.

THE FUTURE OF SOGOSHOSHA

After the 1960s, Japanese material-producing industries reached maturity, and assembly industries took over as the leaders of Japanese industry.

Sogoshosha, by nature, are not especially adept in marketing consumer-oriented, service-requiring durable products such as automobiles and electric appliances; nor are they in a position to play a significant part in the development of such industries as semiconductors and information processing — the most promising growth sectors for Japan.

    With the nation's economic growth slowing and its industrial structure changing, Sogoshosha have been concentrating their efforts on some selected areas. They have been giving great priority to exports of plants — an area particularly suited to Sogoshosha, with their access to source materials, technologies, and marketing outputs world-wide. Sogoshosha also are increasing overseas direct investments to integrate their operations in such areas as energy, chemicals, and foods. In addition, they are expanding third-country businesses by transferring more resources — both personnel and money — to their overseas subsidiaries.

QUESTIONS

In the future it will become increasingly important for Sogoshosha to serve the interests of other nations. They have the ability to do so, and a growing number of foreign governments and enterprises have been using their services to their advantage.

    In order for Sogoshosha to evolve into true multinationals with futures, they will have to overcome certain problems. First, Sogoshosha must succeed in changing the "home-bound" mentality of their management and employees, who feel that any overseas appointment, whether it is for three years or ten years, is temporary; they expect that they will eventually return to home offices. Second, any changes in the sociocultural factors behind the success of Sogoshosha — acceptance of status distinctions, lifetime employment, and corporate loyalty — may weaken the foundation of this very Japanese institution.

Part V

COMPARATIVE ANALYSIS OF JAPANESE AND U.S. MANAGEMENT

Although Japanese have learned, borrowed, and imitated many U.S. management approaches, there are substantial differences between Japanese and U.S. management. We believe a comparative analysis of the two management systems can provide much insight into the weaknesses and strengths of each management system. A total of 14 chapters make up this part.

Motofusa Murayama contributes "A Comparative Analysis of U.S. and Japanese Management Systems." The author analyzes a business organization not only as a separate functional entity but also as a part of the social environment with its unique characteristics and constraints. He analyzes American and Japanese management systems from this broad perspective.

Ann C. Seror, in "A Cultural Contingency Framework for the Comparative Analysis of Japanese and U.S. Organizations," discusses how the growing Japanese challenge to U.S. business has stimulated renewed interest in cross-cultural analysis of managerial structures and processes. Research in this area has been characterized by a general lack of theory, particularly regarding the impact of cultural dimensions of the external organizational environment on effective organization design. In this chapter, Seror integrates empirical works in a cultural contingency framework for the comparative analysis of Japanese and U.S. organizations.

James L. Hall and Joel K. Leidecker present "Is Japanese-Style

Management Anything New? A Comparison of Japanese-Style Management with U.S. Participative Models." The authors develop a model of Japanese-style management (JSM) and compare it with important U.S. models of participative management. The authors conclude that, while similarities exist, JSM is more comprehensive and provides both a contribution to the participative management literature and a more effective roadmap for the manager interested in practicing participative management.

In "Motivational Orientation Differences between Japan and the United States: The Key to Worker Productivity Successes and Problems," Matt M. Amano looks at worker motivation issues from a cross-cultural perspective, comparing U.S. and Japanese motivational orientations. Motivational theories in the United States place a heavy emphasis on what may be called "self-centered" motivation, and the culture in general seems to support such an orientation. The Japanese culture, on the other hand, seems to emphasize "others-oriented" motivation and mutual dependence between management and the worker. The author suggests that while "self-centered" motivation may diminish when needs are met, and thus usually is short-lived, "others-oriented" motivation does not suffer from the same motivational problem and may offer a key to understanding the current labor productivity problems in the United States.

Renate R. Mai-Dalton's chapter, "Traditional Japanese Management versus Likert's System 4," describes the characteristics of traditional Japanese management and compares these with the participative approach to management of Likert's System 4. Differences and similarities are pointed out. It is stressed that the successful transfer of Japanese management techniques to corporations in the United States would be difficult because the value systems of American managers are substantially different from those of Japanese managers. Unless a change in the value systems of American managers occurs, traditional Japanese management techniques can be implemented only to a limited extent in U.S. organizations.

William V. Ruch contributes "Techniques of Communication in U.S. and Japanese Corporations: Are They Interchangeable?" This chapter examines and compares the communication systems of U.S. and Japanese corporations to discover what they can learn from each other. Most channels of communication in U.S. firms are also used in Japan; however, several techniques in use in Japan are not and probably could not be used in the United States. Among these is the ringi system of proposal writing for decision making. Americans should learn the value of a strong system of upward communication. The Japanese should acquire a faster process of decision making.

Arlyn J. Melcher and Bernard Arogyaswamy, in "Decision and Compensation Systems in the United States and Japan: Contrasting Approaches to Management," contrast the decision systems and compensation systems typically used in large firms in the United States and Japan. Sharply different strategies are being pursued by U.S. firms and Japanese firms in the management of their organizations. The authors develop a number of the factors that determine the consequences of these systems for organizational performance in U.S. and Japanese settings. The degree to which the contexts are different determines, at least in part, the different effects achieved by these systems in the United States and Japan.

In "Strategic Management in U.S. versus Japanese Firms," Lester A. Digman points out that Japanese success could not have occurred without proper management strategies. He compares the strategic management approaches of U.S. and Japanese firms.

Liam Fahey and Michael Radnor contribute "The Product-Market Strategies of U.S. and Japanese Firms in the U.S. Consumer Electronics Marketplace." The authors contrast U.S. and Japanese firms' strategies for making product-market choices. More specifically, the authors analyze the evolution of the Japanese infiltration and domination of the U.S. consumer electronics market.

Lee J. Krajewski, Barry E. King, Larry P. Ritzman, Nan Weiner, and Danny S. Wong present "A Comparison of Japanese and U.S. Systems for Inventory and Productivity Management: A Simulation Approach." The chapter discusses a simulation approach to the analysis of inventory and productivity management systems. Often the "system" is thought to be the key factor in improvement in inventory levels and productivity; however, there are other factors that may even be more important than the system itself. This chapter analyzes these factors and various inventory and productivity management systems, and shows how they are evaluated by a simulation model.

Manjulika Koshal and Rajindar A. Koshal, in "Productivity and Labor Turnover: A Comparative Analysis of the United States and Japan," consider the changes in labor turnover rates and labor productivity in Japan and the United States for the period 1970–78. The statistical analysis reveals that during 1970–78, Japan experienced a higher reduction in labor turnover rates than did the United States. In addition, there was a slower growth in productivity in the United States than in Japan. This study presents several possible causes of these changes in labor turnover rates and labor productivity.

"Program for Research on Organizations and Management: The United States-Japanese Electronics Industries Study," by William G. Ouchi, Jay B. Barney, and David Ulrich, reviews a long-term research project that describes and analyzes the electronics industries of the United States and Japan. The research is based on an organizational theory application of an efficiency model. The project's long-range purpose is to describe and understand a firm's strategic relations with other firms so that more efficient, equitable, and effective transactions can be determined and implemented. This chapter reviews six components of this project with preliminary results that indicate structural differences between the electronics industries of the United States and Japan.

Frank H. Clarke and Masako N. Darrough contribute "Income Security or Employment Security? An Economic Analysis." Two unique characteristics of modern Japanese labor management practice are lifetime employment and biannual bonuses. While prevalent in Japan, these practices are relatively infrequent in the United States. Many of the explanations offered so far attribute the difference to cultural, political, or institutional differences between the two countries. In this chapter, the authors present a different point of view, one that provides an economic rationale for various practices, based on the framework of principal-agent relationship.

John W. Goebel presents "The Social Audit: Japanese and U.S. Concepts." During the last decade the concept of the social audit has attracted considerable attention. Extensive study of this notion in the United States and comparison with similar efforts in Europe have yielded no consensus on what is to be done, for what purpose, and by whom. This chapter is the initial stage of a study in which the evolution of similar reporting techniques in Japan will be examined with the expectation that such work will aid in bringing discussion to an end so that implementation can begin.

16

A Comparative Analysis of U.S. and Japanese Management Systems

MOTOFUSA MURAYAMA

PRECONDITIONAL SETTINGS AND MANAGERIAL FUNCTIONS IN THE LOCAL BUSINESS SYSTEM

Introduction of Objectives, Functions, and Preconditions

There exists a scientific concept of a rational organization unit as a functional whole. In addition, a business entity shares some characteristics of a social unit, since it is precontrolled as well as preconditioned by the environmental constraints generated from the integrated totality consisting of multilateral subsystems of the society — such as law, culture, customs, and education. The business organization cannot exist independently of the environmental settings that are defined as local preconditions for management functions.

Two spheres, made up of internal and external factors, can be said to exist in the local business system. The former can be defined as "managerial functions," which are directed by management principles or attitudes on business functions or technique. The latter, "preconditional settings," are both the foundation and the influencing forces that affect managerial functions. This integrative relation is illustrated in Figure 16.1.

FIGURE 16.1   Integration of Managerial Functions with Preconditional Settings toward Business Objectives

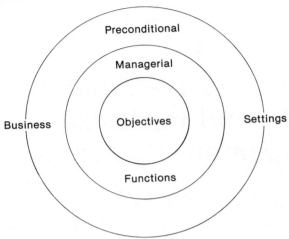

Source: Compiled by the author.

The elements of managerial functions are molded as both the components and factors of business, science, technology, efficiency, productivity, organization, functions, control, prebehavior, and so on. These are the accepted common disciplines that support the framework of business operations with the clear-cut goal of maximizing the value of resources available to any company. At times the framework of business operations might be described as the integrated subsystems including multilateral functions and principal rules of organizational behaviors such as marketing, accounting, production, structure, and personnel. The elements of managerial functions can be characterized as more tangible and formal disciplines.

In contrast to managerial functions, the elements of preconditional settings are various nonbusiness factors, such as humanity, culture, convention and law, motivation, creativity, emotion and religion, language and education, and race distribution. These are preconditional elements; they normally are "givens" that any business entity must consider before it can operate with the desired business-goal-oriented behavior. Preconditional settings tend to be nonsystematic units or informal summings of subsystems, set the environmental conditions under which management works toward maximum efficiency. In sum, the aforementioned elements can be defined as the intangible forces that generate environmental influences and constraints upon the managerial system of rationalism.

The business value system (Murayama 1971a) is the leading environmental factor in the local business, linking the multilateral subsystem or nonmanagerial system of culture, motivation, custom, competition, and so on with the norms of management functioning. The ethical system (the value premises) of local business form the basis for business establishment and its operations. For example, the motivational environment in which management functions is known as a national asset of the Japanese local business system. Motivational factors are introduced by means of the accepted ethical support of Japanese society, which must be integrated with Japanese management efficiency. These factors could be called nonbusiness elements, but, alternately relate to the foundation of higher work moral, creative planning, more reliable management system, and better job relationship in the theoretical framework of the Japanese management functions. Management is supported by such preconditional factors. But in a country like Japan these factors have been built into the society and has not been taken into consideration as major problems in management per se. For example, the internal accounting control system in a business entity represents one of the "managerial functions" in a theoretical sense, and the quality of a good internal accounting control system* is absolutely preconditioned or precontrolled by the quality of ethical forces in a society. Where a suitable situation in the precontrol system of the society is observed, more efficiency is available to the control mechanism and spirit in the management organization. Thus, the author clarified the concept of "premanagement" (Murayama 1971b) which is disciplines to precondition studies of the national business system.

Between managerial functions and preconditional settings, we can recognize integration of subsystems and environmental factors in the total business system. They are correlated in terms of input and output relationships. Intricate relationship between and among them can be seen as subsystem effects on environments or environmental effects on subsystems.

For example, general ethics in the Japanese society is input factors to the Japanese managerial system with the character of both "maintenance force" and "performance force" (Misumi 1969) in an organization. These factors are represented by human characteristics as generally described in the expression of "diligence" and "competition." The output factors in relation to general ethics of Japan is the group management peculiarity, such as a strong sense of belonging to the company.

Thus, we must include the ethical nonbusiness factors or environmen-

---

*The internal accounting control system is more sophisticated in the Western hemisphere due to recognition of both graduate-distrust in the society and emphasis on an automatic control system desired by the management staff who can early separate the human and manpower aspects of a person in an organization.

tal system of premanagement factors in this phase of developing a Japanese management theory that will function as the comparative standards in analyzing business and management systems on both the quantitative and qualitative basis.

Environmental Impact on Business Modernization

The business ethical system serves as the maintenance force as well as performance force for any type of corporation. The developing process of Japanese business ethics will be considered here. Any society stands on a system of ethics, but we must search for any reorientation of the ethical system in response to reformation of or changes in the social structure. *Reorientation for the Japanese business ethical system took place in the Meiji Reformation period, when Japan was forced into contact with foreign nations and different cultural systems. From this perspective, we can study the reorientation process that occurred to meet the need for business modernization about 100 years ago.

Pre-Meiji Japan, with its inferiority complex, faced a critical situation in the form of a threat of a takeover that might make Japan into a colony of the Western countries; added to this was the surge of nationalism in preparation for modernization. The modernization of Japan was apparently colored by trust in and dependence on the materialistic civilization of advanced countries. In reality, however, the denouncing of the industrial civilizations and the movement against modernization were always an undercurrent in Japan. This undercurrent was revealed often among the people, forcing controversy and opposition among the leaders in the development of Japan. The sudden modernization and the capitalistic reorganization of Japan were results of the forced, energetic pressure of the political power under the new Meiji government. The modernization, which depended on the Meiji constitution, was achieved by the ethos of the warriors of the feudal and village community families. The frame of the modernization of agriculture as the establishing foundation of a country and the mercantilism embodied the ethos of the warriors (Sakata 1965).

One environmental problem during the Meiji Reformation was how to motivate the confused nationals to cope with the industrial civilization of the European nations and the United States. A reorientation of the traditional Japanese cultural system became necessary when the Japanese were

---

*The social structure is remodeled by the business structure or is the influential source to revise the latter. Both have input and output relations for integration and interaction.

abruptly brought into contact with the heterogeneous culture of the industrial West. Fortunately, the setting for industrialization was favorable to the Japanese society and entrepreneurs. The objective and subjective environmental factors consisted mainly of the feudalistic system of social ethics and psychological make-up of the people that prevailed in those days of changes. An analysis of the need for modernization must consider the mental background among the Japanese nationals of the Meiji era.

This situation can be more objectively evaluated by the foreign observer. Ruth Benedict writes, in *The Chrysanthemum and Sword* (1946), that "the Japanese culture is a shame culture, not a guilt culture." The standard judgment of behavior among Westerners is that one changes one's behavior if there occurs mental suffering. In other words, one's behavior is changed if it involves a personal recognition of sin. On the other hand, the Japanese move according to social prestige. In short, they are always conscious of what others may say in regard to their behavior. The Japanese are satisfied when they make decisions in agreement with others and play the same game under the same rules as others. To control themselves in this manner is a mental burden; but the guilty consciousness of being individualistic is at the base of their decision.

The people avail themselves of the grace of God and at the same time skillfully utilize nature to meet their demand. A unique quality of the Japanese is to harness nature and thereby create a special sense of the esthetic. On the other hand, the abstract distinctions among gods, human beings, animals, and plants created low ethics and overconfidence in manpower for the Japanese. This ideology produced the separation of oneself from others and the disunion. This ideology is the essence of general comprehension. However, the output of "shame culture" and "group favoritism" are, in the meantime, the input to the Japanese business system and all other organizational units.

The principles of favor, self-sacrifices, and a sense of obligation upheld feudalism, which was the means of supporting and reinforcing the position of the upper classes. This sense of obligation is one of the outstanding characteristics of the Japanese, one known to the rest of the world. The signing of a contract or payment of a debt reveals the Japanese sensitivity to an insult and the sense of obligation to society in protecting one's name. These are all important factors in the moral standards of the Japanese, but the essential point to be noted is that the sense of obligation does not require any reward.

The idea of physiocracy developed the sense of nature and God, which were in turn developed by the characteristic climate, lands, and religions, as the social ethic of Japan. The principal influences in the village community were Shintoism, seniority, the family, class distinctions, and exclusiveness. The village community, which considered the consciousness of families as the principal axis, was a vertical structure based on the family and the ranks of families. Each person took the role of "relay racer" rather than "swimming racer" in the family. The network of human relations was suited to the community, and residents were insured of a happy life in that community. This means that the Japanese do not wish isolation.

The preconditional aspects of each organization are reflected by the generally accepted social system of a nation. In short, the social order of an organization is one part of the order of a nation. The relation between the society and enterprises in Japan can be described in the following way. First, during the Meiji Restoration, the modern industries of Western countries forced their way into the Japanese economy and developed under the protection of the government. This was very new to the Japanese. Second, the human relationships in the small enterprises were based on the feudal family system, wherein the father was the head of the family. These small enterprises were insufficiently equipped and had little experience in the field of business. Third, giant enterprises were established and organized to meet the interest of the government. This national interest was one of the motivations for industrialization in Japan.

There were no industrial leaders as could be found in the Western countries, although the Japanese had to endure bitterness and make sacrifices for industrialization. The strong family system in which the father was the undisputed head endured throughout this industrialization period prior to World War II. This is a typical example of ingrained continuance of the Japanese culture.

In Japan, the valuation of employees depends on their human nature and not on their ability. The foundation and the purpose of the organization policy are to form community life and to have the group work harmoniously. This is referred to in Japanese as Wa,* which means the strength of human unity. This spirit of unity of the family system of organization corresponds to the social order and system of Japan. This system of organization is called the family enterprise. The family enterprise is formed by one's feeling of love and obligation to the employer, the spirit of respect for the old, and the security of lifetime employment.

In reality, the family enterprise during modernization was a reorganization of the management system of the feudal society. After the reorganization and development, the family enterprise, keeping its old characteristics, accepted the new society. Although this family enterprise had some persistent feudal elements, it was a rational management approach of adapting to the society.

---

*Wa implies "harmony" in vertical stratification of human society. Wa provides the discipline that guides all the company staff and workers toward cooperative behavior.

Devotion and service, harmony and respect, and discipline (*shitsuke*) and culture were the creeds of the family and of one who served an employer with devotion. Harmony and respect meant that one should respect human unity. Discipline and culture meant understanding one's social position and acting accordingly. These elements of feudalism still exist in family enterprises. They also had historical and social rationality during the modernization after the Open Door policy and the Meiji Restoration. Japanese psychology and the weakness of Japanese capitalism still exist in the family enterprise and will continue to keep their characteristics.

The management philosophy that tried to oppose labor movements with the traditional family system that depended on favor, the human unit, and feudalism had the same quality of logic that industrialized Japan under the Meiji constitution. The characteristics of human relations in the Japanese organization were the formal class distinctions and informal equality developed through feudalism, as compared with the formal equality and the informal class distinctions of Western countries.

World War II struck a blow to the management system and also to the employment field and the materialistic foundation of the family enterprise. Since the modernization of Japan developed within the Meiji constitution the social mores continued relatively unchanged. The proponents of modernization fell into two different schools of thought, represented by the mercantilism of the warriors and the physiocracy of the lower-class people. The family enterprise was the rational management system and philosophy that embodied those two different ideas in the field of organization.

The system of an organization behavior of Japan in the postwar period outwardly appeared to take on the new management philosophy. But in reality, such a behavior represented the egoism of business administration which was based on private logic and ethics during the disorder right after World War II. The existence and continuance of feudalism made the egoism of business administration possible. The principle of the family enterprise and the egoism of business administration was the group system.

Although the feudalism of Japan was damaged by World War II, it still exists in modern enterprises. For example, in any giant enterprise, such as Mitsui, Mitsubishi, or Sumitomo, important positions were filled by individuals through some exclusive human relationships. Therefore, it is still almost impossible for one who possesses a special ability to be appointed to a directorship in an enterprise if that individual has no relationship with the executives of the enterprise. It can be seen that while the Japanese have a special ability to assimilate anything new in a short time, they also have a strong desire to protect their own traditional ways and culture. Therein is encompassed the characteristic Japanese management philosophy. This greatly depends upon the education in the home (*Katei kyoiku*, which has developed for centuries under feudalism) and public education, as conceived in the Meiji period and based on a fusion of feudalism and Western education.

In summary, the environmental impact of the Meiji Reformation generated a shift involving reorientation and increased sophistication of the Japanese business ethical system. The revised system was basically influenced by the traditional cultural framework, but reoriented or reeducated toward the national interest goals. These coincided with the goals of the business system as it surged toward modernization.

THE LOCAL BUSINESS SYSTEM COMPARED WITH THE INTERNATIONAL BUSINESS SYSTEM—MANAGEMENT NORMS AND PARTICULARITIES

Each nation has developed its own business system, either peculiar to the regional and local settings or common to internationally accepted business settings. The local business settings consist of unclassified and accumulated experiences of traditional business value judgment that are different from the other, foreign criteria.* Thus, the local business system is a complex of particular and multilateral components found in any society in which one is involved.

The international business system is an extended area of the national business system beyond the borderline of nations. The methods of extension from the domestic business system to the international business system vary in accordance with constraints of both internal and external influence toward maintenance of a business entity under competition for survival and prosperity. Before characterizing Japanese business systems that have been founded upon cultural determinants within the national organizational structure, we must set certain standards and criteria for recognizing and measuring the Japanese local business systems that are objectively compared with them or analyzed on their logical basis.† This requires us to build theoretical frameworks or frames of reference as universal substructures in order to construct the expected system of Japanese local business and the internal or external factors within it.

Under such methodological assumptions, we must somehow acquire

---

*The foreign criteria cannot always be the base standards for judgment, but can be applied as major source references and guidelines for the initial stage of the decision-making process.

†In addition to the sociological approach to analysis, a quantitative approach using more-scientific methods has been sought since theorization of Japanese managerial system began.

"norms," that is, common values, expectations, standardized views, or objective scales of judgment, so that "particularism" in the Japanese business system can be logically reviewed and presented to the world outside the Japanese domestic business sphere. These norms can be defined as universally accepted management thoughts and techniques that can be transplanted from one country to others with some adjustments or without any revision or transformation of the original. In pure theory of functions and technologies or in model settings of abstract concepts as well as quantitative approaches, the norms will serve as the guidelines and rules for constructing theories of local business administration. Norms also form the bridge between two domestic business systems in terms of internationalized, standardized, conventional, and agreed-upon behaviors of transboundary firms. Norms are sometimes viewed as the common communication values among the business people of heterogeneous origins.

Figure 16.2 is a geographical presentation of norm factors, which are transferable and included in the internationally accepted system, compared with heterogeneous (particular) factors of the domestic system, which are usually excluded from the aforesaid norms of the international system.

Proposition 1: The Convergence Hypothesis

The convergence hypothesis is shown in Figure 16.2, (A). Norms have been ideologically as well as empirically recognized by heterogeneous systems, which stand on equal platforms. Factors with opposite ideologies-originated leaderships once denied each other, but failed to practice the pure theory of each belief. Each factor found the advantageous components and disadvantageous components in each system sophistication process through the empirical approach, and there appears to be an agreement that human nature and human dignity should be the most important determinants. The means of covering up the weakness of one system may be copying the merits of other systems.

Under the above conditions, and if both systems have an opportunity for integration and interaction, complementary efforts can be available from both factors so that progress can be made in both social organizations, in areas including unemployment, consumer satisfaction, life standards, and work motivation.

Therefore, particular tendencies in each system must be corrected or adjusted toward the direction of other systems, success motivation and patterns. This attitude for corrections and adjustments toward the norms that both particularities recognize as a target of re-theorization toward action is

FIGURE 16.2   Relationship between Norms and Particularities

(A) The Convergence Hypothesis

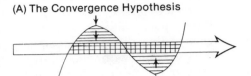

(B) The Natural-Agreement-or-Disagreement Hypothesis

(C) The Superiority Hypothesis

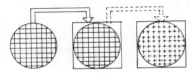

(D) The Intermediary Hypothesis

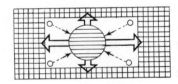

Legend:

▦	Homogeneity; generalization; universal, international norms
≡	Heterogeneity, particularity; individual, domestic norms
⇒	Movement of cultural, business, and management system

Source: Compiled by the author.

referred to as "convergence hypothesis." This means that both traditional value systems are willing to reframe their particular behaviors and ideologies toward more efficiency for the society, so that the common and objective value of homogeneous factors set down and developed by both heterogeneous factors can function to implement the management goals.

According to the convergence hypothesis, U.S. and Japanese management particularities can be illustrated as in Table 16.1.

The table shows that the same context of business system are identified with the different approaches and ideologies. The goal is the same but forces to achieve the goal are contradictory. However, as long as we retain an understanding of norms and particularities, we will not deviate from the fundamental trait of international business systems and Japanese or U.S. systems.

Proposition 2: The Natural-Agreement-or-Disagreement Hypothesis

The natural-agreement-or-disagreement hypothesis is represented by Figure 16.2, (B). In most instances, norms and particularities are not classified, rather comingled until they are evaluated with the foreign-based criteria. The individual domestic system consists of norm and particularity com-

TABLE 16.1   Tendency toward Convergence

U.S. PARTICULARITY	NORMS BY CONVERGENCE	JAPANESE PARTICULARITY
Direct approach	Profit-motivated behavior	Indirect approach
Vocational approach	Management education at university level	Cultural approach
Employment system based on high wages and job satisfaction	Stability of qualified staff	Lifetime employment system
Professionalism in the individual's experience	Executive development	Amateurism in the group experience
Individual responsibility	Management responsibility	Group responsibility
Victory concept: team in sports and players	Organizational goal and behavior	Survival concept: maintenance of family and family members
Managers for a team	Roles of the presidents	Father for the family
Dividend approach: profit distribution; capital stock issued	Security in financing	Interest approach: expense distribution; loans (banks) granted
Rationalism Materialism Individualism	Business attitude	Irrationalism Spiritualism Collectivism

ponents without any distinction or definition. Thus, the domestic system is balanced by the equilibrium between the norm factors (foreign-accepted elements) and particularity factors (foreign-rejected elements), after the value of the domestic quality is reflected in and measured by the objectively transferable value of internationally accepted foreign systems.

The natural-agreement hypothesis is defined as the agreement of different systems by coincidence without adjustments or with few adjustments. This means that the norm factors of two or more than two heterogeneous systems can be matched as they were duplicated in terms of international business operations such as foreign trading, joint ventures, and acquisitions of foreign corporations. The norm factors pull other heterogeneities and coincide as if according to the law of gravity. However, the particularity factors are like the brake of the automobile: they always tend to stop and pull back the movement of norm factors due to unfamiliarity heterogeneous to the potential strength of the foreign-based norm factors. This idea can be called the natural-disagreement hypothesis. "East is East and West is West" if we look only at the peculiarity factors in the natural-disagreement hypothesis.

The author hereby intends to clarify only the norm factors in matching the national business system with the international business system to find the common values (see Table 16.2 for summary).

Proposition 3: The Superiority Hypothesis

The superiority hypothesis (see Figure 16.2, [C]) is the bargaining and dominating impact by which the superior system of more-advanced nations can suppress the inferior system of less advanced nations, if the two cultural systems are mixed by forces or transplantations from the former to the latter. The inferior system has certain characteristics due to incomplete modernization. This is also viewed from comparative analysis. Relative superiority can be expressed in terms such as progress rate in industrialization, disposable personal income, per capita literacy and frequency of higher education, and recognition of human dignity.

The superiority hypothesis may be denied by the egalitarian society, but in reality we cannot ignore the historical background within the local framework. The conventional rules state that civilization flows from the higher to the lower; this could be termed a "society gap," generated by heterogeneous factors of cultural heritage, environmental framework, or historical trends. Candid recognition of inequality in progress in areas like the structure of society is most essential for refining the national business system and consolidating it with the international business system.

According to the superiority hypothesis, the handicapped nations

TABLE 16.2   Natural Norms Matching

U.S. NORMS	U.S. AND JAPANESE NORMS MATCHING	JAPANESE NORMS
Seniority system (lay-off-motivated)	Ultimate management efficiency	Seniority system (pro-motion-motivated)
Professional skill-development attitude (money-motivated)	Standard level of quality control in production	Professional skill-development attitude (Kimochi-motivated)
Common law system (flexibility framework)	Authority based in and respect for the legally governed organization	Roman law system (rigidity framework)
Manpower (religious foundation)	Productivity conscious-ness with diligence and work moral	Belief in a group
Competition (radical atmosphere)	New-project and new-product development	Competition (mild atmosphere)
Participation theory (tactics-driven)	Management leadership	Participation theory (personality-driven)
Controllership (steward-ship or trusteeship-based)	Demand for reporting	Controllership (depend-ence and loyalty)

whose culture differs must rely on the progressive nation for development or copying. Therefore, this is a one-way-flow system with less rejection, because there is no expectation of evaluation of the foreign influences, which are directly transplanted into the nonsystem condition.

The transferred superior system can change or remodel the inherent core character of any local system. In other words, the Western system turns into the local system or the local system is remodeled by the imported system without preservation of the original. From this point of view, the more industrialized nations' managerial systems can be compared with the less industrialized nations' as shown in Table 16.3.

Proposition 4: The Intermediary Hypothesis

The intermediary hypothesis is illustrated in Figure 16.2 (D). Even in the national or domestic system, there is the two-fold stratification of domes-tic-oriented nationals and the foreign-oriented nationals. This classifi-cation is based not only on race distribution, but also on educational back-

TABLE 16.3   Accepted and Displaced or Remodeled Factors in the Less Industrialized Nations from the More Industrialized Nations

TRANSPLANTED FACTORS	DISPLACED FACTORS	REMODELED FACTORS
Management philosophy	Religious belief	Social stratification revised
Mangerial control mechanism	Traditional leaders authenticity	Personal relationship and productivity revised
Automation and technology	Racial and class prejudice	Labor relationship and productivity movement revised
Management development	Dependence on masters	Educational system leadership revised
Marketing management	Exploitation by middlemen	Intermediary system installation
Financing management	Dictatorship by clergy and tribal elite	Opportunity for creation and expansion increased
Production management	Subservience to natural phenomena	Urbanization and process-ing method innovated
Personnel management	Master-and-servant relationship	Human dignity in organi-zation incremented

ground or ways of thinking. The latter group is minor in number but
major in leadership of the relevant environment of input information
without actual performance leadership due to the aforementioned "society
gap" which has been beneficial to those people educated in the more industrialized nations. The foreign-oriented nationals are the intermediaries
in the "culture-mixing" function. For this purpose one need not speak
foreign languages; skill and knowledge are required in digesting or adapting the foreign sources to the domestic sources. Yukichi Fukuzawa,* who
lived in the Meiji Reformation period of Japan, is an ideal figure to illustrate the role of cultural intermediary in Japanese history.

At present, there are quite a large number of domestic nationals ex-

---

*Yukichi Fukuzawa was born in 1935 and died in 1901. He is respected as the foremost edu-
cator, scholar, and writer during and after the Meiji Reformation period. He established
Keio University in Tokyo. His major contribution to Japan was the role he played in changing
the traditional society to the modernized society (Ishikawa 1968).

posed to foreign cultural influences. They may be with international joint ventures as business people, in universities as scholars, in government as specialists or officials, in the press or publishing business as journalists, in the business firms as managers, and so forth.

These individuals act as buffering agents between the foreign and domestic elements, facilitating the smooth flow of direct importation while lessening the confusion. The successful transplantation of the foreign cultural factor to the domestic business system must be conditioned through efforts of traditional value recognition for comparison and adaptation and also by the attitude of societal interest rather than self-interest.

The intermediary persons with buffering functions sometimes monopolize their advantages when more than two races reside in the same community or country. This is not favorable from the long-run viewpoint because they lose access to the international communication channel derived from the foreign-based cultural factors. The intermediary people in the culture mix are the bridge between the national system and international systems. The link between the two systems can be attempted by those who can understand both the foreign and domestic characteristics. This implies that there exists a need for development of international business people and international-minded society leaders in the local environment as the first stage of internationalization of the local firm and business group. In Table 16.4, some approaches to developing or reeducating the international go-betweens are summarized, as suggestions for implementing the internationalization process discussed here.

TABLE 16.4 Some Ideas on Development Methods for International Intermediaries in Cultural Mixing

---

Foreign students' programs at the university
International tourism promotion
Foreign professor exchange programs
Mission for research or studies to the target nation
Training in the foreign home office
Development of international language or promotion of bilingual educational system
Mobility of educational institutions, staff, curriculum, and accreditation
Establishment of joint-venture business
Foreign aid in education
International conferences
Self-development in international marketing and research activities
Establishment of new educational organization for international business development

---

COMPARATIVE MANAGEMENT SYSTEM
AND CONCEPT VARIANCES

System Variance-Quantitative Approach

At the first stage of comparative management research, the total system of each local managerial structure must be determined by incorporating the business value system; the framework of managerial functions; and the already existing setting, which presents the environmental constraints on formation of management functions.

The total system of managerial structure in the individual business system is conceptualized as the standards in comparative management research.

If we compare total system A with total system B of the two different managerial structures which have heterogeneous origins of two local business systems at the second stage of comparative studies, five types of variances can be found:

- (x)   variance: Business value system variances
- (y)   variance: Functional system variances
- (z)   variance: Environmental system variances
- (xz) variance: Value and functions mixed variances
- (yz) variance: Environments and functions mixed variances

The above five variances are illustrated in the Figures 16.3 and 16.4.

Before measuring each comparative variance of x, y, z, xz, and yz, the following must be specified:

1. system scope and contents of each X, Y, Z
2. uniform analytical method and standards developed to systematize X, Y, Z
3. clarification of X and Y, Y and Z correlations and interdependence

The first chart shows the nonintegrated comparisons of XA and XB, YA and YB, ZA and ZB, which are all independent from other integrated systems like XY, YZ, or XYZ. The second chart is intended to indicate the integrated comparison of (A)XYZ and (B)XYZ systems as the shell-shaped chart is closed. x, y, z variances are more independent and static comparison results, while xy and yz variances are dependent and dynamic comparison results. x, y, and variances are useful and focus on the preliminary fact-finding, and xy and yz are directed toward the more intensive fact-findings after the initial fact-findings.

FIGURE 16.3   Comparative Management (I)

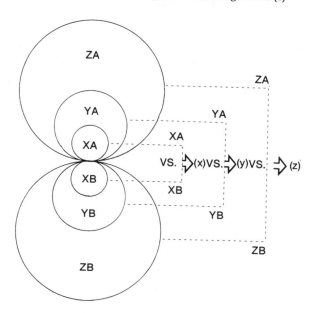

Notes: X is the business value system; Y is the functional management system; Z is the preconditional management system; A and B are the total system of the two different local managerial structures.

Source: Compiled by the author.

Concept Variances — Qualitative Approach

Management functions, including local management methods in production, distribution, personnel, and finance, must be studied along with the sociocultural, legal-political, educational, economical, and other environmental factors. Each function of Japanese management can be cross referenced to the cause factors of the environmental areas. This will be discussed as management concept variances, which will be studied in parallel with management system variance. In the course of developing concept variances in comparative management theories between the United States (A) and Japan (B) in Figure 16.4, the following hypotheses can be proposed:

1. Between English and Japanese expression, there is no exact translation or definite correspondence of concepts in management terminologies.

FIGURE 16.4 Comparative Management (II)

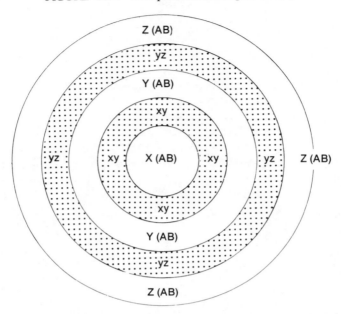

Notes: X (AB) is the business value system agreement of A and B; Y (AB) is the functional management system agreement of A and B; Z (AB) is the preconditional management system agreement of A and B; xy is variance due to the ideological constraints from X to Y; yz is variance due to the environmental constraints from Z to Y.

Source: Compiled by the author.

2. Variances in conception are caused by variances in environments.
3. Management functions in both nations share the characteristic of being goal-motivated, but are implemented within the constraints of local conception in each management setting.
4. The local concept of management is created by the local people's thinking, which in turn is influenced by local environmental factors. This is an assumption for the structure of Japanese management theories.
5. Management functions can be defined with a universal agreement, but the local concept of the individual nation's management must be separately qualified in conformity with the analysis of local management environmental factors.
6. Definite local management concepts serve as a basis for comparison with the standardized concepts of international business administration or other systems of local management.
7. Comparison variance due to environmental and conceptual fac-

tors must also be considered by international business executives and management scholars. These are sources of communication variances to be eliminated in the mass-culture movement.

The basic concepts in the Japanese managerial system can be primarily defined from the socioanthropological approach and comparative study methods. Referring to the above hypotheses, the major concepts applied in U.S. and Japanese management are comparatively summarized in Table 16.5 as the preliminary analysis for further discussion.

The concept variances of the qualitative approach can serve to interpret the system variances of the quantitative approach. Therefore, the concept variances are more objectively and rationally examined when we conduct comparative research.

From Table 16.5, it can be seen that the analytical results of the Japanese management structure always circle around the traditional con-

TABLE 16.5   Major Concepts in the Comparative Analysis of U.S. and Japanese Management

COMPARATIVE FACTORS OF EXPRESSION IN MANAGEMENT	LEADING DETERMINANTS OF DEFINITION — PRINCIPAL MEANINGS	
	UNITED STATES	JAPAN
Company	Team in sport	Family in village
President (employer, owner, professional executive)	Manager in team	Father in family
Business goal	To win	To survive
Employees	Players in team	Children in family
Human relations	Functional	Emotional
Competition	Cut-throat	Cooperation or sin
Profit motivation	By all means	Means to an end
Sense of identification	Job pride	Group prestige
Work motivation	Individual income	Group atmosphere
Law and regulation	Defensive	Trusting, "gentlemen's Agreement"
Accounting	Controllership and strategies	Clerical and honesty
Sales	Personality and skill	Sociability
Production	Productivity	Training and diligence
Personnel	Efficiency	Maintenance
Promotion	According to abilities	According to years of service
Payroll	Service and results	Considered an award for patience and sacrifice

cept of *Kazoku* (family) and *Shudan* (group), which are the fundamental social units from which patterns of existence and expectations are formed in Japanese society. The family and group are the most basic sources, from which all theorization of Japanese local management peculiarities can be made. Therefore, these family and group systems should be researched more thoroughly prior to studies of comparative management and in conjunction with studies of the Japanese management system.

SUMMARY

The most difficult task of comparative management research lies in the quantitative approach of evaluating or measuring the local business, management, and value systems of the relevant countries prior to a comparative analysis. We must search for quantitative standards that are internationally accepted, so that comparative management can be more definitely and scientifically established as a multinationally transferable management theory. This need was not met adequately in this chapter, because in the first stage of comparative management more emphasis must be given to the qualitative approach. Also, the author intended to stress the creation of a new theoretical framework of comparative management whereby theory can be developed for local (national) business, management, and value systems according to each environment or nation.

The author is aware that many questions may have been left unanswered; however, it is hoped that the readers may have gained a different insight into this subject. Any criticism and comments regarding this study will be appreciated as the author pursues further research and clarification in this area.

REFERENCES

Benedict, Ruth. 1946. *The Chrysanthemum and Sword.* Cambridge, Mass.: The Riverside Press.

Ishikawa, Kanmei. 1968. *Fukuzawa Yukichiden (Autobiography of Yukichi Fukuzawa).* Tokyo: Iwanami Shoten.

Misumi, F. 1969. *Atarishi Leadership (New Leadership)*, pp. 117–99. Tokyo: Diamond.

Murayama, M. 1971a. "Japanese Business Value System." *Sophia Economic Review* 17:1–28.

_____. 1971b. "Preconditional Theory of Asian Management." *Humanities and Social Sciences (Jimbun Kiyo* – Chiba University) 3:37–62.

Sakata, Yoshio. 1965. *Shikon Shosai (Samurai Spirits and Merchant Talents).* Tokyo: Miraisha.

17

A Cultural Contingency Framework for the Comparative Analysis of Japanese and U.S. Organizations

ANN C. SEROR

INTRODUCTION: CULTURE DEFINED

There has been a recent resurgence of interest in the cross-cultural analysis of managerial structures and processes and their impact on aspects of organizational effectiveness such as productivity and innovation. Much of this renewed interest has been inspired by the growing Japanese challenge to U.S. business. Child (1981) points to a general lack of theory guiding research efforts on cultural differences among organizations, particularly regarding the relevance of cultural dimensions of the external organizational environment.

This literature review examines recent research contributions to a contingency theory of organization based on comparative analyses of U.S. and Japanese organizations. In this framework, culture is considered to have a decisive impact on managerial structures and processes through characteristics of individuals and social systems. The distinction between these two levels of cross-cultural analysis has most recently been discussed by Parsons (1973). According to Parsons, culture may be defined as a system of meaning, including patterns of ideas and values that contribute to shaping individual and collective behavior. The social system is a means of "organizing human action which is concerned with linking meaning to the conditions of concrete behavior in the environmentally given world" (Parsons 1973, p. 36). The most important aspect of the interaction between cultural systems of meaning and the organization of human action, according to Parsons, is the moral-evaluative function of meaning. While Parsons considers the moral-evaluative function of a system of meaning apart from the institutional organization of action, the perspective of this chapter defines the moral-evaluative function as inherent in both patterns of meaning and the larger social system. Culture is expressed at the individual level in needs, attitudes, values, and perceptual tendencies of the organizational participant. An example of an individual cultural value is the work ethic, or the importance and priority attached to expenditure of effort in the accomplishment of work (Cole 1979). At the level of the social system, culture is manifested through institutions supporting organizational endeavor. The Sogoshosha, Japan's multinational trading companies, which express the close cooperation between Japanese business and government, are important examples of an institutional factor in Japan. These examples show how cultural factors have an impact on managerial structures and processes at two levels of cross-cultural organizational analysis.

The following general propositions form a basis for development of the literature review as suggested below in Figure 17.1.

Proposition 1: Organizational structures and processes are a function of the organization's external cultural environment, including social, economic, and political institutions (Child 1981; Sethi 1975).

FIGURE 17.1   A Cultural Contingency Framework

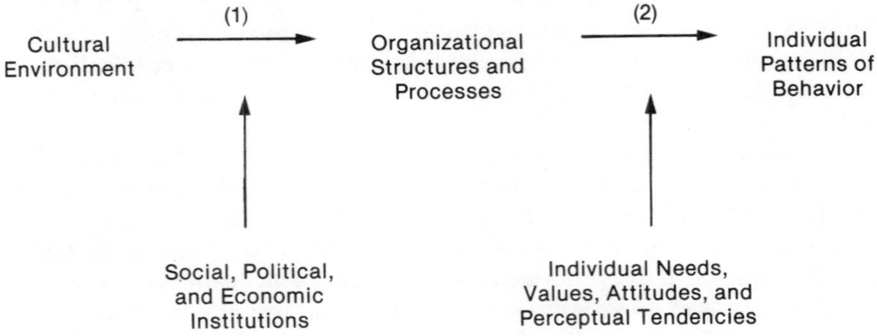

Source: Child (1981) and Parsons (1973).

Proposition 2: Individual behavior patterns in organizations are a function of the congruence between individual needs, values, attitudes, and perceptual tendencies and organizational structures and processes (Lincoln, Hanada, and Olson 1981; Marsh and Mannari 1976).

The objective of this literature review is to define culture as an empirical construct at the institutional and individual levels and to integrate recent theoretical and empirical works on comparative Japanese/U.S. organizational analysis in the cultural contingency framework described. This literature review is divided into four parts. The first part reviews recent theoretical and empirical works contributing to an understanding of the impact of culture on organizational structures and processes in Japanese and U.S. firms. This section identifies directions for future research efforts. The second section focuses on the relationship between the organization and its cultural environment; and the third section considers the cultural needs, values, attitudes, and perceptual tendencies affecting individual and group behavior in organizational settings. The fourth section summarizes the implications of the cultural contingency framework developed from the literature review.

THE IMPACT OF CULTURE ON ORGANIZATIONAL STRUCTURES AND PROCESSES

Recent descriptive literature on Japanese organization has attempted to define the dimensions of Japanese managerial style distinguishing it from U.S. management practice. Drucker (1981), Hatvany and Pucik (1981), Ouchi (1981), Ouchi and Jaeger (1978), Ouchi and Price (1978), Pascale (1978b), and Sethi (1975) have identified a number of such dimensions. Ouchi (1981) has presented the most comprehensive framework in the description of the Type J organization. The structural dimensions determining this organizational mode are (1) lifetime employment, (2) consensual or group decision making, (3) collective responsibility, (4) slow evaluation and promotion, (5) implicit and informal methods of control, (6) the nonspecialized career path, and (7) concern for the member of the organizational community that includes his or her personal life.

Hatvany and Pucik (1981) have identified general strategies and specific techniques defining a model of Japanese management. The focus of this model is on human resource management. Three general strategies are (1) development of an internal labor market, (2) definition of a unique company philosophy and identity, and (3) intensive socialization of organ-

izational participants. The specific techniques contributing to these strategies are (1) job rotation and slow promotion, (2) evaluation of individual
personality and behavior, (3) emphasis on work groups and (4) open communication, (5) consultative decision making, and (6) concern for the general well-being of the employee. These strategies and techniques corre-
spond to the descriptive dimensions distinguishing the Type J organization
from other organizational modes.

While these descriptive approaches provide a framework for the
comparison of Japanese and U.S. organizations, they do not consider the
relationship between management style and organizational technology,
nor do they consider the dimensions of organizational structure commonly
under study in the literature on contingency theory of organizational effectiveness. These dimensions include (1) organizational size, or number
of employees and scale of operations, (2) division of labor, (3) vertical and
horizontal differentiation of organizational units, (4) hierarchy of authority, (5) centralization of decision making, (6) span of supervisory control,
and (7) formalization of rules and procedures. A final criticism of the descriptive approaches is their general tendency to view Japanese and U.S.
organizations as two distinct types of organization, with little attention giv-
en to the analysis of environmental factors or characteristics of the individual organizational participant having an impact on the effectiveness of a
particular mode or style of management.

The following review of the empirical literature on comparative Japa-
nese/U.S. organizational analysis is an attempt to address the research
needs identified above. Recent empirical research (published since 1975)
contributing to this cultural contingency framework may be classified in
three broad categories: (1) studies with the objective of validating contingency theories of organizational structure in the Japanese industrial environment (Marsh and Mannari 1981; 1976; Tracy and Azumi 1976); (2)
studies with the objective of testing hypotheses on comparative Japanese
and U.S. organizational analysis (Lincoln, Hanada, and Olson 1981; Lincoln, Olson, and Hanada 1978; Pascale 1978a); and (3) studies exploring
cross-cultural differences through comparative data analysis, but without
the formulation of a priori hypotheses (Cole 1979).

The first group of studies (Marsh and Mannari 1981; 1976; Tracy and
Azumi 1976) have as their objective the validation of contingency theories
of organizational structure in the Japanese industrial environment. Each
of these studies derives its hypotheses from previous research on contingency theory.

Marsh and Mannari base their hypotheses concerning individual job
satisfaction, work values, and performance on the work of Abegglen (1958).
Abegglen hypothesizes a positive causal relationship between the paternalistic type of social organization in Japanese firms and their performance.

Marsh and Mannari (1976) find that Japanese social organization variables, including preference for paternalism, company housing, participation in company activities, company identification, and lifetime commitment have less causal impact on performance than more universal social organizational variables such as employee status in the company, sex, job satisfaction, and knowledge of organization. They conclude that performance in Japanese firms apparently has the same determinants as demonstrated by research on Western firms.

In another study by Marsh and Mannari (1981), the theoretical basis for the competing hypotheses tested is the work of Woodward (1965) and Pugh et al. (1969). The aim of this research is to clarify the ongoing debate on the relative importance of size and technology as determinants of organizational structure. Marsh and Mannari (1981) find more support for Woodward's hypotheses than for the hypotheses tested by the Aston Group (a group of researchers from the University of Aston in England). Technology emerges as a more significant determinant of organizational structure than size. Marsh and Mannari further conclude from this study that culture is not evident as an explanatory factor for two reasons: (1) "Most analysts would presumably agree that recurrence of the same systematic relationships between properties of organizations in different societies suggests the cross-cultural invariance of these relationships" (1981, p. 53). (2) If culture means patterns that are relatively constant within a society, then culture cannot explain significant variance among Japanese factories on such organizational characteristics as centralization and span of control.

Tracy and Azumi (1976) also formulate hypotheses based on the work of Woodward and the Aston Group. The authors find evidence to support both sets of hypotheses. (These hypotheses are not formulated to set the two approaches in competition.) Tracy and Azumi find that contextual factors, defined as plant size and task variability resulting from unstable relationships between the organization and its environment, are related to automaticity and formalization in the same ways as hypothesized for Western organizations. These authors conclude in the same way as Marsh and Mannari (1976) that relationships between context and structure may remain relatively stable across cultures.

The arguments advanced by these authors to reject culture as an explanatory variable are inadequate. First, the recurrence of the same systematic relationships in different societies does not permit conclusions regarding the absolute levels of the observed variables under consideration. These absolute levels may be quite different. Second, culture cannot be excluded in a contingency framework as explaining significant variance in organizational dimensions such as centralization and span of control among Japanese factories, since such variance may be a result of culture-based contextual factors. Third, Marsh and Mannari (1981) and Tracy and

Azumi (1976) do not consider the relationship of structure to organizational effectiveness outcomes. The dimensions of organizational structure may be related to organizational effectiveness in very different ways in Japan and the United States. Fourth, the authors of these studies reject culture without having formulated an a priori definition of this construct, and without having conducted a cross-cultural organizational analysis.

The second group of studies is designed to test hypotheses on comparative Japanese and U.S. organizational structure (Lincoln, Hanada, and Olson 1981; Lincoln, Olson, and Hanada 1978; Pascale 1978a). Lincoln, Olson, and Hanada (1978) formulate their hypotheses largely based on the work of Azumi and McMillan (1974). Japanese organizations in the United States are hypothesized to be less specialized, more centralized, more vertically differentiated, and less formalized than U.S. organizations. The Aston scales are used to measure these organizational variables. The authors find support only for the hypothesis that functional specialization varies inversely with the proportion of Japanese and Japanese-Americans in the organizational population. Lincoln et al. (1978) interpret these results as having two possible explanations. First, the sociocultural environment may determine organizational structure for both U.S. and Japanese firms in the United States. Second, Japanese and U.S. organizational styles may converge. The first explanation is consistent with the perspective of this chapter. The importance of the external cultural environment has been underestimated as a determinant of organizational structure.

In another study, Lincoln, Hanada, and Olson (1981) examine the effects of individual cultural origin on paternalistic value orientation, job satisfaction, and social integration in the organization. They find support for the hypotheses that Japanese employees are more likely than Americans to express a paternalistic value orientation, and that they are generally less satisfied with their organizational involvement. The analyses also show that, consistent with the Japanese need for vertical social structure, vertical differentiation is positively related and horizontal differentiation is negatively related to social integration and job satisfaction of Japanese and Japanese-Americans, while vertical and horizontal differentiation are not related to these outcomes for Americans. In conclusion, the authors formulate a view that organizations are determined by individual values and attitudes and institutional arrangements characterizing their cultural environments.

Pascale (1978a) examines the communication and decision-making patterns characterizing a sample of U.S. and Japanese operating units. He finds that the number of face-to-face contacts is greater among managers in Japanese than in U.S. units. Subordinates initiate more communication with management in Japanese than in U.S. units. No differences are found in use of the consultative approach to decision making, but the perceived quality of decision implementation is greater in Japanese than in U.S. operating units. Pascale considers that the data demonstrate important areas of similarity between Japanese and U.S. communication and decision-making styles. The author appropriately notes that the measures employed in the study focus only on observable and measurable aspects of the processes under study, ignoring aspects of communication implicit to the cultural context. Further, Pascale reports that no significant differences are identified between Japanese subsidiaries and U.S. organizations in the United States, while Japanese subsidiaries differ from their parent companies in the use of face-to-face, written, and upward communication and in perceived decision quality. These differences are in the directions hypothesized for Japanese and U.S. firms. As suggested by Lincoln, Olson, and Hanada (1978), this Americanization of the Japanese firm in the United States may be due to the impact of the sociocultural environment on organizational structures and processes. Another possible explanation is the set of work values and attitudes of the American organizational populations in Japanese subsidiaries in the United States. Both of these possible explanations are consistent with the contingency perspective presented in this chapter.

The second group of studies shows some evidence in support of a cultural contingency view, at both institutional and individual levels of analysis. A weakness common to these approaches is the inadequate definition of the concept of culture. Culture is defined at the level of the organization as Japanese or U.S. ownership or control, and at the level of the individual as Japanese, Japanese-American, or American cultural origin. These operationalizations of the concept of culture have two major deficiencies. First, the dimensions of Japanese or American culture are not identified. Second, the framework offered is not useful to comparative analysis of organizations in other cultures.

One major study by Cole (1979), focusing on workers in the automotive industries of Detroit and Yokahama, falls in the third category of research. Its objective is to explore cross-cultural differences through comparative data analysis without testing of a priori hypotheses. The aim of Cole's study is to develop a better understanding of Japanese and U.S. labor market practices. Three major propositions concerning Japanese and U.S. organization emerge from Cole's analyses. First, the social organization of a Japanese firm is characterized by broader and less explicit definition of job duties than is the organization of the U.S. firm. Second, the social organization of the Japanese firm is characterized by a stronger internal labor market, in which employees demonstrate high career commitment to the company. Third, the Japanese organization places a stronger emphasis on the development of human resource assets than does the U.S. organization. According to Cole, the major insights of the study concern the permeability of boundaries between organizations and between jobs. The characteristics of one boundary are closely related to the characteristics of the other. This general proposition suggests the importance of the external environment in determining organizational structure.

These comparative propositions suggest hypotheses that need to be tested in future comparative organizational analyses. Cole's work presents a wealth of qualitative as well as quantitative information on the comparisons drawn. Such an exploratory approach allows the cross-validation of qualitative and quantitative observations. A possible weakness of exploratory data analysis is the lack of focus for statistical inference.

In summary, the conclusions presented in the empirical studies reviewed in this section suggest the cultural invariance of organizational structures and processes in Japan and the United States. However, examination of the methodologies employed reveals inadequate attention to the definition of this construct at the institutional, organizational, and individual levels. The impact of the cultural environment on organizational structures and processes is suggested by some of the data, but this level of analysis has not been pursued in any of the literature on Japanese/U.S. comparative organizational analysis. It is a major premise of this chapter that organizational structures cannot be understood without careful analysis of the impact of culturally determined institutions on such structures. The studies in the first group conclude that, where systematic relationships existing in Western organizations are also found to exist in Japanese organizations, those relationships should be considered invariant across Japanese and U.S. cultures. This conclusion is in error, since significant differences in levels of observed variables under study may exist. Further, the measures applied, such as the Aston scales, may not be adequately adapted for use in Japanese organizations, or they may not tap the structural dimensions relevant to cross-cultural organizational analysis.

The studies in the second group define culture based only on organizational ownership and control of the organization or individual cultural origin. Culture as an empirical construct needs to be examined to identify its dimensions and to extend its usefulness to a general theoretical framework for cross-cultural organizational analysis. Cross-cultural studies need to be designed to explore the qualitative and quantitative nature of cultural differences; to develop valid and reliable measures of dimensions of cultural environments, organizational structures and processes, and individual attitudes, values, and perceptual tendencies; and to generate and test propositions such as those elaborated by Cole (1979).

The next two sections of this chapter focus on elaboration of a theoretical framework including (1) the impact of cultural institutions on organizational structures and processes and (2) the effects of individual attitudes, values, and perceptual tendencies on individual and group behavior patterns within the organization.

CULTURAL INSTITUTIONS

Child (1981) has emphasized the lack of theory to guide research efforts on cross-cultural analysis, particularly regarding the identification of cultural aspects of the external organizational structures and processes. Child suggests that there may be three major variables to be considered in the cultural environment of the organization. First, the degree of interrelationship between the organization and the national state affects the centralization of planning and control processes. Second, the general level of industrialization of the culture under study affects organizational technology. Third, the extent of differentiation in the economic system between the ownership of capital and the managerial function may affect the setting of organizational goals and the means of achieving them. Similarly, Meyer and Rowan (1977) emphasize the importance of the external social environment for organizational survival. They criticize the assumption expressed in the work of many organization theorists that success of the formal organization is determined primarily by the coordination and control of internal activities: "formal structures of many organizations in post-industrial society dramatically reflect the myths of their institutional environments instead of the demands of their work activities" (Meyer and Rowan 1977, p. 341). Myths generating formal organizational structure are defined as rationalized and impersonal prescriptions that identify certain social purposes and specify the appropriate means of accomplishing these purposes beyond the discretion of individuals or organizations.

Two major propositions define the importance of the external environment for organizational structure. First, as rationalized institutional rules evolve in work activity, formal organizations form and expand by incorporating these rules as structural elements. The results of this process for the organization are maximization of legitimacy and an increase in resources and survival capacity. Second, "the more modernized the society, the more extended the rationalized institutional structure in given domains and the greater the number of domains containing rationalized institutions" (Meyer and Rowan 1977, p. 345). Modernization may be defined in this context as the process of rationalization of social systems encompassing and surpassing processes of industrialization. This approach strongly substantiates the importance of institutions in the external cultural environment, but does not provide a focus for the identification of relevant institutional arrangements affecting organizational structures and processes.

Crozier (1964), in his discussion of French organizational tendencies, considers the importance of established national institutions: the educational system, the labor movement, and political and national administrative systems, as determinants of bureaucracy. Based on the work of Emery and Trist (1965), Katz and Kahn (1978) develop a comprehensive framework for the analysis of the impact of organizational environments. This framework includes four descriptive dimensions: (1) degree of environmental stability, (2) degree to which the environment is organized, (3) extent of diversity of structures and processes in the environment, and (4) the extent of resource availability. These dimensions describe the dynamic functional relationships of the organization to its environment.

The organization maintains four types of functional relationships to its cultural environment. The organization must function within the value patterns of its cultural environment, within the political and legal structures defining its formal legitimacy, within the economic constraints of competitive markets and sources of inputs such as labor force and materials, and within the informational and technological environment. The identification of these environmental sectors aids in the specification of social and political institutions relevant to the cultural determination of organizational structures and processes. Little theoretical or empirical work has elucidated the first proposition of the cultural contingency framework presented above. The following discussion is intended to suggest the effects of certain institutional arrangements on the structure of organizations in Japan and the United States. Before beginning the discussion, we repeat Proposition 1:

Proposition 1: Organizational structures and processes are a function of organization's external cultural environment, including social, economic, and political institutions (Child 1981; Sethi 1975).

Societal Values

Since 1970, consumerism has developed in Japan in a way comparable to the evolution observed in the United States, stimulated largely by the realization among the Japanese that their standard of living has not increased at the same rate as their national productivity (Sethi 1975). The impact of the consumer movement on organizational structure and process can be assessed by analysis of organizational response strategies. According to Sethi, important differences exist between the U.S. and Japanese organizational responses to consumerism. While U.S. organizations use media campaigns to familiarize the public with their position and change their image to fit public expectations, Japanese firms design mechanisms to allow their positions to be expressed by outside groups, such as committees including local residents, scholars, and employees (Sethi 1975). By such boundary-spanning mechanisms, Japanese firms can maintain closer relationships to consumers and the community.

> *Proposition 1a:* The greater the emphasis on information exchange between consumer and community interest groups and the business organization, the more frequent the use of boundary-spanning structural mechanisms to manage the exchange.

The Political Sector

An important feature of the functional relationship between the organization and its political environment is the nature of its relationship to national government. According to Tsurumi (1981), the character of this relationship is cooperative in Japan, while it is adversarial in the United States. The promotion of targeted growth industries is an indication of the Japanese government's economic planning process; this promotion is expressed through governmental cooperation and guidance. The United States does not guide the development of selected industries, but must resort to rescue of certain key enterprises, such as the failing automotive industry. A high level of cooperation in business-government relations means a general reduction of environmental uncertainty experienced by the organization and increased reliance on a centralized national strategic planning process.

> *Proposition 1b:* The greater the cooperation between business and national government, the greater the reliance of the organization on a centralized national strategic planning process.

The Economic Sector

The Sogoshosha (Japanese trading companies) are a unique institution in the Japanese economic environment. The ten leading trading companies generate annual sales equivalent to about 30 percent of Japan's gross national product (Young 1979). These trading companies offer important financial services to their clients, including extension of credit, loans, loan guarantees, and venture capital. Information services offered include current data on product markets throughout the world. These institutions serve as a channel connecting supply and demand, and they also create long-range supply and demand to promote business stability and new opportunities for growth. The organizational result of reduced environmental uncertainty due to increased information is a corresponding reduction in information-gathering mechanisms and a decreased need for differentiation of certain finance and marketing functions within the organization.

> *Proposition 1c:* The greater the institutional structure to support exportation, the greater the information available regarding foreign markets and the greater the activity of the business organization in foreign trade.

Another example of a unique functional relationship in the economic environment is the relationship between the business organization and the labor union. The nature of this relationship is less adversarial in Japan than in the United States. The role of the union is to absorb the ideas and demands of employees and to represent them (Cole 1979). Unions may negotiate for better working conditions, but they consider work assignment to be a managerial prerogative. The emphasis in company and union attitudes is on the exchange of information. This open exchange of information is possible because each company has its own union organization.

> *Proposition 1d:* The greater the common identity of the business organization and the union, the greater the worker participation and the greater the flexibility of the work force in accomplishing organizational goals.

The Technological Sector

The Japanese educational system reinforces the structure of the internal labor market of the Japanese firm. Education may predict whether an individual will be a white-collar or a blue-collar worker within the organization. Based on 1970 census data, 76 percent of employed American males over 25 years of age with 13 or more years of education hold white-collar jobs. Similar data from the 1970 Japanese national census show a parallel percentage when 12 or more years of education are considered. However, in the United States the percentage drops to 69 percent when 12 or more years of education are considered (Cole 1979). These percentages suggest that the high school diploma in Japan is a more consistent predictor of category of occupation than in the United States.

> *Proposition 1e:* The more homogeneous the educational level within each occupational category, the more effective the group-oriented

organizational style, including consensual decision making at the managerial level and quality control circles at the operational level.

The foregoing propositions suggest possible systematic relationships between organizational structures and their institutional environments. The next section of this chapter will describe cultural needs, values, attitudes, and perceptual tendencies that shape individual and group behavior in organizations.

INDIVIDUAL DIMENSIONS OF CULTURE

We repeat here the second proposition of the cultural contingency framework presented above:

> *Proposition 2:* Individual behavior patterns in organizations are a function of the congruence between individual needs, values, attitudes, and perceptual tendencies and organizational structures and processes (Lincoln, Hanada, and Olson 1981; Marsh and Mannari 1976).

Several writers on cross-cultural organizational analysis have described the impact of Japanese culture on organizational structures and processes through individual needs, values, attitudes, and perceptual tendencies (Child 1981; Lincoln, Hanada, and Olson 1981; Marsh and Mannari 1976; Yamamura 1975). The following discussion identifies dimensions that differentiate Japanese and U.S. cultures at the individual level of analysis in interpersonal relationships. Propositions are developed concerning the implications of these individual dimensions for the effective structuring of organizations (Galbraith 1973).

Need for Vertical Social Organization

According to Yamamura (1975) and Sethi (1975), the Japanese have a strong need for an established social rank order. Lincoln, Hanada, and Olson (1981) find that vertical differentiation in the organization is positively related and horizontal differentiation is negatively related to social integration and job satisfaction expressed by Japanese and Japanese-Americans in organizational settings, while vertical and horizontal differentiation are not related to these outcomes for American employees. This aspect of the Japanese character affects organizational structure, manifesting itself in strong departmentalism constructed along functional vertical lines, grouping together a section head and that individual's subordinates, or a university professor and the professor's lecturer, assistant, and students (Yamamura 1975).

> *Proposition 2a:* The greater the individual need for vertical social organization, the more efficient the clear definition of hierarchy, vertical task differentiation, and vertical communication systems in organizational design.

Preference for Groupism

The Japanese sociopsychological tendency toward groupism emphasizes the "us-against-them" perspective (Lincoln, Hanada, and Olson 1981; Sethi 1975; Yamamura 1975). This preference means that Japanese employees may value the company, department, or section of which they are a part over any other social unit. The preference for groupism is expressed through the paternalistic institution of lifetime employment and is reinforced through such organizational practices as welfare programs, company housing for employees, and group sessions before work for exercise and recitation of company mottoes (Sethi 1975).

> *Proposition 2b:* The greater the individual preference for groupism, the more feasible the design of work groups for self-contained tasks and quality control functions.

Need for Dependence and Affiliation

According to Cole (1979), Ouchi and Jaeger (1978), and Sethi (1975), the need for dependence and reliance on others is an important basis of the Japanese social system. This need is related to the indistinct and permeable boundaries between the "self" and "other" characterizing the Japanese self-concept. The need for dependence or affiliation is expressed in cooperative and conforming group behavior (Sethi 1975) and high levels of internalization of organizational and personal goals (Cole 1979).

> *Proposition 2c:* The greater the individual need for dependence and affiliation within the organization, the greater the identity among individual, group, and organizational goals, the greater the cooperative behavior in achieving those goals, and the greater the effectiveness of implicit organizational control systems.

The propositions developed in this section are intended to show the implications of culture-based individual factors affecting interpersonal relationships for the design of organizational structure. The next section of the chapter summarizes the implications of the literature review and the proposed theoretical framework.

CONCLUSION

Recent concern about the growing Japanese challenge to U.S. business has inspired much interest in Japanese managerial style and its applicability in the U.S. business environment. Descriptive approaches to understanding Japanese managerial style have identified the major characteristics of this style distinguishing it from U.S. practices. However, these approaches tend to conceptualize Japanese and U.S. modes of organization as two distinct types, with little attention to the institutional and individual contingencies through which culture affects the applicability of these modes of organization.

A review of the empirical literature published since 1975 contributing to a cultural contingency theory for the comparative analysis of Japanese and U.S. organizations reveals, according to the authors of the research, a lack of evidence to support culture as an empirical construct useful in explaining cross-cultural variance in organizational structures and processes. Three types of empirical studies have been reviewed:

1. studies with the objective of validating contingency theories of organizational structure in the Japanese industrial environment
2. studies with the objective of testing hypotheses concerning comparative Japanese/U.S. organizational analysis at the work-unit or individual level
3. studies with the research aims of contributing to the available data base on Japanese and U.S. organizations, exploring cross-cultural differences through comparative data analysis, and generating research propositions for future empirical testing

Examination of the analytical methods applied in these studies reveals the inadequacy of the conclusion that culture should be rejected as an empirical construct. First, no a priori definition of the dimensions of culture is offered at the institutional, organizational, or individual level of analysis. Second, correlational analyses conducted in the research reviewed often do not justify the conclusion that important structural relations to organizational size or technology remain invariant between Japanese and U.S. organizations and among organizations across cultures in general.

The absolute levels of the observed variables may vary significantly, and they may have differing effects on organizational outcomes such as individual job satisfaction and performance. Variables hypothesized to be culture-based, such as Japanese social organization variables, may not explain variance in organizational structures within a single culture, since they may not vary significantly. Third, very little cross-cultural organizational analysis has in fact been conducted. This important construct cannot be rejected based on research conducted in single cultural settings.

In summary, the defining and testing of culture has not been adequate to justify rejection of culture as a valid empirical construct. It is the premise of this chapter that the definition of the construct is essential to future research on the applicability of the Japanese managerial style in the U.S. business environment, as well as to research on managerial approaches used in other countries. A set of theoretical propositions has been developed in an attempt to contribute to a cultural contingency framework for the comparative analysis of Japanese and U.S. organizations. The greater aim of this framework is to contribute to a general cultural contingency theory of organization.

REFERENCES

Abegglen, J. 1958. *The Japanese Factory*. Glencoe, Ill.: Free Press.

Azumi, K., and C. J. McMillan. 1974. "Management Strategy and Organization Structure: A Japanese Comparative Study." Unpublished paper, Center for Japanese and Korean Studies, University of California, Berkeley.

Child, J. 1981. "Culture, Contingency, and Capitalism in the Cross-National Study of Organizations." In *Research in Organizational Behavior*, ed. L. L. Cummings and B. M. Staw, Vol. 3, pp. 303–52.

Cole, R. E. 1979. *Work, Mobility, and Participation: A Comparative Study of American and Japanese Industry*. Berkeley, Calif.: University of California Press.

Crozier, M. 1964. *The Bureaucratic Phenomenon*. Chicago: University of Chicago Press.

Dore, R. 1973. *British Factory — Japanese Factory*. Berkeley: University of California Press.

Drucker, P. F. 1981. "What We Can Learn From Japanese Management." *Harvard Business Review* (March–April):110–22.

Emery, F., and E. Trist. 1965. "The Causal Texture of Organizational Environments." *Human Relations* 18:21–32.

Galbraith, J. 1973. *Organization Design*. Reading, Mass.: Addison Wesley.

Hatvany, N., and V. Pucik. 1981. "An Integrated Management System: Lessons from the Japanese Experience." *Academy of Management Review*, 6, no.3: 469–80.

Katz, D., and R. Kahn. 1978. *The Social Psychology of Organizations*. New York: John Wiley.

Lincoln, J. R., M. Hanada, and J. Olson. 1981. "Cultural Orientations and Individual Reactions to Organizations: A Study of Employees of Japanese-Owned Firms." *Administrative Science Quarterly* 26:93–115.

Lincoln, J. R., J. Olson, and M. Hanada. 1978. "Cultural Effects on Organizational Structure: The Case of Japanese Firms in the United States." *American Sociological Review* 43:829–47.

Marsh, R., and H. Mannari. 1981. "Technology and Size as Determinants of the Organizational Structure of Japanese Factories." *Administrative Science Quarterly* 26:33–57.

———. 1976. *Modernization and the Japanese Factory.* Princeton, N.J.: Princeton University Press.

Meyer, J. W., and B. Rowan. 1977. "Institutional Organizations: Formal Structure as Myth and Ceremony." *American Journal of Sociology* 83:340–63.

Ouchi, W. G. 1981. *Theory Z: How American Business Can Meet the Japanese Challenge.* Reading, Mass.: Addison-Wesley.

Ouchi, W. G., and A. M. Jaeger. 1978. "Type Z Organization: Stability in the Midst of Mobility." *Academy of Management Review* (April):305–14.

Ouchi, W. G., and R. Price. 1978. "Hierarchies, Clans, and Theory Z: A New Perspective on Organization Development." *Organizational Dynamics* (Autumn): 25–44.

Parsons, T. 1973. "Culture and Social System Revisited." In *The Idea of Culture in the Social Sciences*, ed. L. Schnieder and C. M. Bonjean. Cambridge: Cambridge University Press.

Pascale, R. T. 1978a. "Communication and Decision Making Across Cultures: Japanese and American Comparisons." *Administrative Science Quarterly* 23: 91–109.

———. 1978b. "Zen and the Art of Management." *Harvard Business Review* (March-April):153–62.

Pugh, D. S., D. J. Hickson, C. R. Hinings, and C. Turner. 1969. "Dimensions of Organizational Structure." *Administrative Science Quarterly* 14:211–28.

Sethi, S. P. 1975. *Japanese Business and Social Conflict: A Comparative Analysis of Response Patterns with American Business.* Cambridge, Mass.: Ballinger.

Tracy, P., and K. Azumi. 1976. "Determinants of Administrative Contol: A Test of a Theory with Japanese Factories." *American Sociological Review* 41:80–93.

Tsurumi, Y. 1981. *Comparative Teaching Modules on Japan: Business-Government Relations.* New York: Japan Society.

Vogel, E. F. 1979. *Japan as No. 1: Lessons for America.* Cambridge, Mass.: Harvard University Press.

Woodward, J. 1965. *Industrial Organization: Theory and Practice.* London: Oxford University Press.

Yamamura, K. Y. 1975. "A Compromise with Culture: The Historical Evolution of the Managerial Structure of Large Japanese Firms." In *Evolution of International Management Structures*, ed. H. F. Williamson. Newark: University of Delaware Press.

Young, A. K. 1979. *The Sogo Shosha: Japan's Multinational Trading Companies.* Boulder, Colo.: Westview Press.

18

Is Japanese-Style Management Anything New? A Comparison of Japanese-Style Management with U.S. Participative Models

JAMES L. HALL *and* JOEL K. LEIDECKER

INTRODUCTION

Considerable attention has been focused recently on the Japanese style of management, due to the growth of Japanese productivity compared with that of the United States. One set of studies has centered on Japanese management as practiced in Japan (Bowen 1977; Drucker 1971; 1981; Rehder 1979; Whitehill and Takezawa 1978). Such studies describe how Japanese companies are organized and managed and, to some extent, discuss the feasibility of exporting parts or all of the Japanese systems to the West.

A second set of studies, more relevant to U.S. managers, describes the use of Japanese management techniques in the United States (Hatvany and

We acknowledge with thanks our colleagues Dennis Moberg and Barry Posner, who provided helpful reviews of an earlier draft of this study.

Pucik 1981; Johnson and Ouchi 1974; Kraar 1975; Krisher 1981; Tavernier 1976). These studies suggest that Japanese managers have increased the productivity and satisfaction of American employees by using the Japanese management style.

Third, Ouchi (1981), Ouchi and Jaeger (1978), and Main (1981) have described a management style, Type Z, that is in effect a version of the Japanese style but one that has evolved simultaneously in a few U.S. organizations without the involvement of Japanese managers or ownership.

We have drawn upon these three sources to develop a model we call Japanese-style management (JSM — see Figure 18.1), and will use this model in the comparative analysis that follows in the second section of this chapter.

Japanese-style management, whether in Japan or abroad, typically has several distinguishing characteristics. Above all, however, Japanese management is probably best described as a participative management style. The term "participative management" has become a catchword in the United States and has lost specific meaning. Consequently, it is important to identify the precise similarities and differences between the Japanese style of participative management and other specific models of participative management.

Making such a comparison is important for two reasons. First, communication between and among managers and scholars is often frustrated by a lack of comparisons. As Lorsch (1979) has pointed out: "Different scholars use different labels to mean the same thing. Because no one relates his ideas to those of others, an academic Tower of Babel develops" (p. 176). Second, a thorough analysis and comparison of similar theories minimizes the danger of oversimplification (which may involve inaccurate conclusions as to content and use), a trap both practitioners and academicians may fall into. In this context, the question is whether JSM is anything more than the participative management techniques introduced in the U.S. management literature. If our analysis supports, reflects, or raises new issues relating to this question, then the result will further the understanding and application of the participative management literature.

Is JSM anything more than an old package with new wrapping paper? This study explores this question. First we will summarize the salient characteristics of JSM. Then we will compare prominent U.S. models of participative management with JSM.

JAPANESE-STYLE MANAGEMENT (JSM)

Bottom-up Process

JSM emphasizes information flow and initiative from the lower levels of the organization to the top level. The apparent assumption is that change and

FIGURE 18.1 Japanese-Style Management: Sources and Characteristics

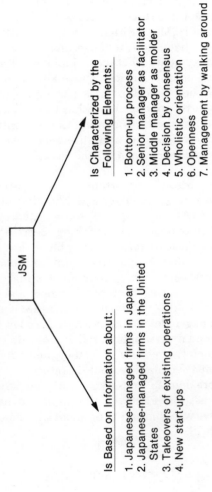

Is Based on Information about:

1. Japanese-managed firms in Japan
2. Japanese-managed firms in the United States
3. Takeovers of existing operations
4. New start-ups

JSM

Is Characterized by the Following Elements:

1. Bottom-up process
2. Senior manager as facilitator
3. Middle manager as molder
4. Decision by consensus
5. Wholistic orientation
6. Openness
7. Management by walking around

Type Z Firms:

1. Naturally evolved U.S. operations
2. Evolved via "Z" change agents

Source: Compiled by the author.

initiative should come from those closest to the problem, whatever the organizational level (Johnson and Ouchi 1974). In support of this assumption, each employee has access to all managerial levels — a real open-door policy that runs counter to the typical lines of authority and the formal communication channels in most U.S. firms. Indeed, in Japanese-run plants, senior managers often visit the shop floor on "rounds" to make themselves more accessible (Tavernier 1976).

The Senior Manager as Facilitator

Senior managers do not perceive their task to be one of setting objectives and issuing orders. Instead they do respond actively to the ideas resulting from the bottom-up process. Such a response requires large amounts of time spent in interactions with lower levels within the organization. Typically the senior manager asks questions, makes suggestions, provides encouragement, and may send subordinates who have made proposals back for more information. Thus the manager performs a teaching function.

Often U.S. managers have difficulty working within this perspective, and feel frustrated at the lack of explicit directions from senior management. The Japanese, however, emphasize the importance of "knowing the company": understanding the company's philosophy, having a sense of its corporate strategy, and knowing what type of behavior is valued. Thus each employee understands what the company is trying to do and can determine, in each situation, what is best for the company even if no one tells the employee what to do. Such a philosophy is, of course, very consistent with the bottom-up process (Johnson and Ouchi 1974).

The Middle Manager as Molder

A key role for middle-level managers is helping subordinates and colleagues shape a composite plan before presenting it to superiors. As noted earlier, junior managers are not perceived as functional specialists who carry out bosses' directives. They are expected to be perceivers and identifiers of problems, and are expected to formulate tentative solutions to such problems. A critical aspect of this role is developing coordination with other departments affected by any problem or solution. Thus the Japanese place great emphasis on *lateral communication* at all organizational levels.

Many American managers feel uncomfortable with this emphasis. While a Japanese manager might view a day on the telephone as productive, an American manager is apt to view such a day as unproductive. Indeed, the Japanese are often critical of American managers' communication skills.

The Japanese often use an open office plan to encourage communication across all organizational levels. This structure provides a setting in which several managers and their subordinates can easily converse. Furthermore, in the open work setting almost all information becomes "public" information, thereby helping all employees to attain the objective of "knowing the company" (Johnson and Ouchi 1974).

Decision by Consensus

Consensus does not necessarily mean unanimity. It does indicate, however, that each participant in the decision-making process feels satisfied that his or her point of view has been fairly heard; consensus also means that each participant is willing to go along with *and support* the decision (Hatvany and Pucik 1981). This technique is closely related to the lateral communication emphasis of JSM. It is an attempt to reach a consensus based on close coordination of the activities of each functional area affected by an issue. Typically, the consensus process will involve much time and numerous meetings. Many people, at several organizational levels, will review and discuss a problem before a decision emerges.

A key assumption of this consensus decision-making process is that, while in most cases there are many viable alternatives, consensus creates commitment of all participants to the chosen solution. Thus, acceptance of the decision is stressed. At the same time, the review process and the open dialogue help to insure high-quality decisions as well as commitment (Johnson and Ouchi 1974). In addition, the process is a means to signal and reinforce the value the organization places on cooperative effort by its members.

Wholistic Orientation

JSM includes a concern for the welfare of all employees, and is exemplified on the job by managers' concern for the total employee, not just those facts about the employee that affect today's performance. Employees and managers know more about each other and engage in a wider range of work and nonwork activities than is usual in the West. There is an opportunity to accomplish work objectives with friends. The wholistic orientation emphasizes and fosters an egalitarian atmosphere. This atmosphere is a central feature of Type Z organizations and implies the presence of trust: trust that employees can work autonomously, without close supervision (Ouchi 1981).

JSM stresses the importance of shaping and influencing employees' attitudes toward the job. Attitudes are considered crucial to productivity and quality control. Japanese managers demonstrate concern for the whole employee in several ways. One way is by knowing the names of all employees. In a small firm of 100 employees, the president would be expected to know all the employees. In large organizations, it is expected that at least two levels of management above foreman will know the employees by name and be familiar with personal details such as when an employee's baby is due (Kraar 1975). The objective is to let people know they count.

Japanese managers try to create a positive attitude in the workforce by providing a role model, through diligence and long working hours. Japanese executives become personally familiar with the jobs at all levels by making rounds and by working on shop/floor jobs occasionally. Another practice helps generate worker commitment: an employee who has made an honest mistake is rarely fired. Executives believe that employees will become more productive by learning from mistakes (Kraar 1975).

Consensus decision making and the bottom-up process also support a wholistic orientation, by demonstrating that the company values the employees' contribution to decision making.

Openness

In JSM there is a strong norm of openness; there is a place for honesty and criticism in an atmosphere of trust. This trust is based on the assumption that, in the long run, everyone shares fundamentally compatible goals (Ouchi 1981). Another aspect of openness, which reinforces the discussion of communication above, is the use of the open office plan to encourage communication across all organizational levels. This structure provides a setting in which several managers and their subordinates can easily converse. Furthermore, the open office setting allows most information to become "public" information, thereby helping all employees attain the objective of "knowing the company" (Johnson and Ouchi 1974).

Management by Walking Around

Ouchi (1981) developed the concept of "management by walking around" in his description of Type Z organizations. This management practice is also evident in reports on Japanese-managed organizations (Hatvany and Pucik 1981; Krisher 1981). Management by walking around involves two aspects: (1) career development — managers may be moved laterally or even to apparently lower-level jobs to provide new exposure; and (2) a rather informal day-to-day style of managing — including moving the desk of a top manager to the center of a problem area and frequent visits by top management to the production line to discuss problems with workers or even to work occasionally on the production line.

Both aspects underscore the importance of getting out into the organization to become familiar with personnel and their tasks at all levels and from many perspectives. It is one method by which cooperation and openness are encouraged.

U.S. MODELS OF PARTICIPATIVE MANAGEMENT

In this section, we compare five important U.S. models of participative management with JSM. Each U.S. model is examined to determine whether it includes the JSM elements and, if so, to what extent. The models chosen are:

1. Human relations model
2. Tannenbaum and Schmidt's leadership continuum
3. Greiner's participative management characteristics
4. Likert's System 4
5. Blake and Mouton's 9, 9 style

Table 18.1 provides a summary assessment of these models according to specific dimensions of JSM.

Human Relations Model

Various interpretations of the human relations model can be found. They include: (1) an attempt to modify the classical or bureaucratic approach by recognizing the existence of individual needs and behavioral patterns—that is, of factors other than economic rationality (Scott 1967); (2) an emphasis on politeness, with "pleases" required to reflect the proper attitude toward subordinates, followed by sensitivity training (Herzberg 1968); (3) an attempt by managers to use behavioral science research in a limited and manipulative way to obtain compliance with managerial authority (Miles 1965).

One central theme in these diverse interpretations leads to the conclusion that the human relations model calls for interest in the employee's psychological state. Thus, the human relations model shares with JSM an emphasis on a wholistic, or personal, concern for the employee. The wholistic orientation of JSM goes well beyond the "concern for employee" prescription of the human relations model, by providing a linkage between attitudes and

TABLE 18.1 An Assessment of U.S. Models of Participative Management According to Elements of Japanese-Style Management (JSM)

U.S. MODELS	JSM ELEMENTS						
	BOTTOM-UP PROCESS	SENIOR MANAGER AS FACILITATOR	MIDDLE MANAGER AS MOLDER	OPENNESS AND HONEST CRITICISM	DECISION MAKING BY CONSENSUS	WHOLISTIC ORIENTATION	MANAGEMENT BY WALKING AROUND
Human Relations Model	Low	Low	Low	Moderate	Low	Moderate	Low
Tannenbaum and Schmidt's Leadership Continuum	High	Low	Low	Moderate	Moderate	Moderate	Low
Greiner's Participative Management Characteristics	High	Moderate	Moderate	Moderate	Low	Moderate	Low
Likert's System 4	Moderate	High	High	High	High	Moderate	Low
Blake and Mouton's 9,9 Style	High	High	High	Moderate	Moderate	Moderate	Low

Note: Low = little if any mention; Moderate = some discussion; High = an important part of the model.

productivity, stressing the equalitarian atmosphere as a means of establishing trust, and placing greater emphasis on the depth of involvement between employees and management in work- and nonwork-related activities.

Openness is another dimension found in some of the writing on human relations. Certainly openness is an important tenet of sensitivity training. Other elements of JSM seem to be missing from the human relations model, however. Little emphasis is given to the bottom-up process. The supervision role remains primarily one of problem finder and decision maker rather than facilitator of decision making and shaper/molder of ideas. Attention is not given to consensual decision making or to management by walking about.

Tannenbaum and Schmidt's Leadership Continuum

Tannenbaum and Schmidt's (1973) model of leadership is presented in Figure 18.2. In this model, the authors describe a range of leadership styles, from highly autocratic to highly participative. Movement to the right along the continuum indicates a more participative approach. The leadership styles on the extreme right resemble JSM in their bottom-up style of decision making.

> [The extreme right] represents an extreme degree of group freedom only occasionally encountered in formal organizations. Here the team of managers or engineers undertakes the identification and diagnosis of the problem, develops alternate proceedings for solving it, and decides on one or more of these alternative solutions (Tannenbaum and Schmidt 1973, p. 7; emphasis added).

This description indicates the presence of the lower-level initiative and responsibility characteristic of the bottom-up decision-making process. In fact, the degree of low-level initiative may exceed JSM, since under JSM the decision would not be made by one level alone.

The manager's role, however, does not seem to be the same as in JSM.

> If the boss participates in the decision-making process, he attempts to do so with no more authority than any other member of the group. He commits himself in advance to assist in implementing whatever decision the group makes (Tannenbaum and Schmidt 1973, p. 7).

This role differs substantially from the facilitator and molder roles of JSM, because it seems to abrogate the teaching function present in JSM.

FIGURE 18.2 Tannenbaum and Schmidt's Leadership Continuum Model

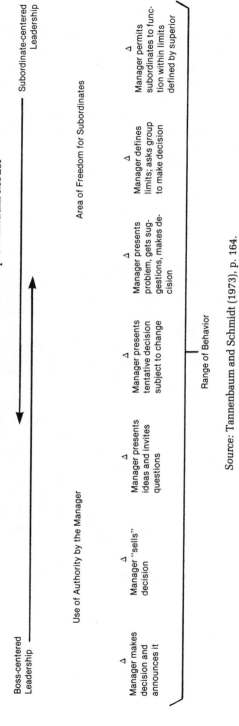

Source: Tannenbaum and Schmidt (1973), p. 164.

Any discussion of consensus decision making in the Tannenbaum and Schmidt model is limited to intragroup decision making. No attention is given to intergroup consensus or to the lateral communication stressed in JSM. The atmosphere of trust and open communication and the career-development orientation that are prevalent themes in JSM are not mentioned with any degree of specificity in the Tannenbaum and Schmidt model. Finally, the Tannenbaum and Schmidt model does not directly discuss the "personal concern" stressed in JSM, with its wholistic orientation although such concern may be implied.

Greiner's Participative Management Characteristics

Greiner (1973) has been included because his research identifies the characteristics that U.S. managers attribute to participative management. Managers attending the Harvard Business School Executive Development Program were asked to specify the leadership characteristics that they most closely associated with a participative management style. Table 18.2 identifies the characteristics rated as the top ten.

The inclusion of subordinate involvement in decision making could reflect a bottom-up approach, although it is not clear whether the initiative element of a bottom-up approach is assumed or stressed. Keeping subordinates informed (Number 2) and being easily approachable (Number 4), however, are certainly integral aspects of a bottom-up approach.

Counseling and developing subordinates might be consistent with the molder role of JSM. However, we lack a clear indication of how much counseling and development is to be accomplished. Do managers have in mind the questioning, Socratic mode of JSM; or is the counseling and development to be accomplished with a "tell and sell" technique? A wholistic orientation is indicated, as managers include "thoughtfulness and consideration of others" (Number 7), and "doing everything possible to make the organization's morale high" (Number 3), as dimensions of participative management. There is little indication that decision making by consensus and lateral communication are stressed, nor is the specific career-path orientation (management by walking around) of JSM discussed.

Likert's System 4

Likert's (1967) research on organizational effectiveness has provided us with a comprehensive model of participative management. He identifies organizational characteristics such as leadership style and communication

TABLE 18.2   Greiner's Participative Management Characteristics

THE TEN HIGHEST-RATED PARTICIPATION CHARACTERISTICS	AVERAGE SCALE RATING
1. Manager gives subordinates a share in decision making.	6.08
2. Manager keeps subordinates informed of the true situation, good or bad, under all circumstances.	5.69
3. Manager stays aware of the state of the organization's morale and does everything possible to make it high.	5.45
4. Manager is easily approachable.	5.38
5. Manager counsels, trains, and develops subordinates.	5.34
6. Manager communicates effectively with subordinates.	5.22
7. Manager shows thoughtfulness and consideration of others.	5.19
8. Manager is willing to make changes in ways of doing things.	4.96
9. Manager is willing to support subordinates even when they make mistakes.	4.92
10. Manager expresses appreciation when a subordinate does a good job.	4.80

Note: On the scale, 1 equals low degree of participation and 7 equals high degree of participation.
Source: Greiner (1973), p. 114.

patterns to determine the extent to which a participative management approach is used. Likert identifies a range of management styles specified as Systems 1 to 4, with System 4 being the most participative. As indicated in Table 18.1, System 4, of the U.S. models reviewed so far, approximates the JSM approach most closely. An overview of Likert's System 4 model is provided in Table 18.3.

Freedom to talk to superiors about one's job is an important prerequisite for a bottom-up system of decision making. It is not clear, however, whether such freedom is intended to extend as high as it does in JSM (that is, to the president of a company). The suggestion that subordinates' ideas are sought and used constructively also is supportive of the bottom-up element. The term "sought," however, does not seem to emphasize the importance of subordinate initiative, which is a key part of bottom-up decision making in JSM.

Under System 4, the manager's role is "supportive" (Likert 1967, p. 48). This includes helping subordinates think through problems and helping subordinates to think for themselves, dimensions that seem consistent with JSM's conception of the manager as a molder and shaper of ideas.

Likert states that decision making by consensus is part of System 4

TABLE 18.3   Characteristics of System 4 Management

1. A great deal of confidence and trust is shown in subordinates.
2. Subordinates feel free to talk to superiors about job.
3. Superiors frequently seek and constructively use subordinates' ideas.
4. Group involvement and rewards are a focus of leadership and motivation in the organization.
5. Responsibility for achieving organizational goals extends to all levels within the organization.
6. A great deal of cooperative teamwork exists.
7. Information flows in the organization are both vertical and lateral.
8. Downward communication is accepted with a receptive mind.
9. Upward communication is almost always accurate.
10. Superiors are very aware of and knowledgeable about problems faced by subordinates.
11. Decisions are made at all levels within the organization, but are well integrated.
12. Subordinates are fully involved in decisions related to their work.
13. The decision-making process contributes to motivation of subordinates.
14. Organizational goals (except in crisis situations) are established by group action.
15. Very little covert resistance to goals is present.
16. Review and control functions are widely shared throughout the organization.
17. The goals of the informal organization are the same as those of the formal organization.
18. Productivity and cost information and other control data are used for self-guidance and problem solving.

Source: Adapted from Dowling (1973), p. 35.

management. He develops the linking pin concept, which states that group-to-group relationships exist in organizations, with individuals serving as a linking pin. Thus lateral coordination, which is an important part of JSM decision making by consensus, is included in System 4 (Dowling 1973). Also, the emphasis on "cooperative teamwork" and on integrated decisions made at all levels of the organization seems consistent with the JSM consensus approach. Some concern for the whole person is present in System 4: "How much is your superior really interested in helping you with your personal and family problems?" (Likert 1967, p. 48). Likert does not expand on this theme, however, to the extent found in JSM, with its wholistic orientation. Finally, System 4 does not state or imply the importance of or the strategy for an individual's career path in an organization; System 4 has no component like the management by walking around of JSM.

Managerial Grid: 9, 9 Style

In the managerial grid, Blake and Mouton (1964) provide a model for thinking about managerial behavior in terms of two dimensions: (1) concern for production and (2) concern for people. Emphasis is placed on the degree of concern, recognizing that a wide variety of behavior is possible. Figure 18.3 identifies five types of behavior based on varying combinations of concern for production and concern for people. The most open, participative style is a combination of high concern for production with a high concern for people (9, 9). Blake and Mouton's evidence indicates this style is more effective than the others (1964, p. 248).

There seem to be several similarities between the 9, 9 style and JSM.

FIGURE 18.3   Blake and Mouton's Managerial Grid: 9, 9 Style

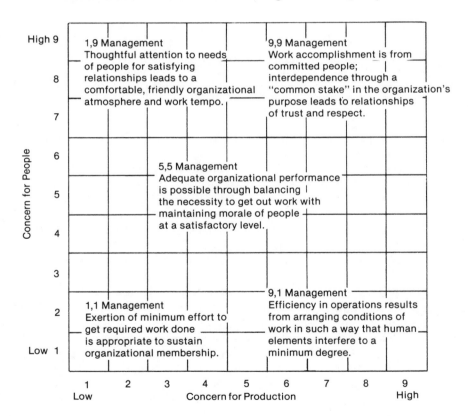

Source: Blake and Mouton (1966), p. 31.

Overall, there is a comparable emphasis on gaining commitment to the organization by "creating conditions of work where people understand the problem, have stakes in the outcomes, and where their ideas make a real contribution to the result obtained" (Blake and Mouton 1964, p. 144).

The 9, 9 style recognizes the potential contribution of individuals at all levels to effective decision making. In this respect, the 9, 9 style does include a bottom-up approach, but without the emphasis on initiative from below. It is critical to the bottom-up approach, however, that all employees understand the organization's purpose and direction; such understanding facilitates initiative from below. The 9, 9 style does stress understanding and awareness both of the total organizational purpose and of how that purpose affects one's own area of concern (section, department, and so on).

The 9, 9 style is consistent with the shaper/molder role and with the facilitator role, as indicated by the following quotations:

> My job is not necessarily to *make* sound decisions, but it surely is my job to see to it that sound decisions are made . . . .
>
> I keep familiar with major points of progress and exert influence on subordinates through identifying problems and resolving goals with them as necessary. I lend assistance when needed by helping to remove road blocks (Blake and Mouton 1964, p. 143).

Like JSM, the 9, 9 approach is very concerned with generating worker commitment to organizational goals by "creating conditions of work where people understand the problem, [have a stake in the outcome], and where ideas then make a real contribution to the result obtained."

However, the descriptions of the 9, 9 approach do not refer to the wholistic orientation, the "personal" involvement approach, that in JSM shapes attitudes toward such commitment. We find, for example, no mention of knowing details about employees' children.

However, JSM and 9, 9 are similar in their philosophy about and reaction to mistakes. As in JSM, mistakes are corrected in such a way that the *cause* is dealt with. The manager might say, "Tough luck. It's embarrassing, but the thing is to study the problem and to learn from it" (Blake and Mouton 1964, p. 148).

The 9, 9 style identifies several decision-making options as desirable (group, pair, solo), and does not focus on decision making by consensus as the JSM model does. Like JSM, however, the 9, 9 approach does stress the importance of coordination (and lateral communication), regardless of whether this leads to decision making by consensus. Critical to 9, 9 is the development of shared responsibility; the goal is to avoid situations where areas of responsibility "fall into the cracks."

CONCLUSION

During the decade of the 1970s, and now into the 1980s, management theorists and practitioners in the United States continue to observe and study Japanese management techniques and their application to U.S. management. Some have hailed these techniques as revolutionary and a major breakthrough in dealing with productivity problems. In this chapter, we have referred to this phenomenon as Japanese-style management (JSM). We have summarized and briefly discussed the major components of this managerial and organizational style, and have attempted to answer the question, Is JSM really different from U.S. views of participative management? Is JSM "old hat"? We have analyzed several contributions to U.S. management literature and compared these approaches with JSM.

Table 18.1 highlights our assessment of five U.S. models of participative management with respect to the seven elements of JSM. It is clear that there are similarities between JSM and U.S. models of participative management. At first glance, it may seem that U.S. managers and academics are becoming excited about an approach already described and espoused by U.S. theorists. To some extent it may be that Japanese managers are practicing what U.S. theorists and models have preached.

However, as Table 18.1 indicates, we believe that none of the U.S. models is as comprehensive as JSM in either breadth or depth. Although all of the U.S. models contain at least one JSM element, none of the U.S. models includes substantial discussion of all seven JSM elements. It is clear that, overall, the U.S. models lack the breadth of JSM. Furthermore JSM has more depth; that is, it is more fully developed than any of the U.S. models. In JSM, the development of each element is more thorough. The description of each element is often more elaborate; greater emphasis is place on the importance of each element. This contrast is indicated in Table 18.1 whenever "moderate" or "low" appears. Such comprehensiveness differentiates JSM from U.S. models of participative management, and may well provide the manager with a more effective road map with which to use a participative management technique.

Is JSM anything new? We think so. It provides a very comprehensive and effectively integrated model of participative management. It is a contribution from which U.S. managers can benefit.

REFERENCES

Blake, Robert R., and Jane Arygley Mouton. 1964. *The Managerial Grid*. Houston: Gulf.

Bowen, William. 1977. "Japanese Managers Tell How Their System Works." *For-*

tune, November, pp. 126–38.

Burck, Charles G. 1981. "Working Smarter." *Fortune*, June 15, pp. 68–73.

Dowling, William F. 1973. "An Interview With Rensis Likert." *Organizational Dynamics* (Summer):32–50.

Drucker, Peter F. 1981. "Behind Japan's Success." *Harvard Business Review* (January–February):83–90.

———. 1971. "What We Can Learn from Japanese Management." *Harvard Business Review* (March/April):110–22.

Greiner, Larry E. 1973. "What Managers Think of Participative Leadership." *Harvard Business Review* (March–April):111–17.

Hatvany, Nina, and Vladimir Pucik. 1981. "Japanese Management Practices and Productivity." *Organizational Dynamics* (Spring):4–21.

Herzberg, Frederick. 1968. "One More Time: How Do You Motivate Employees?" *Harvard Business Review* (January–February):53–62.

Johnson, Richard T., and William G. Ouchi. 1974. "Made in America (Under Japanese Management)." *Harvard Business Review* (September/October):61–69.

Kraar, Louise. 1975. "The Japanese Are Coming — With Their Own Style of Management." *Fortune*, March, pp. 116–64.

Krisher, Bernard. 1981. "How the Japanese Manage in the U.S." *Fortune*, June 15, pp. 97–103.

Likert, Rensis. 1967. *The Human Organization*. New York: McGraw-Hill.

Lorsch, Jay W. 1979. "Making Behavioral Science More Useful." *Harvard Business Review* (March/April):171–80.

Main, Jeremy. 1981. "Westinghouse Cultural Revolution." *Fortune*, June 15, pp. 74–93.

Miles, Raymond E. 1965. "Human Relations or Human Resources." *Harvard Business Review* (July–August):150–56.

Ouchi, William. 1981. *Theory Z: How American Business Can Meet the Japanese Challenge*. Reading, Mass.: Addison-Wesley.

Ouchi, William G., and Alfred M. Jaeger. 1978. "Type Z Organization: Stability in the Midst of Mobility." *Academy of Management Review* (April):305–15.

Rehder, Robert R. 1979. "Japanese Management: An American Challenge." *Human Resource Management* (Winter):21–27.

Scott, William G. 1967. *Organization Theory*. Ill.: Richard D. Irwin.

Tannenbaum, Robert, and Warren H. Schmidt. 1973. "How to Choose a Leadership Pattern." *Harvard Business Review* (May–June):162–80.

Tavernier, Gerard. 1976. "Applying Japanese Techniques in the West." *International Management* (June):35–40.

Whitehill, Arthur M., and Shin-icki Takezawa. 1978. "Workplace Harmony: Another Japanese Miracle?" *Columbia Journal of World Business* (Fall):25–39.

19

Motivational Orientation Differences between Japan and the United States: The Key to Worker Productivity Successes and Problems

MATT M. AMANO

A recent government publication reports that the labor productivity in the United States has steadily been decreasing during the past three decades. Especially recently, the annual productivity increase has been minimal at best; in the worst cases productivity has dropped. Some other industrial nations, on the other hand, have been reporting consistently high productivity gains (*Handbook*, p. 582; *Monthly Labor Review:* 96).

This poor showing by the United States in the area of labor productivity progress seems somewhat incongruous in view of the fact that an increasingly greater number of behavioral scientists have been engaged, during the same period, in trying to discover keys to worker motivation and organizational effectiveness.

This chapter tries to look at this motivation issue from a cross-cultural perspective, especially comparing the U.S. and the Japanese motivational orientations. In brief, it seems that U.S. theories of motivation place a heavy emphasis on what may be called "self-centered" motivation; the culture in general seems to support such an orientation. The Japanese culture, on the other hand, seems to emphasize what may be called "others-oriented" motivation.

This chapter will look into these two motivational orientations in some detail and will suggest a new direction the organizational behaviorists may pursue in their search for keys to greater worker motivation and higher worker productivity.

SELF-CENTERED MOTIVATION

A Pandora's box of worker motivation was opened when longitudinal research was conducted at the Hawthorne Works of the Western Electric Company in the late 1920s and the early 1930s (Roethlisberger and Dickson 1939). Ever since, many scholars have looked into worker motivation issues in an effort to describe the keys to worker motivation and improved productivity (Hampton et al. 1973, pp. 3–23).

When various pieces of research are looked at together, an interesting characteristic common to them emerges. They all seem to subscribe to the same basic motivational theme: an emphasis on self-interest. An individual behaves in certain ways because these behaviors are of greatest benefit to that individual. This orientation is self-centered and immediately self-serving. Given this premise, it may be easier to understand why there has been so much emphasis on the "carrot in front of the donkey" in worker motivation. In every theory presented, whether it is Maslow's (1954) need hierarchy, the two-factor theory of Herzberg et al. (1959), or McClelland's (1961) needs theory, the basic pattern seems to be to find what workers want and provide what is wanted, to motivate them to work harder.

This emphasis on self-centered motivation is often seen even in daily use of the English language. A passenger who wishes to have the driver of a car turn to the right at the next corner may say, perhaps without much thought, "Now *you want* to turn to the right." Obviously, it is the passenger's wish and not the driver's to turn to the right. Yet, through this expression, the passenger conveys the message that it is the driver's choice to turn to the right, thus serving his own interests and not the passenger's. In a similar fashion, daily encounters often include questions such as "Would you like to do this?" or "Are you interested in doing that?" In most cases these expressions are pleas for help. The U.S. culture, as exemplified by these daily expressions, must be oriented toward self-centered motivation.

Yet, as Maslow pointed out, when a need is satisfied, one shifts toward other need(s) (1954, pp. 80–106). In other words, needs can be satisfied, and those needs that have been satisfied cannot be much use in motivating an individual. In this sense, carrot-in-front-of-the-donkey motivational practices have their own built-in limitation. Besides, workers may realize management is eager to cater to their current needs only to have them work more productively; they may also see that management is the party to benefit from the changes. In such a situation, the workers not only understand that they are being exploited but also resent such managerial exploitation. If U.S. management utilizes available motivational theories and practices to exploit unsuspecting workers so that management gains, the tactic may be effective in the short run but perhaps not in the long run.

Consider an employee who is given a challenging job. The person may work hard, if the two-factor theory of motivation is correct (Herzberg et al. 1959, pp. 113–19). That employee is contributing toward organizational effectiveness. Theoretically speaking, such an employee does not need to be appreciated or rewarded; that individual has excelled when challenged, and done what he or she wanted to do.

With this self-centered motivation, a society does not require anyone to be obliged to anyone else; thus it is unnecessary for one to thank others. U.S. society can be called, from this point of view, a thankless society. The assumption that we do things because we want to, of course, serves us well, especially at the beginning. We have freedom of choice and we allow no one to restrict our choices. Yet, in order to make a living, we may do what our work requires over and over again for a long time. A dentist may pull hundreds or thousands of teeth during a lifetime practice. An assembly-line worker may tighten the one-millionth bolt. A lawyer may read tens of thousands of pages of legal proceedings. No interest bug can survive under these circumstances. There can be no intrinsic satisfaction left in the job itself.* Yet the job must be carried on. This societal assumption that people work because they want to, nevertheless, makes it necessary for people to seek rewards from what they are doing, since they cannot expect appreciation from others. When there is no more reward from the job itself, therefore, there cannot be any more motivation for one to excel.

OTHERS-ORIENTED MOTIVATION

In Japan, the societal view of personal motivation seems "others-oriented." That is, individuals who serve the needs of others know that they are of value to the society, and are rewarded by that knowledge. The basic as-

---

*This thought may contradict what is said by Robert N. Ford (1969).

sumption in Japan is that one does things not because one wants to, but rather because things have to be done to fulfill others' needs.

This others-oriented motivation is expressed in Japanese as *ikigai* (pronounced "iky-guy"), which may be translated into English as "reason for being" (Mita 1970). In plain language, it means the reasons for one's existence: "Why do I live, or what is the value of my living to the society?" With this type of motivational assumption, rewards come, as was mentioned before, from the awareness that one is useful to others. Workers work hard because working hard is productive and useful for the organization to which they belong and for the society in general. In return, management is expected to put serving the needs of its workers first. Japanese management is expected to provide, as a moral and not legal obligation, lifetime employment for workers. This expectation seems to be rooted in the societal assumption that actions are undertaken because of the needs of others. Thus the concept of mutual support between management and labor is heavily emphasized in daily behavior.

Under the Japanese system, individuals allow others to serve them. Yet this very act of receiving services from others makes each individual immediately obliged to others. Because society assumes that the others-oriented motivation is present, appreciation for others' services is always expected from the recipients of the services, even when such services have been rendered for purposes of business gains. Even if one no longer finds doing the job itself rewarding, one can at least receive the reward of appreciation from the recipients of one's services.

It can be said that in Japan management exists to protect the welfare of workers and workers exist to serve the needs of the organization and its management. A mutual support and dependence relationship, therefore, exists in the Japanese place of employment. Because of this, one may find in Japan another interesting institution called *amae* (pronounced "a-ma-ye") (Doi 1972). There is no English equivalent for this word. It may be most closely translated as "dependence on parental indulgence." Workers show *amae* by entrusting their future to management. It then becomes the responsibility of management to look after the welfare of each worker by studying his or her personality, interests, past performances, and other characteristics, and to find for him or her the most appropriate career path in the organization. When a worker is not doing well, it is again considered the superior's responsibility to help the worker to become a productive and self-respecting member of the organization. From time to time, workers may slip in their performance, yet they may not feel insecure because they know that they are allowed to depend on *amae*, this parental indulgence of management.

This mechanism of *amae* provides security for workers and makes them feel comfortable even when they are in error or in a slump. Sooner or later they will be out of it. This feeling of security seems to help them discharge their productive energy on their assigned tasks. The Japanese workers know that when they take care of their management by producing results, they can be assured that management will take care of them.

This system of mutual support and trust is considered the major reason that management does not lay off workers during times of economic recession, even when everyone knows that there is a surplus of labor in the organization. Once even one person is laid off, the basic premise of mutual dependence and trust will be broken, and the foundation of the others-oriented motivation will be violated. As a result, in a serious business recession, Japanese management often cuts its own wages first, then asks for volunteers to resign, offering substantial financial incentives, and only finally resorts to lay-offs.

THE MOTIVATION PROBLEM IN THE UNITED STATES

PART V

In the United States, management seems to coddle workers when business is booming. At such times, management apparently is eager to provide whatever incentives are necessary. Yet workers are often laid off without proper advance warning as the business cycle turns downward, and at such a time a position elsewhere may be difficult to find. It often seems as if management lays off workers without giving the matter a second thought. This managerial act, in itself, reinforces the workers' self-centered motivation. They must act solely based on their own interests. When business is good, they may feel that they should demand the highest rewards in terms of wages and benefits yet produce the least, conserving their energy. With whatever energy is conserved, they can search for other sources of income, making themselves independent from the employer's whims. While employed, they may think, they should gain as much experience and knowledge as possible; then they can leave the position as soon as another, more attractive job opportunity appears.

The recent emphasis on "self-fulfillment" seems to endorse this self-centered motivation. One is looking for a self-fulfilling job, whatever that means. Many may think a self-fulfilling job is a job that satisfies their own needs, allowing them to feel self-respecting and comfortable, and to enjoy great social prestige. To gain a self-fulfilling job, people may even try to exploit others, without any feeling of empathy (Kernberg 1978). Such an orientation, however, may only enhance the feeling of mutual distrust and exploitation between workers and management and among workers. High productivity can not be expected from workers under such circumstances.

REEXAMINATION OF THE PAST

When one rereads some of the original writings of familiar authors — Frederick W. Taylor (1947) or Abraham H. Maslow (1954), for instance — one may get impressions different from what one might have been led to believe. Consider, for instance, Taylor, the father of scientific management. He is often described as advocating the application of scientific methods to finding the best way to do a job; each worker was then to follow this best way like a robot. This idea of robotizing the worker created much concern in the United States (Taylor 1947, pt. 3). Yet, if one reads Taylor's original writings, his motivation becomes clear immediately. He observed that a healthy and sturdy worker who ran from home to work moved slowly as soon as he reached his workplace and produced little. When quitting time came, he again ran back to his home and worked hard to do his farm work until darkness prevented him from continuing (Taylor 1947, pt. 1). Taylor realized that what was needed was a sense of sharing between management and the laborer.

Through the application of scientific methods, he knew, labor productivity would easily be improved. He knew at the same time that management must share the increased profits with the labor. He called this idea the "mental revolution." If profits were truly shared by workers and management, who had both contributed to the gaining of profits, then the workers would understand that producing profit was to their own benefit also. In this sense, Taylor was stressing the importance of *mutual support* between management and labor. History tells us, unfortunately, that many employers sought Taylor's scientific methods to improve worker productivity, but few remembered his other emphasis, the mental revolution.

Abraham Maslow seems to have been misunderstood and misinterpreted also. Indeed, he used "self-fulfillment" in his explanation of the final and most important human need, self-actualization (1954, pp. 91–92, 199–239). He explained what he meant by self-actualization in detail. Yet many writers on organizational behavior have been very vague in discussing this concept. The self-actualization concept was first popularized by Douglas McGregor:

> Self-fulfillment needs: . . . there are the needs for self-fulfillment. There are the needs for realizing one's own potentialities, for continued self-development, for being creative in the broadest sense of that term . . . (1957, p. 27).

Many writers who followed McGregor reproduced similar phrases of Maslow's concept. This type of writing tends to give the impression that self-actualization means self-fulfillment, which in turn means "doing one's own thing."

When one goes back to the original writings of Maslow, one may immediately encounter him telling about love in relation to self-actualization, and the mother as the potentially most powerful self-actualizer when she is caring for her child (1954, pp. 199–234). An examination of nature may be useful in understanding this Maslow concept. A plant, for instance, takes nourishment from the earth, the air, and the sun to fulfill its own needs. Yet, at its maturity, it bears fruit and provides food for others to consume. A plant demonstrates two distinctive behaviors. One is taking in and consuming resources from its environment. The other is bearing fruits and providing resources to its environment.

In a similar fashion, human beings need to receive basic necessities from their environment to support their life and growth. They may also feel the necessity of fulfilling other needs — for security, social needs, and self-esteem, for example. After taking what they need and reaching their full maturity, however, individuals may feel the need to understand the true meaning of their being by discharging their accumulated energy in such a way that they are contributing to the needs of others. It seems that Maslow is talking about self-actualization in these terms. It is not self-fulfillment in terms of satisfying one's own needs. Rather, when one starts serving others, acting from others-oriented motivations, one may feel that one is discharging the obligation to humanity for which one has been brought up. When one has this experience of serving, one has a feeling of surging fulfillment, or a feeling of self-fulfillment. When this point of view is taken, what type of job one is engaged in becomes immaterial.

If the above interpretation is accepted, Maslow's concept is not very different from either Taylor's ideas or the Japanese *ikigai*. In this instance, there will be no diminishing returns of rewards from doing whatever one is doing. With this insight, a careful reassessment of Maslow's original concepts, as well as various other motivational theories, may be needed.

CONCLUSION

In this chapter, U.S. motivational orientations and Japanese motivational orientations have been compared. If the U.S. approach is termed "self-centered" motivation, the Japanese one can be considered "others-oriented" motivation. It was noted that the "others-oriented" motivation seemed to provide a better chance of long-lasting worker motivation and productivity. When such classic writers as Taylor and Maslow were examined, it was found that they were basically advocating the others-oriented motivational approach. Self-actualization, because of Maslow's unfortunate use of the term "self-fulfillment," seemed to have been misinterpreted and misunderstood by people who came after him.

It seems that behavioral scientists may now have to go back to Maslow's original writings and reassess his concepts to develop a more effective motivational theory and practice for both management and the worker.

REFERENCES

Doi, Takeo. 1972. *Amae no Kozo (The Structure of Amae)*. Tokyo: Kobundo.

Ford, N. 1969. *Motivation Through the Work Itself*. New York: American Management Association.

Hampton, David R., Charles E. Summer, and Ross A. Webber, 1973. *Organizational Behavior and the Practice of Management*. Glenview, Ill.: Scott, Foresman.

Handbook of Labor Statistics. 1978; 1979. Washington, D.C.: U.S. Department of Labor.

Herzberg, Frederick, Bernard Mausner, and Barbara Block Snyderman. 1959. *The Motivation to Work*. New York: John Wiley and Sons.

Kernberg, Otto. 1978. "Why Some People Can't Love." *Psychology Today*, July, pp. 55–59.

Maslow, Abraham H. 1954. *Motivation and Personality*. New York: Harper and Row.

McClelland, David C. 1961. *The Achieving Society*. Princeton, N.J.: D. Van Nostrand.

McGregor, Douglas. 1957. "The Human Side of Enterprise." *The Management Review* 46, no. 11 (November):22–28.

Mita, Munesuke. 1970. *Gendai no Ikigai (Today's Ikigai)*. Tokyo: Nippon Keizai Shinbun.

Monthly Labor Review. 1980. 103, no. 8 (August).

Roethlisberger, F. J., and William J. Dickson. 1939. *Management and the Worker*. New York: John Wiley and Sons.

Taylor, Frederick W. 1947. *Scientific Management*. New York: Harper and Row.

20

Traditional Japanese Management versus Likert's System 4

RENATE R. MAI-DALTON

INTRODUCTION

During the past 20 years, business contacts between the United States and Japan have become more frequent. As a result, each culture has become exposed to the other's management techniques and procedures. Lately, U.S. businesses have attempted to transfer the traditional Japanese management system to U.S. corporations that have already experimented with U.S.-developed participative management approaches, such as Theory X and Theory Y (McGregor 1960) and Likert's Systems 1 to 4 (Likert 1967). The latter has some parallels to the traditional Japanese management style. This chapter will compare the traditional Japanese management system and Likert's System 4. However, such a comparison can be undertaken only when the underlying cultural assumptions of each society are taken into consideration. Thus, this study will discuss the basis of each management system and list its characteristics. Then the two approaches will be compared and recommendations on their applicability to U.S. corporate management will be made.

This research was partially supported by the University of Kansas General Research Allocation 3532–20–0038.

THE BASIS AND CHARACTERISTICS OF
TRADITIONAL JAPANESE MANAGEMENT

The hiring process for managerial personnel in Japan is distinctly different from the hiring process in the United States (Johnson and Ouchi 1974). In Japan, an applicant is screened in terms of family background and personality. Interviewers consider how the potential employee, as a person, would fit into the corporate ranks of upper management. The applicant's particular skills and abilities play a less important part in the hiring decision than they do in the United States. Instead, a potential employee is evaluated on the level of commitment that can be expected from him or her toward the company, since employment is expected to last for a lifetime.

The well-educated Japanese manager is expected to have internalized traditional Japanese values, which include placing the well-being of the company above the manager's own goals, and striving toward harmony within the working environment rather than operating aggressively. Under those circumstances, only a minimum of formal controls over employee behavior is necessary. The traditional Japanese system of decision making, termed *Ringi*, further facilitates corporate harmony and allows for lower-level input without conflict. In this form of decision making, a proposal is circulated by middle management to all units in the company that would be affected by the proposed action. Employees can then review and revise the suggested procedures and become well informed on intended changes. The final decision about the actions to be taken, however, remains in the hands of middle or upper management.

Employee compensation is based on seniority, personal need, and status rather than on the particular job contribution. Employees are motivated not primarily by monetary rewards, but give their best efforts to the company in exchange for lifelong security. This security can be provided by Japanese companies because they enjoy considerable government protection from foreign competition and feel responsible for their managerial personnel. In contrast to Western business philosophy, the main objectives of the Japanese corporation are economic stability and the well-being of the employees (Fox 1975; Dutton, 1975). To avoid lay-offs and unemployment, managers are frequently placed with other corporate plants in times of slow work. Consequently, management training is geared toward all-around ability rather than specialization. Training further serves the purpose of establishing close relationships with co-workers in other departments, enhancing the employee-employer relations, and instilling a feeling of commitment and belonging. Job descriptions are frowned upon because each manager is interested in smooth functioning across departmental lines and levels of authority, and a distinct separation of jobs would disturb this objective. The close interweaving of relationships is also expressed in the physical set-up of Japanese offices. Few dividing walls exist. Employees with different statuses work together around one table or in one general area. Therefore, communication flows easily through the whole company, and most subordinates have easy access to superiors.

Thus, Japanese managers consider themselves "part of the family" at their place of employment. They enjoy in exchange strong protection from the adversities of life. The manager's attitude toward work is based on a value system that was established early in life and is a "given" when any employee enters the company for lifetime service. Some younger-generation Japanese, however, feel that the traditional type of management, with its security and protection, is possible only at the expense of lower-level and temporary employees, who have virtually no union protection or insurance against unemployment. Dissenting voices against the traditional Japanese method seem to be multiplying among younger workers. The younger generation demands government involvement to promote individual rights, and protection against unemployment in order to distribute employee benefits to all Japanese workers rather than a relatively small group (Fox 1975).

THE BASIS AND CHARACTERISTICS OF LIKERT'S SYSTEM 4

Likert's System 4 is basically a participative, humanistic approach to management, which is in contrast to the earlier, authoritative approach common in the Western world (Dowling 1975). Likert contends that employees who are informed about corporate processes are also interested in the well-being of the company and are, therefore, effective performers. He stresses participation, communication, trust, and teamwork. The main objective of Likert's approach is still increased output (as it is in most other Western managerial systems), but additional emphasis is placed on increased employee morale and satisfaction.

To change a company from an authoritative management system to a participative one, Likert assesses the characteristics of the particular company and then proceeds to induce behavioral changes in all employees, but primarily in managerial and supervisory personnel. Behavioral change is brought about by intensive and prolonged training that includes communication improvement, job definitions, goal setting, and team-building techniques. The responsibility for the performance and smooth functioning of a unit lies with each unit member, and the self-assertiveness and initiative of the individual are encouraged. Continuous feedback to the employee about behavior and performance is an integral part of Likert's System 4 and has proven effective. Likert (1967) further proposes decentralization as a cost-cutting device and advocates cross-functional teams to deemphasize the sharp separation of individual departments in large corporations.

Thus, Likert attempts to motivate management and lower-level employees through an increase in their involvement in their work, fairness in departmental procedures, and adequate compensation for performance. He expects a build-up in worker morale, group cohesiveness, and higher output to result. System 4 has several drawbacks that must be recognized, however. The attempt to improve the human components in an organization requires high initial investments in the form of training expenditures and often instrumentation improvements to accommodate labor demands. Although improvement in morale can frequently be observed fairly soon after training has begun, the improvement of the performance record can be shown only after a long time — from three to eight years. It is doubtful that many corporations and their stockholders are willing to wait such a long time for tangible results. Furthermore, Likert makes the assumption that individuals can change their behavior permanently, an assumption not borne out by the literature. Campbell et al. (1970) report that the longest time behavioral changes have held up was eight months. After this period, most employees returned to their former behavioral modes unless given additional training. Likert's major validation study employed a typical System 4 manager who had been successful in the past and obviously did not have to learn to change his style during the time of the study. One wonders what the outcome would have been if a new manager who had to adjust to the System 4 style had been studied. Nevertheless, Likert's System 4 has merit in some situations, and its positive influences will be discussed below.

COMPARISON OF THE TRADITIONAL JAPANESE MANAGEMENT SYSTEM AND LIKERT'S SYSTEM 4

The traditional Japanese system and Likert's System 4 have the following similarities. Both systems pay close attention to individual employees and their personal well-being. Both systems stress teamwork and cooperation rather than competition and conflict. Also, Likert's cross-functional teams using participative decision making approximate the Japanese *Ringi* system, with its close group interaction and intertwined intracorporate relationships.

There are, however, a number of dissimilarities between the two systems. System 4 holds individual workers responsible for their work. Traditional Japanese management, on the other hand, gives the responsibility for corporate success to the employees as a group. This is possible in Japan because commitment to the company is an internalized value. This is not the case with American workers; in the United States, commitment to the organization needs to be built up and cannot be assumed.

The two systems differ as to organizational goals. An important goal of the Japanese approach is creating and continuing jobs and providing security for employees, while the goal of the System 4 approach is increased production, with employee satisfaction used as a means of obtaining higher profits.

System 4 encourages open discussion of problems. Japanese management discourages this type of openness to preserve harmony in internal relationships and to avoid a "loss of face." In addition, while System 4 is open to and understanding of cultural differences, traditional Japanese management seems to show less understanding for the idiosyncracies of business managers in other countries and often expects to be accommodated on its own terms.

RECOMMENDATIONS FOR U.S. MANAGEMENT

The traditional Japanese management system and Likert's System 4 management seem to be relatively successful in their respective environments. However, it is difficult to imagine that traditional Japanese management strategies could be easily transplanted to U.S. companies, because the Japanese system is based on a philosophy of work that differs radically from that held by the average American worker. Japanese management is similar to System 4 in some aspects, though, and these could be valuable for U.S. corporations. These include commitment to the employer, nonaggressiveness, and cooperation across departmental lines. Because these concepts are relatively new to American workers, the necessary behaviors must generally be taught from scratch. This might explain why the System 4 approach requires so much time before it translates into higher profits. Nevertheless, stress on these values should be continued; the resulting atmosphere respects the dignity of the individual employee, who seems to respond to this treatment in a favorable manner. The modern technology of the 1960s, 1970s, and 1980s, which has resulted in large conglomerates and corporations, has often alienated the employees from their place of work by treating them as numbers rather than as individuals. System 4 and the traditional Japanese system, with their emphasis on employee participation, could be the way to stop and partially reverse this trend of worker alienation.

Participative leadership appears particularly desirable when (1) members of the organization possess valuable, decision-related information; (2) high-quality decisions are required; and (3) the support and acceptance of the group are needed for the implementation of the decisions at hand. In addition, participation seems to be successful only when the worker feels that his or her voice makes a difference. Workers must clearly understand the organizational contingencies and have a say in goal-setting procedures. A worker's interest in obtaining a particular outcome is thereby increased and the worker becomes more involved in the decision-making process. This results in higher motivation and commitment to the employer.

However, there is still the question the extent to which managers can learn to change their behavior permanently from an authoritative to a participative leadership style. If replications of earlier research confirm the suspicion that behavior cannot be changed and maintained in the desired direction, a contingency approach to management might be preferable. Thus, authoritative managers might be given subordinates who respond to clearly given directives, while participative managers should be matched with subordinates who show initiative, creativity, and a drive toward innovation.

The complete application of Likert's System 4 and traditional Japanese management in the United States might require a new breed of managers. This new breed would be a group of individuals who had learned early in their careers to cooperate with co-workers across departments, and who had shifted their primary focus from profits to a balance between the profit motive and a concern for the well-being of the individual worker. This type of approach seemingly violates the traditional drive for success and achievement of the individual in the United States. Such a transition of values could take considerable time. These comments notwithstanding, it is clear that *parts* of the above systems — such as consultative decision making and tenure — have been successfully instituted in U.S. corporations (Hatvany and Pucik 1981). These efforts should continue whenever appropriate.

REFERENCES

Campbell, D. T., M. D. Dunnette, E. E. Lawler, and K. E. Weick. 1970. *Managerial Behavior, Performance and Effectiveness*. New York: McGraw-Hill.

Dowling, William F. 1975. "System 4 Builds Performance and Profits." *Organizational Dynamics* 3 (Winter):23–28.

Dutton, Richard. 1975. "Japanese Management Philosophy and Buddhism: An Interrelationship." Paper presented at the annual convention of the Academy of Management, New Orleans.

Fox, William M. 1975. "Traditional Japanese Management: Upside Down and Inside Out." Paper presented at the American Psychology Association, Division 14, Symposium ("An International View of Motivation"), Chicago.

Hatvany, N., and Pucik, V. 1981. "An Integrated Management System: Lessons from the Japanese Experience." *Academy of Management Review* 6, no. 3: 469–80.

Johnson, R. T., and W. G. Ouchi. 1974. "Made in America (Under Japanese Management)." *Harvard Business Review* 52, no. 5:61–69.

Likert, Rensis. 1967. *The Human Organization.* New York: McGraw-Hill.

McGregor, D. 1960. *The Human Side of Enterprise.* New York: McGraw-Hill.

21

Techniques of Communication in U.S. and Japanese Corporations: Are They Interchangeable?

WILLIAM V. RUCH

INTRODUCTION

Twenty years ago, while I was teaching English in a high school in the small, agricultural town of Matsuyama in southern Japan, I learned that the Japanese approach to some aspects of life is exactly the opposite of what I, as an American, was used to. For example, someone might ask me, "Aren't you going to the faculty meeting today?" If I answered "Yes," meaning that I was going, the questioner thought I meant, "Yes, I am not going to the faculty meeting today."

Also, the Japanese at that time very seldom smiled in photographs; and I found that the greatest compliment I could give someone about a picture was that it looked just like anyone else. Americans smile broadly, and like it best when someone says a photograph looks just like them.

Since 1962, when I returned from Japan, I have been working in and teaching others about corporate communications. I have often wondered how many of these kinds of opposites exist in the communication programs of U.S. and Japanese corporations. Some of them are described by writers such as Peter Drucker. Drucker (1971) stated that the American manager's view of the Japanese method of decision making by consensus is that it leads "only to indecision or politicking, or at best to innocuous compromise which offends no one but also solves nothing." (p. 111). A contrary view was expressed by Yoshi Tsurumi (1978) in *Japanese Business:* "Most Japanese managers find it comical to see American managers exchanging memos even when they have adjacent offices and share a secretary" (p. 110).

Such opinions prompted an examination of both systems of communication to discover not only what differences there were between them but also what U.S. and Japanese corporations have to teach each other about communicating in corporations. After a general discussion of organizational communication, we describe internal communication, both formal and informal, in U.S. and Japanese corporations. Then we compare the communication systems in these companies, seeking any communication techniques that are interchangeable.

ORGANIZATIONAL COMMUNICATION

Communication in organizations is described by the direction in which it flows; thus, there is downward, upward, and horizontal communication, as shown in Figure 21.1.

A superior communicates with subordinates in downward communication. Channels for downward communication are usually numerous and opportunities for using them unlimited. Through these channels the lead-

FIGURE 21.1   The Formal Communication System in Any Organization

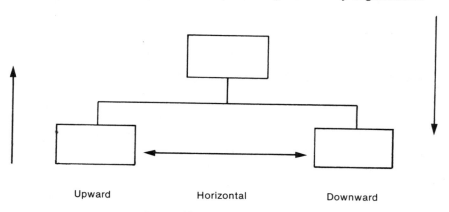

Source: Compiled by the author.

ers of organizations tell subordinates whatever the leaders feel the others need to know about the organization.

In upward communication, the members of the organization communicate with their leaders. Channels for upward communication are usually fewer in number than those for downward communication. Apparently there is less need to hear what members of the organization have to say than to say things to them.

Finally, lateral or horizontal communication takes place between persons in the organization who operate on the same level. Least attention is paid to this type of communication in an organization.

The above are types of formal communication. In addition, organizations cannot avoid informal communication between members. The informal system provides additional communication channels through which members send and receive messages.

This is the framework within which organizational communication occurs. Specific channels of communication take different forms according to the organization and the country in which that organization is located.

James Abegglen, in his now classic *Japanese Factory*, notes that the interpersonal relationships that will be effective in economic activity in a given country depend on the country's culture. Principles of business administration are not absolute; they are relative to the culture of the society (Abegglen 1958, p. vii). Given the considerable differences between the cultures of Japan and the United States, therefore, we can anticipate major differences in corporate life and methods of communicating as we examine companies in both countries, not merely to list the differences but to discover techniques that might be exchanged between them.

U.S. CORPORATIONS

The communication program in the U.S. business organization, as shown in Figure 21.2, is designed for speed and efficiency. As can be seen, more emphasis is placed on downward communication channels.

Personal contact plays an important part in all three types of communication, and memos are a part of everyday life. Important as forms of upward communication are reports (since the primary purpose of that form of communication is to inform superiors about work of the organization) and interviews of all kinds. All of these, including employee councils and suggestion systems, are used in Japanese corporations.

Horizontal communication, usually for the purpose of coordinating work between lateral units in the organization, has few channels: personal

FIGURE 21.2   Internal Communication Channels in the American Business Organization

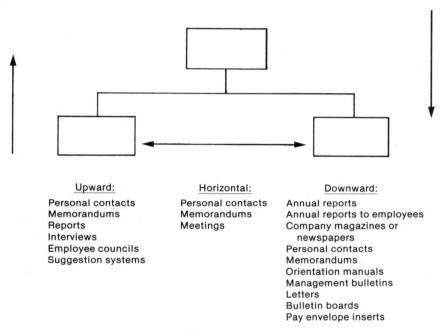

Upward:	Horizontal:	Downward:
Personal contacts	Personal contacts	Annual reports
Memorandums	Memorandums	Annual reports to employees
Reports	Meetings	Company magazines or
Interviews		newspapers
Employee councils		Personal contacts
Suggestion systems		Memorandums
		Orientation manuals
		Management bulletins
		Letters
		Bulletin boards
		Pay envelope inserts

Source: Compiled by the author.

contacts, memos, and meetings. Finally, downward communication, which both directs employees in their work and apprises them of important company information, receives the most attention in American firms. The most important piece of business communication, the annual report, is included here because most companies use it to communicate with employees and other important groups. Again, it is likely that all of the channels listed in Figure 21.2 are used in varying forms in Japanese business organizations.

In addition to that formal system of communication, any U.S. corporation has an informal system, usually called the grapevine. We think of the grapevine as supplementing the formal system — which is a little misleading, as studies have shown that more than half and sometimes as much as 85 percent of the information circulating in an organization is transmitted via the grapevine. Research also has shown that information passed along within this informal network is from 75 to 95 percent accurate (Davis 1973, p. 46).

JAPANESE CORPORATIONS

Although the basic structure of the Japanese organization is similar to that of the American organization, there are fundamental and important differences. Those differences perpetuate a different purpose of communication and different methods of communicating. William Ouchi reports in *Theory Z* that because of Japanese customs such as providing lifetime employment for workers, an organizational culture develops that facilitates communication: "Employees have a broad array of common experiences as touchstones through which to communicate with a great deal of subtlety. . . . This commonality provides them with a shorthand form of communication" (Ouchi 1981, p. 42).

The Japanese customarily maintain long-term relationships in daily associations that also support this shorthand form of communication. American employees move from organization to organization a great deal, thus losing these benefits for themselves and their organizations.

Americans also tend to look for personal relationships in horizontal associations in the organization; Japanese managers feel the same way about their vertical associations. This is an important distinction because, in the large organization, vertical relationships reinforce authority while horizontal ones challenge them (Rohlen 1974, p. 265). There are other important differences in internal corporate communication in Japan and the United States.

Language

First there is the language. Japanese as a language includes different levels of speech — low, common, and high — representing the status of the speakers. That quality of the language can impede or improve communication.

Until two Japanese business people know each other's position, for example, they find it difficult to communicate. That is why it is often easier for a Japanese to converse with a foreigner than with another Japanese to whom formal introductions have not been made. Americans, on the other hand, tend to seek a feeling of equality in status and deemphasize age differences (Rohlen 1974, p. 122).

Once status has been established between two Japanese business people, however, communication flows easily, particularly vertically. A relationship of senior-junior interdependence and support (called by the Japanese *sempai-kohai*) develops that focuses on the relationship rather than, American style, on the individuals in the relationship (Pascale and Athos 1981, p. 136).

A superior addresses his subordinates in familiar terms that express his acceptance of and affection for them. This suggests a paternalistic warmth, and kindly concern for the future of the junior, his training and his welfare in general.
The junior accepts this, is respectful and works hard (Craig 1969, p. 12).

Thus communication in Japan serves not only to transmit ideas between individuals but also to provide what one writer called an "emotional massage"
(Bairy 1969, p. 54).

In addressing the superior, a subordinate uses high-level language
with its more honorific expressions. Information is transmitted between
different levels of the hierarchy much more easily than it is in the American
corporation.

This is not to say that horizontal communication in the Japanese firm
is ignored. Because the work of the Japanese corporation is conducted in
groups, a good relationship among group members is nurtured. The Japanese philosophy is that the company with good human relations will succeed, while the company with bad human relations will fail (DeMente
1975, p. 69). It is in everyone's best interest to establish open communication among group members, particularly when those employees will be in
the same company for the rest of their working lives, and when much of
their decision making will be through consensus. Section leaders are called
upon to improve communication within their sections (Fürstenberg 1974,
p. 32). If there is a negative side to this system, it is that the success of interpersonal relationship within groups sometimes makes communication
between groups difficult (Abegglen 1973, p. 92).

The Formal System

Downward communication

Downward communication in Japanese firms is very similar to that in
American corporations. There are print media—company magazines,
newspapers, and newsletters. There are also bulletin boards, which are
called information boards in Japan and are used to communicate with employees much more extensively than they are in U.S. companies.

Upward communication

Much more important to the Japanese corporation is upward communication.

Meetings. Meetings of all kinds (called *kaigi* in Japanese) (DeMente
1975, p. 89) are an excellent form of upward communication. They are

longer and more frequent in Japanese corporations than they are in the United States, as is necessary for decision making by consensus. They allow coordination of work by those on the same managerial level and communication between those on different levels.

The style in which meetings are conducted in the two countries differs too. Americans invite open and honest confrontation at meetings. Japanese, as they are culturally trained to do, avoid open confrontation. Any subject likely to cause disagreement is discussed in advance of the meeting, and agreement is reached on a solution. During the meeting, then, everyone understands how the issue will be settled; and no one disagrees or loses. In fact, the meeting can provide a formal approval of a decision reached during informal consultation (Craig 1969, p. 23). The term for this system in Japanese was reported by Edwin Reischauer in *The Japanese* to be *haragei*, roughly translated as "the art of the belly" (Reischauer 1977, p. 135) or, as one of our faculty members in Japan used to call it, "reading stomachs."

When there is a problem to be settled at a meeting or alternative solutions to a problem, decisions are made through consensus. Each person at the meeting may take any desired amount of time to express views on the subject. Afterwards, the leader of the group makes a decision based on the wishes of the group, even when that is contrary to the leader's own preference.

A requirement of this system is the sort of active listening that most Japanese are good at and most Americans are not. In *The Art of Japanese Management*, Richard Pascale and Anthony Athos describe the differences in listening between Americans and Japanese at meetings. Americans listen in an evaluative way, accepting or rejecting ideas presented, which leads to fatigue and listening short cuts, so that they actually absorb only about 30 percent of the message. The Japanese, the authors explain, practice "less-ego listening." "They hold 'principle' in abeyance, regard themselves as one among others in the situation, and thus achieve easy accommodation with the circumstances of the meeting. . . . This situational ethic enables the Japanese to aid different views without falling into a duel of personalities" (Pascale and Athos 1981, pp. 131–32). This process is called *nemawashii*, meaning literally "binding the roots of a plant before pulling it out" (Vogel 1975, p. xxiii).

This process stands in contrast to the American drive for a decision, which, as Pascale and Athos observe, "often prompts managers to choose prematurely, based on conceptual analysis and substantive merit but without due regard for implementation feasibility" (Pascale and Athos 1981, p. 112).

The functions that occur in the meeting in the United States are performed in Japan through the broad, informal system of consultation just described, the formal meeting, and, to some extent, the *ringi* system (Craig 1969, p. 24).

Ringi. *Ringi* is a system of proposal writing used in decision making that is unique to the Japanese corporation. It is believed to have been used in the civil bureaucracy in the early Meiji Era and to have been adopted later by private corporations (Yoshino 1968, p. 265). According to M. Yoshino in *Japan's Managerial System*, *rin* means "submitting a proposal to one's superior and receiving his approval"; and *gi* means "deliberations and decisions" (Yoshino 1968, p. 265). The *ringi* system includes all of these. The written proposal itself is called the *ringisho*.

One employee, usually on a lower echelon of the management hierarchy, is assigned the task of preparing the *ringisho*. The employee is not likely to know all there is to know about the subject, and so is forced to consult with others, on the same management level and on higher levels, to be sure that a complete and acceptable proposal is prepared. Through informal consultation and formal meetings, an agreement is reached. Only then is the *ringisho* prepared for circulation among the executives for their approval. Those who do approve apply their seal and pass the document along. Others, who have disagreements, apply their seal but add their opinions.

The *ringi* system is not used for all issues but only for those that are complex and require a high degree of coordination. For unimportant matters, the system serves to circulate information about decisions already made (Craig 1969, p. 24).

The president is responsible for ultimately approving or not approving the *ringisho*. In most cases, the *ringisho* is approved without modification because of the long process of approval that created it. The president's role is to legitimize decisions made by group consensus.

Koichi Hamada has described the difference between Japanese communication and Western communication as that between the "logic of adaptation" and the "logic of choice." The Western pattern of communication or negotiation is to specify the possible alternatives and then to choose one strategy. "The Japanese pattern of communication or negotiation is to adapt its attitude depending on the attitude of other parties" (Hamada 1976, p. 194). The system of *ringisho* illustrates well the Japanese approach.

The technique is time-consuming and maybe a little cumbersome, but the benefits are many. Shared information allows the *ringisho* to reach a level of perfection that would otherwise be impossible. The system plays an important part in downward communication (Fürstenberg 1974, p. 71). Involvement of executives on various levels ensures fast implementation of the subject of the *ringisho*. Ezra Vogel reports in the popular *Japan as Number One* that "occasionally top Japanese bureaucrats talk enviously of their Western counterparts who can simply give out orders or directives or plans, but when pushed they acknowledge that the Japanese system works better in the long run" (Vogel 1979, p. 95). To that I would add that the Japanese system works better in the long run *for the Japanese.*

Voluntary reporting system. Another form of upward communication is a frequent survey of employee attitudes, usually administered by the personnel department and called by some the voluntary reporting system (Fürstenberg 1974, p. 72). At least annually and frequently more often, questionnaires are distributed to employees, asking for their opinion on almost everything in their corporate lives, including satisfaction, office leadership, and personal problems on the job (Rohlen 1974, p. 101). There are also questions on many aspects of employees' personal lives, such as rent paid, size of living quarters, hobbies, and desire for a transfer (Clark 1979, p. 181). The results are the basis for changes in the corporation and provide a profile of the morale of each office (Rohlen 1974, p. 101). It has been said that this system is needed because of the social distance between managers and employees.

Suggestion system. The suggestion system is used for upward communication purposes in Japan, just as it is in the United States; however, its use by the Japanese is more intensive. Committees of employees and managers evaluate suggestions submitted by individuals or groups. Some companies exhibit on information boards accepted suggestions, which may also be reported in the corporation's print media (van Helvoort 1979, p. 120).

Joint councils. A system that is used in both Japan and the United States is one of consultation between employees and managers, for the purpose mainly of upward communication. Friedrich Fürstenberg reported that a 1968 study by the Japanese Productivity Center showed that the most widely mentioned objectives of joint councils were the improvement of understanding and the harmonious running of the business (Fürstenberg 1974, pp. 57–58). A similar study of joint councils in the United States would undoubtedly draw a different response.

The Informal System — The *Habatsu*

The informal system of communication in the Japanese corporation is quite different from the grapevine in the U.S. firm. It is comprised of *habatsu* (cliques).

Yoshino reports that, because the traditional culture of Japan included no notions of the large organization, Japanese tended to feel uncomfortably isolated in them. In response, Japanese created "narrow social groupings offering particularistic and emotional ties within the impersonal formal organization" (Yoshino 1968, p. 208).

Although a part of the informal system, *habatsu* are highly goal-oriented — the major goal being to enhance their own power and influence in the organization. Membership in *habatsu* is not the result of the random associations found in informal communication in the United States. Instead, membership is based on a specific common unchangeable tie, such as place of birth or school. Membership is nonoverlapping; here the system again differs from the U.S. system, which allows employees to belong to several informal groups. Members of a *habatsu* are drawn from various management levels, and the *habatsu* themselves are hierarchically organized.

Habatsu have their own highly effective network of communication. They can be very beneficial or deleterious to an organization's operations. *Habatsu* provide a valuable means of bypassing an occasional blockage in vertical communication. They also allow lateral communication with a high level of trust (Craig 1969, p. 14).

On the other hand, in extreme cases approval by *habatsu* is required before a new policy can be implemented. Also, inter-*habatsu* rivalries develop, and the outcome may present a morale problem for those members of *habatsu* that are not dominant.

A model representing the Japanese communication system looks very similar to a model of the U.S. system. (Figure 21.3 presents the Japanese system.) However, the differences are considerable. In the U.S. system, downward communication is dominant and horizontal communication is a distant third. In Japan, upward communication is dominant, followed closely by horizontal communication. Also, because the informal system (the *habatsu*) is semiorganized and extremely influential in the Japanese organization, it is shown in Figure 21.3. The informal system in the U.S. corporation functions separately and totally randomly, and thus was not shown on Figure 21.2.

NONVERBAL COMMUNICATION

Japanese and U.S. corporations also differ in communication that uses no words. Americans almost totally ignore nonverbal communication; Japanese are keenly attentive to it. Reischauer (1977) observes that, because Japan's society is homogeneous, "nonverbal forms of communication may have been easier to develop than in countries in South and West Asia and the Occident where greater cultural diversity made verbal skills more necessary and therefore more highly prized" (p. 136). Today, Reischauer re-

FIGURE 21.3   Internal Communication Channels in the Japanese Business Organization

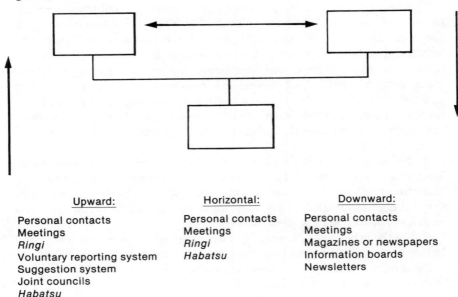

Upward:	Horizontal:	Downward:
Personal contacts	Personal contacts	Personal contacts
Meetings	Meetings	Meetings
Ringi	*Ringi*	Magazines or newspapers
Voluntary reporting system	*Habatsu*	Information boards
Suggestion system		Newsletters
Joint councils		
Habatsu		

Source: Compiled by the author.

ports, the Japanese "have a positive mistrust of verbal skills, thinking that these tend to show superficially, in contrast to inner, less articulate feelings that are communicated by innuendo or nonverbal means" (p. 135).

Language in Japan is sometimes intentionally vague, report Pascale and Athos (1981), "to hold strained relations together and reduce unnecessary conflict" (p. 94). They feel that efforts by Americans toward clear communication between people only make things worse, especially when disagreements are substantive.

In the United States, communication without words includes body language, touching, space, time, clothing, appearance, and voice tones. It is impossible not to communicate; when no words are used, nonverbal messages are being transmitted. However, most Americans are not aware that such messages exist.

In Japanese corporations, as in Japanese life generally, nonverbal communication between two or more people is constant. Many important aspects of Japanese life are rarely, if ever, verbalized, report Paul Norbury and Geoffrey Bownas (1980) in *Business in Japan*. "Even if verbalizing something, there is often a large element of understatement, and silence is valued for its powers of communication" (p. 194). Words are often considered unnecessary to Japanese, in cases where Americans might feel the need for lengthy explanations.

In Japan, nonverbal communication often indicates status. Many Americans do not know, for example, that the bow can indicate difference in status. The person of lower rank bows lower and longer.

There is less eye contact in Japan; subordinates avoid looking superiors in the eye. In the United States, we believe that someone who does not look us in the eye during conversations is being dishonest.

Also, since samurai days, the expressionless face in Japan has been considered important to hide one's feelings from one's adversaries. Americans send a myriad of messages through facial expressions.

Clothing in Japan communicates. Uniforms in all aspects of Japanese life are used to communicate status and position, making conversations with the proper honorifics possible even between strangers.

Finally, intonation or voice tones communicate in Japan. Certain words, for example, can be expressions of mild reproach or the worst possible insult, depending on the tone with which the words are uttered.

CONCLUSION

Communication in Japanese and U.S. companies reflects the respective cultures in which the corporations function. For U.S. firms that means communication that is direct, efficient, and honest. For Japanese business organizations that means communication that is informal, indirect, emotionally gratifying, and often intentionally vague.

Table 21.1 compares the two systems in other respects. Because of decision making by consensus, frequent meetings are needed in Japan. Meetings in the United States are fewer and shorter; they serve the same function as informal consultation and, in part, the *ringi* system.

Internal communication in the United States employs, in general, downward communication. Horizontal communication is deemphasized, and upward communication is in the middle. The Japanese system emphasizes upward communication, closely followed by horizontal communication. Downward communication is not far behind.

Most communication techniques in use in U.S. firms are also used in Japan; some techniques in use in Japan are not used in the United States and probably could not be. What, then, can corporations in the two countries learn from each other with regard to communication? The answer is, not a great deal. Perhaps there is one important lesson that each can learn from the other.

For Americans, that lesson is the value of a strong upward communication system. Who is more familiar with the operations of the company than those working in them? They must have important things to say about

TABLE 21.1   Comparison of Internal Communication in Japanese and U.S. Corporations

JAPANESE CORPORATIONS	U.S. CORPORATIONS
Communication transmits information and provides emotional gratification.	Communication transmits information.
Informal communication system is strong.	Formal communication system is strong.
Upward communication is strong.	Downward communication is strong.
Horizontal communication is strong.	Horizontal communication is weak.
Nonverbal communication an important part of any message.	Nonverbal communication is almost totally ignored.
Indirect communication is preferred.	Direct communication is preferred.
Strong group-nurturing system exists because of decision making by consensus.	Individuals are nurtured.
Meetings are frequent and long.	Meetings are fewer and shorter.
Compromise and conciliation are preferred at meetings.	Confrontation is invited at meetings.
Communication shorthand is established by long-term associations.	High mobility of employees eliminates communication shorthand.

their work; American managers might learn to ask the right questions and then learn to listen to what workers have to say.

For the Japanese, the most important lesson is one they are well aware of — the value of a fast-working system of decision making. The *ringi* system is anachronistic in the modern large organization, and a faster system is needed. As one executive put it, Japanese management must transform itself from management by seals to management by objectives (Yoshino 1968, p. 262).

Some companies are already altering the *ringi* system by using it only for medium- to long-term projects. Others currently restrict its use to information disseminating and approval instead of decision making (Fürstenberg, p. 34).

> Some companies have standardized and simplified formats of *ringi* documents, clarified routes for their circulation and reduced the number of individuals who examine a proposal. . . . Another procedural improvement is to allow *ringi* proposals to be submitted directly to top management in cases of urgency (Yoshino 1968, p. 263).

In some firms, executives discuss proposals in executive committee meetings, rather than having each executive individually act on them.

There is one component of corporate life that will force additional changes in the *ringi* system, as in many other communication processes in both U.S. and Japanese corporations through the 1980s and beyond. That component is computerization. The prospect is absolutely beguiling.

REFERENCES

Abegglen, James C. 1973. *Management and Worker, the Japanese Solution.* Tokyo: Kodansha International.

———. 1958. *The Japanese Factory.* Glencoe, Ill.: The Free Press.

Bairy, Maurice. 1969. "Motivational Forces in Japanese Life." In *The Japanese Employee,* ed. Robert Ballon. Tokyo: Sophia University.

Clark, Rodney. 1979. *The Japanese Company.* New Haven: Yale University Press.

Craig, Albert M. 1969. "Functional and Dysfunctional Aspects of Government Bureaucracy." In *Modern Japanese Organization and Decision-Making,* ed. Ezra Vogel. Berkeley: University of California Press.

Davis, Keith. 1973. "Care and Cultivation of the Corporate Grapevine." *Dun's Review* 102 (July):46.

DeMente, Boye. 1975. *Japanese Manners and Ethics in Business.* Phoenix: Simpson-Doyle.

Drucker, Peter F. 1971. "What We Can Learn from Japanese Management." *Harvard Business Review* (March-April):110–22.

Fürstenberg, Friedrich. 1974. *Why the Japanese Have Been So Successful in Business.* New York: Hippocrene Books.

Hamada, Koichi. 1976. "Japan's Role in the World Economy." In *Japan, America and the Future World Order,* ed. Morton A. Kaplan and Kinhide Mushakoji. New York: The Free Press.

Norbury, Paul, and Goeffrey Bownas, eds. 1980. *Business in Japan.* Boulder, Colo.: Westview Press.

Ouchi, William. 1981. *Theory Z.* Reading, Mass.: Addison-Wesley.

Pascale, Richard T., and Anthony G. Athos. 1981. *The Art of Japanese Management.* New York: Simon and Schuster.

Reischauer, Edwin O. 1977. *The Japanese.* Cambridge: Harvard University Press.

Rohlen, Thomas P. 1974. *For Harmony and Strength.* Berkeley: University of California Press.

Tsurumi, Yoshi. 1978. *Japanese Business.* New York: Praeger.

van Helvoort, Ernest. 1979. *The Japanese Working Man: What Choice? What Reward?* Vancouver: University of British Columbia Press.

Vogel, Ezra F. 1979. *Japan as Number One.* Cambridge: Harvard University Press.

———, ed. 1975. *Modern Japanese Organization and Decision-Making.* Berkeley: University of California Press.

Yoshino, M. Y. 1968. *Japan's Managerial System.* Cambridge: The MIT Press.

22

Decision and Compensation Systems in the United States and Japan: Contrasting Approaches to Management

ARLYN J. MELCHER *and* BERNARD AROGYASWAMY

INTRODUCTION

The U.S. challenge of the 1950s and 1960s has been replaced by the Japanese challenge of the 1970s and 1980s. Management practices were viewed as contributing to and determining the superiority and dominance of U.S. firms in the postwar era. The management style and approaches of the Japanese are viewed as a key part of the success Japanese firms have subsequently enjoyed in the United States and elsewhere. Managers and scholars are studying Japanese practices, and many are presenting these approaches as models to be emulated (Cole 1980; Hattori 1978; Marengo 1979; Ouchi 1981; Pascale and Athos 1981; Vogel 1979a). A great deal of uncritical description and many enthusiastic prescriptions are being offered to improve the position of U.S. firms and U.S. industries that are being overwhelmed by the competitive intensity of the Japanese.

A growing literature, including studies of Japanese culture and industrial development, case studies of firms and industries, surveys, and essays by observers of the American scene and the Japanese setting, has emerged in the last two decades (Bieda 1970; Clark 1979; Drucker 1981; Furstenberg 1974; Gold 1978; Ishida 1971; Kahn and Pepper 1979; Long and Seo 1977; Reischauer 1979; Seo 1977; Whitehill and Takezawa 1978; Yoshino 1968). A basis exists for beginning to synthesize and codify descriptions of practices, the consequences associated with these practices in the Japanese setting, the conditions that enable the practices to achieve positive results in the Japanese setting but negative consequences in other settings, and the practices that are transferable to the United States or other contexts.

A number of problems confound this process of codification. First, many of the studies have dealt with the practices of the large, leading firms in Japan. The stratification of firms into prestige levels based upon such factors as their size, importance in the Japanese economy, and the scope of their satellite network affects the practices followed. The generalizations that can be made about the large, dominant firms probably will not hold for the smaller firm that is at an economic and political disadvantage.

Second, other factors besides management practices determine the success or failure of firms. Tax laws and subsidies transfer resources from business firms to other groups. Governmental policies, regulations, and programs shift costs to private firms from the government or community at large, affecting areas such as pollution controls, safety standards, and so-cial security welfare systems for the retired and handicapped. Policies asso-ciated with facilitating social change, such as upgrading conditions for per-sonnel who traditionally have been discriminated against in the society, shift costs to or away from private firms. Other public policies may impose substantial costs on businesses, making it more difficult for them to operate or compete on an international basis. Monetary and fiscal policies may cre-ate pressures for inflation that place a country at a substantial advantage or disadvantage in world markets, or in domestic markets when competing against foreign firms.

Public policies may impose substantial costs or restrictions on firms, affecting considerably their ability to generate internally, retain, or obtain financial and other resources. Markets may be distorted through price con-trols, allocation mechanisms, special taxes, or subsidies. The power of par-ticular groups may be enhanced in a way that constrains the actions of a firm and affects its costs; an important example is legislation that supports the formation and functioning of strong national unions, consumer groups, or community groups that may be able to block any action perceived as ad-versely affecting their interests. A firm may be successful because of a sup-portive climate of economic, political, and community factors that provide a substantial competitive advantage; a firm may be successful despite its management practices rather than because of them.

It is necessary to examine closely the nature of management practices in Japan and other countries, to identify carefully the degree of similarity or difference between such practices, and then to puzzle out the consequences of these practices for the functioning of firms. We cannot assume, because a firm is successful, that the practices followed led to that success. Many other factors in the environment may be contributing factors to success; management policies may even impede the functioning of the firm. It may be that where specific conditions hold certain management policies will contribute to success; perhaps under different conditions the policies are harmful. A careful investigation must begin by tracing out the character of management practices; then the issue of the way that those practices affect the functioning of firms can be pursued. The accumulated literature on Japanese organizations and the extensive set of studies done in the United States on the effects of particular organizational forms provide a basis for analysis.

This chapter focuses upon two aspects of management approaches in Japan and the United States — the nature of the decision-making systems and the nature of the reward-penalty systems in large corporations in the two countries. Attention will be given only to the management structure. The degree to which the system is implemented and the nature of the effects on operating personnel will be explored in another study. In this chapter, the similarities and differences between these systems are identified. The consequences of the systems for the functioning of organizations in each country are then explored, and the conditions that enable the systems to function in the two contexts are set forth. Next, certain questions are considered: To what extent are the systems transferable? What are the consequences of applying the U.S. system in Japan and the Japanese system in the United States?

The analysis being presented here is set forth in Table 22.1 The general cultural characteristics of Japan approach the Gemeinschaft form

TABLE 22.1 Combinations of Cultural Conditions with Decision-Making and Reward Systems in the United States and Japan

DECISION-MAKING AND REWARD SYSTEMS	CULTURAL CONDITIONS	
	GEMEINSCHAFT	GESELLSCHAFT
Individual decision process Graded rewards and penalties; no ultimate sanctions	U.S. subsidiary in Japan	U.S. firm in the United States
Group decision process Ungraded rewards; ultimate sanctions	Japanese firm in Japan	Japanese subsidiary in the United States

of social system; those of the United States more accurately reflect the values of a Gesellschaft-like social system, as described in Charles Loomis's (1960) insightful *Social Systems*. The decision and reward systems in Japan and the United States differ sharply, as summarized in Tables 22.2 and 22.3. The issue is, what are the separate and combined effects of different cultural conditions and different decision and reward systems on the performance of organizations? A U.S. firm may carry its practices over into the Japanese cultural setting; a Japanese firm may carry its management practices over into the U.S. setting.

CONTRASTING CHARACTERISTICS OF DECISION-MAKING AND REWARD SYSTEMS

Table 22.2 contrasts several properties of decision-making systems in large U.S. firms and Japanese firms. These include clarity, focus, and amount of responsibility and authority exercised by middle and top-level management; the degree of involvement in decision-making processes; amount of consensus achieved before a decision is implemented; and the discretion exercised by higher-level management. Other properties of the decision-making process that are contrasted include the clarity and process of formulating standards and the degree of formal enforcement. Another aspect explored is the role of management in conflict resolution in U.S. and Japanese settings. These properties of decision-making systems have been discussed in the literature. Table 22.2 summarizes the contrasts between U.S. and Japanese systems.

A number of properties of reward-penalty systems are contrasted: the continuity of employment in U.S. and Japanese firms under varying economic conditions and performance levels, the emphasis given to seniority in rewarding and promoting personnel, and the response to disruptive behavior and to advancing age. Firms in the two settings differ in the values involved in these aspects of rewarding and penalizing individuals and groups. Compensation was contrasted with respect to the degree that salaries are related to individual performance, the differentials that are provided, the salary levels, and the proportion of compensation given as salary or bonuses. These aspects of compensation figure importantly in the structure of the motivation system that is established. The criteria for promotion, demotion, and termination are other important properties of a reward-penalty system. Related to the promotion system are the recruitment and training of the managers or potential managers. Educational qualifications and breadth of training are contrasted in Table 22.2.

These properties of the reward-penalty systems and decision-making

TABLE 22.2   Properties of Decision-Making and Reward Systems in the United States and Japan

DECISION-MAKING SYSTEMS	UNITED STATES	JAPAN
Authority and Responsibility		
Clarity of authority and responsibility	*Clear statement:* Limits are often codified in policy manuals and organizational charts.	*Vague statement:* Limits of authority and responsibility are unspecified.
Focus of authority and responsibility	*Office:* Authority and responsibility are assigned to the office and the individual is held responsible for performance.	*Group:* Authority and responsibility is assigned to the unit. Groups are delegated authority and are held jointly responsible for performance.
Top management's responsibility	*Extensive:* Higher-level managers are held responsible for actions and decisions of subordinates.	*Limited:* Group is held responsible; higher-level management accepts symbolic responsibility when things go wrong.
Decision-Making Process		
Degree of involvement and participation	*Limited:* Top management initiates the statement of problems and proposes solutions.	*Broad:* Top managment initiates the statement of problems; there is broad involvement of all those affected in approaches to dealing with the problem.
Degree of consensus formally required on decision	*None formally required:* A judgment is made on strength of opposition, but the official has authority to make the decision without consensus.	*Unanimity required:* All involved parties must agree they have had the opportunity of being fairly heard; consensus is formally documented.
Discretion exercised by higher-level management	*Extensive:* The manager makes the final decision.	*Limited:* The manager codifies the final decision.

TABLE 22.2   *(continued)*

REWARD-PENALTY SYSTEMS	UNITED STATES	JAPAN
Performance Standards		
Clarity and process of setting standards	*Clear and set by management:* Specific performance standards are set for the individual; standards are jointly set, or established by higher-level management.	*Vague and set by the group:* Vague performance standards exist for the group; standards are generated from the group and formalized by management.
Nature of reward-penalty systems	*Regular performance review:* Rationalized system of individual performance review by higher management exists; graded rewards and penalties are based upon performance.	*Group processes with self-evaluation:* These are supported by group bonus systems and "ultimate" individual penalties.
Management involvement in conflict resolution	*High:* Issues are referred to higher management for resolution.	*Low:* Conflicts are referred back to individuals or groups for resolution.
Continuity of Employment		
With varying economic conditions	*Discontinuous:* Employment varies with economic activity; there is a higher degree of continuity for "senior" personnel, but few jobs are secure.	*Continuous:* Lifetime employment is the norm for "permanent" personnel; employment is discontinuous for "temporary" personnel.
With varying performance levels	*Partial continuity:* Some consideration is given to years with the company even if performance declines over time.	*Continuous:* Little differentiation is made on the basis of performance; all "permanent" employees qualify for continuous employment.

(continued)

TABLE 22.2   *(continued)*

REWARD-PENALTY SYSTEMS	UNITED STATES	JAPAN
With disruptive behavior	*Low continuity:* Individual who is identified as disruptive is fired.	*Moderate:* Individual is pressed to resign or modify behavior, but seldom fired.
Age criteria	*High continuity:* Early retirement is optional from 55; retirement at 65 or 70 is required.	*Limited:* All personnel except promotable supervisors are required to retire at 55.
Degree of benefits	Lifetime benefits of high percentage of salary.	One-time bonus payment, equivalent to several years' pay, is made.
Employment potential after retirement	Potential varies, but generally employment is widely available until abilities decay.	Large firms place personnel in satellite firms for a ten-year period; employment potential is sharply limited beyond these conditions.

Compensation

Relation of salary benefits to individual performance	*High:* Attempts are made to reward outstanding individual performance directly.	*Low:* Individual performance is not formally evaluated for ten years after entering the firm; salary progression is automatic.
Compensation differentials	*Large:* The combinations of salaries, fringes, and "perks" of office sharply differentiate rewards among supervisors at different levels.	*Small:* There are small differences in salary levels, and few "perks" of office.
Salary levels	*Relatively high:* Salaries, compared with those in nonbusiness firms, are high.	*Relatively low:* Fringe benefits are liberal fringes, but salary bases are low.
Degree to which group bonuses and profit	*Relatively limited:* Bonuses and profit shar-	*Extensive:* Bonuses can be sizeable; they are

TABLE 22.2   (continued)

REWARD-PENALTY SYSTEMS	UNITED STATES	JAPAN
sharing are used	ing are a small part of total compensation except for chief executive officer and division managers.	paid every six months or year.

Promotion

Criteria for promotion	Criteria are relative performance and minimum educational degree (such as B.S. or M.B.A.).	Criteria are ranks, seniority, education, successful passing of examinations.
Rate of promotion	*Rapid:* Where performance is outstanding, rapid advancement is the rule.	*Slow:* Only time is considered; first review may be after ten years.
Demotion criteria	*Performance:* Failure in performance, or decline in business activity, is cause for demotion.	*None:* Personnel are not demoted except under exceptional circumstances.
Termination criteria	*Multiple factors:* Weak performance, disruptive behavior, economic conditions, reorganization, and personal conflicts are some of the reasons for termination.	*Few factors:* Even disruptive behavior is rarely cause for dismissal; supervisors have job security until age 55.

Recruitment and Training

Entering educational qualifications	*Professional education* consists of technical or business education with B.S., M.B.A., or Ph.D./D.B.A.	*Limited professional grounding:* About one-half of personnel have technical, economic, or business education at the B.S. level.
Degree of specialization	*High:* Extensive specialization and education, with limited experience across specialties, is usual.	*Low:* Generally there is little specialization and education; extensive experience across specialties is usual.

TABLE 22.3   Cultural and Operating Conditions Affecting the Functioning of
Decision-Making and Reward Systems in the United States and Japan

CULTURAL AND OPERATING CONDITIONS	UNITED STATES	JAPAN
Socialization		
Norm of cooperation	*Limited:* One is socialized to promote individual interest; cooperation is viewed instrumentally, rather than affectively.	*Intensive:* One is socialized to cooperate within the work group; cooperation is both instrumentally and affectively valued.
Norm of competition	*Extensive:* Competition is supported within groups as well as between groups.	*Partial:* Competition and winning in a zero-sum outcome is valued between groups (such as among companies), but not within groups.
Legitimacy of conflict	*High:* Conflict is accepted as long as social rules of behavior are observed.	*Low:* Conflict is rejected except between benefit groups.
Enforcement of Norms		
Power of group over time—shunning, withdrawal of group support, disapproval	*Limited:* Group sanctions and approval is valued, but are not essential.	*Extensive:* Power of the group is great, because of the importance of "face" and the importance of group support in work activity.
Availability of formal graded sanctions	*Extensive:* Compensation, promotion or demotion, termination, and "perks" of office are used to recognize performance.	*Limited:* Emphasis is upon equality; rewards are related to rank, seniority, and education achieved.
Availability of "ultimate" sanctions	*Limited:* There is a possibility of escape from all penalties. An individual can leave, transfer, or openly	*Extensive:* Escape potential is low. An individual cannot leave the organization or escape the surveillance

TABLE 22.3   *(continued)*

CULTURAL AND OPERATING CONDITIONS	UNITED STATES	JAPAN
	confront; alternatives to bending to the organization's pressure have bearable costs.	and sanctions of the group. Employment, status in the community, and self-esteem are all tied in with the job and the firm.

systems are associated with a set of consequences in the two countries. The effects that have been highlighted in the studies include the speed of implementing decisions, friction and resistance encountered in implementing decisions, the degree of acceptance of responsibility, and the amount of cooperation within and among groups. The speed of formulating decisions, the scope of factors considered, the subordination of group interests to organizational interests, loyalty to the firm, and the time horizon of decisions have also been discussed as products of the systems. While little attention has been given to degree of inbreeding, it has also been contrasted in the two sets of firms. These effects are summarized in Table 22.4.

As these consequences are examined, both systems reveal strengths and weaknesses. It is an open question whether the gains of the Japanese systems are offset by high costs. The literature provides examples of applications of modified forms of the Japanese system in the United States, but not of the U.S. system in Japan (Amano 1979; Johnson and Ouchi 1974; Kraar 1975; Ouchi 1981; Pascale and Athos 1981). The case studies are suggestive but hardly definitive on the issue. Alongside the success stories stand the stories of failures (Van de Ven and Ferry 1980).

CONTRASTING CONDITIONS IN THE UNITED STATES AND JAPAN

The literature provides a basis for assessing conditions that facilitate the functioning of the two types of systems. Some of the cultural and operating conditions have been summarized in the literature (Emi 1963; Haitani

TABLE 22.4   Characteristics and Consequences of Decision-Making and Reward Systems in the United States and Japan

CHARACTERISTICS AND CONSEQUENCES	UNITED STATES	JAPAN
Decision-Making Process		
Speed of decision making	*Rapid:* Decisions can be made and transmitted in a day.	*Slow:* The complete cycle of the *ringi* process may take months.
Scope of factors	*Limited:* The scope is highly variable, but limited in the typical case.	*Extensive:* All affected parties have opportunity for input.
Degree to which the group's interests are subordinated to the organizational goals	*Limited:* Each group promotes its own interest; higher-level management must make the trade-offs to support overall organizational goals.	*Extensive:* Groups tend to subordinate their interest to the overall interest; issues are reconciled by groups instead of by higher-level management.
Scope of perspective	*Departmental perspective:* Personnel evaluate issues primarily from the standpoint of each department.	*Company perspective:* Issues are viewed broadly, largely as a consequence of *ringi system.*
Time horizon	*Short:* There is a need to show immediate results, and the tendency to be involved in operating problems creates short-term perspectives.	*Long:* The longer review period and the release of top management from operating problems support longer planning horizons.
Loyalty to the firm	*Low:* Zero-sum nature of the decision-making process tends to alienate the losers; often they resign for positions in other firms.	*High:* Broad involvement, joint pay-off view, and lack of opportunities elsewhere elicit high loyalty.
Implementation of Decisions		
Speed of implementation; friction and re-	Those affected by decisions often have lim-	Broad consensus promotes rapid imple-

TABLE 22.4   *(continued)*

CHARACTERISTICS AND CONSEQUENCES	UNITED STATES	JAPAN
sistance to implementation	ited agreement and understanding; unintentional errors, subverting of decision by passive resistance, or subverting of decision when operationally feasible may occur.	mentation with little friction and with active support of all parties.
Acceptance of responsibility	Responsibility is rejected when decision is initially opposed.	All parties accept responsibility for making the decision work.
Behavioral Consequences		
Degree of inbreeding	*Limited:* Some on-the-job training may be given; further education is primarily outside the firm. Recruitment is from a multiplicity of universities, firms in the industry, and other industries.	*Extensive:* Training is primarily within the firm, and on the job; promotion is entirely within. Recruitment is from a few universities, or within a set of firms within the industry.
Individual motivation	*High:* Individuals aggressively seek higher rewards, promotion, and recognition.	*High:* Individuals seek group approval, bonuses, and consideration for moving to higher management.
Amount and timing of costs and gains of employee turnover	*High and continuous:* Personnel leave or are fired as they seek to escape organizational pressures or find better opportunity; low-performing personnel are fired or forced to resign. Late retirement age permits long con-	*Low and at end of work career:* There is little chance of personnel leaving until retirement. Major costs occur as highly trained personnel in their prime are retired; there are relatively high training costs with

(continued)

TABLE 22.4 (continued)

CHARACTERISTICS AND CONSEQUENCES	UNITED STATES	JAPAN
	tributions from those that stay. Recruitment at all levels supports infusion of new ideas and reduces inbreeding; there is potential for rapid upgrading where changing environment requires new skills.	short periods of pay-off. Personnel changes are possible only at beginning and end of career, which creates rigidities in meeting new conditions.
Cooperation of different groups	Rivalry and cooperation are low where other groups are adversely affected by decisions; zero-sum-type situations tend to elicit rivalry, competition, and confrontation.	There is a high degree of cooperation among affected groups; the situation is identified as a joint pay-off rather than as a zero-sum situation.

1976; Ishida 1971; Long and Seo 1977; Mochizuki 1980; Patrick and Rosov-sky 1976; Reischauer 1979; Seo 1977; Yoshino 1968). They include the different values placed upon the norms of cooperation, competition, and legitimacy of conflict. The enforcement of the norms on those who have only partially internalized them can also be highlighted, by assessing the availability of graded sanctions and the ability of the firm to apply ultimate sanctions to those that do not conform or respond.

These conditions determine to a large degree the way in which these systems operate, and sharply affect the transferability of the Japanese system to U.S. subsidiaries or other firms. The key factor that differentiates the two settings is the availability of ultimate sanctions. An ultimate sanction is a penalty applied that the individual cannot ignore or recover from. The "scarlet letter" in Hawthorne's famous novel is an example; the disgraced lady was required always to wear the letter announcing her adultery to the world and to herself. The ultimate sanctions need not be used often; a few dramatic cases are sufficient to work their influence. In Japan, dismissal for cause or the possibility of dismissal for cause would approach an ultimate sanction. The combination of employment conditions and social values creates a pervasive condition where it is extremely difficult to escape from the penalties associated with dismissal. The graded hierarchy of firms, the recruitment of only junior personnel from outside, promotion entirely from within, and the degree of esteem that position provides both within the firm and in the general society, plus the lack of a vested pension system or any governmental retirement system, provide the dismissed employee little opportunity to recover his or her fortunes. When this system of sanctions is combined with a work ethic that values a high level of work commitment, minimizes the legitimacy of conflict, and stresses cooperation, a powerful social system operates.

The social system in Japan supports a decision-making system that requires all to accept a decision even if the interest of a particular person or group does not seem to be supported. Disruptive behavior and confrontation have high risks. A reward system can operate that removes most graded incentives and the tie of incentives to individual performance. The physical setting of open offices enables everybody to be under constant observation. Those who are not pulling their weight can be identified and instructed by other group members who may fear their group will falter in meeting expected performance standards. Goals can be elicited from the group. Standards of performance can be set by the group that can be expected to tax their abilities and energies substantially. All groups are in a position to check on each other.

If the availability of ultimate sanctions is removed, the entire system can be expected to change its processes. A Japanese firm operating in the U.S. setting or U.S. firm operating in the U.S. setting has few penalties approximating these ultimate sanctions that condition and shape behavior. In the United States, the lack of a clear-cut hierarchy of firms, the recruitment from multiple sources at all levels, and vested pension systems, unemployment insurance, and social security benefits sharply reduce the importance of continuous employment with a firm. It is awkward financially to lose one's job and for a few it may be a disaster economically and socially. For most employees, however, the loss of a job is an inconvenience from which they can readily recover.

If ultimate sanctions are not available, then graded rewards and sanctions assume much greater importance. Decision-making processes that require complete consensus are likely to be used by intransigent individuals and groups as leverage for greater power. The trust and confidence that management may anticipate may be replaced by truculence and power politicking. Vague statements of responsibility and ambiguity of authority are likely to support wheeling and dealing of ambitious supervisors and escape from accountability when things go wrong. Managers who abandon the careful design of formal structure and count upon intervention techniques to facilitate group processes are likely to be too busy solving problems to do much planning, or to have much productivity.

There are lessons to be learned from the management of Japanese plants — but we can easily learn the wrong ones. Japanese managers have demonstrated the immense productivity that can be elicited from a work force. They have capitalized upon some special characteristics of the Japanese setting and culture. There are high costs associated with part of their system; it rests upon a relatively fragile base that requires existing social arrangements to be largely maintained. Continuity, prosperity, and growth of their industry are also necessary. Perhaps these conditions will remain as they have been. If so, it will be one of few such examples in human history.

CONCLUSION

As organization theorists, we have been concerned with the degree to which the theory being presented in U.S. textbooks is culturally bounded. The theory may be applicable in the U.S. setting, but not, for example, in the Mexican, German, or Japanese context. Most of the systematic research on organizations traditionally has come out of U.S. or British universities. The literature developing in different countries in the last decade provides a basis for assessing the general applicability of theories. Descriptions of management practices in Japan and behavior associated with these management practices directly confront the issue of transferability of existing organization theory.

This chapter compares two sets of practices commonly followed in large firms in the United States and Japan. The contrasts reflect sharply different judgments on the most efficient way of designing organizations and intervening in organizational processes. The values of each approach cannot be demonstrated by examining what happens when Japanese approaches are introduced into a poorly managed U.S. plant or firm. Any change that gave systematic attention to resolving the problems, rather than maintaining the status quo or reinforcing destructive practices, would improve the functioning of the firm. Systematic application of existing theory would also be expected to improve the situation. Many instant cures for problems of organizational functioning are available in tidily presented consulting packages, training seminars, attitude surveys, and lists of do's and don'ts. Most of these do little good, but also are harmless in that they do not make the situation worse.

Our experience with fads and the quick fix should make us cautious about discarding a systematic body of theory and rigorous research on the design of organizations (Hagesfeld and Jones 1981; Melcher and Falcone 1980; Melcher and Melcher 1978; Minzberg 1979; Van de Ven and Ferry

1980). If we are to modify or discard the existing theory, let us do so only after careful examination of all the facets of the proposed alternatives.

The Japanese have made tremendous strides in improving the productivity of their organizations. One reason may be their management practices, including the elements of decision-making and reward systems described in this study. The thrust of this analysis, though, is that the systems are likely to work only where a special set of conditions exists. Those conditions that have been identified are largely absent in the U.S. setting, and rest on a relatively fragile base in Japan.

We can learn from the Japanese; aspects of their approach that may prove useful are the emphasis that they give to quality throughout the organization, and the factors that facilitate group processes, including broader training of specialists and use of group bonuses. Other aspects of this system have little likelihood of being effective in the U.S. setting. Vague authority and responsibilities, and nonperformance reward systems promote inefficiency and low productivity in the U.S. setting (Melcher 1966; Van de Ven and Ferry 1980).

If we wish to learn more about the factors supporting the productivity and competitiveness of Japanese firms, we need to look at public policies that have an impact upon the cost structure, operating constraints, and general support of private enterprise. Under the Reagan administration, the United States is taking part in a mass economic experiment involving changing the costs imposed on organizations from various regulations, giving emphasis to competitive pressures rather than governmental constraints, reducing the tax burden on organizations, and changing the nature of incentives in the society at large. We can learn from the Japanese — about public policy as well as management approaches.

REFERENCES

Amano, Matt M. 1979. "Organizational Changes of a Japanese Firm in America." *California Management Review* 21, no. 3 (Spring):51–59.

Bieda, K. 1970. *The Structure and Operation of the Japanese Economy*. Sydney: John Wiley and Sons.

Clark, Rodney. 1979. *The Japanese Company*. New Haven: Yale University Press.

Cole, Robert E. 1980. "Learning from the Japanese: Prospects and Pitfalls." *Management Review* (September):22–28.

Drucker, P. F. 1981. "Behind Japan's Success." *Harvard Business Review* 59:83–90.

Emi, K. 1963. *Government Fiscal Activity and Economic Growth in Japan: 1868–1960*. Tokyo: Kinokuniya Book-Store Co.

Furstenberg, F. 1974. *Why the Japanese Have Been So Successful in Business*. London: Leviathan House.

Gold, Bela. 1978. "Factor Stimulating Technological Progress in Japanese Industries: The Case of Computerization in Steel." *Quarterly Review of Economics
and Business* 4 (Winter):47–57.

Hagesfeld, Bonita, and Robert E. Jones. 1981. "The Effects of Organizational Design on the Delivery of Rehabilitation Services: Implications for Improving
Administrative Effectiveness." *Journal of Rehabilitation Administration* (August):95–105.

Haitani, Kanji. 1976. *The Japanese Economic System*. Lexington: Lexington Books.

Hashimoto, Masanori. 1979. "Bonus Payments, On-the Job Training, and Lifetime
Employment in Japan." *Journal of Political Economy* 87, no. 5:1086–1104.

Hattori, Ichiro. 1978. "A Proposition on Efficient Decision-Making in the Japanese
Corporation." *Columbia Journal of World Business* (Summer):7–15.

Ishida, T. 1971. *Japanese Society*. New York: Random House.

Johnson, Richard T., and W. G. Ouchi. 1974. "Made in America (Under Japanese
Management)." *Harvard Business Review* 52, no. 5:61–69.

Kahn, Herman, and Thomas Pepper. 1979. *The Japanese Challenge*. New York:
Harper and Row.

Kraar, Louis. 1975. "The Japanese Are Coming — With Their Own Style of Management." *Fortune*, March, pp. 116–120.

Long. W. A., and K. K. Seo. 1977. *Management in Japan and India*. New York:
Praeger.

Loomis, Charles P. 1960. *Social Systems: Essays on Their Persistence and Change*.
Princeton, N.J.: D. Van Nostrand.

Marengo, F. D. 1979. "Learning from the Japanese: What or How." *Management
International Review* 19, no. 4:39–46.

Marsh, R., and H. Mannari. 1971. "Lifetime Commitment in Japan: Roles, Norms,
and Values." *American Journal of Sociology* 76:795–812.

Melcher, Arlyn. 1966. *Structure and Process of Organizations*. New York: Prentice-Hall.

Melcher, Arlyn, and Tom Falcone. 1980. "Escape Potential of Personnel: Implications for Mental Health and Organizational Productivity." Paper presented
at the International Congress on Applied Systems Research and Cybernetics,
Acapulco.

Melcher, Arlyn, and Bonita Melcher. 1978. "Organizational Diagnosis: An Application of a Structural-Process Organizational Model." Paper presented at the
ORSA/TIMS meeting, Los Angeles, November 13–15.

Minzberg, Henry. 1979. *The Structuring of Organizations*. New York: Prentice-
Hall.

Mochizuki, K. 1980. "Government-Business Relations in Japan and the United
States: A Study in Contrasts." In *U.S. — Japanese Economic Relations: Co-
operation, Competition, and Confrontation*, ed. D. Tasca, pp. 85–93. New
York: Pergamon Press.

Ohkawa, K., and Y. Hayami, eds. 1973. *Economic Growth: The Japanese Experience Since the Meiji Era*. Vol. 1. Homewood, Ill.: The Japan Economic Research Center.

Ouchi, William G. 1981. *Theory Z — How American Business Can Meet the Japanese Challenge*. Reading, Mass.: Addison Wesley.

Pascale, Richard T., and Anthony G. Athos. 1981. *The Art of Japanese Management*. New York: Simon and Schuster.

Patrick, H., and H. Rosovsky, eds. 1976. *Asia's New Giant: How the Japanese Economy Works*. Washington, D.C.: The Brookings Institute.

Rehder, Robert R. 1979. "Japanese Management: An American Challenge." *Human Resource Management* (Winter):21–27.

Reischauer, Edwin O. 1979. *The Japanese*. Cambridge: Harvard University Press.

Seo, K. K. 1977. *Management in Japan and India*. New York: Praeger.

Tsurumi, Yoshi. 1978. "The Best of Times and the Worst of Times: Japanese Management in America." *Columbia Journal of World Business* (Summer):56–61.

Van de Ven, Andrew, and Diane Ferry. 1980. *Measuring and Assessing Organizations*. New York: Wiley.

Vogel, Ezra F. 1979a. *Japan as Number One: Lessons for America*. Cambridge: Harvard University Press.

————, ed. 1979b. *Modern Japanese Organization and Decision-Making*. Berkeley: University of California Press.

Whitehill, Arthur M., Shin-ichi Takezawa. 1978. "Workplace Harmony: Another Japanese 'Miracle'?" *Columbia Journal of World Business* (Fall): 25–39.

Yoshino, M. Y. 1968. *Japan's Managerial System: Tradition and Innovation*. Cambridge: MIT Press.

23

Strategic Management in U.S. versus Japanese Firms

LESTER A. DIGMAN

INTRODUCTION

Much has been written recently about the success of Japanese management. Japan's growing productivity, plus its growing market share in automobiles, electronics, steel, and other industries in world markets — particularly in the United States — have attracted growing interest, speculation, and comment (Ouchi 1981; Ouchi and Price 1978; Pascale and Athos 1981; Vogel 1979).

Much of the comment and literature focuses on anthropological or sociological factors present in Japan that influence its management philosophy and processes. Frequently mentioned are lifetime employment, *ringi* group decision making, bottom-up approaches, company unions, the importance of seniority, diffused responsibility, attention to detail, and quality control circles (Hayes 1981; Kagono et al. 1981; Kono 1980).

Conspicuous by its absence, however, is a discussion of strategic management as practiced by the Japanese. Serious students of strategic management are likely to conclude that the frequently discussed facets of Japanese management may perhaps be necessary conditions for recent successes, but what of the sufficient condition — effective strategic management? It is difficult to believe that the Japanese phenomenon could have occurred without the development and implementation of the proper strategies, even though certain writers have suggested that the effective tactics of the Japanese have given them a strategic advantage — that more-effective management of operations gives the Japanese an important competitive advantage (Hayes 1981; Wheelwright 1981). Is this in fact the case, or is the conventional wisdom true — that the United States has adopted a short-sighted, profit-oriented approach, while the Japanese are more successfully focusing on longer-term results?

Adding to the confusion are statements by certain writers to the effect that the Japanese have copied and adapted the U.S. style of management. For example, Yoshino concludes that "in organizational structure and ownership policies, Japanese multinational enterprises have begun to manifest signs of convergence toward the pattern established by United States firms." Further, "Japan's distinctive managerial system, which was nurtured in the home environment and proved effective in that setting, is an important factor inhibiting the growth of Japanese multinational enterprise" (Yoshino 1976, p. 161). The editors of the journal *Management Japan* agree, stating that "the methods learned from America were adapted and developed for use in the Japanese environment" ("Editorial," p. 5). These opinions are substantiated by the fact that Japan's often cited quality control systems are built upon the theories of two American pioneers — W. E. Deming and J. M. Juran. Also, Japan is not alone in the use of quality circles — it has been reported that, in the United States, Westinghouse, for example, "has over 700 quality circles at more than 150 locations. Well over 10,000 employees are expected to participate in such programs" ("Federal Beat" 1981).

Further confusing the conventional wisdom is Drucker's (1981) conclusion that the U.S. focus on the short term has given its firms a definite advantage over the Europeans. This orientation, according to Drucker, has enabled U.S. firms to protect their profitability during periods of rapid change (in this case, wild currency fluctuations and a sharp recession), while the Europeans tend to delay adjustments too long, sticking to the long-range plan "come what may" (Drucker 1981). Is it possible that the frequently mentioned short-range approach puts the United States at an advantage vis-à-vis the Europeans but at a disadvantage vis-à-vis the Japanese? Does the answer lie in the planning process? Is the seeming Japanese phenomenon a temporary one or the result of a combination of environmental factors? Is the current competitive advantage of the Japanese the result not of strategic management but of superior operations (tactics)? Perhaps an investigation of Japan's strategic management practices can shed additional light on these and other questions.

JAPANESE STRATEGIC MANAGEMENT

Writing in 1968, Yoshino states that the formal concept of planning was first introduced into Japanese corporations in the form of budgets, which resemble closely those found in large U.S. corporations. In the late 1950s, the concept of strategic (long-range) planning was adopted by leading Japanese firms, largely as a result of two factors: the influence of U.S. management thinking; and the aggressive expansion and diversification in Japanese firms. This soon led to the creation of an organizational unit to serve as the focal point in developing long-range plans. Progress has been slow, however, because the concept of long-range planning is contrary to the *ringi* (bottom-up) system of decision making. The value of strategic planning has been reduced because top management has found it difficult to take the initiative in defining corporate goals and objectives. Over time, however, planning has tended to overcome some of the basic shortcomings of the *ringi* system (Yoshino 1968).

Current Studies

Three current studies were discovered that, given the above historical perspective, provide important information on current Japanese strategic management practices. Horvath and McMillan (1980) investigate planning from a national or macro perspective, drawing their conclusions from an analysis of economic data. Kagono et al. (1981) conducted a questionnaire survey of approximately 1,000 Japanese and U.S. firms, with a response rate of 25 percent from the firms questioned. Kono (1980) conducted personal interviews at 30 selected U.S. and Japanese firms, and also conducted a mail survey of 152 southern California and 536 Japanese firms, with a response rate of 15 percent. While response rates are low for both the Kagono et al. and the Kono studies, they were the only pertinent data-based studies located. The combined results of these three studies are described below.

Strategic Management at the National Level

The Horvath and McMillan (1980) study concludes that Japan employs the growth-share matrix concept at the national level. The growth-share matrix, as utilized in the United States, is a device for evaluating and analyzing the component businesses (or strategic business units — SBUs) of a diversified organization. It provides a framework that enables the firm to portray the portfolio of businesses in which the company competes. It is a key device in formulating corporate-level strategy that deals with which businsses the firm should be in, including how the firm's set of businesses should be integrated to maximize the firm's ability to attain its objectives (Hofer et al. 1980). By evaluating the SBUs according to measures of industry attractiveness on one axis and measures of the firm's competitive or business strengths on the other axis, the firm is able to segment its component businesses. Commonly used categories include stars, cash cows, question marks, and dogs. The successful corporation needs a mixture of types of SBUs — the declining businesses (dogs) are candidates for elimination or divestiture, successful mature businesses (cash cows) provide the funds to develop future growth areas (stars), and so on. The Boston Consulting Group and General Electric are credited with developing this concept in the early 1970s.

According to Horvath and McMillan (1980), Japan uses this concept on a national level, to indicate which industries to enter and invest in, which to "milk," and which to drop. Instead of industry attractiveness and competitive strength, Japan substitutes production growth and relative productivity of labor as measures to analyze its industries on a national scale by sectors of the economy. On this basis, Japan provides favored treatment for its stars and potential future stars (question marks), maintains its cash cows (while realizing that they are currently competitive but in long term decline because of the industry life cycle), and prepares to replace its dogs or "throw-away" industries.

The following table lists Japanese industries or sectors considered to comprise the four sectors of the matrix (Horvath and McMillan 1980).

Stars

Chemical fibers
Pharmaceuticals
Cosmetics
Autos
Office machinery
Iron and steel
Organic chemicals
Commerical equipment
Agricultural machinery

Question Marks

Computers
Aircraft
Textile machinery

Cash Cows

Inorganic chemicals
Chemical fertilizers
Home electric appliances
Cutlery

Dogs

Textiles
Toys
Optical instruments
Paper

FIGURE 23.1   Japan's Growth-Share Matrix

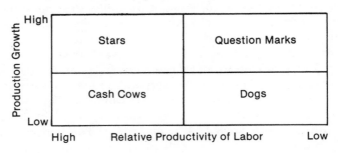

Source: Compiled by the author.

Thus, Japan seems to employ effective corporate-level strategic management on a national level so that its economic "portfolio" of industries is managed for continued and efficient future growth.

In implementing its national-level strategy, Horvath and McMillan observe, Japan employs a second strategic management concept found to be effective by U.S. firms — again at the national level, however. This concept is the "experience curve" or learning curve. The concept of the learning curve has been effectively employed in the U.S. aircraft industry since World War II, and most recently has been utilized in the U.S. electronics industry, most notably by Texas Instruments. In recent years, the Boston Consulting Group has renamed the concept the experience curve, and suggested that its use can provide a definite competitive and strategic advantage.

Experience has shown that growth in exports from Japan frequently precedes growth in production for the Japanese domestic market. The Japanese situation thus differs from the conventional approach, in which an industry develops domestically and subsequently turns to exports as the domestic market becomes sufficiently saturated and as a comparative cost advantage accrues to firms in the industry because of learning effects. Strategically, however, the firm (or industry) that reaches a high level of production early has a continuing cost advantage over its followers because of experience curve effects. The firm that prices its products low enough early in the process (anticipating learning effects) should experience higher demand and production, accelerating its movement down the learning curve "ahead of the pack." Most of us are familiar with the dramatic experience curve effects on the costs (and prices) of calculators, computers, and microprocessors. Again, Texas Instruments has used this strategy quite effectively.

In Japan, penetration of export and domestic markets in star and potential future star industries occurs in parallel, incorporating experience curve pricing. Thus, the industry reaches higher levels of production sooner, placing it farther out on the experience curve, giving it a distinct cost and competitive advantage from which the competition may never recover. This approach permits long production runs and large productivity gains from economies of scale (Horvath and McMillan 1980).

Strategic Management at the Firm Level

Having seen that Japan effectively utilizes modern strategic management concepts (developed in the United States) at the national level, we will now consider what the Japanese employ at the level of the individual firm. Attention will be directed to the areas of organizational mission and objectives, environmental analysis, strategy formulation, and strategy content (including corporate-level, business-level, and functional strategies).

Organizational mission and objectives

Kono (1980) found that financial goals are more important to U.S. firms, while productivity and efficiency are more important to Japanese firms. Kagono et al. (1981) found that stockholder gain is a significantly more important goal to U.S. firms than to the Japanese, while the reverse is true for new product development. Table 23.1 ranks the relative importance of various goals to the U.S. and Japanese firms participating in the two studies. While there are clear differences in the rankings between the two countries, perhaps surprising in view of conventional wisdom are the relative importance given to financial performance by the Japanese and the lack of importance of measures of financial health.

Environmental analysis

The Kagono et al. study (1981) asked Japanese and U.S. managers to rate certain environmental factors, using a semantic differential scale. The results (shown in Table 23.2) indicate that U.S. managers consider their markets to be more diverse in terms of geographical dispersion, products, promotional strategies, and competitiveness. They also perceive greater governmental constraints and labor mobility. The Japanese see more volatile markets, higher barriers to entry, and constraints imposed by customers, distributors, suppliers, and subcontractors. On the other hand, competition, sources of capital, profitability, and information exchange are not perceived as significantly different. Whether the perceptions are accurate is, of course, open to question.

TABLE 23.1   Two Rankings of Corporate Objectives

UNITED STATES	JAPAN
KONO RANKING[a]	
1. Debt/equity ratio	1. Sales
1. Growth policy	2. Profit level
3. Sales	3. Growth rate
3. Growth rate	4. Return on sales
5. Profit policy	5. Labor productivity
6. Profit level	5. Growth policy
6. Return on equity	7. Market share
8. Return on assets	7. Value added
8. Earnings per share	9. Dividends
10. Market share	9. Profit policy
KAGANO RANKING[b]	
1. Return on investment	1. Market share increase
2. Stockholder gain	2. Return on investment
3. Market share increase	3. New product ratio
4. Product portfolio	4. Logistics efficiency
5. Logistics efficiency	5. Product portfolio
6. Debt/equity ratio	6. Debt/equity ratio
7. New product ratio	7. Public image
8. Public image	8. Working conditions
9. Working conditions	9. Stockholder gain

[a]Source: Adapted from Kono (1980).
[b]Source: Adapted from Kagono et al. (1981).

Strategy formulation

An important ingredient in strategy formulation is the top management of the firm, including the board of directors. Kono (1980) states that the typical Japanese board consists of 16 members, with only 11 percent outside members, and performs the minimum number of jobs, only those legally required. The typical U.S. board, in contrast, is composed of 60 percent outsiders or former officers, and performs a number of functions over and above those required by law. These include financial advice, closer monitoring of managerial decisions, and ratification of corporate strategies.

It is not uncommon in the U.S. firms to have a top management group decision-making body of three to five top people, which may be called the office of the president, management committee, senior executive committee, or planning committee. Japan adopted the management committee concept in the 1950s. In its Japanese form, the management committee comprises eight to ten senior executives, with sole responsibility for general management and strategic decisions (and little responsibility for operational decisions).

In addition to this body, the average Japanese firm has a planning department consisting of 12 people and acting as a strategic staff. The planning department works closely with top management and participates in the initiation and formulation of strategies. In the United States, on the other hand, this body typically numbers three to five people and functions more as a coordinator of the strategic planning process, with the planning decisions made by heads of operating divisions and top management. Thus corporate planning departments play different roles in the two countries.

Kono further found that long-range planning is widely used by large firms in both countries — 85 percent in the United States and 77 percent in Japan. The plan is formal and written in about 75 percent of these firms in both countries, and the components of the plans are also very similar. However, preparation of the plan is another matter. In the United States, planning is largely a bottom-up process; in fact, two-thirds of the firms rely upon operating units to prepare plans, with the bulk of the remainder using

TABLE 23.2   Perceptions of Environment

DIMENSION	PERCEIVED AS GREATER IN	SIGNIFICANCE LEVEL
Entry barriers	Japan	.001
Geographical diversity	United States	.001
Governmental constraints	United States	.001
Inability to influence market	United States	.001
Distributor/customer constraints	Japan	.001
Supplier/subcontractor constraints	Japan	.001
Managerial mobility	United States	.001
Mobility of technical experts	United States	.001
Market rivalry	United States	.001
Product diversity	United States	.01
Rate of technological change	Japan	.01
Promotional strategy diversity	United States	.05
Rate of demand change	Japan	.05
Exchange of product information	Japan	Not significant
Market profitability	United States	Not significant
Bank/stockholder constraints	Japan	Not significant
Competitor constraints	Japan	Not significant

Source: Adapted from Kagono et al. (1981).

an interactive process between managers of operating units and corporate-level managers. Japan, contrary to what might be expected with the *ringi* system, relies primarily on top-down or interactive processes, depending heavily on the planning department. In fact, the planning department prepares the long-range plan in 86 percent of the Japanese firms, versus 39 percent in the United States Division management performs this task in 87 percent of U.S. firms, versus 39 percent in Japan (overlap occurs due to shared responsibility). Plans are reviewed by planning departments in 57 percent of U.S. firms (versus 7 percent in Japan), by corporate management in 70 percent of U.S. firms (versus 12 percent in Japan), and jointly by the chief executive officer and division executives in 61 percent of U.S. firms (versus 14 percent in Japan). In contrast, plans are reviewed by the management committee in 63 percent of Japanese firms (versus 22 percent in the United States). The final decision on the long-range plan is made by the chief executive officer in 61 percent of U.S. firms (versus 40 percent in Japan) and by the board of directors in 35 percent of U.S. firms (versus 9 percent in Japan). In Japan, this decision is made by the mangagement committee in 52 percent of the firms (versus 22 percent in the United States). Thus, significant differences exist between the two countries regarding responsibilities for the preparation, review, and final approval of long-range plans (Kono 1980).

Further, Kagono et al. (1981) found that U.S. firms rely upon the intuitive judgment of experienced executives to a significantly greater degree in formulating strategy than do the Japanese. However, the use of systematic research data and sophisticated analytical methods does not differ significantly. The Japanese, however, seek a significantly broader range of information (even on markets unrelated to present businesses) than do the Americans.

Strategy content

Strategy content is analyzed from three perspectives — corporate-level strategies, business-level strategies, and functional strategies.

Corporate-level strategies. This level of strategy deals with the mix or portfolio of businesses in which the firm competes (Hofer et al. 1980). Kono found a higher level of diversification in U.S. firms than in the Japanese companies, with U.S. firms diversifying primarily through acquisitions. The Japanese, however, seldom acquire other companies for diversification, but use internal development or joint contract ventures to diversify (Kono 1980). Kagono et al. (1981) also found very significant differences between the two countries in previous acquisition behavior, differences that favored the Americans. The Americans were also found to be much less hesitant to drop questionable businesses, which substantiates the statements previously attributed to Drucker (1981). Kagono et al. (1981) found little difference between the countries concerning diversification directions — both Japanese and U.S. firms prefer to diversify into products with technology similar to the firm's existing base and into areas where existing marketing strengths can be applied.

No difference existed in the degree of activity in developing foreign markets; however, the Americans appear to be significantly more active in investing in foreign production subsidiaries. Perhaps this reflects domestic labor costs more than any other factor.

Interesting significant differences were found between the countries in the areas of resource accumulation and utilization. The Japanese were more likely to base recruitment of managerial and technical people upon long-range as opposed to immediate needs. They also were more likely to try to accumulate a diverse knowledge base than to make better use of existing expertise. From the reverse perspective, this means that the Americans favor using existing skills and abilities to a greater degree. As a final point on resource utilization, U.S. firms showed a significantly stronger preference for concentrating resources in a few strategic market segments (Kagono et al. 1981). Whether this reflects actual practice or perception, it seems to conflict with the diversification findings of Kono (1980).

Lastly, Kagono et al. (1981) develop a growth-share matrix for the responding U.S. and Japanese firms. Industry attractiveness was measured by growth rate of the market, with "high" defined as 10 percent or more, and "low" as less than 10 percent. Competitive position was measured by market position, with "strong" defined as first or second in market share, and "weak" being third or lower. The results, shown in Table 23.3, indicate that the U.S. firms contain a significantly lower percentage of dogs and a significantly higher proportion of stars than do the Japanese. The percentages of cash cows and of question marks are not significantly different (Kagono et al. 1981). While this may be surprising in light of the popu-

TABLE 23.3   United States versus Japanese Market Portfolio

STARS[a]	QUESTION MARKS	CASH COWS	DOGS[b]
United States 30.7 percent	United States 18.2 percent	United States 36.2 percent	United States 14.9 percent
Japan 25.1 percent	Japan 19.5 percent	Japan 34.0 percent	Japan 21.3 percent

[a]Significant at .05 level.

[b]Significant at .01 level.

Source: Adapted from Kagono et al. (1981).

lar opinion of Japanese performance, it confirms Kagono's previous findings on resource deployment. Perhaps U.S. firms are less hesitant to get rid of dogs, while the Japanese are less likely to drop unprofitable industries as rapidly at the corporate level. The previously discussed hypothesis of Horvath and McMillan (1980) indicates that this may not be true at the national level, however. Different national growth rates and market structures could also affect the results of this type of analysis.

Business-level strategies. Business-level strategies deal with how a firm should compete in a given business, industry, or market. Included are the questions of how the firm should position itself and allocate its resources, as well as how to integrate the firm's various functional activities (Hofer et al. 1980).

A comparison of the importance of five types of business-level strategies is shown in the rankings in Table 23.4. The definition of each of the strategies is as follows:

Product — product planning, market research for new products, research and development, etc.

Production — economies of scale, cost reduction, production systems, etc.

Pricing — pricing policy, pricing decisions, etc.

Promotional — advertising, sales management, personal selling, market communication, etc.

Distribution — channels, inventory programs, etc. (Kagono et al. 1981)

The rankings show that the Japanese favor a production strategy to a greater degree than do the Americans. This corresponds with Wheelwright's (1981) conclusions. While the U.S. firms favor a product strategy,

TABLE 23.4   Importance of Business-Level Strategies

UNITED STATES	JAPAN
1. Product strategy	1. Production strategy
2. Production strategy	2. Product strategy
3. Pricing strategy	3. Pricing strategy
4. Promotional strategy	4. Promotional strategy
5. Distribution strategy	5. Distribution strategy

Source: Adopted from Kagono et al. (1981).

the rankings do not show the strength of importance of each strategy. For example, the U.S. firms rated distribution fifth, as did the Japanese, but mean importance given to the strategy was very significantly higher for the U.S. firms. The Americans also rated pricing strategy as significantly more important than did the Japanese, with the reverse being true for production strategies.

With regard to specific strategic approaches, U.S. firms perceived that they competed head-on with competitors to a significantly greater degree than did the Japanese. No difference existed concerning selection of advantageous market segments or pursuit of coexistence with competitors. Also, none of the following areas showed any difference: follower behavior to avoid risks; innovator/leader behavior and assumption of risk; and production of high-quality, high value-added products relying on nonprice strategies.

However, the Americans perceived themselves as consistently seeking higher market share and trying to exploit cost efficiencies to a greater degree than did the Japanese. These perceptions conflict with the corporate objectives rankings in Table 23.1, and perhaps reflect perceptual differences and/or methodological weaknesses (Kagono et al. 1981).

Functional strategies. This level of strategy deals with integration of subfunctional activities of the firm and relating functional-area policies to functional-area environmental changes (Hofer et al. 1980). Focusing on the functional area of research and development, Kagono et al. (1981) found no significant differences in two important respects: the ratio of research and development expenditures to total sales; and the percentage of sales accounted for by products introduced since 1973. However, the Japanese considered both basic research on new technologies and development of new products significantly more important than did the Americans.

The U.S. firms, however, consider research on improving and updating existing products significantly more important than do the Japanese companies. It appears that the Japanese favor basic research, invention, and new products, while the Americans favor applied research, innovation, and product improvement. Again, these findings appear to run counter to stereotyped impressions. No difference was found concerning the importance of new production methods and processes.

In the production area, the Japanese derive a significantly larger percentage of their output from custom technology than do the Americans, with the reverse holding for large-batch technology. No significant differences exist between output from continuous-process technology, mass-production technology, or small-batch, job-shop technology (Kagono et al. 1981).

No data were located concerning other functional areas.

CONCLUSIONS

Many of the findings either do not support or conflict directly with commonly held opinions of Japanese management as compared with U.S. management. In addition, there is some contradiction within these findings. While one cannot put a great deal of confidence in the results, because of the use of survey and questionnaire methodology and because of low response rates, validity, and reliability, the studies do provide the groundwork for interesting speculation. Perhaps the strategic differences between U.S. and Japanese firms are not as great as we might have imagined; perhaps Japanese firms have adapted American approaches and improved upon them somewhat (as with the role of the planning committee). Perhaps the main difference is that Japanese management is slightly more thorough in a number of areas (such as quality control); perhaps culture is important; or perhaps Japan is enjoying the successes the Americans experienced a generation ago and will experience our malaise as their economy matures. Perhaps the most significant difference discovered is the use of corporate planning frameworks at the national level; if so, is the price of Japan's success a little less freedom and equal opportunity at the corporation, industry, or sector level? One thing is certain — a number of interesting and important areas for further research remain.

REFERENCES

Drucker, Peter F. 1981. "Some High Marks for American Management." *Wall Street Journal*, August 17.
"Editorial." 1980. *Management Japan* 13, no. 2 (Autumn):5.
"Federal Beat." 1981. *Journal of Industrial Engineering* (August):14.
Hayashi, Kichiro. 1980. "Corporate Planning in the Japanese Cultural Milieu." *Management Japan* 13, no. 2 (Autumn):6.
Hayes, R. H. 1981. "Why Japanese Factories Work." *Harvard Business Review* 59, no. 4 (July-August):56.
Hofer, C. W., E. A. Murray, Jr., Ram Charan, and R. A. Pitts. 1980. *Strategic Management*. St. Paul, Minn.: West.
Horvath, Deszo, and Charles McMillan. 1980. "Industrial Planning in Japan." *California Management Review* 23, no. 1 (Fall):11.
Kagono, T., I. Nonaka, A. Okumura, K. Sakakibara, Y. Komatsu, and A. Sakashita. 1981. "Mechanistic vs. Organic Management Systems: A Comparative Study of Adaptive Patterns of U.S. and Japanese Firms." *Annals of the School of Business Administration, Kobe University*, no. 25:115.
Kono, Toyohiro. 1980. "Comparative Study of Strategy, Structure, and Long-Range Planning in Japan and in the United States of America." *Management Japan* 13, no. 1 (Spring):20.

O'Leary, L. K. 1981. "Theory Z." *Bell Telephone Magazine* 60, no. 3, p. 8.

Ouchi, William. 1981. *Theory Z*. Reading, Mass.: Addison-Wesley.

Ouchi, William, and R. L. Price. 1978. "Hierarchies, Clans, and Theory Z: A New Perspective on Organization Development." *Organizational Dynamics* 7, no. 2 (Autumn):24.

Pascale, R. T., and A. G. Athos. 1981. *The Art of Japanese Management*. New York: Simon and Schuster.

Vogel, E. F. 1979. *Japan as Number One: Lessons for America*. Cambridge: Harvard University Press.

Wheelwright, S. C. 1981. "Japan—Where Operations Really Are Strategic." *Harvard Business Review* 59, no. 4 (July-August):67.

Yoshino, M. Y. 1976. *Japan's Multinational Enterprises*. Cambridge: Harvard University Press.

———. 1968. *Japan's Managerial System: Tradition and Innovation*. Cambridge: MIT Press.

24

The Product-Market Strategies of U.S. and Japanese Firms in the U.S. Consumer Electronics Marketplace

LIAM FAHEY *and* MICHAEL RADNOR

Business, government, labor, and other public voices are becoming increasingly concerned with what is frequently referred to as the "Japanese challenge" to the United States ("Mitsubishi" 1981; "What It Takes" 1979; "How Japan Does It" 1981; Vogel 1979). Japanese firms now dominate many product-market or industry sectors in the United States ("Japan Takes Over" 1981; "What It Takes" 1979). This study provides an overview of the evolution of the Japanese infiltration and domination of one such product market: the U.S. consumer electronics industry, with specific reference to the television receiver sector (Radnor et al. 1980).

The purpose of the chapter is to compare, contrast, and explain U.S. and Japanese firms' strategies in terms of product-market choices, modes of competition, and their management over time in the television receiver industry sector. The chapter begins with a short account of the background of the industry in the United States. The principal components of the U.S. and Japanese strategies are then highlighted. Many of these elements are further elaborated upon in the next section, in which specific emphasis is placed upon isolating and understanding the variety of forces and conditions that have contributed to these choices and strategies. Finally, some implications for our understanding of Japanese business strategy are noted.

BACKGROUND OF THE INDUSTRY

Consumer electronics is a $12.5 billion sector of the U.S. economy, which rises to $17 billion when software is included. Traditional products — television, radio, and audio — and the new video recorder/players, home computers, and electronic games are rapidly improving and evolving into integrated home information and entertainment systems that may have revolutionary technology, market, and service implications.

Many product-market sectors of the industry have been heavily penetrated by foreign (largely Japanese) competition, and foreign competition has established a strong foothold in other sectors. The extent of this penetration is dramatically illustrated by the following figures: in 1978, imports accounted for 18 percent of color television receivers; 85 percent of monochrome sets; 100 percent of video tape recorders, video discs, AM home radios, audiotape recorder/players, and home television cameras; 43 percent of phonographs and stereo sets; 64 percent of hi-fi components; 50 percent of electronic calculators; and 90 percent of CB radios. This position of strength is now being buttressed by the establishment of manufacturing and assembly plants in the United States by many Japanese producers. The decline of the U.S. industry is further reflected in a negative balance of payments of approximately $5 billion in 1978. Employment fell from 130,000 in 1966 to 74,000 in 1978 for the industry as a whole, and from 62,000 in 1966 to 28,000 in 1978 for the television manufacturing sector. These employment trends are due partly to technology changes. In comparison with many other industries, profits have been generally low in U.S. firms in the consumer electronics industry, and they have been declining for many years.

The decline of the U.S. consumer electronics industry and the emergence of strong foreign competition are thus relatively recent; yet in some areas the industry demonstrates considerable vibrancy. A number of U.S. firms are still at the forefront of research and development, technology development, and product design. We now turn to a brief description of the U.S. and Japanese strategies.

THE U.S. STRATEGY

With an enormous and affluent domestic market to satisfy, the U.S. television industry during the 1950s and early 1960s did not feel pressure to pursue foreign markets aggressively; many of these, in any case, presented numerous tariff and nontariff barriers. Thus, the domestic market was almost entirely the focus of U.S. television manufacturers. It must also be noted that the U.S. industry, because of its postwar technological and capital advantages, was able to develop and market its products in the United States without significant foreign competition. Television quickly became a highly visible, high-growth industry segment, with comfortable margins available to the leading competitors.

The product-market strategy of U.S. firms in both monochrome and color sectors was characterized by a number of general features. Their product strategy from the beginning was to concentrate on large, high-value, high-priced products that permitted the addition of "step-up" features, and for which profit margins were quite high. This product strategy was eminently reasonable and successful until the advent of intense competition among U.S. manufacturers themselves in the mid 1960s and increasing penetration of the market by foreign competitors. As the color television market exploded in the early and mid 1960s, the fierce competition that developed among U.S. manufacturers caused their early nonaggressive pricing tactics to give way to what the *Wall Street Journal* referred to on its front page as a "price war."

U.S. firms placed heavy emphasis upon the development of brand identification and awareness. The private-label market, which offered lower profits as well as competition with brand names, was largely the domain of smaller firms. The larger firms engaged in heavy advertising directly to consumers, projecting brand name and image and emphasizing product-quality features.

Another very significant feature of the product-market strategy of U.S. firms was that, to gain mass market penetration, they sold through extensive distribution networks supported by well-established service systems. The two-tier system of well-entrenched distributors and retailers was utilized by all U.S. manufacturers for all but extremely large-volume accounts, with the notable exception of General Electric. The emphasis upon national advertising and brand differentiation to engender "demand pull" contributed to lower distribution and dealer margins than if the strategy had been "product push." In summary, the U.S. strategy was to develop nationally advertised brand-name products, using extensive distribution and service networks, and pushing high-end, high-profit merchandise such as big consoles.

THE JAPANESE STRATEGY

While the U.S. television industry was growing rapidly, Japan was not standing idly by. In the 1950s, consumer electronics in Japan became a high-priority sector. The Japanese government put together a package of promotional policies to encourage its development. These policies included government support for research and development and the acquisition of foreign technology, support for export activities, and support in the form of protection of the home market.

In developing a consumer electronics industry, and particularly in its efforts to penetrate the U.S. market, Japan was confronted with some formidable disadvantages. It initially faced both capital and technological disadvantages. Other factors included transportation costs, lack of familiarity with the market, lack of distribution systems and service networks, nonexistent brand-name recognition, and a residual reputation for poor quality.

The Japanese product-market strategy also demonstrates a number of key features. The initial market focus of the Japanese strategy was the Japanese domestic market. Televisions were developed for and tested in the Japanese market, a market quite well protected from foreign competition. The domestic market thus served to debug products that were then directed toward foreign markets, particularly the United States. The Japanese product-market strategy was highly market-oriented and, unlike the U.S. approach, world-wide in scope.

A significant reflection of this market orientation is the product-market strategy adopted by the Japanese to enter and develop a strong position in the U.S. marketplace. This strategy can be summarized as follows: focus upon market segments not being addressed by U.S. manufacturers, develop high-volume products, dominate the product segment, and then move up the product line. In both monochrome and color segments, the Japanese initially entered the U.S. market with much smaller products than those of U.S. firms. Indeed, when the Japanese first marketed small black-and-white television sets in the United States, most U.S. firms felt that the market for these sets was very limited; they accordingly had been producing very limited quantities.

To develop high-volume products, the Japanese not only addressed markets being neglected by U.S. manufacturers but also used a double price structure to penetrate the U.S. market. They charged inflated prices in Japan — which was essentially closed to foreign competition — thus generating high profits. These profits allowed them to sell at very low prices in the United States to undercut the prices of U.S. sets, a practice known as "dumping." As will be discussed later, both a heavy emphasis upon driving costs down early in the product life cycle and lower labor costs facilitated this aggressive pricing policy.

Attainment of market share did not come quickly to Japanese firms. It took them 15 years to capture 15 percent of the monochrome market; but in 1970, only ten years from the time they began production, and well before U.S. demand had peaked, they captured close to 17 percent of the U.S. color market. Once significant market penetration was achieved, they extended the product line upward, increasing features and raising prices. Having gained dominance of the "second-set" market — with small, basic, reliable color televisions at a relatively low price — and a significant share of the medium-sized market, Japanese firms are currently extending into sets with more advanced features, including large consoles. A similar strategy was evident in the Japanese introduction of the three-transistor radio at $14 when U.S. firms were marketing higher-quality six-transistor radios at $60. Japanese firms eventually dropped the price to $3.75; then, when U.S. firms abandoned the home radio market, they extended the product line to include portable multifunctional radios that cost up to $250.

Critical to the Japanese product-market strategy has been a particularly heavy emphasis upon product quality: reliability, durability, and (later) product features. These quality dimensions result from specific manufacturing policies, process innovation, and research and development commitments (which are discussed below).

Unlike U.S. manufacturers, Japanese firms choose private labels, rather than branded products, as the most effective means of overcoming existing barriers to entry. However, while Japanese producers increased their combined share of the private-label market in the 1960s, in the 1970s they also developed their own brand-name markets. Japanese and other foreign brands now represent a significant share of many consumer electronics areas, with several foreign firms having branded sales volumes approaching those of U.S. firms.

Complementary to private labels and aggressive pricing was the utilization of one-step distribution systems (direct from manufacturer to retailer) by the Japanese as an economical method of serving a relatively small number of high-volume accounts and thus achieving relatively quick market penetration. Mass merchandisers have internal warehouses and inventory and distribution systems in place, which eliminate the need for a second step in the distribution chain. Retail chains make it possible to reach smaller-volume brand franchises.

Japanese producers have also employed their distribution arm to promote their products by offering relatively higher profit margins to dealers, causing dealers to support these brands at the point of sale. Thus, rather than the demand-pull approach of U.S. firms, Japanese manufacturers have typically employed a product-push strategy.

In summary, the Japanese strategy has been to enter the U.S. marketplace in market segments not served by U.S. firms, with high-quality products. High-volume products are developed through aggressive pricing, private labeling, and use of the distribution arm as a promotional tool; once significant market position is established, Japanese manufacturers move up the product line.

EXPLAINING THE STRATEGIES

The previous two sections briefly describe product-market strategies, but do not explain how and why they came to be. The intent of this section is to identify and discuss what we believe are the critical factors underlying the choice of these strategies. While we stress the obvious interconnection among the factors identified, for purposes of illustration we compare and contrast the U.S. and Japanese positions along each factor.

The Macroinstitutional Framework: Government-Industry Relations

The dominant ideological tenet of U.S. government and industry has been its commitment to "the free market system." This has resulted in open U.S. markets, the export of U.S. leadership technology, and few, weakly enforced import regulations. Foreign competitors thus had relatively unimpeded access to the U.S. market until the mid 1970s. Perhaps of more critical importance, U.S. firms began to license monochrome television technology to Japan in 1952–53, and the Japanese began production that year. In 1960, just as mass production of color sets was beginning in the United States, RCA licensed color technology to the Japanese.

Furthermore, U.S. government and industry have had fragmented, uncertain postures and an adversary relationship with regard to industry development, competitiveness and other national policy issues. U.S. firms, various governmental agencies, and unions see themselves as representing different constituencies, as part of a system of checks and balances. The battles among them are fought in a milieu where competitiveness within and between domestic firms is highly prized. These dimensions of U.S. government and industry, by contributing to an open and poorly coordinated economy, facilitated the infiltration of the U.S. marketplace by foreign competition, particularly foreign competitors as well organized and dedicated as the Japanese.

By contrast, Japanese government and industry function largely as a partnership with respect to industry development and export trade. The Japanese strategy begins with the concept of a "targeted" industry: government and industry mutually recognize important or potentially important industries (typically capital-intensive and characterized by high technology, low use of metals and energy, and low costs of transport) as high-priority areas for national resource commitments. Targeted industries receive priority in terms of capital and personnel allocation, technology development, and government support programs.

Thus, in the mid 1950s, the government of Japan put together a package of promotional policies to encourage the development of its consumer electronics sector. Laws were enacted under which the government provided grants and long-term, low-interest loans to stimulate acquisition of foreign technology and to underwrite research and development, particularly in targeted growth industries. It also allowed extra depreciation based on increased exports, and provided tax exemptions for expenditures to develop overseas markets. Behind a strong "protectionist" regime that imposed controls on foreign direct investment, set import quotas, and put restrictions on import and currency exchange licenses, the Japanese government thus intervened directly in the domestic environment of its electronics firms so as to encourage the development of an internally competitive consumer electronics sector.

Industry Fragmentation

It is our contention that a "fragmentation mentality" has pervaded the U.S. consumer electronics industry with respect to business perspectives, operations, and business-government relations; and that it has greatly contributed to the success of foreign competition in the U.S. marketplace. Largely because of legal prohibitions, joint research and development and other technology-related collaboration is almost unheard of within the U.S. industry. Industry supplier and customer relations, within as well as between firms, have often been described as poor. Even in response to rising imports, industry members adopted quite different stances in their demands (or lack of demands) for governmental action. Again, in part due to legal factors, unity of industry purpose and commitment, as manifested in cooperative and collaborative relations, has been notably absent in the United States, while in Japan the opposite has been an often noted characteristic.

Two outcomes of this fragmentation mentality are worthy of mention. First, U.S. firms could rely only on their own individual resource bases to fend off or respond to foreign competitive moves and threats. Thus, when Japanese firms entered the U.S. market with small televisions, each U.S. firm had to design its own response. Second, partially as a reflection of the broader political economy previously discussed, U.S. firms as a whole — the industry — were not in a position to engage in any form of collaboration with the U.S. government, either to react to foreign competitors or to develop a base from which to attack them.

Intrafirm Decision Making

In conjunction with these features of the broader political economy, two corporate decision-making characteristics that differentiate U.S. and Japanese firms — degree of internal cooperativeness and strategic decision-making time horizon — help explain their product-market choices and behaviors. The U.S. tradition of individual, departmental, divisional, and company independence, as reflected in such concepts as decentralization and profit centers, spurs competitiveness rather than cooperation among organizational units. A central theme of most of our U.S. industry interviews was that competitiveness within firms (such as between divisions or functional areas) is a common incentive-creating mechanism but one that hampers many necessary forms of collaboration — and collaboration becomes even more necessary in a context of rapid product, market, and technology change. For instance, even in the late 1970s, none of the U.S. firms had integrated planning of supply or product design between television and components divisions, even in firms with semiconductor or tube capability. In contrast, all the leading Japanese firms have in-house sources of components, developed in close collaboration with end-user requirements.

It is also typically the case in Japanese firms that marketing, product development, engineering, and manufacturing are tightly linked. This linkage involves not only optimization of components in product systems (leading to improvements in performance, costs, and product reliability), but also control. The mutual control of products and critical components could be the key in many sectors of consumer electronics: component technology is the source of significant present and future innovation, and end-product control is an important determinant of component sources and innovation.

With regard to the temporal dimension of strategic decision making, the institutional financial structure in the United States, both within firms and outside them (that is, the financial markets), has emphasized short-run profits and deemphasized investments that require long-run pay-offs. This tendency on the part of U.S. firms has been noted frequently (Rappaport 1978). U.S. firms, in tending to concentrate on short-term profit requirements, palliatives, and "fire fighting," inevitably deal with symptoms rather than with underlying causes of problems. For instance, the decision by many U.S. firms to take large parts of their television production "offshore" can be seen as valid in the short run. Nevertheless, in the absence of a concurrent and intensive effort aimed at technology improvement, it also limited future automation potentials by locking firms into existing technologies.

By contrast, the Japanese response to rising wages at home was to combine offshore moves with vigorous efforts to retool and automate. The policy yielded not only cost efficiency, but product innovation, compact design that had high consumer acceptance, low shipping costs, little need for service networks, and a quantum jump into new technology. The decision to go offshore could be a viable short-term strategy if it were used to buy time to make fundamental changes.

In Japan, lifelong employment for many employees, long-term financing, and government-supported programs in research and development encourage a longer-term view. This longer-term perspective is evident in many ways. It underlies the entry strategy of Japanese firms: they seek learning curve gains to permit aggressive product modifications, product-line extensions, and market development as an integrated package over extended time periods (Kotler and Fahey 1981). Similarly, from a technological and production perspective, it is evident that the Japanese planned ahead for the maturity phase of television by developing solid-state technology and automatic insertion.

Market Focus

Perhaps nothing distinguishes U.S. firms from the Japanese and accounts for their different success records as clearly as their respective market foci. U.S. consumer electronics firms traditionally have focused on the domestic market, while foreign firms — Japanese, European, and (more recently) other Far Eastern — employ a world-wide marketing strategy and, in fact, depend on foreign markets for a large part of their business. In general, foreign firms frequently develop products specifically for export markets, adapting them to national tastes and language requirements.

To concentration on the domestic market must be added some implications of the "fragmentation mentality" noted previously with regard to the product-market choices of the U.S. industry. While it is clearly not reasonable to suggest that each major consumer electronics firm needs to manufacture a full range of products and lines, there are also reasons to question the "cherry picking"-based product-market strategy employed by the dominant U.S. firms. While the choice of larger-screen, higher-priced, and higher-profit products may have been initially appropriate, the commitment and devotion of U.S. firms to this product-market sector opened up windows of opportunity for overseas competitors. From a strategic product-market management perspective, this short-term "cherry picking" approach is not sufficiently broad or responsive in a context of very rapid product, market, and technology change. Among other things, it leads to underconsideration of the advantages of scale and the foregoing of synergies among products and markets; in addition, it provides little incentive for longer-term forecasting, analysis, and planning.

In consumer electronics, this strategy led to the virtual ceding of the transistor radio, monochrome television, small-screen color television, and audio markets to the Japanese as each, incrementally, failed to demonstrate a *current* profit expectation when compared with seemingly better alternatives. Thus, when the Japanese first marketed small black-and-white television sets in the United States, most U.S. firms felt that the market for these sets was very limited and did not treat the market seriously for a number of years. The pattern was repeated in the color television market. The Japanese, therefore, developed the second-set market.

New Product Development

Central to the Japanese product-market strategy is the availability of the domestic market for new product introduction and development prior to efforts to penetrate foreign markets. What often goes unnoticed is that Japanese firms have been much more involved in new product introduction than is indicated by the number of products they have commercialized abroad. Thus, when smaller-screen monochrome and color televisions were launched in the U.S. marketplace, their quality in terms of reliability, durability, and picture had been severely tested in their domestic market. These were new products to the U.S. marketplace but not to the Japanese firms promoting them. This product introduction and development posture is currently evident in video recorders and video cameras.

High-Volume Products

The goal of establishing high-volume products is central to the Japanese world-wide product-market strategy. High-volume products are essential to reaping the benefits of economies of scale, experience curves, enticing distribution system support, and aggressive pricing. Here the world-wide scale of some Japanese firms, such as Matsushita, Sony, and Sanyo, must be emphasized. The international focus of these companies has led to benefits in vertical integration, international component sourcing, and funds for research and development. Fixed costs with world-wide application, such as research and development spending and process design, can be spread across a large number of units produced and sold.

Integration and Relative Importance of Functional Areas

The product-market and competitive strategies of Japanese and U.S. firms and their relative degrees of success defy explanation unless we take into account their different emphases upon functional areas, such as marketing and production. Marketing and sales expenditures, product innovation, process improvements, and manufacturing costs are emphasized different-ly by Japanese and U.S. manufacturers. Briefly, U.S. firms follow an ap-proach based on the life cycle of a typical product: they initially focus upon product innovation, and then on marketing through the maturation phase, with increasing emphasis upon manufacturing costs through maturation and decline. As previously noted, Japanese producers in their efforts to ex-ploit learning curves focus initially upon manufacturing costs and process innovations in order to become extremely cost-competitive in the early phases of the product life cycle. Price rather than other marketing and sales variables (such as advertising, promotions, and distribution) becomes the dominant competitive weapon.

The Japanese have been much more incisive than U.S. firms in inte-grating production and manufacturing management with their product-market strategies. As a prerequisite to this integration, manufacturing is accorded a much higher status within Japanese firms. In the United States, design engineering is regarded as basically a product-development func-tion and manufacturing engineering is low in status; technical effort and input are directed primarily to product activity. Due to the tighter linkage of the functional areas in Japanese firms, manufacturing management is often intimately involved from the initial stages of new product develop-ment, and the final product reflects significant manufacturing and engi-neering input.

IMPLICATIONS

It is evident from the previous discussion that the relative success and fail-ure of Japanese and U.S. firms in the television reciver product market are the result of many complex and interrelated factors. Thus, single-factor ex-planations, such as market-entry controls, government supports, labor costs, and decision-making style, overly simplify this complex reality. While many implications for our understanding of Japanese success might be noted, three points will be emphasized.

First, central to the Japanese way of doing business are some key deci-sion-making characteristics that are reflected in the strategy choices and modes of implementation of Japanese firms. These firms emphasize above all else systematic product-market choice and development. This emphasis contrasts sharply with an apparent tendency on the part of most U.S. firms to concentrate on product development to the relative neglect of market development. The Japanese strategy (especially the Japanese global strategy) revolves around the development of products for unserved or relatively neglected market sectors; the penetration of these product-market sectors via competitive strategies that typically are dissimilar to those of their dominant competitors; and, as soon as a substantial degree of penetration is achieved, development of product-line width to pursue broader (usually higher-profit) markets.

Second, U.S. firms, at least as evidenced by the history of the consumer electronics industry, seem to possess a much narrower conception of product-market development. Although in many respects they outdid the Japanese in the development of new product features (early technology leads and the first solid-state technology utilization, for example) a similar conclusion cannot be reached with regard to the focus and success of their market-development efforts. While it is true that U.S. firms bore the brunt of the initial development of the U.S. market for both monochrome and color television sets, it was the Japanese firms who came in and provided the impetus or leadership for major new market development through the introduction of smaller products utilizing private labels and one-tier distribution systems. In effect, the Japanese developed the second-set market. All this took place while U.S. firms were busy "milking" their profitable current product offerings.

Third, the Japanese have adopted a systemic orientation toward management. By "systemic" we mean concerned with the management of the various interconnections that may arise among strategy-related variables. This orientation can be illustrated by mentioning some of its main characteristics. One, product-market and operating (that is, production and manufacturing) linkages are accorded high priority. Experience gains, automation, reduction of components count, and so on are oriented toward achieving specific product-market advantages. Two, in a similar vein, product and process technologies are not treated as unrelated phenomena. Both areas are viewed as potential contributors to product-market advantages; both receive heavy resource commitments in terms of capital and personnel; and both are exhorted to work in close liaison with each other. Three, all phases of the corporate transformation process — raw material and components acquisition, product design and development, manufacturing, marketing, and after-sales service — are viewed as interrelated and interdependent activities. Thus, a high premium is placed upon integration in the design, planning, and implementation of these activities. Four, some Japanese firms have especially focused upon the development of synergistic benefits across product lines and markets. This is the opposite of the fragmentation that seems to characterize so many U.S. firms.

In short, Japanese success in the television receiver marketplace is a consequence of many factors internal and external to Japanese firms. This study has emphasized strategy-related factors — factors that have frequently been omitted in explanations of Japanese business success.

REFERENCES

"How Japan Does It." 1981. *Time*, March 30, pp. 54–60.

"Japan Takes Over in High-Speed Fax." 1981. *Business Week*, November 2, pp. 104–8.

Kotler, Philip, and Liam Fahey. 1981. "The World's Champion Marketers: The Japanese?" Northwestern University, November, manuscript.

"Mitsubishi: A Japanese Giant's Plans for Growth in the U.S." 1981. *Business Week*, July 20, pp. 128–32.

Radnor, Michael, Barbara Collins, Liam Fahey, Robert Beam, and Bala V. Balachandran. 1980. *The U.S. Consumer Electronics Industry and Foreign Competition*. Washington, D.C.: U.S. Department of Commerce, May.

Rappaport, Alfred. 1978. "Executive Incentives vs. Corporate Growth." *Harvard Business Review* (July-August):81–91.

Vogel, Ezra F. 1979. *Japan as Number One: Lessons for America*. Cambridge: Harvard University Press.

"What It Takes to Meet the Japanese Challenge." *Fortune*, June 18, pp. 104–20.

25

A Comparison of Japanese and U.S. Systems for Inventory and Productivity Management: A Simulation Approach

LEE J. KRAJEWSKI, BARRY E. KING, LARRY P. RITZMAN, NAN WEINER, *and* DANNY S. WONG

INTRODUCTION

Although it may not be obvious to the average person in the street, the United States is once again at war with Japan. This time the weaponry is economics, yet the threat is just as serious now as it was several decades ago. Recent increases in the prime lending rate, international shortages of oil, and spiraling inflation rates are but a few of the reasons that manufacturing management in the United States has looked to the East to see how the Japanese have coped with these problems and still been able to produce a high-quality product at a competitive price. Perhaps it came as no surprise that there was not much written about Japanese manufacturing management methods. In any case, many U.S. management teams visited Japan to see their methods first-hand.

Recently a number of articles have appeared in the literature describing various aspects of the "Japanese method." They can be separated into two basic categories: management style and system techniques. The articles on management style (exemplified by Pascale and Athos 1981; Drucker 1981; 1971; Johnson and Ouchi 1974; Kraar 1975; Ouchi 1981; Ozawa 1980) describe the Japanese lifestyle and how concepts like "bottom-up management" and quality circles are effectively put to use. The system technique articles (such as Monden 1981a; 1981b; Sugimori et al. 1977) concentrate on the information flow and various technical aspects of the so-called just-in-time manufacturing system of the Japanese. In reality, one cannot separate the behavioral issues from the technical issues, as even the technically oriented articles will admit. Whatever successes can be credited to the Japanese came about through a total technical and behavioral effort.

Supposing that a manager wishes to improve his or her inventory, productivity, and service position, which elements of the total Japanese approach to manufacturing management will yield the most benefit if applied here in the United States? There seem to be two approaches to answering this question. The first is to read all there is available on Japanese manufacturing methods and then visit a Japanese firm in a comparable industry. Many Japanese firms are eager to set up reciprocal visiting arrangements because they are skillful technology importers and much of what they apply today was developed in the United States years ago. Members of the U.S. management team, on the other hand, learn how the Japanese manage their production and then go home to apply the concepts in their own plants.

On the surface this approach sounds reasonable. However, it can be very costly if the factors that make the system work so well in Japan are not present in the U.S. plant environment. At present, there is a lot of speculation about which factors are critical to the improvement of inventory, productivity, and service positions. The literature does not provide much insight into this area.

The second approach is to identify the factors that may be critical and then to analyze them systematically to determine which ones (singly or in combination) have the most impact on inventory, productivity, and service. Experiments are run on computer models rather than in an actual plant to condense the time required for each experiment and to avoid the cost of making mistakes in the real plant. In this approach, the technical factors are modeled, while the behavioral factors are dealt with separately. The results of the technical analysis will then indicate the largest benefit expected from the adjustment of a technical factor under ideal behavioral conditions. The behavioral study assesses the degree to which the technical factor can be changed in the U.S. labor environment.

The study described in the remainder of this chapter follows the second approach described above. The next section discusses the U.S. and Japanese production systems to be analyzed. Then we discuss the other factors affecting inventory, productivity, and service. Next, the methodology is presented. A discussion of the model validation process follows.

U.S. AND JAPANESE INVENTORY AND PRODUCTIVITY MANAGEMENT SYSTEMS

Often the "system" is presented as the key factor to successful inventory, productivity, and service management, provided that the behavioral problems of implementation can be overcome. Whether or not this view is correct, it seems evident that the system does play an important role. A number of U.S. and Japanese systems have enjoyed considerable attention in the literature over the past several years. The ones analyzed in this study are described in this section.

Material Requirements Planning (MRP) System

A material requirements planning (MRP) system uses bills of material, inventory on-hand data, open order data, and a master production schedule to calculate time-phased requirements for materials. It also makes recommendations to release replenishment orders for materials or to reschedule open orders when due dates and need dates are not in phase.

Much has been said about the benefits of MRP. Improvements in inventory turnover, delivery lead time, percentage of time delivery promises are met, and split orders due to lack of material have all been reported for successful MRP users. It is difficult to fault the pure logic of MRP; however, there have also been a considerable number of failures or improper applications of the system. It seems it is not a panacea for the ills of all manufacturing organizations.

Traditional Planning System

Many firms use reorder point (ROP) and lot requirements planning (LRP) logic to launch orders to the shop and suppliers. ROP is used for all make or buy to-stock items, whereas LRP is used for make or buy to-order items. The logic of ROP indicates that a replanishment order of some predetermined fixed quantity is released whenever the inventory on hand plus the inventory on order falls below the reorder point. LRP for a to-order item releases lot-for-lot orders for the parent item and all to-order components that do not have a to-stock item as an immediate parent. The order release mechanism stops when a to-stock item is encountered. It is assumed that there will always be a supply of the to-stock items since these items will trigger replenishment orders whenever their reorder points are reached.

The planned lead time to use for each item depends upon its components. The lead time for a parent item that has to-stock items for its immediate components is merely the sum of the processing time, the set-up time, and slack for queue and component delay time to process the immediate components. If the parent item has to-order components, the lead time for the parent item includes the maximum cumulative planned lead time of the to-order components in contiguous parent-component relationships in the parent's bill of materials until a to-stock item is encountered. Thus when the reorder point of the parent is reached, orders for the parent as well as the to-order components are released.

Although there are variants of the system just described, the major differences between it and MRP are the lack of time-phased requirements planning and the ability to replan orders. However, the system is simpler than MRP, and under certain conditions may perform reasonably well compared with an MRP system.

Just-In-Time System

The Japanese system that has caused so much interest recently is the just-in-time system. Perhaps the most discussed system of this type is Toyota's Kanban system (Monden 1981a; 1981b; Sugimori 1977). The order release mechanism is relatively simple. It is effected by the use of an order card (Kanban) on the shop floor. There are two basic types of Kanban cards — a conveyance card and a production card. Production quantities of an item are conveyed from one process to another in containers equal to approximately 10 percent of the daily demand for that item. When the contents of a container are consumed, the conveyance Kanban is removed from the container by a worker and taken to the stocking point of the previous process to pick up another container of this part. The conveyance Kanban is attached to this new container. The production Kanban attached to this container is removed and becomes the order for the previous process to produce another container of parts. The entire production process, from the final assembly to preceding processes, subcontractors, and raw material suppliers, is linked through just-in-time production to result in a system that keeps work-in-process inventories at a minimum.

In the Kanban system, no defective parts are sent to later manufacturing stages. Earlier manufacturing stages manufacture only the quantity taken by later manufacturing stages. Materials cannot be received without a Kanban, and only the amount written on the Kanban can be withdrawn. Changes in production rates are accommodated by changing the number of Kanban in process or, in the case of rate increases, using overtime.

The just-in-time system, in the proper environment, reduces inventory investment dramatically. The factors that contribute to the proper environment will be discussed in the next section; however, the just-in-time system requires a stable master production schedule and, coupled with machine grouping and small lot production, produces a daily production schedule that changes only infrequently. Forward planning of component production as in MRP is not as critical, since it is relatively stable on a day-to-day basis. Of course, products that do not have a large annual demand or are produced to customer order are difficult to incorporate into the just-in-time system.

ENVIRONMENTAL ELEMENTS

The inventory and productivity management system is not the only factor that can affect inventory, productivity, and service positions. In fact, a number of environmental elements may prove to be even more important than the system itself.

Table 25.1 contains a list of various environmental elements that have an impact on inventory, productivity, and service. Since most of these elements are familiar, we will define only two of them here. Factor 14, ± zero

TABLE 25.1 Environmental Elements Affecting Inventory, Productivity, and Service

1. Small lot production
2. Single-digit setups
3. 100 percent quality
4. High machine reliability
5. Balanced work flow between stations
6. Stable master production schedule
7. Low-cost automation
8. One-worker-multiple-machine (OWMM)
9. Group technology
10. Focused factories
11. Few bills-of-material changes
12. Vendor reliability
13. Short vendor lead times
14. ± zero performance to schedule
15. Flexible workforce
16. Short manufacturing cycle times
17. High-volume demands
18. Quality circles
19. Bottom-up management

performance to schedule refers to finishing the daily production schedule each day, even if it takes overtime to do it. Bottom-up management, factor 19, is at the base of Japan's productivity achievement. Decisions are made by committee and consensus at lower levels rather than by top-down edict as in the United States. Operating decisions are made at the lower levels of the organization, thereby involving the foremen and workers who must implement the decisions.

Japan's successes can at least in large part be traced to its commitment of time and resources to establish an environment characterized by the elements listed in Table 25.1. In fact, the just-in-time system is merely a logical extension of production planning in such an environment. That is why these elements may even be more important than the system itself. Perhaps many of these elements cannot be realized in a U.S. environment due to differences in the customer and labor markets as well as geography. Nonetheless, two pertinent questions can be asked relative to these elements.

First, what inventory and productivity management system is best for a given factory environment? For example, for a given plant with 10 percent scrap loss factor, relatively unstable master production schedule, and vendor lead uncertainty, which system would yield the best inventory, productivity, and service positions? Second, which elements, when improved singly or in combination, will yield the greatest benefit for a given inventory and productivity management system? Consider single-digit set-ups. What improvement in inventory, productivity, and service can be expected if an engineering effort is instituted to reduce set-up times from four hours to 15 minutes? The study described in the remainder of this chapter is intended to develop the ability to answer questions such as these.

THE EXPERIMENTAL FACTORS AND THE MODEL

In this section, we will describe the experimental factors used in the study, the various programs and files needed as input to the simulator, and the simulator itself.

Experimental Factors

To study this problem analytically, it was necessary to devise a set of experimental factors to represent quantitatively the environmental elements in Table 25.1. This was accomplished with the help of a group of managers representing six plants of the sponsor organization. In a marathon meeting, the research team and the managers agreed to the factors given in Table 25.2.

TABLE 25.2   Experimental Factors Used in the Study

1. Inventory record accuracy
2. Master production schedule stability — time fence
3. Master production schedule stability — lumpy lot sizes
4. Forecast accuracy
5. Percentage time to-order
6. Vendor lead-time average
7. Vendor lead-time variance
8. Vendor product quality
9. Reject rate (internal)
10. Equipment downtime
11. Bills-of-material levels
12. Parents per component
13. Components per parent
14. Material flow pattern
15. Worker flexibility
16. Set-up-to-process time ratio
17. Items per work station
18. Percentage fabrication departments
19. Capacity slack
20. Capacity imbalances
21. Number of operations in routings
22. Lot sizes
23. Safety stock and lead time
24. Lot splitting
25. Static or discrete lot sizing
26. Priority rules
27. Material requirements planning system
28. Traditional system
29. Just-in-time system
30. Hybrid systems

Several of the factors need elaboration. The material flow pattern, factor 14, describes the degree to which the typical routings represent a flow shop arrangement. Factor 17 describes the degree of specialization at a work center. An environment that has a large number of unique items per work center has more general-purpose production equipment than one that routes only a few items through each work center. Capacity slack, factor 19, is the percentage of time for set-up, machine breakdowns, and idleness, and is used experimentally to generate processing times. Factor 20 can be used to create imbalanced workflows between departments. Finally, factor 30 addresses the possibility of combinations of the three systems described earlier. In this study we will create two hybrid systems — MRP/ROP and MRP/just-in-time. Both these systems have precedents in practice, and under certain environmental settings may outperform any of the pure systems.

Input Stream Generation

The large number of experimental factors makes the input data preparation for the simulator extremely difficult. To ease this burden, a number of programs and data files were created to prepare the data in the proper format for the simulator. Figure 25.1 shows the programs and files used in this study.

The input stream generator program requires two input files. The first is created by the factor input generator, which is an on-line program operated from a computer terminal. The user manually enters the values of a series of parameters that quantitatively describe the factors in Table 25.2. The program then creates a file for use by the input stream generator and an optional hard-copy report depicting the values in the file, which can be printed at the terminal. The user has the option of modification of an existing file (rather than manual input) to create a new file.

The second input file required by the input stream generator is the bills-of-material (BOM) file. This file is created by the BOM generator, which has the capability of generating bills of material from experimental factor inputs such as the number of end items, intermediate items, and purchased items desired; the average number of components per parent and parents per component; and the number of levels desired in each end item's bill of materials. The program uses a heuristic with random sampling to create the bills of material with the desired characteristics. Since random sampling is involved, several sets of bills of materials can be generated with the same characteristics, to permit experimental replication of the simulations. In addition to the BOM file, the program generates a single-level BOM listing for verification. The BOM generator is operated from a computer terminal, thereby permitting user interaction when the program cannot generate a BOM file with the desired characteristics.

There are actually two forms of the input stream generator. Version 1 uses the factor input file and the BOM file to create an experimental plant that conforms to the experimental factor settings. In addition to passing many factor values directly to the simulator, it creates new parameters including item lead times, total departments broken out as fabrication or assembly, number of machine groups within each department, number of machines within each machine group, item routings, number of workers per department, item-processing and set-up times, and independent demand rates. It also estimates average lot sizes for each item, the average inventory turns, and the total time spent by each department for set-ups, pro-

FIGURE 25.1 The Manufacturing Simulation System

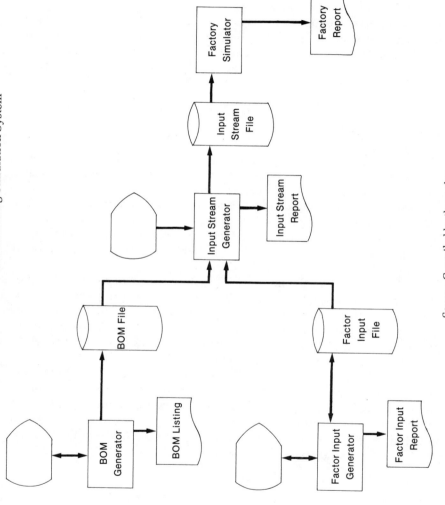

Source: Compiled by the author.

cessing, breakdowns, and idleness. These estimates are made assuming steady-state conditions and serve as a check on the reasonableness of the simulator output.

Version 2 bypasses the factor input and BOM files and accepts real factory data, thereby allowing the simulation of an actual factory. In this case, the input stream generator checks the input for consistency and prepares it for input to the simulator.

The printed output consists of 31 pages summarizing the parameters generated for each item produced or purchased by the plant and each department and machine group. The output serves as a record of the input for a particular simulation experiment and provides the research team or plant manager with a chance to judge the reasonableness of the inputs before the simulation is conducted.

The Simulator

The input stream generator provides the input file for the Fortran-based, discrete-event factory simulator. The model launches orders using any one of the inventory systems described earlier and processes them through a shop specified by the input stream generator file. It can simulate virtually any bill of material or shop configuration. Computer core storage is the only limitation on size. At present, the factory simulator requires 1000K bytes of memory and can handle approximately 800 production orders in process at any one time.

The output from the simulation is voluminous and consists of aggregate and individual statistics. The aggregate statistics on system performance include percentage of on-time delivery, average weeks of supply in inventory, and average weeks of backlog for finished goods, intermediate goods, raw materials, and total inventory. Aggregate facility utilization and worker utilization data are also available.

Individual statistics provided by the factory simulator include average cycle time, queue time, process time, component delay time, tardiness, weeks of supply in inventory, weeks of backlog, and number and size of orders for each inventory item. Individual statistics on utilization and queuing are generated for each machine group. Most of the individual statistics are also gathered on an aggregate basis.

MODEL VALIDATION

Two approaches to validating the factory simulator are being used. One involves an internal audit of the program, its inputs, and the results it provides. The other approach is an external check that amounts to using actual plant data from one of the sponsor's plants and verifying with the plant manager that the model is an adequate representation of the plant's operation.

Internal Validation

The factory simulator is a very complex program, and validating it is a tedious process. The internal validation process began by using the factor input generator, BOM generator, and input stream generator to create an experimental plant to be simulated by the simulator. The experimental plant environment is extremely benign. For example, inventory record accuracy is 100 percent, the master production schedule is stable, there are no forecast errors, no vendor problems, no rejects, and so on. This plant environment is called VANILLA, for obvious reasons. The simulator was executed with the VANILLA environment and the output was checked for reasonableness. In this regard, the predictions of the input stream generator were very useful as an independent check.

After the research team was confident that the VANILLA run was correct, separate files were created whereby each factor successively was initiated, leaving all the others as they were in the VANILLA file. For example, one file that was created initiated the vendor variance factor, allowing the vendor lead time to vary according to a normal distribution with the planned lead time as its average and its standard deviation 20 percent of its average. All the other factors were the same as in the VANILLA file.

The factory simulator was then executed with these experimental files, and the outputs were compared with the VANILLA output. A number of input errors and simulator program errors were uncovered in this process. As each error was discovered, all experimental settings that were affected by the corrections had to be redone.

External Validation

Perhaps the most crucial test of the methodology is its validation using actual plant data. Two members of the research team visited one of the sponsor's plants and, with the plant manager, specified the data requirements for the simulator. The plant manager and his staff developed the data, which included (among many other items) bills of material for 31 finished goods, routings, department and machine group specifications, and lot sizes. In total, settings for all of the experimental factors had to be specified.

The "status quo" plant environment was simulated; then several factor settings, of the manager's choosing, were adjusted to provide several simulations to study. All performance statistics were within the range of reasonableness and the model passed the test. If the runs had been off the mark, the research team and the manager would have had to work together to see where the simulator was failing to capture the plant's environment.

CONCLUSION

Now that the factory simulator has been validated, it will be used to analyze the experimental factors systematically. A fractional-factorial design will be used to eliminate the factors that do not have a significant impact on inventory, productivity, and service. The remaining factors will be subjected to a full-factorial design to capture the effects of interactions among the factors. The final report will discuss the effects these factors, including the various inventory and productivity management systems, have on inventory, productivity, and service.

REFERENCES

Drucker, Peter F. 1981. "Behind Japan's Success." *Harvard Business Review* (January–February):83–90.

———. 1971. "What Can We Learn From Japanese Management?" *Harvard Business Review* (March–April):110–22.

Johnson, Richard Tanner, and William G. Ouchi. 1974. "Made in America (Under Japanese Management)." *Harvard Business Review* (September–October): 61–69.

Kraar, Louis. 1975. "The Japanese Are Coming — With Their Own Style of Management." *Fortune*, March, pp. 116–21, 160–64.

Monden, Yasuhiro. 1981a. "Adaptable Kanban System Helps Toyota Maintain Just-in-Time Production." *Industrial Engineering* (May):29–46.

———. 1981b. "What Makes the Toyota Production System Really Tick?" *Industrial Engineering* (January):36–46.

Ouchi, William G. 1981. *Theory* Z. Reading, Mass.: Addison-Wesley.

Ozawa, Terutomo. 1980. "Japan's Industrial Groups." *MSU Business Topics* (Autumn):33–41.

Pascale, Richard T., and Anthony G. Athos. 1981. *The Art of Japanese Management*. New York: Simon and Schuster.

Sugimori, Y., K. Kusunoki, F. Cho, and S. Uchikawa. 1977. "Toyota Production System and Kanban System — Materialization of Just-In-Time and Respect-for-Human System." *Proceedings of the 4th International Conference on Production Research (Tokyo)*. London: Taylor and Francis.

26

Productivity and Labor Turnover: A Comparative Analysis of the United States and Japan

MANJULIKA KOSHAL *and* RAJINDAR K. KOSHAL

Labor turnover has traditionally been studied with respect to the labor-management relationship in a firm or industry. Labor turnover has been defined as a balance between a worker's inducement utilities and contribution utilities (March and Simon 1958, p. 93). A higher state of equilibrium between the two utilities means a healthier future for the labor-management relationship in a firm, a lower level of dissatisfaction in the labor force, and fewer strikes and grievances. A large number of studies in this area are based on the measurement of labor turnover, specifically on the methodology of data collection. These discussions revolve around the concepts of the stability index, stability curves, the turnover index, and replacements (Bowey 1969; Kilbridge 1961; Knox 1961). Recently the concept of labor turnover has been directly related to productivity studies. Such studies examine "labor turnover" as a study of the "committed labor force" (James 1960) or a study of the "leavers" (Stoikov and Raimon 1969), which provides management insight into the ability of the firm to retain its labor (Bowey 1969, p. 79). The larger the committed labor force in a firm, the higher the firm's commitment toward its stable labor force and the greater the future productivity of the firm. Unfortunately, the studies on labor turnover indicated that there is not one single variable (Cole 1979, p. 88) that can explain a high or a low turnover rate in a firm or industry.

Most of the studies on labor turnover are at the micro level and are based on sample surveys of a firm or group of workers. Thus there can be variations in the data from one firm to another. A macro study attempting to test empirically all the possible variables should provide an overall perspective on the problem. One such study by Stoikov and Raimon (1969) is based on 52 industries in the United States.

A macro study of labor turnover should be a valid approach to the analysis of productivity for a country as a whole. However, when one tries to make comparisons between the productivity and labor turnover rates of two developing countries, other variables become significant. Some of these variables may be the economic and political history of the country and the role of labor, the laws relating to industrial relations, the sociocultural characteristics of the society, the role of labor in the decision-making process, the future of the labor market, and the future of business in general. In the case of Japan, some sociocultural variables have played an important role in boosting Japan's productivity. This may not be true for the United States. However, both countries (the United States and Japan) can be labeled developed countries that have excelled in productivity during the last five years.

Because of the vast difference between the employment systems in the two countries, it is most interesting to study, compare, and contrast the trends of (labor) productivity in Japan and the United States. The basic difference is significant. First, in Japan the labor-management relationship is basically rooted in traditional social structure. This social structure is characterized by emphasis upon vertical human relationships as exemplified in the parent-child or superior-subordinate pattern (Evans 1972). Such a pattern stands in contrast to Western Europe and North America, where primary emphasis is upon horizontal relationships (Evans 1972). As a result, different weights have been assigned in the two countries to factors such as financial rewards, the quality of work, work experience, and merit. All these factors have a great impact on labor turnover, which in turn influences productivity.

In addition, some basic institutions characterize the system in Japan. These are (1) age- and seniority-based rewards; (2) "lifetime employment" (shusin koyo); and (3) the "enterprise union" (kigyo kumiai) (Evans 1972, p. 4). The Japanese system has resulted in labor cost flexibility (Haitaini 1978). Large numbers of young people work at low wages relative to their productivity. They are hired with the implicit promise that wages will rise as they grow in seniority and age. This results in greater labor stability and worker satisfaction, lower labor costs, a boost in worker morale, and higher productivity. Japan's economy achieved phenomenal growth during the 1950s and 1960s. The system of lifetime employment and seniority-based promotion and wages led to a surplus of labor with very few older workers — in fact, the age structure of employees is a pyramid (Haitaini 1978, p. 1032). The system of "union enterprise" results in long hours of work and shorter vacations and holidays, but almost no absenteeism. Shorter vacations and fewer holidays are accepted voluntarily by workers in Japan. Japanese workers enjoy their work because they regard it as a family venture or a group activity enabling them to spend more time together. The average Japanese man worked 54 hours a week, compared with 44 hours for American men, in 1965–66 (Hideaki 1971). The difference of ten hours per week amounts to almost 2.5 months of standard eight-hour days each year (Evans 1972, p. 5). During the same period, the average number of vacation days per worker per year was 130 in the United States and 70 in Japan.

In the United States, historically there has been a shortage of labor. Wages in the United States are based on merit, not age. It is never taken for granted that employment is for the employee's working lifetime. The workplace is for working, not social visiting. The satisfaction derived from working is not comparable to a feeling of communal harmony or family enjoyment.

The two countries exhibiting such differences in labor market patterns and tradition, degrees of industrial concentration, growth experience, value judgments, and occupational and industrial structures have experienced a surplus of labor and stability on the one hand (Japan) and a shortage of labor and instability on the other (United States), yet both have had tremendous productivity in the early 1950s and 1960s. Table 26.1 provides a comparative analysis of the various characteristics existing in both countries (Clark 1979a, pp. 140–79; Ouchi and Jaeger 1978, p. 308).

Today the Japanese employment system has changed. Factors responsible for this change are the sluggish economy, a rise in the average age of the Japanese worker, and an increase in the size of the educated labor force. The lower rate of growth of the national economy has been due largely to the 1973 oil crisis, the 1973–75 recession, and the increasing rate of inflation in the 1980s. The average age of Japanese workers has been rising rapidly, perhaps the result of better medical facilities. There also has been an increasing proportion of college graduates in the labor force (Haitaini 1978, p. 1029). The last two factors are the direct result of the systems of *nenko joretsu* (age- and seniority-based wages) and *shushin koyo* (lifetime employment). The growing number of older workers in the labor force has resulted in declining birth rates, a steadily rising life expectancy of the population, and an increase in the total wage bill every year. All these factors mean tremendously rising labor and retirement costs for a large number of older workers for a long period. The bottom of the "age pyramid" is

TABLE 26.1 A Comparison of Some Characteristics of Employment Systems in the United States and Japan

	UNITED STATES	JAPAN
Employment	Short-term employment; no ideal of lifetime employment	"Lifetime employment" (shu-shin koyo) an ideal
Decision making	Individual decisionmaking	Consensual decisionmaking
Responsibility	Individual responsibility	Collective responsibility
Relationship	Horizontal	Vertical (parent/child, teacher/student
Promotion	Rapid evaluation and rapid promotion	Slow evaluation and slow promotion; promotion based on age and seniority
Control	Explicit, formalized control	Implicit, informal control
Wages	Wages based on productivity; financial rewards based on merit	Age- and seniority-based wages; age the only criterion for financial rewards
Career path	Specialized career path	Nonspecialized career path
Concern	Segmented concern	Holistic concern
Unions	Segmented unions for blue- or white-collar workers (trade unions)	Enterprise union, with all employees belonging to one group
Mobility	More intrafirm mobility	Greater interfirm mobility (recent phenomenon)
Characteristics of mobile and immobile groups		Mobile: (1) young men, aged 25 years or less, with sufficient education; (2) young women; (3) temporary and irregular employees Immobile: (1) older men in larger firms; (2) graduates; (3) older women in family firms
Working hours	Shorter hours	Longer hours

Source: Some of these characteristics are given in Clark (1979b), p. 154, and Wheelwright (1981–82).

shrinking and a bulge is developing at the lower middle-age level. In fact, the male life expectancy has increased from 43 years in the 1970s to 72 years in the 1980s (Haitaini 1978). In addition, the college-age population has increased from 10 percent of the total population in 1960 to 38 percent in 1975. This indicates a declining number of young (aged 20–29) job seekers, an oversupply of university graduates, and competition for managerial positions among graduates (more supply and scarce demand)

The *nenko* system has also affected the promotion system. With a decreasing number of managerial positions, there is the "problem of inflation of managerial ranks." Promoting managers to satisfy their desire for "status" or "title" may lead to too many titles with "attendant inefficiency;" on the other hand, failing to give them positions would lower morale and productivity. This has recently been one of the vexing problems of Japan. Only about 10 percent of male college graduates 45 years of age and older will be able to occupy high positions in the year 2000, as compared with 70 percent from 1975 to the 1980s (Haitaini 1978, p. 1041).

All this would mean an increasing blue-collar labor shortage in Japan in the coming years. Japan might have to take other drastic measures to solve its future problems — measures that may not be compatible with the traditional values of the Japanese society. Some of these measures may be: compulsory retirement at the age of 60, linking wages to productivity rather than age, demoting managers from functional positions, rotating administrative positions, abolishing the system of automatic increase in wages, shorter work weeks, and hiring more part-time workers, especially women (Clark 1979a, pp. 248–57).

With too many available graduates, the concept of "enterprise union" — a union of a single enterprise or plant — would fade away (Clark 1979a, pp. 248–57). This would lessen the dependence of employees upon one single employer. All this would mean a changed Japan — a Japan with an increasing number of labor strikes, more grievances, a horizontal relationship among management and employees, high turnovers, and shortage of labor.

The characteristics of Japan's emerging economy resemble the characteristics of the U.S. economy of the 1970s. It seems interesting to study the productivity trends of two developed nations of today that will face similar changes but are wide apart culturally, socially, and historically.

The United States has been experiencing an imbalance in which the ratio of white-collar workers, the shortage of labor, and increasing labor unrest all play a part. As a result, greater emphasis is being put on increasing productivity and on adding more women to the labor force. A recent study on management efficiency in the refining industry of the United States indicated that the measure of management efficiency is not related to the size of the corporation. However, the elasticity of the scale of the enterprise is positively related to management efficiency. The most surprising result of this study is that the value of the marginal contribution of labor to output is negative except for the smallest corporation in the study. This indicates that in general the scale of the enterprise in refining has gone beyond the optimal point (Koshal and Koshal 1981).

QUANTITATIVE ANALYSIS

As pointed out earlier in this chapter, a few studies have suggested that labor productivity is negatively related to turnover rate. The main reason for such a relationship is that an increase in turnover rate suggests that workers are dissatisfied with present working conditions. If other conditions are held constant, a dissatisfied worker will produce less output than a satisfied worker. Dissatisfied workers are involved in more accidents — other things equal, the higher the turnover rate, the higher the accident rate (Koshal and Koshal 1972; Koshal, Koshal, and Shukla 1972). When a worker leaves, the company has to hire a new, inexperienced worker, who will produce less than the experienced worker. As more workers leave, the total cost of hiring increases, which in turn results in lower productivity per worker.

To examine the extent of the relationship between productivity and labor turnover rate, we provide in Table 26.2 coefficients of correlation between productivity indexes and turnover rates in Japan. Three productivity indexes have been selected: the index of total productivity for the economy as a whole, the index of productivity for the mining sector, and the index of productivity for the manufacturing sector. Turnover indexes are of three types: separation, accession, and overall turnover. The data are for 1970 and 1974–78. The selection of these years is dictated by the availability of data for Japan.

TABLE 26.2   Coefficients of Correlation between Turnover Rates and Productivity Indexes in Japan, 1970 and 1974–78.

	PRODUCTIVITY INDEXES		
TURNOVER RATES	ECONOMY AS A WHOLE	MINING SECTOR	MANUFACTURING SECTOR
Separation	− 0.9449[a]	− 0.9277[a]	− 0.9434[a]
Accession	− 0.8885[b]	− 0.9051[a]	− 0.8862[b]
Turnover	− 0.9175[a]	− 0.9193[a]	− 0.9155[a]

[a]Significant at the 1 percent level.
[b]Significant at the 5 percent level.
Source: Japan Statistical Yearbook (1979).

An examination of Table 26.2 will convince the reader that there is a strong negative relationship between productivity and turnover rates in Japan. Of the nine coefficients of correlation, seven are statistically significant at the 1 percent level, while the remaining two are statistically significant at the 5 percent level.

Table 26.3 provides the coefficients of correlation between turnover rates and productivity indexes in the United States. The data on productivity indexes for manufacturing in the United States are of two types: the output per man-hour and the output per employed person. Turnover rates are for total manufacturing, the durable goods sector, and the nondurable goods sector. An examination of Table 26.3 reveals that the coefficients of correlation between turnover rates and productivity are negative. This suggests that a reduction in turnover rates would be followed by an increase in productivity. However, for the United States, separation rates and productivity indexes show statistically significant coefficients of correlation at the 20 percent level. For the accession rates and productivity indexes, though, none of the coefficients of correlation are statistically significant. This might be because, in the United States, a larger proportion of new hirelings consists of younger workers. On the other hand, in Japan new hirelings represent a smaller proportion of the labor force. In fact, an analysis of the growth in the population and labor force in Japan and in the United States confirms these trends.

Table 26.4 gives the growth of population between 1970 and 1978 in Japan and in the United States. Table 26.5 gives the growth of the labor force for 1970–78 in Japan and in the United States. It is interesting to note that, although during 1970–78 in the United States the population grew by only 6.6 percent (against 11.0 percent in Japan), the labor force increased during the same period by 19.3 percent (against 6.2 percent in Japan). Thus a higher growth in the labor force in the United States contributed to a proportionate increase of younger and inexperienced workers in the labor force. Such a shift in labor composition would inevitably lower the growth of productivity in the United States.

This assertion is confirmed by an examination of the changing age distribution in the labor force in these two countries. Table 26.6 gives for 1970 and 1978 the age distribution of the Japanese labor force. Similarly, Table 26.7 gives for 1970 and 1978 the age distribution of the U.S. labor force. Table 26.7 suggests that, in the United States, the labor force 34 years old or younger, as a percentage of the total labor force, has increased from 43.8 in 1970 to 50.7 in 1978. On the other hand, in Japan the labor force 29 years old or younger decreased from 68.4 in 1970 to 61.3 in 1978. Considering the group aged 45–54 years in the United States, one sees a decrease of 16.6 percent. In Japan, there has been an increase of 30.3 percent in the proportion of the workers between the ages of 45 and 54 years. The net im-

TABLE 26.3   Coefficients of Correlation between Turnover Rates and Productivity Indexes in the United States, 1970–78

	PRODUCTIVITY INDEX	
TURNOVER INDEX	OUTPUT PER MAN-HOUR	OUTPUT PER EMPLOYED PERSON
Total manufacturing		
Separation	– 0.7652[a]	– 0.7400[a]
Accession	– 0.1009	– 0.0200
Turnover	– 0.5565[b]	– 0.4986[c]
Durable goods sector		
Separation	– 0.8269[a]	– 0.8189[a]
Accession	– 0.0874	0.0451
Turnover	– 0.5998[b]	– 0.5484[b]
Nondurable goods sector		
Separation	– 0.5177[c]	– 0.4684[d]
Accession	– 0.1184	– 0.0467
Turnover	– 0.3500	– 0.2867

[a]Significant at the 1 percent level.
[b]Significant at the 10 percent level.
[c]Significant at the 15 percent level.
[d]Significant at the 20 percent level.
Source: Handbook of Labor Statistics (1980).

TABLE 26.4   Growth of Population in Japan and in the United States, 1970–78

	JAPAN		UNITED STATES	
YEAR	TOTAL (THOUSANDS)	PERCENTAGE CHANGE OVER PREVIOUS YEAR	TOTAL (THOUSANDS)	PERCENTAGE CHANGE OVER PREVIOUS YEAR
1970	103,720	—	204,900	—
1971	105,145	1.37	207,100	1.07
1972	107,595	2.33	208,800	0.82
1973	109,104	1.40	210,400	0.77
1974	110,573	1.35	211,900	0.71
1975	111,940	1.24	213,600	0.80
1976	113,089	1.03	215,200	0.75
1977	114,154	0.94	216,900	0.79
1978	115,174	0.89	218,500	0.74
Percentage increase, 1970–78		11.04		6.64

Source: Japan Statistical Yearbook (1979) and Handbook of Labor Statistics (1980).

TABLE 26.5   Growth of Labor Force in Japan and the United States, 1970–78

YEAR	JAPAN		UNITED STATES	
	TOTAL (THOUSANDS)	PERCENTAGE CHANGE OVER PRE-VIOUS YEAR	TOTAL (THOUSANDS)	PERCENTAGE CHANGE OVER PRE-VIOUS YEAR
1970	51,530	—	85,900	—
1971	51,780	0.49	86,900	1.16
1972	51,820	0.08	89,000	2.42
1973	n.a.	n.a.	91,000	2.25
1974	52,370	n.a.	93,200	2.42
1975	52,230	− 0.27	94,800	1.72
1976	52,710	0.92	96,900	2.22
1977	53,420	1.35	99,500	2.68
1978	54,080	1.24	102,500	3.02
Percentage increase, 1970–78		6.16		19.32

Note: n.a. = not available.
Source: Japan Statistical Yearbook (1979) and Handbook of Labor Statistics (1980).

TABLE 26.6   Age Distribution of Labor Force in Japan

AGE (YEARS)	1970	1978	PERCENTAGE CHANGE, 1970–78
Under 20	27.4	20.9	− 23.72
20–29	41.0	40.4	− 1.46
30–44	21.3	25.3	18.78
45–54	6.6	8.6	30.30
55 and over	3.7	4.8	29.73
Total	100.0	100.0	—
Average age (years)	28.89	30.66	6.13

TABLE 26.7   Age Distribution of Labor Force in United States

AGE (YEARS)	1970	1978	PERCENTAGE CHANGE, 1970–78
Under 20	8.9	9.6	7.87
20–34	34.9	41.1	17.77
35–44	19.5	18.4	− 5.64
45–54	19.8	16.5	− 16.67
55 and over	16.8	14.3	− 14.88
Total	100.0	100.0	—
Average age (years)	38.67	36.91	− 4.56

pact of these changes in age composition is that the average age of the worker in the United States is declining while in Japan it is increasing. For example, in the United States the age of the average worker decreased from 38.67 years in 1970 to 36.91 years in 1978, a decline of 4.6 percent. However, in Japan the average age of the worker increased from 28.89 years in 1970 to 30.66 years in 1978 (an increase of 6.1 percent). These figures suggest that the slower growth in productivity in the United States than in Japan might be partly explained by changes in the age composition of the labor force in the two countries.

Finally, for Japan and the United States, Tables 26.8 and 26.9 give the percentage changes in labor turnover rates of various sectors of the economy for the period 1970–78. An examination of Table 26.8 reveals that during the period 1970–78 in Japan, both accession and separation rates declined. This factor has had a large impact on the overall declining turnover rate in all the sectors of the Japanese economy. However, an examination of Table 26.9 suggests that during the same period in the United States, some categories of the manufacturing sector indicate a downward trend in the accession and separation rates. On the whole, for the durable goods sector during this period, the accession rate increased by 8.57 percent but the separation rate declined by 27.66 percent. Thus, for the durable goods sector in the United States, the overall turnover rate declined by only 12.20 percent, compared with a 39.08 percent decline (in the labor turnover rate) in Japan.

A comparison of Tables 26.8 and 26.9 further suggests that, on the average, there has been a much larger decline in the turnover rates in all the sectors of the Japanese economy than there has been in the turnover rates in the U.S. economy. Such a difference in change in turnover rate, as suggested earlier in this chapter, would be automatically reflected in slower growth in productivity in the United States. Many cultural and sociological factors are also responsible for these trends, as explained earlier.

SUMMARY

In this chapter we have examined for the period 1970–78 the changes in labor turnover rates and labor productivity in Japan and the United States. A statistical analysis suggests that there is a negative relationship between the labor turnover rates and labor productivity. Further analysis reveals that during 1970–78 Japan experienced a higher reduction in labor turnover than did the United States. This higher reduction in labor turnover rates may be explained partly by the changes in the age composition of the labor force in the two countries and partly by the cultural and sociological practices that influence the hiring and rewarding practices of labor. Fur-

TABLE 26.8 Turnover Rates in Japan, 1970 and 1978

SECTOR	ACCESSION			SEPARATION			TURNOVER		
	1970	1978	PERCENTAGE CHANGE	1970	1978	PERCENTAGE CHANGE	1970	1978	PERCENTAGE CHANGE
Total	22.92	13.47	−41.23	21.54	14.06	−34.74	22.23	13.77	−38.08
Mining	13.80	12.30	−10.81	22.64	15.92	−29.69	18.22	14.11	−22.56
Manufacturing	22.85	11.28	−50.65	21.28	13.04	−38.71	22.07	12.16	−44.89
Wholesale and retail	26.76	17.66	−34.01	25.45	18.32	−28.02	26.16	17.99	−31.09
Finance and insurance	23.58	14.47	−38.65	20.50	12.82	−37.48	22.04	13.65	−38.09
Real estate	33.09	15.76	−52.36	31.43	19.54	−37.85	32.26	17.65	−45.29
Transport and communication	17.47	10.03	−42.61	16.95	10.57	−37.63	17.21	10.30	−40.15
Electricity, gas, and water	4.50	4.45	−1.03	4.70	3.85	−18.08	4.60	4.15	−9.78
Services	24.06	15.44	−35.82	22.31	13.60	−39.05	23.19	14.52	−37.37

TABLE 26.9 Turnover Rates in the United States, 1970 and 1978

SECTOR	ACCESSION			SEPARATION			TURNOVER		
	1970	1978	PERCENTAGE CHANGE	1970	1978	PERCENTAGE CHANGE	1970	1978	PERCENTAGE CHANGE
Durables, total	3.5	3.8	8.57	4.7	3.4	− 27.66	4.1	3.6	− 12.20
Lumber and wood products	5.8	6.0	3.45	6.7	5.9	− 11.94	6.3	6.0	− 4.80
Furniture and fixtures	4.9	5.8	18.37	5.7	5.7	0	5.3	5.8	8.49
Stone, clay, and glass	4.3	4.1	− 4.65	4.8	4.0	− 16.67	4.6	4.6	− 10.99
Primary metal	3.1	2.9	− 6.45	4.1	2.5	− 39.02	3.6	2.7	− 25.00
Fabricated metal	4.5	4.7	4.44	5.0	4.5	− 10.00	4.8	4.6	− 3.16
Machinery	2.6	3.0	15.38	3.7	2.5	− 32.43	3.4	2.8	− 12.70
Electrical equipment	3.1	3.5	12.90	4.4	3.2	− 27.27	3.8	3.4	− 10.67
Transportation	3.8	3.6	− 5.26	5.5	3.0	− 45.45	4.7	3.3	− 29.03

Instruments	2.6	2.8	7.69	3.4	2.5	−26.47	3.5	2.7	−24.29
Miscellaneous manufacture	5.6	5.8	3.57	6.6	5.8	−12.12	6.1	5.8	−4.92
Nondurable, total	4.6	4.5	−2.17	5.0	4.5	−10.00	4.3	4.5	−6.25
Food	6.7	6.4	−4.48	6.8	6.3	−7.35	6.8	6.4	−5.93
Tobacco manufacture	5.0	3.4	−32.00	4.9	3.5	−28.57	5.0	3.5	−30.30
Textile mill products	4.9	4.6	−6.12	5.5	4.7	−14.55	5.2	4.7	−10.58
Apparel and other textiles	5.4	5.6	3.70	6.1	5.8	−4.92	5.8	5.7	−0.87
Paper	3.2	2.9	−9.38	3.7	2.8	−24.32	4.0	2.9	−17.39
Printing and publishing	3.2	3.5	9.38	3.4	3.2	−5.88	3.3	3.4	1.52
Chemicals	2.2	1.8	−18.18	2.5	1.7	−32.00	2.4	2.8	−25.53
Petroleum	2.3	2.2	−4.35	2.5	2.1	−16.00	2.4	2.2	−10.42
Rubber	4.7	5.0	6.38	5.6	4.8	−14.29	5.2	4.9	−4.85
Leather products	5.8	7.3	25.87	6.5	7.6	16.92	6.2	7.5	21.14

ther, a relatively slow growth in productivity in the United States as compared with Japan is due partly to changing age composition of the labor
force and partly to the relatively low reduction in labor turnover rates in
the United States. Further studies considering separately each sector of the
economy might provide further insight. However, necessary data for such
comparisons are not available at this stage.

REFERENCES

Bowey, A. M. 1969. "Labor Stability Curves and a Labor Stability Index." *British Journal of Industrial Relations* 7, no. 1 (March):71.

Clark, R. 1979a. *The Japanese Are Coming*. New Haven: Yale University Press.

_____. 1979b. *The Japanese Company*. New Haven: Yale University Press.

Cole, R. E. 1979. *Work, Mobility, and Participation*. Berkeley: University of California Press.

Evans, R., Jr. 1972. "Japan's Labor Economy—Project for the Future." *Monthly Labor Review* (October):3.

Haitaini, K. 1978. "Changing Characteristics of the Japanese Employment System." *Asian Survey* 8:1031.

The Handbook of Labor Statistics. 1980. Washington, D.C.: U.S. Government Printing Office.

Hideaki, O. 1971. "Work and Leisure in Japan." *Labor Bulletin* (October):5–8.

James, R. C. 1960. "The Casual Labor Problem in Indian Manufacturing." *Quarterly Journal of Economics* 74, no. 1 (February):114–16.

The Japan Statistical Year Book. 1979. Tokyo: Bureau of Statistics, Office of the Prime Minister.

Kilbridge, M. D. 1961. "Turnover, Absence, and Transfer Rates as Indicators of Employee Dissatisfaction with Repetitive Work." *Industrial and Labor Relations Review* 15, no. 1 (October):21–32.

Knox, J. B. 1961. "Absenteeism and Turnover in an Argentine Factory." *American Sociological Review* 26, no. 3 (June):424–28.

Koshal, M., and R. K. Koshal. 1981. "Management Efficiency and Optimal Size of Enterprise: A Case of Gasoline Industry." Paper presented at the annual meeting of the Midwest Business Administration Association, Chicago, April.

_____. 1972. "Industrial Accidents in Japan: An Empirical Analysis." *Keio Economic Studies* 9:97–103.

Koshal, M., R. K. Koshal, and V. Shukla. 1972. "Industrial Accidents in the United States—A Macro Approach." *Indian Journal of Industrial Relations* 1:393–402.

March, J. G., and H. A. Simon. 1958. *Organizations*. New York: Wiley.

Ouchi, W. G., and Alfred M. Jaeger. 1978. "Type Z Organization—Stability in the Midst of Mobility." *Academy of Management Review* 2:308.

Stoikov, Vladimir, and R. L. Raimon. 1969. "Determinants of Differences in the Quit Rates Among Industries." *American Economic Review* 58 (December):1283.

Wheelwright, S. C. 1981–1982. "Operations as Strategy Lessons from Japan." *Stanford GSB* (Fall):3–7.

27

Program for Research on Organizations and Management: The United States-Japanese Electronic Industries Study

WILLIAM G. OUCHI, JAY B. BARNEY, and DAVID ULRICH

INTRODUCTION

Recent publication of several books on Japanese industry (Vogel 1979; Ouchi 1981; Pascale and Athos 1981) has sparked widespread interest throughout the United States in Japanese management and its relation to productivity. While these and other works are important in describing the style of many Japanese managers, they may not tell the whole story of apparent Japanese efficiency, effectiveness, and productivity. A recent review of some of this work in the *Asian Wall Street Journal* (1981) noted the importance of understanding management practices and their relation to productivity, but suggested that Japanese success could not be fully under-

We gratefully acknowledge the assistance of Guido Krickx, Sharon Stevens, Mary Kay Stout, and Shin Watanabee in the reported research. This work is supported by grants from the Office of Naval Research, the Alcoa Foundation, General Electric Foundation, AMP, Inc., and the IBM Corporation.

stood without also considering relations between Japanese firms and between industry and government in Japan. This review noted that

> in focusing exclusively on the role of management in Japan's success, [we] may neglect to mention many other contributing factors. Among these are the relatively weak Japanese anti-trust laws; government sponsorship of favored industries; a high rate of savings in Japan, which makes capital cheap, and the large shareholdings in major corporations by Japanese banks, which are often willing to forego fat dividends until the firm has carved out an unchallengeable market share (p. 11).

The primary purpose of this chapter is to describe a research project that is being undertaken at the Graduate School of Management at UCLA. This project, entitled the Electronics Industry Study, has a long-range purpose of understanding strategic relations between firms. This chapter reviews this project in several sections. We begin by introducing a general theoretical framework that guides this research. Next, we present a brief historical review of the U.S. and Japanese electronics industries. Following this, several specific research studies that together form the bulk of the project are reviewed. The first three of these studies have progressed more quickly and will be discussed in more detail. As appropriate, empirical results will be reported.

THEORETICAL FRAMEWORK

An emerging organization theory framework that generates important insights into the analysis of cooperative relations between firms and between industries and government was originally developed in economics by Williamson (1975). Known by various names, including the transaction costs framework and the organizational failures framework, this perspective on organizations will be the conceptual base for our empirical comparisons of the U.S. and Japanese electronics industries. This framework and its relevance to the research described below are discussed in some detail elsewhere (Ouchi 1981; Barney and Ulrich 1981). We will introduce and briefly describe this conceptual framework with an example of the application of the model.

Consider a typical U.S. example of firm relations with other firms. Suppose a computer manufacturer became aware of a new and powerful semiconductor chip uniquely manufactured by a particular large-scale integration (LSI) company and wished to design this new chip into its next generation of computers. The computer firm in the United States may be reluctant to design its new machine around this new device, fearing that once this takes place, the firm will be at the mercy of its sole supplier of this chip. Once the computer firm makes the design investments, they often cannot be changed to incorporate new LSI devices without considerable expense. Under these conditions, the chip manufacturer could raise prices, lower quality, or provide poor service, all without unduly jeopardizing the sale of its device to the computer manufacturer.

Three alternatives immediately present themselves to the computer manufacturer. First, the manufacturer may decide not to incorporate the new chip into its design, and thus avoid any sole-supplier relations. Unfortunately, this may also lead to an inferior product on the market. Second, the computer firm may acquire the chip manufacturer. Such vertical integration seems likely to insure stable, low-cost supplies of the device to the computer firm, but may have some secondary negative consequences. For example, the computer firm may not have LSI manufacturing competence, which would cause a rise in manufacturing costs. Also, whereas the sole interest of the separate semiconductor firm was LSI research and development, LSI development in the vertically integrated firm may be only a small percent of total research and development expenditures. Under such conditions, the vertically integrated firm may be less innovative in LSI technology than the separate semiconductor firm was. Finally, the computer firm may require the semiconductor manufacturer to license another firm to manufacture the new device also, in exchange for a guarantee that the computer firm will buy most of the new devices it uses from the original semiconductor firm. Such second sourcing, though common in the United States electronics industry, is fraught with difficulties. First, it is often difficult to find a semiconductor firm willing to manufacture the new device under such restrictions. Second, because these devices are so complex, it may be difficult to transfer all the knowledge and understanding necessary to the second source for it to manufacture a high-quality product. Moreover, the original semiconductor firm may choose not to transfer all the relevant information, thus insuring that the second source manufactures an inferior product. Also, because of the complexity of the manufacturing process and the amount of proprietary information, the computer firm may not be able to police the development of a second source adequately to assure high quality.

In Japan, computer manufacturers facing a similar situation could also adopt one of these three alternatives. It appears that vertical integration is a common solution to this particular single-sourcing problem. However, two additional alternatives may be available to the Japanese firm that may not be available to U.S. firms. First, Japanese computer manufacturers might be able to call on a third party, such as the Ministry of International Trade and Industry (MITI), to mediate the exchange and insure that both parties were dealt with equitably. This third party would have to have intimate knowledge of both parties to the exchange. It would also have to be trusted to decide ambiguous and complex issues in ways that would assure long-term equity in the exchange. Lifson (1981) shows how this third-party guarantor helps assure equitable relations within large Japanese firms. At the firm level, this third party could be the government, but is more likely to be a bank that has substantial holdings in both firms and enjoys a long-term, stable, and intimate relation with both firms. If either actor behaves so as to jeopardize an equitable exchange, the bank may take appropriate action. Second, the potential problems associated with single-source relations could be considerably lessened in the two firms in Japan if they had mutual interests in maintaining a long-term equitable exchange. This could occur, for example, if each firm held substantial amounts of stock in the other firm, thus increasing the likelihood of cooperation between firms.

In the above example, we have described five ways an exchange can be governed: through no exchange, through a common hierarchy (vertical integration), through a quasi-market mechanism (second sourcing), or through one of two "intermediate" forms of governance. These governance mechanisms are depicted in Figure 27.1.

These last forms of governance are basically markets in nature, but are assisted by hierarchies or clans (that is, cooperative mechanisms). In the intermediate case, firms remain separate, but ambiguous or complex exchange issues are mediated by a third party with an interest in maintaining an equitable relationship — the bank, or firms that recognize their joint interest in maintaining such a relationship due to interdependent ownership. This extended example summarizes the theoretical context underlying the research project.

HISTORY OF THE UNITED STATES AND JAPANESE COMPUTER INDUSTRIES

Our study includes ten major product-market segments of the electronics industries, of which "computers" is one. This brief historical overview is meant to indicate the range of research questions that we are pursuing.

The United States computer and semiconductor industries have grown rapidly since their inception in the early 1940s. The industry originated with the first modern digital computers, Mach I and ENIAC. In the 1940s, leading electronics technology included vacuum tubes and was applied principally to information processing in the military. In the 1950s, transistors were the major technical innovation. Products such as silicon transistors were developed by Texas Instruments in 1954 and continued to serve predominantly the military and aerospace markets. Throughout the

FIGURE 27.1   Example of Efficiency Hypothesis
U.S. Case of Computer and Semiconductor Firms

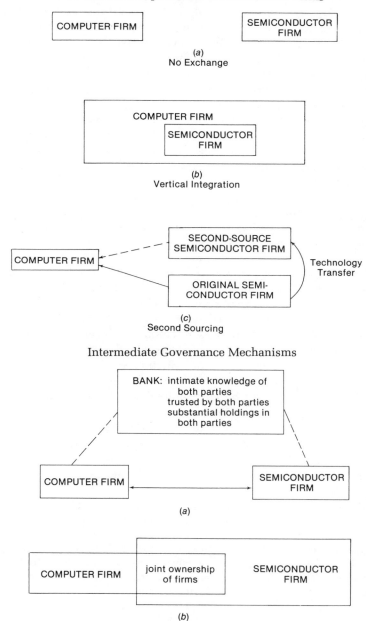

Source: Compiled by the author.

1960s, technical innovations such as the integrated circuit (IC), medium-scale integration (MSI), and large-scale integration (LSI) became dominant technologies, often used in both military and nonmilitary computer markets. In the 1970s and into the 1980s, Intel maintained a technical lead in a rapidly evolving market with very-large-scale integration (VLSI). Such semiconductor devices are currently used in a variety of applications from automobiles to office machinery (U.S., Dept. of Commerce 1979; Brittain and Freeman 1980). Current projects indicate that the electronics industry should remain one of this country's most valuable assets and critical industries through the 1980s (U.S., Congress 1981).

Fairchild Publications reports annually on the U.S. electronics industry by summarizing the reports filed by public firms (10-K, corporate reports) in *The Electronic New Financial Fact Book and Directory*. In the 1980 edition, this text included summary information on 680 firms.

The Japanese computer industry began in the mid 1950s with MITI sponsoring electronics research. MITI founded the Research Committee on Computers, comprised of prospective manufacturers, industry leaders, and research scientists, to study Japan's investment in the electronics field. However, real growth in the Japanese electronics industry began in the mid 1960s. By this time, IBM had developed the System 360 computer. This machine highlighted both the future relevance of electronic technology and Japan's lack of technological development vis-à-vis the U.S. industry. As the importance of the electronics industry became clear, MITI began to allocate resources to firms' research and development and manufacturing. Firms such as the Japan Electronic Computer Corporation (a joint venture of seven computer manufacturers) and the Japan Software Company (a joint venture of Fujitsu, Hitachi, and Nippon Electric) received government support for electronics development. As a result, these firms began to invest great amounts of time and resources to develop, manufacture, and market new electronics technologies. In the 1970s, the Japanese electronics industry continued to grow rapidly. In 1974, MITI published *Japan's Industrial Structure — A Long Range Vision*, which reviewed Japan's commitment to the electronics industry:

> The computer, which will form the core of informationalization, will probably record an especially large expansion in demand as informationalization progresses in industry, in society, and in the people's lives. . . . The role played by imported technology centering on technology in the electronics industrial fields has been very important, but now that Japan has reached the same general technological level as Europe and America, the self-development of technology will be a big issue for the future" (pp. 71–72).

Japanese firms have been successful in their endeavors to develop technology and capture world market share in electronics. Their world market share has increased significantly in the last decade. Robert Noyce, vice-chairman of Intel Corporation, testified before the Subcommittee on International Finance of the Committee on Banking, Housing, and Urban Affairs of the United States Senate that one of the major challenges the U.S. electronics industry faces in the 1980s is the rapid technological and market growth of the Japanese industry (U.S., Congress 1980).

The Oriental Economist publishes *Japan's Company Handbook*, a book similar to one published by Fairchild Publications. The handbook includes summaries of public information on approximately 125 Japanese electronics firms.

Two relevant points should be highlighted from the above brief historical overview of the U.S. and Japanese electronics industries. First, both industries have become very complex. The number of products produced by the industries and the number of firms in each industry have grown very rapidly with new applications of electronics technology. Second, despite their parallel growth, the U.S. and Japanese industries have evolved very differently. While the U.S. industry has grown through technological developments taking place in independently acting firms, the Japanese industry has grown with close cooperation between government and business and, in addition, cooperation across firms in the industry.

ELECTRONICS INDUSTRY STUDY PROJECTS

The above analysis lays the foundation for a group of hypotheses that remain to be tested in our analysis of the U.S. and Japanese electronics industries. To test these hypotheses, several specific research studies have been designed. These are discussed below.

Taxonomy of U.S. and Japanese Electronics Industries

Recent work in organization theory (McKelvey [forthcoming]) and competitive strategy (Porter 1980) recognizes the importance of classification of firms into populations or strategic groups. Classification schemes group similar firms into populations. McKelvey argues that taxonomies will help develop the science of organizations, provide a basis for data retrieval about organizations, increase the generalizability and predictability of organization studies, and provide a basis for sampling in organization studies. Porter, in a more practical vein, proposes that managers who recognize their strategic group (population) can make improved strategic decisions. These strategic decisions include selecting suppliers, customers, and employees; recognizing competition; and identifying alternative operating decisions on product mix, speed of entry into a market, and evaluation of barriers to entry. In brief, the population concept helps firms assess their niche within an industry (Ulrich 1981).

In the UCLA Electronics Industry Study, data are being collected on 680 U.S. and 125 Japanese firms. These data, when analyzed, will yield a taxonomy of firms into populations in both the U.S. and Japanese industries. The data for this taxonomy come from firms' public reports (10-K, corporate reports) over three years (1978, 1979, and 1980), as reported in the Fairchild and *Oriental Economist* publications. The information was coded from these reports by a team of researchers at UCLA. After this information had been coded, each firm was contacted by telephone, and key informants verified the information derived from secondary data. Because of the process of coding secondary data and then contacting the firm for verification of the coded data, confidence is high that the information in the data is accurate and reliable.

These data will yield a taxonomy that will provide a comprehensive and detailed description of the two industries. The taxonomy will be based on information outlined in Table 27.1. These data have been placed in a firm-by-variable matrix so that a classification of firms has been derived using appropriate clustering algorithms (see Figure 27.2). The cluster analysis groups firms with similar characteristics. Commonalities and subtle differences between firms will be identified via the clustering programs. For example, the sole relationship of some U.S. firms (such as Silicon Systems Incorporated) to the electronics industry is through the design and manufacture of components that are then sold to customers outside the firm (General Electric, for example). Firms in this supplier category are likely to be clustered into one population, while firms operating in more markets and more-complex technologies (such as Westinghouse) are likely to be clustered into another population.

The taxonomies of the U.S. and Japanese industries should show some interesting differences. Since the U.S. industry began with individual firms competing for resources, while Japanese firms collaborated through the government support for development of the industry, one hypothesis is that more diverse populations of firms exist in the United States than in Japan. The U.S. electronics industry will be likely to have more populations of firms that specialize within the electronics industry. This diversity will probably reflect the "arms-length" competitive markets that often underlie U.S. industry in general. By contrast, the Japanese electronics industry will quite likely be grouped into more distinct, large populations. The identification of these will be one of the foremost analytical efforts made to describe in depth a major industry of the United States and Japan. It should begin to clarify some of the structural differences between industrial development in the two cultures. The populations will also serve as a

TABLE 27.1   Information Gathered on 680 U.S. and 125 Japanese Electronics Firms

Location	U.S. state
	Japanese province
Size of Firm	Number of employees (in 1978, 1979, and 1980)
	Sales volume (in 1978, 1979, and 1980)
	Number of plants
Structure of Firm	Specialization ratio (used by Wrigley [1970] and Rumelt [1974])
	Number of divisions
	Number of divisions in electronics
Market/Technology Matrix	Yes/no questions on ten alternative electronics markets (such as components, power generation/ transmission, instruments and so on)
	Yes/no questions on given alternative technological activities within each market (such as manufac- turers, markets, and so on)
Financial Data (for 1978, 1979, and 1980)	Revenues (sales)
	Net income (profits)
	Number of common shares
	Current assets
	Total assets
	Current liabilities
	Long-term debt
	All debt
	Shareholders' equity
Transfer Agent/Bank References	Banks that firms transact with
Ownership Data	Beneficiary owners (those who own more than 5 per- cent of stock) and owner states (such as internal officer, member of board of directors, bank, indus- try, and so on)

sample frame for future research, which will describe in more detail trans- actions between firms in the industry.

Ownership Patterns

In addition to structural, market, and technology information, which will be used in defining populations, data have also been collected on patterns of stock ownership in the U.S. and Japanese electronics industries. In the

FIGURE 27.2   Overview of Variable-by-Firm Clustering Matrix

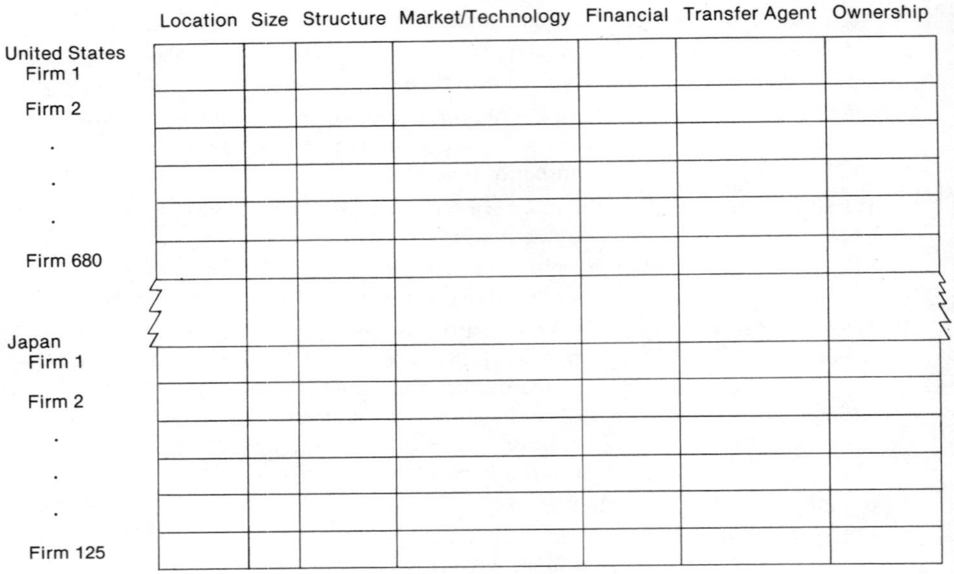

	Location	Size	Structure	Market/Technology	Financial	Transfer Agent	Ownership
United States Firm 1							
Firm 2							
.							
.							
.							
Firm 680							
Japan Firm 1							
Firm 2							
.							
.							
.							
Firm 125							

Source: Compiled by the author.

United States, all beneficiary owners (those who own more than 5 percent) are required to file with the Securities Exchange Commission. For Japanese electronics firms, information on major shareholders is also public. Ownership information has been compiled for all 680 U.S. and 125 Japanese firms.

The ownership data should begin to reveal some significant differences between the U.S. and Japanese electronics industries consistent with our theoretical framework outlined above. First, since many of the U.S. firms were developed by technological entrepreneurs, our research should find much of the stock ownership maintained by those inside the firm, either as members of the firm's board of directors or as officers of the firm. By contrast, since the Japanese firms have more and longer-term relationships with other firms and financial sources, we would expect to find ownership patterns more widely dispersed.

Second, closer analysis of the ownership patterns will test the "Japan, Incorporated" hypothesis that has often been described. Firms that have major ownership in Japanese firms are likely to be those that either supply important resources or are supplied resources by the focal firm. For example, Aritsu Electric, an independent firm that produces telecommunications equipment, is owned by Nippon Electric (32 percent), its major customer, and by Sumitomo Bank and Insurance Companies (18 percent), its financial suppliers. The tight ownership relationships of supplier, producer, and customer may be indicative of long-term, cooperative relationships within the Japanese industry (Ouchi 1980).

These hypothesized ownership patterns may begin to reveal some industry-level phenomena that support and foster Japanese management systems, which are receiving so much attention currently. For example, since firms share ownership with suppliers and customers, often with banks as the mediators or guarantors, managers may feel more secure, because they know that their firm is likely to acquire the necessary resources to be productive over time. In addition, such ownership patterns are likely to indicate that many suppliers and customers have a vested interest in cooperating with each other. Firms with such incentives may share sensitive information about costs and prices; collaborate to maximize both firms' performance; and develop other characteristics of cooperative relationships, such as goal congruence, symbolic representation of values, and control based on traditions.

Interbank and Bank-Firm Relations

As mentioned above, many of the supplier, firm, and customer relationships in the United States are kept "at arms length" and separate; it appears that, in Japan, these relationships are linked through ownership patterns and other relationships. Japanese firms may be linked through bank relationships in addition to joint ownership. Historically, large Japanese banks have been at the center of the *zaibatsu*, or the more current *keiretsu*. The *keiretsu* emerged after World War II legislation against concentrated holding companies. The *keiretsu* do not have formal control over their members, but may affect member-firm behavior through mutual exchange of ownership shares, swapping of members of boards of directors, and financial advice and assistance from the bank that is at the center of the *keiretsu*. Firms affiliated with a *keiretsu* may be able to receive preferred credit from the central financial institution. This preferred credit should allow the affiliated firms to assume more long-term debt, as the financial institution that links the *keiretsu* need not receive immediate return on its investment in the firm.

The UCLA Electronics Industry Study assesses, for the United States and Japan, relationships between banks and between banks and electronics firms. In one study, we examine ownership patterns of banks and insurance companies in Japan and New York City.* New York banks were se-

---

*Again, the data for this analysis are under development. The ownership of Japanese banks comes from *Japan's Company Handbook*. The ownership of U.S. banks is more complex and is

lected for comparison with Japanese banks because New York represents a geographical area that parallels the Japanese bank systems. In addition, the New York banks represent the center of commercial banking in the United States. All banks headquartered in New York City were included in the sample.*

The following data have been collected: First, a list of all Japanese banks was developed. Using information summarized in *Japan's Company Handbook*, ownership patterns among banks were recorded. It soon became obvious that marine and fire insurance companies, as well as life insurance companies, were important types of owners in this network. These organizations were also included in the analysis. A 114 by 114 matrix, called OWN, was formed. Each cell (i,j) of OWN listed the percentage of stock of bank/insurance company j that was owned by bank/insurance company i. For example, Nippon Credit Bank stock is owned by Dai-Ichi Kangyo Bank (2.9 percent), Nippon Life Insurance (2.3 percent), Sumitomo Marine Life Insurance (2.0 percent), Asahi Marine Life Insurance (1.8 percent), Dai-Ichi Marine Life Insurance (1.8 percent), and Mitsubishi Bank (1.7 percent). This network is depicted in Figure 27.3.

Information on a second network of relations among banks was also collected. This network, called REF, listed the number of times two banks were co-listed as references by the same electronics firms. This network is also depicted in Figure 27.3.

The two networks, OWN and REF, were then subjected to a multiple network blockmodel analysis (White, Boorman, and Breiger 1976). The clustering algorithm used was CONCOR (Breiger, Boorman, and Arabie 1975). A graphic representation of the obtained blockmodel image matrices is shown in Figure 27.4.

A brief review of Figure 27.4 reveals a three-tiered hierarchical structure. At the top of the figure (block 9), insurance companies have major holdings in all three tiers. One block of banks (block 3), made up of large, national banks in Japan (such as Daiwa, Industrial Bank, and Bank of Tokyo), also has substantial holdings in second- and third-tier banks.

---

being compiled from Federal Reserve information and from New York City and New York State information.

*The alternatives to selecting and working with one geographical locale in the United States is to work with all banks in the United States, which is too large a data set, or to work with the 100 largest banks in the United States. This latter option was not taken because the 100 largest U.S. banks are not comparable with all banks in Japan; the Japanese sample includes both local, smaller banks and larger, national banks. New York City banks are a comparable data set in terms of composition of the banks, number of banks, and geographical dispersion of the banks.

FIGURE 27.3   Bank/Bank Relationships

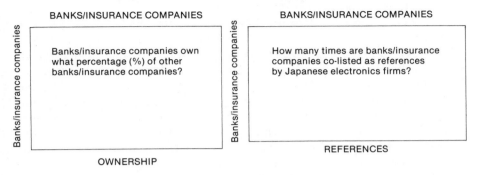

Source: Compiled by the author.

Second-tier banks, including some national and regional banks, have substantial holdings in third-tier banks. One of these blocks of third-tier banks (block 8) is made up almost exclusively of Japanese savings banks. Third-tier banks do not have substantial stock investments in any banks.

Turning to the co-listing of electronics firm references, it appears that blocks 2, 3, and 4 specialize in the electronics industry. Block 3 is likely to be a specialist in not only the electronics industry but other industries,

FIGURE 27.4   Structure of Japanese Banks

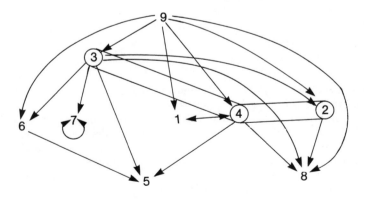

Source: Compiled by the author.

because it is made up of large national banks. Blocks 3 and 4 represent banks that specialize in electronics firms.

While these findings are still tentative, the shape of the graph in Figure 27.4, when compared with a formal organization chart, is suggestive. It appears that Japanese banks may be subject to some degree of centralized control or coordination. This relationship, manifested through patterns of ownership, exists despite the fact that each bank included in the study is a separate, incorporated entity. Thus, apparently, banks in Japan are organized in a manner that, in terms of classification, lies somewhere between market relations (each bank a separate entity) and bureaucratic/clan relations (centralized coordination or control). This type of organization has been referred to previously as an intermediate governance mechanism.

Further research must address several questions. First, how does the structure depicted in Figure 27.4 differ from the structure of interbank relations in other countries? Early analysis of the structure of interbank relations in the United States indicates that few intermediate-form relations exist. Rather, banks in the United States appear to be wholly owned subsidiaries of the same bank-holding company or financially not interdependent. Second, we must consider the dynamics that underlie the banking structure in Japan and the United States. A structure apparently exists in Japan that would facilitate interbank coordination, but it is still not clear whether such coordination takes place. We also need to consider what impact these patterns of interbank relations might have for firms in the Japanese electronics industry. Similarly, if our tentative U.S. analysis holds, the effect of U.S. interbank relations also needs to be considered.

The interlocking banking system in Japan has several important potential implications for firm behavior. One of the fears that Noyce raised in testimony before the Senate Subcommittee on International Finance (U.S., Congress 1980) was the significantly higher debt/equity ratio in Japanese electronics firms than in U.S. electronics firms:

> The key concern of the [semiconductor] industry is its severe disadvantage in competing with aggressively-growing government subsidized foreign companies which have assured sources of capital and thus can price their products without concern for current earnings. The profitability of U.S. semiconductor firms is double or triple the profitability of the Japanese and European firms and the U.S. return on equity is double its foreign competition, despite almost exclusive U.S. reliance on equity capital. The U.S. companies raise most of their capital from retained earnings and equity investments while the average Japanese and European companies are able to borrow heavily, as evidenced by the higher debt to equity ratios. This is what U.S. semiconductor executives

call the "leverage gap." In simplest terms, these data reflect the reasons why the U.S. semiconductor industry may grow less rapidly than our foreign competitors in the decade ahead.

	1978 Average After Tax Return on Equity	1978 After Tax Earnings As $ of Sales	1978 Debt/equity Ratio
Six U.S. companies	16.3%	6.4%	16%
Four Japanese companies	8.0%	1.9%	345%
Two European companies	9.6%	2.4%	47%

The above statement represents a common concern in the U.S. electronics industry—that the higher debt/equity ratio in Japanese industry favors long-term investment. The bank data described above may help us to understand why the Japanese bank system can seem to assume such high risk. The regional bank that specializes in electronics may not need to assume the entire risk of a firm borrowing heavily. That bank, which has stock owned in significant percentages by banks in a higher tier (either large central banks or insurance companies), may be able to pass some of the risk on to its owner banks. This sponsorship may allow the regional banks that specialize in electronics to allocate larger loans to electronics firms. This may be even more the case since it may often occur that the financial institution that is loaning the money is at the center of a *keiretsu* and has ownership interests of its own in the electronics firm. This infusion of money supports the electronics firm in its commitment to growth, without undue short-term demands for immediate profits.

U.S. firms, by contrast, are generally faced with monthly or quarterly profit reports and demands from dispersed owners. Financial institutions, not backed by more-powerful banks, are unable to finance firms with higher debt/equity ratios. As a result, the U.S. electronics firms may not have access to financial support of the same type that is available to Japanese firms. As Noyce indicates, this financial support may be a key factor in the future of the electronics industry:

> Given the increasing capital intensity in our industry and the need to increase R & D . . . the U.S. semiconductor industry in the 1980's will have to increase after tax earnings from an average of 4.3% during 1968–1977 to 13.5% (or obtain equivalent tax or other financial incentives). . . . Foreign government subsidies to semiconductor research and capacity were estimated at $2.0 billion. . . . In the last analysis . . . access to capital may be the decisive factor in determining the world market share leader by the end of this decade (U.S., Congress 1980).

FIGURE 27.5

May 1981

ELECTRONICS INDUSTRY STUDY
Secondary Data Code Sheet

_____ (1-4) Company name:

_____ (5-6) Address:

Phone number:

PRODUCT CATEGORIES (check = 1; blank = 0)

	Produces/ Manufactures; Fabricates	Sells/ Markets	Distributes; Services; Installs	R & D; Design; Testing	Leases; Rents	Other
1. Electronic components	(7)	(8)	(9)	(10)	(11)	(12)
2. **Power generation/transmission**	(13)	(14)	(15)	(16)	(17)	(18)
3. Industrial/manufacturing electronics	(19)	(20)	(21)	(22)	(23)	(24)
4. Instruments	(25)	(26)	(27)	(28)	(29)	(30)
5. Communications equipment and systems	(31)	(32)	(33)	(34)	(35)	(36)
6. Consumer/business electronics	(37)	(38)	(39)	(40)	(41)	(42)
7. Computer and computer devices	(43)	(44)	(45)	(46)	(47)	(48)
8. Government/military electronics	(49)	(50)	(51)	(52)	(53)	(54)
9. Transportation	(55)	(56)	(57)	(58)	(59)	(60)
10. Other, nonelectrical	(61)	(62)	(63)	(64)	(65)	(66)

_____ (67-68)   Total number of operating divisions
_____ (69-70)   Number of divisions in unrelated industries (nonelectronics)
_____ (71-72)   Number of plants and facilities
_____ (73-74)   Number of acquisitions listed

Put a "1" in column 80 and skip to column 7 of card 2

Transfer Agents: (Card 2) _____ (7–9) _____ (10–12) _____ (13–15) _____ (16–18)
_____ (19–21) _____ (22–24) _____ (25–27) _____ (28–30)

	1978	1979	1980
Number of employees	(31–36)	(37–42)	(43–48)
Revenues (sales) (000s)	(49–55)	(56–62)	(63–69)
		CARD 3:	
Net income (profit) (000s)	(70–76)	(7–13)	(14–20)
Number of common shares (000s)	(21–27)	(28–34)	(35–41)
Current assets (000s)	(42–48)	(49–55)	(56–62)
			CARD 4:
Total assets (000s)	(63–69)	(70–76)	(7–13)
Current liabilities (000s)	(14–20)	(21–27)	(28–34)
Long-term debt (000s)	(35–41)	(42–48)	(49–55)
All debts (000s)	(56–62)	(63–69)	(70–76)
	CARD 5:		
Shareholder's equity (000s)	(7–13)	(14–20)	(21–27)
Specialization ratio	(28–29)	(30–31)	(32–33)
Electronics specialization (yes = 2/no = 1)	(34)	(35)	(36)
Electronics related ratio	(37–38)	(39–40)	(41–42)

Ownership Information

1. _____ (43–46)
2. _____ (47–50)
3. _____ (51–54)
4. _____ (55–58)
5. _____ (59–62)
6. _____ (63–66)
7. _____ (67–70)
8. _____ (71–74)
9. _____ (75–78)

Categories of Ownership

1 = Industry
2 = Bank/trust/finance company
3 = Insurance company
4 = Internal employees (stock plan)
5 = Internal employees (officer)
6 = Internal employees (Board of Director)
7 = Internal employees (officer/Board of Director)
8 = Private investor
9 = Management firm

Source: Compiled by the author.

A Trade Association Study

From preliminary discussion with trade association personnel in the United States and Japan and with industry leaders in the electronics field, the role of trade associations in the two cultures appears to differ. In the United States, when government agencies attempt to enact new legislation, the more powerful firms send representatives to interact with those agencies to lobby for industry interests. Noyce's testimony in presenting Intel's point of view to the Senate subcommittee represents this type of action. It is possible that the intense but uncoordinated efforts of numerous firms in the United States could cause more confusion than direction in the relevant government agencies. (There is some evidence that firms in the United States are discouraged from cooperative lobbying because of some potential antitrust violations.)

In Japan, individual firms seldom interact directly with government agencies. Instead, the firms work with other firms through associations to interact with government agencies. This more coordinated industry lobbying effort may have its rewards, as the government agency is able to discuss industry needs reasonably and identify legislation that benefits both industry and government.

The trade association project discussed here will deal with the role of trade associations in the two cultures. Initially, it will describe the various activities that trade associations undertake, as well as the size of and relationships among the trade associations. As the study progresses, we hope to define some of the specific alternative trade association activities that can be pursued to enhance industry-government relations in both the United States and Japan.

Efficiency of Electronics Firms and Suppliers

Economists have recently made attempts to define the boundaries of a firm from an efficiency perspective. This perspective argues that a firm can place its boundaries better if it understands the nature of the transactions that it must undertake and applies appropriate governance mechanisms to those transactions (Williamson 1979; 1975). As briefly discussed above, organization theorists (Ouchi 1980) have begun to apply the efficiency model to an analysis of organization/supplier relationships.

In the efficiency model, three pure forms of governing supplier relationships exist: market, bureaucracy, and clan. The market governs relationships by price, with firms keeping "an arms length" from each other. Markets are not efficient under many circumstances (see Barney and Ulrich [1981] for a summary of these and related arguments). Markets are often replaced by bureaucracies, or organizations, which are governed by rules. In these cases, the supplier firm is likely to become a part of the manufacturing firm, and the supplier complies with the rules set by the parent firm. Again, under certain transaction conditions, bureaucracies are not efficient, and they are replaced by clans. Clans govern behavior by shared values and traditions.

The efficiency model is a powerful alternative in explaining firm strategies for interacting with other firms. The model begins to identify the circumstances under which markets, bureaucracies, or clans are efficient means of governing transactions. This model is particularly useful in studies of U.S. and Japanese industries because Japanese industry is more likely to follow a clan or hierarchical approach to governance between firms. Such hierarchical intermediate forms were discussed above. In the efficiency study of suppliers, we hope to identify when the market, bureaucracy, clan, or intermediate governance mechanisms are appropriate. This information can be central to issues of regulation and of potential economies of scale and/or antitrust implications of size.

The relevance of the efficiency of alternative governance mechanisms in the study of supplier relations in the electronics industry can be highlighted by the following incident. When representatives of the American Automobile Manufacturers visited Japan in spring of 1981, they noticed the robots, work groups, quality circles, and other commonly discussed characteristics of the Japanese work force. They were most struck, however, by one instance in which a supplier drove his van up to the loading dock of the manufacturing firm. Unaided, he parked the truck, unloaded the supplies, and looked around to find a broom; then he cleaned the area he was working in so that it was cleaner than when he had arrived. The visitors were impressed. They speculated that if a supplier's delivery person in the United States had done the same thing, the plant's union would quite likely have reacted negatively to an outside person working in the plant.

The efficiency descriptions of Japanese industrial structure explain the supplier behavior as reasonable. It is likely that the supplier firm had worked for many years with the manufacturing firm. The two firms probably shared some degree of stock ownership. They also probably had dealings with the same bank. With these close associations, even the truck driver of the supplier firm might realize that his interests were well served by helping the manufacturing firm to be profitable. It was only reasonable that he unload his supplies and clean the dock area.

Efficiency of Relationships between Electronics Firms and Banks

The logic of applying an efficiency model to firm-supplier relationships also fits with the firm-bank relationship. Those firms that govern transactions with their bank efficiently are more likely to prosper. Detailing efficient relationships between suppliers, banks, and firms will provide a thorough description of the electronics industries in the two countries.

CONCLUSION

This chapter has briefly described a long-term study of the U.S. and Japanese electronics industries. This study should provide some insights into the nature of the Japanese and U.S. industries and begin to explain how the industrial structure allows U.S. and Japanese management techniques to operate effectively. Two further points need to be made. First, while we are excited about the potential results of applying taxonomy analysis and efficiency models to the two industries, we realize that these are relatively new tools to the organization theorist. Because of their newness, we have been extremely careful to verify our study methods and conceptual frameworks with experts in the industry. Only through such academic industrial interchanges can practical, yet conceptually sound, models of industry structure and firm relationships develop. Second, one common criticism and interpretation of current research on the U.S. and Japanese industrial systems is the tendency among some to suggest that U.S. firms adopt Japanese management styles. We are in no way proposing this universal adoption of another culture's industrial structure or management practices; nor are we suggesting that one management style is universally better than another. Rather, we hope our research provides insights to both American and Japanese managers in the operation of their firms. It is our belief that both countries can benefit from the appropriate adoption of efficient and effective management systems.

REFERENCES

Asian Wall Street Journal. 1981. June 29, p. 11.

Barney, J. B., and D. O. Ulrich. 1981. "Models in Organization Theory: Resource Dependence, Efficiency, and Ecology." Paper under review.

Breiger, R. L., S. A. Boorman, and P. Arabie. 1975. "An Algorithm for Clustering Relational Data, with Applications to Social Network Analysis in Comparison with Multidimensional Scaling." *Journal of Mathematical Psychology* 12: 328–83.

Brittain, J. W., and J. H. Freeman, 1980. "Organizational Proliferation and Density-dependent Selection: Organizational Evolution in the Semiconductor Industry. In *The Organization Life Cycle*, ed. J. R. Kimberly, R. H. Miles and Associates, pp. 291–338. San Francisco: Jossey-Bass.

Electronic News Financial Fact Book and Directory. 1980. New York: Fairchild.

Japan's Company Handbook. 1981. Tokyo: Oriental Economist.

Japan's Industrial Structure—A Long Range Vision. 1974. Tokyo: Ministry of International Trade and Industry.

Lifson, T. B. 1981. "Sectoral Systems Management: A Theoretical Model of Japan's Sogo Shosha (General Trading Firms)." Paper presented at the Academy of Management in San Diego.

McKelvey, W. W. Forthcoming. *Organizational Systematics: Taxonomy, Evolution, Classification.* Berkeley: University of California Press.

Ouchi, W. G. 1981. *Theory Z: How American Business Can Meet the Japanese Challenge.* Menlo Park, Calif.: Addison Wesley.

———. 1980. "Markets, Bureaucracies, and Clans." *Administrative Science Quarterly* 25:129–41.

Pascale, R., and A. G. Athos. 1981. *The Art of Japanese Management.* New York: Simon and Schuster.

Porter, M. 1980. *Competitive Strategy.* New York: Free Press.

Ulrich, D. 1981. "Managerial Implications of Ecology Models." Paper presented at the Academy of Management in San Diego.

U.S., Congress, Office of Technology Assessment. 1981. *U.S. Industrial Competitiveness: A Comparison of Steel, Electronics and Automobiles.* Washington, D.C.: Office of Technological Assessment.

U.S., Congress, Senate, Committee on Banking, Housing and Urban Affairs, Subcommittee on International Finance. 1980. Statement by R. R. Noyce, Jan. 15.

U.S., Department of Commerce. 1979. *A Report on the U.S. Semiconductor Industry.* Washington, D.C.: Government Printing Office.

Vogel, E. F. 1979. *Japan as Number One: Lessons for America.* Cambridge: Harvard University Press.

White, H.C., S. A. Boorman, and R. L. Breiger. 1976. "Social Structure for Multiple Networks. I. Block Models of Roles and Positions." *American Journal of Sociology* 81:730–80.

Williamson, O. E. 1979. "Transaction Cost Economics: The Governance of Contractual Relations." *Journal of Law and Economics* 22:233–61.

———. 1975. *Markets and Hierarchies: Analysis and Antitrust Implications.* New York: Free Press.

28

Income Security
or Employment Security?
An Economic Analysis

FRANK H. CLARKE *and* MASAKO N. DARROUGH

INTRODUCTION

Two unique characteristics of modern Japanese labor management practice that are often cited in the literature (Hashimoto 1979; Galenson 1976)
are the prevalence of lifetime employment and of biannual bonuses.* Lifetime employment provides job security to the workers but implies employment rigidity for the firm. On the other hand, the bonus, since it is variable
in magnitude, gives rise to flexibility in the compensation scheme.† In contrast, these practices are relatively infrequent in the United States. For example, job mobility is generally very high and wages/salaries tend to be
fixed over (relatively short) contract periods. Many of the explanations

---

Nenko-Jeretsu (the seniority system) is another feature much discussed by scholars. In this
study, we treat the seniority wage payment system as an integral part of lifetime employment.

†Ohkawa and Rosovsky (1973) discuss the modern Japanese system as "an institutional device
gradually developed by modern firms at the beginning of this century. Its purpose has been to
assure an adequate flow of qualified workers. . . ." They claim that Japanese enterprises attempt to maintain a long-run normal wage bill, since the wage bill under the lifetime employment system resembles fixed cost. Ohkawa and Rosovsky, however, do not discuss bonus payments as a means of compensating for rigidity in employment.

that have been offered attribute the difference to cultural, political, and institutional differences between the two countries.*

We adopt in this chapter a different point of view, one that provides an economic rationale for various practices.† We shall first develop a general model using the framework of the principal-agent relationship (Harris and Raviv 1976; Holmström 1979; Mirrlees 1979; Ross 1973; and Shavell 1979, among others). We shall see that this model focuses attention on a variety of factors that bear upon contract length and the degree to which bonuses are used. Among these are uncertainty, (the employee's) risk aversion, the relative significance of productivity and/or disutility of effort, and an "averaging" effect of long-term contracts that may be beneficial to the principal. As we shall demonstrate with numerical examples, these factors can combine to yield a variety of optimal employment policies. In particular, we shall identify the factors that would seem to lead to the Japanese and the U.S. policies described above.

In the chapter's second section, we give a brief survey of relevant employment practices. We conclude that, despite the patterns mentioned above, there is more diversity than commonly believed. This may be an indication that rather than being culturally or philosophically predetermined, employment practices may be a result of rational reaction to economic conditions. In the third section, we describe a mechanism that will be used to show how these rational reactions take place; this is the principal-agent model alluded to above. The fourth section contains six numerical examples illustrating various types of optimal employment policies that can arise as various factors are increased or decreased in relative importance. The final section summarizes our results and draws some conclusions.

LIFETIME EMPLOYMENT AND BONUSES

Exactly how wide-spread are these systems practiced in Japan? Is every worker expected to work for only one employer? What about American workers? A look at statistics tells us, contrary to the belief of many, that

---

*For example, Haitani (1976) attributes the origin of lifetime employment, seniority wage systems, and elaborate fringe benefits to Tokugawa employment institutions. The modern corporations, however, adopted these practices (often called "corporate paternalism") as "calculated responses" to the problem of skilled-labor shortage and high labor turnover.

†Hashimoto (1979) discusses lifetime employment and bonus payments as a result of optimizing behavior. His entire analysis is based upon the assumption that "the practice of lifetime employment is a result of a high profitability of investment in firm specific skills."

lifetime employment is not necessarily a norm for *all* workers in Japan. The so-called temporary workers and many female workers are excluded from the lifetime employment track. Many of these temporary workers never achieve regular status.

The percentage of those "temporary workers" (perhaps "permanently temporary") among the employed is not trivial. It varies from one industry to another, with construction having the most temporary workers (over 30 percent in 1975). The overall industry average was almost 10 percent. The percentage, however, decreases as the size of the establishment increases.

The average duration of employment increases as the size (in terms of both number of employees and assets) of the establishment increases. For example, firms with over 5,000 employees had workers who, on the average, were 37.2 years of age and had been with the firm for 14.3 years, whereas the comparable figures were 39.4 years of age and 9.4 years of service for firms with 30 to 99 employees. Thus it seems evident that the so-called dual structure (Bieda 1970; Galenson 1976) in Japanese industry also manifests itself in the employment compensation practice.* Only the larger firms provide lifetime employment to most of their employees. Not only salaries and wages, but also the bonuses, vary significantly according to the size of the establishment.

Bonuses, however, are a significant portion of income for all workers in Japan, although the magnitude fluctuates from year to year, from industry to industry, and from firm to firm. Between 1963 and 1979, employees were compensated on the average with bonuses (paid in June and December) that amounted from 3 to 4.6 times the value of their regular monthly salary. The difference due to the size of firms is not trivial: for example, in 1979, firms with 30 to 99 employees on the average paid bonuses equivalent to 3 months' salary, whereas firms with 500 or more employees paid bonuses equal to 4.2 months' salary.

In summary, large firms seem to employ a higher percentage of workers as regular employees who will stay longer with the firms. In addition, these workers tend to be better educated and as a result are better paid, but with a larger portion in flexible compensation. In this case, lifetime employment is reducing flexibility in employment, whereas the bonus payment is compensating for the lack of flexibility.

Bonuses serve another purpose: they can be an incentive for achieving a desirable goal. For example, bonuses may be a way of inducing employees to work exceptionally hard. It is often impossible to sort out var-

---

*The dual structure, however, seems to be on the decline (Galenson 1976, p. 605).

ious reasons for a profit increase and to identify the marginal product of each worker. Hence compensation according to each individual's contribution may not be feasible. In such a situation, bonuses may be viewed as similar to what stockholders receive in the form of dividends and capital gains. However, to the extent that workers' efforts influence the outcome, a profit-sharing scheme will increase the effort. Of course, there will exist the problem of moral hazard (the "free rider" problem) and monitoring.

Among American workers, top managers with large responsibilities are often compensated with perquisites in addition to regular salaries. Among them is profit sharing in the form of stock options and/or bonuses. Moreover, some of these people do stay with the same firm for a long time. However, neither the payment of bonuses nor lifetime employment is a norm in the United States, even for well-educated college graduates. In rewarding employees for superior performance, salaries are increased and promotions are given. However, these changes are usually downward-inflexible; this is one difference between increases in base pay and changes in bonuses.

Thus "the U.S. system" and "the Japanese system" may indeed exist in each country as frequently observed phenomena; however, it should be emphasized that they are not the only forms of employment practices. Various forms do exist in each country, however different the distributions may be. This existence of various practices in both countries suggests that mere cultural or philosophical explanation is insufficient. We shall argue in this chapter that all such practices can simply evolve as an economically rational response to certain conditions. We show this through the model to which we turn now.

DESCRIPTION AND ANALYSIS OF THE GENERAL MODEL

In this section, we describe and analyze a general model of the optimal employment contract between the employer and the employee. The framework for the model has been developed in the context of the principal and agent relationship. The principal (the employer) in general offers the agent (the employee) a "contract." This contract specifies: (1) the term (length) of the contract, (2) a wage rate (predetermined but possibly time-dependent), and (3) a prescribed share of the ensuing profit during the term of the contract. The agent in turn accepts this contract if and only if (through some appropriate level of effort) this contract provides an expected utility (totaled and discounted to the present) that exceeds the utility obtainable through specified alternate means. The appropriate level of effort is chosen by the agent so as to maximize the expected utility, given the contract. In this construction, it should be noted that the principal cannot *specify* the effort level (due to, for example, exorbitant monitoring cost). The effort level supplied is, therefore, a "conditional" (but calculated) response on the part of the agent.

A more formal description of the model follows using the following notations:

$$
\begin{aligned}
t &= \text{time} \\
w &= \text{wage} \\
M &= \text{term (length) of a contract} \\
s &= \text{the agent's share of the profit} \\
\varrho &= \text{measurement of effort} \\
\theta &= \text{state of the world} \\
R_t(\theta, \varrho) &= \text{revenue} \\
I &= \text{income} \\
\delta &= \text{the principal's discount rate} \\
\gamma &= \text{the agent's discount rate} \\
U_t(I, \varrho) &= \text{the agent's utility function at time } t \\
A_t(\theta) &= \text{the agent's alternate utility at time } t
\end{aligned}
$$

Thus each contract specifies M, w_t, s_t. Corresponding to a choice of effort profile ϱ_t, the expected present value of the agent's utility over the term M of the contract is given by:

$$
EU = E \sum_{t=1}^{M} e^{-\gamma t} u_t(I, \varrho) \tag{1}
$$

where E denotes expectation over θ, γ is the agent's discount rate and where

$$
I_t = w_t + s_t[R_t(\theta, \varrho_t) - w_t] \tag{2}
$$

The agent chooses his/her effort profile ϱ_t so as to maximize this quantity EU. The expected present value of utility from the agent's alternate employment, AU, is given by

$$
AU = E \sum_{t=1}^{M} e^{-\gamma t} A_t(\theta) \tag{3}
$$

The contract is acceptable to the agent precisely when EU (for the maximizing effort) is at least as large as AU. The expected profit, $E\Pi$, to the principal is then seen to be:

$$
E\Pi = E \sum_{t=1}^{M} e^{-\delta t}[(1 - s_t)(R_t(\theta, \varrho_t) - w_t)] \tag{4}
$$

where δ is the principal's discount rate. The state of the world represented by θ may be viewed by the principal as possessing a probability distribution that is different from that seen by the agent. Since the principal is risk-neutral, she or he wishes to maximize $E\Pi$. If the term M were fixed, the principal's concern would simply be to choose the wage and share profiles so as to maximize $E\Pi$; this is the case that has been studied so far. Our situation here is a new one, however, since the principal's concern extends over a given horizon of length H, and the principal's problem is to determine an optimal sequence of contracts spanning H. (Of course, in some cases it may be optimal to have a single contract of length H.)

Determining this optimal sequence of contracts is in general a highly nontrivial task, since the expected return from future contracts must be calculated by means of probabilities conditioned by the events that happened during preceding contracts. An assumption that greatly simplifies the problem is that the state of the world varies independently from period to period. That is, we suppose that θ consists of H independent, identically distributed random variables (one for each unit of the planning period). This implies that there is no gain in information as the time progresses (the future is independent of the past).

In this context, the principal's problem is to select some number k of contracts spanning the planning period ($t = 0$ to H) so as to maximize:

$$\sum_i e^{-\delta t_i} E\Pi_i - k\tau \qquad (5)$$

where $E\Pi_i$ is the expected return from the ith contract as calculated above, t_i is the period in which the ith contract begins (hence $t_1 = 0$), and τ is a fixed cost associated with any new contract (for example, transaction or training cost).

An analysis of the model in this generality is still a formidable task. We shall adopt two further simplifying hypotheses: First, over the term of a contract, the wage profile is of the form w, we^α, $we^{2\alpha}$, and so on. That is, wages exhibit mandatory seniority increases during a given contract period at a constant rate α, where α is predetermined. Second, during any given contract period, share and effort levels are constant.

The principal's maximization problem is now summarized below:

$$\max_{k, w_i, s_i, M_i} \sum_{i=1}^{k} e^{-\delta t_i} E\Pi_i - k\tau \qquad (6)$$

subject to $EU_i \geq AU_i$ for each i, where the effort level in each contract is the one that maximizes the agent's utility, and where

$$\sum_{i=1}^{k} M_i = H$$

Given the model above, we now analyze the optimizing behavior of the principal and the agent, assuming that the principal faces only one agent as a potential employee. The two main issues focused upon here are the magnitude of bonuses used and the length of contract. Under what conditions do long contracts result as the solution to the optimizing problem? What are the advantages of having short contracts? To what extent and when should bonuses be paid?

Bonus versus No Bonus

Essentially, bonuses should be used to induce more effort. A risk-neutral agent will be indifferent between a bonus and a higher wage (of equal value) for the same amount of effort supplied. However, this agent might find it worthwhile to work harder, if (and only if) disutility of additional effort is more than compensated for by additional income. This is also the case for a risk-averse agent. In fact, there exists only one reason for which a bonus payment should be made to a risk-average agent. That is to induce effort. If the agent is risk-averse, it is less costly for the principal to pay the agent a (fixed) wage than to offer a bonus (profit sharing) in order to provide the same expected utility. This follows from risk aversion (or strict concavity of the utility function in income). A certain wage payment is preferred to an uncertain bonus payment of the same expected value. We then expect that a wage payment is used as a means of securing an agent's service away from the alternative opportunity (by guaranteeing, at least cost, utility at least as good as the agent's alternate opportunity) and a bonus payment as a means of inducing more effort. Of course, the principal will find it profitable to offer a bonus up to the point where the expected marginal revenue product (over the contract period) is equal to the expected marginal cost (in the form of a bonus) of compensation for resulting disutility of effort. In general, the more productive effort is and the less the agent minds effort, the more effective bonuses will be in generating more effort.

Risk aversion and disutility of effort, although very different in origin, do affect expected utility in a somewhat similar manner. Figure 28.1 shows how they interact. The agent, of course, chooses the optimal effort level by calculating his or her expected utility for each effort level, given wage, and share. Illustrated in the figure are three strictly concave utility functions corresponding to three levels of effort $(0 < \varrho_1 < \varrho_2)$, two possible incomes for each effort level (for given w and $s > 0$), and corresponding expected utilities. Future uncertainty is incorporated by two possible outcomes from the agent's effort. If the share level were to increase, the resulting pairs of income would move to the right for each effort level. Exactly how the expected utility changes depends upon (1) the shape of the utility

FIGURE 28.1   Expected Utility, Given w and s

One Period
Two States (with Equal Probability)
Three Effort Levels

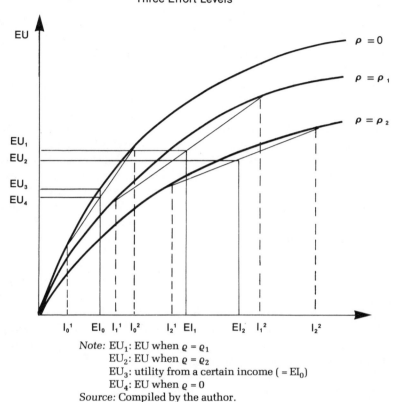

Note: EU_1: EU when $\varrho = \varrho_1$
EU_2: EU when $\varrho = \varrho_2$
EU_3: utility from a certain income ($= EI_0$)
EU_4: EU when $\varrho = 0$
Source: Compiled by the author.

function (that is, the degree of risk aversion) and (2) the degree to which utility is lowered by effort (that is, the magnitude of disutility).

Short- versus Long-Term Contracts

It seems apparent that short contracts provide more flexibility. The principal is free to hire or not hire, to package different wage/share combinations. This type of flexibility may be advantageous, especially when exogenous variables fluctuate wildly (as in the case of a fluctuating revenue function). Labor in this case is left as a variable (rather than fixed) factor, possibly over the entire planning period. On the other hand, with long-term contracts, the principal is committed to a specific employment structure, that is, to lack of flexibility. However, since a long-term contract guarantees the agent's service, it has been argued that it is an appropriate method of securing an agent. This concern seems critical, especially during a period of labor shortage. "Flexibility" and "security," therefore, seem to be important. However, a glance at the model shows that neither flexibility nor security of employment per se has any intrinsic merit. Optimizing policy is planned over the entire planning period and these prior decisions are precisely what we are concerned with.

To understand how various factors influence the length of optimal contracts, we shall examine the following: transaction or training costs, the seniority wage increase, risk aversion, and discount rates. The first two are easily understandable, while risk aversion and discount rates are more complex. We shall later discuss "averaging effects" due to risk aversion or differential discount rates between the principal and the agent. The transaction cost is incurred every time a new contract is agreed upon, thus the principal has no reason to hire, fire, and rehire an agent with the same compensation package, other things being equal. It may be worthwhile to negotiate for a new contract if the economic condition calls for a different package (by increasing or decreasing wage or share in order to change the total income, and/or to induce a different level of effort). Of course, short contracts may be justified if the automatic wage increase is high. In some situations, the principal may weigh the wage increase against the transaction cost.

Since a risk-averse agent will prefer a contract with a certain wage income to uncertain alternate opportunities with the same expected present value, as has been discussed a fixed wage (rather than profit sharing) is a less costly method of securing the agent. This is true whether the contract period is short or long. If labor is scarce (and thus the alternate opportunity may be improving rapidly), a long-term contract may secure an agent who would be very expensive if hired later. The principal can, however, always outbid the alternate opportunities by offering higher wages for each of the sequence of short contracts. After all, there is no reason that the agent should prefer a long-term contract to a sequence of short ones with the same compensation package. The "length" per se is of no value for the agent even if she or he is risk-averse.

With short contracts, the wage offer for each period will have to trace out the movements in the alternate utility ($EU_t \geq AU_t$ for every t). On the other hand, if a long contract is chosen, the principal offers a package that gives the agent an expected utility that is on the average just as good as or better than the alternative

$$(\overset{M}{\Sigma}EU_t\, e^{-\delta t} \geq \overset{M}{\Sigma}AU_t\, e^{-\delta t})$$

That is, the agent might have done "better" in some periods in the alternate opportunity. The agent does not have to be made better off in every period, but only on the average. We shall call this phenomenon an "averaging effect" and proceed to argue that averaging can be profitable for the principal for two reasons. Suppose the alternate opportunity is nonconstant, then the risk-averse agent will be better off with a steady income stream than with fluctuating alternate utilities of the same expected present value. In other words, the principal can obtain the agent's service with a labor cost whose expected present value is less than that of the alternate opportunity. This is the case of profitable averaging due to risk aversion. Of course, averaging is of no advantage if the alternate opportunity is constant. When the alternate changes over time, however, the principal may offer a long-term contract and get away with paying the agent less some of the time.*

Even if there is no risk aversion, the "averaging" possibility can be exploited to the principal's advantage, when the two parties value future monetary returns differently. We call this an averaging due to differential discount rates. For example, if $\delta < \gamma$ (that is, the principal's discount rate is lower than that of the agent), and the alternate opportunity improves rapidly for the agent, the principal can hire the agent with an income stream good enough to entice the agent's employment, but the present value (cost) to the principal will be less.† In summary, we point out that advantages associated with long contracts are: (1) the averaging possibility and (2) the reduction of transaction or training cost.

The above discussion shows that various forms of contracts have both advantages and disadvantages. The optimal contract can, thus, take on almost any combination in the compensation packages offered to the agent. When viewed as optimizing behavior, various practices cannot be judged on a priori grounds without an investigation of the particulars relevant to each situation. It is simple, however, to produce the extremes of behavior. For example, consider the following situation: the agent is risk-averse; the agent's effort has no effect on the revenue stream; there is no automatic wage in-

---

*As a simple illustration, consider a case in which the agent's alternate opportunity provides her or him with an expected income stream of (1, 2, 3), a stream that would have to be matched precisely (or improved upon) if there were three short contracts. On the other hand, the principal can offer one three-period contract with the wage/period of less than 2, the average of the stream (assuming that the discount rate is 0), to leave the agent indifferent. Due to a strictly concave utility function (risk aversion), (2, 2, 2) is strictly preferred to (1, 2, 3).

†Assume that the alternate opportunity provides an income stream to the agent of (1,2,3,) over three periods. If $\delta = 0$ and $\gamma > 0$, then the agent will prefer (2,2,2) to (1,2,3) whether or not there is risk aversion. For the principal, however, these two streams are equivalent. Thus the principal can pay *less* than 2 per period in a three-period contract.

crease ($\alpha = 0$); there is a positive training cost ($\tau > 0$); and $E\Pi(t,\theta,s,w,\varrho) \geq$ 0. In this case, as we would expect, the optimal policy consists of one long contract with a fixed wage. Alternatively, consider the situation in which the wage increases over the contract period due to seniority ($\alpha > 0$); there is no training cost ($\tau = 0$); and the alternate opportunity is constant over the horizon. In this case, the optimal policy will be a series of short contracts (to avoid the seniority wage increases).

NUMERICAL TEST CASES

In this section, we discuss our numerical model and report some test cases of interest. The functional forms to be specified are the revenue, the agent's utility, and the alternate utility functions. First we will discuss the general features that should be incorporated in these functional forms.

For the revenue function, $R(t,\varrho,\theta)$, a specific form may include time variables to represent a secular trend and/or cyclical trend. The variable ϱ can be incorporated to represent productivity of effort, which may be subject to an increase (or decrease) over time. In addition, a stochastic element must be specified to represent an uncertain future. For the agent's utility, we have $U_t(I,\varrho)$ where, as usual, $U_I > 0$, $U_{II} \leq 0$, and $U_\varrho < 0$. For the alternate utility function, AU, there do not exist any a priori restrictions. For our experiment, we use the following forms for the three functions:

$$R(t,\varrho,\theta) = \{r_1 + r_2 e^{r_3 t} + r_4 \sin(r_5 t)\}(r_6 + r_7 e^{r_8 t}\varrho)(r_9 + r_{10} z) \tag{7}$$

$$U_t(I,\varrho) = I^{u_1}(u_2 + u_3\varrho) \tag{8}$$

$$AU = A_1 e^{A_2 t}(A_3 + A_4 z) \tag{9}$$

where z represents the state of nature with some underlying probability distribution. All coefficients are nonnegative except u_3 and u_4. u_3 is nonpositive, since it represents disutility of effort. The sign of A_4 is not restricted, and is dependent upon whether the agent's alternate opportunity improves (or deteriorates) with the state of nature. In addition, we have $0 < u_1 \leq 1$. If the agent is risk-averse, $u_1 < 1$.

We now turn to six test cases. Details for each case are found in the appendix. The first part of each table shows the optimal employment policy for successive planning periods of lengths 1 through 10. The numbers under "TERM" indicate the length of the first contract of the optimal beginning at that value of T. The numbers under "WAGE," "SHARE," and "EFFORT" refer to levels rather than values (the latter are listed later in each case). "PRES VALUE EXP PROFIT" represents the present value of the expected net profit corresponding to the optimal package starting at each T.

The second part of each table shows the optimal (nondiscounted) stream for the entire horizon, while the last part shows the values used for calculation in each case.

Case One

In this case we see maximum lengths for contracts no matter when contracts are negotiated, due partly to high training cost partly to an ever increasing expected alternate utility. Labor productivity starts high and also increases over time; therefore, maximum effort is induced by the maximum level of profit sharing. The averaging of expected utility (as well as income) is clearly visible, with expected utility being higher than the expected alternate utility in only four out of ten periods. Since the wage rate increases automatically at 12 percent per period, the wage rate would have increased to 1.767 the original wage by the last period. However, it should be noted that this is still much lower than what an agent who had been given a new contract in the last period would have been paid. In that case the wage rate would be 3.0 the starting wage.

Case Two

Basically, the situation is identical with Case One, with the exception that the growth rate of labor productivity is less (2 percent instead of 5 percent per period). The resulting optimal contract is very similar, although the starting wage rate at $T = 0$ is made higher to compensate for lower bonus income (since a lower labor productivity growth implies lower bonuses even with the same share levels). It is interesting, however, to note that the optimal policy would be quite different had the principal gone into negotiation at $T = 3$ (or later). For example, as we see from the first table of Case 2, the optimal policy for a seven-year planning period beginning at $T = 3$ would consist of a contract of term 5 followed by one of term 2. Similarly, we see that the optimal policy starting at $T = 6$ is to issue three contracts of lengths 2, 1, and 1. The wage rates required for these short contracts are quite high even though the share given is the highest possible. At $T = 0$, the agent would be offered the longest possible contract. Under this contract, the agent's expected utility for each of the last four periods is consistently less than the agent's alternative.

Case Three

Another change has been added to the first two cases. In this case, the alternate utility increases but more slowly. As a result, the principal is now able to secure maximum effort with bonuses, and they alone turn out to be sufficient income. If a contract had to be made later, however, say, at T = 2, the wage/share combination does change to one with a positive wage and a lower share. An interesting observation to be noted is that the agent is worse off at the beginning (that is, at T = 0, 1, and 3) than with the alternative, but then becomes significantly better off in later periods. Thus we see and averaging taking place here. Another point to be noted is that, if the planning period consisted of the last nine periods (T = 1 to T = 10), then, as we see in the first table of Case 3, the optimal policy would be two contracts, the first for six periods and the second for three periods.

Case Four

In this case, parametric values are such that the resulting revenue stream is rather low. In fact, the principal's net profit for T = 1 and for T = 3 is negative. Despite these downturns, the principal finds it more profitable to hire the agent for the entire periods if the negotiations take place at T = 0. The agent is risk-averse and, in addition, has to be compensated for additional effort. The principal does not find it worthwhile to induce more effort in this case, hence pays the agent a fixed wage and no bonus. Notice if the planning had started at T = 1, then the principal would have offered a nine-period contract even though the revenue in the first period is less than the agents's wage. Since the alternate opportunity is improving for the agent, the principal finds it optimal to secure the agent's service at the (relatively low) wage level 8 rather than waiting for another period and paying the agent a higher wage level.

Case Five

In this case, the principal does not hire the agent for the first two periods, because the revenues are too low to warrant an agent. There is no reason to hire an agent then for the sole purpose of securing one immediately, since the alternate opportunity remains the same over the horizon.

Case Six

Zero training cost coupled with an automatic wage increase in this case gives rise to a series of ten one-period contracts. The marginal rate of profit (MRP) of effort is too low relative to the marginal cost (MC) of effort to warrant any bonus payment. If the training cost were positive, it would have to be balanced against the automatic seniority wage increase. For a small training cost, the optimal policy may be a series of short (but not necessarily one-period) contracts. For example, when the training cost is 0.03, the optimal policy consists of three three-period contracts followed by one one-period contract.

SUMMARY AND CONCLUSION

In this study, we have focused on the issues of employment security versus flexibility, and of fixed wages versus bonus or incentive plans. Long-term employment and bonuses are frequently viewed as characteristics of Japanese labor practice, while U.S. labor practice has favored shorter terms and has placed relatively less emphasis upon bonuses. However, as discussed, various mixes of these labor practice ingredients do exist in the two countries. This indicates to us that the labor practices are probably more a response to economic conditions than a simple matter of cultural or philosophical influence.

Our main goal, then, is to demonstrate how these various labor practices could result from economic factors. We carry out this demonstration by means of a model incorporating the familiar principal-agent relationship. In contrast to previous analyses, our model allows a *sequence* of contracts spanning a given planning period.

We find that the main factors influencing the extent to which bonuses figure in the optimal policy are labor productivity, the agent's effort, and the degree of risk aversion of the agent. The factors influencing contract length turn out to be transaction and training cost, the extent of seniority wage increases, and the degree to which "averaging" of wages is beneficial to the principal. The last of these is by far the most subtle of all these factors, and the one that seems to have escaped scrutiny. As we discussed, this averaging effect can allow the principal to exploit (through long-term contracts) the agent's risk aversion, as well as differentials in the principal's and agent's discount rates. In some cases, it also serves to secure the service of an agent who may be much more expensive later.

By judiciously combining these factors, it is possible to produce situations in which any specified type of employment policy becomes optimal. We illustrate this by means of six numerically solved examples. The implications for the Japanese experience may be that long-term employment with bonuses has evolved as a rational reaction to, for example, a growth economy, a labor force exhibiting high risk aversion and low disutility of effort, and/or a high training cost. In the case of the U.S. economy, our model would explain its labor practices as a rational reaction to, for example, a fluctuating economy, a labor force with relatively low risk aversion and high disutility of effort, and/or a low transaction cost.

APPENDIX

Case One

Time	Hire?	TERM	WAGE LEVEL	SHARE LEVEL	EFFORT LEVEL	PRES VALUE EXP PROFIT
9	Yes	1	16	3	3	73.6806
8	Yes	2	18	3	3	112.6345
7	Yes	3	13	3	3	154.7494
6	Yes	4	11	3	3	173.9164
5	Yes	5	9	3	3	184.6552
4	Yes	6	7	3	3	196.6285
3	Yes	7	7	3	3	187.2033
2	Yes	8	5	3	3	191.1089
1	Yes	9	5	3	3	178.0157
0	Yes	10	4	3	3	168.6020

Optimal Stream for the Largest Horizon

Time	Cont Yr	W	S	E	A's Income	Exp Util	Exp AU	Revenue	Exp Profit
0	1/10	4	3	3	1.2900	1.3987	1.3500	7.5000	6.2100
1	2/10	4	3	3	1.2853	1.3979	1.4580	6.8053	5.5200
2	3/10	4	3	3	2.9284	1.7842	1.5746	22.5107	19.5822
3	4/10	4	3	3	1.9503	1.5828	1.7006	11.9161	9.9658
4	5/10	4	3	3	4.0951	1.9723	1.8367	32.4541	28.3590
5	6/10	4	3	3	4.0344	1.9644	1.9836	30.8271	26.7928
6	7/10	4	3	3	4.9647	2.0899	2.1423	38.9886	34.0239
7	8/10	4	3	3	7.1708	2.3317	2.3137	59.7702	52.5994
8	9/10	4	3	3	6.8734	2.3034	2.4988	55.3642	48.4908
9	10/10	4	3	3	10.5398	2.6163	2.6987	90.4229	79.8832

Parameter Values for This Run

Effort:	0	0.5	1.0						
Share:	0	0.05	0.1						
Wage:	0	0.2	0.4	0.6	0.8	1.0	1.2	1.4	1.6	1.8
	2.0	2.2	2.4	2.6	2.8	3.0	3.2	3.4	3.6	3.8
	4.0	4.2	4.4	4.6	4.8	5.0	5.2	5.4	5.6	5.8
	6.0	6.2	6.4	6.6	6.8	7.0	7.2	7.4	7.6	7.8
	8.0								
States:	0	(probability of 0.5)	1	(probability of 0.5)					

Revenue Function:	0.5	2.5	0.2	2.5	10.0	1.0	2.0	0.05	0.7	0.6
Alt. Utility Fn:	0.9	8.0	1.0	1.0						
Utility Function:	0.3	1.5	−0.2							
P's Discount Rate:		10.0								
A's Discount Rate:		10.0								
Wage Increase Rate:		12.0								
Training Cost:		5.0								

Case Two

Time	Hire?	TERM	WAGE LEVEL	SHARE LEVEL	EFFORT LEVEL	PRES VALUE EXP PROFIT
9	Yes	1	25	3	3	57.4594
8	Yes	1	23	3	2	70.4622
7	Yes	1	12	3	3	103.3353
6	Yes	2	11	3	3	122.5257
5	Yes	5	12	3	3	153.0568
4	Yes	6	9	3	3	165.8440
3	Yes	2	6	3	3	154.1788
2	Yes	8	7	3	3	163.0663
1	Yes	9	6	3	3	153.4478
0	Yes	10	5	3	3	145.8974

Optimal Stream for the Largest Horizon

Time	Cont Yr	W	S	E	A's Income	Exp Util	Exp AU	Revenue	Exp Profit
0	1/10	5	3	3	1.4700	1.4557	1.3500	7.5000	6.0300
1	2/10	5	3	3	1.4733	1.4574	1.4580	6.6690	5.1957
2	3/10	5	3	3	3.0640	1.8103	1.5746	21.6081	18.5441
3	4/10	5	3	3	2.1315	1.6270	1.7006	11.1991	9.0676
4	5/10	5	3	3	4.1179	1.9776	1.8367	29.8501	25.7319
5	6/10	5	3	3	4.0425	1.9678	1.9836	27.7366	23.6941
6	7/10	5	3	3	4.8514	2.0778	2.1423	34.3020	29.4506
7	8/10	5	3	3	6.7315	2.2905	2.3137	51.3985	44.6670
8	9/10	5	3	3	6.4343	2.2610	2.4988	46.5164	40.0821
9	10/10	5	3	3	9.4165	2.5322	2.6987	74.1993	64.7828

Parameter Values for This Run

Effort:	0	0.5	1.0							
Share:	0	0.05	0.1							
Wage:	0	0.2	0.4	0.6	0.8	1.0	1.2	1.4	1.6	1.8
	2.0	2.2	2.4	2.6	2.8	3.0	3.2	3.4	3.6	3.8
	4.0	4.2	4.4	4.6	4.8	5.0	5.2	5.4	5.6	5.8

	6.0	6.2	6.4	6.6	6.8	7.0	7.2	7.4	7.6	7.8
	8.0									
States:	0	(probability of 0.5)		1		(probability of 0.5)				
Revenue Function:	0.5	2.5	0.2	2.5	10.0	1.0	2.0	0.02	0.7	0.6
Alt. Utility Fn:	0.9	8.0	1.0	1.0						
Utility Function:	0.3	1.5	−0.2							
P's Discount Rate:	10.0									
A's Discount Rate:	10.0									
Wage Increase Rate:	12.0									
Training Cost:	5.0									

Case Three

Time	Hire?	TERM	WAGE LEVEL	SHARE LEVEL	EFFORT LEVEL	PRES VALUE EXP PROFIT
9	Yes	1	2	2	3	65.2994
8	Yes	2	4	2	3	102.1215
7	Yes	3	4	2	3	140.5163
6	Yes	4	4	2	3	159.1145
5	Yes	5	4	2	3	169.7191
4	Yes	6	4	2	3	181.3008
3	Yes	7	4	2	3	174.0430
2	Yes	8	4	2	3	177.2643
1	Yes	6	1	3	3	162.7322
0	Yes	10	1	3	3	153.7160

Optimal Stream for the Largest Horizon

Time	Cont Yr	W	S	E	A's Income	Exp Util	Exp AU	Revenue	Exp Profit
0	1/10	1	3	3	0.7500	1.1808	1.3500	7.5000	6.7500
1	2/10	1	3	3	0.6669	1.1400	1.4040	6.6690	6.0021
2	3/10	1	3	3	2.1608	1.6220	1.4602	21.6081	19.4473
3	4/10	1	3	3	1.1199	1.3318	1.5186	11.1991	10.0791
4	5/10	1	3	3	2.9850	1.7871	1.5793	29.8504	26.8651
5	6/10	1	3	3	2.7737	1.7482	1.6425	27.7366	24.9629
6	7/10	1	3	3	3.4303	1.8632	1.7082	34.3020	30.8718
7	8/10	1	3	3	5.1399	2.1036	1.7765	51.3985	46.2587
8	9/10	1	3	3	4.6516	2.0415	1.8476	46.5164	41.8648
9	10/10	1	3	3	7.4199	2.3485	1.9214	74.1993	66.7794

Parameter Values for This Run

Effort:	0	0.5	1.0							
Share:	0	0.05	0.1							
Wage:	0	0.2	0.4	0.6	0.8	1.0	1.2	1.4	1.6	1.8

2.0	2.2	2.4	2.6	2.8	3.0	3.2	3.4	3.6	3.8
4.0	4.2	4.4	4.6	4.8	5.0	5.2	5.4	5.6	5.8
6.0	6.2	6.4	6.6	6.8	7.0	7.2	7.4	7.6	7.8
8.0									

States:	0	(probability of 0.5)	1	(probability of 0.5)					
Revenue Function:	0.5	2.5	0.2	2.5	10.0	1.0	2.0	0.02	0.7	0.6
Alt. Utility Fn:	0.9	4.0	1.0	1.0					
Utility Function:	0.3	1.5	−0.2						
P's Discount Rate:	10.0								
A's Discount Rate:	10.0								
Wage Increase Rate:	12.0								
Training Cost:	5.0								

Case Four

Time	Hire?	TERM	WAGE LEVEL	SHARE LEVEL	EFFORT LEVEL	PRES VALUE EXP PROFIT
9	Yes	1	12	2	1	7.2914
8	Yes	1	16	1	1	9.1953
7	Yes	3	16	1	1	14.4148
6	Yes	4	14	1	1	16.3072
5	Yes	1	6	2	1	17.5260
4	Yes	6	7	2	1	20.4196
3	Yes	7	10	1	1	18.7288
2	Yes	8	9	1	1	20.8730
1	Yes	9	8	1	1	19.0628
0	Yes	10	7	1	1	18.1678

Optimal Stream for the Largest Horizon

Time	Cont Yr	W	S	E	A's Income	Exp Util	Exp AU	Revenue	Exp Profit
0	1/10	7	1	1	0.3500	1.6206	1.5000	0.9000	0.5500
1	2/10	7	1	1	0.3500	1.6206	1.5300	0.2206	−0.1294
2	3/10	7	1	1	0.3500	1.6206	1.5606	4.0534	3.7033
3	4/10	7	1	1	0.3500	1.6206	1.5918	0.3418	−0.0082
4	5/10	7	1	1	0.3500	1.6206	1.6236	4.8191	4.4691
5	6/10	7	1	1	0.3500	1.6206	1.6561	3.1435	2.7935
6	7/10	7	1	1	0.3500	1.6206	1.6892	3.6541	3.3041
7	8/10	7	1	1	0.3500	1.6206	1.7230	6.7036	6.3536
8	9/10	7	1	1	0.3500	1.6206	1.7575	3.3667	3.0167
9	10/10	7	1	1	0.3500	1.6206	1.7926	8.2751	7.9251

Parameter Values for This Run

Effort:	0	0.5	1.0

Share:	0	0.05	0.1							
Wage:	0	0.10	0.15	0.20	0.25	0.30	0.35	0.40	0.45	0.50
	0.55	0.60	0.65	0.70	0.75	0.80	0.85	0.90	0.95	1.00
	1.05	1.10	1.15	1.20	1.25	1.30	1.35	1.40	1.45	1.50
	1.60	1.70	1.80	1.90	2.00					

States:	0	(probability of 0.5)		1	(probability of 0.5)				
Revenue Function:	0.1	0.2	0.1	0.5	10.0	1.0	1.0	0.01	4.0	1.0
Alt. Utility Fn:	1.0	2.0	1.5	0					
Utility Function:	0.1	1.8	−0.24						
P's Discount Rate:	10.0								
A's Discount Rate:	10.0								
Wage Increase Rate:	0								
Training Cost:	0								

Case Five

Time	Hire?	TERM	WAGE LEVEL	SHARE LEVEL	EFFORT LEVEL	PRES VALUE EXP PROFIT
9	Yes	1	4	1	1	4.1557
8	Yes	2	4	1	1	6.2760
7	Yes	3	3	1	1	11.3002
6	Yes	4	3	1	1	13.0483
5	Yes	5	3	1	1	14.1663
4	Yes	6	3	1	1	16.6546
3	No	1				15.1405
2	Yes	8	3	1	1	16.6219
1	No	1				15.1108
0	No	2				13.7371

Optimal Stream for the Largest Horizon

Time	Cont Yr	W	S	E	A's Income	Exp Util	Exp AU	Revenue	Exp Profit
0	1/2						1.5000		
1	2/2						1.5000		
2	1/8	3	1	1	0.1500	1.4890	1.5000	3.6030	3.4530
3	2/8	3	1	1	0.1680	1.5059	1.5000	0.3038	0.1358
4	3/8	3	1	1	0.1882	1.5231	1.5000	4.2837	4.0955
5	4/8	3	1	1	0.2107	1.5404	1.5000	2.7942	2.5835
6	5/8	3	1	1	0.2360	1.5580	1.5000	3.2481	3.0120
7	6/8	3	1	1	0.2644	1.5758	1.5000	5.9588	5.6944
8	7/8	3	1	1	0.2961	1.5937	1.5000	2.9927	2.6966
9	8/8	3	1	1	0.3316	1.6119	1.5000	7.3557	7.0241

Parameter Values for This Run

Effort:	0	0.5	1.0

Share:	0	0.05	0.1						
Wage:	0	0.10	0.15	0.20	0.25	0.30	0.35	0.40	0.45	0.50
	0.55	0.60	0.65	0.70	0.75	0.80	0.85	0.90	0.95	1.00
	1.05	1.10	1.15	1.20	1.25	1.30	1.35	1.40	1.45	1.50
	1.60	1.70	1.80	1.90	2.00					

States:	0	(probability of 0.5)	1	(probability of 0.5)

Revenue Function: 0.1   0.2   0.1   0.5   10.0   1.0   1.0   0.01   4.0   0
Alt. Utility Fn: 1.0   0   1.5   0
Utility Function: 0.1   1.8   −0.24
P's Discount Rate: 10.0
A's Discount Rate: 10.0
Wage Increase Rate: 12.0
Training Cost: 3.0

Case Six

Time	Hire?	TERM	WAGE LEVEL	SHARE LEVEL	EFFORT LEVEL	PRES VALUE EXP PROFIT
9	Yes	1	4	1	1	7.1937
8	Yes	1	4	1	1	9.3704
7	Yes	1	4	1	1	14.3153
6	Yes	1	4	1	1	16.1000
5	Yes	1	4	1	1	17.2686
4	Yes	1	4	1	1	19.8204
3	Yes	1	4	1	1	18.1604
2	Yes	1	4	1	1	19.9504
1	Yes	1	4	1	1	18.1709
0	Yes	1	4	1	1	17.1570

Optimal Stream for the Largest Horizon

Time	Cont Yr	W	S	E	A's Income	Exp Util	Exp AU	Revenue	Exp Profit
0	1/1	4	1	1	0.1620	1.5005	1.5000	0.8000	0.6380
1	1/1	4	1	1	0.1620	1.5005	1.5000	0.1961	0.0341
2	1/1	4	1	1	0.1620	1.5005	1.5000	3.6030	3.4410
3	1/1	4	1	1	0.1620	1.5005	1.5000	0.3038	0.1418
4	1/1	4	1	1	0.1620	1.5005	1.5000	4.2837	4.1217
5	1/1	4	1	1	0.1620	1.5005	1.5000	2.7942	2.6322
6	1/1	4	1	1	0.1620	1.5005	1.5000	3.2481	3.0861
7	1/1	4	1	1	0.1620	1.5005	1.5000	5.9588	5.7968
8	1/1	4	1	1	0.1620	1.5005	1.5000	2.9927	2.8307
9	1/1	4	1	1	0.1620	1.5005	1.5000	7.3557	7.1937

Parameter Values for This Run

Effort: 0   0.5   1.0

```
Share:               0    0.05  0.1
Wage:                0    0.10  0.15  0.162 0.20  0.25  0.30  0.35  0.40  0.45
                     0.50 0.55  0.60  0.65  0.70  0.75  0.80  0.85  0.90  0.95
                     1.00 1.05  1.10  1.15  1.20  1.25  1.30  1.35  1.40  1.45
                     1.50 1.60  1.70  1.80  1.90  2.00
States:              0    (probability of 0.5)    1    (probability of 0.5)
Revenue Function:    0.1  0.2   0.1   0.5   10.0  1.0   1.0   0.01  4.0   0
Alt. Utility Fn:     1.0  0     1.5   0
Utility Function:    0.1  1.8   -0.24
P's Discount Rate:   10.0
A's Discount Rate:   10.0
Wage Increase Rate:  12.0
Training Cost:       0
```

REFERENCES

Bieda, K. 1970. *The Structure and Operation of the Japanese Economy*. Sydney: John Wiley and Sons.

Clarke, Frank H., and Masako N. Darrough. 1977. "Optimal Incentive Schemes: Existence and Characterization." *Economics Letters* 5:305–10.

Galenson, Walter. 1976. "The Japanese Labor Market." In *Asia's New Giant*, ed. Hugh Patrick and Henry Rosovsky. Washington, D. C.: Brookings Institution.

Haitani, Kanji. 1976. *The Japanese Economic System*. Lexington, Mass.: Lexington Books.

Harris, Milton, and Arthur Raviv. 1976. "Optimal Incentive Contracts with Imperfect Information." *Journal of Economic Theory* 20:231–59.

Hashimoto, Masanori. 1979. "Bonus Payments, On-the-Job Training, and Lifetime Employment in Japan." *Journal of Political Economy* 87, no. 5:1086–1104.

Holmström, B. 1979. "Moral Hazard and Observability." *Bell Journal of Economics* 10:74–91.

Levine, Solomon B. 1965. "Labor Markets and Collective Bargaining in Japan." In *The State and Economic Enterprise in Japan*, ed. W. W. Lockwood. Princeton: Princeton University Press.

Mirrlees, James A. 1979. "The Optimal Structure of Incentives and Authority Within an Organization." *Bell Journal of Economics* 7:105–31.

1975 Establishment Census of Japan. Bureau of Statistics, Prime Minister's Office, Japan.

1977 White Paper on Labor. Ministry of Labor, Japan.

Ohkawa, K., and H. Rosovsky. 1973. *Japanese Economic Growth*. Stanford: Stanford University Press.

Ross, Stephen A. 1973. "The Economic Theory of Agency: The Principal's Problem." *American Economic Review* 63, no. 2:134–39.

Shavell, S. 1979. "Risk Sharing and Incentives in the Principal and Agent Relationship." *Bell Journal of Economics* 10:55–73.

29

The Social Audit: Japanese and U.S. Concepts

JOHN W. GOEBEL

INTRODUCTION

For over a decade, the notion that business firms should clearly indicate the manner in which they are meeting social needs has seemed to be an idea whose time has come. A great deal has been written about the subject, a number of approaches to the problem have been developed, surveys have been conducted to assess the reality of the need, and an examination of work in the field has been undertaken to categorize and enumerate the methods used to accomplish the objectives sought. However, in spite of all these efforts, consensus does not seem to be close at hand. It appears that a look at the issues from another perspective might be fruitful in attempting to narrow the considerations a bit, and stimulate thinking that will lead to a meeting of the minds. To that end, this study of the evolution and current status of suggested reporting formats for social responsibility in two countries is being undertaken.

The members of society in the United States and in Japan have recently evidenced concern about the manner in which business interacts with society at large. Although numerous articles have been written in the United States about attempts to deal with this issue, a relatively small number have been written in the U.S. periodical literature about Japanese efforts in this area. A meaningful comparison of the approaches to the problem in these two countries will require a long-range effort.

The propriety of such a study may well be questioned. After all, if more than a decade has passed with seemingly little movement in the United States toward one central approach, or at least an acceptance of a fairly limited number of techniques, it might be said that the topic does not any longer warrant further study. However, it may very well be that the current political climate and the consequences of current governmental policies will focus much greater attention on the actions of business with regard to problem areas in society. As governmental support is withdrawn from areas that many perceive as areas of social need, it seems quite likely that there will be increased demand for socially responsible action on the part of the business community. As such pressure on business increases, the need for a meaningful reporting format will become painfully clear. Both external and internal users will require useful comparative data upon which future decisions will be based, and upon which to judge the merits of past programs. Further study of the complex issues that arise in attempts to report socially responsible activities will provide additional information with which to establish an appropriate reporting format.

This chapter is the first step in a process that will continue for some time. "Social audit" concepts that have surfaced in the United States in the last decade are today being refined to some extent, but, at this time, there is no clear indication of the direction to be taken as far as the reporting format is concerned. Because of some of the unique cultural considerations that exist in Japan, social responsibility can be viewed from a different perspective, a point of view that should yield very fruitful insights. Such an approach, involving examination of practices in other countries, certainly is not new. In the early days of the "social audit" concept, it was believed that much could be learned from the requirements for social accounting that existed in Europe at that time, a notion that at first seemed likely to yield significant benefits but now, in retrospect, seems not to have been as productive as was hoped. As noted above, while there is some literature in which the commonality of ideas relating to social responsibility in the United States and Japan is discussed, more work dealing with the reporting format will be useful.

This study is intended to lay the foundation for what is to follow. The history of the so-called social audit concept in the United States will be summarized, and some current developments examined. Also, a brief review of the Japanese concept of social responsibility will be undertaken, with some consideration of reporting formats. Finally, future steps and expectations will be outlined.

SOCIAL RESPONSIBILITY REPORTING
IN THE UNITED STATES

A few years ago, in the late 1960s and early 1970s, scholars from a variety of disciplines were excitedly discussing a field that seemed to be developing rapidly, a field they hoped would be envisioned by a suddenly socially responsible society as an endeavor that would yield the answers anxiously sought to many questions, a field that seemed to many to require no special expertise for entry or practice. This field was given a variety of labels: social accounting, social responsibility accounting, socioeconomic accounting, corporate social measurement, and social auditing, to list some of the more often used terms. Discussing the need for the information that would be provided by such reports, and preparing scholarly tomes relating to the justification for the dissemination of such information, were academicians and practitioners alike from many fields, including economics, psychology, sociology, management, law, and accounting. Many possible reporting formats were proposed by scholars from each field and, to a great extent, the only expertise required to implement the reporting process was that of the discipline embraced by the individual offering the suggested approach.

To put these fairly recent developments in proper perspective, it is necessary to outline briefly the evolution of the "social audit" concept from its origins in the notion of social responsibility. While a casual reading of current literature on the subject of social responsibility would lead the reader to believe that this concept is a product of the turmoil of the 1960s, historians date concern for this area as far back as early Greece (Bauer and Fenn 1972, p. iii). Examination of the charters of the early English corporations indicates that socially responsible objectives were prime requisites for incorporation, and similar socially justifiable purposes were required in many jurisdictions in the early days of the corporate form in the United States. It must be admitted that these altruistic objectives were not long deemed important for the corporate form, and that for many years, from the late 1800s to the present time, the creation of the corporate form has not necessarily been limited to creation solely for noble purposes. However, in the United States, events like the Great Depression of the 1930s did create an awareness of the social consequences of business activity (Heald 1970, p. 103); and rising expectations resulting from changing standards of living after World War II did usher in new societal attitudes toward business, along with heightened requirements for the business sector in terms of meeting society's needs. Social responsibility of business is not the product of recent thought, but has been a consideration of philosophers and business people alike, in varying degrees of intensity, since very early times.

The first problem encountered in attempting to deal with the question of the "social audit" is a nomenclature problem. All sorts of confusion has attended the use of the phrase "social accounting." As noted earlier, this language conjures up a variety of notions, ranging from macroeconomic measurement devices, to the behavioral connotation of human resource accounting, and finally to the "social audit" concept, with many other possible detours along the way. Whether it is an expression of the broader field of economic measurement, a newly developed separate field of endeavor, or, as one writer has suggested, a very broad area comprising at least five subfields (Cowen and Segal 1981), it seems at this stage of development to be of little significance, in spite of the fact that much has been written to substantiate each of the above claims. What is currently sought is a meaningful method of reporting corporate social performance. The term currently used by many to describe this reporting format is the "social audit." This title will be used in the remainder of the chapter to describe the system designed to accomplish the goal of reporting the contribution of the firm to social objectives.

Specific definitions of the social audit abound. For example, it may be the "systematic assessment of, and reporting on, some meaningful, definable domain of a company's activities that have a social input" (Bauer and Fenn 1973) or an "investigation of an enterprise's performance as a member of the community in which it has its primary input" (Dilley 1974). Doris and Bromstrom (1975:13) have formulated a comprehensive statement that seems to embody most of the dimensions found in a variety of definitions:

> A social audit is a systematic study and evaluation of an organization's social performance, as distinguished from its economic performance. It is concerned with possible influence on the social quality of life instead of economic quality of life.

Professional organizations in the field of accounting recognize the concept, and in attempting to define the role of the accountant in this area contribute to the plethora of conceptual frameworks available. The American Institute of Certified Public Accountants, the National Association of Accountants, and the American Accounting Association have created committees to deal with the issue. While these units seem to be no closer to agreement on technique and format than academics and others who write in this field, there does seem to be a common recognition of objectives evidenced in their comments, and an appreciation for the role to be played by the professional accountant in the development of a meaningful social audit report (American Institute 1977; Ratcliffe and Munter 1972–73:34).

The identification of the proper party to render this statement indicating corporate support of social progress has yet to be satisfactorily ac-

complished. Because of their familiarity with the concept of social indicators and skills in forecasting, economists are often perceived as filling this
role. The point of view and training of sociologists has been said to prepare
such specialists well for work on these reports. Management experts, law-
yers, and psychologists, as well as accountants, have all been suggested as
those best equipped to perform the task. This issue may be best resolved, as
suggested by some writers, by creation of an interdisciplinary team to do
the work, a team made up of representatives from a variety of fields such as
management, accounting, law, economics, and physical and behavioral
sciences (Linowes 1972–73:40; Britoff 1972–73:47). Of course, whether the
report was prepared internally or externally would also be likely to have
some bearing on the identity of the preparer. No doubt economic considerations, as well as the desired objectives, would affect the decision made by
the firm.

There are indeed a wide variety of social audit formats available for
discussion. An attempt to cover all the options in this study would unneces-
sarily extend its scope at this time. Instead, it seems appropriate to provide
an overview of the basic considerations involved, with specific examination
of a few of the more often discussed techniques to provide the reader with
some examples of proposed approaches.

Suggested mechanisms for reporting fall basically into two broad general categories: those generated externally and those generated internally
(Sethi 1972–73:34). Whether the report is intended for internal or external
use may affect the choice of the means of preparation by the firm, but the
intended purpose will not necessarily affect the result. Whether the report
is an attempt to comply with indicators (standards) established by the firm
or by someone outside the firm may have a bearing on what is reported, but
if there is reasonable consensus on social needs that can be met by business,
the product should be essentially the same. A very important issue is the
type of format used. The determination of presentation format, quantitative or qualitative, will influence the extent to which the summary is narrative in form. A desire for complexity and detail, as opposed to breadth and
general discussion, will have an impact on readability and effectiveness.
An excellent sense of the range of possibilities is contained in Table 29.1.

Internally generated reports, such as those that were conceived, prepared, and published by firms in the early period of development of the social audit concept, disclose a great deal of the rationale underlying the social reporting. The Abt Associates Annual Report and Social Audit of 1977
contains the following note, which sheds some light on the intent of those
who prepared the report.

The company believes that its performance should be judged on both financial and social grounds because in reality the two are always linked. Manage-

TABLE 29.1　A Summary of Business Social Accounting Models

MODEL	TYPE OF DISCLOSURE ADVOCATED	DEGREE OF COMPREHEN-SIVENESS	IMPLEMENTABILITY
Corcoran and Leininger	Nonmonetary quantification —several different value scales advocated	Partial—lacks development and detail	Immediate—little difficulty, although perhaps somewhat confusing
Beams	Monetary—add accounts to present financial accounting model	Extremely limited—applies only to pollution and to certain industries	Immediate—little additional disclosure
Linowes	Tabulation of monetary expenditures	Relatively comprehensive—lacks measurement detail	Could be implemented with some development
Abt	Monetary statement presentation	Extremely comprehensive for the particular industry utilized	Has been used for one particular industry
American Accounting Association	Narrative disclosure	Extremely limited	Immediate, but of questionable usefulness
Marlin	Nonmonetary quantification —compares performance with standards	Extremely limited—applies only to pollution controls	Immediate—a fairly good indicator of pollution abatement performance
Dilley and Weygandt	Monetary and nonmonetary disclosures	Somewhat—focuses on pollution, health and safety matters, and minority recruitment	Has been used for particular industry
Seidler	Monetary disclosures to derive social profit	Limited—lacks sufficient detail to appro-	Impossible without further development

TABLE 29.1 (continued)

MODEL	TYPE OF DISCLOSURE ADVOCATED	DEGREE OF COMPREHEN-SIVENESS	IMPLEMENTABILITY
		priately evaluate	
Estes	Monetary and nonmonetary disclosures	Extremely comprehensive in detail and development	Not immediate – serves as standard – a good long-range goal
Dillon	Nonmonetary disclosures	Somewhat – focuses on managerial decision making	Could be implemented with thorough advance planning
Anderson	Monetary or non-monetary disclosures	Extremely comprehensive in detail and development	Less complex levels could be implemented. Further development needed for more complex levels

Source: Ratcliffe and Munter (1972–73):57.

ment needs the tools to assess the financial consequences of social investment and policy decisions, and the social consequences of financial decisions, which, in turn, lead to further financial results.

The Abt report is prepared in a traditional format, with a balance sheet, income statement, and statement of changes in position. Dollar values are assigned rather arbitrarily and there is considerable use of footnotes for further elaboration. As an early effort, the Abt report did much to show the way for later undertakings.

Another approach that has received considerable attention is the so-called social-economic statement. This statement attempts to assess the impact on a community of inaction as well as action, and to indicate a socioeconomic gain or loss for the period. Only expenditures voluntarily undertaken for the benefit of society are considered in this approach (Linowes 1972–73). Socially detrimental actions would necessarily be reported in this statement, thus decreasing the likelihood of its widespread use for any purpose other than internal comparisons. Of course, if such a report were mandated by some authority, the technique could yield great benefit when used for comparison of a firm with similar firms.

A very early approach to the problem of measuring the contribution of a firm to society was that undertaken in the banking industry by the First National Bank of Minneapolis. For some reason this process has received relatively little attention when compared with other formats that seem to have no more to offer. This approach depends upon selection of social indicators that reflect in some way the effect of the firm's action on the community (Hetland 1974, p. 2). This use of the social indicator concept makes it possible to relate the standards used to those that might be developed at the national level, as was anticipated in the early 1970s (American Institute 1977, p. 8). The bank identified a number of factors that could be said to be significant quality-of-life factors in the community, factors that would reflect in some way the firm's response to social needs in the community, with the intent that subsequent comparisons would provide useful insights internally. Although later changes have modified the approach somewhat, this approach may warrant further study as those interested in this field move toward some relatively common reporting format.

It should also be noted that the frequently found narrative approach to reporting socially responsive actions by the firm continues to find support in many circles. From a brief narrative footnote, to mention in a letter from the firm's president to employees, or to the rather extensive narrative disclosures recommended by the American Accounting Association (1973), the descriptive, nonquantitative disclosure provides what many feel is adequate communication.

As Table 29.1 suggests, there are many other suggested alternatives for reporting corporate responses to social needs — indeed, several fairly well known proposals are not even mentioned in the table. The problem is not a lack of ideas. Rather, as suggested in a prize-winning paper on the subject, the "major problem has been absence of generally accepted and widely applicable methodology for identifying and measuring a firm's social cost" (Szepon 1980:80).

Just a few years ago, proponents of more-rapid implementation of some form of social audit report had been given an indication that greater progress might be made as a result of increased political, bureaucratic, and legislative attention to the issue. An interesting parallel can be drawn here. As any reader of business history knows, financial reporting improved vastly after the implementation of the Securities Act of 1933. Before then, the attitude of many firms toward financial reporting was not unlike that found today toward social reporting. Many concerned with the slow progress of the social reporting concept hoped for some similar legislative support; and, while there had never been a mandate that socially relevant information be reported by business, a few events in the late 1970s pointed toward the possibility of such requirements in the future. A regulatory agency, the Securities and Exchange Commission, required that all filings include information relating to environmentally sensitive issues when a material amount of money was involved and was such that an average prudent investor should be informed (Cowen and Segal 1981).

The Community Reinvestment Act of 1977 also had an impact on the financial community, but in a much different way. As a result of the act, the comptroller of the currency issued regulations that required covered banks to report some socially responsive data, namely, participation in socially desirable activities through credit policies (U.S., Department of the Treasury 1978). In 1977, it seemed that additional impetus was about to be provided, when Juanita Krepps, then secretary of commerce, clearly indicated her commitment to creation of a "social index." It was her belief that such a mechanism would provide a basis for comparison of performance in the social area and, presumably, stimulate greater participation by business.

Unfortunately for supporters of more-rapid development of the social audit concept, Krepps left government, and it seems that no one is now prepared to pick up the gauntlet. Further, it appears that compliance with the new regulatory provisions mentioned above is being left to the initiative of the firms who might be affected by the specific rule. Although dormant legislation can be revived quickly, or new rules proposed with seemingly little additional effort, the current legislative climate does not augur well for immediate action in this area. What seemed to be a spate of political and legal incentives for firms to provide information related to social performance now seems, at best, to be held in abeyance; at worst, action in this area may not surface again for some time.

In spite of the lack of a governmental mandate, many business firms have for some time been attempting to provide social audit types of information in one way or another. The results of a 1972 survey indicated that almost 60 percent of the Fortune 500 companies were providing stockholders and others with information in their annual reports on socially relevant actions (Beresford 1974). A perusal of the Ernst and Ernst (Ernst and Whinney today) *Social Responsibility Disclosure 1978 Survey* provides a great deal of information on methods of disclosure used by Fortune 500 companies. Although that survey does disclose a slight decrease (2 percent) in the percentage of firms including socially oriented information in their annual reports, the steady growth in such reporting from 1973 through 1976 seems a much more important harbinger of things to come. Some of the shifts over the years presumably reflect changing attitudes in society about the importance of one item as compared with another (for example, community involvement versus energy conservation). Other shifts apparently reflect the dissatisfaction of those reporting with the format used in the past. Overall, the incidence and meaningfulness of the reports has increased significantly in recent years.

While some see the societal support indicated for recent budget reductions as reflective of a mood in society that portends decreasing expectations in the area of social needs, it does not necessarily follow that there will be less need for the social audit. Indeed, as government funds are less available to meet society's needs in the sensitive areas reported on by social audits, it is likely that business will bear a greater burden in this area. As demands increase, the need for information on utilization and effectiveness, both externally and internally, is likely to be greater than before.

SOCIAL RESPONSIBILITY REPORTING IN JAPAN

Undertaking to trace the evolution of the concept of social responsibility in another country is a task involving considerable risk. Lack of thorough knowledge of the cultural differences that influence the actions of the people of a nation can lead to serious distortion in the perception of what has happened and why it happened. There is available a wealth of literature explaining the awakening of other countries to the notion of social responsibility, with some studies more attuned than others to the importance of cultural differences. Current evidence clearly indicates that Japan, as a nation, falls into the camp of those who recognize the social responsibility of business. However, the route taken by the citizenry of that country toward a strong commitment to this notion is inextricably interwoven with cultural and moral implications, and is a path not easily outlined by those unfamiliar with some of the more subtle differences between peoples.

The issues that attracted attention to the question of social responsibility in the United States, and that helped to coalesce this concern into what can be described as the social responsibility movement in this country from the late 1960s to date, are essentially the same as those that prompted growth in this area in other countries, including Japan (Preston, Rey, and Dierkes 1978). Such issues as consumer protection, adequacy of business response to social needs, and, especially, environmental pollution served as focal points for recognition of the need for socially responsible action by business in many countries (Duerr 1974). In Japan, concern about environment, the quality of life, business behavior, and related subjects "had been becoming more salient since the mid-1960s" (Nagashima 1976: 21).

It appears that environmental pollution has been a critical issue in recognition of corporate social responsibility in Japan. While the negative effect of industrial activity in Japan has been so great that it has been suggested that Japan engage in "exporting of pollution" by locating certain types of refining and processing functions in South Korea and Taiwan (Sherk 1974), a more positive approach seems to be the general rule. For example, the president of Kawasaki indicated that an appreciation of the firm's social responsibility played a major role in that organization's decision to spend 10 to 15 percent of its annual capital expenditure on pollution-control equipment in 1975. (This $8 million outlay is said to be small by comparison with that of some other Japanese firms, but really quite large in comparison with the size of Kawasaki's pollution problem [Clatterbuck 1974].) That the failure by Japanese business to recognize the consequences of socially irresponsible actions was becoming a significant internal concern was well explained by S. Prakash Sethi (1974–75). The social responsibility of business is recognized as important in Japan today, and proposed solutions will continue to come forth.

As in the United States, the identification and implementation of a means of reporting how these needs are met has been and will continue to be a center of discussion. Although an examination of a small number of randomly selected annual reports of Japanese firms for 1979 and 1980 yields little if any information on social issues, activities by Japanese firms in the early 1970s seemed to indicate a positive response to the social audit concept: "even in the early 1970's many corporations — approximately 25 percent of those in Japan and the United States — felt the need to make a report to the stockholders on their social performance . . ." (Abt 1977, p. 7). Although excerpts of Abt's discussion with Japanese executives included specific reference to the social audit concept, little information indicating purpose and format has subsequently appeared in the literature of the U.S. business community that is related to this field.

CONCLUSION

Business institutions, especially large corporations in the United States and Japan, have been given a large part of the credit for the remarkable growth and dynamism of their respective economies. Yet in both these countries business institutions have been beset by a high degree of public hostility and criticism — for contributing to a general deterioration in the quality of life, being insensitive to changing socio-political needs, and subverting decision making in the public domain through undue influence on governmental bureaucracies and political parties (Sethi 1978, p. 27).

The above statement handily makes the connection that is the basis for this chapter and the study to follow: "an evaluation of corporate performance or the performance of any other social institution must be to a large extent culturally and temporally determined" (Sethi 1975, p. 15).

Sethi has noted elsewhere that "the practical result" of having corporate response to social need met on a voluntary basis, with the extent and fashion determined by each firm "has been to make corporate social responsibility mean what anyone wants it to mean, thereby making some type of public accountability all but impossible" (Sethi 1978, p. 27). The idea that many might view this task as impossible is what prompts the remainder of this study.

Neither budget reductions nor economic slowdowns will reduce the pressure from citizens more acutely attuned to social problems than were their predecessors. The increasingly better educated constituency in the United States and Japan will continue to press firms for the details of their participation in the tasks of meeting societal needs in their own sphere and in the larger society in which they participate. Such a report will be forthcoming. The identity of those who will prepare it, the scope and nature of the coverage, and the basic form in which the report will be presented will be determined in the near future.

REFERENCES

Abt, Clark C. 1977. *The Social Audit for Management*. New York: AMACOM.

American Accounting Association. 1973. "Report of the Committee on Environmental Effects of Organizational Behavior." *Accounting Review* (supp. to vol. 48): 72.

American Institute of Certified Public Accountants. 1977. *The Measurement of Corporate Social Performance*. New York: Author.

Bauer, Raymond A., and Don H. Fenn, Jr. 1973. "What *Is* a Corporate Social Audit?" *Harvard Business Review* (January-February):37.

———. 1972. *Corporate Social Audit*. New York: Russell Sage Foundation.

Beresford, Dennis R. 1974. "How Companies are Reporting Social Performance." *Management Accounting* (August):41.

Britoff, Abraham J. 1972–73. "Commentary on 'Lets Get on With the Social Audit.' " *Business and Society* (Winter):47.

Clatterbuck, David. 1976. "Kawasaki Stresses Its Environmental Responsibilities." *International Management* (April):14.

Cowen, Scott S., and Mitchell G. Segal. 1981. "In the Public Eye: Reporting Social Performance." *Financial Executive* (January):12.

Dilley, Steven C. 1975. "Practical Approaches to Social Accounting." *CPA Journal* (February):17.

———. 1974. "What Is Social Responsibility: Some Definitions for Doing the Corporate Social Audit." *Canadian Chartered Accountant* (November):26.

Doris, Keith, and Robert C. Bromstrom. 1975. "Implementing the Social Audit in an Organization." *Business and Society* (Fall):13.

Duerr, Michael G. 1974. *What Troubles the World Business Leaders.* New York: The Conference Board.

Heald, Morrell. 1970. *The Social Responsibility of Business.* Cleveland: The Press of the Case Western Reserve University.

Hetland, James C., Jr. 1974. "The Social Audit: First National Bank's Experience." Paper presented at the 1974 Public Affairs Conference, Bank Marketing Association/American Bankers Association, February 11.

Linowes, David F. 1972–73. "Let's Get on With the Social Audit: A Specific Proposal." *Business and Society* (Winter):40.

Nagashima, Yukiniri. 1976. "Response of Japanese Companies to Environment Changes." *Long Range Planning* (February):21.

Preston, Lee E., Francoise Rey, and Meinoff Dierkes. 1978. "Comparing Corporate Social Performance: Germany, France, Canada, and the U.S." *California Management Review* (Summer):40–49.

Ratcliffe, Thomas A., and Paul Munter. 1972–73. "The Development of Social Accounting Models: A Comparative Analysis." *Business and Society* (Winter): 34.

Sethi, S. Prakash. 1978. "An Analytical Framework for Making Cross Cultural Comparisons of Business Responses to Social Pressures: The Case of the United States and Japan." *Research in Corporate Social Performance and Policy,* ed. Lee E. Preston, Greenwich, Conn.: JAI Press.

———. 1975. *Japanese Business and Social Conflict.* Cambridge, Mass.: Ballinger.

———. 1974–75. "Why Japanese Business Is Losing Its Halo." *Business and Society* (Winter):35–43.

———. 1972–73. "Getting a Handle on the Social Audit." *Business and Society* (Winter):34.

Sherk, Donald R. 1974. "Foreign Investment in Asia: Japan vs. the U.S." *Columbia Journal of World Business* (Fall):98.

Social Responsibility Disclosure 1978 Survey. 1978. New York: Ernst and Ernst.

Szepon, Susan B. 1980. "Corporate Social Responsibility—An Update." *Journal of Accountancy* (July):80.

U.S., Department of the Treasury, Comptroller of the Currency. 1978. *Banking Circular No. 120: Community Reinvestment Act of 1977.* October 6.

Part VI

THE TRANSFERABILITY
OF JAPANESE
MANAGEMENT SYSTEMS
TO THE UNITED STATES

The primary purpose of studying Japanese management systems is to ascertain whether some of the systems that have proven effective in Japan could be transferred to U.S. organizations. In this part, we include nine chapters that discuss some of the ways to adapt Japanese systems to U.S. corporations.

Tony Hain, in "Japanese Management in the United States," presents the results of a study of 20 Japanese-U.S. organizations. The study strongly suggests that management practices are a key factor behind the Japanese success and that they can successfully be applied in the United States. This chapter presents 15 strategic organizational and managerial characteristics of Japanese firms managed in the United States.

John D. Blair and Jerome V. Hurwitz contribute "Quality Circles for U.S. Firms? Some Unanswered Questions and Their Implications for Managers." In this chapter, the authors thoroughly review the Japanese management technique of quality circles (QC). They point out the difficulty of adequately measuring the success of QC programs, even in blue-collar jobs. Thus, the basic issues for American managers to consider are whether QCs can be effectively utilized in U.S. industries, particularly those with predominantly white-collar work forces, and whether the anticipated results are worth the anticipated costs of implementation. The conclusion drawn is that quality circles can be useful in some U.S. industries under certain circumstances, but that they should be considered only one additional element in the U.S. managerial arsenal and employed judiciously.

The next chapter, by Ken I. Kim and Harold I. Lunde, is "Quality Circles: Why They Work in Japan and How We Can Make Them Work in the United States." To understand the "quality circles phenomenon," the authors assess societal values in Japan, facilitating elements in Japanese firms' immediate environment, and internal management practices favorable to quality circle activities in Japanese firms. The chapter also takes a look at aspects of the U.S. corporate environment and management practices to determine the transferability of this unique Japanese participative management technique. Ways in which U.S. management can create the facilitating organizational climate are then discussed, along with practical suggestions for implementing the program in U.S. companies.

Michael J. Cleary et al. contribute "The Quality Circle Process: The ASQC Model for Success." This chapter is the final product of the American Society for Quality Control Technical Subcommittee on How to Achieve a Successful Quality Circle Process. It presents a detailed description of the quality circle process of the ASQC model.

Robert J. Barbato and Richard E. Drexel, in "Americanizing Quality Circles," present a case study involving a Fortune 500 organization in the northeastern section of the United States. A program introducing quality circles has been launched. To ensure that the program will be successful and will spread effectively throughout the organization, several innovative steps have been taken. These steps are thoroughly discussed.

In "The Experiential Approach to Organizational Training and Development Programs: Application in Japanese Universities," M. Tom Basuray and Stephen E. Blythe investigate the use of simulation in business administration courses in Japanese universities. The results of questionnaires sent to 50 Japanese business professors are analyzed in this chapter.

David T. Methé, contributes "The Japanese Way of Management: Does It Make Sense for U.S. Firms?" This study analyzes the success of current Japanese managerial techniques in light of several cultural and organizational components of Japanese industry. The argument is put forth that the answer to the high level of productivity exhibited in Japanese industry does not lie only in the culture or the current organizational structure of Japanese industry, but in the interaction of the two. The implications of the interaction of culture and organization for application to U.S. industry are outlined. It is concluded that it will be difficult to adopt the Japanese techniques directly and that they must be adapted to the U.S. cultural and organizational milieu.

"Theory Z — Question Y: A Conceptualization on the Application of the Product Life Cycle Approach to the Theory Z Concept," by P. K. Shukla, considers Theory Z and Japanese management methods. These have received increased interest and exposure recently; yet several questions remain as to the present position and future of transference of Japanese concepts to U.S. corporations. This chapter applies the product life cycle approach to the Theory Z concepts. Based upon empirical data and qualitative analysis, a conceptualized curve is developed. Using the curve, five phases (introduction, growth, maturity, decline, and revision) are identified and analyzed as to time frame; academic, research, and consulting implications; and managerial orientations.

Kenneth D. Ramsing contributes "The Easy Answer Isn't Here." As one effort to bolster the productivity decline, U.S. industry has been tempted to launch into a rapid use of Japanese management concepts and techniques. In this chapter, the author suggests that the temptation to jump on the bandwagon must be tempered by taking into account many of the current attitudes and practices of U.S. management. Of great importance is an understanding of the adversarial relationship of management, government, and unions. That relationship is quite different in Japan, and is of critical importance to the success of many Japanese management processes.

30

Japanese Management in the United States

TONY HAIN

Much has recently been written about Japan's outstanding economic success. Cars, televisions, motorcycles, cameras, watches, and semiconductors are six examples of products where Japanese companies have become dominant. How did a tiny island nation — possessing limited natural resources, located far from export markets, and with a population only one-half of our own — become such a formidable economic force?

To explain this "economic miracle," many U.S. executives and business analysts have pointed to "Japan Inc." as the basis for this success. Japanese firms, according to this view, have a close, cooperative relationship with unions, banks, and the government, which has given them a comparative advantage over their competitors. Other experts have pointed to their ancient island culture and homogeneous society as the basis for their success.

While it is true that all of these factors constitute important reasons behind the Japanese success, another significant reason often goes unnoticed. Consider these examples:

1. Matsushita Company purchased Motorola's television plant in 1974. Under Motorola management, workers were building television sets with 150 defects per 100 units. Seven years later, with largely the same work force, the same plant is producing televisions with three defects per 100 sets. At the same time, production volume has increased by over 40 percent.

2. Sony Corporation in San Diego set a U.S. record by operating 200 consecutive days without a major quality defect. This year the San Diego plant will turn out 700,000 color television sets, one-third of Sony's total world production. This success led Sony to build another facility in Dothan, Alabama. This new facility started with a work force of 200 in 1977 and now employs 1,500. Sony's sales in the United States have more than doubled from 1977 levels of $500 million to nearly $1.3 billion in the latest fiscal year, and U.S. employment currently stands at about 4,500 people. Sony recently announced a major restructuring of its operations that will significantly add to its manufacturing base in the United States.

3. Nissan Corporation has begun building a truck assembly facility in Smyrna, Tennessee. Over 800 acres of land have been purchased with a capital investment of over $500 million — the largest direct foreign investment that any Japanese firm has ever made in the United States. Company executives fully expect product quality at this location to be equal to, if not better than, product quality at Nissan in Japan.

4. Honda of America currently produces about 4,000 motorcycles each month at the Marysville, Ohio, facility, with quality ratings that are the envy of many U.S. firms. Additionally, Honda recently announced groundbreaking for a 900,000 square-foot car assembly plant, where it plans to build 10,000 Honda Accords a month, starting in 1983.

5. Hitachi, Kikkoman, Yamaha, Toshiba, Sanyo, YKK, Sharp, and Kawasaki provide further examples of Japanese firms that have set up successful U.S. operations.

In these U.S. operations, it must be remembered, Japanese firms have had to deal with *our* workers, *our* governmental regulations, *our* diverse culture, *our* workers' values, and even — in some cases — *our* unions. Many American managers said it couldn't be done, but the Japanese have done it.

Have the Japanese firms developed a magic management formula or a new economic calculus that gives them a strategic advantage over their competitors? My investigation of these firms revealed that they had not. What they have done — as described in the following sections — is to develop a synergistic organizational paradigm in which all strategies and managerial methods fit into a remarkably well integrated system. The firm's strategy is highly congruent with the way tasks are organized, and with the managerial methods employed. Such a fit results in a high degree of effectiveness that can serve as a role model for U.S. firms to follow.

My study disclosed a set of 15 characteristics of Japanese-owned firms operating in the United States. The main characteristics that emerged are discussed under three headings — strategy, structure and organization, and managerial practices (See Table 30.1). While no single firm had all, or even half, of these characteristics, they did, in general, employ them to a greater extent than U.S. firms I am familiar with.

The reader should note that my investigation was not a scientifically, highly controlled, and explicitly defined study. Instead, I chose a case study procedure to understand better the subtleties and nuances of these firms. During my study, I interviewed over 100 Japanese and American managers, from 20 different U.S. facilities.

STRATEGY

Longer Planning Horizons

One of the most consistent features of the Japanese-U.S. manufacturing strategy — one shared by U.S. and Japanese managers — was the longer time horizon that is used to evaluate and judge company performance. I found Japanese firms consistently evaluating their U.S. operations with five- to ten-year time horizons. Taking a longer view of their businesses, these managers are less driven by short-term profit concerns and thus are

TABLE 30.1 Characteristics of Japanese Firms Operating in the United States

---

Strategy:
  Longer planning horizons
  Quality as key business value
  Avoidance of unions
  Preference for rural plant location
  Manufacturing emphasis on excellence

Structure and organization:
  Building small plants
  Flexible organizational structure and emphasis on coordination
  Reduced number of organization levels
  Egalitarian emphasis
  Company-sponsored social events

Managerial practices:
  Emphasis on employment security
  High information density
  Management by *wa* (harmony)
  Selection, placement, and training emphasis
  Limited use of quality circles

---

more able to make investment decisions that lead to future growth. One Japanese manager observed that he did not want to entertain any business decision that had less than a five-year operating impact — "My operating managers should take care of these," he said. Another chief executive — an American with 37 years of experience as a key executive in a major U.S. firm — offered this comparison: "At Ford the bottom line was always king. You had to produce higher earnings quickly, or you were out." At Nissan, he said, "It is not whether you make the budget that really matters, but rather how hard you *try*."

The Japanese firms place more emphasis on the balance sheet than on the profit-loss statement, and consider market share more important than rate of return. As a result, they are more willing to make important investments in new plants, equipment, and manufacturing processes.

Many Japanese managers interviewed felt that too many top corporate positions in U.S. firms are filled by people who are financial wizards, but who know very little about the fundamentals of the businesses they run. Additionally, Japanese managers question the efficacy — if not the validity — of a number of commonly used yardsticks, such as "discounted cash flow" and indecipherable "hurdle rate" formulas, all biased toward the short term. What is needed, they argue, is less financial detachment of "the fourteenth floor" and more nuts-and-bolts understanding of the factory floor.

An interesting finding becomes immediately apparent to anyone who visits Japanese-U.S. firms: there is, to my knowledge, no financial person holding down the key executive position in any of the facilities I visited.

Quality as Key Business Value

Another important strategic feature of these firms is their almost fanatical concern with product quality. Product quality is pursued with an almost religious zeal, and product quality is perceived as a strategic weapon for increasing market share and financial performance. A theme often heard in these facilities is "if we make a better-quality product than our competitors, customers will buy it." This simple business principle has great importance in shaping not only firm strategy but also managerial attitude on the factory floor.

Concern for quality has become a part of the culture in these firms. Nearly all managers interviewed — down to the lowest level — had illustrations of how they had improved quality. "You cannot inspect quality into the product," said a Japanese manager, "you have to build it into the product from the beginning." As these managers move up the corporate ladder, no doubt they will become role models for newcomers and their concern for quality will continue.

Avoidance of Unions

While the work force in Japan is highly unionized—more so than in the United States—Japanese firms are extremely reluctant to have their U.S. facilities organized. My research suggests that fewer than 10 percent of the 110 Japanese manufacturing facilities in the United States are organized at present.

Japanese-U.S. firms go to great lengths to avoid unions, which they see as hampering their flexibility and "family style" of dealing with their employees. "We want to keep the union out to maintain our corporate philosophy," says a Japanese key executive. "We want to keep our family whole and not have a third party interfering."

What is the primary advantage that these firms gain from operating without unions? Many might answer that the biggest advantage is lower wages and benefits. My study suggests otherwise. The greatest benefit that such companies derive from not being unionized is increased flexibility in improving their productivity in both the short and the long run.

It is interesting that Ford Motor Company, in an effort to improve operating performance, has recently asked the United Auto Workers for substantial work-rule concessions to keep Ford plants productive and viable. The goal of these concessions is to give management more operating flexibility and, presumably, to facilitate productivity improvements.

A U.S. labor relations executive of a major Japanese motorcycle firm offered this comparison between his nonunionized firm and a comparable unionized U.S. competitor: "Our hourly work force is almost exactly the size of their (the U.S. firm's), yet we have only 20 different job descriptions versus 150 for them. This reduction in job classifications gives us a significant competitive advantage with respect to labor force utilization that they do not have." It is worth observing that, shortly after these remarks were made, the U.S. motorcycle firm went out of business. A manager of the U.S. firm noted, "We can't compete with them."

As Japanese companies open more and more U.S. operations, they are finding that it is becoming increasingly difficult to keep their operations union-free. U.S. unions that were unable to organize a number of Japanese plants that opened here in the early 1970s are now, through intensified campaigns, beginning to succeed.

In 1980, three Japanese firms have been organized by three different unions. Perhaps the most significant of these union takeovers occurred at the San Diego plant of the Sanyo Electric Company. Earlier this year, 540 workers voted, by a 55 percent margin, to join the Communications Workers of America (CWA). This union success is remarkable, since the California electronics industry is about 99 percent union-free ("Japanese U.S. Plants Go Union," 1981, p. 70). The International Brotherhood of Electrical Workers (IBEW) won the right to represent 630 workers at the Sharp

Manufacturing Company in Memphis, Tennessee, earlier this year. The United Auto Workers (UAW), which had tried unsuccessfully to organize the Honda of America motorcycle plant in Marysville, Ohio, was recently successful in gaining a small foothold in the company by organizing a handful of employees in the boiler operation.

The most important test of U.S. labor versus Japanese-American management is likely to occur in 1983, when the UAW will attempt to organize the work force of over 3,000 employees at the Nissan facility in Smyrna, Tennessee.

Management at Nissan and in other Japanese-U.S. operations are working hard to avoid the "we versus them," adversarial attitude that they believe hampers quality and productivity. These companies project a sense of caring to the worker, have established elaborate employee communications programs and built family recreational facilities, and conduct extensive training programs in an effort to instill intense loyalty and trust in the work force. "We are not antiunion," notes Marvin T. Runyon, president of Nissan U.S.A., "we are proworker. What we are going to do at Nissan is to create a working environment where everybody will want to pull in the same direction. We need to close the needlessly adversarial and counterproductive atmosphere that often separates management and labor in the U.S."

During my study, it became apparent that the union-organized Japanese facilities were more American in character, were less productive, and had a lower quality of work life than those without a union.

Preference for Rural Plant Location

Japanese companies initiating operations in the United States almost always choose rural or suburban plant sites — mostly in the South or Southwest. While transportation, distribution, and logistical factors play a role in selection of plant sites, several other situational factors are also important. These factors include the quality of the work ethic and the chances of remaining nonunion.

Japanese managers have found the work ethic to be stronger in rural than in urban areas. They feel that worker commitment in rural areas is stronger and that employees are less alienated from work in general. Yuzaburo Magi, executive vice-president of the Kikkoman Soy Sauce plant at Walworth, Wisconsin, made this observation regarding the quality of U.S. labor:

> I believe work ethic is closely related to environment. Walworth is an agricultural community. Farmers look at their crops from beginning to end; trans-

planted to the factory, it's following the product from the input of raw materials to the finished goods. People close to agriculture know they must work hard in order to gain a good crop or profit. Our Japanese plants also happen to be situated in farming areas, and our workers there bring the same attitude toward their work (Magi 1981, p. 98).

Not only do many of the companies carefully choose rural plant sites, but they frequently locate them in southern states in an effort to avoid unions. As mentioned, Japanese managers prefer to keep their operations union-free.

Manufacturing Emphasis on Excellence

While my study did not initially focus on manufacturing methodology, it quickly became evident that superior manufacturing performance is a key factor behind the Japanese success in the United States. Contrary to popular opinion, the factories I observed did not use any exotic or magical manufacturing techniques; the techniques used are also present in many U.S. operations. My observations of these facilities led me to the same conclusion that Robert H. Hayes (1981) reached in his investigation of Japanese firms in Japan: The Japanese have achieved their present level of manufacturing excellence not from using advanced technologies like robots, but from doing simple things very well and by looking continually for ways to improve their operation. My observations suggest that the Japanese strive always to do the basics a little better by paying close attention to every step in the manufacturing process. "The nail that sticks up is hammered down," says the Japanese proverb.

Another surprising characteristic of Japanese-U.S. manufacturing methodology was its relative simplicity. Complex and sophisticated operations are often managed in simple, human ways that seem to work extremely well. Machine up-time, for example, was reported to be much higher than in typical U.S. operations. "We are not choking in our own bureaucracy," said Clinton Michaelis, general manager of Sony Magnetics. "We don't manage complexity with even more complexity."

Japanese-U.S. firms try to simplify their operations to a level at which production difficulties are minimized; if difficulties occur, they are easily corrected. My observation is that too many U.S. firms have become so enamored of complex production and material control procedures that they create control systems that are reasonable but, unfortunately, often do not work well.

Other areas to which the Japanese direct special consideration are creating a clean, pleasant work environment for employees; carrying out preventative machine maintenance; and paying close attention to materials management issues. Careful attention to these manufacturing basics has resulted in greater machine up-time, reduction of work-in-process inventory, and higher levels of quality and productivity than in comparable U.S. operations that I am familiar with.

STRUCTURE AND ORGANIZATION

Building Small Plants

A very important similarity between Japanese operations in the United States and those in Japan is the propensity for building small plants. A recent study of Japanese employment revealed that a significant majority of the work force — approximately 70 percent — was working in firms with fewer than 500 employees (Mead 1981). Similarly, the companies in my study were far smaller than typical U.S. firms. For example, the following distribution of size for 25 Japanese firms operating in the United States was found by Mark Fruin (1980).

Size of Sites	Number of Firms
Less than 100 employees	13
100 to 300	10
300 and over	2
	25

Japanese managers have found that smaller plants provide a higher quality of work life, along with a reduced rate of absenteeism, lower turnover, and less grievance behavior. The combination of these factors translates directly into higher productivity and satisfaction levels simultaneously.

Even where the number of employees working at a particular location is large, Japanese managers — in their effort to maintain a focus in the factory — typically parcel this group of employees into a number of smaller units, to promote personalized management attention for better labor relations. They keep their plants small — usually between 200 and 500 employees — to maintain closer management contact with employees.

Flexible Organizational Structure and Emphasis on Coordination

"The right hand must know what the left is doing": this is a widely shared value among the firms I visited. These firms' leaders think that effective coordination among different functional units is absolutely essential to successful operating performance. If there is any one characteristic of these firms, it may be their constant emphasis on organizational commitment, inculcation of a sense of duty, and the need to have everyone "pull in the same direction." As a result of this emphasis, these firms have evolved an extremely flexible organizational form where line and staff distinctions, manual of job descriptions, and status differentials are minimized. In fact, in quite a few firms I visited, the ambiguity of line and staff distinctions resulted in having the same person occupy both line and staff positions. This usually occurred at higher levels in the organization, where, for example, the vice president of production often may also serve as the vice president for research and development.

This flexibility in organizational structure is not without its "downside" risks. Doubling up of assignments or unclear reporting relationships often created tension and consternation among American managers. One high-level American manager complained that he never knew who from Japan might call and give him a new directive or change in assignment. "It's frustrating," he noted, "never to know who might call from Japan and tell you to do something. I'm not sure I know to whom I report half of the time."

An extremely difficult assignment for anyone visiting one of these facilities is to get one of the Japanese managers to bring out the organizational chart or to provide job descriptions for different functions. These managers would usually respond, "Yes, we do have job descriptions and organizational charts, but we really don't use or need them very much." "Around here," they said, "flexibility in assignment and ease of cooperation is expected and, therefore, did not have to be written down. We try to instill into the work force that anything and everything that makes the product better is their responsibility."

Reduced Number of Organizational Levels

In an effort to facilitate vertical communication flow and reduce the amount of indirect labor, Japanese operations tended to have fewer salaried layers than the U.S. organizations I am familiar with. Many of the firms, for example, would often not have a general foreman position; instead, a "team leader" would assume both first- and second-level supervisory responsibilities. This combination of duties, along with the doubling-up procedure mentioned earlier, allows Japanese operations to reduce their indirect employment and simultaneously to improve their ability to communicate with workers, because they have removed at least one barrier to good communication flow.

Egalitarian Emphasis

Driving into the parking lot of most Japanese firms, one immediately becomes aware of the conspicuous absence of preferential parking for key executives. Upon entering the plant, the visitor is also struck by the absence of many customary symbols of corporate rank and status. Everyone — from the vice-president to the janitor — not only competes for the same parking spaces, but eats in the same cafeteria, receives the same fringe benefits, and has his or her office in the same "bull-pen" area. In some firms, this egalitarian attitude goes even further. For example, in a few firms, everyone is referred to as an associate of the firm, or everyone — including the vice-president — punches the time clock when coming to work, or wears the same company uniform.

Numerous other examples of the egalitarian orientation can be found. In one case, an American-born president of a major Japanese firm agreed to sit on a dunking platform during a company picnic. Employees were asked to take turns throwing balls at a target that, when hit, would cause the president to be dunked into a tank of cold water. "It was important for me to show these people that I put my pants on the same way as they do," said the president. In another company, a major trading firm, the main lobby has only a "corporate family album" for visitors to read. "We want our customers and guests to know that our company is the people we employ and that we consider them to be our most important resource," remarked the vice-president of this firm. A final example is that executive offices are extremely spartan by U.S. standards. In one firm, the production manager had his desk located immediately next to the main assembly line, right on the factory floor.

Management commitment to employees is demonstrated not only symbolically, but also through certain policies and practices. Most firms are committed to job security, extensive training programs, promotion from within, and sponsorship of many social events. "Everyone swims in the same pot," said one Japanese manager.

Company-Sponsored Social Events

In an effort to instill a family atmosphere within the work force, firms place much emphasis on company-sponsored social and recreational activities involving employees and their families. Company-sponsored athletic teams, picnics, banquets, recreational facilities, and extensive excursions are actively used to promote good will and a sense of belonging among employees. "These activities are very important to our managerial formula," said an executive of a large electronics facility. "They foster not only harmony among workers, but they help convey the idea that management is keenly interested in them, and also in their families."

Driving into many of these facilities reminds one of driving into a recreational complex, as baseball diamonds, golf courses, and fabricated lakes are often present. The additional cost of these activities and facilities is significant — averaging approximately 1 percent of payroll, according to one estimate. In one facility of approximately 450 employees, the labor relations director had a budget of $100,000 earmarked for company-sponsored social activities. This amounts to over $2,200 per employee.

MANAGERIAL PRACTICES

Emphasis on Employment Security

"How could anyone expect good teamwork, group loyalty or a common interest in raising productivity when almost half of the work force will either quit or be laid off within twelve months?" asks Lester C. Thurow, a distinguished American labor economist (Thurow 1981, p. 66). New labor-saving machines that lead to improvements in productivity will not be acceptable to workers who feel that their job security is threatened. "Who would be willing to raise productivity if it means that they would be out of a job?" asks a Japanese executive. Recent statistics reveal that, in 1980, labor force turnover — due to layoffs and quits — averaged four percent per month in U.S. manufacturing firms ("Where Management Fails" 1981). "Who can build a high-quality work force interested in long-term growth and prosperity," asks a Japanese manager, "when almost 50 percent of the labor force either quits or is laid off every year?"

While no Japanese-U.S. firm in my study guarantees lifelong employment to employees, the firms studied all strive to make the workers feel psychologically secure in their jobs. They have not committed themselves to guaranteed employment, nor have they said that workers will never be laid off, but they go to great lengths before considering lay-offs. For example, during the 1974-75 recession, a worried American manager of a new Sony subsidiary in this country contacted the chairman of the board in Japan. The American manager explained that the subsidiary was "drowning in red ink," as the warehouse was full and no one was buying the products. The American manager suggested that a lay-off was necessary to bring costs in line with declining sales. The Japanese response was an emphatic no: "Think of this as a blessing," the chairman suggested. "If our workers see that we will not lay them off under these severe economic conditions, we will be the beneficiary of their increased motivation and commitment in the future." Employee morale and performance there are currently "sky-high."

During the present economic showdown, the Kawasaki motorcycle plant in Lincoln, Nebraska, found that it needed only 270 of its 320 hourly work force. Rather than lay any workers off, the plant put the extra employees on special project jobs within the plant.

Another example comes from YKK, the world's number-one maker of zippers. Tadahiro Yoshida, the senior managing director, said, "At our U.S. plants we've adopted a mixed American-Japanese style. We do not practice the lifetime system. Instead, we call it 'stable employment.' If we face difficulty, we first proportionately reduce wages of all employees from general manager down to the lowest-paid employee. Only if we can't manage do we resort to a lay-off."

Japanese managers believe strongly that job security has a positive impact on quality of work life and productivity, limits employee turnover, and improves the morale of the total organization. As a result, they are more willing to increase their costs temporarily and accept a temporary negative impact of carrying all employees.

Most of these operations — because of their rapid growth — have not yet had to deal with this problem, although the Kikkomon company had to institute across-the-board wage cuts in an attempt to stabilize employment during the last recession. In this study, only one Japanese firm (whose leaders wished not to be identified) has ever had to lay off employees.

If U.S. operations truly want a loyal labor force, interested in raising productivity and with high morale, lay-offs, it seems to me, have to become the last, rather than the first, resort when the firm is facing an economic downturn.

High Information Density

Perhaps the most striking contrast between Japanese and U.S. firms lies in the greater volume of information available to employees. My study led me to conclude that the average hourly employee in Japanese-U.S. firms has approximately the same information base — with respect to company affairs — as middle-level managers in the large U.S. manufacturing firms with which I am familiar.

Not only are data on product quality and manufacturing performance available, but detailed financial data for the firm and industry are also provided — often in extremely explicit form. Once, after visiting a Hitachi plant, I went into a local drinking establishment that was frequented by Hitachi employees after work. Sitting next to me were two hourly employees who began talking about international currency risk, market share, and other industry-related issues that might have an impact on Hitachi's success. These workers, to my surprise, were talking about topics normally limited to executives or MBA students at top business schools. When I asked where they learned about such topics, they replied, "These issues were discussed at our recent quarterly business meeting."

Most firms in my study had weekly meetings between supervisors and workers, quarterly meetings with top-level executives, and, in some cases, yearly meetings that included even the chairman of the board. In one facility, even retirees were invited back once a year for a yearly business update. While the content of these meetings varied from providing industry, production, or operating data to merely listening to employee concerns, these meetings did project a sense of caring and provided an excellent forum for communication among workers at all levels.

In a recent study of 3,000 employees over a three-year period, a significant correlation was found between management communication and such performance measures as absenteeism, grievances, medical visits, and efficiency (Hain 1982).

Management by *Wa* (Harmony)

While management is an integral aspect of every characteristic thus far discussed, the emphasis placed on promoting harmony and good will among all corporate units deserves individual mention.

Japanese managers strive to treat their American employees more as members of the corporate family than as mere hired hands. Emphasis goes toward managing through shared values rather than through complicated procedures and rigid company policies. Mutual trust and confidence are developed by creating an environment where all employees work well together, with minimal procedures and a powerful sense of direction. Japanese managers emphasize teamwork and group performance — even, in some cases, over direct individual contributions. For example, at the Yamaha musical products factory, an American employee turned in a suggestion that resulted in considerable savings to the company. In turn, he received a polite letter from the firm's chairman that said, "Congratulations, you have just contributed to your own security and to the security of the company." The employee was incensed because his individual suggestion was not more directly rewarded, according to the personnel director.

How do Japanese and American managers differ? According to the co-founder of Honda Motor Company, "[they are] 95 percent the same and differ . . . in all important aspects" (Pascale and Athos 1981).

One important difference is that U.S. managers tend to be tough, macho and bottom-line-oriented. The winners in U.S. firms are "tigers, executives who play 'hardball' ". In the United States, apparently, decisiveness is valued, and decisions based on rational analysis and concrete facts are demanded. Bonuses and promotions supposedly motivate and emphasize individual performance. Japanese managers, on the other hand, can be tough, but do not admire toughness. They prefer to delay decisions, often waiting for more data. They realize that there are times when it is better to wait and accept the ambiguity inherent in situations rather than strive for logic, clarity, and immediate action.

While teamwork, consensus, and harmony are all desirable attributes that Japanese-U.S. firms strive to obtain, these characteristics do carry some "downside" risks. American employees may resent the time it takes to make decisions, and may thus be less patient with a longer decision-making process. At the Sharp Manufacturing Company in Memphis, for instance, the communications director believed that slowness in decision making was responsible for the union's success in organizing that facility. "Employees were particularly upset at the slowness of decisions on revising the company's medical plan, adopting a pension plan, and deciding whether to let employees buy Sharp products at a discount," he said. "Japanese executives just don't make rash statements" ("Japanese U.S. Plants Go Union" 1981, p. 75).

Even though decision making via *wa* may often be tedious and sometimes interminable process of compromise, Japanese managers believe that, in the end, the organization benefits because all members are in agreement with organization's goals.

Selection, Placement, and Training Emphasis

Since employees are considered the firm's most valuable asset, it follows that great care is taken to select the best employees. At Honda, for example, every employee is hired after screening by two three-person panels of employees — representing all levels in the plant — who determine if the employee fits in with the others already hired. All six must agree that the person should be hired.

At Sony, prospective employees, after making formal job applications, were invited to attend classes conducted by the company at the local high school. Those attending were then evaluated in terms of their aptitude and positive attitude. Those who displayed these characteristics were subsequently hired.

Japanese managers prefer to hire young employees, because they find them more malleable and group-oriented. The average age at Kawasaki, for example, is 27 years. "Older employees tend to be more independent and set in their ways," said the plant manager.

A high level of education also is characteristic of Japanese-U.S. firms. The average educational level — even on some of the assembly lines — may include one year or more of college.

In talking with Mitsuyo Hanada, a Japanese management recruiting consultant, I was struck by the criteria he used to select American managers for Japanese-U.S. operations. "I am looking for three qualities — shyness, seriousness, and hard working," he said. "The Japanese firms want up-front people who don't play management games, and we love people who are hard-working." Shyness, however, was such a surprising quality I asked him to explain. "We don't want the independent macho man up there making all the decisions, tearing things up. We prefer quiet, sensitive men who take a softer, gentler approach to things. We prefer management by *wa*," he said.

Extensive training is conducted to inculcate company philosophy and to increase job and product knowledge. At the Nissan site in Tennessee, for example, a 30,000 square-foot training center is being built at the same time as the plant. In addition, over 400 employees will be sent to Japan for up to four months of training, according to the firm's president. Other firms in my study also make extensive use of training and often send large numbers of workers to Japan to increase job skills and to show U.S. employees what work commitment, motivation, and performance are really like.

The firms in my study conduct intensive training for four primary reasons: (1) to improve job-related skills; (2) to introduce new recruits to high performance standards; (3) to instill company philosophy; and (4) to foster dedication to continuing self-improvement as a way of increasing one's value to the company and work group.

Management training is also widely conducted — especially in the new firms — as a way of instilling company philosophy and developing future managers. A vice-president of a major trading company remarked, "We feel that the distribution of managerial talent is much greater than what is commonly thought in the U.S. Our feeling is, given the appropriate training, a large number of employees — rather than a selected few — are capable of performing management functions."

Job rotation and careful employee placement are also stressed. My study suggests that Japanese-U.S. firms are quicker to rotate employees through jobs *at the same level*, but are more reluctant to promote managers vertically. The Japanese promotional strategy is designed to make more employees feel that they are slated for top positions. The public identification of "winners," "water walkers," or "high-pots" is delayed so as not to increase the resentment of the losers — who greatly outnumber the winners. The feeling of Japanese managers is that by not making early or quick promotional decisions, they can capitalize more fully on the total work force, which more than compensates for any decrease in motivation that may result from not promoting the "water walker" group quickly. Young American managers I interviewed, however, seem to resent this procedure, at least judging from our conversations; they feel their advancement would be more rapid in a traditional firm. These same employees also think that in too many cases the top jobs are held by Japanese managers.

Limited Use of Quality Circles

What I fully expected, but did not see, was the use of quality circles — even on a limited basis. Much to my surprise, the Japanese-U.S. firms did not use this much publicized technique. Only one firm was seriously considering introducing quality circles. "It's not that we are against QCs," said a Japanese manager, "in fact, we consider them to be an important technique for improving worker morale and productivity simultaneously. We feel, however, that you just don't start up QCs until the organization is ready for it."

Japanese managers point to rapid growth rates of their U.S. subsidiaries, increased job mobility and shift changes, a more independent and less group-oriented work force, narrow job descriptions, union resistance, and lack of middle management commitment to QCs as major roadblocks that need to be overcome.

CHALLENGE TO MANAGEMENT

Certainly there are important differences between Japan and the United States in culture, government policy, relationships with unions, and capital markets. Yet, despite these differences, my study strongly suggests that the key elements of Japanese management practice at not unique to Japan but can successfully be applied in the United States as well.

My purpose in studying these firms was not to provide a recipe for organizational success; nothing would be more of a mistake than merely "plugging in" these characteristics in the hope of alleviating organizational ills. My goal, rather, was to describe the variety of ways that Japanese firms have been able to create a work environment where employees take an active interest in raising productivity and in the firm's success. Japanese-U.S. firms are successful because they have recognized the synergistic value of combining all of the firm's resources — technical, financial, and, especially, human — into a well-integrated pattern.

REFERENCES

Fruin, Mark. 1980. "Japanese Manufacturing Enterprises in the U.S." Paper presented at the Japanese Investment Conference, San Francisco, March 21.

Hain, Tony. 1982. "Productivity and Communication." In *Organizational Communication*, ed. Calvin W. Downs. International Communication Association.

Hayes, Robert. 1981. "Why Japanese Factories Work." *Harvard Business Review* (July-August):57–66.

"Japanese U.S. Plants Go Union." 1981. *Business Week*, October 5, pp. 70–75.

Magi, Yuzaburo. 1981. "How Japanese Manage in U.S.?" Interview in *Fortune*, June 15, p. 98.

Mead, Christopher. 1981. "Small Business in Japan." *Inc.* (November):67.

Pascale, R. T., and A. G. Athos. 1981. *The Art of Japanese Management: Applications for American Executives*. New York: Simon and Schuster.

Thurow, Lester C. 1981. "A Plague of Job Hopper." *Time*, June 22, p. 66.

"Where Management Fails." 1981. *Newsweek*, December 7, p. 78.

31

Quality Circles for U.S. Firms? Some Unanswered Questions and Their Implications for Managers

JOHN D. BLAIR *and* JEROME V. HURWITZ

INTRODUCTION

The success of the Japanese economy in recent years has generated among American managers a growing fascination with the Japanese style of management. Recent research has attempted to analyze carefully the Japanese approach and to show in what ways, if any, such approaches can be transplanted or adapted for U.S. firms (Cole 1979b; Ouchi 1981; Pascale and Athos 1981).

Although they constitute only one part of the broader Japanese approach to corporate management, quality (control) circles have begun to spread rapidly throughout U.S. industry. Perhaps because of their apparent low cost and ease of implementation, they have become for many American managers the concrete representation of the Japanese art of management.

The main purposes of this chapter are threefold: first, to review the quality circle (QC) concept; second, to raise a series of significant questions that at this point remain unanswered; and, third, to discuss some of the managerial implications of these questions for the implementation of quality circles in the U.S. work force.

BACKGROUND

Interest in quality circles has continued to increase in recent years (Juran 1980, 1967; Papst 1972; Yager 1980; Cole 1980b, 1979a, 1979b). Quality circles represent an organizational intervention whose primary objective is to increase an organization's productivity and the quality of its products through direct employee participation. The underlying assumption is that such participation will result in useful suggestions for improving work methods and/or quality control, and in employee commitment to implementing change based on the suggestions. The name "quality circles" is derived from the basic process, wherein a small group of employees, doing similar work, volunteer to meet periodically to discuss their production and quality (as well as quality-related) problems, investigate causes, recommend solutions, and take corrective actions to the extent of their authority. The technique generally includes the following:

1. A company-wide steering committee of both union and management representatives decides where quality circles should be introduced within the organization and what types of problems are appropriate for the quality circles to work on.
2. Approximately ten employees from a work unit meet voluntarily with their immediate supervisor for one hour a week to discuss ways of improving productivity and related issues.
3. The group and its leader are trained in group dynamics, problem solving, data analysis, quality control, and presentation of information and recommendations to management.
4. The quality circle meetings are held on company time and at company expense.
5. The decision to implement any of the group's suggestions remains ultimately with management.
6. External facilitators, usually company employees, offer guidance and assistance to the quality circle group.

This technique, originally developed from U.S. quality control and management techniques, has reportedly been used with great success by Japanese industry since the early 1960s (Juran 1967; Cole 1979b; Ouchi 1981). The technique was experimentally tested in the United States by Corning Glass and other companies; then Lockheed Missile and Space

Company became, in 1974, the first U.S. corporation to initiate a large-scale quality circles program. By 1977, Lockheed estimated, quality circles had saved the company approximately $3 million. The ratio of savings to cost of operating the circles was reported to be six to one. The number of defects caused by manufacturing process problems had dropped 67 percent. Lockheed later directed its efforts toward helping other U.S. companies start QC programs. Today several large corporations, including General Motors, Honeywell, and Westinghouse, employ this technique. Westinghouse, for example, started with the approach developed at Lockheed, but has developed its own program and currently has over 800 circles in operation (Obringer and Dent 1981).

SOME UNANSWERED QUESTIONS

The reported success of quality circle programs, such as those at Lockheed and Westinghouse, with the increased interest in the reasons behind Japanese productivity, has generated considerable interest by American managers in the possible utility of quality circles for increasing lagging productivity. While reports of success are typical, several questions remain to be answered before the large-scale introduction of quality circles can be recommended for U.S. companies. These questions include the following.

How much must quality circle programs be adapted to the U.S. workplace, given the fundamental differences between Japanese and U.S. cultures and management philosophies? Although quality circles have been successfully introduced not only in Japan but within several segments of U.S. industry, their potential broader effectiveness for U.S. industry remains in question. U.S. management and the U.S. work force differ in many respects from their counterparts in Japan. The most fundamental question here is whether quality circles can survive as an alien graft or transplant that may be just another isolated program within many used by American managers, or whether it must be the impetus for broader changes in corporate management philosophy in order to have any substantial impact. Can QCs be successful as a limited program or must they be incorporated into a more broadly defined solution to the problems faced by American managers, as argued by Pascale and Athos (1981)?

> The problem isn't simple, and neither is its solution. No quick introduction of uncoordinated parts will address the whole problem. Quality control circles, "Theory Y" reorganizations, team building, two-week organizational development programs, etc., etc. — each has its uses, but unless there is an overall *fit* of all the managerial parts across time there will be little sustained leverage and few results. (p. 201)

Must American managers strive for Ouchi's Theory Z-type organization (or observe the "Seven S's" of Pascale and Athos) to use QCs successfully, or can they effectively stand alone?

How effective will quality circles be with a predominantly white-collar work force? Most quality circle programs in the United States and Japan have dealt primarily with blue-collar production employees. Mixed success has been reported in Japan in programs tested with its white-collar work force. Since a large proportion of the U.S. work force is white-collar, it is essential that we carefully determine, before the widespread operational implementation of quality circles programs, their potential impact on these employees. The self-initiated nature of much white-collar work, the difficulty of establishing precise performance measures, and attitudes of individualism may serve as barriers to effective quality circles programs with white-collar workers. It is possible, of course, that some of these same characteristics could facilitate the performance of QCs. How to turn what many see as barriers into positive factors that would contribute to QC success is still not known.

What are the underlying motivational and social processes in QCs that are responsible for their success? Although there are a variety of published reports of success with this technique, there has been little systematic attention given to what aspects of the QC process are responsible for its success. There are three potential reasons for the success of QC programs: (1) the attention given by management to production employees, perhaps for the first time (for example, the Hawthorne effect); the facilitation of the group's interaction by virtue of the process-oriented aspects of the team-building and employee participation component of QCs (such as the emphasis on improving group dynamics); the unique productivity-, task-oriented nature and methodology of the QC program (for example, the focus on data analysis and problem-solving techniques).

Our understanding of these processes is more incomplete because QC programs are much more recent in the United States than in Japan, and the possibility of the Hawthorne effect is greater. In addition, the consensus-oriented, participative approach and the quality control training for lower-level employees are new to most U.S. companies that have introduced QCs.

A better understanding of these processes is essential for successful implementation or modification of QC programs in the United States. However, it is also important to understand what is making the greatest contribution, to ensure that QCs are the most cost-effective way to achieve desired productivity changes or to decide whether, for example, management attention alone would have nearly the same effects without the sizeable cost of QCs.

How successful have QC programs actually been? As indicated above, measuring the success of QC programs in the white-collar sector will probably be difficult. However, even in blue-collar jobs, the reported successes probably exceed the actual effectiveness of programs in three basic ways: first, there is a clear bias toward reporting successes, not failures, so it is difficult to estimate the relative probability of success; second, cost savings are often estimated through savings in employees' time, which is then assumed (but not demonstrated) to be spent in being more productive rather than in resting or in some other nonproductive way — thus the actual extent of success is unclear; and, third, the cost of the program — including the facilitators, their supervisors, general program management, coordination time, training materials, and the work of the steering committee — is often underestimated or not all-inclusive.

How effective are quality circles in relation to other, more conventional organizational interventions? Is the specific task-oriented quality circle process more effective in increasing productivity than other methods, such as team building, that emphasize improving interpersonal relations within the work group and between supervisors and subordinates? Alternatively, would an even more explicit attempt to match the technical and social systems, as in the sociotechnical system approach, prove to be a superior method? Indeed, would the U.S. companies be made substantially more effective through increased capital expenditures for office automation among their white-collar workers rather than through QCs? These different approaches are, of course, not mutually exclusive, but their relative effectiveness should be considered. A recent comparison with other types of organizational intervention has looked at the common and unique aspects of QCs (Blair, Hurwitz, and Sokol 1981). U.S. firms need not see QCs as the only option for productivity improvement.

How can quality circles be most effectively introduced? Should a quality circle program be implemented directly through ongoing work groups? Alternatively, are quality circles more likely to be effective if they are implemented as a second phase of organizational intervention — for example, only after a first phase that has focused on improving the existing interpersonal processes within the work group so that levels of distrust are minimized and positive feelings between supervisors and employees and among fellow workers have been facilitated? This would be consistent with past observations of quality circles that have indicated that such programs work best when there are already good management-employee relationships, and that they are more likely to fail when such conditions do not exist.

How can the programs be sustained over time? The initial success of many kinds of innovative productivity and quality-of-work-life programs has not been sustained. Recent research shows that as many as 75 percent of initially successful programs were no longer in operation within a few years (Goodman 1980). Even Lockheed, the initial QC proponent in the United States, has reportedly moved away from quality circles. Perhaps most sobering is the following quotation from Robert Cole (1980b), one of the leading authorities on the Japanese labor force:

> The fact is that the circles do not work very well in many Japanese companies. Even in those plants recognized as having the best operating programs, management knows that perhaps only one-third of the circles are working well, with another third borderline and one-third simply making no contribution at all. For all the rhetoric of voluntarism, in a number of companies, the workers clearly perceive circle activity as coercive. Japanese companies face a continuing struggle to revitalize circle activity to insure that it does not degenerate into ritualistic behavior (p. 30).

Thus, even if there were no significant differences between Japanese and U.S. systems of employment and levels of organizational commitment that make the Japanese work environment considerably more suitable for such a participative technique, one would find such an evaluation of the actual long-term success of QCs in Japan in marked contrast to the reports of consultants and others who advocate the immediate and widespread implementation of this "proven" technique.

With several years of QC experience behind them, the managers of Westinghouse's program are attempting to find innovative solutions to the problem of sustaining their program over the long term (Obringer and Dent 1981). Research is clearly needed to find ways to keep QCs viable and productive in the long run if they are to justify their financial and organizational costs.

SOME IMPLICATIONS FOR MANAGERS

In addition to raising these unanswered questions, one should also think carefully about the potential negative as well as positive implications of the widespread introduction of QCs. The point is to find ways not only to increase the probability that the program will do what it is expected to do, but also to increase the probability that the program will not lead to unanticipated consequences that are harmful.

It is widely recognized in principle (but easy for managers to forget) that there are two fundamentally different ways in which organizational interventions of any kind can fail. The first of these is that the program itself does not work at all or does not work as effectively as anticipated. The second type of program failure occurs when the program, whether successful or not, produces a series of other problems that were not anticipated. This latter type is most easily overlooked in planning for organizational change. Of course, experiencing both types of program failures can have quite negative consequences for the organization that introduced the program. Both of these types of program failures are possible when QCs are implemented.

The first type of program failure might be represented by a QC program that simply failed to get many volunteers or that failed to produce useful suggestions for quality or productivity improvements. One example of the second type of program failure could be a QC program that was perceived by the union or middle management to be a major threat, and that exacerbated existing union-management conflict or affected the implementation of other programs because of resistance or low morale on the part of anxious or resentful middle managers.

An example of simultaneously experiencing both kinds of program failures could be a QC program that greatly raised expectations of improved productivity on the part of top management, but did not fulfill those expectations. This could occur in a program that was either ineffectively implemented or implemented in an inappropriate situation. The program could generate fear and hostility on the part of workers as well as middle managers. Such a set of program failures would result in an organization that did not receive the expected benefits of QC-induced productivity improvement, but did suffer from worsened worker and supervisor morale and heightened union-management conflict — which in turn lowered overall productivity.

Some of the implications to be drawn from the above considerations, as well as from the unanswered questions raised earlier in this chapter, include the following.

Managers should first conduct a careful organizational diagnosis to ensure that an organizational development intervention is appropriate. That is, they should be sure that their problem is not caused primarily by general problems of organizational design, out-of-date equipment, or technical design, rather than by group processes or other types of problems addressed by organizational development interventions. Such a diagnosis may require consulting with those inside or outside the organization who are knowledgeable about various sources of and solutions to organizational problems.

If such an intervention is needed, managers should be sure that quality circles are the most appropriate type of intervention. Other types of organizational interventions, such as team building, job enrichment, sociotechnical approaches, or even alternative work schedules, may be more suitable and potentially more effective in a specific organization or situation.

Managers should not have inflated expectations of what quality circles are likely to do. Expectations should be reduced in terms of both scope and time. Quality circles may lead to a significant cost saving or some other major productivity improvement, but in any particular organization they are unlikely to do more than make minor improvements. They may even do no more than improve the group dynamics of the work group or improve job satisfaction without improving productivity. (This, of course, may be a major goal of the manager, but it is a different issue from productivity improvement per se.)

Whatever the improvements that may result from a QC program, they are not likely to occur quickly. Even under the best of circumstances, there is a long period of planning, organizing, and training before the circles are able to operate efficiently. In addition, the actual solution to any problem (or even the suggestions for changes that the group is likely to arrive at) will probably take some time to materialize and even longer to implement beyond the immediate work group.

Managers should not introduce QCs into organizations that are under extreme stress. Organizations in trouble, especially where acrimonious union-management conflicts or high levels of distrust between employees and management exist, will not generally be good candidates for QCs. QCs are not effective substitutes for healthy labor-management relations; neither are they miracle cures for management problems that actually require fundamental changes in organizational policies and new strategic directions.

Managers should be concerned about the financial and organizational costs of large QC programs throughout the entire organization. The financial costs of introducing and maintaining a QC program and a separate staff of facilitators are sizeable. The costs of extensive coordination and resolving potential conflict between departments and work groups may also be great for the organization and its managers.

Managers should probably expect, first, that a substantial proportion of the quality circles will fail from the start and, second, that an even higher proportion of those that are initially successful will not continue to be successful over the long run. Unless very carefully introduced — with strong support from top management, through an effective steering committee, and with well trained and committed facilitators — QC programs will generally encounter strong resistance from middle mangers and distrust from unions and workers. Even with skillful implementation, resistance and distrust may still exist and can lead to circles that fail. In addition, competing management pressures for increased production during the peak period of the month or the year may result in infrequent meetings and deterioration in interest and effectiveness. Some programs are likely to deteriorate as different policy emphases appear, as personnel change both among management and among members of the work groups, as the rewards of participation and recognition becomes less attractive over time, or as overt labor-management conflict allows adversarial rather than cooperative arrangements to reemerge.

Managers should start a QC program only after they have openly and candidly considered whether they are willing to make a commitment to changing their management style and to expanding the nature of employee participation. Since QC programs represent "bottom-up" management, their widespread and long-term success within an organization will require a commitment on the part of management to a more fundamental change away from a "top-down" management style, greater responsiveness to workers, and a reconceptualization of workers' capabilities and the value of their participation. A lack of prior commitment to making these changes may lead to the sudden termination of the program when pressure for broader change develops. Eliminating programs defined as successful by the participants will probably lead to considerable organizational stress and conflict. QCs raise the expectations of workers (and first-line supervisors) with regard to changes in responsiveness to their contributions and in management's style. Pulling out of a QC effort may make the situation far worse than if the effort had not been started at all. Managers can probably expect, at a minimum, decreased employee commitment and morale combined with increased cynicism and resistance to future change. Of course, these attitudes may have a considerable, negative impact on productivity and product quality — the reverse of the apparent impact of positive attitudes resulting from participation in a successful QC effort.

If there is widespread introduction of QCs, there should be not only careful procedures for program evaluation, but also an explicit commitment to developing research projects that can answer some of the questions that remain unanswered. Thus, if there are operational programs (subject to the managerial considerations suggested above), there should also be experimental programs were careful research is being conducted to ensure that answers are generated for the questions we have raised here. The purpose of that research would be to try to change the probabilities of both types of program failure by more clearly understanding the group and organizational processes that lead to program success.

It would be unrealistic and inappropriate to expect that introduction of operational programs into U.S. firms will cease until all the research answers are in. Such a realization, however, should not preclude organizations from conducting systematic research to answer these questions about QCs at the same time that some programs are introduced.

CONCLUSIONS

Quality circle programs can and do work both in the United States and in Japan — but not all the time, nor in all places, nor necessarily as well as expected. In this chapter, we have raised some troubling questions and looked at some of their implications for American managers.

QCs should be viewed in the broader context of organizational change and productivity improvement. They are clearly a potentially valuable addition to the repertoires of American managers — but only when they are used with realistic expectations, by managers committed to responding to the broader organizational changes they may lead to, and are introduced into appropriate organizational settings, where success will be more likely.

REFERENCES

Blair, J. D., J. V. Hurwitz, and M. B. Sokol. 1981. "Comparing Quality Circles with Other Organizational Interventions: A Model for Managerial Decision-Making." Paper presented at the Annual Meeting of the Academy of Management, San Diego, Calif., August.

Cole, R. E. 1980a. "Learning from the Japanese: Prospects and Pitfalls." *Management Review* 69, no. 9 (September):22–28, 38–42.

_____. 1980b. "Will QC Circles Work in the U.S.?" *Quality Progress* (July):30–33.

_____. 1979a. "Made in Japan: Quality Control Circles." *Across the Board* 16, no. 11 (November):72–78.

_____. 1979b. *Work, Mobility and Participation: A Comparative Study of American and Japanese Industry.* Berkeley: University of California Press.

Goodman, P. S. 1980. "Quality of Work Projects in the 1980s." *Labor Law Journal* (August).

Juran, J. M. 1980. "International Significance of the QC Circle Movement." *Quality Progress* (November):18–22.

_____. 1967. "The QC Circle Phenomenon." *Industrial Quality Control* 23 (January):329–36.

Obringer, V. G., and D. L. Dent. 1981. "Quality Circles: Innovative Elements Are Vital to Long-Term Success." Unpublished paper from Westinghouse, Integrated Logistics Support Division.

Ouchi, William. 1981. *Theory Z: How American Business Can Meet the Japanese Challenge.* Reading, Mass.: Addison-Wesley.

Papst, W. R., Jr. 1972. "Motivating People in Japan." *Quality Progress* (October):14–18.

Pascale, R. T., and A. G. Athos. 1981. *The Art of Japanese Management: Application for American Executives.* New York: Simon and Schuster.

Yager, E. 1980. "Quality Circles: A Tool for the '80's." *Training and Development Journal* 34, no. 8 (August):60–62.

32

Quality Circles: Why They Work in Japan and How We Can Make Them Work in the United States

KEN I. KIM *and* HAROLD I. LUNDE

A quality circle consists of a leader and usually eight to ten members participating voluntarily to identify problems (usually related to quality) and to find and implement solutions. The first quality circle was organized in Japan in 1962 under the leadership of the Japanese Union of Scientists and Engineers (JUSE) and especially K. Ishikawa, often called the father of quality circles in Japan (Dewar 1976). There are about 1 million registered and unregistered quality circles in Japan (Gryna 1981). As of December 1975, 500 quality circle conferences had been held in Japan (Asao 1976). The first quality circle in the United States was organized in 1974 in the Lockheed Missiles and Space Company, Inc. under the leadership of Wayne S. Rieker, manufacturing manager, and Doland L. Dewar, quality control circle coordinator in the Missile Systems Division Manufacturing (Rieker 1976). Although quality circles got off to a slow start in the United States, the number of U.S. companies applying this concept is estimated to approach 1,000 and the number of circles, 10,000 (Diener 1981).

In Japan, billions of dollars of savings have been achieved through millions of quality circle projects, and tremendously improved worker motivation and communication have been realized as a result of the quality circle movement (Juran 1978). Can we be part of this success story? Some observers are optimistic (Gryna 1981); some are more cautious (Cole 1980). We do not believe, however, that the issue is whether quality circles can or cannot be used in the United States. The transferability of quality circles to U.S. corporations is believed to hinge upon understanding how they work, building a facilitating climate, and, finally, careful planning and implementation. The purpose of this chapter is to address these three questions:

1. What makes quality circles work in Japan?
2. Which elements of the Japanese system are transferable and how can we create the facilitating organizational climate in the United States?
3. How should we implement the program in U.S. companies?

WHAT MAKES QUALITY CIRCLES WORK IN JAPAN?

According to the internationally known quality control expert J. M. Juran (1967), the quality circle movement in Japan is "a brilliant achievement — a tour de force in management leadership." It is not that the Western industrial world has not had experience with somewhat similar worker participation programs. The Scanlon plan, Zero Defects (ZD) programs, the system of Stakhanovism and its derivatives as practiced in Eastern Europe, and the familiar suggestion boxes are just a few of the better-known programs. Japanese quality circles are distinguished from the rest, however, by their spectacular accomplishments, which were realized by "harnessing the interest, the time, and the ingenuity of the work force." This use of the employee's maximum energy and productive contribution, well above the minimally acceptable level of job performance, is at the heart of the effectiveness of quality circles in Japan. It appears that it took a unique fusion of a highly motivated, highly trained work force and a facilitating internal organizational climate for quality circles in Japanese companies to obtain such phenomenal results. The profiles of the organizations and the employees involved in successful quality circle operations in Japan may be summarized as follows:

Organizations:

1. High quality awareness throughout the entire organization
2. High priority accorded to quality control and quality circles

3. A wholistic philosophy of employee development
4. A sense of goal congruency between management and workers, and between management and labor unions
5. Relatively stable, long-term employment practices

Employees:

1. Loyalty and commitment to the work group and the organization
2. Good training both in jobs and in quality circle tools
3. Intrinsic work values and preferences for learning, mastery of craft, creative accomplishments, and recognition through work

How have the Japanese companies acquired these sets of organizational and employee characteristics? To answer this question, we will analyze the facilitating factors existing in Japan on the following three levels: (1) societal values; (2) immediate environment of firms; and (3) internal management practices of firms. Figure 32.1 summarizes these three sets of factors, their interrelationships, and subfactors comprising these factors.

 ## Societal Values

As both Japanese and Japanologists agree, the influence of Zen Buddhism and Confucianism on Japan and its people has been pervasive. Zen Buddhist contemplation and self-discipline had a great impact on the early ruling class — the samurai, or warriors — as early as the Kamakura era (1185–1333). This influence laid the groundwork for *bushido* (the way of the warriors), and still remains as a distinct strain in Japanese *kokuminsei* (national character). However, it was the rationalism and pragmatism of Confucianism that helped establish during the premodern Tokukawa era (1603–1867) the basic structure of political, social, and economic institutions in Japan. During this prosperous, peaceful period spanning two and a half centuries, the basic Japanese value system is believed to have been formed (Burks 1981). Three components of this value system will be discussed.

Wa

Wa (harmony) can be dated back to the Confucian perspective of natural law. An ideal society should be run on the basis of natural law. *Wa* represents the proper relationship, dictated by this natural law, between the ruler and the ruled, and also between individuals. Individuals should strive to develop harmonious relationships with others, groups, and the ruler. Individuals are valuable to the extent that they contribute to the harmonious

FIGURE 32.1   Factors Contributing to Quality Circle Success in Japan

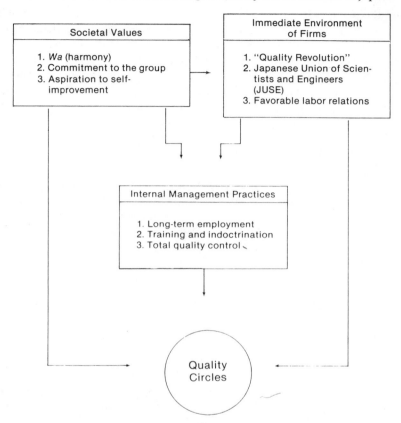

Source: Compiled by the author.

functioning of the whole (Riggs and Seo 1976). The first article of the "Seventeen Article Constitution," issued by Prince Shotoku in 604, summarily attests to the centrality of *wa* to Japanese society when it reads: "*Wa* is a virtue, and make it a rule not to dispute" (Krieger and Lee 1981).

Commitment to the group

This component is closely related to *wa*. Groups are seen to provide a continuous flow of nourishment and blessings to individuals. These benefits, in turn, establish obligations for individuals. Group commitment is considered the most fundamental value in Japanese society and permeates practically all social institutions (Burks 1981).

Aspiration to self-improvement

Confucian emphasis on ethical conduct planted in the Japanese a strong desire for self-improvement and education, which heavily influenced the attitudes of the Japanese toward work. Work is considered not only a means to
compensation, but a way to grow and achieve high ideals in life. One may
argue that this Confucian work ethic is not unique; the Protestant work
ethic of the West may be similar as far as the impact on worker motivation
is concerned. However, one important difference should be noted. While
prosperity and secularism have eroded the Protestant work ethic in the
minds of many workers in the West, the Confucian work ethic has strongly
survived *kindaika* (modernization) of Japan, and thus far shows little if any
sign of abatement.

Quality circles have been enormously successful in Japan mainly because of the circle members' will to learn and grow, and to apply what they
have learned for the good of the organization. Japan's value system provided Japanese workers with a fertile soil for cultivating this will. Now we turn
to the more immediate environment of Japanese firms, which is more directly related to the development of quality circles.

Immediate Environment of Firms

"Quality revolution"

The first environmental element is the way in which the Japanese approached
their quality problems. This approach may best be described by the term
"quality revolution" (Juran 1978; 1974). Japan's industrialization has only
about a century's history. It was started as part of broad social reform inspired by the Meiji Restoration of 1868. Although Japan had achieved fast
industrialization and quickly emerged as a world power between the two
world wars, it was faced with serious product-quality problems during the
reconstruction period after World War II. The national policy of establishing an export-driven economy, which was necessitated by a lack of natural
resources, was threatened by the widely publicized poor quality of the
country's products. As a counter measure, Japanese industrial and governmental leaders carved out a revolutionary approach to this problem.

As many Japanese quality experts acknowledge, the awareness of the
importance of quality control can also in part be attributed to the work of
two American quality control consultants in Japan in the early 1950s. W.
Edwards Deming conducted lectures in statistical methodology starting in
1950, and J. M. Juran taught training courses in the management aspect of
quality control starting in 1954 (Gryna 1981). However, it should be remembered that, after this initial stimulus, Japanese industry carried out
the necessary steps for fully developed quality control programs.

Among the policies developed by Japanese industry is the complete debugging or scrub-down of new products before they reach markets (Juran 1978). This policy poses a sharp contrast to the common Western practice of pushing products to the market without complete debugging. This Western practice assumes that good field service will be provided to compensate for the field failures, and that a follow-through will be made to complete the scrub-down after the model has gone to market. In practice these assumptions have rarely proven valid.

Another example illustrating the Japanese quality revolution is total quality control. In a nutshell, this is a quality control system designed to build in quality rather than "inspect it in." Details on this system are discussed later in conjunction with the internal management practices of Japanese firms.

Japanese Union of Scientists and Engineers (JUSE)

The second facilitating environmental factor in Japan has been the pioneering role of the Japanese Union of Scientists and Engineers (JUSE). Since 1962, when JUSE founded quality circle programs, it has been heavily involved in various activities to promote the quality circle movement (Asao 1976; Rieker 1976). JUSE operates the Quality Control Circle Headquarters, and through its national organization (eight regions and 30 sections), various promotional programs are carried out. Some of the activities of JUSE are:

1. Serving as a registration center for quality circles
2. Holding symposiums and conferences, organizing training sessions, and administering quality circle awards
3. Publishing journals and training materials
4. Financially supporting quality circle conferences

Although the American Society for Quality Control was the chief promoter of quality circles in the United States in the early 1970s, it has failed to become a JUSE equivalent. More recently, the International Association of Quality Circles, with headquarters in Midwest City, Oklahoma, has published training materials and a journal and sponsored conferences and training sessions.

Favorable labor relations

The last facilitating environmental factor for quality circles in Japan is favorable labor relations, which are considered by many quality circle experts a key to the success of quality circle programs (see Cole 1980, for example). Unions tend to view unfavorably any management effort toward greater efficiency on the work floor. In Japan, the spirit of *wa* largely guides the interinstitutional relationships and helps to effect a harmonious, symbiotic unity. (This unique aspect of Japanese society has been recently popularized in the phrase "Japan, Incorporated.") Within the firm, management and labor generally enjoy a similar cooperative relationship. Reinforcing this relationship are certain aspects of labor union organization and employers' relationships with unions. In Japan, union organization parallels company organization — from home office down to regional and plant organizations — and union ties between companies in the industry are weak. Thus, Japanese unions have inherently weaker organized power than their U.S. counterparts, which are organized across many companies, usually by industry or craft.

Apart from the organizational aspect, Japanese companies use tactics to neutralize union power. A common practice in Japan is illustrated by an example at the Kawasaki Iron Mill of Nihon Kokan, one of the largest steel mills in Japan (Tsuda 1974). Management influences the election of union officers by working through key employees, who are loyal to the company and also are influential union members, to ensure that only employees acceptable to management will be elected. Management also stays at the hub of the company-worker communication system by sponsoring a myriad of informal groups. At the Kawasaki Iron Mill, these informal groups are set up in each unit of the company organization, often even at the *han* (crew) level. These groups may also be organized on the basis of school graduated from, length of service, or job status — for example, in the Toyota Automobile Manufacturing Company, separate meetings of *kumicho* (section chiefs) and of *hancho* (crew leaders) are organized. In these informal meetings, formal issues such as additional overtime work are often discussed and the leaders of these groups work to persuade employees to accept plans agreeable to management, thus bypassing costly union negotiations.

So far we have discussed facilitating factors existing in the immediate environment of Japanese firms that have contributed to the phenomenal growth of quality circles in Japan. Next, we will analyze the facilitating factors within Japanese firms, namely, the internal management practices of Japanese companies that have been favorable to the development of quality circles.

Internal Management Practices of Firms

Within Japanese companies, three unique management practices define the internal climate of work and favorably influence quality circle activities.

Long-term employment

It is estimated that about one-third of the Japanese work force is under the *nenko* (permanent employment) system (Oh 1976; Tsuda 1974). Under *nenko*, the employer guarantees employment until the usual retirement age at 55. *Nenko* is adopted only by large companies as a measure to secure a committed, loyal work force. Employees in small and medium-sized companies are not protected by *nenko* and may be called, at best, medium-term employees. Temporary, subcontract, and retired workers hired by both *nenko* and non-*nenko* companies are the first ones laid off during market slumps. This may lead one to conclude that the notion of guaranteed employment in Japan is an overstatement. However, even non-*nenko* companies retain their regular employees (as opposed to temporary employees) much longer than in the United States, and the employees are more committed to long-term relationships with their employers.

Long-term commitment and employee loyalty are most notable among *nenko* employees. *Nenko* is a product of both cultural heritage and economic necessity. Culturally, it is an extension of the Confucian family concept; economically, it is a solution to persistent labor shortages, which accompanied rapid industrialization, especially after World War I (Sumiva 1965).

Nenko employees are hired mostly directly from schools and farms at a relatively low beginning compensation level. Subsequent wage and salary increases are based largely upon the length of service, with the large increases that occur during the later period of employment creating a deferred reward system (Fujita 1962). Although in some industries compensation based upon job classification is playing an increasingly larger role (for example, in the Japanese steel industry, it accounts for as much as 20 percent of a worker's monthly earnings), the length-of-service payment system is still dominant (Tsuda 1974). Along with basic wages and salaries, employees are paid a variety of allowances, for almost fully meeting their total needs, and a large lump-sum payment upon retirement. Guaranteed employment, deferred compensation based upon the length of service, and the employer's holistic concern for the employee's total needs create a tremendous amount of loyalty and dedication on the part of *nenko* employees (Ouchi 1981). Albeit to a lesser degree, the same is true among non-*nenko* employees.

Training and indoctrination

Along with the practice of long-term employment, a major feature of Japanese personnel management is intensive on-the-job training. Because of employers' preference for youthful workers, newly hired recruits usually lack needed job skills. That situation creates the need for training at work. Training in the form of job rotation is widely practiced. A variety of job experiences is considered a necessary qualification for assuming managerial responsibilities.

Along with job training, the typical Japanese company utilizes a complex system of employee indoctrination to imbue employees with company values and loyalty. This indoctrination involves both formal and informal processes. Formal processes include group meetings, company songs, slogans, and publications, company picnics, group calisthenic practice sessions, and so on. Employees also participate in informal group activities, such as after-hours parties and group tours. Interested readers are referred to Ouchi (1981) and Pascale and Athos (1981) for further details. Burks' (1981) observation of a unique behavior pattern of Japanese managers succinctly illustrates the powerful effect of this socialization process in Japan. He found that Japanese bank employees who were attending training sessions at Rutgers University usually introduced themselves by family name followed by the company affiliation, while the American participants usually specified their functional specialties after introducing their names. Essentially, the typical Japanese employee is a "Sony man" or some other "company man," and that is considered before his other attributes.

Total quality control

As was briefly mentioned earlier, total quality control (TQC) in Japan is designed to "build in" quality. In U.S. companies, quality control is usually the responsibility of a separate quality control department. However, in Japanese companies, quality control is primarily the responsibility of production line management. Furthermore, it involves all functions — not only production, but research, development, design, purchasing, sales, and accounting (Juran 1967). In all of these functional areas, all levels of management — from top management down to the individual employees — are responsible for quality control.

As a result, the level of quality awareness is very high at all levels of management in Japanese companies. Cole (1980) illustrates the essentiality of quality awareness as a precondition for quality circles by citing what a Japanese manager of a U.S.-based operation of Matsushita Electric of Japan had to say about his experience. Although Matsushita is well known for its successful quality circle operations in Japan, Nakai, the Japanese co-manager of quality at the Matsushita-owned Quasar television plant outside Chicago, did not feel that he should start quality circles at Quasar, largely because of the extremely low quality awareness among his American employees. Needless to say, in Japanese companies, the importance of quality is deeply instilled throughout the entire corporate hierarchy. It is clearly understood in Japan that quality is seldom, if ever, a trade-off issue — if quality and efficiency requirements collide with one another, quality generally wins. In Toyota's Kanban production and inventory control system, a worker can stop the entire production line if he or she finds it necessary to do so to correct a problem (Monden 1981). The Japanese concept of quality and related management practices strike a sharp contrast to the predominant U.S. industry practice of putting efficiency and volume before quality.

EXPLORING TRANSFERABLE ELEMENTS OF THE JAPANESE SYSTEM AND CREATING THE FACILITATING ORGANIZATIONAL CLIMATE IN THE UNITED STATES

So far we have reviewed some factors believed to be responsible for the remarkable achievements of Japan's quality circle movement. More specifically, we have examined the facilitating factors at three levels: societal values, immediate environment of firms, and internal management practices. It is clear that some of the Japanese values, institutions, and management practices are not compatible with the cultural, economic, and institutional realities in the United States. The philosophies of *wa* and total commitment to a group do not go well with Western individualistic values, and can even be dysfunctional by stifling creativity (Tsuda 1974). Practices such as guaranteed employment and employee indoctrination are probably, at best, economically difficult or culturally aversive in the United States.

We do not recommend blind emulation or adoption of Japanese ways. However, we recognize the need to learn selectively from the Japanese and to create consciously in U.S. industry a supporting mechanism for quality circles that is compatible with our values and institutions. Fortunately, there have been a few significant developments in recent years in the internal and external environment of U.S. corporations that signal remarkable changes favorable to the implementation of quality circles.

First, an increased concern for product quality has been shown by both consumers and businesses. This is in part attributable to the inroads made in U.S. markets by Japanese products such as cars, color televisions, and other consumer electronic products. Along with the American consumer's quality perceptions and experiences, a number of published reports have confirmed the view that some Japanese products have better track records in terms of defects and frequency of repairs. Consumer resistance to poor quality has been evidenced recently by the car-buying behavior of the many Americans who paid more for imports than they would have for comparable Detroit models, and waited longer for delivery. One may argue that the lack of fuel-efficient domestic models played a role here, but no one can deny that dissatisfaction with the perceived quality of some U.S. cars was in the minds of many car buyers. In response to consumer pressure and harsh economic reality, many U.S. manufacturers, notably the Big Three automobile manufacturers, appear to have adopted a policy that represents a major shift toward giving a higher priority to product quality (Cole 1981a; 1981b; Potter 1981).

Second, an era of improved management-labor relationships seems to be in the offing. Threats from foreign competition, widespread lay-offs in key industries, and the realization that labor's share cannot grow if productivity growth remains low appear to have prompted both labor and management to reassess their traditional antagonistic stance toward each other. General Motors' Quality-of-Worklife program, which is jointly promoted by GM management and the United Auto Workers, is an example of renewed labor-management cooperation (Gryna 1981; Potter 1981).

The third development is U.S. management's increasing awareness of worker dissatisfaction with demeaning, repetitious jobs. In U.S. industry today, the predominant task design is characterized by highly specialized, simplified jobs. Since Taylor's formulation of the concept of strict division of labor between managers and workers, workers have been expected to carry out simplified tasks designed by managers and engineers. This system, unfortunately, is not compatible with today's workers, who are better educated, more sophisticated, and pursuing more diverse life goals than in the past (Juran 1980; Mortimer 1979). Management has become more aware that increased worker participation in management, which allows a stronger sense of accomplishment on the job, is a necessary measure to reduce worker alienation (Potter 1981).

Despite such favorable developments, efforts still need to be concentrated in certain areas to create the facilitating climate for the successful transfer of quality circles to the United States. Many prudent observers conclude that Western organizations have failed to make the most of what an employee is able to offer to an organization (Pascale and Athos 1981). Japanese companies have demonstrated that they can harness a much higher level of employees' energy — physical, mental, and even spiritual (in the nondeified sense). Quality circles are a prime example of such total application of employee ability.

The concept of quality circles is unique in that the ability of relatively unskilled, uneducated production floor workers is fully utilized. This approach is counter to the traditional simplistic view of workers held by many American managers. While "Japanese employers appear strongly committed to developing the skills of their employees fully, American employers tend to think that increased efficiency comes not from workers' initiatives or commitment but from guidance offered by an educated management and from better technology" (Cole 1979). By and large, U.S. management has not had high expectations of workers, and this has, to some extent, become a self-fulfilling prophecy. The necessary first step toward establishing a favorable environment for quality circles in U.S. industry is to change traditional management assumptions about workers and expect them to be partners in management.

A second step needs to be an increased emphasis on worker training and development. The relative lack of concern for training is due in part to the widely held assumption that most quality problems are motivational problems — "they can but they won't." Many problems, however, will remain unresolved even when worker motivation has been improved, if workers have not received proper training (Juran 1967).

Third, U.S. management needs to operate with a longer time horizon. Compared with volume increases or cost reductions, quality improvements may take longer to obtain. They may take longer to show up favorably on the income statement, but they will show up eventually. Also, quality circles bring about many intangible and hard-to-measure benefits, such as favorable changes in worker morale and communication. It may be all but impossible to measure the financial impact of these intangible benefits on a short-run basis, but they affect the survival and well-being of the company in the long run. In fact, U.S. industry's overemphasis on short-term objectives — the relentless drive to maximize earnings per share every quarter of the year — has been blamed by a number of observers for many of our current economic and business problems (for example, Lohr [1981]).

IMPLEMENTING THE PROGRAM IN U.S. COMPANIES

The effective implementation of quality circle programs in U.S. companies, like any other new management program, must be tailor-made, to some degree, to fit the specific situation in each company. Obviously, the development of detailed plans for implementing quality circles in specific companies is beyond the scope of this chapter. We have attempted here to discuss three broad areas — planning, training, and administration. It is hoped that this discussion will help to provide an outline or starting point for the development of specific plans for implementing quality circles in U.S. companies.

Planning

Management should first assess the economic and behavioral reality of the organization to see if the minimum requirements for quality circles are present. Substantial instability in the work force due to frequent lay-offs and highly antagonistic attitudes of workers toward the company may be indications that the company is not ready for quality circles. Many companies spend about six months planning before they start their quality circle programs (Gryna 1981). Planning usually involves the following phases (but not necessarily in this order):

1. Select coordinator(s) who are capable in both technical and interpersonal aspects, well respected by both management and workers, and, most of all, personally interested in quality circles.
2. Study other quality circle programs through a review of the literature, visits to other companies, and assistance from consultants.
3. Educate and gain commitment from upper management and union leaders.
4. Prepare or obtain training material. The International Association for Quality Circles and companies with quality circle experience may be contacted.
5. Expose all employees to the quality circle concept.
6. Organize a steering committee, and select facilitators, circle leaders, and members.

A typical circle organization is illustrated in Figure 32.2, using the example of Federal Products Corporation (Hanley 1980).

The following is a brief description of quality circle organization:

1. Circle members. The size of circles may vary from three to 15, but the typical size is about ten. For effectiveness, large circles are often divided into subcircles. Circle members participate voluntarily. Unwilling or uncommitted members only hamper the circle's effectiveness.
2. Circle leaders. Circle leaders are either elected by members of the circle or appointed by management from the rank of first-line supervisors or foremen. Since circle leaders play a key role in training and leading circle members, it is essential that they be able to learn new concepts and lead and relate to others. They must have task-related knowledge and skills as well. They should also be team players — quality circles do not need "stars."
3. Facilitators. Facilitators supervise circles and often train circle leaders. They also act as liaison between circle leaders and the

FIGURE 32.2   Quality Circle Organization

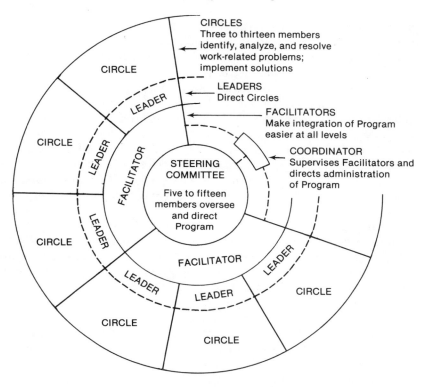

CIRCLES
Three to thirteen members
identify, analyze, and resolve
work-related problems;
implement solutions

LEADERS
Direct Circles

FACILITATORS
Make integration of Program
easier at all levels

COORDINATOR
Supervises Facilitators and
directs administration
of Program

STEERING
COMMITTEE

Five to fifteen
members oversee
and direct
Program

CIRCLE

LEADER

FACILITATOR

Source: Hanley (1980). Copyright 1980 by American Society for Quality Control, Inc. Reprinted by permission.

steering committee. Since solutions devised by circles should clear upper management, facilitators should possess an ability to deal effectively with upper management, job experience, and communication skills. A facilitator should also be flexible, creative, and adaptive.

4. Steering committee. This is the highest-level coordinating body for quality circles. Usually, it is composed of department managers, upper-level engineers, general foremen, personnel managers, and union leaders. The head of the steering committee usually acts as the quality circle coordinator. The function of the steering committee is to plan, organize, and provide management support for quality circle activities.

Training

Training is the most crucial aspect of quality circles. The first phase involves training of circle leaders and facilitators. The second phase is the training of circle members by circle leaders and facilitators. The success of Japanese quality circles may be, in large part, attributed to their strong philosophy of employee training and development, and to their thorough and rigorous training programs. Unlike most of their U.S. counterparts, Japanese managers seem to subscribe to the belief that "workers will if they know how." Assisted by the practice of long-term employment (which renders training less costly because of low turnover) and the value attached to learning, the Japanese appear to have developed highly the art of employee training. Ishikawa (1972) sums up the importance of training and education by saying, "Quality control starts with education and ends with education."

Training involves relatively simple quality circle concepts and tools. U.S. quality control engineers probably have used most of these tools over many decades. What is most remarkable about Japanese training programs is that they teach the use of relatively sophisticated concepts and tools to production floor workers who do not normally have much formal education. Specific tools often taught are:

1. Pareto maldistribution charts to identify "vital few" problems
2. Cause-effect diagrams or Ishikawa fishbone diagrams to analyze causes of problems (Ishikawa 1976; Juran 1978; 1974)
3. Histograms, graphs, and control charts
4. Stratification
5. Binomial probability

Administration

A few of the points that need to be addressed in the administration of quality circle programs are discussed below.

Meetings

Meetings are usually conducted outside of regular working hours, normally with overtime pay, to minimize disruption of on-going operations. (In Japan, 44 percent of meetings are held outside of working hours, and 83 percent of participants receive overtime pay (Nakazato [1976]). Meetings should be held in a relaxed, freewheeling atmosphere. Often the brainstorming technique is utilized to get as many creative solutions to a problem as possible. Team play is to be emphasized.

Compensation

Intrinsic rewards are the primary compensation for participating in a quality circle. Examples of intrinsic rewards for quality circle participants are (1) recognition through company publications, awards, banquets, and so on; (2) opportunity to attend quality circle conferences and workshops and meet other workers involved in quality circle activities; and (3) opportunity for presenting projects to upper management.

Although monetary rewards are downplayed, and usually no payments are made beyond overtime pay for the period spent in circle meetings, Cole (1980) suggests that some form of sharing by circle members of gains may be advisable, in view of U.S. workers' high propensity for immediate rewards.

Scope of projects

Circles usually deal initially with quality problems in production operations; but ultimately the project scope expands far beyond this. Currently, Japanese quality circles have expanded circle activities to (1) productivity, cost, maintenance, and safety; (2) service operations such as warehousing, transportation, purchasing, and telephone use; and (3) subsidiaries and suppliers (Gryna 1981). Even some company chauffeurs have quality circles in Japan.

CONCLUSION

The quality circle technique appears to present profitable opportunities for the productivity and quality drive undertaken by many U.S. industrial organizations. However, whether the full potential benefits will be realized remains to be seen. The key to successful implementation of the program appears to be a proper understanding of the environmental, motivational, and behavioral dynamics involved.

REFERENCES

Asao, M. 1976. "Role of JUSE for QC Circle Movement." In *QC Circles: Applications, Tools, and Theory*, ed. D. M. Amsden and R. T. Amsden. Milwaukee, Wisc.: American Society for Quality Control.

Burks, A. W. 1981. *Japan: Profile of a Postindustrial Power.* Boulder, Colo.: Westview Press.

Cole, R. E. 1981a. "Analysis of U.S. and Japanese Automotive Technology." In *The Japanese Automotive Industry: Model and Challenge for the Future?*, ed. R. E. Cole. Ann Arbor, Mich.: Center for Japanese Studies, University of Michigan.

_____. 1981b. "Quality Control Practices in the Auto Industry: United States and Japan Compared." In *The Japanese Automotive Industry: Model and Challenge for the Future?*, ed. R. E. Cole. Ann Arbor, Mich.: Center for Japanese Studies, University of Michigan.

_____. 1980. "Will Quality Circles Work in the U.S.?" *Quality Progress* (July):30–33.

_____. 1979. "Made in Japan—Quality Control Circles." *Across the Board* (16):72–78.

Dewar, D. L. 1976. "Foreword." In *QC Circles: Applications, Tools, and Theory*, ed. D. M. Amsden and R. T. Amsden. Milwaukee, Wisc.: American Society for Quality Control.

Diener, R. D. 1981. Personal communication to K. I. Kim. August. Diener is executive director of the International Association of Quality Circles.

Fujita, W. 1962. *Labor Union Organization and Activities (Rohdo Kumiai no Soshiki to Undo)*. Kyoto: Minerva.

Gryna, F. M., Jr. 1981. *Quality Circles*. New York: AMACOM, Division of American Management Association.

Hanley, J. 1980. "Our Experience with Quality Circles." *Quality Progress* (February):22–24.

Ishikawa, K. 1976. "Cause and Effect Diagram—CE Diagram—Tokusei Yoin Zu—Ishikawa Diagram." In *QC Circles: Applications, Tools, and Theory*, ed. D. M. Amsden and R. T. Amsden. Milwaukee, Wisc.: American Society for Quality Control.

_____. 1972. "Quality Control Starts and Ends with Education." *Quality Progress* 5 (August):18.

Juran, J. M. 1980. "International Significance of QC Circle Movement." *Quality Progress* 13 (November):18–22.

_____. 1978. "Japanese and Western Quality—A Contrast." *Quality Progress* (December):10–18.

_____. 1967. "The QC Circle Phenomenon." *Industrial Quality Control* (January):329–36.

_____, ed. 1974. *Quality Control Handbook*. 3d ed. New York: McGraw-Hill.

Krieger, J. L., and J. W. Lee. 1981. "Genesis of Japanese Management Success." In *Academy of Management Proceedings '81*, ed. K. H. Chung. Academy of Management.

Lohr, S. 1981. "Overhauling America's Business Management." *New York Times Magazine*, January 4, pp. 14–17, 42–45, 51–53, 58, and 62.

Monden, Y. 1981. "What Makes the Toyota Production System Really Tick?" *Industrial Engineering* (January):36–40, 42–44, and 46.

Mortimer, J. T. 1979. *Changing Attitudes toward Work*. Scarsdale, N.Y.: Work in America Institute, Inc.

Nakazato, H. 1976. "The Present Status of the QC Circle Activities in Japan." In *QC Circles: Applications, Tools and Theory*, ed. D. M. Amsden and R. T. Amsden. Milwaukee, Wisc.: American Society for Quality Control.

Oh, T. K. 1976. "Japanese Management—A Critical Review." *Academy of Management Review* (January):14–25.

Ouchi, W. G. 1981. *Theory Z*. Reading, Mass.: Addison-Wesley.

Pascale, R. T., and A. G. Athos. 1981. *The Secret of Japanese Management.* New York: Simon and Schuster.

Potter, D. S. 1981. "The American Automobile Industry and the Japanese Challenge." In *The Japanese Automotive Industry: Model and Challenge for the Future?*, ed. R. E. Cole. Ann Arbor, Mich.: Center for Japanese Studies, University of Michigan.

Rieker, W. S. 1976. "What is the Lockheed Quality Control Circle Program?" In *QC Circles: Applications, Tools, and Theory*, ed. D. M. Amsden and R. T. Amsden. Milwaukee, Wisc.: American Society for Quality Control.

Riggs, J. L., and K. K. Seo. 1976. "Wa: Personnel Factor of Japanese Productivity." *I. E., Industrial Engineering* (April):32–35.

Sumiva, M. 1965. "The Impact of Technological Change on Industrial Relations in Japan." In *The Changing Patterns of Industrial Relations: Proceedings of the International Conference on Industrial Relations.* Tokyo: Japan Institute of Labor.

Tsuda, M. 1974. "Personnel Administration at the Industrial Plant Level." In *Workers and Employers in Japan: The Japanese Employment Relations System*, ed. K. Okochi, B. Karsh, and S. B. Levine. Princeton, N.J.: Princeton University Press.

33

The Quality Circle Process: The ASQC Model for Success

AMERICAN SOCIETY FOR QUALITY CONTROL
TECHNICAL SUBCOMMITTEE ON GUIDELINES
FOR A SUCCESSFUL QUALITY CIRCLE PROCESS*

INTRODUCTION

Quality circles represent a logical process that allows for management and labor to join forces in the attainment of organizational goals. A process differs from a program, which typically has a beginning, middle, and end; rather, a process will be ongoing in the organization. If quality circles are properly implemented, both management and labor will benefit, and in turn so will the organization.

Although quality circles have most recently come from Japan, the basis for them was developed in the United States. In general, the quality circle concept rests on two arms of general management theory. The first is the behavioral aspect, which describes the ways in which people think and operate in their work environments. Some important contributors to this area were Abraham Maslow, who addressed the hierarchy of needs; Frederick Herzberg, who expounded the value of job enrichment; and Douglas

*Chairman: Michael J. Cleary; members: Jill P. Kern, David R. Schwinn, Robert Amsden, Davida Amsden, Joyce McDonald, Price Gibson, Gordon Constable, Wendy Fencl, David H. Ransom.

McGregor, known for his "Theory Y," which assumed that people inherently want achievement and responsibility through work. The second precursor to the theory of Quality Circles was work on the quantitative aspect of management. Individuals associated with this area are W. Edward Deming and Joseph M. Juran, both quality control engineers who went to Japan after World War II. K. Ishikawa has been given credit for the development of the circle model in Japan.

The U.S. contribution to the development of the concept is very real. Many U.S. firms facing serious questions of employee-management relationships and productivity are ready to consider adapting the quality circle process to this nation's needs. Many such firms have already implemented the process successfully.

A quality circle is a small group of employees (between three and 13) who work in the same area or do similar types of work. The circle members participate regularly on a voluntary basis, typically meeting for one hour per week during working hours. The size of the group remains small so that people are comfortable and effective in communicating their ideas during the circle meetings. People in the group usually come from the same work area so that they can discuss concerns of common interest. The circle leader is typically the foreman of the circle members. Circles generally are voluntary, to encourage workers rather than force them to become involved in the problem-solving and decision-making aspects of their organization. This concept of volunteerism is critical to the success of the circle.

Except for matters of wages and salaries, personnel, and other agreed-upon exceptions, the circle members can discuss any aspects of their work process about which they are concerned. These include the environment in which they work, the production process, operating procedures, or any other aspect of their job. The determination of what is to be discussed is entirely under the control of the circle itself. Management does not dictate to the circle what it is to address, although in some organizations it may make suggestions. The circle is not just a vehicle to provide a list of concerns or suggestions; rather, it sets out to solve the problem that its members have decided to address. Circles, therefore, must receive training in a variety of problem-solving techniques. These techniques allow the circles to come up with potential solutions to their problems. Once these solutions have been identified, the circle will analyze and select what it feels to be the best solution to the problem. The circle then formally presents the potential solution with its supporting documentation to management for its consideration. Management will consider the solution and decide either to implement it or not to. Feedback from management, whether positive or negative, should be provided to the circle. If possible, the circle will be involved with the actual implementation of the solution. The administration of the quality circle is done by the facilitator, who is responsible for training, liaison, resources, and so on.

There has been a great deal of concern on the part of many members of the American Society for Quality Control (ASQC) with respect to the introduction of quality circles into organizations in the United States. Quality circles began in the United States in 1974 at Lockheed, and have spread rapidly throughout the country. Because of the dramatic success and rapid spread of the concept, concern has been expressed about attempts to install quality circles without adequate preparation, thereby undermining the process and potentially leading to failure. In their eagerness to find solutions to company problems, managers have at times seized upon quality circles as a panacea to solve specific problems that they face, rather than installing circles as an ongoing process for the long-term benefit of the organization and its employees. ASQC has attempted to address the concomitant problems by forming a committee of practitioners, consultants, and academicians who have had extensive experience with quality circles. The committee is charged with spelling out to organizations that have not yet embarked upon the quality circle process the steps necessary to insure the success of quality circles within their own structures. The development of these steps may be considered, therefore, as a model against which organizations may check their progress along a continuum from very little understanding to a more complete knowledge of the working of the quality circle process. Additionally, the model includes information about what factors organizations must consider before implementing the quality circle process. Without the proper preparation, the quality circle process has little chance for success.

Figure 33.1 indicates the sequence of steps, from discovery to adjustment and improvement, through which an organization will move as it adopts the quality circle process. It should be noted that the process is a never-ending one. (Table 33.1, at the end of the chapter, shows the steps in outline form.)

DISCOVERY

The process of discovery is a simple one. Many have heard about quality circles from reading articles in *The Wall Street Journal, Fortune, Business Week*, or other widely circulated publications. Others have become acquainted with quality circles through communication with organizations like their own that have adopted the process, or through trade journals. Finally, a number of consulting organizations are actively soliciting opportunities for helping to install quality circles. Whatever the source, more than 1,000 organizations within the United States now use quality circles,

FIGURE 33.1   The Quality Circle Process: The ASQC Model for Success

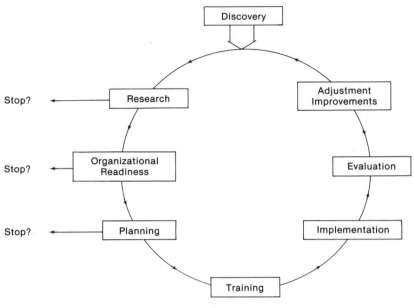

Source: Compiled by the author.

and literally tens of thousands of others have heard about and are considering the installation of quality circles.

RESEARCH

Once an organization has discovered the potential for quality circles in its own operation, there are a variety of methods by which it may undertake research on the process. The first is to examine the literature available in the area. While at present there is no single authoritative reference on the subject, ASQC has provided a bibliography of books, articles, and other readings that are available. Another potential area for research is seminars offered by consultants, university faculty, or practitioners explaining what the quality circle process involves. Another way to gather information about quality circles is through visits to organizations that are utilizing them, to see first-hand how the process functions.

The final step in research would be to offer an opportunity for those within the organization who are interested in quality circles to meet and discuss their own perceptions and research about the program, and to suggest ways in which their own organization would profit from further study of quality circles. As Figure 33.1 indicates, at this point or during the next two steps, members of the organization may determine that the quality circle process will not function properly in their organization. It is much better that the organization reconsider the idea of implementing the quality circle process, rather than continue ahead only to face eventual failure. On the other hand, members of the organization may feel that the idea of quality circles is good, but that their organization will have to undergo some changes in its own basic managerial style and structure before beginning the quality circle process.

ORGANIZATIONAL READINESS

The quality circle process is not a panacea that can be quickly patched onto an organization to solve every problem it faces. It is a carefully considered process that must be nurtured with adequate understanding and realistic expectations. For circles to run successfully, management must provide both its support and its personnel commitment. Management support means that management outwardly supports the theory of quality circles and, additionally, believes that workers throughout the organization can contribute to the goals of that organization. In addition, the organization must express management commitment to the quality circle process — through willingness to provide time for circles to meet, proper training of circle members, and resources to implement suggestions made by the circles when appropriate, and by providing timely and rational responses to circle recommendations. One way to express this commitment is through a well-thought-out, published statement of policy regarding the quality circle process. Another visible sign is the creation of an effective steering committee (see section on planning). Support and commitment at the various management levels must be present without the expectation of financial returns. Group problem solving is a very difficult and lengthy process. A year may go by before a given quality circle yields any monetary return to the company. Thus, management support and commitment must be established before an organization can move forward to a long-term successful quality circle process.

Where there are unions, organizations should also consider, with respect to readiness, the union's cooperation. In most instances, unions will at least allow quality circles to be installed if they are given complete information about the process before it begins. The union should be invited to become actively engaged in the process of evaluating and developing the process in the very beginning. If the union shows no interest, it should be actively informed of progress. If the union shows strong resistance, then management should consider the wisdom of proceeding with the quality circle process without some additional development of its union-management relationships.

The organization should undertake a realistic evaluation of its own formal and informal organizational structure to assess potential constraints offered by this structure. For instance, the organization may have developed a structure that allows only for top-down communication or decision making, which is incompatible with the quality circle process. In some cases, lack of cooperation among various departments and department members can impede the quality circle process. Thus, the organization should review its existing structure to determine fully where and if the quality circle process can be grafted smoothly onto the operation.

In addition, the organization must examine its internal climate prior to moving forward with a quality circle process. That is, effort should be expended to evaluate management style, honesty, communication style, receptivity, and morale. Quality circles will not in themselves correct major attitudinal problems faced by an organization, nor will they reverse faulty employee-management relationships. On the contrary, these serious problems of atmosphere may preclude success of the process. In the process of evaluating the internal organizational climate, one should look at the organization's experience with programs such as MBO and zero defects. The success of such programs may have influenced employee and management attitudes regarding the potential success of quality circles. In addition, previous training affects the internal climate. Valuable interpersonal and problem-solving skills may already exist in the work force. On the other hand, a prior inability to use these skills in the organization may cause a suspicion of the whole quality circle process. Although these attitudes are difficult to evaluate, they may be examined through interviews or questionnaires. Frequently, an outside consultant is valuable at this stage. This step will supplement the organization's ability to evaluate its own readiness for the introduction of quality circles.

Another factor important to the adoption of quality circles in an organization is external climate. A good example is the U.S. auto domestic industry; the industry was facing such difficult problems and pressures from outside the industry and from overseas competition that it was willing to become involved in quality circles and quality-of-work-life programs. It has been demonstrated that organizations facing difficult times not because of their own ineffectiveness but because of external pressures are excellent candidates for quality circle programs.

Finally, the organization should examine employee commitment and support. Even though employees are often eager to become involved in quality circles, these employees themselves should also become involved in the evaluation and planning of the program as early as possible, so as to include their input and commitment as the program is developed.

PLANNING

The planning unit for the quality circle process is typically called the steering committee. This committee is made up of representatives from various strata of the organization, from top management to hourly workers. It should also include representation from the various departments of the organizations. Experience has shown that union involvement at this point is invaluable.

This committee has the overall responsibility for the quality circle process. The first committee function is the establishment of the goals for the quality circle process. These should encourage the achievement of individual goals and work satisfaction through the achievement of clearly defined organizational objectives. These goals must also include items such as:

improved communication

improved technical training

reduced scrap and rework

improved quality

improved working conditions

increased productivity

reduced absenteeism

improved working hours

To allow these goals to be accomplished, the steering committee must provide the resources and support mechanism. This mechanism usually includes an effective internal or external consultant. In addition, the steering committee should act as a model for the quality circle process itself. Decisions within the steering committee should utilize a participative style and problem-solving techniques.

The second overall goal of the steering committee is to establish the responsibilities of the quality circle process. This involves determining a structure for the process, which might include defining the role of a facilitator, analyzing the process's relationships with extant systems such as the suggestion system, exploring the role of the union, finding a name for the program, examining ways to publicize the program, and other such matters. Limitations of the circle should be defined. Areas such as labor negotiations, salaries, or personnel matters are normally not topics with which circles deal. Next, the steering committee must determine the types of measurements to be used in evaluating the quality circle process. This involves, first, examining what measurements of quality, productivity, and employee morale are already used in the organization; and, secondly, deciding on what additional measures would be used. Since many organizations do not fully utilize their internal data bases, this process could involve a great deal of time. In addition, the committee should establish baseline measurements for all segments of the organization. This will allow proper monitoring of the progress of the quality circle process.

The third responsibility of the steering committee is the development of an implementation plan. The first step is establishing a training program — determining who will be trained, who will do the training, what training materials to be used, and what the timetable for training will be. Next, a pilot program will be initiated. The steering committee must determine how many circles will begin, what the locations of those circles will be, and how circle leaders and facilitators will be selected. As noted above, participation of both management and hourly workers in the program should be voluntary. In addition, the future needs of the process should be considered, with respect to horizontal expansion of the program — that is, establishing additional circles in the same areas as the pilot program, and vertically — establishing circles in the other levels of the organization. The rate of expansion should also be determined.

The committee's final responsibility is setting up a process to monitor circle activities. This involves documentation of the results, involving both people improvements and productivity improvements from the baselines that were established during the planning stage. In addition, the steering committee should be ready to review the goals of the program on a continuing basis and to provide support to the circles as required.

TRAINING

The training steps generally begin with a familiarization of all the management and union representatives with the quality circle process. This orientation should be complete, so that both management and union representatives truly understand the nature of the quality circle process. After the decision has been made to proceed with implementing the circle process, the organization should insure that all the groups that will be involved in the implementation — steering committee, facilitators, leaders, and members — are properly trained in the process. All of these groups should be made up of individuals who have volunteered to participate in the circle process. Top-down training is important to assure that all members of the management chain understand the process. In addition, all members of management and the union leadership should be encouraged to go through the training.

Quality circle training starts with the training of the circle leaders and facilitators. It involves four or five days of material, and is most effective when the training is spread over a four- or five-week period, so that the participants can use their own data in learning the problem-solving techniques. These techniques include brainstorming, cause-and-effect diagrams, Pareto analysis, histograms, check sheets, and other statistical techniques. The training also includes information on other topics — for example, group problem solving, how to run circle meetings, and how to make management presentations. It is important that the organization give complete support to this phase of the program in the form of effective and thorough training for all of these groups. Complete support generally requires an understanding of the process and its tools and techniques, along with a willingness to utilize the results and recommendations coming out of the circles.

The organization should also begin to train the support personnel around the circles in tools and techniques and encourage their vendors to become involved in quality circles.

IMPLEMENTATION

Once the people associated with the implementation process have been properly trained, the pilot program is initiated. Typically, there should be a reasonable minimum number of circles (three to six) in a pilot program, to increase the likelihood of success; but the organization should not begin too ambitiously. With only one or two circles, problems such as the poor choice of a circle leader or interference by middle management might lead to negative feelings about the process before it had had a chance to blossom. On the other hand, beginning with too many circles raises the possibility of inadequate support and training for the process. Some organizations have successfully started with as many as 50 circles, but they have had solid management support and extensive training. As the pilot program begins, the steering committee should communicate to those not in the program all details of the program. This is extremely important, since employees outside the circle process should be made aware of what quality circles are, as well as how, why, and when the organization plans to implement these circles and when additional circles will be implemented. Other matters that should be addressed during the implementation stage are how those responsible for administering the program can communicate with other companies that have quality circles, and what forms of recognition and reward should be provided for the circles.

Finally, during the implementation stage, management should be continually reminded by the steering committee of its important role in the success of the program. As indicated above, management should be both supportive of the program, with awareness and a positive attitude toward it, and committed to providing it with resources required to maintain the process. Support and commitment should be also shown by managers' attendance at circle presentations and by timely, rational response to problem solutions proposed by circles.

EVALUATION

After the pilot program has been established, the steering committee should monitor the process to evaluate the results. As previously mentioned, this should include the documentation of results of the pilot program. The measurements established by the steering committee should cover both employee-related and organization-related goals. Evaluating employee-related goals is the more difficult of these two, but the organization may examine such indicators as absenteeism, grievances, and turnover to observe what effect circles are having on the organization. A number of companies have used a before-and-after attitude survey to help evaluate the effect of quality circles. For product-related goals, the organization may examine baseline measurements established by the steering committee to see how and where improvements in quality and productivity have occurred.

Even after the organization has been involved in circle operation for a year or two, it cannot be assumed that the quality circle process is perfected. One way to evaluate a mature circle process is periodically to carry out a review by top management of the activities of the steering committee and of the process as a whole. One purpose of such a review is to keep top management completely involved in and committed to the goals of the quality circle process. Such a review should minimize the possibility that the steering committee will pursue tangents of its own creation, or pursue the wrong objectives through a lack of communication with top management. In organizations where there has been effective interaction and communication between the steering committee and top management, this review can be viewed as a self-examination by the steering committee.

ADJUSTMENT AND IMPROVEMENT OF THE CIRCLE PROCESS

As the circle process matures, expansions will take place both horizontally and vertically throughout the organization. At some point, if the program continues to expand, quality circles should become a way of life within that organization. This can happen only when quality circle philosophy includes not only the hourly workers but also the management structure of the organization. A number of organizations have been able to reach this goal through the use of middle managers in support of the circles. This has been accomplished by establishing quality circles of managers and also by utilizing managers as part-time facilitators. Some organizations have become so involved in quality circles that they view the process as a way of life.

As the quality circle process continues, there will be a need for more-advanced techniques. This need will have two sources. The first will be those circles that have been successful in problem solving and are interested in securing additional tools to solve more-complex problems. These advanced techniques might include regression, analysis of variance, control charts, experimental design, and other statistical quality control techniques used by quality control professionals. The proper use of these techniques increases as the organization becomes more adept at utilizing its internal data sources. The second circumstance that will cause a need for these techniques is higher levels of education among middle management. Such people are almost immediately capable of considering the application of advanced techniques. Additional training in group dynamics, communication, and presentation skills is also appropriate for both leaders and facilitators.

CONCLUSION

The American Society for Quality Control has been concerned about the adequate preparation of organizations that undertake the implementation of the quality circle process. While this model in no way guarantees success for a quality circle effort, it includes the steps that a number of organizations have employed in successfully implementing the quality circle process.

Finally, it should be emphasized that the steps in the ASQC model, as shown in Figure 33.1, are an ongoing process. The quality circle process is not something to be tried for a year or so and then abandoned, or arbitrarily assigned to only one department or another. It is a change in management style and the attitude of management toward the employees of an organization, with an altered perception about these employees' involvement in and contribution to the decision-making process of that organization.

TABLE 33.1   The Quality Circle Process: The ASQC Model for Success

  I. Discovery

 II. Research
     A. Reading
     B. Seminars
     C. Visits
     D. Discussion meeting — internal

III. Organizational readiness
     A. Management support
     B. Management commitment
     C. Union involvement
     D. Internal organizational climate
     E. External climate

 IV. Planning (steering committee)
     A. Determination of goals
     B. Establishment of responsibilities
        1. Structure of program
        2. Establishment of baseline measures
     C. Developing of implementation plan
        1. Training
        2. Pilot program planning
        3. Expansion of process
     D. The monitoring process

  V. Training
     A. Training groups
        1. Top management
        2. Facilitators, leaders, members
        3. Support groups — vendors, etc.
     B. Training methods
        1. Time period for training
        2. Training materials
        3. Who will do training

 VI. Implementation
     A. Pilot program
     B. Communication — to those not yet involved in the process
     C. External involvement
     D. Follow-through by management

VII. Evaluation
     A. Measurement

(continued)

TABLE 33.1 *(continued)*

    B. Documentation of results
       1. People
       2. Product
    C. Review by top management and/or steering committee

VIII. Adjustment and improvement of the circle process
    A. Expansion
       1. Horizontal
       2. Vertical
    B. A Way of Life
    C. Advanced techniques
    D. Total quality assurance

34

Americanizing Quality Circles

ROBERT J. BARBATO *and* RICHARD E. DREXEL

INTRODUCTION

The purpose of this case study is to describe the steps taken by one organization to ensure the successful introduction and diffusion of a quality circle (QC) program. It was believed that a successful QC program had to accomplish three things. First, an impressive track record was needed for those initial quality circles that would serve as pilots to precede the eventual system-wide involvement with quality circles. Second, support from top management, seen as a critical element in the long-term success of the program, had to be established. Finally, it was felt, the cooperation and support needed for successful diffusion had to be developed in those areas that would be directly or indirectly affected by the QC program.

BACKGROUND

This case study involves a Fortune 500 organization in a medium-sized city in the northeastern section of the United States. The organization uses skilled and semiskilled employees to manufacture precision products. Quality circles are being implemented to improve productivity and morale.

SIX GUIDELINES

To accomplish these goals, six guidelines were developed. These guidelines
are based on the notion that quality circles are a Japanese innovation. To
introduce quality circles successfully into a U.S. organization, an understanding of the differences between Japanese organizations and U.S. organizations is required.*

A commonly accepted difference centers around the cooperation that
exists in Japan among management, labor, and government. The history of
the U.S. labor movement, on the other hand, depicts a much more adversarial relationship between unions and management. A second difference
between Japan and the United States lies in cutural values and their impact
on management. A Japanese manager is likely to see himself as a father,
and the workers as an extension of his family. In this sense, cooperation,
consensus, and trust are givens in the Japanese system. In the United States,
the relationship between a manager and the workers is a contractual one
that emphasizes a certain pay for certain work. In this system, the dominant values are individuality and entrepreneurship. Cooperation, consensus, and trust are not givens; instead, they have to be obtained.

It was felt that this quality circle program should recognize these differences by adapting certain aspects of quality circles to this U.S. organization. The following were guidelines for the attempt to do so.

Obtaining Enthusiasm and Support from
Top Management

Too often, innovations fail because they lose support from top management. This happens because management often has unrealistic expectations about the program's ability to affect performance indicators in the
early stages. Top management support was generated at the beginning of
the QC program through seminars designed to provide top management
with a realistic orientation.

Involving Line Managers in All Aspects
of the Program

Unlike other intervention strategies, quality circles are intended primarily
to increase productivity. Success is more likely when line managers, through
education and involvement, perceive a QC as an aid to getting their job

---

*The authors owe special thanks to Dr. Paul Bernstein for his helpful comments outlining these
differences.

done rather than as an annoying and unproductive human relations program.

Implementing Programs in Each Division Independently

The probability of acceptance of a QC program can be increased when managers and employees feel ownership of the program. This is accomplished by allowing each division to begin a QC program independently of other divisions. Since a different facilitator is involved in each division, the QC program in each division can take on a different atmosphere. This contributes to feelings of ownership and acceptance.

Creating a Steering Committee To Deal with Interfaces among Affected Areas

For the program to diffuse successfully throughout the organization, it is necessary to elicit support from areas that are affected by the QC program. A steering committee that includes members from all these areas as well as the QC facilitator is built into the structure, to deal with potential conflicts in a way that ensures the integrity of all programs involved. At this organization, the steering committee included members of engineering, quality assurance, manufacturing management, and the employee suggestion program.

Selecting Facilitators and Group Leaders on the Basis of Their Adaptability and Knowledge of Modern Management Theory

A group leader's managerial style is often different from the managerial style common to many production areas in large organizations. It is recognized that program success requires a proper fit between a manager's style and the requirements of a group leader. A manager's ability to change and his or her recognition of modern management theories are important characteristics for ensuring program success.

Measuring Effectiveness Using Baseline Measurements

Diffusion of the QC program will occur only if it is perceived as successful. Consequently, it is important to measure and report success in terms that are directly related to productivity. A pilot program has been set up to do this. The pilot program consists of three quality circles. In each case, effectiveness will be tested using the following baseline measures: the amount of scrap, the amount of rework, rate of absenteeism, rate of turnover, and attitude change. Expansion of quality circles depends on the success of the pilot program.

SUMMARY

Quality circles are an innovation that exists in over 1,000 organizations in the United States. For this innovation to succeed and spread, it is felt, U.S. companies must recognize cultural differences that exist, and must adapt QC programs to these differences. This case study offers six guidelines that have been successfully implemented in a U.S. company.

35

The Experiential Approach to Organizational Training and Development Programs: Application in Japanese Universities

M. TOM BASURAY *and* STEPHEN E. BLYTHE

INTRODUCTION

A review of available literature on simulation and experiential learning, and the number of scholarly papers presented on these topics at various academic gatherings are testimonies to the efficacy of the experiential teaching/learning method as practiced in the institutions of higher learning in the United States. Evidence relating to the influence of simulation and experiential learning in U.S. business education seems to be conflicting, however. The increasing number of published simulation materials and the heightened interest among business educators in creative dialogues through professional associations seems to support a contention that simulation's influence in business education is on the ascent.

On the other hand, recent research has noted that the degree of utilization of simulation in U.S. business education is not as great as previously thought. Goosen (1977) commented that "probably less than 2 percent of all business courses involve the use of a business simulation. The number of students who actually participate in business simulations is less than 10 percent of all business students. The number of teachers who use business simulations probably does not exceed 800, which number represents about 4 percent of all business teachers" (p. 214). Therefore, in relative, temporal terms, the degree of utilization of simulation/experiential methods appears to be on the rise in U.S. business schools; absolutely, however, it seems that still only a small minority of business students in the United States are being exposed to these innovative methods.

Until now, not much effort seems to have been expended in identifying the interest in and the commitment to the experiential learning methods among the educators in other cultures. A search of the relevant literature fails to indicate either substantial participation by educators from other countries or research conducted by educators from this country. Considering the extent to which the template of business administration education, as developed in the United States, has been duplicated in other countries, the absence of research on the degree to which the simulation techniques are in use in other cultures is quite striking.

The thrust of the research effort reported here is to initiate the preliminary steps toward bridging the knowledge gap that currently exists in this area. This chapter discusses the results of a pilot study conducted in the summer of 1980 on the use of simulation material in business administration education in the Japanese universities.

Therefore, the principal null hypothesis to be considered in this study may be stated thus: there is no significant difference between Japanese and U.S. business schools in terms of their degree of utilization of experiential/simulation pedagogical methods.

THEORETICAL FOUNDATION FOR SIMULATION-USE BEHAVIOR

Theoretical statements explaining and predicting use of simulation and experiential exercises are mostly at the developmental stage. The few available researches tend to derive cause-and-effect relationships between a limited set of variables that preclude valid generalizations pertaining to a process that is generally perceived as complex. Estes (1979) indicated that the utilization of computer-based simulation is appropriate when learning of the application of specific skill or tool to business problem situations is the major objective. The efforts of Burns and Gentry (1980, p. 17) to conceptualize a number of the process variables relevant to decisions on use of simulation exercises, and their efforts to cast these variables into a functional cause-and-effect linkage set are most noteworthy.

The basic model postulated by Burns and Gentry is that:

Games Used (Nature, Conduct) = f (Concepts Taught) modified by (Student Attributes, Instructor Considerations)

Each of these variables was then operationalized along a number of dimensions. These variable sets were then connected by conceptualized cause-and-effect relationship flowcharts described as hypothesized propositions.

A more comprehensive framework describing and explaining the elements and sequencing of educational process within the psychosocial context has been presented by Mogar (1969). His model (see Table 35.1) clearly depicts the fundamental interaction in the educational process — that in which the person undertaking the learning experience is exposed to a specific learning situation with certain characteristics. In this case model, Mogar looks at various personality characteristics of the learner, including his/her motivations, values, beliefs, life style, and perception/judgment configurations. The intriguing feature of the model is the acknowledgment made by Mogar of the peripheral influences exerted by the antecedent conditions from which the learner evolves as well as the life stage of the learner.

The Burns and Gentry model of experiential learning system and the psychosocial theory of the educational process by Mogar indicate some very important aspects of teaching/learning activities, experiential or otherwise, that are quite often overlooked in research that attempts to evaluate effectiveness of specific teaching methodologies. These are the concepts that (a) the outcome of the teaching/learning process is caused by complex interactions of a number of variables that are extremely difficult to control; (b) the sociocultural influences probably determine the teaching/learning methodologies that would be undertaken in a given learning situation; and (c) no one single criterion is capable of assessing learning effectiveness.

Until now, most of the assessment research focused on the experiential learning process has been partial. A survey of the literature reveals that approaches to assessing experiential learning have taken one of the following forms. One approach to evaluating experiential learning through use of simulation and games has been to teach several sections of the same course under different conditions and to compare the performance of students across the various sections on a test administered to all sections (Catalanello and Brenenstuhl 1977; Mancuso 1975). Another approach to evaluation research attempted to compare students' performance (by grades) in the simulation gaming part of a course with their performance on other "traditional" examinations and assignments in the course (Estes 1979; Wolfe 1979). A third approach has been to ascertain the usefulness of simulation games by obtaining written feedback from students who took

TABLE 35.1 Elements and Sequencing of the Educational Process

A		B		C		D		O
ANTECEDENT CONDITIONS	produce}	A PERSON WITH CERTAIN CHARACTERISTICS	who interacts with	A SITUATION (EDUCATIONAL SYSTEM) WITH CERTAIN CHARACTERISTICS	during	LIFE STAGE	to produce}	OUTCOMES
Heredity		Abilities		Capacities required		Infancy		New abilities
Culture		Aptitudes		Needs assumed		Preschool		New satisfactions
Family structure		Needs		Values required		Elementary school		New values
Parental attitudes		Motives		Interpersonal environment		Secondary school		New behavior patterns
		Values				High school		New attitudes
		Beliefs				College		New motivations
		Life style						
For example, egalitarian-socialistic cultures		For example, verbal and nonverbal abilities		For example, cognitive, affective, and domain-oriented educational systems				For example, psychosocial adaptation, self-actualization
Patriarchal and matriarchal families		Security achievement – self-actualizing motives		Leader and leaderless work systems				
Lower, middle, and upper classes		Promethean, Dionysian, and Buddhistic values		Directive and nondirective therapy techniques				
Authoritarian and permissive parents		Sensing, feeling, intuitive, and thinking life styles						

Source: Mogar (1969):18.

a course in which a simulation game was used (Chisholm, Kumar, and Clay 1978; Mancuso 1975). The results of these evaluations have not provided conclusive evidence as to the merits of experiential learning vis-à-vis traditional methods.

Despite the absence of empirical evidence supporting the superiority of experiential teaching/learning methods, use of experiential games, simulations, and similar techniques in business education has grown significantly in the United States. One reason for such growth could be that evaluative research has not established experiential methods as inferior to other, traditional methods. The positive aspects resulting from use of experiential teaching techniques, such as increased student interest (at least initially) and greater student participation, may have caused the rapid spread of their use.

Since the present research attempting to examine the use of experiential and simulation exercises in a cross-cultural teaching/learning environment is designed to be a pilot study, the scope of data collection was limited to a few variables. However, the authors feel that, despite the simplified research design, the data gathered would provide indirect support of the relationships postulated by Burns and Gentry and by Mogar.

METHODOLOGY

A survey questionnaire on simulation utilization was developed for the purpose of gathering information from business college faculty members in Japanese universities. The questionnaire was designed to gather information under two major categories. The first data category was termed "demographic." Respondents were asked to provide the following information:

1. Respondent's number of years of teaching experience at the college/university level
2. The highest academic degree held by the respondent
3. The respondent's major field of concentration in the highest academic degree program
4. The country where the highest academic degree was earned
5. The proportion of teaching time spent by the respondent in one or more of the business disciplines
6. In each of the business disciplines (management, marketing, economics, etc.), the proportion of time spent in graduate and/or undergraduate teaching.
7. The average number of students in the classes taught by respondent

The second data category was titled "simulation usage information." The respondents were asked to provide data on:

1. The proportion of time the respondents devoted to simulation and nonsimulation methods of teaching
2. For a specific business discipline (such as management, marketing, economics, etc.), the proportion of simulation-oriented instruction that the respondent utilized in teaching
3. The titles of the courses where the respondent utilized simulation and the proportion of time devoted to simulation
4. The frequency and the method of evaluation conducted by the respondent to assess the effectiveness of simulation-centered courses

A list of 50 business administration faculty members currently teaching in Japanese universities was obtained from current membership directories of the Academy of Management and the Academy of International Business. The survey questionnaires, along with postage-guaranteed return envelopes, were mailed to the respondents from Tokyo. A total of 20 responses was received (40 percent returned rate). The responses were coded and were subjected to Statistical Analysis System (SAS) package treatment.

RESULTS

The results of the analysis of the first category of data (demographic information) are summarized below:

1. 50 percent of the respondents had been teaching for 18 or more years (average number of years taught by all respondents was 15.5 years).
2. 60 percent of the respondents had a master's degree as the highest academic degree.
   40 percent of the respondents had a Ph.D. as the highest academic degree.
3. 50 percent of the respondents had management as the major field of concentration in their highest academic degree program.
4. 80 percent of the respondents earned their highest academic degree in Japan; 15 percent of the respondents earned their highest degree in the United States; and 5 percent of the respondents earned their highest degree in Germany.
5. 80 percent of the respondents reported teaching responsibilities in the area of management, and, of these, 50 percent reported devoting at least 60 percent of their time to teaching management sub-

jects. In comparison to this, only 30 percent of the respondents reported some teaching responsibilities in the area of marketing; 10 percent of the respondents reported having some teaching responsibilities in the area of accounting; and 25 percent of the respondents reported some teaching responsibilities in the area of economics. Only 10 percent of the respondents had some teaching responsibilities in the area of finance.

6. Of the 80 percent of the respondents involved in teaching management courses, half devoted 40 percent or more time to teaching graduate-level courses. By contrast, only 20 percent of the respondents who were teaching some marketing courses had any graduate course responsibilities. This was the same percentage of respondents who were involved with graduate courses in the economics area.

7. Half of the respondents reported teaching classes of 65 or more students. The average number of students in classes taught by all of the respondents was 89.

The results of the analysis of the second category of data (simulation usage information) are summarized below:

1. Half of the respondents did not use any simulation in their teaching methodology. The other half indicated some use of simulation in their instructions (range of usage was from 10 to 85 percent).

2. Of the respondents who are teaching in management classes, 31 percent reported using some simulation. In comparison, of the respondents who were teaching in the area of marketing, 50 percent reported using some simulation. Of the respondents who were teaching in the area of economics, 80 percent reported using some simulation.

3. Of the respondents reporting use of simulation in teaching, all used student evaluations to assess the effectiveness of courses they taught.

Of the respondents reporting use of simulation in teaching, 60 percent used evaluation from faculty colleagues to assess the effectiveness of the courses they taught.

4. The specific courses where some of the respondents reported using simulation are international business management, multinational enterprises, seminar in international business, economic development, economics, business games, productivity measurement, application of programming, marketing management, and marketing seminar. No use of simulation was reported in personnel management, industrial relations, or human relations courses.

Other results of interest are summarized below:

1. Of the respondents with the Ph.D. as the highest earned academic degree, 21 percent reported using some simulation, while among the respondents with the master's degree as the highest earned degree, only 18 percent reported using some simulation.
2. No significant correlations were detected among any of the variables generated through the questionnaire, though the relations were, in all instances, in the directions hypothesized a priori. For example, the use of simulation in classes with more students was low (negative, though not significant, correlation).

DISCUSSION

The results of the pilot study failed to establish any statistically significant correlation between certain demographic variables and the use of simulation exercise by business administration faculty members in Japanese universities. The absence of statistically significant correlation notwithstanding, some interesting patterns do emerge that may be indirectly explained by the hypothesized cause-and-effect framework of Burns and Gentry.

Half of the respondents in this study did not use any simulation in their teaching methodology. It appears, therefore, that experiential simulation methods are far removed from being a pervasive phenomenon in Japanese business schools. Based upon this (admittedly scanty) evidence, the null hypothesis is not rejected because: (1) although the utilization of simulation/experiential methods seems to be increasing in Japanese universities, (2) these methods do not seem to have attained a status of widespread popularity. These conditions approximate the status quo of simulation/experiential learning in U.S. business schools.

In the context of this finding, two of the results obtained in the demographic variable section appear to be quite noteworthy. First, the average number of students enrolled in the Japanese business classes reported on by the respondents was 89. Compared with class sizes in the United States, this appears to be high. Second, 50 percent of the respondents had been teaching for 18 or more years. Burns and Gentry (1980) hypothesized that (1) the number of students in the class will negatively affect their ability to participate in the exercise; and (2) the user's familiarity with the business topics being taught and teaching philosophy will affect the user's motive for using games or exercises. These two propositions may help explain why half of the Japanese business faculty (who had begun their teaching careers 18 or more years ago) decided against the use of simulation exercises in classes where, on the average, 89 students were enrolled.

Another Burns and Gentry proposition states that accountability and autonomy will positively affect participant involvement in the exercise. The formality of the Japanese societal structure and the Japanese cultural orientation toward formalized interactions between the older and younger members of the society may lead to an assumption of low accountability and autonomy vested in the Japanese students. The results of this study indicated that all of the respondents using simulation in teaching conducted student evaluations to assess the effectiveness of the courses. It may be speculated that those faculty members who did not use simulation exercises in their teaching methodology were, by conducting fewer student course evaluations, providing less accountability and autonomy to the students in their classes. This would indirectly support the last proposition of Burns and Gentry cited above.

Estes (1979) reported that greater effectiveness of simulation exercises is expected in courses that attempt to impart a skill orientation for specific problem solutions. The courses for which the use of simulation exercises was reported by the respondents were of this type.

Catalanello (1980) indicated that an important variable in a discussion of the use of experiential exercises was the cost and benefits accruing to the instructor as a result of the decision to use such techniques. The benefits to be gained from use were listed by Catalanello as (1) increased instructor interest in teaching, (2) increased status due to innovative quality of teaching, and (3) greater teaching effectiveness. Costs associated with use of experiential techniques were (1) greater time demands placed on the instructor, (2) increased frustration experienced by a portion of the students, and (3) lack of peer support. In a society such as ours, where academic freedom acts as a powerful infrastructure for support, cost items (2) and (3) may not carry much weight. However, in a traditional society such as Japan, these may be significant barriers to (costs associated with) implementation of innovations such as simulation and experiential techniques. Only 15 percent of the respondents had earned their highest academic degree in the United States. It may be assumed that the overall teaching/learning climate among the respondents would be along traditional Japanese lines.

CONCLUSIONS

This pilot investigation of the intensity of the use of simulation techniques by business college faculty members in Japanese universities failed to provide any conclusive evidence regarding cause-and-effect relationships among variables. Nevertheless, the trends exhibited are quite interesting and revealing in some respects. The obvious limitations of the study are the narrow scope and the absence of comparative data from other countries. The authors are fully aware that a comparative analytical framework would be necessary to identify the cultural influences that may help explain the greater use of simulation and experiential techniques in one environment than in another. The analysis of the use of experiential techniques in the United States must, of necessity, be the cornerstone as far as business education is concerned. The authors hope that such research efforts would provide the necessary linkages toward the establishment of a true theory, which is so conspicuous by its absence.

REFERENCES

Burns, Alvin C., and James W. Gentry. 1980. "Moving Toward a 'Theory' of the Use of Simulation Games and Experiential Exercises." In *Experiential Learning Enters the Eighties*, ed. Daniel C. Brenenstuhl and William D. Biggs, pp. 17–20. Proceedings of the Seventh Annual Conference of the Association for Business Simulation and Experiential Learning. Tempe, Ariz.: Bureau of Business and Economic Research, Arizona State University.

Catalanello, Ralph F. 1980. "To Use or Not to Use Experiential Techniques, That is the Question." *Experiential Learning Enters the Eighties*, ed. Daniel C. Brenenstuhl and William D. Biggs, p. 106. Proceedings of the Seventh Annual Conference of the Association for Business Simulation and Experiential Learning. Tempe, Ariz.: Bureau of Business and Economic Research, Arizona State University.

Catalanello, Ralph F., and D. C. Brenenstuhl. 1977. "The Assessment of the Effect of Experiential, Simulation and Discussion Pedagologies Used in Laboratory Sections of an Introductory Management Course." *New Horizons in Simulation Games and Experiential Learning*, ed. Carl C. Nielsen, pp. 51–58. Proceedings of the Fourth Annual Conference of the Association for Business Simulation and Experiential Learning. Wichita, Kansas: Wichita State University.

Chisholm, Thomas A., Parameswar Krishn Kumar, and James P. Clay. 1978. "An Exploratory Investigation of Student Perceptions of Computer Simulation as an Educational Tool." *Exploring Experiential Learning: Simulations and Experiential Exercises*, ed. Samuel C. Certo, pp. 330–36. Proceedings of the 4th Annual Conference of the Association for Business Simulation and Experiential Learning, Denver, Colorado.

Estes, James. 1979. "What's In It For Me? Over, Under, and Around, Using A Computerized Business Simulation." *Journal of Experiential Learning and Simulation* 1, no. 1 (January):65–89.

Estes, James E. 1979. "Research on the Effectiveness of Using a Computerized Simulation in the Basic Management Course." *Insights into Experiential Pedagogy*, eds. Samuel C. Certo and Daniel C. Brenenstuhl, pp. 225–28. Proceedings of the Sixth Annual Conference of the Association for Business Simulation and Experiential Learning. Tempe: Arizona State University.

Goosen, Kenneth R. 1977. "An Analysis of ABSEL: Its Past Achievements and Future Prospects." *New Horizons in Simulation Games and Experiential Learning*, ed. Carl C. Nielsen, pp. 207–14. Proceedings of the Fourth Annual Conference of the Association for Business Simulation and Experiential Learning. Wichita, Kansas: Wichita State University.

Mancuso, Louis C. 1975. "A Comparison of Lecture-Case Study and Lecture Computer Simulation Teaching Methodologies in Teaching Minority Students Basic Marketing." *Simulation Games and Experiential Learning in Action*, ed. Richard H. Bushart, pp. 339–46. Proceedings of the Second Annual Conference of the Association for Business Simulation and Experiential Learning. Bloomington, Ind.: Indiana University.

Mogar, Robert E. 1969. "Toward a Psychological Theory of Education." *Journal of Humanistic Psychology* 9, no. 1 (Spring):17–52.

Wolfe, Joseph. 1979. "Correlations Between Academic Achievement, Aptitudes, and Business Game Performance." *Exploring Experiential Learning: Simulations and Experiential Exercises*, ed. Samuel C. Certo, pp. 316–24. Proceedings of the Fifth Annual Conference of the Association for Business Simulation and Experiential Learning, Denver, Colo.

Part V

36

The Japanese Way of Management: Does It Make Sense for U.S. Firms?

DAVID T. METHÉ

The West's fascination with the philosophies of the East has taken many turns since it was decided that "never the twain shall meet." Faced with ever stiffening competition from the Japanese and with new markets opening up in China and throughout Asia, the American business person is taking a keener interest in the Orient. Among management academicians and practitioners, much talk is heard of adopting Japanese styles of management. Further, as more U.S. firms locate in Japan and more Japanese firms locate in the United States, the need for understanding each other's ways of thinking and acting in the area of management increases (Cook 1981, pp. 119–28; Ginsberg 1981, pp. 44–46; Ouchi, 1981; Pascale and Athos 1981). This chapter describes such key Japanese management techniques as quality control circles, and investigates the values that underlie them.

Because these management techniques evolve in a particular coun-

The author would like to thank the following people who helped in acquisition of material and in editing: Laurel Battaglia, Judy Glickman, Michael Spendolini, James Perry, and David Krackhardt.

try and are supported by cultural characteristics of that country, it seems likely that their transfer to organizations of a different culture would be less than problem-free. In light of cultural differences, then, the transferability of the Japanese techniques to U.S. firms is discussed. Table 36.1 provides an appropriate basis for examining their transferability.

Several management practices are outlined in Table 36.1 in relation to instrumental and affective aspects of the Japanese industrial system. Instrumental characteristics are those found in a specific institution and not ubiquitous in the society. These characteristics are usually consciously brought into being by the members of an institution. An example is incentive systems. Affective characteristics, on the other hand, are ubiquitous in the society, and their origins are usually unknown or shrouded in myth. Values and attitudes are examples of affective characteristics.

The reinforcing effect of social institutions upon values is an important aspect of culture.* One of the most important social institutions is the work place. The characteristics of the work place, such as employment conditions and wages, do have an effect on the work patterns exhibited. To launch this discussion of transferability, some of the prominent characteristics of the Japanese industrial system and how they affect work patterns are examined.

CHARACTERISTICS OF JAPANESE INDUSTRY: THE INSTRUMENTAL COMPONENT

The discussion in this section will focus on the instrumental elements in Table 36.1. The locus for the discussion will be characteristics internal to the firm and characteristics external to the firm. Internal characteristics are concerned with the relationship of the firm to its employees. External

---

*Initially it would be useful to outline, in general terms, what culture is. While the question of what culture is is important, a full discussion of it is beyond the scope of this study. Therefore, a brief definition is offered. Culture is determined by a group of individuals and consists of the collective programming of the mind; that is, the ways of thinking, feeling, and reacting to the environment of the group, which have been historically derived and selected. In modern societies, these ways of thinking, feeling, and reacting — or, in other words, cultural values — become formalized in institutions such as the family and the educational process. These institutions serve to reinforce the dominant cultural values in a society. The stimulus for change in these values usually comes from outside these institutions, through forces of nature, such as drought or earthquake, or forces of human endeavor, such as trade, conquest, or scientific discovery. Thus, while these institutions may help transmit a change in cultural values throughout a society, they are seen essentially as stabilizing devices that reinforce the current dominant values. Only when the dominant values are no longer regarded by a majority of people in a society as helpful in the survival of the society are they changed or abandoned (Hofstede 1980, pp. 25–26).

TABLE 36.1 Comparison of Major Differences in Management Practices and Instrumental and Affective Support, for Japan and the United States

	JAPAN			UNITED STATES		
	PRACTICES	INSTRUMENTAL CHARACTERISTICS	AFFECTIVE CHARACTERISTICS	PRACTICES	INSTRUMENTAL CHARACTERISTICS	AFFECTIVE CHARACTERISTICS
INTERNAL TO FIRM						
	Quality control circles	Lifetime employment system	Group orientation: in-group versus out-group; hierarchical; intimacy within in-group	Production quotas	Mobile work force	Individual orientation
	Career building	Nenko (length-of-service wage system)	Obligation/dependency (on, giri, amae)	Job specification	Job-classification wage system	Independence and skill acquisition
	Ringi decision-making process		Consensus decision making within in-group in conflict resolution	Top-down decision-making-process		Analytic and adversarial conflict resolution
						Goal achievement
EXTERNAL TO FIRM						
	Long-term arrangements with suppliers and customers	Funding through industrial group bank	Dedication to long-term goal achievement	Market orientation toward arrangements with suppliers and customers	Funding through external sources, such as stock market	
	Growth of firm through market share maximization	Close government-industry cooperation		Maximization of shareholders' wealth through profit maximization	Regulation of business by government	

characteristics are concerned with the firm's relationship to its environment — in this case, its interaction with government and its acquisition of
funding for investment purposes.

Internal Instrumental Characteristics

Any modern industrial society has many characteristics relevant to the internal workings of its firms. Among them, the wage and tenure systems are
particularly important to employees. Employees, both white-collar and
blue-collar workers, in turn are the essential ingredients that allow all internal operations to function. Thus, how a firm treats its employees with
regard to wages and tenure will have important consequences for the efficiency and effectiveness with which other activities are carried out. Two
internal characteristics that address these matters in Japanese firms are the
lifetime employment system and the length-of-service wage (*nenko*)
system.

The lifetime employment system — working with one firm during
one's entire working lifetime — addresses the matter of tenure. The arrangement is not specified in a legal contract, and there is no guarantee that
a worker will not be laid off or fired. Rather, there is an understanding between employer and employees that as long as employees work diligently,
every attempt will be made not to lay them off during an economic
downturn. The system had its beginnings in the early 1900s (Cole 1979,
chap. 1). It was initiated as a response to management's need to maintain
control over labor, especially skilled labor. The need for skilled labor was
acute and turnover was high. Management established the system to
stabilize the work force.

The lifetime employment system is also closely related to other aspects
of employee/firm relations, and facilitates a very high level of involvement
by the Japanese firm with many facets of its employees' lives. A large
number of company dorms house employees, and company-sponsored
recreational activities offer them entertainment. The focus of the system is
tenure, however (Rohlen 1974a).

The system of lifetime employment affects about one-quarter of the
work force in Japan today* (Tomoko 1980, p. 397). These are essentially
male workers in the larger firms. The system excludes female, temporary,
or seasonal workers and many employees of small and medium-sized firms
(Cole 1971, pp. 113–19). This is the genesis of the dual labor force, which

---

*The figures are difficult to compute accurately, since the definition of "permanent employee"
is vague.

has a core of full-time, career employees supplemented by a large number of temporary employees. The dynamics of this dual labor phenomenon are far too intricate to explain here in any detail. The importance of the temporary employees is that they provide a cushion for Japanese firms during times of economic contraction, since their hours can be cut back or they can be laid off without affecting the core. It is important to note that support for the system by the Japanese labor force is quite high, and it appears that it will remain so, at least for the near future (Economic Planning Agency 1981, p. 223).

Closely linked to the lifetime employment system is the *nenko* wage system, which was established concurrently with the employment system. In its original form, the *nenko* system used length-of-service or seniority criteria to determine the wage of the employee. In response to changes in the sophistication of the equipment used by workers, the *nenko* wage system began to shift toward a performance basis for wage determination (Cole 1971, pp. 78–79). This change began after 1945, and the number of firms shifting to it has steadily increased (Tomoko 1980, p. 219). However, even with this change, length of service is still an important component (Cole 1979, p. 176).

External Instrumental Characteristics

The two external characteristics of Japanese industry that are of greatest consequence are the close link to government in terms of support and guidance, and the interlinking of firms from different industrial and financial sectors of the Japanese economy. Both of these characteristics had their origins in the dissolution of the Tokugawa Shogunate and the subsequent restoration of the imperial system. Confronted with the possibility of domination by the West, the Japanese government took a strong role in promoting industrialization. This included the establishment of government enterprises that were turned over to private industry (Lockwood 1954; Smith 1955). This was also when the *Zaibatsu* (business cliques) had their beginnings. Many of the government enterprises that were turned over to private industry went to the *Zaibatsu*.

Although the *Zaibatsu* were dissolved at the end of World War II, many of the links still exist, albeit weakly and informally (Drucker 1981, pp. 83–90). This is seen especially in the type of funding received by Japanese firms. A heavy reliance on debt, common in the capital structure of Japanese firms, and on the type of stockholders who hold oustanding equity indicates that the connections still exist (Clark 1979, pp. 98–104; Flanigan 1981, pp. 42–46). This type of funding also has a consequence for the time frame that characterizes management investment decisions. Compared with the Western manager, the Japanese manager is not as tied to equity and thus to the maximization of shareholder wealth. Since dividend payment is not as important, quarterly and yearly profits do not figure as large among their goals. Thus the Japanese manager can concentrate more on long-term goals such as market-share growth (Flanigan 1981, p. 46).

Further, while the role of government may not be as strong as it was at the beginning of industrialization, it is still pervasive and very much proindustry. It has been a crucial component of the postwar recovery and growth of the Japanese economy (Takafusa 1975, pp. 410–12). As a consequence, the amount of industrial concentration and interlinking of firms between industries in Japan is high. One example of this is seen in the general trading firm (sogoshosha) (Drucker 1981; Lifson 1981, pp. 69–73).

These two factors — the link to government and the interlinking of firms — act to lessen the constraint placed on managerial decision making. As in the case of funding, the manager can focus on maximizing long-term growth. The manager of the Japanese firm is likely to view the government as benevolent and therefore an aid to him in confronting the turbulent environment of international trade.

Thus, the internal and external characteristics create a framework in which industrial activities take place. These instrumental characteristics are consistent with the predominant behavioral patterns and values outlined in Table 36.1. These behavioral patterns are elaborated next.

BEHAVIORAL PATTERNS: THE AFFECTIVE COMPONENT

Through their interaction with the instrumental characteristics described above, certain behavioral patterns provide the "social grease" necessary for the functioning of those characteristics in the Japanese economy. Socialization into these patterns has its roots in the family. The dynamics of the socialization process in the family and in society in general are extremely intricate. The primary concern of this section is the outcomes of these processes — the patterns of behavior that result (Zigler and Child 1969).

In the family the child is first introduced to the Japanese group (Craig 1979; Lebra 1976; Lebra and Lebra 1974; Yamamoto and Ishida 1971). Here the child learns how to operate in a hierarchical environment that also calls for intimacy (Okada and Kawahara 1979, p. 2; Vogel 1971, pp. 208–11). The emphasis is on harmony and cooperation among group members. The sense of "in-group versus out-group" is an important outcome of this process (Nakane 1970).

The interaction of the individual within a group characterized by hierarchical intimacy is extended to selected non-family members by the educational process. In education, interpersonal competitiveness is not encouraged; instead, competitive tendencies are focused on passing nationally administered examinations for advancement into higher education (Kiefer 1974, pp. 342–56). Consequently, group cohesiveness is not sacrificed to competitive pressure for grades. Further, the examination system is talent-oriented. Usually, a child's family status does not determine what schools the child will attend (Brown 1974, pp. 174–91; Sumiya 1971, pp. 146–66).

The emphasis on the group is especially apparent at the university level. It is very difficult to be dropped from a university because of failing grades, and much time is devoted to formal and informal group activities (Clark 1979, pp. 161–62; Kasahara 1974, pp. 323–31). Thus, the lessons of the family group are reinforced and extended in the educational process (Kiefer 1974, p. 342–56). The group becomes the focal point for all of the patterns described below (Nakane 1970, chap. 2).

The next pattern stems from the concept of obligation (*on/giri*) and its relationship to the concept of dependency (*amae*). These concepts have been dealt with extensively in other works (Doi 1974, pp. 145–55; Lebra 1974, pp. 192–207; Nakane 1970, p. 65). It is important to note that, while these concepts have not remained static in their interpretation in Japanese society, they do still exist. One aspect of them is the reciprocal nature of obligation and dependency between superior and subordinate (Doi 1974, pp. 151–52; Lebra 1974, p. 199). This is demonstrated in the relationship between mother and child, especially a male child in the family. The success of the mother is measured by the success of the child. The child, in return, is given support, especially throughout the grueling examination process (Lebra 1974, pp. 199–200). Consequently, a reciprocal sense of obligation develops between the two, and the child is dependent on the mother for much emotional support (Lebra 1974, p. 204).

This pattern is again generalized in the educational process to non-family members. It is exemplified in the *sempai-kohai*, the upper classman-lower classman relationship (Lebra 1976, p. 34; Nakane 1970, pp. 26–27). This relationship is extremely important, especially in the club activities that are prevalent throughout Japanese school life. The hierarchical intimacy of the group is further enhanced by these concepts of obligation and dependency.

Another behavioral pattern is conflict resolution. Frustration and differences exist in Japan as in any other society; in fact, in many cases the Japanese orientation toward groups can magnify conflicts (Nakane 1970, chap. 2). However, the way in which the conflict is handled is important. First, there is a strong sense that conflict can be resolved and that it is up to the people involved in the conflict to do so; the actions of the people, as opposed to the circumstances, are important (DeVos 1974, pp. 117–44;

DeVos, Hauswald, and Bordes 1979, pp. 214–75). Further, conflict is resolved in relation to the group and group goals. Again, this pattern is seen with the family. A child may leave the family because of differences in aspirations, but the child is then motivated to become a success in society, thus satisfying a major goal of the family (DeVos, Hauswald, and Bordes 1979, pp. 242–43, 245–46). In this sense, the child has never left the family.

The above is closely related to the final behavioral pattern discussed here: achievement. Achievement in Japan is oriented toward long-term goals. The individual, through individual effort and sacrifice, will achieve his or her goals. This is the attitude fostered in the family (DeVos, Hauswald, and Bordes 1979, pp. 220–28). It is reinforced in practice in the educational system, where getting into the most prestigious university can be dependent on which kindergarten the child attended* (Sumiya 1971, p. 155). Attending an elite university is crucial to obtaining work in the most prestigious Japanese companies. The company one works for determines to a great extent the status that society accords one.

In the work place, the affective and instrumental components described here interact with one another and form a support system for the management practices outlined in Table 36.1. The quality of this interaction and how it supports these practices is the subject of the next section.

AFFECTIVE-INSTRUMENTAL INTERACTION

In this section, the three internal practices presented in Table 36.1 — quality control circles, career building, and the *ringi* decision-making process — are examined in light of the discussion above. Although these three practices are internal to the firm, it should not be assumed that a similar analysis could not be carried out for the external practices presented in the table (Cole 1981:32). The internal practices are emphasized because of the current interest in their use in U.S. industry.

How does the quality control circle (also known as quality circle or QC) operate in Japan (Cole 1979, pp. 137–41; Kondo 1981)? The QC is a relatively autonomous group that is concerned with improvements on the shop floor. It operates on a continuing basis and is responsible for implementation of its suggestions once they have been approved by management. QCs make strong use of the foreman. His role is likely to be that of a facilitator providing guidance rather than a task-oriented leader. There is strong support for the QC from middle and upper management. Finally,

---

*This can occur because the college one enters depends on the high school attended; that in turn depends on the middle school; and so on back to the kindergarten.

although individual members do receive recognition, usually of a nonfi-
nancial nature, the emphasis is placed on the functioning of the group.

The process of career building begins for employees, both blue-collar
and white-collar, when they enter the company as new recruits (Cole 1979,
pp. 170–73, 212–15; Rohlen 1974b, pp. 332–41). Career building means
progressing within one's company in the context of lifetime employment.
Most companies have an orientation session that stresses the familial relationship that exists between company and worker, as well as introducing
the more technical aspects of the company's operations. These socialization
seminars emphasize the lifelong relationship it is hoped will exist between
the employee and the firm, and the benefits that will accrue to the employee. This initial training session is followed up by continual training, often
using the QC as an educational device. This training covers not only the
most recent technologies relevant to the work process, but also leadership
and group communication techniques. Career building also can, but does
not always, include involvement by the company in employees' lives outside work. Most companies have employee dormitories and sponsor recreational activities; areas of outside interest for the employee are developed in
the context of the employee's ongoing training. Most of the training
courses, whether or not they relate to company activity, are paid for by the
company.

The final practice to be discussed is the *ringi* (consensus decision-
making) process (Clark 1979, pp. 126–34; Yoshino 1968, pp. 254–62). It
should be noted that not all decisions made in a Japanese company are
made by this process. In fact *ringi*, as it is used here, will refer more to the
aspect of contacting those affected by a decision than to the affixing of a
personal seal to the *ringi* document. In this sense the *ringi* decision-making
process is that process whereby a document or a suggestion originates in the
middle or bottom level of the firm and is circulated through and up the
levels of management until it is either approved or rejected by upper management. Upper management might have been the initiator of the idea, but
it is still sent through the company. Thus the consensual aspect of decision
making is given weight. However, since there is often no comparison of
competing alternatives, little analysis is required. Finally, the process
tends to be ad hoc rather than systematic in its approach to planning. There
have been attempts recently to incorporate analysis and to link the process
to more-systematic planning schemes.

Now that the workings of these management practices have been in-
spected, it is appropriate to elaborate on how the instrumental and affective components of the Japanese industrial system interact and what effect
this interaction has on the functioning of the practices. The lifetime employment system and the *nenko* wage system help to minimize employee
turnover by offering workers the expectation of improved conditions as

they continue with the company. This responsiveness to the employees is enhanced by the capital structure of Japanese firms. Managers are not solely responsible to shareholders, since shareholder power is weak. Further, management can expect support from the government in most endeavors and views government as an aid. Consequently, management can concentrate on longer-term goals and can view the employee as a whole human being rather than solely as a part of the production process. This is not to imply that management is completely altruistic in its approach to its employees. It is not; that is why management practices are termed an instrumental component. Management expects that the worker will improve the quality and quantity of production as a result of these practices.

The affective component acts to legitimize the instrumental. The concept of the firm as a family is still strongly held in contemporary Japan (Rohlen 1974b; Yoshino 1968, pp. 65–84). In this legitimizing function, the affective component also serves as a check on the instrumental, in that the rhetoric is believed only for so long if it does not have some grounding in the reality of the situation. Further, the instrumental provides a framework in which the affective component can operate. Bureaucratic organization is hostile to any vagueness in the managerial process. The Japanese manager works in a highly vague environment with regard to job description and responsibility in decision making. This higher level of vagueness is supported by the instrumental component of the Japanese system, which tends to counter some of the more hostile elements of the bureaucratic process and thus allow the existence of patterns of behavior that at first glance may seem outmoded. Thus, the two components act to reinforce one another.

Change when it occurs is introduced from outside the system. For example, the introduction of a new technology that utilizes less labor, or the advent of a recession in the economy, can bring about change. The system must adjust. In the case of the Japanese, the importance of maintaining the system was exhibited during the 1974 recession. During that time the government passed the 1974 Employment Insurance Act, which helped subsidize firms so that they would not have to lay off their lifetime employees (Cole 1979, p. 256; Salmano 1980, pp. 62–65).

Some examples from these three internal practices may help to illuminate the above discussion. The operation of the QC is affected by both the instrumental and the affective. On the instrumental side, workers are not in fear of losing their jobs. Further, they have visible evidence of improvement of their skills. Affectively, they have worked in groups and toward group goals, and know that because of the strong sense of group cohesiveness, there is little chance that either the "free-rider" or the "grandstander" effect will develop.

In the case of career building in the lifetime employment and *nenko* wage system, the employee is placed in a very dependent position vis-à-vis the firm. This dependency is very useful to the firm. It can be manipulated to enhance the goals of the firm at the expense of those of the employee. It is countered to some extent by the sense of reciprocal obligation that exists on the affective side.

The lifetime employment system is instrumental to the *ringi* system in that it provides a core of employees who have worked with one another over a long period of time. The ability to function in an environment where responsibility is unclear and there is a need to stress nonadversarial types of conflict resolution is provided by the affective component.

Given that the practices have both an instrumental component and an affective component, the question arises of the applicability of these practices in a culture whose instrumental and affective components differ from the Japanese. This is especially relevant today, with the intense interest in these practices exhibited by U.S. business. No simple scheme such as the one presented above can capture the subtle and involved interactions between the practices and the components. A framework can be provided, though, for determining what we do know and what we do not know about how comparable the United States is to Japan, and perhaps what we can change and what we cannot.

APPLICATION TO U.S. INDUSTRY

If the instrumental and affective components of the U.S. industrial system were the same as or very similar to those of the Japanese system, then the practices could be adopted without any modifications. Few would argue, however, that there is strong similarity between the Japanese and U.S. industrial systems. Thus the direct adoption of practices seems unlikely. If, on the other hand, the components as they existed in their respective cultures were completely different and static, unable to be changed, then there would be no reason to attempt to learn from another culture. The Japanese provide an example that is hardly static and unchanging. While they have rarely simply adopted components of other cultures, they have adapted into their own culture what was considered best from others (Bennett and McKnight 1971, pp. 225–36; Hall and Beardsley 1965, pp. 149–53, 160–66). The U.S. system is also very dynamic and oriented toward progress. Further, concepts like team play are not foreign to the U.S. social system. Thus, it seems likely that some form of adaptation of the practices of the Japanese is possible in the United States.

The QCs, as discussed above, represent a major adaptation in the Japanese work place. The concept of quality control originated in the United States. The Japanese seem to be more predisposed to working in groups, and, given the structure of their industry, QCs spread very rapidly. The United States has been slow: the more legalistic way of conducting business, labor-management animosities, and the emphasis on technological improvements to improve productivity were major factors in the slow implementation of QCs (Cole 1979, pp. 253–55). However, with a strong consumer market force for improved quality of products, there is motivation for change. This is further enhanced by the knowledge that QCs can help reduce costs and improve profit margins. It remains to be seen whether the rewards will go only to management. Unless management can offer some inducement to labor, there will be difficulty in implementing any scheme that could potentially reduce the number of jobs needed to carry out some process.

Career building is very similar. The way it is practiced in Japan, in conjunction with the lifetime employment system, has reduced the cost of turnover. The training of employees gives them a better understanding of their jobs and results in less alienation, which in turn lessens absenteeism. The worker as a whole human being is considered by management, and there is no attempt to improve technology without improving worker skills. In the United States, technology places constraints on the utilization of worker skills because of U.S. design engineers' attempts to make machines "idiot proof" (Cole 1979, pp. 226–27). Also, in the U.S. system, as an employee gains experience and skills incentives favor moving to other companies (Krackhardt and Porter 1981). This "brain drain" can be extremely costly in terms of the search for and training of replacements.

Another lesson we can learn from the Japanese is that these two practices, QCs and career building, can act in tandem. They also complement the *ringi* system. While implementation of the *ringi* system is not advocated in U.S. industry (even if it would be possible), one of the important components of it could be implemented. The utilization of all levels of the company in the decision-making process, from initiation through evaluation and implementation, is a procedure well worth exploring. One immediate advantage would be that decisions once made would be implemented very rapidly.

Again the successful operation of these practices in Japan is due to the instrumental and affective systems that support them. Given the U.S. instrumental and affective systems, the practices would have to be modified for U.S. business. The only other course would be to modify the instrumental and affective systems themselves. At the very least, some sort of lifetime employment system would have to be implemented. Perhaps a movement away from short-term profits and toward growth would also be necessary. If these were implemented, the question would become whether the indigenous affective component would support the imported instrumental one. As yet there is no conclusive answer. However, some evidence indicates that by changing incentives and thus behavior, values can be changed (Hofstede 1980, p. 27).

Where might the changes take place in the United States? There are two likely candidates in terms of industries. The first would be in the high-growth sectors of the economy. This would be especially likely if the industry represented new technologies, such as electronics. The high and sustained growth would provide a supportive environment for the lifetime employment system and attract those investors interested primarily in growth. Further, since the industry is a new one, the patterns of labor-management interactions most likely would not be solidified, and new forms of cooperation could be attempted.

The other candidate for implementation would be industries in which a major reevaluation of the existing industrial process is under way. These would be such industries as steel and automobiles. There is a need for retooling and for regaining market share lost to competition; this is a growth-oriented goal. Further, the current industrial relations in these industries are under evaluation and new forms could be tried.

There is already some evidence of experimentation in the electronics industry with policies oriented more toward the needs of employees. This is especially true at Texas Instruments and Hewlett-Packard. Also, the developments at Chrysler indicate that traditional labor-management relationships can be altered. If an attempt were made to further these changes in the context of a lifetime employment system and growth-oriented corporate goals, the consequences might be very exciting.

REFERENCES

Bennett, J. W., and R. K. McKnight, 1971. "Approaches to the Japanese Cultural and Technical Change." In *Selected Reading on Modern Japanese Society*, ed. G. K. Yamamoto and T. Ishida. Berkeley: MacCutchan.

Brown, W. 1974. "Japanese Management: The Cultural Background." In *Japanese Culture and Behavior*, ed. T. S. Lebra and W. P. Lebra. Honolulu: The University Press of Hawaii.

Clark, R. 1979. *The Japanese Company*. New Haven: Yale University Press.

Cole, R. E. 1981. "The Japanese Lesson in Quality." *Technology Review* 38, no. 7 (July):28–40.

_____. 1971. *Work, Mobility, and Participation: A Comparative Study of American and Japanese Industry*. Los Angeles: University of California Press.

_____. 1971. *Japanese Blue Collar: The Changing Tradition*. Berkeley: University of California Press.

Cook, J. 1981. "A Tiger by the Tail." *Forbes*, April 13, pp. 119–128.

Craig, A. M., ed. 1979. *Japan: A Comparative View*. Princeton: Princeton University Press.

DeVos, G. 1974. "The Relation of Guilt Towards Parents to Achievement and Arranged Marriage Among the Japanese." In *Japanese Culture and Behavior*, ed. T. S. Lebra and W. P. Lebra. Honolulu: The University Press of Hawaii.

DeVos, G., L. Hauswald, and O. Bordes. 1979. "Psychocultural Comparison of Chinese and Japanese." In *Japan: A Comparative View*, ed. A. M. Craig. Princeton: Princeton University Press.

Doi, T. L. 1974. "Amae: A Key Concept for Understanding Japanese Personality Structure." In *Japanese Culture and Behavior*, ed. T. S. Lebra and W. P. Lebra. Honolulu: The University Press of Hawaii.

Drucker, P. F. 1981. "Behind Japan's Success." *Harvard Business Review* (January-February):83–90.

Economic Planning Agency, Japanese Government. 1981. *Economic Survey of Japan (1979–1980)*. Tokyo: The Japan Times.

Flanigan, J. 1981. "The Wrong Bottom Line." *Forbes*, May 25, pp. 42–6.

Ginsberg, S. 1981. "Beating the Japanese in Japan." *Forbes*, April 27, pp. 44–6.

Hall, J. W., and R. K. Beardsley. 1965. *Twelve Doors to Japan*. New York: McGraw-Hill.

Hofstede, G. 1980. *Culture's Consequences: International Differences in Work-Related Values*. Beverly Hills, Calif.: Sage.

Kasahara, Y. 1974. " 'Graduation Phobia' in the Japanese University." In *Japanese Culture and Behavior*, ed. T. S. Lebra and W. P. Lebra. Honolulu: The University Press of Hawaii.

Kiefer, C. W. 1974. "The Psychological Interdependence of Family, School, and Bureaucracy in Japan." In *Japanese Culture and Behavior*, ed. T. S. Lebra and W. P. Lebra. Honolulu: The University Press of Hawaii.

Kondo, Y. 1981. "Company-Wide Quality Control and Human Motivation in Japanese Industries." Paper presented at Princeton Seminar on Quality Control, September 3.

Krackhardt, D., and L. Porter. 1981. "Careers and Commitment: A Retrospective Study." Working paper, Graduate School of Management, University of California, Irvine.

Lebra, T. S. 1976. *Japanese Patterns of Behavior*. Honolulu: The University Press of Hawaii.

Lebra, T. S. 1974. "Reciprocity and the Asymmetric Principle: An Analytical Reappraisal of the Japanese Concept of On." In *Japanese Culture and Behavior*, ed. T. S. Lebra and W. P. Lebra. Honolulu: The University Press of Hawaii.

Lebra, T. S., and W. P. Lebra, eds. 1974. *Japanese Culture and Behavior*. Honolulu: The University Press of Hawaii.

Lifson, T. B. 1981. "A Theoretical Model of Japan's Sogo Shosha." *Academy of Management Proceedings '81* (August 2–5, San Diego, Calif.), pp. 69–73.

Lockwood, W. W. 1954. *The Economic Development of Japan 1868–1938, Growth and Structural Change*. Princeton: Princeton University Press.

Nakane, C. 1970. *Japanese Society*. Los Angeles: University of California Press.

Okada, K., and T. Kawahara. 1979. "New Living Arrangements Emerge." *The Japan Times*, January 5, p. 2.

Ouchi, W. 1981. *Theory Z: How American Business Can Meet the Japanese Challenge*. Reading, Mass.: Addison-Wesley.

Pascale, R. T., and A. G. Athos. 1981. *The Art of Japanese Management*. New York: Simon and Schuster.

Rohlen, T. P. 1974a. *For Harmony and Strength: Japanese White-Collar Organization in Anthropological Perspective.* Berkeley: University of California Press.

Rohlen, T. P. 1974b. "Sponsorship of Cultural Continuity in Japan: A Company Training Program." In *Japanese Culture and Behavior*, ed. T. S. Lebra and W. P. Lebra. Honolulu: The University Press of Hawaii.

Salmano, S. 1980. "How Mazda Was Rotated." *Management Today*, February, pp. 62–65.

Smith, T. S. 1955. *Political Change and Industrial Development in Japan: Government Enterprise, 1868–1880.* Menlo Park: Stanford University Press.

Sumiya, M. 1971. "The Function and Social Structure of Education: Schools and the Japanese Society." In *Selected Reading on Modern Japanese Society*, ed. G. K. Yamamoto and T. Ishida. Berkeley: MacCutchan.

Takafusa, N. 1975. "The Tarnished Phoenix." *The Japan Interpreter: A Quarterly Journal of Social and Political Ideas* 9, no. 4 (Spring):410–12.

Tomoko, H. 1980. "Winds of Change: Economic Realism and Japanese Labor Management." *Asian Survey* 20, no. 4 (April):397–406.

Vogel, E. F. 1971. *Japan's New Middle Class.* 2d ed. Berkeley: University of California Press.

Yamamoto, G. K., and T. Ishida, eds. 1971. *Selected Readings on Modern Japanese Society.* Berkeley: MacCutchan.

Yoshino, M. Y. 1980. *Japan's Managerial System: Tradition and Innovation.* Cambridge: The MIT Press.

Zigler, E., and I. L. Child. 1969. "Socialization." In *The Handbook of Social Psychology*, ed. G. Lindzey and E. Aronson. 2d ed., vol. 3. Reading, Mass.: Addison-Wesley.

37

Theory Z—Question Y: A Conceptualization on the Application of the Product Life Cycle Approach to the Theory Z Concept

P. K. SHUKLA

INTRODUCTION

Japanese management systems have received greater attention and interest in recent years, and several important questions have been raised about the potential for transferability of such systems to U.S. corporations. One of the major contributors to this increased interest has been Ouchi's (1981) *Theory Z—How American Business Can Meet The Japanese Challenge.* The book and the term "Theory Z" received an avalanche of publicity during 1981. Even Ouchi comments upon the popularity of the methods in the text of the book: "So popular are they right now that they are in danger of becoming the management fad of the eighties, replacing such previous fads as Zero-Based Budgeting and Management by Objectives . . . " (p. 261).

This chapter elaborates upon the view of Theory Z concepts as a fad phenomenon. Those who hold such a view would conclude that the concepts have a natural period of interest and decline, which is not subject to manageability or marketing efforts. The intent of this chapter is to apply the product life cycle approach to the Theory Z concept. Based upon ranking data of the book on the national best-seller list, a proxy for actual sales is obtained. The empirical data in conjunction with qualitative analysis supports a conceptualized product life cycle. Analysis of this life cycle includes descriptions of the phases involved and their lengths, research implications, academic implications, consulting implications, and managerial orientations.

There are several potential gains from the application of the life cycle approach to the Theory Z concept. Many individuals have different views on the present position of the concepts in U.S. corporate practices and on the potential of the concepts. There are also those individuals who already criticize the notion of transferability. Through the development of a conceptualized life cycle, a greater consensus may be reached on the present position of the concepts and the extrapolated changes in interest in the concepts. Premature criticisms may be delayed until the appropriate phase of the cycle, at which time they may be considered. Management and marketing efforts may provide the concepts with greater longevity, and a premature, faddish abandonment may be avoided.

CONCEPTUALIZED PRODUCT LIFE CYCLE

Empirical Data

For the purposes of this study, Ouchi (1981) *Theory Z* was utilized as a proxy for interest in and exposure to Japanese management systems in general. Other measures were considered, such as the number of articles written on the concepts, the number of seminars offered in the concepts, and other such approximations; these were not explored because of difficulties in data gathering, time lags involved in publishing and seminar set-up, and interpretation problems with peripheral topics.

Data were obtained from rankings of the book on the national best-seller list for nonfiction material. The rankings were published weekly in the *Los Angeles Times Book Review* section and are based upon surveys by *Publishers Weekly*. Figure 37.1 displays a chart of the ranking of the book on the best-seller list for 26 consecutive weeks. The book first appears on the list May 31, 1981, and is placed within the top 15 books for every week until November 22, 1981. Data were not available on the position of the book either before its appearance on the top-15 list or after its departure from the list. *Theory Z* has not reappeared on the list since November 1981.

The rankings do provide some proxy for sales of *Theory Z* and a gener-

FIGURE 37.1　Placement of Theory Z (Ouchi 1981) on National Best-Seller List

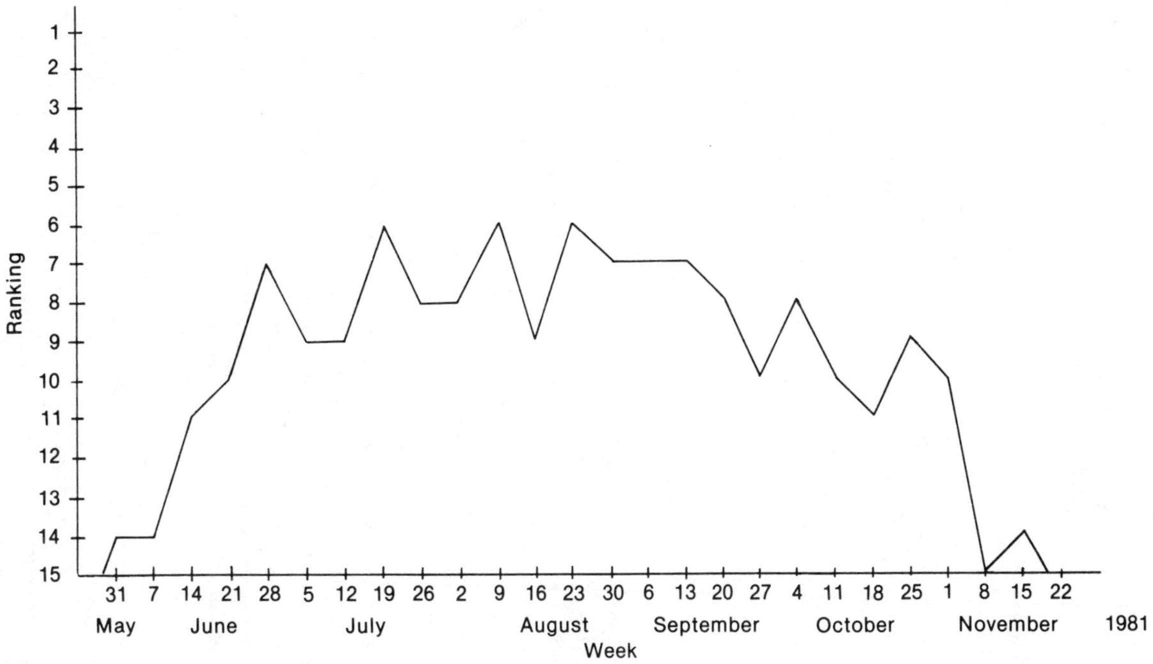

Source: Publisher's Weekly National Best-Seller List 1981.

al indicator for interest in Japanese management concepts. However, there are limitations that should be recognized: it is not clear, based upon the data, what percentage of the sales are attributable to repeat purchase, what percentage of purchasers actually read and comprehend the notions, or what percentage of readers actually follow the recommendations provided.

The data support the conceptualized product life cycle presented in Figure 37.2. The ranking of *Theory Z* on the best-seller list is viewed as a leading indicator for future applications of the concepts to U.S. corporations. The period of 25 weeks during which *Theory Z* was among the top 15 best-selling books indicates the period of rapid growth in the life cycle before the inflection point of the growth phase. The departure from the best-selling list may be viewed as the approach toward the inflection point, with continued growth forecasted, but at a decreasing rate.

Description of Conceptualized Product Life Cycle Curve

Based upon the empirical data obtained, information was insufficient to depict a life cycle for Japanese management concepts in general. To compensate for this lack, qualitative analysis was undertaken. This analysis took the form of a literature review of prior works on Japanese management systems, a review of the literature on other, comparable management models (such as the Yugoslavian model), and interviews with corporate managers on their views on the future of Japanese concepts.

With the addition of the qualitative analysis, a conceptualized product life cycle was developed, as shown in Figure 37.2. Figure 37.2 displays time on one axis against an axis equivalent to sales of, interest in, and/or exposure for Theory Z concepts. Five major phases are identified: introduction, growth, maturity, decline, and revision. These individual and sequential phases are analyzed in the following sections for their implications for research, academic interests, consulting, and managerial orientations. Two additional curves are depicted in the figure: Z' and ZII. Z' represents the efforts of critics who are engaging in efforts to present evidence in support of their beliefs that Japanese-type systems are nontransferable, invalid, or unnecessary. It is important for persons who are interested in the future of research into Japanese management systems to recognize the existence and forecasted growth of this segment. ZII represents the predicted necessary revisions in original presentations of Japanese methods due to the availability and feedback of evaluative research studies of transferability. Such revision will be necessary to further the longevity of the concepts as the decline phase appears. Everyone would agree that Theory Z and Japan-

FIGURE 37.2 Conceptualized Product Life for Theory Z Concept

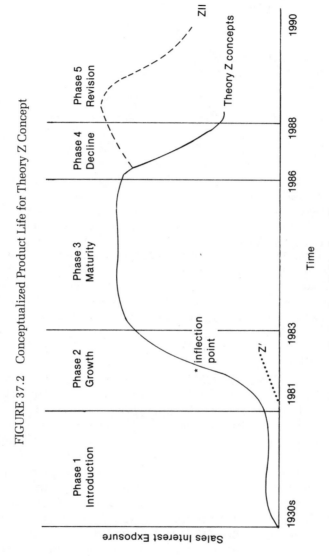

Source: Compiled by the author.

ese management methods are not the final or only solution to the problems faced by U.S. corporations. The figure displays the inflection point, which is on the time axis at the start of 1982.

Phase 1: Introduction

The concepts of the Japanese type of management were developed many years ago. *Nenko*, the Japanese system of lifetime employment, was firmly established after World War I. In 1958 James Abegglen's *The Japanese Factory* appeared, and in 1968 *Japan's Managerial System*, by M. Y. Yoshino, was published. These two books (published, respectively, 23 and 13 years before *Theory Z*) did not create the force necessary for the growth phase of the life cycle. Several explanations may be provided of why these earlier works did not receive the same degree of interest. At the time of the introduction phase, management displayed confidence in U.S. practices and procedures and a lack of comprehension of Japanese procedures. Also, economic activity levels did not necessitate a search for alternative methods. Research in this phase was primarily descriptive; the Japanese methods were described without much elaboration, explanation, or evaluation of transferability. This low-level phase was also characterized by the virtual nonexistence of courses, topics in courses, seminars, or consulting activity dealing with Japanese management systems. Gradual development occurred during the 1970s, with more studies, articles, and communication exchange between the United States and Japan.

Phase 2: Growth

According to the empirical data gathered, Japanese management concepts experienced the start of a growth phase in 1980, which accelerated in 1981 with the release of Ouchi's book. The managerial orientation in this phase may be described as curiosity. American managers witnessed the growth of Japanese industry on a global basis, and many managers viewed Japan as the leading foreign competitor in the markets of the future. With the decline in U.S. productivity and the reports of Japan's gains in efficiency, curiosity increased about the differences between U.S. and Japanese methods. A major contribution to the growth phase was research oriented more toward explanation rather than simple description; this type of research, though not fully tested or theoretical, aided managers in gaining a beginning understanding of what the Japanese management concepts are and what their rationale is. This phase of growth has created opportunities in consulting and presentation of seminars on how to apply the Japanese concepts to U.S. environments. One risk of this fast "cashing-in" is that there may be misapplications, misunderstanding, and insufficient testing of the concepts. These problems may lead to increased criticism of the concepts and a premature decline phase. The risk can be avoided only through self-restraint and appropriate warnings by consultants in the field. This phase has implications for teaching, as the concepts have become buzz-words in industry, and yet complete testing of results has not been completed. In this phase, students should be exposed to the concepts; they should be mentioned where appropriate during courses, along with some arguments of critics to balance the presentation. Few schools would have the resources, faculty, or need to present term-long course offerings in Japanese management methods. The inflection point has been reached but growth will continue due to word-of-mouth introduction and late adopters.

Phase 3: Maturity

It is expected that, by the start of 1983, the maturity phase will be reached, and that it will continue until a decline phase starting in 1986. This phase will occur through the saturation of the marketplace with the concepts; the only category of adopters newly exposed to the concepts will be laggards. At this phase, to counter the mounting numbers of critics and to provide the foundation for ZII, evaluative research will be necessary. The greatest needs will be for measurements, operationalizations, hypotheses, and testing of the concepts; these efforts will permit evaluation of the effectiveness of transference of Japanese methods. At this stage, academic opportunities would be available for the presentation of courses on Japanese methods and the utilization of students to aid in the gathering and analysis of findings. Consulting opportunities will decline, because managers will have adopted a speculative attitude. By the time the maturity phase is reached, many organizations will, to varying degrees, have implemented some Japanese methods. They will be monitoring the incomplete feedback and results. Further commitments will not be undertaken until the waiting for results of earlier efforts is completed.

Phase 4: Decline

With Theory Z, as with all products, a decline phase may be delayed but will be inevitable. Based upon the feedback and results of long-term efforts undertaken by corporations, many reports of unsatisfactory results and unfulfilled expectations will be produced. A rapid decline will occur in consulting opportunities, and only the most firmly established consultants in the field may survive to provide their services. As the negative reports (of misapplications and nontransference) emerge, they should be presented in teaching and in the adjustment of the developed paradigm. With a managerial orientation of resistance, the research needs will include case study

TABLE 37.1   Summary Matrix of Forecasts and Recommendations

| | | PHASE | | | |
ITEM	1 INTRODUCTION	2 GROWTH	3 MATURITY	4 DECLINE	5 REVISION
Year phase starts	1930s	1980	1983	1986	1988
Managerial orientation	Apathy	Curiosity	Speculation	Resistance	Reexamination
Research type	Descriptive	Explanatory	Evaluative	Case studies; field studies	Repeat studies with revisions
Academic implications	Minimal	Exposure to concepts and criticisms	Providing of theoretical paradigm	Testing of paradigm's accuracy and relevance	Presentation of modified paradigms
Consulting	Limited	High demand	Moderate	Low	Moderate

analysis and field studies to determine the causes of failures of applied Japanese methods.

Phase 5: Revision

It is possible that Japanese management methods may become just another fad and will reach a decline phase and disappear. Those who believe that marketing efforts may avert such a scenario would recommend research efforts at revision of original concepts, alterations in the paradigm, multivariate analysis, and the introduction of intervening variables. The goal of such an effort is to prevent the abandonment of all Japanese concepts as invalid and to further a theory and managerial view of convergence between U.S. and Japanese methods. If the efforts are successful, they will permit continued relevance in the teaching of courses in the area and renewed opportunities for consultants. Theory Z and ZII may be seen as analogous to the earlier views toward Matrix management and later descriptions of organizations with Matrix Type II and Matrix Type III.

CONCLUSIONS

The purpose of this report was to examine the application of the product life cycle approach to the Theory Z concept. With a conceptualized curve and understanding of the present position on the curve, the subsequent phases and their risks may be clarified for academics, researchers, and consultants. Table 37.1 summarizes the forecasts and recommendations made in this report. With management of the cycle and appropriate marketing efforts, increased longevity for the concepts may be gained and a premature faddish abandonment may be avoided.

REFERENCES

Abegglen, James. 1958. *The Japanese Factory.* Glencoe, Ill.: Free Press.

Ouchi, William G. 1981. *Theory Z: How American Business Can Meet The Japanese Challenge.* Reading, Mass.: Addison-Wesley.

Publishers Weekly National Best-Seller List. 1981. *Los Angeles Times Book Review,* May 31–Nov. 22. Los Angeles: Times-Mirror.

Self, Thomas M. 1981. "Theory Z." *The Executive of Orange County* 6, iss. 7 (July): 23–24.

Yoshino, M. Y. 1968. *Japan's Managerial System: Tradition and Innovation.* Cambridge, Mass.: MIT Press.

38

The Easy Answer Isn't Here

KENNETH D. RAMSING

It is a foregone conclusion that the United States has been a leading force in world business and trade. This country has been recognized for its entrepreneurial activity, its innovations in both products and management thought, and its marketing procedures. However, during the past few years, these strengths have waned to such an extent that U.S. business has experienced a significant deterioration of its competitive position and ranking as a world power. It is discouraging to observe that during the period 1960–78, the United States had the lowest growth in its manufacturing/labor productivity of the major countries of the world. In this period, the United States experienced an average annual growth of only 2.8 percent, while the United Kingdom showed slightly better and Japan had a whopping 8.2 percent average annual growth (Council on Wage and Price Stability 1979).

One argument set forth by American managers and the American public is that the Japanese have had the opportunity to use far more modern equipment than U.S. industry. Further, it is often said that the cost of labor in Japan is less than here. However, these two arguments do not explain the relative and absolute low productivity experienced in this country. Robert Hayes stated recently that the "modern Japanese factory is not, as many Americans believe, a prototype of the factory of the future." He points out that, for the most part, Japanese factories are not the modern structures filled with highly sophisticated equipment that Americans expect. The few "intelligent" robots encountered were largely still experimental. The general level of technological sophistication observed was not superior to (and was usually lower than) that found in comparable U.S. plants (Hayes 1981).

Although the Japanese at one time experienced significantly lower labor costs than U.S. manufacturers, this balance has been rapidly changing. With offshore production and assembly, many U.S. producers of television sets even share the same low labor cost. These often touted factors certainly have not been responsible for the U.S. productivity decline.

Perhaps as important as the productivity decline itself is the response of many U.S. managers today. Because of the relative success of Japan during the same period that U.S. productivity levels have suffered and some U.S. companies have neared bankruptcy, there has been a tendency to look to Japan for solutions. The literature is full of the managerial techniques and concepts being used by Japanese industries to produce more with better quality at lower costs. It is no accident that American managers have reached out to Japanese ways as possible solutions for our own illnesses. Thus, we see a dramatic upsurge in the number of articles, short courses, seminars, and applications of Kanban, just-in-time inventory systems (JIT), and quality circles. Yet we find that many companies trying these "new" and borrowed production techniques are not prepared to use them. The result is continued frustration, continued slipping of productivity levels, and an increasing U.S. trade deficit.

COMMON REQUIREMENTS

Without undertaking a thorough analysis of these various approaches to production system improvement, there are some points that should be addressed as the most common elements. None of the concepts is totally workable or capable of being implemented without the proper environment. Because these approaches, which are borrowed largely from Japan, require the support of the people using and advocating them, out of necessity we must address the human resource.

Worker Flexibility

Perhaps first and foremost is the fact that a new degree of worker flexibility is required. For example, when a company is using repetitive manufacturing, a single stoppage or slowdown at a machine center may cause a chaining effect to ripple through the production process. If a machine goes down, the system also stops. If it is necessary to call the maintenance crew in regularly for repairs, then regardless of the degree of simplicity, valuable time and human resources are wasted. If, instead, the machine operators and those tied to the repetitive manufacturing stream are also able to diagnose difficulties and then adjust and repair their equipment, the system can be more rapidly reinstated.

Worker flexibility must also be a common element to meet the market commitments of the firm. The ability to shift workers around as necessary to meet marketing expectations can give a firm considerable advantages. Market changes of increased and decreased demand must also be accompanied by worker flexibility. For example, workers at Kawasaki and Lincoln Electric are willing to fabricate machines, paint walls, and do other miscellaneous jobs if the market should soften significantly. Likewise, considerable hours of overtime have been incurred by Lincoln Electric during periods of high demand so that additional workers would not have to be hired for short-run fluctuations in demand (Zager 1978). In part, worker flexibility speaks to the second element needed for using these production techniques: worker participation.

Worker Participation

Kanban, JIT, and quality circles all require high levels of worker participation. Its absence strikes the death blow to the techniques used in the firm. To a large extent, this has been dealt with in Japanese firms by a "bottom-up" communications and decision-making process. This form of decision making is not an easy one for many U.S. firms to accept because of education, culture, and unionism.

Reduced Management Hierarchy

Perhaps an important characteristic of the Japanese management structure is a reduced management hierarchy. For example, Anderson (1981) suggests that at Toyo Kogyo (the manufacturing site for Mazdas) there are only five organizational levels between the production-line employee and the vice president in charge of manufacturing. Typical U.S. manufacturing organizations have many more levels or layers. Organizational blockage of communications will tend to occur less when the organizational hierarchy has fewer levels.

Paternalism

The lifelong employment system used by the Japanese has been cited as an indication of the strong degree of paternalism that exists in Japanese business organizations. However, the lifelong employment system affects less than a third of all Japanese workers (Hayes 1981). It should be emphasized that much more than a paternalistic attitude prevails in the Japanese companies. Japanese business has a sincere and honest concern for employees, a concern "for the whole employee — not for just his work performance" (Johnson and Ouchi 1974). O'Toole (1981) has indicated that the real advantage foreign competitors enjoy is workers who feel a greater loyalty toward the company that employs them and a greater commitment to making high-quality products. This, he states, is the case partly because social values abroad are different from those in the United States.

Attitude toward Waste

Waste takes the form of both the product being produced and the human resources entering the production process. The Japanese are concerned about both. They are a small country with very limited natural resources. A significant element is the attitude of the people toward waste. The Japanese goal is to improve the quality of a product constantly, both by design and by process, thus reducing waste.

The Japanese attitude toward the waste of human resources is also significant. The Japanese work ethic is strong and generally derives from company loyalty (Aonuma 1980). This work ethic permeates much of the organizational fabric of which the employee is a part. The Japanese dedication is such that employees show their dissatisfaction or demands for higher employee benefits by wearing arm bands or headbands — while they continue to perform their regular tasks.

WORKER PARTICIPATION IN THE UNITED STATES

Fortunately, management is beginning to recognize a need for change within the sociotechnical fabric of U.S. industry. Nonetheless, this nation certainly has not made significant moves toward the significant worker participation that is so characteristic of Japanese production systems. The classification in Figure 38.1 captures the levels of increased worker participation, from simple, routine, and low-discrimination jobs to the higher-level, self-regulating, enriching jobs where personal growth is emphasized. While this figure describes increased participation, it also shows the political and economic participation of workers in the organization, and illustrates worker power.

The numbers in the cells of this sociotechnical participation matrix will be used to describe the evolving characteristics of U.S. industry. Within the United States, most companies, both historically and currently, fall into the classification described by cells 1, 2, and 4. Normally, there is

FIGURE 38.1 Sociotechnical Participation

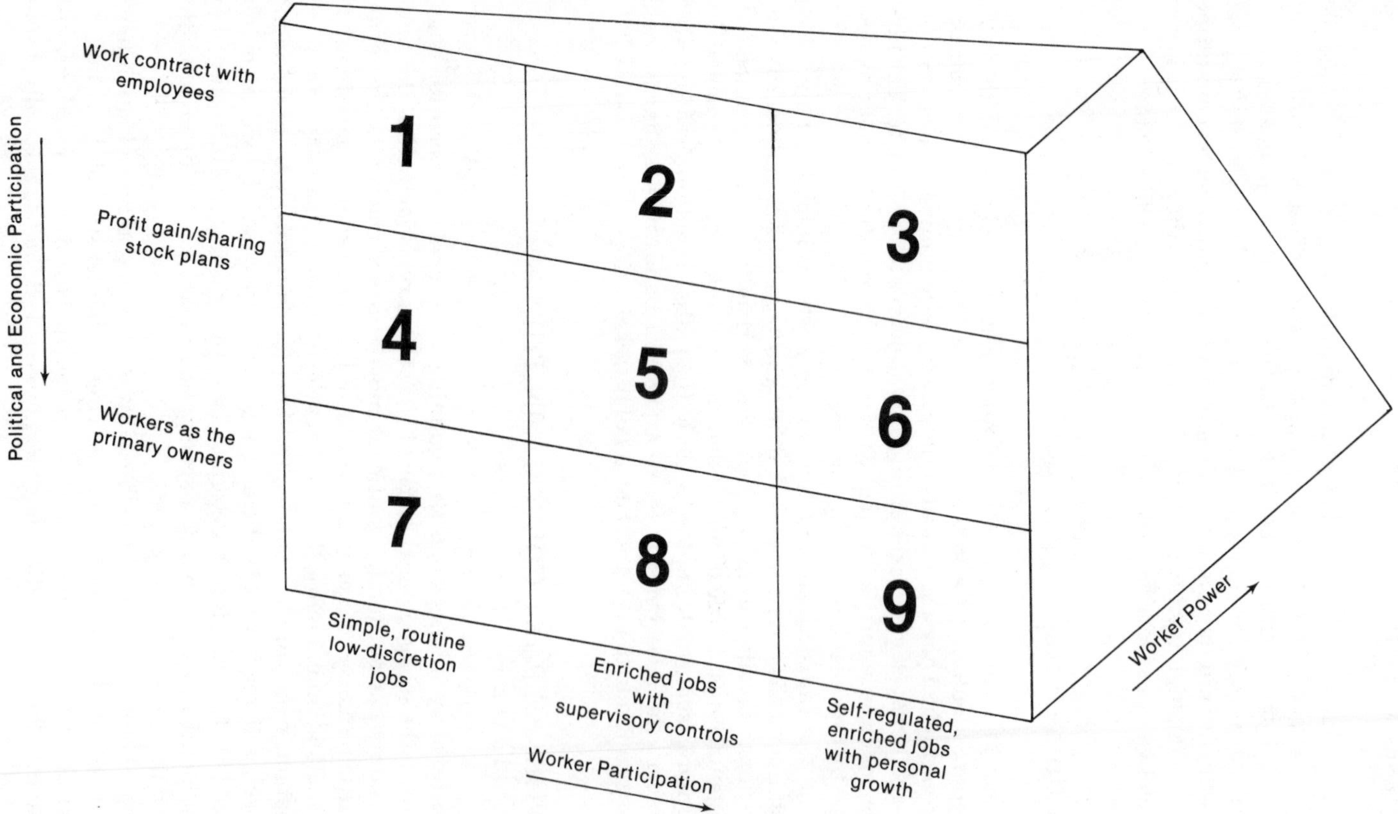
Work contract with employees
Profit gain/sharing stock plans
Workers as the primary owners
Political and Economic Participation
1
2
3
4
5
6
7
8
9
Simple, routine low-discretion jobs
Enriched jobs with supervisory controls
Self-regulated, enriched jobs with personal growth
Worker Participation
Worker Power

Source: Adapted from Fox (1981).

little more than a psychological contract with the workers to produce. Although some job "enrichment" may occur, this often means only an enlargement of the tasks performed by the worker. The "enrichment" usually comes without supervisory controls or participation by the worker. The "Taylorism" exemplified by cell 1 is far too evident in the United States today.

There has been considerable clamor during the past few years about the quality of working life (QWL) of American workers. The QWL has been espoused within industry circles, but the response has been narrow: worker participation has been increased through enriched jobs. Yet the development of QWL has generally been limited to cell 3, with little more than the basic work contract. Although worker participation is increased, political and economic participation remains at its lowest level.

Compensation through systems such as the Scanlon plan has propelled the worker toward cell 4 in this classification scheme. However, even with greater economic participation, the concepts of division of labor and rigid span of control are so dominant that most manufacturing firms remain at the lowest level of worker participation.

The desire of workers to own their own companies has taken many forms, but is perhaps most notable in cooperatives. As an example, the plywood cooperatives are exemplified by cell 7, with very routinized work in companies owned by the workers. One may ask why there is no more activity in cells 7, 8, and 9 by the workers who wish to be their own owners. Worker ownership is a phenomenon in which the labor input to the organization is very visible but the capital is not. Although workers may give indications that they desire self-ownership, they are rarely willing to risk their earnings to obtain this commitment. In such cases, the government generally must become involved as the transfer agent.

Relatively few companies in the United States fall into cell 3, where the worker has a high degree of participation in the governance of the organization. Together with an innovative management and a willing and understanding union environment, great steps have been made. (Many universities with faculty governance may be classified in this category.)

As U.S. industry has moved in an attempt to increase sociotechnical participation, different routes — some easier than others — have been taken. For example, it has generally been easier for companies to move from cell 1, where the organization will have a work contract with the workers, to cell 4, where there is some type of profit sharing. This is normally easier than to move from 1 to 2 to 3. It is rather characteristic of management/owner attitude that it is easier and more expedient to pay to get output than to enrich work and broaden tasks.

Job redesign efforts appear to be moving from cell 1, where the worker is involved with the contract, to cell 4, with profit sharing, and finally to cell 5, with some type of job enrichment and group participation in supervision of the group's work. It is hoped that new job design may at least take on the characteristics of cell 3, with greater degrees of self-regulation and job enrichment.

It should also be observed from Figure 38.1 that as the characteristics of the job move from cell 1 to the higher levels, the amount of individual worker control also increases. Thus, when the worker is at cell 1, there is very little self-control. However, when he or she is in a job position where there is considerable political and economic participation and high degrees of job enrichment, the worker has much more individual control. This is not to be viewed as a negative element, but instead as one that will provide the worker with work of higher intrinsic value and will result in greater commitment to the work place.

PITFALLS FOR U.S. MANAGEMENT

A number of characteristics of U.S. management style and the U.S. social system may be sources of obstacles to a better and more open reception for Japanese management concepts and techniques. Although these characteristics certainly do not permeate all companies, they are widespread enough that they are worth noting. The following are generalities and may not always apply to all companies and conditions.

Adversarial Relationships

Over the years, U.S. management and industry have evolved with a number of checks and balances. Some of these have resulted from misuse of workers, while others have been created by the development of management thought and sometimes even by cultural forces. Without a doubt, an adversarial relationship often exists between management, unions, workers, and government. This relationship exists because of different objective functions for each of the representatives. Unfortunately, this adversarial relationship causes a blockage of communications and processes. It is certainly not always totally negative, but often it does slow down or even prevent relationships that could be positive and productive.

The communications blockage, which is evident between management and unions, has been of great significance. Although there are a number of case histories in which a high degree of cooperation has been present, more frequently than not blockage of communications has hindered creative efforts to provide for greater productivity and worker satisfaction.

Hatvany and Pucik (1981) have suggested that the dominance of craft-based unions in the United States (as contrasted with enterprise-based unions in Japan) precludes the emergence of organizations here using the strategies and techniques found in Japanese corporations. Further, concern has been expressed by the unions that a specific concept, quality circles, is being used as a method of displacing the labor movement. William Roehl, an AFL-CIO assistant director of organization, stated that the quality circle can be part of a company's union-busting strategy (Shaw and Taleghan 1981). However, management also views the unions as a hindrance to the adoption of Japanese management techniques. A vice-president of a small manufacturer of precision parts has indicated that the presence of the union—a third party—can contribute to an adversarial relationship between management and the shopworkers, thus complicating cooperation (McClenahen 1981).

Middle Management

A very critical sector in the typical organization has been middle management. The middle manager has played an important role in the fluid movement of the organization in the United States for years. However, this same level is perhaps intimidated when such activities as "bottom-up" decisions and communications or management by consensus become apparent. This may to some degree be a function of the U.S. business schools or the organizational structure that is so prevalent in this nation. Regardless of the cause, middle management may inadvertently hinder the acceptance or development of innovative management techniques designed to increase productivity.

It is the belief of some managers that the middle management level of their organizations is critical to success or failure in the use of Japanese management techniques. Some believe that middle management often has a "we-they" relationship with the workers and unions because middle management has to translate top management's orders into action.

Several executives stated in an interview series for *Industry Week* (McClenahen 1981) that middle management is important in the successful use of the techniques. Executives felt that middle management must "be receptive to change—even when the proposed changes aren't its ideas," and mentioned managers' concern over "plummeting productivity when workers left their machines for an hour each week to attend a QC meeting."

Attitude toward Quality

As stated previously, waste involves both the product and the human resource associated with the production process. U.S. industry has for years looked at quality control with the view that there must be an acceptable number of good units in a "batch." This is to say that there will be an acceptable or tolerable level of defects. This attitude suggests that a company is tolerant of some defects, the number usually to be determined by contract. With this in mind, additional units are produced for a given order to insure that enough "good" units will be available after inspection to meet the level of demand that has been established. To some degree, this attitude has created an insidious but undeniable feeling among workers that a certain level of defectives is acceptable. Indeed, they may have to be repaired but they will be present nonetheless. On the other hand, the Japanese strive for a level of perfection that is not natural within the U.S. conceptual framework of quality.

Hayes (1981) refers to a Japanese scholar who articulated the concept of the worker's quality program thus: "If you do an economic analysis, you will usually find that it is advantageous to reduce your defect rate from 10 percent to 5 percent. If you repeat that analysis, it may or may not make sense to reduce it further to one percent. The Japanese, however, will reduce it. Having accomplished this, they will attempt to reduce it to 0.1 percent. And then 0.01 percent. You might claim that this obsession is costly, that it makes no economic sense. They are heedless. They will not be satisfied with less than perfection."

In this country, we have not in most cases been able to address quality to the same degree as the Japanese. The difference between the U.S. attitude of operating with a 95 percent level of acceptance and that of the Japanese, where "a defect is a treasure," is staggering. This attitude toward quality is an all-encompassing one not limited to a "quality control department" making periodic checks for defects.

Identity with the Work Place

The social structure of the Japanese business organization suggests that the worker may feel a stronger commitment toward the company than exists in the United States. This articulated and unique company philosophy frequently describes the firm or company as a "family" (Hatvany and Pucik 1981). In this "family" relationship, the employing firm is unique and distinct from any other firm. It serves as a social group, and the worker is selectively admitted but not expected to leave.

According to Aonuma (1980), prewar Japan was shattered in national direction and purpose. The society, which had previously been united for a common purpose, no longer had a common cause. The response to the shattered goals of the nation was that the Japanese turned for their identity to the companies. "The 'public interest' shifted from nation to company, and once it gained widespread acceptance as a social ethic, the Japanese sense of the individual as an employee was the prime thought-pattern promoted" (Hatvany and Pucik 1981). In part, because of this shift of public interest, many Japanese workers regard their work as the most important part of their lives. A certain element of self-denial became linked to company loyalty. According to Aonuma (1980), out of this grew a sense of purpose regarding work — work was not drudgery, but a kind of sacred duty.

This purpose associated with the company has additional aspects that affect the worker. The manager is expected to motivate the average worker to perform well. If not, the company will not achieve the excellent business results that it requires.

It has become apparent that Japanese workers are not better than workers in the United States. However, it is becoming obvious that the workers feel a greater loyalty toward the company that employs them and thus have a greater commitment to making high-quality products and increasing productivity.

Operations Strategy

U.S. manufacturing firms have long been recognized and praised for their ability to make short-term decisions. However, this emphasis on the short-term results may be one of the major shortcomings of the planning systems frequently used in U.S. manufacturing firms today.

One must consider the following three levels of business strategy: corporate, business, and functional. At the corporate level, one identifies what business is desired and how the capital and human resources must be allocated. The second level, business strategy, is the plan for the individual business unit. These strategic business units or divisions have as their goal the maintenance of a competitive advantage. The third level in the U.S. form of strategy is functional planning. This is the strategy for each of the primary functions of the firm. Manufacturing finds itself at this level of the organization.

Table 38.1 provides a list of the decision areas for manufacturing strategy. Wheelwright (1981–82) has suggested that this classification of levels for manufacturing strategy is typical of most U.S. firms today. However, he states, in Japan the view of manufacturing strategy is quite different. Group I of the manufacturing strategy classification is perceived quite similarly in the two countries, but, as Wheelwright points out, the Japanese do not view the second category as strictly tactical or operations-oriented as do U.S. companies:

> While the U.S. typically sees work force, production quality and production planning and materials control as tactical issues, the Japanese, by contrast,

TABLE 38.1   Decision Areas for Manufacturing Strategy

GROUP	UNITED STATES	DECISION AREAS	JAPAN
I: (Long-term, capital-budget-oriented)	Strategic	Capacity — amount, timing, type Facilities — size, location, specialization Vertical integration — sources, distribution, balance Production processes — skills, equipment, automation	Strategic
II: (Short-term, operational)	Tactical	Work force — tasks, union status, incentives Quality — testing, product assurance Production planning/materials control	
III: (Implementation)	Means of implementation	Organization — plants, staff work force	Implementation

Source: Adapted from Wheelwright (1981–82).

view the same issues as being every bit as strategic in their impact on competitive advantage as the more capital-oriented decision of Group I (Wheelwright 1981–82; see also Wheelwright 1981).

THE AMERICAN CHALLENGE

The Japanese have successfully adapted the strength of the management concepts and techniques of other nations to their own style and organizational structure. They have introduced product innovation that has been highly effective in the global marketplace. This small but dynamic country has even captured the attention of a larger but more sluggish country — the United States — and has encouraged it to look more critically at management processes and techniques of operations management.

This may suggest that the United States has nowhere to go but into decline. This need not be the case at all! The United States has been able to maintain the competitive edge in a number of areas of great importance. For example, the U.S. educational system has been studied by the Japanese and others. It has been found worthy of "borrowing" because of its strength as a system for generating concepts. The U.S. educational system does produce innovative and concept-oriented graduates who are capable, with the proper organizational, societal, and economic support, of reinstating the competitive edge. However, this competitive element cannot be restored without the support and integration of the educational system, of the corporate sector, and of government. This is not to say that educators ought to ask for a handout; educational institutions need to take up the challenge of working more closely with industry and government to study new ways to increase productivity, innovations in management style and technique, and new methods of studying organizations and sharing ideas.

In a more pragmatic dimension, we also have opportunities today. These are best viewed in terms of the short- and long-term opportunities. It is possible to use many of the short-term solutions as stopgap measures in dealing with the need for more-permanent and longer-term ways of solving our problems. However, many of these short-term solutions will also set the stage for a better environment and management attitude that will make possible more-fruitful results with long-term approaches.

Short-Term Solutions

Already becoming important in U.S. manufacturing are quality circles. They originated in this country, but were little seen here until recent years. This approach to quality control is now proving successful in a number of companies in the United States. However, the success of quality circles is also subject to the organizational commitment of the companies trying to use them. In most companies, unless middle managers are willing to modify many of their attitudes toward the expansion of the workers' roles and the involvement of workers in the decision-making process, and encourage a bottom-up role for workers, quality circles will not be successful.

The idea of quality circles is much more than merely quality improvement. It is a deep-rooted concept that requires a new level of commitment by U.S. workers and management. It requires a commitment to developing a better and stronger labor force, and will require education and worker development programs. The adversarial relationship of management and worker will also have to be diminished to the point where a cooperative, collective relationship can be fostered.

The rudiments of the quality circle actually lead into the next commitment necessary from management. This is the need to view human resources in a new manner. Americans have recognized for the past two decades that the way to advance and receive better pay has been to move from company to company. This has had the effect of reducing a worker's commitment to the company. The "family" has seldom been seen as a part of the corporate structure in this country.

A reduction of the strong forces toward mobility among workers and management can be improved by the generation of a strong internal labor market (ILM). Although in Japan the ILM has as an implicit base the guarantee of job security, this is not absolutely necessary. Better selection processes, development of job openings with proper pretraining or education, and (perhaps most important) an attitude on the part of management that an ILM can exist are necessary ingredients.

Job security does have many advantages for the organization. An important one is the reduction of employee hostility and resistance to the introduction of labor-saving technology. We will continually face the need for greater amounts of automation in our society. Although there is sometimes the cry that we should reverse the trend in this area, once technology is introduced there is no conceivable way of rolling it back.

There is general empirical evidence that a long tenure in a job is positively associated with commitment to the organization. Although commitment is a complex and multifaceted variable, these findings nonetheless suggest that the results of commitment are organizational goal reinforcement, sharing of values, and a willingness to put forth effort on behalf of the organization.

Many U.S. organizations have experimented with "flexitime" concepts, permitting employees to come and go at their own discretion more than according to the organization's rules. What we may need in the near future is greater commitment to the "flexijob," where the worker will be not only encouraged, but expected, to take a more active part in expanding his or her work boundaries, commitment, and levels. For example, this may take the form of educating workers in the maintenance of the equipment under their direction. In this way, the "pride of ownership" is increased.

To see the flexijob concept in action, one merely has to view many of the independent truckers who operate on the nation's highways. It is usually easy to spot those drivers, who have great pride in their rigs. They are willing to haul for long hours (indeed with an economic return), but they also maintain their own trucks. These trucks generally stand out on the highways because of the special care taken to keep them shiny, maintain spectacular paint jobs, and include lots of "extras." This increased job responsibility has been significant in the trucking industry.

Long-Term Approaches

The longer-term approach should not suggest that it is possible to wait longer before beginning to implement a solution. Instead, a longer view is merely an acceptance of the fact that society, organizations, and government are slow to change and accept new processes.

Critical to the implementation of several other stages of a solution is the need for a reduction of the adversarial relationship among the worker, unions, management, and government. With the four vital forces moving against each other, little can be accomplished. This will not be an easy change to make. The adversarial relationship dates from the 1930s. Yet there have been numerous indications that labor and management can work together so long as their cause is open, sincere, and reasonable. The quality-of-working-life efforts have often involved the various factions, with eventual cooperation and consensus.

Coupling the workers' decision-making process with that of management is important. Business schools may need to change the content and methods used to teach students about their roles in the organization. Middle management, in particular, is vulnerable to intimidation by the "bottom-up" decision-making and communications process, which appears to be important in the adoption of many Japanese manufacturing techniques. This new role for management is critical to the success of productivity improvement methods. Involvement of workers in job redesigning is becoming increasingly necessary.

Although we will see new plants coming on line with opportunities for effective new job design, most companies will be able only to redesign. Regardless of how simple or complex the redesign may be, the involvement of the worker is paramount. This role for the worker does have a record of success in the companies using it.

A new view of manufacturing and corporate strategy not only is timely but is an opportunity that U.S. industry cannot ignore. It is no longer possible to view the work force, quality, production planning, and materials control solely as part of the tactical, short-term operating procedures. Instead, it is necessary to move this level of the manufacturing strategy so that it is a part of the strategic process. This will require a strong philosophical commitment to treating operations as strategy, and will have many and varying implications for the education of managers. It will necessitate a change in the attitudes of not only the corporate management but also the stockholders of U.S. companies.

The view of short-term cost reductions and return on investment (ROI) must be supplemented by the longer-term development of technological competitiveness. It will not be an easy chore to turn the corporate view away from the marketplace of the United States and toward a global perspective. National standards must yield to global rules. New strategies for marketing and innovations are now necessary.

Finally, we, as educators and business leaders, must throw off the self-imposed attitude that we are the best in terms of management education, innovation, and practice and look to others for new developments. There will continue to be a need for new managerial understanding. The opportunity is here for us to learn from others! It may be difficult to study other cultures, societies, and business structures in an effort to gain insight into approaches foreign to our own. However, with broad thinking and through longer-term cooperation among government, labor, and management and with foreign nations, many of the expectations that we have may be fulfilled.

REFERENCES

Anderson, William. 1981. "What We Are Learning from Japan." *Nation's Business* 69, no. 3 (March):39–41.

Aonuma, Yoshimatsu. 1980. "A Japanese Explains Japan's Business Style." *Across The Board* 18, no. 2:41–50.

Council on Wage and Price Stability, Report on Productivity. 1979. *Growth in Labor Productivity since 1960 (U.S. and Abroad)*, July. Washington, D.C.: U.S. Government Printing Office.

Fox, Colin. 1981. Paper presented at a meeting of the Western Academy of Management, Monterey, Calif., March.

Greenberger, Robert S. 1981. "Quality Circles Grow Stirring Union Worries." *Wall Street Journal*, September 23, p. 5.

Hatvany, Nina, and Vladimir Pucik. 1981. "An Integrated Management System: Lessons for a Japanese Experience." *Academy of Management Review* 6, no. 3 (July):469–80.

Hayes, Robert H. 1981. "Why Japanese Factories Work." *Harvard Business Review* 59, no. 4 (July-August):55–66.

Hayes, Robert H., and William J. Abernathy. 1980. "Managing Our Way to Economic Decline." *Harvard Business Review* 58, no. 4 (July-August):67–77.

Johnson, Richard Tanner, and William G. Ouchi. 1974. "Made in America (Under Japanese Management)." *Harvard Business Review* 52, no. 5 (Sept.-Oct.): 61–9.

McClenahen, John S. 1981. "Bringing Home Japan's Lesson." *Industry Week*, February 23, pp. 69–73.

"Organizing for Productivity." 1981. *Industry Week*, Feb. 9, pp. 55–60.

O'Toole, James. 1981. "How Management Hinders Productivity." *Industry Week*, August 10, pp. 55–8.

Ouchi, William G. 1980. "Markets, Bureaucracies, and Clans." *Administrative Science Quarterly* (March):129–140.

Ouchi, William G., and Jerry B. Johnson. 1978. "Types of Organization Control and Their Relationship to Emotional Well Being." *Administrative Science Quarterly* (June):293.

Pascale, Richard Tanner. 1978. "Communication and Decision Making across Cultures: Japanese and American Comparisons." *Administrative Science Quarterly* (March):91–110.

Schonberger, Richard. 1981. "The Transfer of Japanese Manufacturing Approaches to United States Industry." Paper presented at the Academy of Management, San Diego, Calif., August.

Shaw, Robert, and Farhad Taleghan. 1981. "How Quality Circles Works." *World* 15, no. 3:10–11.

Wheelwright, Steven C. 1981–82. "Operations as Strategy — Lessons from Japan." *Stanford GSB* (Fall):2–7.

_____. 1981. "Japan — Where Operations Really Are Strategic." *Harvard Business Review* 59, no. 4, (July-August):67–74.

Zager, Robert. 1978. "Managing Guaranteed Employment." *Harvard Business Review* 56, no. 3 (May-June):105–115.

Index

About the Contributors

MATT M. AMANO is Professor of Management in the School of Business, Oregon State University

NORIO AOYAMA is Assistant Professor of Business Administration at Chuo Gakuin University, Japan

BERNARD AROGYASWAMY is a member of the faculty, Graduate School of Business, Kent State University

ROBERT J. BARBATO is currently Assistant Professor of Organizational Behavior at the Rochester Institute of Technology

JAY B. BARNEY is currently Assistant Professor of Management, Strategy and Policy in the Graduate School of Management, University of California at Los Angeles

M. TOM BASURAY is Associate Professor of Management at the University of North Dakota

JOHN D. BLAIR is currently Associate Professor of Management in the College of Business Administration at Texas Tech University, where he is a faculty associate of the Texas Center for Productivity and Quality of Work Life

STEPHEN E. BLYTHE is Assistant Professor of Management at the University of North Dakota

KATHLEEN C. BRANNEN is Assistant Professor of Management at Creighton University

ROBERT E. CALLAHAN is Assistant Professor of Management at the Albers School of Business, Seattle University

PHILLIP L. CARTER is Professor of Management and Chairman of the Department of Management in the Graduate School of Business at Michigan State University

FRANK H. CLARKE is Professor in the Department of Mathematics, University of British Columbia

MICHAEL J. CLEARY* is Professor of Business Administration at Wright State University

---

*Chairman, American Society for Quality Control Technical Subcommittee on Guidelines for a Successful Quality Circle Process.

THOMAS PATRICK CULLEN is at present a doctoral candidate at Cornell University, studying administration, organizational behavior, and human resources management

MASAKO N. DARROUGH is Assistant Professor of Economics at the University of Santa Clara

LESTER A. DIGMAN is Associate Professor of Management, University of Nebraska-Lincoln

RICHARD E. DREXEL is the Quality Circle Facilitator at Bausch & Lomb, and is currently a member of the International Association of Quality Circles

LIAM FAHEY is Assistant Professor of Policy and Environment, J. L. Kellog Graduate School of Management, Northwestern University

JOHN W. GOEBEL is Professor of Accounting and Business Law and currently Interim Vice Chancellor of Business and Finance at the University of Nebraska-Lincoln

RONALD G. GREENWOOD is Professor of Management at the University of Wisconsin-LaCrosse

TONY HAIN is Professor and Department Head of Industrial Administration, General Motors Institute; during the past year, he served as a visiting scholar at the Harvard Graduate School of Business Administration

JAMES L. HALL is Associate Professor and Chairman of the Management Department at the University of Santa Clara

ROBERT W. HALL is Associate Professor of Management at Indiana University

JO ANN HRANAC is a graduate student in the College of Business Administration at Creighton University

KATE E. HUNTINGTON is a Research Assistant in the College of Business Administration of Pennsylvania State University

JEROME V. HURWITZ is a personnel research psychologist for the Productivity Research Division of the U.S. Office of Personnel Management

GEORGE W. JACOBS is Assistant Professor of Management at Middle Tennessee State University

EUGENE J. KELLEY is Dean and Research Professor of Business Administration in the College of Business Administration of Pennsylvania State University; he is president-elect of the American Marketing Association

KEN I. KIM is Assistant Professor of Management at Bowling Green State University, Bowling Green, Ohio; he teaches courses in business policy and organizational behavior

BARRY E. KING is Assistant Professor of Management Sciences at Ohio State University

MANJULIKA KOSHAL is Assistant Professor of Business Administration at Ohio University

RAJINDAR K. KOSHAL is Professor of Economics at Ohio University

LEE J. KRAJEWSKI is Professor of Production and Operations Management at Ohio State University

JOEL K. LEIDECKER is on the faculty at the University of Santa Clara, where he teaches courses in business policy and strategy

HAROLD I. LUNDE is Professor of Management at Bowling Green State University in Bowling Green, Ohio, where he teaches courses in business policy and strategy

RENATE R. MAI-DALTON is Assistant Professor of Organizational Behavior and Administration in the School of Business at the University of Kansas

IAN MAITLAND is Assistant Professor of Business, Government, and Society in the School of Management at the University of Minnesota

ARLYN J. MELCHER is Professor of Management at Kent State University

STEVEN A. MELNYK is Assistant Professor in the Department of Management, Michigan State University

DAVID T. METHÉ is currently working on his doctoral dissertation on strategic management at the University of California, Irvine

MOTOFUSA MURAYAMA is Professor of Management at Chiba University, Japan

JINICHIRO NAKANE is Professor of Business Management at Waseda University, Japan

DICK KAZUYUKI NANTO is an analyst in international trade and finance with the Congressional Research Service, Library of Congress

WILLIAM G. OUCHI is Professor of Management, Graduate School of Management, University of California at Los Angeles

C. CARL PEGELS is Professor and Chairman, Department of Management Science and Systems, at the State University of New York at Buffalo

MICHAEL RADNOR is Professor at the J.L. Kellogg Graduate School of Management, Northwestern University

KENNETH D. RAMSING is Professor of Management at the University of Oregon

C. P. RAO is Professor of Marketing at the University of Arkansas, Fayetteville

ALLAN C. REDDY is an Associate Professor of Marketing at Valdosta State College, Valdosta, Georgia

LARRY P. RITZMAN is Professor of Operations Management in the Management Sciences Faculty, College of Administrative Science, at Ohio State University

ROBERT H. ROSS is Assistant Professor in the College of Business Administration, Wichita State University

WILLIAM V. RUCH is Assistant Professor in the College of Business Administration at San Diego State University

RICHARD J. SCHONBERGER is Professor of Management in the College of Business Administration, University of Nebraska-Lincoln

ANN C. SEROR is Assistant Professor of Management at the Owen Graduate School of Management, Vanderbilt University

P. K. SHUKLA is a lecturer in management at California State University, Long Beach; he is in the doctoral program at the Graduate School of Management at UCLA, with a specialization in management strategy and policy

DAVID ULRICH is currently a graduate student and research associate at the Graduate School of Management, University of California at Los Angeles

NAN WEINER is a member of the faculties of management sciences and labor and human resources at Ohio State University

DANNY S. WONG is Assistant Professor of Production/Operations Management and Quantitative Methods at Ohio State University

About the Editors

Sang M. Lee is a Regents Professor of the University of Nebraska system, the First National Bank Lincoln Distinguished Professor, and Chairman of the Management Department. He received his MBA from Miami University of Ohio and his Ph.D. in management science from the University of Georgia. He is the author or co-author of 17 books, including *Goal Programming for Decision Analysis, Introduction to Decision Science, Linear Optimization for Management*, and *Management Science*. He has published over 130 research papers in various leading journals of management. He has been an expert referee for the National Research Council, National Academy of Sciences, National Academy of Engineering, and National Science Foundation. He is a consulting editor of several book series with publishers and on the editorial boards of 16 journals. He has been a distinguished visiting scholar at Ohio State, University of Minnesota, University of Georgia, Rutgers, Michigan State University, and many other universities in the United States, England, Japan, and Korea. He won the Outstanding Research Award in 1980 and the AMOCO Distinguished Teaching Award in 1982 at the University of Nebraska System. He was the founder and first president of SE AIDS, from which he received the First Distinguished Service Award. He has been a member of the council, chairman of the publication committee, vice-president, secretary, and nominee for the president-elect of the National AIDS. He is a fellow of AIDS. He received the Distinguished Service Award from National AIDS in 1980 for his contribution to AIDS and the management profession.

Gary Schwendiman is Dean of the College of Business Administration and Professor of Management at the University of Nebraska-Lincoln. A specialist in the area of management psychology, he earned his bachelor's degree with honors from Washington State University and his Master of

Science and Ph.D. degrees from Brigham Young University. In 1969 he joined the faculty of Marshall University in West Virginia, where he taught courses in management and psychology. He joined General Motors Institute, the educational and management development division of the General Motors Corporation, in 1972, where he was Associate Professor of Organizational Behavior and Communication. His research and consulting activities have been mainly with financial organizations. He recently completed a survey of the nation's 300 largest banks to determine future directions for the effective management of human resources. He has developed the Individual Assessment Profile, which is used in the development of supervisory personnel and the Organizational Profile, which assesses organizational and management effectiveness. He has published numerous research papers in scholarly journals of psychology and organizational behavior.